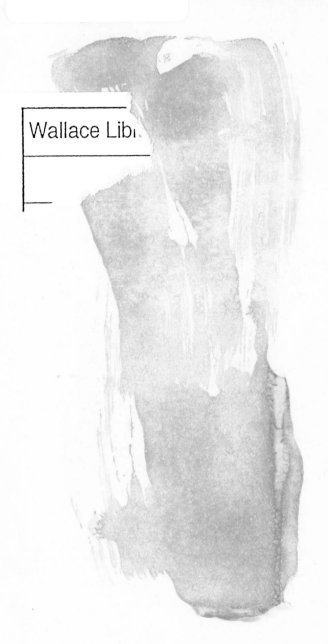

THE ADMINISTRATION OF
THE DIOCESE OF WORCESTER IN
THE FIRST HALF OF THE
FOURTEENTH CENTURY

THE ADMINISTRATION OF
THE DIOCESE OF WORCESTER IN
THE FIRST HALF OF THE
FOURTEENTH CENTURY

R. M. HAINES

Published for the Church Historical Society

LONDON

S·P·C·K

1965

First published in 1965
by S.P.C.K.
Holy Trinity Church
Marylebone Road
London N.W.1

Made and printed in Great Britain by
William Clowes and Sons, Limited
London and Beccles

PUBLISHED WITH THE HELP OF
THE MARC FITCH FUND

TO MY MOTHER

APPENDIX C. "SEDE VACANTE" DOCUMENTS

APPENDIX D. SOME WORCESTER MANDATES

ABBREVIATIONS

Knowles & Hadcock	Knowles, D., and Hadcock, R. N., Medieval Religious Houses (1953)
L.A.	Liber Albus (of Worcester unless otherwise stated)
L.C.S.	*Lincoln Cathedral Statutes*, ed. Bradshaw and Wordsworth (Camb., 1892–7)
L.R.S.	Lincoln Record Society
Landboc Winch.	*Landboc sive Registrum monasterii de Winchelcumba*, ed. Royce (2 Vols., 1892–3)
Lit. Cant.	*Literae Cantuarienses*, ed. J. B. Sheppard, 3 Vols. 1887–9 (R.S.)
M.	Magister (Master)
O.H.S.	Oxford Historical Society
P.B.A.	Proceedings of the British Academy
P.H.E.	*Political History of England*
P.S.A.	Proceedings of the Society of Antiquaries
R.H.S.T.	Royal Historical Society Transactions
R.S.	Rolls Series
R.S.V.	Registrum Sede Vacante (of Worcester)
Seld. Soc.	Selden Society.
Som. R.S.	Somerset Record Society
Surt. Soc.	Surtees Society
Suss. R.S.	Sussex Record Society
V.C.H.	*Victoria County History*
Vetus Lib. Arch. Elien.	*Vetus Liber Archidiaconi Eliensis*, C.A.S. 8° xlviii, 1917 (see p. 367)
W.H.S.	Worcestershire Historical Society
Westm. Abb. Mun.	Westminster Abbey Muniments
Y.A.J.	*Yorkshire Archaeological Journal*

Episcopal Registers of sees other than Worcester are referred to by diocese and name of bishop: for example, *Heref. Reg. Orleton*, p. 21. It has been thought unnecessary to list these publications which can be readily identified.

A NOTE ON THE
TRANSCRIPTION OF DOCUMENTS

The scribes of the Worcester registers in some respects allowed themselves considerable latitude. Thus "p" and "b" are often interchangeable, as in "publicare" (puplicare). So too are "m" and "n" in certain cases (imperpetuum, inperpetuum), "c" and "s" (cituato, situato), "d" and "t" (sicud, sicut), "e" and "i" (deaconi, diaconi: faciat, faceat), "y" and "i" (Wygorn', Wigorn') etc. An "h" is sometimes added, as in "inibi" (inhibi), or omitted, as in "heres" (eres). No rule seems to have been observed with regard to the duplication of medial consonants. Thus we find "ellectus" and "electus", "littera" and "litera" etc. Other variations include the insertion of a "c" in "exercendum" (excercendum), "sumptibus" written as "sumptubus" and the not infrequent use of the present infinitive active where we might expect the passive form. "Excercicium" is often rendered "excercium"; "infra" is sometimes used with the ablative, and "in" with the accusative or ablative regardless of construction. It is frequently difficult to extend the enigmatic "prox" of the MS. and "proximo" seems to have been used as an adverb rather than "proxime". It is clear that "c" was written in many cases where we might expect "t", as in "circumspeccio", "eleccio" etc. It is difficult if not impossible to distinguish "v" and "u", so that it has been found convenient to follow modern practice in this respect. With regard to "i" and "j", the latter has been used in the case of proper nouns "Johannes", "dies Jovis" etc. In general, scribal peculiarities of construction and spelling have been preserved and only an occasional [sic] has been inserted to indicate the more unusual of these.

One cannot be certain about the use of gerunds and gerundives. The evidence suggests that the scribes were not dogmatic about the matter and sometimes used either in entries having the same common form. In extending the enigmatic "end" or "and" of the MS. the gerund has been preferred except where there are indications that such was not the scribe's intention.

As for punctuation, the rule has been to follow that of the MS. as far as possible, only adding or emending to establish the sense of a passage. The irregular use of capitals in the MS. has not been adopted.

Additional words, the extension of the more doubtful contractions, the editorial "etc." as distinct from that of the MS, as well as other emendations, have been enclosed within brackets in the usual way.

Dates have been rendered in the New Style.

The footnotes contain, for the most part, material which is not available in print. The editions of Worcester registers, save that of Bishop Cobham, include little of the text of the original MSS.

ACKNOWLEDGEMENTS

I should like to thank all those who, in various ways, have made possible the writing of this book: particularly the staff of the Diocesan Registry and later that of St Helen's repository, for their assistance over a number of years; the Reverend D. R. Pocock and subsequently the Very Reverend R. L. P. Milburn, Dean of Worcester, for making the cathedral MSS. so readily available; the County Archivist, Mr E. H. Sargeant, for his interest and co-operation; Dr K. Major, for her help and advice; Professor E. F. Jacob, for his kindly supervision, encouragement, and long-continued support; Professor C. R. Cheney and Mr W. A. Pantin, F.B.A., for their constructive criticism of the original D.Phil. thesis; Sir Hugh Chance, whose generosity made practicable a pleasant and, it is hoped, not unprofitable stay in Oxford; and finally my wife, who so courageously coped with the bulk of the typing and did much to improve the readability of the work.

Generous help towards publication was received from various sources, including the Bishop of Worcester, the Dean and Chapter of Worcester, the Provost and Fellows of Worcester College, Oxford, the Worcester College Society, and the Church Historical Society. Publication was finally assured by a British Academy award of £300 following a grant of £400 by the Marc Fitch Fund. I am happy to record my gratitude to the Council of the Fund for such substantial assistance, and would also like to thank Mr Francis Steer, the Honorary Secretary, for his help and interest.

M. I. Ross, a colleague of mine at Westminster, has kindly produced the map of the diocese and the two visitation itineraries.

The Worcestershire County Council, on the recommendation of its Records Committee, made a much appreciated grant towards the cost of making the index.

Westminster School, S.W.1   R.M.H.

PREFACE

The following study is based principally on the diocesan and prioral records at Worcester. In origin an Oxford D.Phil. thesis, it has been modified in detail, and to a lesser extent in scope. It is basically an examination of the developed administrative system at Worcester in the first half of the fourteenth century, but looks both backwards to the thirteenth and forwards to the later fourteenth and the fifteenth century. Moreover, on Professor Cheney's advice, it has with advantage been made comparative, though the material relating to dioceses other than Worcester is derived almost entirely from printed sources.

In the general field of episcopal administration and diocesan organization the writer owes a substantial debt to the pioneer studies of Dr Churchill, Professor Cheney, and Professor Hamilton Thompson. It was the last named who first gave him an enthusiasm for things medieval and directed his initial historical researches.

1

RECORDS AND SEALS

RECORDS

Essential to the continuity of diocesan administration were numerous
records. For the Worcester diocese[1] there survive from the fourteenth
century only the registers, episcopal and prioral, and a large number of
loose manuscripts which for the most part are concerned with the lands
of the priory.[2] All manner of charters, indentures, chantry confirmations, and administrative documents were originally preserved. They
must have been readily accessible, for many were copied into registers
of a much later date.[3] There were the rolls of the consistory courts
which at every vacancy were demanded by the prior in his capacity of
official *sede vacante*.[4] The sequestrator also kept records[5] and
doubtless other episcopal officers did the same. There must have been
many account rolls, acquittances, visitation records,[6] and other documents. Locally there were the records of archdeaconry and deanery.
Ready to hand were the taxation lists. A royal writ of 1346 demanded
information as to whether the church of Claverdon, which was annexed
to the Worcester archdeaconry, was charged with a pension to the

---

[1] Useful comparison can be made with the Lincoln records catalogued by K. Major
in her *Handlist*; R. Hill, intro. to *Rot. & Reg. Sutton* 3, pp. xxvii–xxix, and "Bp.
Sutton and his Archives", *J.E.H.* Vol. 2, No. 1, pp. 43–53.

[2] These constitute Class B MSS. in the cathedral library. Some of them, probably
on the grounds that they concerned the diocese rather than the priory, were handed
over in recent years to the diocesan registrar and were kept in a box marked "Miscellaneous Charters". They are now, with the rest of the diocesan muniments formerly
housed in St Michael's church at Worcester (lately demolished), in the care of the
County Archivist.

[3] A number were copied into Reg. Bransford, the earliest dating from Baldwin's
episcopate (1180–5).

[4] See Chap. 5 below. On fo. 135 of the R.S.V. is a form of citation for the production
of the register of causes of the consistory.

[5] In 1317 Stephen de Northeye, Maidstone's sequestrator, was ordered by the prior,
the official *sede vacante*, to surrender the register, rolls, and muniments of his office.
R.S.V., fo. 98v.

[6] In 1335 Montacute visited at Bromsgrove church "eandem et alias prout in
rotulis visitacionis plenius continetur". Reg. Montacute 2, fo. 48r.

prior of Wootton.[1] Bishop Bransford certified that the registers and other memoranda had been searched,[2] and that in the register containing the taxes of ecclesiastical benefices within the diocese he had found Claverdon to be assessed at 6½ marks according to the Norwich taxation,[3] 10 marks by that of Stroud,[4] and 15 by that of Vienne.[5]

Leaving aside for the moment the episcopal registers, we may usefully consider the evidence for the housing of those records the importance of which merited permanent preservation. From a number of chance references in the registers it would seem that such records were kept in the priory treasury. For instance, an original of the Kempsey chantry ordination of 1316 is described as being in the bishop's treasury within the priory.[6] A charter recording the endowment of the chapel of St Katherine, Campden, during Baldwin's episcopate (1180-4), was copied into Register Bransford when it was said to be "sub cera in thesauro ecclesie cathedralis Wygorn'".[7] This seems to have been the practice in other dioceses.[8] At Lincoln an inventory was made in 1284 of all the MSS. in the cathedral treasury which contained material relating to the see. These were systematically stored in baskets and chests, perhaps under the supervision of John de Scalby who was registrar at the time.[9]

No doubt a number of current records were carried about by the

---

[1] Reg. Bransford, ff. ccxliii v. al. 174– ccxliiii r. al. 175 (1261, 1262). It may be noted that the bishop pointed out that the case was pending in his consistory court and that its cognizance and decision belonged to him.

[2] These taxation records have disappeared. In a box of "unindexed papers" in the cathedral library is a single roll entitled "Rotulum Wigorn. quinti anno [sic]". This, R. L. Poole suggested, dated from 1301/2, the fifth year of the tenth granted in 1291 by Nicholas IV to Edward I (letter attached to MS.).

[3] Called so after Walter Suffield, bishop of that see, who was closely connected with it. See Lunt, *Valuation of Norwich* (1254), and Rose Graham, "Taxation of Nicholas IV", in *English Eccles. Studies*.

[4] John de Strodes, canon of Shrewsbury, was one of the assessors of the tenth for the Holy Land raised in the Worcester diocese (1276). Lunt, *Papal Revenues in the Middle Ages* (1934) 2, pp. 173-4, and *Financial Relations of the Papacy with England to 1327* (1939), pp. 318. 630.

[5] A tenth was imposed by the Council of Vienne in 1311. See Lunt, op. citatis, 1, pp. 40, 243; 2, pp. 124-7; 395-404. This fifteen marks approximates to the £10 6s. 8d. of the 1291 *Taxatio* (p. 218).

[6] Reg. Maidstone, fo. 54r. ". . . et unum originale comprehendens omnes tenores infrascriptos sub sigillo communi prioris et capituli Wyg' est in thesauro domini episcopi Wyg' in prioratu Wyg'."

[7] Reg. Bransford, fo. 121r. al. cxxii (905).

[8] For a Durham instance see *Reg. Palat.* 3, p. 261. At Hereford there is record of a deposit "in ii pixidibus, in arca in capitulo ecclesie Herefordensis . . . sub signo [? sigillo] episcopi Thome". *Reg. Cantilupe*, pp. 40-1 (1276).

[9] *Rot. & Reg. Sutton* 3, intro. p. xxviii. See also W. O. Massingberd in *A.A.S.R.P.* XXIV, p. 313, who gives a translation of a seventeenth-century copy of the inventory.

bishop's clerks in chests, others may have been stored in the episcopal manors, as they were in Lincoln diocese,[1] but of a registry for the deposit and writing of documents we learn nothing at this period.[2]

The study of Worcester diocesan administration must rest almost entirely, in view of this paucity of other material, upon the episcopal registers, supplemented by the priory's Liber Albus and, during vacancies of the see, the "Sede Vacante" Register. Covering the first half of the fourteenth century are eight episcopal registers from that of Gainsburgh (1303–7), the second in the Worcester series, to that of Bransford (1339–49), the ninth.[3] Orleton's register (1328–33), number six, is the first in two volumes.[4] Montacute's register (1334–7) is similarly divided, and so is Bransford's, but Hemenhale occupied the see for so brief a space that his register (1337–8) does not extend beyond one slim volume. The reason for such division is by no means clear. It could hardly have been prompted by the excessive bulk of the material, for only Register Bransford can be called large.[5] Moreover, it resulted in much duplication of entries in the registers of Orleton and Montacute, particularly the latter. There is, indeed, a logical division of subject matter between the first and second volumes of the Orleton register,[6] but quite a different system was adopted by the compilers of Register Montacute, and even that was not strictly adhered to.[7] The second

[1] *Rot. & Reg. Sutton* 3, intro. pp. xxviii, xxix.

[2] Only in the sixteenth century is there mention of a royal charter of confirmation being "in custodia episcopi Wigorn' in scrinio in domo registrarii in palacio episcopi sub sigillo . . ." (D. & C. MS. Vol. A XII, fo. 67).

[3] Register Giffard overlaps somewhat at the beginning of the century. Giffard died 26 January 1302. His register (1268–1302) is the first of the series. Thoresby, who was translated to Worcester in September 1349, did not assume the administration until January 1350.

[4] Originally, that is. These are now bound in a single volume as are the others mentioned below.

[5] The number of folios at present in the registers is as follows: Gainsburgh, 57; Reynolds, 111; Maidstone, 56; Cobham, 126; Orleton, vol. 1, 43 (the last fo. cut to a third), Vol. 2, 57; Montacute, Vol. 1, 66, Vol. 2, 49 (two blank); Hemenhale, 36; Bransford, Vol. 1, 222 (including 36 folios now bound after Vol. 2), Vol. 2, 18.

[6] Vol. 1 contains Ordinations, Institutions, and Inductions, followed by Appropriations, Letters Dimissory and Dispensations. Vol. 2 has Papal Bulls etc., Commissions, details of Enthronement, Acquittances, Inquisitions, Mandates, then Presentations and Inquisitions, Institutions, Inductions, Institutions during the bishop's absence, followed by various routine entries, commissions etc. *ad finem*.

[7] Volume 1: Introductory rubric, Commissions, Institutions, the Crowle Indenture, Dispensations, Royal Writs, Various, Letters Dimissory, Ordinations—the last interrupted by a "special register" about the appropriation of Stratford church. Volume 2: Outgoing Letters etc. (Quaternus de Emanantibus), Licences and Dispensations, Papal Bulls, a Will, the Appropriation of Longdon, Inhibitions and certifications thereof, Royal Writs.

volume of Register Bransford is really a self-contained register for the last few months of the episcopate. The exceptional circumstances of 1349, when the Black Death was at its height in the diocese, may well have had an influence on its composition.[1]

The registers were current compilations. That is not to suggest that entries were made daily, which was certainly not the case, but that large sections were written up at intervals.[2] The lapse of time between the event and the recording of it is sometimes indicated by an editorial "tunc temporis" added to the description of a clerk as the holder of some benefice or office.

The registers probably went with the bishop on his progress through the diocese for they were an essential source of reference. Reynolds, on his return from abroad in 1309, had his register—together with those of his predecessors, Giffard and Gainsburgh—sent to him at Saw-bridgeworth in Hertfordshire.[3] Similarly, in Lincoln diocese, Bishop Sutton (1280–99) took with him not only his own registers and rolls, but also the rolls of his four immediate predecessors.[4]

Although there are many references to the registers, it is noteworthy that there is no mention of a register earlier than that of Godfrey Giffard (1268–1302) which is to-day the earliest in the Worcester series.[5] This suggests strongly that the bishops prior to his time did not have registers though, of course, they did have other records. Bishop Baldwin (1180–4), for instance, because of the contradictions "in matricula antecessorum suorum episcoporum" had inquiry made throughout the diocese "de personatibus, de vicariis, de decimis, et omnibus

[1] There are five sections, each carefully headed: Memoranda, Ordinations, Royal Writs (for the time of Bransford's successor, Thoresby), Register of the Audience Court, Institutions etc. (at the time of the Black Death).

[2] Thus, at the beginning of Register Montacute the scribe prefaced the entries with a summary of contents. "In primis commissio vicariatus et citaciones ad prestand[um] obedienciam dicto electo et confirmato a subditis dicti Wygorniensis diocesis prestandam facte, et commissiones ad obedienciam huiusmodi admittendam inde subsecute. Et commissio ad excercendum officium sequestratoris in diocesi Wygorn' predicta domino Johanni de Stannford facta et alie commissiones quamplures ac mandata et littere diverse et varia. De quorum tenore forma et data inferius continetur" (fo. 1r.).

[3] "Memorandum quod XI⁰ Kalen' Augusti anno domini M⁰CCCᵐᵒ nono apud Sabrichesworth recepit dominus episcopus registra sua tam de tempore Godefridi et Willelmi predecessorum suorum quam de tempore suo per manus Willelmi de Drax clerici sui sibi transmissa a magistro Benedicto de Paston . . ." (Reg. Reynolds, fo. 12r., pp. 10–11). Reynolds was rector of Sawbridgeworth. His own register must have been very small as it had been begun little more than a year before.

[4] Rot. & Reg. Sutton 3, intro. p. xxvii.

[5] Cheney, Bishops' Chanceries App. II, lists the earliest surviving registers of English dioceses.

episcopalibus".[1] The outcome of this inquiry seems to have been the "scrutinium" consulted between 1213 and 1228 by Maurice of Arundel, archdeacon of Gloucester, for details of the church of Mickleton.[2]

Physically the registers are made up of quires of parchment containing various numbers of sheets placed one on top of the other and folded over to form twice as many folios. These quires or quaternions do not necessarily correspond with the divisions of the subject matter, though sometimes they do so. During the construction of a register they probably lay loosely one on top of another, which enables us to comprehend— to take only one instance—the direction for finding the appropriation of Compton Magna in Register Maidstone "in xvii folio secundi quaterni istius registri a capite computando", where now the beginning of the quire can be discovered only by close inspection of the binding.[3] The original covers of the registers, or what remains of them, are in most cases bound within the present binding.[4] Few traces of pagination within the quires can now be found. For an appreciable period the folios were left unnumbered in some if not all of the registers.[5] Thus, the index notes on the fly-leaf of Register Bransford refer vaguely to the appropriation of a church as being in the next quire immediately after the present one,[6] while other items were to be sought in a quire headed 1340.[7] It could not have been long, however, before the folios received their Roman numerals, and in the late Middle Ages they were renumbered with Arabic ones.[8]

This double pagination is invaluable because it gives us some idea of the number of folios which were lost during the medieval period, as

[1] *Landboc Winch.* i, pp. 69–70.

[2] *Eynsham Cart.* i, pp. 137–8. Professor Cheney, *Bishops' Chanceries*, pp. 115–17, comments on the Worcester "matriculae".

[3] Reg. Maidstone cover. See also note 6 below.

[4] The cover of Register Gainsburgh probably dates from the sixteenth century. That of Hemenhale's register was somehow transferred to Register Morgan (see p. 134 below). It is not clear whether the covers were loose or stitched to the folios.

[5] The present eighth quire of Reg. Reynolds (ff. lxi–lxviii) was originally contiguous to the tenth (ff. lxxvii–lxxxiv), as the catchword and continuity of subject matter show clearly. Some time before the addition of the Roman numerals another quire, now the ninth (ff. lxix–lxxvi), was interpolated. This explains why the entry on fo. lxxvii (in the tenth quire) refers back to another "in precedenti quaturno", though the latter, which is on fo. lxiiii v., is now in the quire before the preceding one.

[6] "in proximo quaterno presentem quaternum immediate subsequentum [*sic*]." To-day this entry is to be found on folio 13v. which is in fact in the second quire.

[7] "Require infra in quaterno intitulato anno domini MCCCXL^{mo}."

[8] Probably in the late fifteenth century at the time of the compilation of the index volume which takes account only of the Arabic pagination.

well as of subsequent losses.[1] Further, it tends to support the theory that the quires were loose for some considerable period—though doubtless they were kept within the covers mentioned above. For example, the whole of the ordination lists slipped out from the middle of Register Bransford and the Arabic numeration continues straight on to the folios of royal writs. The ordination lists were then given a separate Arabic pagination of their own, though meanwhile some thirty-five folios had gone astray. In 1881 the surviving folios were restored to the register after they had been discovered among some transcripts in the Registry. Unfortunately, they were not put back in their proper place or in their correct order, but were added after the second volume. The Roman pagination enables us to establish their original position in front of the quire of royal writs and also to rearrange them in their proper order. It may well be significant that there is no quire of royal writs in the registers of Maidstone, Cobham, or Orleton,[2] while the second volume of Bransford's register contains writs which should be in that of Thoresby.[3]

It must have been a difficult matter to decide what was to be recorded in an episcopal register and what omitted. We cannot say for certain whose decision it was, though it may have been that of the bishop's registrar or scribe.[4] Numerous documents of all kinds were kept folded up[5] with some descriptive title on the outside. They were probably stored in chests, but only a proportion of them was ever registered.[6]

Though there were attempts to divide the registers according to subject matter, the rubrics prefacing such tentative divisions[7] are seldom more than a rough guide to their contents and invariably there were omissions[8] and interpolations. It is sometimes assumed that blank

[1] There is a certain amount of information about the chequered career of the Worcester records in the post-Reformation period. An original letter of 1673 interleaved between folios 35 and 36 of Price's *Notitia* tells us of the damage caused by a recent fire: "Most of those register books which the late fire in our Audit-house had not quite consumed were so scorched and disfigured that 'twas not easy to find out what they were or without much tearing to turne to what was in them. . . ."

[2] The editor of Reg. Cobham states (p. v) that "the *registrum brevium* begins on fo. 37 and continues till the close of f. 44". In fact, there are only a few writs in this section. The bulk of them must have been kept separately and were subsequently lost.

[3] See above, pp. 3, n. 5. 4, n. 1.   [4] See below, pp. 133 et seq.

[5] Class B MSS. in the cathedral library have now been opened out and laid flat in boxes, but the original arrangement is quite clear.

[6] Some of those in a "miscellaneous" box in the diocesan registry have *inscribitur* or *registratur* written on the dorse in a contemporary hand, sometimes both words.

[7] Usually termed "Registrum" or "Quaternus".

[8] The scribe of Reg. Reynolds (fo. xxxi r.) frankly admitted: "Hic deficiunt nomina eorum qui fuerunt presentati per episcopum Lond' ad ordines suscipiendos."

quires were set aside for certain classes of entry and then filled up at intervals. No doubt this did happen, particularly in the case of royal writs, but such homogeneity is rare and normal practice could not have been so methodical. The scribe usually wrote up a mass of variegated material which had been roughly sorted into chronological order. As he wrote he passed through several quires[1] and added others as he thought fit. Sometimes he prefaced the entries with a special heading, but this did not necessarily coincide with any physical division of the register.

One can generalize to a certain extent about this matter of registration. It is very noticeable that an attempt was made to keep a separate quire of royal writs which was invariably placed at the end of a register.[2] It was of particular importance to have a copy of such writs because the originals were sent back with the bishop's return on the dorse. Moreover, new writs frequently referred back to earlier ones and it was necessary to know how a writ had been returned on a former occasion. When entering them in the register the scribe usually added the return underneath, but sometimes only the writs themselves were registered and spaces left for details of the returns. The ordination lists are scattered throughout the earlier registers, but they are grouped together in Register Orleton (1328–33), and this is the regular arrangement in subsequent registers. Apart from these two classes of entry there is much variation and not a little confusion. Commissions, licences, dispensations, and institutions are generally lumped together. Ordinations of vicarages and of chantries are often written out at great length, at other times omitted altogether,[3] and much the same can be said of the lengthy processes of monastic elections. In the fourteenth century the searcher of a Worcester register had to rely, apart from the very few sub-divisions of material, upon the chronological arrangement[4] and the frequent marginal rubrics. Only the massive register of Giffard and that of Cobham have rudimentary indexes of more or less contemporary date.

All this leads naturally to the question of the function and purpose of the registers. It may be said at once that they served not one purpose

[1] The word "quaternus" is used of the physical quaternion or quire as well as of the divisions of subject matter: for example, "quaternus de dimissoriis". The two seldom coincided.

[2] This is so in the registers of Gainsburgh, Reynolds, Montacute (Vol. 2), Hemenhale, Bransford (Vol. 1). The writs have slipped out of or were omitted from the registers of Maidstone, Cobham, and Orleton.

[3] Many of those omitted from the registers are recorded in the Liber Albus of the priory.

[4] Hence, many folios have the year A.D. or that of the bishop's consecration at the top.

but several. They are not formula books though they do enshrine much common form.[1] Doubtless, there were formula books for the use of episcopal clerks, and sometimes formal entries from some such source are to be found in the registers.[2] It is true that detailed commissions and processes recorded "in extenso" were invaluable as precedents, but the registers are not primarily precedent books. The fact that the marginal rubrics are impersonal should not be taken to imply that the clerks who wrote them were interested only in the general character of documents without reference to persons or places.[3] Otherwise, it would be hard to explain those of quite disproportionate length which are to be seen by the side of the most cryptic memoranda. Such *marginalia* were a practical expedient. Without them the task of finding any particular entry in a register would be extremely tedious, and there can be no doubt that this fact had much to do with their original purpose. The medieval clerk searching through a register was not, it may be suggested, so much interested in a person or place as in an entry about him or it. The marginal "Commissio", "Dimissorie" etc. told him at a glance what any particular entry was about, and if it was in the right category he looked more closely, if not, he passed on quickly to the next relevant rubric. This contemporary reliance on *marginalia* is particularly noticeable at Lincoln during Sutton's episcopate. Scalby, the registrar, wrote the rubrics himself and devised what Miss Hill describes as "an elaborate system of cross-referencing, by roll or by quire and folio, . . . sometimes reinforced by pen-and-ink drawings in the margin".[4] Worcester registers, however, have comparatively little cross-referencing and only occasional marginal signs.

Had the registers been primarily precedent books they would have borne an entirely different aspect and much needless repetition and duplication would have been avoided. Letters, charters, papal bulls,[5]

[1] The register of Romeyn, Archbishop of York, is prefaced by an index of such of its contents as might prove useful for common formulas: "Kalendarium registri domini J. Eboracensis archiepiscopi, de omnibus formis litterarum cursoriarum contentarum in eo." (*Reg. Romeyn* 2, pp. 179–90). See Hamilton Thompson, "Registers of the Archbishops of York", *Y.A.J.* 32, pp. 245–63 (esp. p. 249). Miss Hill suggests that the idea may have been inspired by a similar calendar in Sutton's register, for Romeyn had held the prebend of Nassington in Lincoln prior to his elevation. *Rot. & Reg. Sutton* 3, intro. p. xxxiv.

[2] For instance, the three letters at the end of Reg. Reynolds: "Littera de forma", "Littera formalis", and "Littera deprecatoria pro clerico beneficiando" (marginal rubrics).

[3] *English Clergy*, p. 8.

[4] *Rot. & Reg. Sutton* 3, intro. p. xxix.

[5] Some copies of bulls were carefully collated with the originals and a marginal note added to that effect. See, for instance, Reg. Montacute 1, ff. 11r., 12r.

wills[1], and other originals were copied because of their intrinsic importance, though the selection made was dependent, not upon any rigid system, but to a large extent upon the relative significance attached to particular documents by the person or persons responsible for each individual register. Doubtless, too, the bishop, and also his greater officers, directed that certain entries were to be made.[2] On the other hand, all ordination lists, institutions, licences, letters dimissory, and royal writs had to be recorded for both immediate and future factual reference,[3] although as every searcher of registers knows only too well, there are many lacunas due to inadvertence or carelessness.

Speculation should not be allowed to obscure the fact that a register was essentially a current compilation reflecting the multifarious acts of the diocesan:[4] a many-sided record, a repository of form as of fact, a reference book, and a means whereby administrative continuity was maintained.

SEALS

Sir William St John Hope, in an article on episcopal seals,[5] distinguished three main types commonly used for diocesan business: seals of dignity—for which there were sometimes counterseals, private seals or "secreta", and seals "ad causas". In the first category was the bishop's great seal which was appended to charters and important documents affecting the property or rights of the see. The "secretum" was reserved for deeds concerning the private estate of the bishop and the "signet" for sealing his personal correspondence.[6] Seals "ad causas" were used for documents of a transitory nature such as those connected with court business, letters testimonial or of orders, probates,

1 The number of wills to be found in the registers is small and declines rapidly during our period. There are none in Register Bransford (1339–49).

2 See p. 170 below, for an example of this.

3 There are many allusions to the searching of the registers for entries of this type. Letters testimonial were often issued after a successful scrutiny.

4 The debts of Maidstone no less than the money which Reynolds received as royal chancellor. To this day the term "Act Book" is used of an episcopal register.

5 *P.S.A.* XI (1887), pp. 271–306. Articles on episcopal seals are scattered, but for Durham see *Archaeologia* 72, pp. 1–24; for Salisbury, *Arch. Jnl.* 45, pp. 22–42; for Carlisle, ibid. 48, pp. 341–53; for Bath and Wells, *Som. Arch. & Nat. Hist. Soc.* 36, pp. 29–39. See also *English Bishops' Chanceries*, pp. 47–51; H. S. Kingsford, "The Epigraphy of Medieval English Seals", *Archaeologia* 79, pp. 149–78. J. H. Bloom gives an incomplete list of Worcester episcopal seals in *Official Seals of the Diocese of Worcester* (1922), pp. 1–8.

6 Examples from Durham diocese of all these types of seals are illustrated in *Archaeologia* 72, pp. 1–24.

and others for which no special seal was in use. But these divisions were not always rigidly observed. For instance, it has been suggested that two fifteenth-century bishops of Durham, Thomas Langley and Robert Neville, made their seals "ad causas" do duty for seals of dignity.[1]

That the bishops of Worcester had at least three seals in the four-teenth century is clear from the registers. Thus Bishops Gainsburgh and Reynolds, in accordance with regular practice, had impressions of their great seals appended to certain letters of caption;[2] while Maid-stone issued an acquittance to his sequestrator, Stephen de Northeye, "sub privato sigillo nostro".[3] Cobham's will was sealed with his great seal and another seal "ad causas", [4] and in 1349, at the end of Brans-ford's episcopate, Thomas atte Mulle had a letter of appointment to the bailiffship of Oswaldslow "sub sigillo domini ad causas".[5]

Ordinarily the chancellor had custody of two of the episcopal seals, but other arrangements must have been made during the not infre-quent absences of this officer. There is a memorandum of the handing of Gainsburgh's seals to Walter de Wotton,[6] and those of Bishop Hemenhale were said to have been carried about by his chancellor, Andrew Offord, who was believed to have taken them out of the diocese after the bishop's death.[7]

The letters which Montacute issued from Oxford and Crookham (Berkshire) prior to his consecration were sealed with the seal of his archdeaconry of Canterbury and later with that of the officiality of Worcester.[8] This latter seal was always claimed by the prior at the beginning of a vacancy and at the end surrendered to the commissaries

---

[1] *Archaeologia* 72, p. 8.

[2] *Reg. Gainsburgh*, fo. 10r., p. 26 (also p. 27); *Reg. Reynolds*, ff. 19v., 22r., pp. 14, 17. The originals of such letters were filed among the Chancery records (P.R.O. Signifi-cavits of Excommunication C.85). In the British Museum are casts of the (great) seals of Bishops Giffard (1278 and 1283), Gainsburgh (n.d.), Cobham (n.d.), Orleton (1333), Montacute (1334), and Bransford (1348). Birch, *Cat. of Seals* 1, Nos. 2279–81; B.M. *Cat. Add. MSS.* 1888–93, p. 380 lxxxvii No. 40; 1900–5, p. 428 cxlvi Nos. 21, 22; ibid., p. 435 cl No. 16.

[3] Reg. Maidstone, fo. 41r.: 23 December 1315.

[4] *Reg. Cobham*, fo. 45, p. 50. "Et vidi testamentum domini T. de Cobeham quondam episcopi Wygorniensis sub sigillis eiusdem magno et alio ad causas cera viridi sub signo magistri Roberti de Checwelle notarii publici ... Ledebury." Richard de Ledbury was Bishop Montacute's notary in 1335, the date of the inspection of the will.

[5] Reg. Bransford 2, fo. 2r. (1332): 30 June 1349.

[6] See p. 125, n. 2 below.   [7] See p. 125, n. 5 below.

[8] "Dat. Oxon. sub sigillo officii nostri archidiaconatus Cantuar."; "Done au Crokeham ... desouz le seal de nostre officiaute de Wyrcestr."; ". . . sigillum officiali-tatis consistorii nostri Wygorn. quo utimur in presenti fecimus hiis apponi" etc. Reg. Mont., *passim*.

of the new bishop.[1] The prior when acting as official *sede vacante* would seem to have had a special seal of office.[2]

Cardinal Otto enumerated certain authentic seals,[3] among them those of officials, of archdeacons and their officials, and of rural deans. He also drew a distinction between the seals of those who held a temporary office and those who held a permanent office or dignity. The seal of a temporary officer, which had to be surrendered to the person from whom it had been received whenever the office was relinquished,[4] incorporated the name of the office only,[5] that of a perpetual officer had in addition a personal name. There is frequent mention in the Worcester registers of the seal of the officiality and of the seals of office used by the archdeacons' officials and by rural deans, but very few impressions have survived.[6] On occasion someone whose seal was not well known, and in the fourteenth century quite humble persons boasted seals of their own, secured the addition of that of a rural dean or archdeacon's official. When, for example, John Freond, a citizen of Worcester, quitclaimed a tenement to the prior and convent there, he appended his own seal and that of the Christianity of Worcester to the document.[7] In the ordination lists titles are sometimes said

---

1 See chapter 5 below.

2 To the commission which he issued in 1339 for the appointment of certain persons to act on his behalf Prior Wolstan appended the "sigillum officialitatis Wygorn' sede vacante". R.S.V. fo. 151v.

3 *Const. Othonis*, tit: "De Sigillis Authenticis" (Athon, pp. 67 et seq.).

4 A point made by Benedict de Paston when he refused to send the seal of the officiality to the prior directly but suggested that the latter should have livery of it through the former bishop, Reynolds, from whom he (Paston) had originally received it. *R.S.V.*, fo. 8ov., p. 138.

5 "Denique illi, qui temporale officium suscipiunt, puta, Decani Rurales & Officiales, sigillum suum, quod tantum nomen officii habeat insculptum, finito officio, ei, a quo habuerint officium, continuo & sine molestia resignent." Op. cit., p. 69. Foster ("The Activities of Rural Deans", pp. 153–4) notes that seven of the seals of rural deans recorded in Birch's *Catalogue* have personal inscriptions contrary to Otto's statute, but suggests that they may have been private ones.

6 The provocation drawn up on behalf of the Worcester priory in 1266 had no fewer than nine pendant seals, including those of the rural deans of Gloucester, Tewkesbury, Stow, and Campden. Only the seal tags remain. D. & C. MS. B. 1612. With the exception of one thirteenth-century seal of an archdeacon and one of a diocesan official (1299: Birch No. 2292, attached to B.M. Cott. ch. viii 23, probate of J. Brommore's will) there is no record of medieval seals from the Worcester diocese, other than episcopal ones, in Birch or the B.M. Add. MSS. catalogues. But J. H. Bloom (*Official Seals of the Diocese of Worcester*, pp. 9, 11), also notes fifteenth-century seals of an archdeacon's official and of the peculiars of Ripple (*c.* 1400), Hartlebury, Stratford, and Tredington.

7 D. & C. MS. B. 1661. ". . . sigillum meum apposui et sigillum officii decanatus Wygorn' procuravi apponi" (1335). The rural dean's seal is damaged but the inscription seems to have been [S]IG[ILLUM] XTI[ANIT]ATIS [W]IGORNIE.

to have been vouched for under the seal of the diocesan official, an archdeacon's official, or a rural dean. But whereas at the time of Otto's constitutions there had been no English notaries public,[1] so that much stress had to be laid on the authenticity of certain seals, this was by no means the case in the fourteenth century. Many documents copied into the registers were originally notarially attested and the names of notaries occur frequently.[2] The "public instrument" had become essential for certain formal processes, such as monastic elections, but for ordinary administrative purposes the authentic seal of a local officer, well known to the bishop and his staff, retained an important place.

[1] "Quoniam tabellionum usus in regno Angliae non habetur propter quod magis ad sigilla authentica recurrere est necesse" (op. cit., pp. 67–8). Athon glosses (ad ver. *non habetur*): "Id est rarus habetur".

[2] See below, pp. 133 et seq.

2

LOCAL ADMINISTRATION

THE EXTENT AND DIVISIONS OF THE DIOCESE

The medieval diocese of Worcester extended for some eighty miles from north to south, its greatest width being about half that distance.[1] It included Worcestershire, save for those parishes in the west of the county which were in Hereford diocese, where they were part of the deanery of Burford in the archdeaconry of Salop;[2] a portion of Warwickshire—the remainder of which formed the archdeaconry of Coventry in the diocese of Coventry and Lichfield; as well as Gloucestershire east of the River Severn.

There were two archdeaconries. That of Worcester comprised the county of that name with its deaneries of Worcester, Powick, Pershore, (Droit)wich,[3] Kidderminster, and Blockley, as well as that portion of Warwickshire within the diocese, divided into the deaneries of Kineton and Warwick. A ninth deanery, of the Vale of Evesham, had become exempt from the jurisdiction of the Worcester bishops by the middle of the thirteenth century. The archdeaconry of Gloucester was divided into the eleven deaneries of Gloucester, Stonehouse, Dursley, Bristol, Bitton, Hawkesbury, Cirencester, Fairford, Stow, Winchcomb, and Campden. Hawkesbury and Bitton were often treated as a single deanery in the fourteenth century and they are amalgamated as Hawkesbury deanery in the sixteenth-century Valor.[4] Within the confines of the Gloucester archdeaconry lay the exempt area of Churchdown.

EXEMPT JURISDICTIONS

In most, if not in all English dioceses, there were areas of "exempt" or

[1] The map which precedes the text has been specially drawn by Ian Ross. Other maps of the medieval diocese are to be found in the *R.S.V.* (before the general introduction) and the *Map of Monastic Britain* (South Sheet), published by the Ordnance Survey (2nd ed., 1954).

[2] For the names of these parishes see *Valor Eccles.* 3, pp. 279–80.

[3] Prior to 1350 few instances of the prefix are to be found. It is said to be derived from ME. "drit" (dirt), possibly because of the low-lying muddy ground, or on account of the salt pans. See *E.P.N.S. Worcs.*, pp. 285–7 and *O.E.D.*   [4] Vol. 2, pp. 491–2.

"peculiar" jurisdiction.[1] There were royal and archiepiscopal or episcopal peculiars, those of deans and chapters, of monasteries, as well as prebendal and rectorial ones.[2] They can be divided broadly into peculiars exempt from episcopal jurisdiction and those exempt only from that of the archdeacon. The number and variety which might exist in a single diocese is well illustrated by Professor Hamilton Thompson's account of the ecclesiastical divisions of Yorkshire,[3] and the same author draws elsewhere an amusing picture of the bishops of Chichester, beset by three peculiars in their own cathedral city.[4] As late as 1832 there were two hundred and eighty-five courts of peculiars in England and Wales.[5]

In the Worcester diocese the peculiars of Evesham and Churchdown were enclaves, geographically within its limits but in no way subject to the bishop's ordinary jurisdiction. Within their confines the officer exercising the peculiar jurisdiction issued letters dimissory and ecclesiastical licences, returned royal writs, and appointed persons answerable to himself to carry out judicial and administrative functions. On the other hand, there were areas, exempt from the archdeacon's authority but subject to the bishop, which had their own deans of jurisdiction, capitular or rural, who exercised powers which were archidiaconal in character and to whom the bishop's mandates were regularly directed. Within this category were the episcopal manors. In addition there were the exempt religious houses. These recognized the bishop as diocesan, their heads taking an oath of obedience to him, but they did not admit him at times of diocesan visitation or permit his interference in their internal affairs.

The total number of exempt churches was considerable. Price in his Notitia listed well over fifty in the Worcester archdeaconry (including dependent chapels and the churches of the Vale of Evesham),[6] and

1 The terms "iurisdiccio exempta" and "iurisdiccio peculiaris" were often used interchangeably.

2 See C. S. Perceval in *P.S.A.* 2nd ser., 5, pp. 238–50.

3 *V.C.H. Yorks.* 3, pp. 80–8. For instance, in the archdeaconry of York and the West Riding, there was the archbishop's liberty of Ripon, various parishes belonging to the dean and chapter of York, others in the jurisdiction of dignitaries and prebendaries of York, and the churches of Selby and Snaith, which were subject to the abbot and convent of Selby.   4 *English Clergy*, p. 75.

5 *Eccles. Cts. Rpt.* 1832, p. 552. They fell into the following categories: royal, 11; archiepiscopal and episcopal, 14; decanal and subdecanal, 44; prebendal, 88; rectorial and vicarial, 63; others, 17; manorial (mainly monastic in origin), 48. Frere, *Visit. Articles* 1, App. 2, pp. 172–86 prints a return of peculiars made in 1563 which omits the dioceses of York, Oxford, Bristol, and Gloucester.

6 Fo. 36 and fo. ii preceding the text. Cf. the 1563 return in Frere, *Visit. Articles* 1, App. 2, pp. 182–3.

there is a list for the southern archdeaconry in Rudder's *New History of Gloucestershire*.[1] In the early nineteenth century there were still five peculiar jurisdictions in the Gloucester (formerly Worcester) diocese,[2] and a further ten, not including Evesham, involving twenty parishes, in that of Worcester.[3]

The peculiars of Churchdown and Evesham

Professor Hamilton Thompson traced the origin and subsequent history of the peculiar of Churchdown, entries about which occur every now and then in the York archiepiscopal registers.[4] It was made up of the parish of St Oswald's in the suburbs of Gloucester with its small prebends and appropriated churches of Churchdown, Norton, Sandhurst, and Compton Abdale, to the north and east of that town. St. Oswald's, which may have been a pre-Conquest minster,[5] became subject to the archbishops of York in the middle of the reign of William Rufus as the result of the settlement of a dispute between successive archbishops and the bishops of Lincoln.[6] It was reconstituted as a house of Augustinian canons in 1153.[7] By the fourteenth century it was considered to be a free chapel under the immediate jurisdiction of the Crown.[8]

The spiritual and temporal officers of the jurisdiction were deputed by the archbishops of York who also appointed the prior of St Oswald's. The spiritual officer was called dean or warden, and was probably the same person as the later official.[9]

[1] 1799 ed., p. 154.

[2] Childs Wickham (although the jurisdiction consisted only in a concurrent right with the diocesan chancellor of granting probate); Bibury, Withington, Bishop's Cleeve (all exempt from archidiaconal visitation); Deerhurst (confined to the right to be visited by the archdeacon within the peculiar). *Valor Eccles.* 2, App. p. 512; cf. *Eccles. Cts. Rpt.* 1832, p. 552.

[3] Nine of the peculiars were ancient episcopal manors, the tenth, consisting of seven parishes, belonged to the Dean and Chapter. *Valor Eccles.* 3, App. p. 512; *Eccles. Cts. Rpt.* 1832, pp. 336, 552. The peculiar jurisdictions were made subject to the diocesan by Order in Council, in accordance with the recommendations of the 1832 Royal Commission. A number of the courts continued to exercise testamentary jurisdiction until this was transferred to the Court of Probate in 1858 (Alvechurch, Bibury, Bishop's Cleeve, Bredon, Evesham, Fladbury, Hampton Lucy, Hanbury, Hartlebury, Ripple, Stratford, Tredington). *Eccles. Cts.* 1954; G. W. Marshall, *Handbook to the Ancient Courts of Probate and Depositories of Wills* (1895).

[4] *Trans. B. & G.A.S.* XLIII (1921), pp. 85–180; cf. the same author in *A.A.S.R.P.* XXXIII, p. 40. R.R. Darlington (*Vita Wulstani, Camd. Soc.* 3rd ser., XL, p. xxvi, n. 4) criticizes Hamilton Thompson's suggestions as to the origin of this jurisdiction.

[5] *Trans. B. & G.A.S.* XLIII, p. 90; *Monasticon* 6, p. 82.

[6] Op. cit., pp. 96–7.   [7] Op. cit., p. 98; *Monasticon* 6, p. 82.

[8] Op. cit., p. 90 and n. 3; *Monasticon* 6 (3), p. 1467.

[9] Op. cit., p. 98; *Monasticon* 6, p. 82.

3

At the beginning of our period the jurisdiction was assailed by both diocesan and metropolitan. Cantilupe seems to have celebrated orders at St Oswald's without opposition,[1] but when in 1300 the bishop of Llandaff attempted to do so on behalf of Giffard, the prior resisted, claiming that it would be prejudicial to the rights of the archbishops of York. Giffard promptly excommunicated the priory's officers.[2] Complaint was made to the king and Giffard was summoned to appear before him, but died meanwhile. His successor, Gainsburgh, also seems to have attempted to exercise his authority there, but a royal prohibition was issued on the grounds that St Oswald's was a royal free chapel exempt from the jurisdiction of the ordinary. The bishop persisted and presented two petitions against the priory at the Carlisle parliament of 1307.[3]

Meanwhile, Archbishop Winchelsey had also become involved in a dispute with St Oswald's. After an unsuccessful attempt to visit the place in 1301, he had launched sentence of excommunication against the recalcitrant prior and canons. Royal aid was again invoked but the dispute was not allayed until 1353 when a compromise was reached by Archbishops Islep and Thoresby.[4]

Giffard's attacks stiffened the attitude of the priory. Since his excommunication of the canons they had boycotted the Pentecostal procession at Gloucester, holding a separate one within the jurisdiction. Moreover, Archbishop Corbridge of York (1300–4) forbade the prior to receive the chrism or oil from the Worcester bishops, a custom that had been adopted for convenience' sake, or to pay Pentecostals or Peter's Pence other than to the dean of the jurisdiction.[5]

St Oswald's remained in the possession of the archbishops of York until 1545, when it was exchanged with Henry VIII for other property.[6]

The Evesham peculiar was much greater in extent. The Benedictine abbey of Evesham had secured exemption from the authority of the diocesan in 1206. The churches of the Vale, with the exception of

---

1 *Ann. Wigorn.*, p. 434.

2 The editor of Giffard's register states that the bishop appointed Robert of Gloucester (his official) and John de Rodberrow "to visit" the priory. In fact they were empowered merely to proceed against its officers for their disobedience. *Reg. Giffard* fo. 425r., pp. 531–2.

3 *C.C.R.* 1296–1302, pp. 191–2; Raine, *Historians of the Church of York* 3, pp. 223–6.

4 Raine, loc. cit.; *Cant. Reg. Winch.*, pp. 810–11; *Concilia* 3, pp. 31–2. See also Rose Graham, "Metropolitical Visit. of the Diocese of Worcester", in *English Eccles. Studies*, p. 347. Douie (*Archbishop Pecham*, pp. 232–3) comments that "after Winchelsey's spectacular failure no archbishop of Canterbury tried to claim jurisdiction over St Oswald's".

5 Raine, loc. cit.   6 *English Clergy*, pp. 3–4.

Abbot's Morton, were finally exempted in 1248.[1] From that date the deanery of Evesham, though nominally within the diocese, went out of the bishops' control.[2] At the Reformation the jurisdiction passed to Christ Church, Oxford, and though challenged on at least one occasion,[3] it survived until 1851 when it was abolished by an Order in Council.[4]

The episcopal manors

Information about the exemption from archidiaconal jurisdiction of the churches of episcopal manors, or those in the bishop's collation, can rarely be found in episcopal registers, although the existence of such exemption may sometimes be inferred from the appointment of special commissaries to carry out induction in place of the archdeacon or rural dean.[5]

In Canterbury diocese the fourteenth-century Black Book of the Archdeacon records twenty-eight exempt parishes.[6] Langton had attempted to subject them to the archdeacon, but Pecham recognized the jurisdiction both of the exempt parishes and of all churches in his collation. In the fourteenth century the number of such jurisdictions varied according to the grants and revocations made by individual archbishops.[7] There were similar autonomous parishes in Winchester diocese. According to the synodal constitutions attributed to Bishop John Gervais (1262–8),[8] archdeacons were forbidden to exact procuration from, or to visit, churches in episcopal collation. The rectors and vicars of such churches were not to attend the archdeacon's chapters

---

[1] *Chronicon Abb. de Evesham.*, pp. xxvi–xxviii and p. 198; Liber Ruber, ff. 49v., 55r., 101–2; Nash 2, pp. 178–9. The abbey conceded to the Worcester bishops the churches of Hillingdon (Middx.), Weston, and Kinwarton. The charter of Henry III confirming this concession, dated 17 November 1265, is now in the custody of the County Archivist (formerly Misc. Charters F. 7 al. 213). An account of the affair is given by Knowles, *The Monastic Order in England*, chap. 19, and another by Coulton, *Five Centuries of Religion* 2, chaps. 24, 25. The papal decisions are incorporated in *Extra.* 5, 33, c.17, and 1, 41, c.3.

[2] Price (Notitia Dioec. Wigorn., fo. 36) lists the following exempt churches in the deanery: Badsey and Aldington; Bengeworth; Bretforton; Broadway; Church Honeybourne; Evesham St Lawrence; Evesham All Saints; Great Hampton; North, Middle, and South Littleton; Norton and Lenchwick; Offenham; Wickhamford.

[3] For example, at the end of the sixteenth century. See Nash 1, pp. 415, 422; Frere, *Visit. Articles* 1, App. 2, p. 182.   [4] *Chron. Abb. de Evesham.*, p. xxviii, n. 1.

[5] In 1832 there were sixty-three courts of peculiars attached to rectories and vicarages in England and Wales: forty-five of them in Winchester diocese, nine (excluding Evesham) in that of Worcester. *Eccles. Cts. Rpt.*, p. 552.

[6] Listed in Churchill 1, p. 109, n. 3. Cf. Woodcock (*Eccles. Cts.*, p. 21) who gives the number as "some twenty-five churches and chapels".

[7] See Woodcock, pp. 21–5; Churchill 1, pp. 83–94.

[8] Cheney, *English Synodalia*, pp. 105–7.

or to respond to his citation. They were to have correction of lesser offences "secundum antiquam consuetudinem" but were not to meddle with matrimonial or other greater causes, or to permit unskilled chaplains or farmers ("firmarii") to deal on their behalf with the lesser ones.[1] At Norwich, according to Blomefield, the bishops appointed a commissary and official of the peculiar jurisdiction of their manors.[2]

Some modern editors of Worcester registers were unaware that similar jurisdictions formerly existed in the diocese.[3] However, as long ago as the late seventeenth century, John Price,[4] who showed a great interest in details of diocesan administration, had written: "It is manifest that the churches belonging to the antient manors of the Bishoprick were never subject to the Archdeacon." He added that this was true of all the churches which the bishop possessed at that time as well as those which had been alienated.[5]

Among the articles of inquiry drawn up by Bishop Giffard in 1276 was one about deans of exempt jurisdictions. It was to be ascertained whether they rendered an account of their perquisites at the appointed times, and whether they carried out corrections without exception of persons as their office required.[6]

The course of such jurisdiction did not always run smoothly. In 1303 Walter, rector of Bredon, complained to Bishop Gainsburgh that when the dean of the place was prepared for the correction of souls and the celebration of the chapter, certain sons of iniquity had burst into the church with vociferous clamour and no little violence and prevented him. They had appointed the dean's official and new apparitors in contempt of God and of ecclesiastical liberty. Not content with that, they had laid violent and sacrilegious hands on certain of his ministers and clerks in the church and graveyard, carried off their

---

1 *Winch. Reg. Pontissara*, p. 234. It may be that the frequent direction of mandates to persons other than the archdeacon or his official commented on (intro. p. xxxii) by the editor of *Winch. Reg. Woodlock* (1305–16) can be partly explained by the existence of these peculiars. Where the bishop was patron the mandate for induction was sent almost invariably either to the rural dean, the diocesan official, a local rector or vicar, or to some other *ad hoc* commissary. In one instance (op. cit., p. 742) the reason is expressly given: "quia exempta est". A large number of Winchester peculiars survived until the nineteenth century: see above, p. 17, n. 5.

2 *Norfolk* 4, p. 554.

3 For example R. A. Wilson in his introduction to *Register Reynolds* (p. iv).

4 Appointed chancellor of the diocese in 1696, he died in 1705. Nash 2, p. clxviii.

5 Notitia, fo. 36.

6 Reg. Giffard, fo. 68r. (out of order): "Item, utrum decani locorum huiusmodi exemptorum de suis perquisitis in generali compoto statutis temporibus plenam sicut decet reddiderint racionem. Et utrum correcciones egerint absque accepcionibus personarum prout eorum officium id requirit."

goods, and in other ways violated ecclesiastical liberty.[1] The bishop ordered the official of the archdeacon of Worcester and the dean of Pershore to pronounce the malefactors excommunicate.[2]

The rector of Stratford is stated to have had special jurisdiction within his parish with the power to institute and remove the incumbents of dependent churches or chapels—the rector of Wilmcote and the perpetual vicars of Bishopton and Luddington. All these rights were reserved to the warden of the newly founded chantry to which Stratford church was appropriated in 1336.[3]

Such references in the episcopal registers to the workings of exempt deaneries are rare, but much more is known about that of Bibury in Gloucestershire owing to the preservation of many relevant documents in the cartulary of Oseney Abbey.[4] The church of Bibury, an episcopal manor, had been given to the canons of Oseney by Bishop John de Pagham in 1151.[5] The grant included the dependent chapels of Barnsley—soon to become a parish church, Winson, Aldsworth, and Arlington. Bishop John de Constantiis (1196–8)[6] allowed the church to be served by one of the Oseney canons who was to be resident and to have the cure of souls together with all liberties, free customs, and jurisdictions enjoyed by other churches of episcopal manors. At each vacancy a canon was to be presented to the bishop for institution.[7]

---

[1] "Querelam domini Walteri rectoris ecclesie de Bredon recepimus continentem, quod quidam iniquitatis filii quorum nomina ignor[antur] ad ecclesiam suam de Bredon cum fastu et impetu quasi furibundo nuper ausu nephario accedentes, ipsam ecclesiam domum dei cum vociferacione clamosa et non modica violencia intraverunt et dec[anum] loci correccionem animarum et celebracionem capituli intendentem quominus in hiis officium suum exequi posset ut deberet impedire dampnabiliter presumpserunt, officialem decani et appparitores novos in contemptum dei et libertatis ecclesiastice preficiendo, et hiis iniuriis non contenti peccata peccatis accumulantes, in quosdam ministros ipsius et clericos in dicta ecclesia et cimiterio eiusdem manus sacrilegias iniecerunt temere viol[entas], bona ad ipsos ministros spectancia ab ipsa ecclesia asportando, ac alias libertatem ecclesiasticam multipliciter violando . . ."

[2] Reg. Gainsburgh, fo. 15v., p. 43. 7 December 1303.

[3] ". . . quorum institucio et destitucio ad rectorem dicte ecclesie de Stretford de consuetudine prescripta pertinuit ab antiquo"; "iurisdiccionem specialem in parochia dicte ecclesie cum potestate instituendi et destituendi rectores et vicarios ecclesiarum seu capellarum dicte ecclesie subiectarum ac beneficia ecclesiastica conferendi sicut easdem iurisdiccionem potestatem et collacionem rectores dicte ecclesie habere et excercere solebant temporibus retroactis." Reg. Montacute 1, ff. 51v., 53r.

[4] Cart. of Oseney Abbey V, ed. H. E. Salter, O.H.S. XCVIII (1935), p. lxxiii and pp. 1–38, nos. 511–48.   [5] Ibid., pp. 1–2, no. 511.

[6] His successor, Bishop Mauger, was not consecrated until 1200 owing to the rejection by the archbishop of his election. This misled H. E. Salter into dating the entries from the episcopate of John de Constantiis 1196–1200 (for example nos. 515B, 520), though the bishop had died 24 September 1198 (Thomas, Account, p. 121).

[7] Op. cit., pp. 9–10, no. 520: ". . . curam animarum parochie dicte ecclesie habere, tam libere, plene & integre, cum omnibus libertatibus & liberis consuetudinibus &

Bibury remained subject to the diocesan in the same manner as other exempt deaneries of its type. In the original grant and in later confirmations his rights were specifically excepted.[1] The bishops of Worcester or their officials were entitled to visit Bibury and to exact procuration there,[2] but it is difficult to find an instance of their having done so.[3]

In 1347 and 1348 Henry de Neubold, Bransford's sequestrator and receiver, acknowledged the receipt of ten shillings from Brother Thomas de Mamesfield, the warden (*custos*) of Bibury.[4] This was stated to be an annual sum due to the bishop for the jurisdiction.[5]

The Oseney Cartulary also contains two thirteenth-century instances of sentences of excommunication inflicted "ordinaria potestate" by the wardens of Bibury because of non-payment of mortuary dues.[6] In each

---

iurisdiccionibus, sicut dicta ecclesia unquam habuit, & sicut alie ecclesie maneriorum nostrorum habere consueverunt temporibus retroactis. . . ." Such institutions are regularly to be found in the episcopal registers. In Register Reynolds there is a rare instance of admission for a limited period only. On 30 January 1312 Bishop Reynolds admitted (there is no mention of institution) Brother Hugh de Compton, a canon of Oseney, to exercise the cure of souls at Bibury "usque ad festum Pentecost' proximo futurum (14 May), nisi interim huiusmodi gracia fuerit revocata; sub hac protestacione, quod dominus protestabatur se per huiusmodi graciam nolle iuri abbatis et conventus Osen' ipsum ad dictam ecclesiam presentancium aut iuri suo in aliquo derogari" (fo. 42v.).

1 Ibid., no. 511, "salvo per omnia iure episcopali"; no. 512, "salvo iure diocesani"; no. 512A, "salvo in omnibus [iure] diocesani episcopi" etc.

2 Ibid., no. 519 (13 November 1276) ". . . salvis nichilominus visitacione & procuracione . . . officialis Wigorniensis qui pro tempore fuerit, quando predictam ecclesiam de Beiburia visitare continget . . ."; and no. 524 (18 October 1285) ". . . in qua & in aliis ecclesiis consimilibus quibuscumque, religiosis appropriatis, episcopus Wigorniensis, qui pro tempore fuerit, de consuetudine hactenus optenta & approbata diucius in sua diocesi ex cura pastorali, que sibi incumbere dinoscitur, visitacionis officium per se vel per suum officialem annis singulis licite poterit exercere. . . ."

3 Willis Bund in his introduction to the *R.S.V.* (pp. viii–ix) assumes that the prior *sede vacante* had no jurisdiction there. This may not have been so in theory, even though there is no record of a prior having visited Bibury. Only chance has preserved a mandate giving warning of the intended visitation in 1302 of the similarly exempt jurisdiction of Alvechurch (L.A. fo. xii v). Moreover, when Stratford church was appropriated to the chantry there, the prior and chapter's jurisdiction was specifically safeguarded: "salva eciam potestate priori et capitulo supradictis sede Wygorn' vacante visitandi capellam et ecclesiam de Stretford predictas ac clerum et populum earundem ac ibidem iurisdiccionem omnimodam excercendi sicut in huiusmodi vacacione dum dicta ecclesia de Stretford dudum per rectorem fuerit gubernata excercere solebant" (Reg. Montacute 1, fo. 53r.). Yet we know that Blockley deanery neither paid procuration nor was visited by the prior between 1300 and 1350. Perhaps, then, such jurisdiction did secure in practice a substantial immunity from priorial visitation.

4 He was instituted 30 November 1339. Reg. Bransford, fo. 11r.–v., (98).

5 *Oseney Cart.* V, p. 9, no. 519A.   6 Ibid., pp. 27–8, 37–8, nos. 539, 548.

case the bishop's official confirmed the sentence "auctoritate ordinaria".[1]

It was usual for the warden of Bibury to exercise the office of penitentiary among his subjects, the bishop issuing his commission at the time of admission to the cure or shortly afterwards.[2]

In 1354 the jurisdiction was challenged when a dispute arose between Richard of Ledbury, the archdeacon of Gloucester, and the abbot and convent of Oseney, about the former's claim to induct the rector of Barnsley by archidiaconal right,[3] although that church lay within the territory of Bibury.[4] The archdeacon, "de iure et possessione antiqua dictorum religiosorum in ea parte plenius informati", renounced his claim to archidiaconal jurisdiction in Barnsley and acknowledged the right of the canons to induct the rector.[5]

It is clear from the Worcester registers that it was customary for mandates for induction to benefices within exempt deaneries, or to those which were in the bishop's collation, to be sent to the dean of the jurisdiction or to special commissaries,[6] rather than to the archdeacons or their officials.[7] None the less, a close study of the registers

---

[1] On the subject of the greater and lesser ordinaries Lyndwood glosses (ad ver. *ordinarii*, p. 16): "Nota quod haec dictio 'ordinarius' principaliter habet locum de Episcopo & aliis superioribus, qui soli sunt universales in suis jurisdictionibus . . . sed sunt sub eo alii ordinarii, hi videlicet quibus competit jurisdictio ordinaria de jure, privilegio, vel consuetudine."

[2] For example, when Brother Hugh de Compton was admitted (see above, p. 19, n. 7). "Et habuit litteras admissionis etc. Et commissum fuit sibi officium penitenciarie verbotenus in parochia sua et de parochianis predictis secundum quod predecessori suo committebatur" (Reg. Reynolds, fo. 42v.).

[3] In 1341 the mandate for induction had been sent as usual to the dean of Bibury: ". . . scriptum fuit decano de Bybury custodi iurisdiccionis exempte eiusdem loci ad ipsum rectorem vel ipsius procuratorem in corporalem dicte ecclesie possessionem inducendum" (Reg. Bransford, fo. 50r. (431).)

[4] ". . . super induccione iure archidiaconali rectoris capelle de Baindesle (*recte* "Barndesle") infra territorium dicte ecclesie de Bibury notorie constitute & a iurisdictione nostra archidiaconali totaliter exempte orta fuisset materia questionis . . ."

[5] *Oseney Cart.* V, p. 29, no. 539A. Ledbury, 28 December 1354.

[6] So far as can be judged from the printed registers of other dioceses—in many of which entries of institutions are summarized in English or tabulated, the practice of appointing special commissaries for institutions to benefices in episcopal collation was not so regularly followed as at Worcester.

[7] Cf. Chancellor Price's seventeenth-century comments (Notitia fo. 77): "Some are of the opinion that where or when the archdeacon has no jurisdiction the mandate for induction should not be directed to him, but to the Vicar General or his surrogate. Such was the practice before the Reformation when the Canon Law was better understood, the mandate being directed either to the Bishop's Vicar General, Sequestrator General, Commissary for Probate of Wills & Corrections, or Official of the Consistory, all of which officers are now united in the Chancellor."

would undoubtedly reveal a number of exceptions to this general rule.[1]

It was also at Barnsley that the testamentary jurisdiction of the Bibury dean was assailed, this time by Bishop Bransford. On 9 August 1341 the will of Thomas de Rysele, rector of Barnsley, was proved before the diocesan official, acting as the bishop's special commissary, and the administration was committed to the executors named therein. Probate before the dean of Bibury and his commission to the executors were declared null "tanquam facta per eum ad quem eadem facere non pertinuit".[2] On the other hand, when John Roger(s), chaplain, died intestate in the parish of Ripple, and no one could be found to exercise the jurisdiction of the rector, the same bishop ordered the dean of Pershore to sequestrate his goods, but he wished it to be made known that it was not his intention to usurp the jurisdiction.[3]

It seems likely that a rector's interest in his rights of jurisdiction was mainly financial in character. Those who, in 1325, inquired into the vacancy of the chapel at Shell could not say whether it was annexed to or dependent upon the church of Hanbury, but they did know that the rector of Hanbury corrected the excesses of the rector and parishioners of the chapel and had the burial rights together with half the mortuary dues.[4] In 1312, one of the articles objected against Robert de Wych, rector of Alvechurch, was that he had received a pecuniary penalty for notorious faults and excesses contrary to the constitutions of the Fathers.[5] When Robert de Chigwell farmed his church of Bredon to

[1] During Bransford's episcopate mandates for induction to the churches of Ripple (in 1343) and Withington (in 1349)—both episcopal manors with deans of jurisdiction—were sent to the official of the Gloucester archdeacon. Ripple, it is true, was in the Worcester archdeaconry, but it is possible that the scribe meant to write "Worcester". If the original mandate was in fact directed to the official of the Gloucester archdeacon it merely provides another *ad hoc* case and not an exception. But it would be hard to find further *ad hoc* mandates of this type addressed to the official of the other archdeacon. Reg. Bransford., fo. 64v.; 2, fo. 19v.; (571, 1566). Bishop Cobham often directed mandates for induction, even to churches of episcopal manors, to the local rural deans, but this was clearly contrary to the usual practice in the diocese. See the printed edition of Cobham's register, App. 1, pp. 228 et seq.

[2] Reg. Bransford fo. 50r. (425).

[3] Reg. Bransford, fo. 27r. (180): 29 April 1339. "Denuncies eciam illis quorum interest quod non est intencionis nostre iurisdiccionem rectoris de Rippel per premissa nobis usurpare sed defectum dicti rectoris suplere ista vice." John Roger(s) himself may have been acting as dean.

[4] "An sit annexa vel dependens ab ecclesia de Hambur' ignorat inquisicio, nisi q[uod] rector ecclesie de Hambur' corrigit excessus rectoris dicte capelle et parochianorum eiusdem [&c.]." (Reg. Cobham, fo. 104r.). Pearce, in his edition of Cobham's register (p. 244, n. 3, q.v.), read "inquirat" for "ignorat" and "quoque" for "quod".

[5] "Obicimus eciam tibi Roberto predicto quod tu in parochia de Alvechirch iuris-

Bishop Thoresby in 1351 he stipulated that the latter should protect the jurisdiction and not permit his officers or ministers to violate it.[1]

Little can be gleaned from the episcopal registers about the appointment or removal of deans of exempt jurisdiction. It is reasonably certain, however, that they were appointed by the rectors to whom such jurisdiction belonged and were removable at their will, though in practice remaining in office during good behaviour. The fact that the mandate for induction to the church of an episcopal manor was sometimes sent to the dean of the jurisdiction, suggests that his tenure of office was not terminated when the rector to whom he owed his appointment vacated the benefice.[2] In all these respects the dean of an exempt jurisdiction was in an analogous position *vis à vis* the rector to that of the ordinary rural dean *vis à vis* the bishop.

We have already noted one instance of episcopal action to ensure the exercise of jurisdiction.[3] Another is recorded in 1340, a time when the church of Blockley was farmed out by its rector.[4] Bishop Bransford appointed John, rector of Hinton and farmer of the church of Blockley, to correct and punish his subjects of the exempt jurisdiction,[5] to hear, take cognizance of, and to terminate all causes and suits moved or to be moved *ex officio* or at the instance of parties, to seek out and to receive proofs of the wills of those dying within the jurisdiction, to approve and insinuate[6] such wills, to commit the administration of the goods of persons dying testate or intestate to executors, to hear the

---

diccionem te habere pretendens penam pecuniarem pro delictis et excessibus notoriis contra sanctorum patrum constituciones recepisti." *Reg. Reynolds*, fo. 54v., p. 47. See also *Extra* 5, 37, c.3 and Lyndwood ad ver. *delicto notorio*, pp. 323–5.

1 Their agreement, in the form of an indenture, is printed in Nash 1, pp. 134–5, from Reg. Thoresby, fo. 27v. "Libertates etiam jurisdictionis, et jura dicte ecclesie, idem episcopus proteget interim et defendet; nec permittet officiales suos vel ministros ipsa aliqualiter violare."

2 Thus, when Alvechurch was collated to Robert de Alne in 1339, the mandate for his induction was sent to the dean of Alvechurch. Reg. Bransford, fo. 30v. (239).

3 See p. 22 above.

4 In 1330 John XXII had provided Gerald de Pristinio, papal notary, to Blockley, which had fallen vacant in the Curia. He was admitted by proxy 17 January 1331 (Reg. Orleton 1, fo. 22r.). The pope appropriated it to the bishopric in 1333, on Orleton's petition. (*C.P.L.* 1305–42, p. 382; Nash 1, pp. 106 et seq.). This was to take effect on the death or resignation of John, bishop of Porto (*ob.* 1348). See pp. 216–17 below.

5 Blockley was not merely the church of an episcopal manor but one of the rural deaneries of the Worcester archdeaconry with its churches and chapels of Batsford, Bourton, Daylesford, Ditchford, Evenlode, Iccomb, Saintbury, Sezincote, and Stretton on Fosse.

6 I.e. to register (*O.E.D.*). Professor Jacob distinguishes the three stages *probacio, approbacio, insinuacio*, which he renders as "proving, declaration of validity, registration". *Cant. Reg. Chichele* 2, introduction p. x.

accounts of such administration, to grant letters of acquittance, with powers of canonical coercion and lawful sequestration, until such time as the commission should be revoked.[1]

A composite picture of the exempt jurisdiction enjoyed by episcopal manors can now be given, with the caution that there may well have been variations of which we have no knowledge. There was a dean of the jurisdiction, probably appointed by the rector, who had his official and apparitors. There may also have been a special penitentiary—as there was at Bibury. The dean held chapters, administered corrections, and exercised testamentary powers. The *custos* of Bibury imposed sentences of excommunication and other deans may have done likewise, but if so the fact is not recorded.[2] A dean was expected to render accounts at certain times—a fixed sum seems to have been paid to the bishop for the Bibury jurisdiction. He had the right to receive the episcopal mandates for induction to benefices within his jurisdiction and consequently such fees as were customary. To him were addressed mandates for inquiry into vacant benefices,[3] ordinarily sent to the archdeacon's official, as well as other mandates which in the absence of peculiar jurisdiction would have been sent to the archdeacon or rural dean. His deanery was not exempt from visitation by the diocesan but in practice it enjoyed a substantial immunity. In short, though an integral part of the diocese, it may be said to have occupied a privileged position outside the regular administrative structure of archdeaconry and rural deanery—a position, moreover, which was seldom, if ever, challenged in the fourteenth century.

The churches of the cathedral priory

In dioceses with secular chapters it was usual for the dean and chapter to exercise jurisdiction over churches appropriated to the Common Fund, while the prebendaries had jurisdiction at least in the ancient prebends, subject to the dean's triennial visitation.[4] The

---

[1] Reg. Bransford, fo. 18v. (129): 15 May 1340.

[2] Lyndwood tells us that not only the deans of cathedral churches but also rural deans had power to excommunicate in some places. "Nam & Decani Rurales in quibusdam partibus habent jurisdictionem, & Apparitores sive Bedellos sibi intendentes" (p. 352 ad ver. *Decanorum*).

[3] For example, in 1349 the dean of the peculiar of Blockley carried out the inquiry into the vacancy of Batsford. Reg. Bransford 2, fo. 15r. (1485).

[4] At Lincoln the exercise of "episcopalia" seems to have begun *c.* 1160 when Bishop Robert de Chesney specifically granted exemption to the dean and chapter similar to that enjoyed by the canons of Salisbury. *Linc. Archives Comm., Archivist's Rpt.* March 1952 to March 1953, p. 58; *Reg. Antiqu.* 1 (*L.R.S.*) no. 287; cf. Edwards, *Secular Cathedrals*, p. 126. It was well established elsewhere by the mid-thirteenth cen-

chapters strenuously resisted episcopal visitation, both of themselves and of the prebends, although they were finally forced to submit at any rate to a restricted form of visitation.[1] In practice then, there were considerable areas within such dioceses which were largely autonomous.[2]

The situation seems to have been different in dioceses with monastic chapters, for although the monks were often equally unwilling to submit to the bishop's unrestricted visitation, their manorial churches were commonly subject to episcopal and sometimes even to archidiaconal jurisdiction. In the diocese of Durham the prior and convent did not exercise undisputed jurisdiction over their appropriated churches in the Durham archdeaconry until about 1377, and they were still in conflict with the archdeacon of Northumberland at the end of the century.[3] Of Norwich, Blomefield wrote: "There is, and from the foundation always was, a peculiar jurisdiction belonging to the prior and convent, and now to the dean and chapter." This was archidiaconal in character and exercised by a dean of the jurisdiction of the manors of the prior and convent.[4]

The claim of the Worcester priory to archidiaconal jurisdiction can be traced at least to the eleventh century. At a synod held by Bishop Wulfstan in 1092[5] it was reported that the only parish in the city of Worcester was that of the mother church (the cathedral), of which St Helen's had been a vicarage since the time of King Ethelred. On the foundation of the cathedral priory St Helen's with other churches had been handed over to the monks, and Bishop Oswald had conceded that Winsy, the first prior, and his successors, should be deans over them to the exclusion of (rural?) dean and archdeacon.[6] After various disputes

tury. But the withdrawal from archidiaconal jurisdiction of prebends which were acquired at a later time was not easy. At Wells in the thirteenth century the canons, fortified by the advice of the dean of Salisbury, were able to secure immunity for all their prebends, although as late as 1319 Bishop Drokensford was threatening to visit them. At Lichfield some prebends acquired in the thirteenth century remained subject to the archdeacon. See *H.M.C.R.* X, App. pt. 1, pp. 30, 31, 189, 203; Jenkins, "Lichfield Cathedral", pp. 34–5, 134–6, 162; Frere, *Visit. Articles* 1, intro. pp. 72–9.

1 Edwards, *Secular Cathedrals*, pp. 129 et seq.

2 Edwards (op. cit. p. 134) speaks of the secular chapters forming "almost autonomous ecclesiastical republics".

3 Barlow, *Durham Jurisdictional Peculiars*, pp. 1–52.   4 *Norfolk* 4, pp. 562–3.

5 *Monasticon* 1, pp. 609–10. R. R. Darlington in his introduction to the *Vita Wulfstani* (p. xxxv, n. 2) describes the record of the synod as "beyond suspicion".

6 "Concessit etiam illi, omnibusque suis successoribus prioribus hujus ecclesiae, decanos esse super omnes ecclesias suas et presbiteros, ita videlicet quod nullus decanus, nullus archidiaconus, de monachorum ecclesiis seu clericis se intromittat nisi per priorem ecclesiae." *Monasticon* 1, pp. 609–10. Cf. *Chron. Abb. de Evesham*, p. 227 (1208): "Et ecclesia Wigornensis habet priorem qui fungitur vice decani. . . ."

St Helen's passed in 1234[1] to the bishop, and the exempt jurisdiction of the rector, which is occasionally mentioned in the fourteenth century,[2] may have been derived from the 1092 synod. This claim was certainly made for the cathedral priory's churches of Broadwas, Grimley, and Hallow.[3] Their *personae*, it was alleged, by authority of St Wulfstan acted as archdeacons within their parishes and received all archidiaconal fees.[4] Some measure of exemption survived the Reformation at both St Helen's and Broadwas,[5] although even in the fourteenth century mandates for induction to both churches were sent to the archdeacon's official in the ordinary way. There seems to be no record, at any rate in the fourteenth century, of a separate jurisdiction of the priory's city churches. However, in the sixteenth century the dean and chapter claimed that the cathedral and the "churches of the borough" (among others)[6] were exempt from the ordinary "in causes of correction and probate of testaments and committing of administrations".[7]

The episcopal registers give no hint of any special jurisdiction at Hallow, but an isolated document preserved at Worcester shows that in the late thirteenth century, possibly after Hallow's appropriation to the priory in 1268,[8] the prior and convent were trying to make good their claim to archidiaconal authority there. The bishop's official declared that, pretending to exemption and the special prerogative of a liberty, they had laid claim to archidiaconal rights, appointed a dean and apparitor, convoked and celebrated chapters, heard causes, corrected crimes—or claimed to have done so, and exacted fines from delinquents and used them for their own purposes. He intended to inquire into the matter and to do what justice required. Unfortunately, there is no record of the outcome.[9]

---

[1] *Ann. Wigorn.* p. 426. See also *V.C.H. Worcs.* IV, p. 410; Nash 2, App. p. cxlv.

[2] For example, Reg. Bransford, fo. 7v. (63): "Decano iurisdiccionis ecclesie Sancte Helene Wyg.".

[3] By the late thirteenth century Grimley was accounted a parish church and Hallow its chapel.

[4] "Ecclesia [Broadwas] libera est, auctoritate Sancti Wlstani, ab omni iurisdictione archidiaconi et decani. Prior patronus: persona tanquam archidiaconus parochiae suae est, et percipit omnia emolumenta archidiaconalia, et nihil solvit." Reg. Prioratus, fo. 32b; and cf. ff. 44a, 50a.

[5] See the 1563 return of peculiars; Frere, *Visit. Articles* I, pp. 182–3.

[6] Including Wolverley where the priory's jurisdiction is mentioned in 1354. See Nash 2, p. 476 (from Liber Pens., fo. 56v.).

[7] Frere, *Visit. Articles* I, p. 182. The peculiar of the dean and chapter comprised seven parishes in 1832: see above, p. 15, n. 3.

[8] Nash (1, pp. 477–8) prints the appropriation document of Grimley with Hallow from Liber Pensionum, fo. 18, instead of from the contemporary entry on fo. 6r. of Reg. Giffard.

[9] "... ius archidiaconale sibi vendicant in eadem, decanum creant, apparitorem

Although the evidence is a little confused, it seems that the Worcester monks were by no means so successful as those of Durham and Norwich in withdrawing their churches from archidiaconal control. Moreover, in the matter of induction such churches were not given the same privileged treatment as the churches of the episcopal manors.[1]

Collegiate churches

Within the diocese there were two major collegiate churches: that of the Blessed Virgin Mary at Warwick, and Holy Trinity, Westbury on Trym.[2]

St Mary's had been founded shortly after 1123 by Roger de Newburgh, the second earl of Warwick. The seven prebends remained in the patronage of the earls of Warwick.[3] The diocesan's right to visit the college had been disputed in Giffard's time by Dean Robert de Plesset,[4] but during the fourteenth century it regularly underwent visitation.

There were disputes between the Worcester archdeacons and successive deans, which affected episcopal rights as well. Prior John de Wyke in a letter to Reynolds, then bishop elect, described Dean Robert Tankard as a roaring lion ("leo rugiens in iurisdiccionem"), for he had held chapters in Warwick and appointed an apparitor, introducing a new jurisdiction where the bishops had formerly enjoyed two parts of the emoluments.[5] In another letter, addressed to the archdeacon, Francis de Neapoli, the prior declared that the archdeacons or their officials had time out of mind exercised the right to celebrate chapters in St Mary's and other Warwick churches, to hear and terminate suits, enjoin penances, and make corrections there. He advised him to secure the citation of Tankard in person to the Curia.[6] The legal struggle continued for a number of years.[7] It flared up again in 1343 between

---

constituunt, capitula inibi convocant et celebrant, causas audiunt, crimina corrigunt, seu corrigere se dicunt, mulctas a delinquentibus exigunt et illas in usus proprios pro suo libito convertunt, exempcionem et libertatis specialem prerogativam pretendentes . . ." D. & C. MS. B. 407a (formerly 41), transcribed by Poole in *Hist. MSS. Rpt.*, p. 191. The document, which is undated, is roughly contemporary with the entries in Reg. Prioratus (see above, p. 26, n. 4).

1 See p. 21 above.   2 See p. 212 below.

3 *Knowles & Hadcock*, p. 344; *V.C.H. Warwicks.* 2, pp. 124–9.

4 *Reg. Giffard*, fo. 136v. (al. cxxxv), pp. 147–8 *et passim*. The dean appealed to Canterbury and this dispute became part of a wider one between Giffard and Archbishop Pecham about the latter's jurisdiction within the diocese.

5 L.A., ff. xxxi v.—xxxii r. Cf. p. 49 below.   6 L.A., fo. xliii r.

7 In April 1311 Tankard was condemned by the Court of Canterbury to pay £20 to the archdeacon's official and the case was remitted to the diocesan official. Shortly afterwards—so the prior (who was farming the archdeaconry) alleged—he secured a bull for certain judges who "clandestine procedentes" pronounced definitive sentence

Dean Robert de Endredeby and Archdeacon Robert of Worcester. In the presence of John de la Lowe, Bransford's official, and Hugh de Pembridge, his adjutor, the dean swore that he would not exercise any archidiaconal jurisdiction within the town of Warwick until the dispute had been settled by amicable composition or legal agreement. Exception was made of his jurisdiction among the canons in matters concerning the "regimen chori" and the "modus conveniendi ad divina".[1]

Westbury had been a pre-Conquest minster of secular clerks. Later it became a collegiate church with six prebends in the patronage of the Worcester bishops.[2] Giffard had attempted to make a number of churches in his collation prebendal to Westbury and apparently planned to elevate it to cathedral rank.[3] The Worcester monks strenuously opposed his schemes, which proved abortive.[4]

The parishes of Henbury and Westbury, of which the dean and canons were collectively rectors, formed a rural deanery exempt from the archdeacon.[5] But like Warwick, Westbury was visited by the diocesan and by the prior *sede vacante*. The failure of the colleges to establish jurisdiction exempt from the diocesan meant that they did not become an embarrassment to the bishops as did more powerful institutions of the kind in other dioceses.[6]

Though the deans were frequently non-resident, from time to time *ad hoc* episcopal mandates were directed to them. The deanery of Westbury, being in the bishops' collation, was not infrequently held by clerks in their service, though seldom for long.[7] Thus Adam of Aylton,

---

to the prejudice of the church of Worcester and the special damage of the archdeacon. L.A., ff.1 v., liii r.

[1] Reg. Bransford, fo. 63r. (556).

[2] *Knowles & Hadcock*, p. 344; *V.C.H. Gloucs.* 2, pp. 106–8; H. J. Wilkins, *Westbury College* (1917), chap. 1.

[3] Giffard's motives are suggested by Hamilton Thompson, *Trans. B. & G.A.S.* XXXVIII, pp. 106, 109–12. One of them was the establishment of a dependent body of episcopal clerks. Similar schemes elsewhere proved more successful. In the last two decades of the thirteenth century Antony Bek, bishop of Durham, established secular chapters at Bishop Auckland, Lanchester, and Chester-le-Street, though on a modest scale. Thompson, "Colleg. Churches of the Bpric. of Durham", *D.U.J.* XXXVI, pp. 33 et seq.; Fraser, *Antony Bek*, p. 115; cf. below, p. 97, nn. 1, 2. Bishop Carpenter refounded Westbury in 1455 and is said on occasion to have styled himself "bishop of Worcester and Westbury.". *Monasticon* 6, p. 1439; Godwin, *De Praesulibus*, p. 519; Wilkins, op. cit., pp. 152, 162, n. 4.

[4] See the documents from Reg. Giffard in Thomas, *App.* 63, pp. 49–54; also ibid., *App.* 67, p. 65, art. 8.   [5] *B. & G.A.S.* XXXVIII, p. 117.

[6] For this problem see *English Clergy*, chap. 3.

[7] The list of deans given in *V.C.H. Gloucs.* 2, p. 108 is far from complete. William Edington and Adam de Aylincton (*recte* "Aylineton") are given as "occurring" in 1335 and there is no mention of another dean until 1395. The deanery was collated to

one of Orleton's clerks, held it for about two years (1333-5), and during that period was dispensed from the obligation of personal residence by a specific apostolic grace conceded by John XXII so that he would be free to serve the bishop.[1]

Exempt monasteries[2]

The most notable exemption, that of the Benedictine abbey of Evesham, has already been mentioned. Other houses of the Order acknowledged the diocesan's right of visitation—save only Great Malvern, but a number of them disputed that of the prior *sede vacante*, as will be shown later.

The priory of Great Malvern was a cell of Westminster Abbey. When Archbishop Pecham attempted to visit the place in 1283 the proctors of the abbot of Westminster asserted that it was so privileged that neither the archbishop nor the bishop of Worcester ought to have any jurisdiction there.[3] Giffard eventually acknowledged the abbey's claims, receiving the manor of Knightwick in return—an arrangement which Pecham denounced as simoniacal and injurious to the rights of Canterbury.[4] The affair was not forgotten by the Worcester bishops, and Orleton, albeit unsuccessfully, attempted to barter his consent to

---

John Stratford, Iuris Civilis Professor, the future archbishop, 14 December 1316, and to Nicholas de Gore, 31 January 1317, when it was said to be vacant by the resignation of Gilbert de Kirkeby (Reg. Maidstone, ff. 49v., 50r.). Nicholas de Gore, one of Cobham's officials, exchanged the deanery in 1323 for the church of Stisted (London diocese) held by Ralph de Lacu (*Reg. Cobham*, fo. 33r., p. 33). Adam of Aylton (MS. "Aylineton") resigned the church of Rock at the Holy See, the pope providing Peter de Hope to that benefice 22 September 1333 (Reg. Orleton 2, ff. 55v., 56r.). He seems to have secured the Westbury deanery at the same time (ibid., fo. 57r.). Adam exchanged it for the church of Middleton Cheney, Northamptonshire, in 1335, and on 3 July in that year William de Edyngton (bishop of Winchester 1346–66) was instituted (Reg. Montacute 1, fo. 16v.). On 26 September 1335 Stephen Baret was instituted to the deanery and on 21 June 1336 it was collated to William of Oxford in exchange for Oddington (ibid., ff. 20r., 22v.). William received licence to be absent until the feast of All Saints (ibid., fo. 23r.). For later deans and for lists of prebendaries, sub-deans, and treasurers, see Wilkins, *Westbury College*, pp. 47–113.

[1] ". . . quibuscumque statutis et consuetudinibus ipsius ecclesie eciam si fuerint iuramento vallata nequaquam obstantibus". Reg. Orleton 2, fo. 57r.: Avignon, 22 September 1333.

[2] For monastic exemption in general see Knowles, *Monastic Order in England*, pp. 474–606 (esp. pp. 585–6), and Frere, *Visit. Articles* 1, pp. 59–69.

[3] *Reg. Epist. Peckham* 2, p. 748, from Reg. Giffard fo. 153 al. cliiii.

[4] *Ibid.*, pp. 527–8, 643–4, 757–8; Thomas, *App.* 67, p. 67, art. 14; *Ann. Wigorn.*, p. 488. For detailed accounts of the dispute see *V.C.H. Worcs.* 2, pp. 138–41; *Reg. Giffard*, intro. pp. xlii–xlvii. Some of the original documents are preserved at Westminster. Among them are two copies of Giffard's recognition of the abbey's rights, sealed with his great seal in green wax and dated 5 November 1283; two copies of the ratification by William of Ledbury, the Malvern prior, of the peace arranged between

the appropriation of Longdon to Westminster Abbey for the lost jurisdiction over Great Malvern.[1]

Houses of the Cistercian Order—Bordesley, Hailes, and Kingswood, and the Premonstratensian abbey of Halesowen, were outside episcopal jurisdiction.[2] So too was the alien priory of Deerhurst, a cell of St Denis.[3]

The effect of exemption was that the bishop lost his right to visit certain monasteries, to levy procuration from them—except for their appropriated churches, to interfere in their internal affairs, and to confirm or quash their elections. He was still acknowledged as their diocesan and was accustomed to receive an oath of subjection, reverence, and obedience from their heads.[4]

THE ARCHDEACONRIES

The appointment of archdeacons

Both archdeaconries were in the bishop's collation, though in practice his rights were seriously curtailed, as was the case in other dioceses, by papal provision and by royal presentation at times of vacancy. Although he rarely did so, the bishop could canonically deprive an archdeacon in the same way as any other holder of a benefice.[5]

On receipt of the episcopal mandate the Worcester prior would install an archdeacon of Worcester in the last stall on the right hand side

---

bishop and abbot after mediation of the king and his council, dated 9 October 1283; royal letters patent with *inspeximus* and confirmation of each of the above; and a summary of the bishop's proceedings against the Malvern monks drawn up on behalf of the priory. Westm. Abb. Mun., nos. 32640, 32641, 504, 32635, 32642, 32643, 32636.

[1] *C.P.L.* 1305–42, pp. 350, 393.

[2] The statements of Willis Bund in his introduction to Reg. Giffard (pp. xcii, xciii, xcvi) to the effect that the bishop visited these houses rests on a misunderstanding of the entries (*Reg. Giff.*, ff. 48r.–v., 59v., pp. 66–7, 81). He misled the writer of *V.C.H. Worcs.* 2, pp. 26, 153, but the writer of *V.C.H. Gloucs.* 2, p. 96, n. 15, rightly repudiates the suggestion.

[3] In the early nineteenth century the peculiar of Deerhurst comprised Deerhurst, Hasfield, Staverton with Boddington Chapel, Corse, Leigh, Tirley, and Forthampton. This points to the existence of an area exempt from the archdeacon in pre-Reformation times. Most of the above churches were being farmed by the priory *temp.* Henry VIII. *Valor Eccles.* 2, App. p. 512; *Monasticon* 4, pp. 666–7.

[4] Usually at the time of their benediction. See, for instance, the oaths of the Cistercian abbots of Hailes (*Reg. Gainsburgh*, fo. 30r., p. 114) and Kingswood (*Reg. Cobham*, fo. 13r., p. 15).

[5] An instance is recorded in 1245. "M[auricius de Arundel] archidiaconus Gloucesstriae sentencialiter, culpis suis exigentibus, auctoritate domini episcopi privatus est omni officio et beneficio." *Ann. Wigorn.*, p. 436. Cf. the temporary deprivation of the archdeacon of Bath in 1341: *B. & W. Reg. Shrewsb.* pp. 427, 429, 436, nos. 1584, 1590, 1619.

of the choir, an archdeacon of Gloucester in that on the opposite side
next to the prior.[1] He would then notify the bishop that he had done
so, at the same time publishing a protestation to the effect that such
installation conferred no right to a voice in chapter.[2]

To the Gloucester archdeaconry were attached certain houses in
Gloucester as well as other rights and appurtenances.[3] The church of
Claverdon in Warwickshire was annexed to the Worcester archdeaconry.[4] It is probable that the archdeacon of Worcester had the
right to appoint the master of the grammar school in the city.[5]

Of the seven archdeacons of Worcester between 1289 and 1352,
three—Francis de Neapoli, Henry Delphini, and John Brucy—were
provided by the pope; one, Adam le Champeneys, though later presented by the king, was first appointed by Bishop Cobham; one other,
Robert of Worcester, secured the archdeaconry by an exchange;
leaving two (apart from Champeneys), John de Orleton and John de
Severleye, who were directly appointed by the diocesan.

It was a similar story in the Gloucester archdeaconry. There were
eight archdeacons between 1295 and 1348—though one, Nicholas
Hugate, was probably not installed. Of these, two, Nicholas Hugate
and M. Hugh de Statherne, were presented by the king. Joceus de
Kynebauton, Roger de Breynton, and Richard of Ledbury secured the
archdeaconry by way of exchange. Only three, Walter Burdon,
William de Birston, and John of Usk, were chosen by the bishop.

---

[1] *Reg. Prioratus*, fo. lxii v. (p. 132a–b).　　[2] For example, Liber Albus, fo. ciii r.

[3] In 1328 the vicar of St Mary's in Broadgate, Gloucester, was ordered to induct the
archdeacon "in possessionem domorum eidem archidiaconatui annexarum apud
Glouc' et iurium et pertinenciarum [sic] ipsarum" (Reg. Orleton 2, fo. 25r.).
Archdeacon's lane ("venella archidiaconi") is mentioned in *Cart. S. Petri Glouc.* 2,
p. 236. In 1366 the archdeaconry was said to be taxed at forty-six marks (£30 13s. 4d.);
in 1535 at £71 13s. gross, from which £3 was paid to the archdeacon's receiver and
£4 3s. to his official. *Cant. Reg. Langham*, p. 35; *Valor Eccles.* 2, p. 493.

[4] A copy of the charter of William, earl of Warwick (1153–84), granting the
advowson of Claverdon to Roger, bishop of Worcester (1164–79), is in Liber Ruber,
fo. cxxxvi. In 1535 the gross income of the archdeaconry was £60 3s. 11d., which
comprised procurations and synodals £50 4s. 8½d., pensions from religious houses
£1 19s. 2½d., and Claverdon church £8. *Valor Eccles.* 3, p. 227.

[5] In August 1312, during the vacancy of the archdeaconry, Reynolds conferred the
rule of the schools on M. Hugh of Northampton "utrum ad nos iure episcopali vel
archidiaconali earundem collacio pertineat..." (Reg. Reynolds fo. 59r.–v.). The
mandate for induction was addressed to the *custos* of the sequestration of the archdeaconry. Cf. the authority exercised by the archdeacons of Ely over the master of
Glomery and his Glommerels in Cambridge. *Vetus Liber Arch. Elien.*, p. 202, Excursus
B, pp. 289–91. A. F. Leach's contention that the bishop ordinarily appointed the
Worcester master is not convincing in view of the fact that the only two recorded
appointments by the diocesan (the other was in 1429) specifically mention the archdeacon's right. See *Early Education in Worc.* (*W.H.S.*), pp. xxiii–xxiv, 77.

4

By the fourteenth century it was somewhat unusual for an archdeacon to be resident. Obviously papal and royal nominees were invariably absentees. Only three Worcester archdeacons, Adam le Champeneys, Robert of Worcester, and John de Severleye, took a prominent part in diocesan affairs, and then only for a limited period. Of the Gloucester archdeacons, Walter Burdon seems to have been resident from time to time and personally to have defended the rights of his archdeaconry against the alleged encroachments of Bishop Giffard. However, he took no part, so far as is known, in diocesan administration. A notable theologian, his interests lay elsewhere. William de Birston, though frequently absent, did act as auditor and commissary-general during Reynolds' episcopate. John of Usk and Roger de Breynton were both prominent in Orleton's administration. Such was the general picture, but we must now study the individual archdeacons in more detail.

The archdeacons of Worcester

On the death in 1287 of Cardinal Hugh of Evesham, by poison as some suggested,[1] Bishop Giffard seems to have collated the archdeaconry to Ralph Hengham, later chief justice of the Common Pleas.[2] Pope Nicholas IV determined to provide Francis de Neapoli, who later became Cardinal of St Lucia in Silice, and threatened Giffard with suspension, and Ralph with excommunication and deprivation, if the archdeaconry were not surrendered.[3] The pope had his way and Francis was installed by proxy on 8 January 1289.[4] In the same year he was licensed to visit his archdeaconry by deputy and to receive procurations.[5] In 1290 he farmed it for 90 marks (£60) to the prior and convent of Worcester, first for a period of one year, later for five years.[6] He promoted the affairs of the church of Worcester at Rome and Bishop Gainsburgh allowed him an annual pension of fifty gold florins.[7]

---

1 *Ann. Wigorn.*, p. 494; *Reg. Giffard*, fo. 290v., p. 333.

2 There is no record of his collation or installation in the printed edition of Reg. Giffard, but he is mentioned as archdeacon on a number of occasions (for example, pp. 317, 343). He was a pluralist (ibid., pp. 487, 493), and the twenty-fourth article of Archbishop Winchelsey's indictment of Giffard accuses the latter of having admitted him, "tunc habentem notorie plura beneficia curam animarum habentia", to the church of Fairford. To which Giffard responded that he had done so under expectation of an apostolic grace. Thomas, *App.* 67, p. 70.

3 *C.P.L.* 1198–1304, p. 495: 4 July 1288.

4 *Ann. Wigorn.*, p 496; *Reg. Giffard*, fo. 286v., p. 323.

5 *Reg. Giffard*, fo. 302r., p. 356. The bull is dated 6 July 1289.

6 *Ann. Wigorn.*, pp. 502, 532. There must have been other grants, for the prior was still farming the archdeaconry in 1311: L.A., fo. liii r., and see above, p. 27, n. 7.

7 *Reg. Gainsburgh*, fo. 22v., p. 75. Henry de Luceby was appointed proctor for

News of the archdeacon's death, which occurred at the beginning of 1312,[1] probably reached Worcester by March, for on the fifteenth custody of the sequestration of the archdeaconry was granted to Adam de Orleton.[2] On the same day Bishop Reynolds directed a mandate to his sequestrator, John de Broadwas, for the livery of the seal of the officiality, together with the rolls and other items which on the occasion of such sequestration belonged to the bishop.[3] However, a marginal note records that these letters were revoked and a similar grant made on the twenty-seventh to M. Henry de la Lee, vicar of Bromsgrove,[4] who had earlier been mentioned as the archdeacon's official.[5] A number of mandates addressed to the *custos sequestri* are to be found in both Register Reynolds and the Liber Albus.[6]

Meanwhile, on 18 January 1312, Clement V, claiming the reservation of all benefices vacated by cardinals, conferred the archdeaconry on Henry "natum nobilis viri Imberti Delphini Vienum".[7] Bishop Reynolds admitted him on 5 September in the person of his proctor, Francis de Balma, canon of Vienne.[8] The new archdeacon was also treasurer of Rouen and beneficed in Cambrai. A papal indult permitted him to retain his benefices for seven years while engaged in the study of civil law.[9] Another enabled him to visit his archdeaconry by deputy for three years and to receive procuration during that time.[10]

The date of Archdeacon Henry's resignation is not recorded in the registers, but it may have been 1319, when he was provided to the

---

pledging the church of Worcester to make payment of this sum to Cardinal Francis and for coming to an agreement with him about the farm of his archdeaconry.

[1] Eubel, *Hierarchia*, p. 12.   [2] *Reg. Reynolds*, fo. 45r., p. 154.

[3] Ibid. "... sigillum officialitatis archidiaconatus predicti una cum rotulis et ceteris occasione dicti sequestri ad dictum episcopum pertinentibus."

[4] Ibid., fo. 45r., p. 35.   [5] Ibid., fo. 13r., p. 12.

[6] For example, Reg. Reynolds, fo. 59v. (see above, p. 31, n 5); Liber Albus, ff. li v.–liii.

[7] Henry de la Tour was the fourth son of Humbert I, Seigneur de la Tour du Pin and later Dauphin de Viennois (Dauphiné). He became first tutor and later regent for his nephew, the Dauphin Guigue VII (1318–33). John XXII provided him to the bishopric of Metz in 1319, but he resigned it shortly after November 1324, assuming the title of Baron de Montauban. He probably died in 1329. *Histoire Généalogique . . . de la Maison Royale de France*, 3rd ed., Paris 1726, p. 20; *La Grande Encyclopédie* (Paris n.d.) s.v. "Dauphiné"; Gams, *Series Episc.*

[8] *Reg. Reynolds*, ff. 61–2, pp. 54–5; Liber Albus fo. lvii r.–v.; *C.P.L.* 1305–42, p. 94.

[9] *C.P.L.* 1305–42, p. 112: 6 April 1313.

[10] Ibid., p. 120: 27 November 1313. Professor Hamilton Thompson suggested (*English Clergy*, p. 61, n. 6) that such indults were "constant from the last decade of the fourteenth century onwards". He quotes that granted to the archdeacon of Sudbury in 1363 as "an early instance". In fact, there are many in *C.P.L.* dating from the first half of the century.

bishopric of Metz. We only know of John Brucy's promotion in his
stead because of the certificate of an inquiry held by the dean of
Arches and dated 23 July 1321. This inquiry, held at Bishop Cobham's
request, revealed that the archdeaconry had been vacant for a year
and more since the death of Brucy who had been buried in the diocese
of Avignon.[1] It is clear that he too had been provided by the pope.

It would seem that at this point king and bishop connived at the
exclusion of a further papal nominee.[2] On 15 May 1321, long before he
had received the official result of the inquiry, Bishop Cobham had
collated the archdeaconry to Adam le Champeneys of Sandwich, one
of his clerks regularly employed on diocesan business.[3] The king
presented the same clerk on 20 July, claiming that the archdeaconry
was in his gift by reason of the late voidance of the see.[4] On the same
day the bishop sent a mandate to the sacrist of Worcester and the dean
of the Christianity there for Adam's induction.[5] He was duly installed
by proxy in August.[6]

In an undated letter to John XXII Cobham pointed out that the
archdeaconry was in the gift of the king for the occasion, and that it had
been given to one of his clerks. Certain royal clerks, he continued,
hearing a rumour that because the archdeaconry had fallen vacant in
the Curia it lay with the pope to make provision, had asked him to give
warning of the king's displeasure were his gift or the promotion of his
clerk to be impeded.[7]

The combination of king and bishop proved successful. The line of
papal nominees was broken at last, and for the first time in the fourteenth century an archdeacon of Worcester was resident in the diocese.

Bishop Orleton collated the archdeaconry to his brother, John de
Orleton, in 1329.[8] Orleton was always careful to make provision for

1 *Reg. Cobham*, fo. 26r., p. 31.

2 Such connivance was not uncommon. Miss Deeley remarks ("Papal Provision
etc.", *E.H.R.* XLIII, p. 505): "Whenever it seemed advisable to forestall a papal
claim, it was done by advancing the king's title to the presentation for that turn."
By English law papal collations and reservations could not affect benefices in lay
patronage.

3 *Reg. Cobham*, fo. 24v., p. 29.   4 Ibid., fo. 26r., pp. 30–1; *C.P.R.* 1321–4, p. 4.

5 *Reg. Cobham*, loc. cit.

6 Liber Albus, fo. ciii r.; *Reg. Cobham* fo. 65v., p. 104.

7 *Reg. Cobham*, ff. 66v.–67r., pp. 106–7: ". . . quia quidam domini regis predicti
clerici speciales audiunt murmurare quod dicitur a quibusdam archidiaconatum
ipsum nunc ultimo in curia vacavisse, et sic vestre sanctitati forsitan suggerendum
quod vestrum esset ipsi archidiaconatui providere, me ex parte domini regis predicti
requirere curaverunt, quod vestre celsitudini intimarem ipsi graviter displicere, si ad
cuiuscunque rogatum esset sua donacio et clerici sui promocio prepedita [etc.]."

8 Reg. Orleton 2, fo. 33r.: 17 October 1329.

his relatives and John was already a pluralist.[1] He seems to have taken little or no part in diocesan affairs. In 1337 he exchanged the archdeaconry with Robert of Worcester for the church of Meonstoke in Winchester diocese, where his patron was already installed as bishop.[2]

The new archdeacon, Robert of Worcester,[3] Iuris Civilis Professor, had been granted licences to study by Bishops Maidstone[4] and Cobham.[5] Presented by Worcester priory to the rectory of Sedgeberrow in 1315,[6] he is to be found acting as the monastery's legal adviser in the 1320s, receiving a corrody and pension upon taking the usual oath of faithful service.[7] He exchanged Sedgeberrow in 1324 for the rectory of East Tilbury, Essex, and became rural dean of Fordham, Norwich diocese, and chaplain of St Julian's chapel, Thetford, two years later.[8] In 1333 he was provided to a canonry in Salisbury cathedral.[9] The date of his institution to Meonstoke is not known.

Bishop Cobham made some use of Robert's services and wrote (1323) to congratulate him on his appointment as an advocate in the Court of Canterbury.[10] In 1334 Montacute made him one of his proctors at the Curia, where he was already acting for the bishop of Bath and Wells, Ralph of Shrewsbury.[11] During Bransford's episcopate he farmed the manor of Letcombe in Berkshire, the property of the abbey of Cluny,[12] and also, for three years, the church of St Michael, Worcester.[13]

In 1346, because of the repeated claims of the prior of Wootton on

[1] A canon of Hereford, he received the prebend of Nonnington in 1322, that of Moreton Parva *in commendam* in 1326 (*Hereford Reg. Orleton*, pp. 388, 389). After his promotion as archdeacon he resigned (3 November 1329) the church of Acle in Norwich diocese (Reg. Orleton, fo. 34r). Cf. pp. 95–6 below.

[2] Reg. Montacute 1, fo. 27v.

[3] Alias "of Himbleton". He should not be confused with the person of the same name who in the first decade of the fourteenth century was granted licences for study totalling six years by Bishop Simon of Ghent and who was associated with the abbey of Hyde, near Winchester, occupying successively its rectories of Laverstock and Collingbourne Kingston. *Salisb. Reg. S. de Gandavo*, pp. 705, 842, 849, 866, 907–8: *Winch. Reg. Pontissara*, pp. 348, 349. See also Emden, *Biographical Reg.*, sub nom.

[4] Reg. Maidstone, fo. 48v.; for two years (1316).

[5] *Reg. Cobham*, ff. 9r., 27r., pp. 253, 258; for 3 years (1318), subsequently (1321) for two.   [6] L.A., fo. lxvi v.

[7] Ibid., fo. cxxiv (1325). For the form of oath see Wilson, *Worc. Liber Albus*, p. 137.

[8] L.A., fo. cxv r.; *Reg. Cobham*, fo. 35r., p. 241; Emden, sub nom.

[9] *C.P.L.* 1305–42, p. 375.

[10] *Reg. Cobham*, ff. 68v., 92v. 117v., pp. 110, 163, 208.

[11] Reg. Montacute 1, fo. 2r.–v.; *B. & W. Reg. Shrewsb.* p. 91, no. 377 (1332). He also acted (1329–30, 1332–3) for St Augustine's Canterbury: Emden, sub nom.

[12] Writs of *levari facias* were issued against him in 1342 and 1343 for arrears of farm. Reg. Bransford, ff. ccxxviii v. al. 159, ccxxix r. al. 160 *bis*, nos. 1174, 1178, 1180.

[13] Ibid., fo. 30r. (234). Licence dated 25 November 1339.

the archdeacon's church of Claverdon,[1] a writ *certiorari* was sent on behalf of Robert of Worcester to Bishop Bransford. In his return the bishop gave details of recent taxation of Claverdon, including a portion (£3 14s. 8d.) paid to the prior of Wootton. After consulting his register of taxes as well as other registers and memoranda, he could not be certain, while the parties remained unheard, whether a pension ought to be paid or not.[2] Two writs of *venire facias* were later issued against the archdeacon on this account.[3]

Apart from this legal dispute there is only rare mention in Bransford's register of Archdeacon Robert who seems to have had little concern with diocesan affairs. He died between 14 and 22 May 1349, at the time of the Black Death.[4]

The archdeaconry was collated to John de Severleye on 22 May 1349.[5] He was one of the more important of Bransford's clerks. At the beginning of the episcopate he had received several licences for absence from his rectory of Billesley.[6] He is mentioned in 1342 as the bishop's chancellor and was empowered to hear and terminate causes in the court of audience as well as to correct and punish faults brought to light at a recent visitation.[7] He was also one of Bishop Bransford's proctors for the parliamentary assemblies of 1343, 1344, and 1346.[8] He was very active towards the end of the episcopate and for the last few months combined the offices of archdeacon and chancellor.[9]

Severleye is mentioned as official in Thoresby's register and was appointed joint vicar-general with the prior of Llanthony by that bishop.[10] In February 1352 he exchanged his archdeaconry for the church of Buxted, Sussex, in the diocese of Chichester.[11] He was present at the profession of obedience to the see of Canterbury made by Regi-

---

[1] Said to have been of the gift of certain progenitors of the king. See above, p. 31, n. 4.

[2] Reg. Bransford, fo. ccxliii v. al. 174 (1261). The return is on fo. ccxliiii r. al. 175 (1262). See pp. 1–2 above.   [3] Loc. cit. (1263, 1264).

[4] He is mentioned as patron of Claverdon on the 14th; the archdeaconry was collated to his successor on the 22nd. Reg. Bransford 2, fo. 11r.–v. (1410–1413).

[5] Ibid., fo. 11v. (1413).

[6] In 1339, 1340, and 1341, the last for two years. The first licence was for study, no reason is given in the other two entries. Reg. Bransford, ff. 29v., 42v., 50r. (223, 344, 429).

[7] Reg. Bransford, fo. 64r. (566) and Vol. 2, fo. 2r. (1330), duplicated on fo. 8r, (1365).

[8] Ibid., ff. ccxxxi r. al. 162, ccxxxiii v. al. 164, ccxxxvi r. al. 167, ccxliii r. al. 174, (1192, 1208, 1217, 1258). These were summoned for 28 April 1343, 18 April 1344, 7 June 1344, and 3 February 1346 respectively.

[9] Bishop Bransford died 6 August 1349.

[10] Reg. Thoresby, ff. 2r., 9r., 12r., 26r., *et passim*. See also *B. & W. Reg. Shrewsb.* p. 684, no. 2631.   [11] *R.S.V.*, fo. 110v., pp. 200–1.

nald Bryan, Thoresby's successor at Worcester, in 1353.[1] In 1356 he is mentioned as a canon of Chichester and one of several commissaries appointed by Archbishop Islep to take cognizance of ecclesiastical causes pending in the court of the late dean of South Malling.[2] Between 1353 and 1355 he acted as auditor and commissary of causes in the archbishop's court.[3]

The archdeacons of Gloucester

The Gloucester archdeaconry was collated to Walter de Burdon on 23 July 1295,[4] though the copy of the mandate for his installation is dated three years later.[5]

Burdon, a distinguished theologian, was elected chancellor of Oxford University in 1306 and resigned the office two years later.[6] He was one of a number of scholars who received Salisbury prebends from Bishop Simon of Ghent, being collated to South Alton in 1298 and to Horton in 1304.[7]

The archdeacon's relations with his diocesan were by no means peaceful, as is evident from articles 32 to 36 of the indictment of Giffard drawn up after Winchelsey's metropolitan visitation in 1301. These concern encroachments alleged to have been made by the bishop on archidiaconal rights, and have reference to the Gloucester archdeaconry.[8] In 1299 Burdon had renounced all the appeals launched by him against Giffard and the following year had formally declared his obedience.[9] However, it seems that the coming of the archbishop gave him fresh opportunity to air all the old grievances.

The archdeaconry became vacant with Burdon's death in 1308 and, on 17 December, Reynolds committed its cure and administration by

---

[1] Churchill 2, p. 132.   [2] Ibid. 1, p. 77.

[3] Ibid. 1, p. 491. See also ibid., pp. 140, 491n., and 2, p. 243.

[4] *Reg. Giffard*, fo. 392v., p. 461; *Ann. Wigorn.*, p. 523.

[5] *Reg. Giffard*, fo. 426v., p. 497: 25 May 1298.

[6] Emden, *Biographical Reg.*, sub nom.; Little and Pelster, *Oxford Theology and Theologians (O.H.S.)*, pp. 256–7 *et passim*; *Snappe's Formulary (O.H.S.)*, pp. 64, 325, 359.

[7] Jones, *Fasti Sarisb.*, pp. 350, 394; *Salisb. Reg. S. de Gandavo*, pp. 10, 148; *Reg. Gainsburgh*, fo. 27v., p. 96. Horton, Bitton, Inkberrow, and Moreton & Whaddon were the only cathedral prebends in Worcester diocese. Bitton was prebendal to Salisbury, Inkberrow and Moreton & Whaddon to Hereford. Letters for induction were issued by Worcester bishops to the official of the appropriate archdeacon on receipt of a mandate from the diocesan concerned. Full details of the process of institution, installation, and induction to the prebend of Horton (the last by the bishop of Worcester "quatenus infra limites nostre iurisdiccionis consistit") are in Reg. Bransford, ff. 119v.–120r. (886–8).

[8] They are printed in Thomas, *App.* 75, pp. 71–3, from Reg. Giffard. See below, pp. 59 et seq.   [9] *Reg. Giffard*, ff. 440v., 447r., pp. 513, 526.

title of commend to M. William de Birston, priest.[1] It was collated to him on 7 June of the following year.[2]

Some details of Birston's activities as auditor and commissary-general of the bishop are to be found in Register Reynolds.[3] He was a notable pluralist and while in possession of two rectories and as many canonries he secured papal dispensation to hold two additional benefices.[4] In the same year (1314) a papal indult enabled him to visit his archdeaconry by deputy for three years and to receive procurations.[5] He died before 13 December 1317 when Cobham cited his executors to show cause why they should not pay 115 marks for dilapidations in his church of Bredon.[6]

Meanwhile, the king, claiming the presentation on account of the Maidstone/Cobham vacancy, granted the archdeaconry to Nicholas Hugate, one of his clerks. The *custos* of the spiritualities (the Worcester prior) was ordered to put him in corporal possession.[7] It is doubtful whether Nicholas was ever installed, and six months later the king presented M. Hugh de Statherne.[8] The latter played no part in Cobham's administration. In 1328 he exchanged the archdeaconry for the precentorship of St Paul's with Joceus de Kynebauton, Iuris Utriusque Professor, who likewise played no part in diocesan affairs.[9]

The archdeaconry was vacant in January 1331,[10] if not before, but it

---

[1] *Reg. Reynolds*, fo. 3v., p. 148.

[2] Ibid., fo. 12v., p. 149. "... cui causa lenocinii archidiaconatum Gloucestriae dudum contulerat" (*Flores Hist.* 3, p. 156).

[3] *Reg. Reynolds*, ff. 52v., 56r., pp. 45, 49.

[4] *C.P.L.* 1305-42, p. 121: 6 January 1314. He was said to be rector of Patrington (Yorkshire) and Bradenham (Norfolk), a canon and prebendary of St Martin le Grand, London, and of Westbury. Hennessy does not include him among the prebendaries of St. Martin's. Reynolds tried unsuccessfully to secure a prebend for him at Hereford (*Heref. Reg. Swinfield*, pp. 482-3). Maidstone collated Bredon to him 6 July 1314 (Reg. Maidstone, fo. 12v.).

[5] *C.P.L.* 1305-42, p. 120: 6 January 1314.

[6] *Reg. Cobham*, fo. 2v., p. 3. During the vacancy of the archdeaconry M. John de Broadwas was appointed to hold the archidiaconal chapters (*Reg. Cobham*, fo. 3v., p. 4) and mandates ordinarily directed to the archdeacon's official were sent to him (for example, for inquiry into the vacancy at Swindon; *Reg. Cobham*, fo. 4v., p. 5).

[7] *C.P.R.* 1317-21, p. 49: 16 November 1317.

[8] Ibid., p. 142: 20 May 1318. He was admitted by proxy in London on the 27th and the induction was committed to John Bloyo (*Reg. Cobham*, fo. 7v., p. 229). The prior sent his certification of installation on 5 June (Liber Albus fo. xc).

[9] Orleton empowered Stephen Gravesend, bishop of London, to carry out the exchange (Reg. Orleton 2, fo. 24r., Dover, 21 May 1328). The archdeaconry was collated to Joceus on 21 August (ibid. 1, fo. 17r.). Orleton's commission to the prior for the archdeacon's installation and his mandate to his subjects in the archdeaconry enjoining obedience are also recorded in the register (ibid. 2, fo. 25r. Cf. L.A., fo. cxxxiii v.).   [10] Reg. Orleton 1, fo. 22r.

was not until 25 May that Orleton collated it to M. John of Usk, one of the clerks of his familia.[1] A month later he exchanged it with M. Roger de Breynton, canon of Hereford,[2] for the rectory of Hanbury.[3] Breynton was one of Orleton's greater clerks and acted as vicar-general in 1331 and 1332.[4] During the bishop's absence abroad in 1331 he was one of his attorneys, and in the following year he accompanied him to France.[5]

After Orleton's translation to Winchester at the end of 1333 Roger Breynton's participation in Worcester affairs was slight. This was because of his increasing activity in the Hereford diocese. Bishop Charlton made use of him, and his successor, Trilleck, appointed him vicar-general and employed him in a variety of other ways.[6] He seems to have contemplated exchanging his archdeaconry for the rectory of Old Radnor in 1339, for Wolstan de Bransford, then bishop elect, empowered the bishop of Hereford's commissaries to carry out such an exchange.[7] However, he remained archdeacon until 1348 when he exchanged with the rector of Doddington in Ely diocese. He resigned on 7 April and his successor, M. Richard of Ledbury, was instituted by proxy on the same day.[8] Richard is not mentioned again in Bishop Bransford's register.

The archdeacons' officials

Absenteeism among archdeacons may well have given rise to the archdeacon's official, certainly to his importance. By the early thirteenth century he is to be found in all English dioceses[9] and at Worcester the statutes of Bishop Blois show that in 1219 he had a recognized place in the diocesan hierarchy.[10]

Although in some dioceses archdeacons were often resident in the late thirteenth and early fourteenth centuries,[11] this was not so at

1 Reg. Orleton 1, fo. 22v.; 2, fo. 41v.; L.A., fo. cxxxviii r.
2 Orleton, then bishop of Hereford, had given him the prebend of Norton in 1326 (*Hereford Reg. Orleton*, p. 389).
3 Reg. Orleton 1, fo. 31r.; 2, fo. 42r.; L.A. fo. cxxxviii v. (21 June 1331).
4 Ibid. 2, fo. 39r.; 1, fo. 27r. and 2, fo. 53r. (duplicated). He petitioned the bishop on account of "quamplures defectus notabiles" discovered in the houses and appurtenances of the archdeaconry at the time of Joceus de Kynebauton's death (ibid. 2, fo. 42v.).   5 *C.P.R.* 1330–4, pp. 42, 277.
6 *Hereford Regs. Charlton*, p. 25; *Trilleck*, pp. 1–2 *et passim*.
7 Reg. Bransford, fo. 2v. (19).   8 Ibid., ff. 121v. al. cxxi, 121 r. al. cxxii (901–4).
9 He may have developed from the twelfth-century vice-archdeacon. See Cheney, *Bishops' Chanceries*, App. 1 (esp. pp. 145n., 145–6).   10 *Concilia* 1, p. 570.
11 For how long it is difficult to be certain. At Lincoln Bishop Sutton was able to make use of all his archdeacons except the archdeacon of Lincoln who was conspicuous by his absence. (*Rot. & Reg. Sutton, passim*).

Worcester.[1] In any case the separation between the archdeacon and his office seems to have been completed by that time. Episcopal mandates were commonly addressed alternatively to the archdeacon or his official, occasionally to the official alone.[2] Comparatively few mandates for ordinary archidiaconal business are to be found addressed to archdeacons even when they were resident,[3] though of course, special commissions to a named archdeacon are common enough.

The appointment of an official doubtless rested with his principal, the archdeacon, subject to the bishop's right to exact an oath of canonical obedience.[4] There is no direct evidence for this in the Worcester registers, but when an archdeaconry fell vacant the bishop's sequestrator took possession of it in the same way as other benefices, together with the seal of the officiality, the rolls, and other items.[5] The diocesan then appointed someone to exercise the jurisdiction. Thus, after the death of Archdeacon Hugh de Fangefos, Giffard empowered Thomas de Stok to exercise archidiaconal jurisdiction and the office of visitation in the Gloucester archdeaconry.[6] This clerk is later mentioned as official of John de Ebroicis, the next archdeacon, and he may also have held that position under his predecessor. Similarly, in 1312, Henry de la Lee, who is known to have been acting as official of the Worcester archdeacon, was appointed *custos sequestri* of the vacant archdeaconry.[7] In January 1331, during a similar vacancy of the Gloucester archdeaconry, Orleton described M. W. de Bosco as his commissary-general there.[8]

[1] See pp. 31–2 above.

[2] The following examples from Bransford's register show the variety of address used in the Worcester diocese: "domini archidiaconi nostri Wyg' officiali"; "officiali domini archidiaconi Glouc."; "dilecto filio archidiacono nostro Wyg' aut eius officiali"; "dilecto filio officiali domini archidiaconi Glouc.". It is rare for the official to be named but there are instances, for example, "dilecto filio magistro R. Maiel rectori ecclesie de Preston super Stoure officiali archidiaconi nostri Wyg'" (Reg. Orleton 2, fo. 54r.).

[3] There are a number in *Linc. Rot. & Reg. Sutton*. There is an instance in *York Reg. Giffard* (p. 89) of a mandate sent to the archdeacon of Nottingham who himself directed his official to carry it out.

[4] For examples of this oath see *Linc. Rot. & Reg. Sutton* 3, p. 93; Churchill 2, p. 12. At Canterbury the archdeacon had an official at least by Pecham's time (1279–92), who undertook on oath to execute the archbishop's mandates. Churchill 1, p. 50 and n.

[5] See p. 33 above.

[6] *Reg. Giffard*, fo. 284v., p. 320 (1288). Cf. the commission in *Heref. Reg. Charlton* (p. 27) for the exercise of jurisdiction in the vacant archdeaconries of Hereford and Salop (1333).

[7] *Reg. Reynolds*, fo. 45r., p. 35. The bishop ordered the clergy of the archdeaconry to obey the custodian (ibid., fo. 45v., p. 36).

[8] Reg. Orleton 1, fo. 22r. "Et scripsit magistro W. de Bosco rectori ecclesie de Twenyng dicti patris in archidiaconatu Glouc' eodem vacante commissario generali

Only occasionally is an archdeacon's official specifically named, and it would be impossible to compile anything approaching a complete list for either archdeaconry.[1] None the less, we can identify a sufficient number of such officials to gain some notion of the type of person who usually held the office.

M. Henry de la Lee is first mentioned as official of the Worcester archdeacon in 1303 when Archbishop Winchelsey ordered him to induct John de Middleton to the church of Dodderhill.[2] In the same year it was perhaps *ex officio* that he was present in the prior's chamber when the latter's jurisdiction as official *sede vacante* was formally terminated.[3] John de Feckenham seems to have replaced him in 1307,[4] but two years later he is again acting as official.[5] As we have seen, in 1312 he was appointed custodian of the sequestration of the archdeaconry. The rectors of Broughton Hacket and Peopleton were licensed to farm their benefices to him in 1302 and 1309 respectively.[6] He had been instituted to St Swithin's, Worcester, in 1297,[7] and a commission for his admission to the vicarage of Bromsgrove was issued in 1310.[8]

There follows a somewhat lengthy gap. In 1330 a M. John de B(?)ude, official of the archdeacon of Worcester, occurs as one of the commissaries appointed by Orleton to ascertain the value of Snitterfield church.[9]

M. Richard Mayel was official of the Worcester archdeacon for a number of years. He seems to have been first mentioned in this capacity in 1329, and subsequently in 1334 and 1336. Obviously an important clerk, he can probably be identified with the Richard "Mahel" whom Bishop Maidstone appointed in 1315 as the deputy of his diocesan

---

pro induccione ipsius" (Inst. of the vicar of Down Ampney, 21 January 1331). At Canterbury it was usual for the archbishop to appoint the diocesan commissary-general to act during a vacancy. Churchill 1, pp. 48–9; 2, p. 11.

1 For Norwich diocese Blomefield compiled useful lists of the officials of the archdeacons of Norwich, Norfolk, Sudbury, and Suffolk (*Norfolk*, pp. 659–61).

2 *R.S.V.*, fo. xviii v., p. 49. The Worcester monks had hoped to complete their appropriation of the church but the archbishop appointed Middleton, claiming the right by lapse of presentation.

3 *R.S.V.*, fo. xv v., p. 38.   4 *Reg. Gainsburgh*, fo. 11r. (*bis*), pp. 29–30.

5 He was appointed, jointly with the sequestrator, to settle a dispute between claimants to the vicarage of Wasperton (*Reg. Reynolds*, fo. 13r., p. 12: 1309).

6 *R.S.V.*, fo. vii r., p. 12; *Reg. Reynolds*, fo. 14v., p. 86.

7 *Reg. Giffard*, fo. 411, p. 484. He probably resigned in 1310 when another clerk was instituted (*Reg. Reynolds*, fo. 22v., p. 151).

8 *Reg. Reynolds*, fo. 22r., p. 150. He was instituted 27 March 1310 (not "1312" as in the printed edition) when he gave proof of his legitimation (ibid., fo. 43v., p. 154). His increase in income was slight. St Swithin's was worth £7 6s. 8d., Bromsgrove £8, according to the *Taxatio* of 1291 (pp. 216, 217).   9 Reg. Orleton 2, ff. 37v.–38r.

official.[1] He was rector of Preston on Stour and, in 1316, was granted licence of absence for three years to enable him to study.[2] In 1329 Bishop Orleton appointed him, as official, to receive the subsidy which he was endeavouring to exact from the Worcester archdeaconry. In 1334 the same bishop directed him, again as official, to inquire about the right of presentation to the church of Morton Bagot, empowering him to institute and induct thereto.[3] The same year he was one of the proctors of the Worcester clergy for the council summoned to meet at St Paul's on the Monday after the Exaltation (19 September).[4] He is again mentioned as official of the archdeacon in February 1336,[5] and three years later was one of those appointed by Bransford to receive the canonical obedience of the diocese.[6] There is no further mention of him in that bishop's register.

Information about the officials of the Gloucester archdeacons is even more sparse. John de Wakerley, Archdeacon Burdon's official, acting as his special commissary, arbitrated in a tithe dispute in 1299.[7] He is mentioned again in 1305[8] and was the archdeacon's proctor for the Carlisle parliament of 1307, although he appointed a substitute.[9] In 1317, when James de Cobham was acting as vicar-general of the newly promoted Bishop Cobham, a M. Robert de Pyrington, official of the Gloucester archdeacon and rector of Kemerton, was granted the sequestration of the fruits of Overbury church.[10]

We have already noted[11] that Orleton described M. William de Bosco, rector of Twyning in Gloucestershire, as his commissary-general in the vacant archdeaconry. He was appointed, on the complaint of the newly collated archdeacon, Roger de Breynton, to inquire into the defects of the archdeaconry.[12] In the same year (1331) he was joined with the sequestrator in a commission for inquiry into the church of Tytherington, being described as official of the archdeacon for the first time.[13] He had earlier been in the service of the monks of Winchcomb from whom he had received a corrody and his rectory of

---

1 Reg. Maidstone, fo. 36v.: 20 September 1315.   2 Ibid., fo. 44v.
3 Reg. Orleton 2, fo. 11r. and fo. 54r.
4 Reg. Montacute 2, fo. 5r. Among the others were M. John de Orleton and M. Roger de Breynton, archdeacons of Worcester and Gloucester respectively, and M. William de Adelynton, official of the Gloucester archdeacon.
5 Ibid., fo. 36r.   6 Reg. Bransford, fo. 1r. (6).   7 Landboc Winch. 2, pp. 344–6.
8 Reg. Gainsburgh, fo. 60v., p. 231. He had been instituted to Great Rissington in 1304 (ibid. fo. 27v., p. 95).
9 Rot. Parl. 1, pp. 190, 191. He is entitled "magister".
10 Reg. Maidstone, fo. 52r.   11 See above, p. 40, n. 8.
12 Reg. Orleton 2, fo. 42v. See above, p. 39, n. 4.   13 Ibid., fo. 43v.

Twyning.[1] It is possible that he continued to act as one of their legal advisors, although he was increasingly occupied with diocesan affairs. He played an important rôle at the beginning of Montacute's episcopate. In 1334 he was appointed, jointly with the sequestrator, to confer benefices in the bishop's collation during his absence abroad.[2] About the same time Montacute's official, John de Clipston, made him his deputy in all causes and legal business.[3] Under Bishop Bransford he was given licence to leave his church provided that he remained in attendance on Robert Stratford, bishop of Chichester.[4] He died shortly before 23 April 1349 when a successor was instituted to his rectory of Twyning.[5] It is certain that he had long ceased to be official of the Gloucester archdeacon. In fact, as early as 1334, M. William de Adelynton is mentioned as such.[6]

Thus little is known of the archdeacons' officials during our period, apart from Henry de la Lee, Richard Mayel, and William de Bosco. What we do learn is that such officials were invariably beneficed locally and that most of them were entitled *magister* which, at this time and in this context, can be taken to mean that they had obtained a master's degree, possibly at Oxford where the university was flourishing in the fourteenth century.[7] They remained in office for long periods which were not always consecutive. Their comparative permanence must have enabled them to play an important part in maintaining the continuity of archidiaconal administration. Quite apart from their normal duties as officials they were frequently used by bishops as *ad hoc* commissaries. Some, like William de Bosco, were taken into episcopal service, for which their education and administrative experience made them eminently suitable.

[1] The corrody was granted 13 March 1321 "pro suis serviciis . . . impensis et in posterum impendendis". He was to have the chamber west of the abbey gate with the chapel and cellar below, a stable, gardrobe, and plot of land between St Peter's church and the chamber. These were to revert to the abbey if he were to be promoted to a benefice too far away for residence. *Landboc Winch.* 1, p. 339.

[2] Reg. Montacute 1, fo. 10v.: 28 June 1334.

[3] Ibid., fo. 9r.: 25 May 1334. "Item, eodem die J. de Clipston officialis Wyg' comisit vices suas magistro Willelmo de Bosco in causis et negociis, quousque eas &c."

[4] Reg. Bransford, fo. 57v. (510): 24 May 1343. Another William de Bosco was also in the service of this bishop. He held a Chichester prebend and died in 1329. See Jenkins, "Lichfield Cath.", App. F sub nom., for a summary of his career. Emden tries to disentangle the biographies of a number of fourteenth-century clerks of this name.

[5] Reg. Bransford 2, fo. 10v. (1390). In 1350 Bosco's corrody was granted to Robert de Alne, rector of Alvechurch. *Landboc Winch.* 1, pp. 262-5.

[6] See above, p. 42, n. 4.

[7] Although only William de Bosco seems to figure in Emden's register, and he is recorded merely as "clerk of Winchcombe abbey".

The office of archdeacon [1]

The division of dioceses into territorial archdeaconries, which had been completed by the early thirteenth century, was a great administrative convenience. In theory the archdeacon exercised a general superintendence, under the bishop, over the clergy of his archdeaconry, but in practice his duties were carried out by a deputy—his official. [2]

The powers of archdeacons varied considerably. [3] At Carlisle where the single archdeaconry was coextensive with the diocese, [4] the archdeacon had no judicial powers in the fourteenth century. [5] The archdeacon of Richmond, on the other hand, as we learn from Archbishop Melton's composition (1331), was exempt from any control other than that of occasional visitation by the archbishops of York. [6] Between these extremes were varying degrees of archidiaconal jurisdiction, some of them defined by compositions drawn up in the thirteenth and fourteenth centuries. [7] Such compositions were the outcome partly of a prominent trend towards legal definition, partly of the related growth of a centralized administrative system in the dioceses.

[1] For a general account see Hamilton Thompson, *English Clergy* (pp. 5, 57–63, 70) and his Raleigh lecture, *Diocesan Organization in the Middle Ages: Archdeacons and Rural Deans* (*P.B.A.* Vol. XXIX). More localized are the same author's comments in his introduction to *York Reg. Greenfield*, pp. xv–xix (pt. 2, *Surt. Soc.* CXLIX, 1934) and in *Arch. Jnl.* 72 (1915), pp. 232–84: "The Will of M. William Doune, Archd. of Leicester." See also E. H. Minns, "The Office of the Archd. of Ely" (intro. to the *Vetus Liber Archidiaconi Eliensis*); Adrien Gréa, "Essai Historique sur les Archidiacres", *B.E.C.* 3me. ser., t. 2, pp. 39–67, 215–47.

[2] The absenteeism of fourteenth-century archdeacons should not be exaggerated. In a number of dioceses they played an important part in episcopal administration. Even so, it is clear that the routine work of the archdeaconries was carried out by their officials (see p. 39 above).

[3] Innocent III (*Extra.* 1, 23, c.7) summed up the canonical rights and duties of the archdeacon's office. See also Lyndwood, lib. 1, tit. 10, "De officio archidiaconi" (pp. 49 et seq.).

[4] Until the nineteenth century there were also single archdeaconries in Canterbury, Rochester, Ely, Llandaff, and St Asaph dioceses.

[5] *Carlisle Reg. Halton* (ed. T. F. Tout), intro. pp. xxix–xxx, and pp. 176–7.

[6] Raine, *Historians of the Church of York* 3, pp. 248–50; *York Reg. Wickwane*, pp. 116 et seq. (1281 visitation). The archdeaconry was not wholly extra-diocesan and the archbishop had concurrent jurisdiction in certain matters. See Hamilton Thompson. "Registers of the Archd. of Richmond", *Y.A.J.* XXV, pp. 129–269; XXX, pp. 1–132; XXXII, pp. 111–45.

[7] For example, the agreement between Bishop Ralph of Shrewsbury and Roger Mortimer, archdeacon of Wells, in 1338 (*H.M.C.R.* X, App. pt. 1, pp. 538–9), or between Aymer of Lusignan, bishop elect of Winchester, and M. Walter of Exeter, archdeacon of Surrey in 1254 (*Winch. Reg. Pontissara*, pp. 2–3). See also Archbishop Arundel's award in the dispute between the bishop and the archdeacon of Ely (*Vetus Lib. Arch. Elien.*, pp. 179–96), and that of Archbishop Melton mentioned above (note 6). For the powers of the archdeacon of Lincoln, see *Arch. Jnl.* 72, p. 242, n. 2 (cf. p. 122, n. 1 below).

Broadly speaking the *ius archidiaconale* was considered to involve the celebration of chapters, the holding of visitations, the oversight of parish churches and their ministers, the hearing of lesser causes, the making of corrections, the levying of fines from delinquents,[1] and the receipt of mandates for induction. At Worcester there is no trace of rights to appoint and amove rural deans and their apparitors, to grant probate of lesser wills, to exercise matrimonial jurisdiction, or to share in the fruits of vacant benefices, some, or all of which powers, we know to have been exercised by archdeacons in a number of other dioceses in the fourteenth century.

Few archidiaconal records survive from pre-Reformation times. Obviously episcopal registers were not intended to provide details of the functions of archdeacons though we do learn something about them incidentally, particularly in cases of disputed jurisdiction. The division into archdeaconries had no effect on the internal arrangement of most registers, being significant only in that a mandate was addressed to the official of one archdeacon rather than to that of another.[2]

Episcopal legislation often throws light on the activities of archdeacons. For the Worcester diocese Bishop Blois issued statutes in 1219 and 1229, the latter being partly a reissue of the earlier series. The statutes which Bishop Cantilupe promulgated in 1240 incorporated many of those of his predecessor, but were much more comprehensive.[3] Although these statutes are not specifically mentioned in fourteenth-century registers it is likely that they continued to be observed.[4]

Bishop Blois' statutes tell us comparatively little about archdeacons, but the explicit instructions for the commemoration of deceased clergy

[1] Lyndwood (p. 52 ad ver. *poena canonica*) discusses the question of the archdeacon's right to inflict a pecuniary penalty.

[2] The material on the thirteenth-century episcopal rolls of Lincoln was mostly divided according to archdeaconries. See K. Major, *Handlist of the Records of the Bishops of Lincoln &c.* At York, Greenfield's register had a separate section for each archdeaconry and this was the usual practice there. *Surt. Soc.* CXLV (1931), pref. p. x; Jacob, *Medieval Registers of Cant. and York*, p. 11.

[3] Cheney, *English Synodalia*, pp. 90 et seq. Bodl. MS. Rawlinson C. 428, which contains all the statutes, was procured for the cathedral priory by Brother Henry Fouke (professed in 1302 and later sacrist). It is in a good state of preservation but shows little sign of having been frequently consulted, and there are very few additional marginalia.

[4] Cheney (op. cit., p. 10) states that "statutes lawfully promulgated in a synod"— as were Bishop Blois' second series and those of Bishop Cantilupe—"were perpetually binding on the subjects of the diocesan and his successors". This was Bishop Ralph of Shrewsbury's contention when, in 1342, his commissary-general republished the statutes of William of Bitton, but the publication was revoked owing to the opposition of some "in and of the church of Wells". *B. & W. Reg. Ralph of Shrewsb.*, p. 458. For Bitton's statutes see Cheney, op. cit., pp. 97 et seq.

in the 1219 series show clearly the hierarchy of bishop, diocesan official, archdeacon, archdeacon's official, rural dean, and rector, vicar, or parish priest.[1] Cantilupe's statutes, on the other hand, give a good idea of what was expected of archdeacons in the mid-thirteenth century although, owing to their eclectic nature, we cannot be sure that they pay adequate attention to variations of function and procedure which may have prevailed in the Worcester diocese.[2]

Archdeacons in their visitations were to observe the statutes of the Fourth Lateran Council and of the Councils of Oxford (1222) and London (1237), and were forbidden to have more than the lawful number of mounted attendants.[3] They were not to extort money from those subject to them; to receive payment themselves, or through their officials, for the concealment of crimes; to excommunicate their subjects without the canonical threefold warning;[4] or to accept anything for the distribution of chrism or oil. Litigants, in cases in which composition was permissible,[5] were to be allowed to withdraw from their suits.[6]

For the appointment of apparitors in the deaneries and for ensuring that adequate vicarages were maintained in churches appropriated to monasteries, the archdeacon was to act jointly with the bishop's official.[7] Either archdeacon or diocesan official was to decide what ornaments, additional to those prescribed for every parish church, were to be kept in the greater churches. To one or other of them priests ordained elsewhere than in the diocese, who wished to celebrate Mass or to look after parishes, were to be presented for approval.[8] In other matters, including the provision of a greater number of clergy for those wealthier churches which had widespread parishes, and making inquiry as to whether any beneficed clergy were married or kept concubines,[9] the archdeacons were associated with the bishop's officers.[10]

---

[1] *Concilia* i, pp. 570–1.

[2] Ibid., pp. 665–78. Cheney, *English Synodalia*, pp. 90 et seq., discusses their provenance. But the later addition to the statutes, with its implication that there were only two archdeaconries, its reference to the synodal constitutions and Cantilupe's treatise on confession, as well as its mention of specific dates, would seem to have been written with individual Worcester conditions strongly in mind. See p. 47 below.

[3] *Extra* 3, 39, c.6 (ed. Friedburg) has "v vel vii" with an alternative reading "v vel vi".   [4] *Decretum*, Causa 24, Qu. 3, C. 6; *Extra* 5, 39, c.48.

[5] These are summarized in Athon's gloss ad ver. *tale negotium* (p. 55).

[6] *Concilia* i, p. 671.

[7] *Concilia* i, p. 674. In the fourteenth century the Worcester bishops appointed the apparitors, and though the archdeacons' officials may have advised them as to the suitability of candidates, there is no evidence that they did so.

[8] Ibid., pp. 666, 675.

[9] *Const. Othonis*, cc. "Innotuit nobis", "Licet ad profugandum" (Athon, pp. 38–41, 41–6).   [10] *Officiales*, apparently in a general sense. *Concilia* i, pp. 671, 672–3.

Appended to the sub-division of the constitutions entitled "De Ordine" is a section which may well have served as a "practical guide to archdeacons in their visitations" and formed "the basis of visitation articles".[1] It is concerned with the behaviour of the clergy, their literacy, orders, residence, and the celebration of Mass. However, the archdeacons and rural deans were forbidden to suspend erring rectors or vicars from the exercise of the divine offices while they could be coerced in person or by their goods.[2]

A later addition to Cantilupe's statutes,[3] most of which seems to be directed to the archdeacons, gives detailed instructions about the admission of parochial clergy and the procedure for dealing with the incontinence of stipendiary priests or incumbents of benefices. Stipendiary priests were to be punished by pecuniary fine for the first offence and to undertake to be of good behaviour under heavy penalty, which was to be exacted at once on the commission of a second offence.[4] If they were found guilty a third time, they were to be removed.[5] To prevent their passing from one archdeaconry to the other, the archdeacons were to keep each other informed of the names of ejected clerks. For the same reason, each archdeacon was forbidden to admit a priest ("capellanus") until inquiry had been made about his behaviour of the archdeacon from whose jurisdiction he had come. Priests from outside the diocese were to bring letters testimonial, and those ordained other than by their own diocesan were to give proof of his dispensation. Stipendiary priests, especially those presented to the cure of souls, were to be examined in the synodal constitutions and the bishop's treatise on confession.

Incontinent rectors or vicars were to be dealt with in much the same way as stipendiary priests. After their initial offence and fine, sureties for their good conduct were to be exacted by the archdeacon and sent to the bishop within a month. Punishment for a third lapse belonged to the bishop alone who imposed it on erring clerks "secundum jura et formam suarum obligationum", and insisted that those who had

---

1 Cheney, *Eng. Synodalia*, p. 90; *Concilia* I, p. 673.

2 See below, p. 66, n. 2.

3 *Concilia* I, p. 676. Cheney, op. cit., p. 94, provisionally dates it between July 1240 and the bishop's death in February 1266.

4 On each occasion the offender was to be moved to another place "propter infamiam et periculum evitandum".

5 Cf. Bishop Blois' 1229 provision (*Concilia* I, p. 625): "Ut sacerdotes annui ministrantes vitio incontinentiae notati chartas suas conficiant quod de caetero honestae conversationis erunt et caste vivent sub poena pecuniaria per cautionem fidejussoriam adhibitam: ita videlicet, quod si de caetero super eodem vitio convicti fuerint, vel quasi convicti, in episcopatu non ministrent."

5

committed offences in their own parishes should not be admitted to purgation except in his presence.

In the absence of archidiaconal records we cannot judge to what extent the archdeacons carried out their obligations, and there are few entries in the episcopal registers which throw light on their activities. But an entry of 1276 in Register Giffard does show signs of the influence of the diocesan statutes.[1] It is entitled "Articles of enquiry to be put by the archdeacon of the place to rectors and vicars of churches."[2] This is not an accurate description of the document for the preamble shows that it was certain offences of the archdeacons themselves— brought to light during episcopal visitation and at other times, which had led the bishop to make investigation. The articles are in the form of questions most of which, it must be admitted, may well have been posed at times of archidiaconal visitation, though others concern the archdeacons themselves and exempt jurisdictions over which they had no authority. In short, they must have been drawn up either for use at an episcopal visitation or for some special inquiry to be carried out by Giffard's commissaries.

In the preamble we learn that complaint had been made of the injuries and palpable molestations inflicted by archdeacons, their officials, or ministers, as well as by others deputed by the bishop. Heavy fines beyond what was permissible had been imposed. It was alleged that the faults of certain persons had been disregarded on some dissembling pretext, while those of others, though notorious, had been allowed to remain—not without grave scandal. Moreover, various defects in both churches and their ministers had sprung up contrary to ancient observances, to the detriment of divine worship.

Following this preamble are nineteen articles of inquiry,[3] the first three of which concern the conduct of archdeacons and their deputies. Were they carrying out corrections as was fitting? What were the names of those who had been sent back from the examination of the archdeacons to the bishop as incorrigible,[4] for what crime, and since when had they been apprehended? If beneficed clergy, had they pledged themselves by charter under penalty of deprivation of their

---

[1] Ff. 67v.–68r.: 13 September 1276. There is a summary in the printed edition.

[2] "Articuli inquirendi per archidiaconum loci versus rectores ecclesiarum et vicarios" (Marginal rubric).

[3] Only seventeen are included in Willis Bund's summary in the printed edition of the register. Visitation articles are discussed by Frere (*Visit. Art.* 1, pp. 95 et seq.) who prints a number of sets.

[4] The composition between Bishop Ralph of Shrewsbury and the archdeacon of Wells (1338) provided that certain cases should belong to the archdeacon to the exclusion of the bishop until a third offence. *H.M.C.R.* X, App. pt. 1, pp. 538–9.

benefices, or in other ways at the determination of the sender, both for incontinency and other crimes for which they were unable to purge themselves, especially if they were widely defamed?[1] Had the officials of archdeacons exacted or received any money from parish priests at the usual time of admission to the cure of souls, or at other times of admission to the celebration of the divine offices, or had they entered into any agreement with them before such admission? Had a proportionate amount of such receipts been paid into the general account? The remaining articles are chiefly concerned with the parishes, and there is no need to enumerate them here.

There is a similar series of articles in Bishop Cobham's register. This comprises no fewer than thirty-five points of inquiry and was intended, so the rubric tells us, to be used at the visitation of secular prelates.[2]

On at least three occasions papal indults permitted visitation and the collection of procurations by deputy.[3] That personal visitation was carried out by Archdeacon Burdon is suggested by the thirty-fourth article of Winchelsey's indictment of Giffard.[4] This asserts that the bishop had extorted two parts of the profits of visitation in the (Gloucester) archdeaconry—those from contumacies and all other procurations excepted, at times when the archdeacon was personally visiting and correcting.[5]

These details of archidiaconal visitation are all the more interesting because such material rarely found its way into episcopal registers. However, they tell us little about the efficacy and nothing about the regularity of such visitation.[6]

[1] Clearly a reference to Cantilupe's careful regulations on this subject (see p. 47 above). Cf. number twenty-nine of the sixty-eight articles printed by Frere (*Visit. Art.* 1, pp. 99–103) from the Burton Annals (*Ann. Mon.* 1, pp. 307–10): "An aliqui convicti vel confessi super incontinencia obligaverint se ad resignacionem beneficii vel aliam penam canonicam si recidiverint: et si quisquam eorum post obligacionem recidiverit" (Frere, p. 101, whose rendering differs slightly from *Ann. Mon.* 1, p. 308). The Burton annalist (*sub anno* 1253) states that the inquiries were made "per singulas et universas dioceses tocius regni Anglie".

[2] *Reg. Cobham,* fo. 126r.–v., pp. 225–6. "Articuli inquirendi in visitacione secularium prelatorum." At least one article is concerned with the conduct of archdeacons: "An archidiaconus vel suus officialis seu decani propter aliquod lucrum accrescens eis dimittant peccata subditorum incorrecta."

[3] According to c. 33 of the Fourth Lateran Council (*Extra* 3, 39, c. 23) archdeacons and others were to receive procurations only when visiting in person. See Archbishop Greenfield's instruction to his official on this point (*York Reg. Greenf.*, pp. 144–5). In the *Vetus Lib. Arch. Elien.* (pp. xvi, 19) is some account of the archdeacon of Ely's *dieta* or daily round while on visitation. [4] See p. 60 below.

[5] Thomas, *App.*, p. 72. For the bishop's two-thirds in the Worcester archdeaconry, see p. 27 above.

[6] Lyndwood (p. 49 ad ver. *visitatione*) tells us that an archdeacon could visit annually—or more often if necessary: "Et nota, quod archidiaconus, etiamsi non subsit

Apart from times of visitation the activities of archdeacons or their officials in the sphere of correction would seem to have taken place in their periodical chapters,[1] as was also the practice in exempt deaneries enjoying quasi-archidiaconal jurisdiction. It is difficult to establish the relationship between these archidiaconal chapters and ruridecanal ones.[2] The most recent worker in this field has shown that in five dioceses—York, Lincoln, Durham, Winchester, and Worcester, there is evidence of the exercise of judicial functions in rural chapters by archdeacons or their officials, but he doubts whether this would justify the assumption that they ordinarily conducted their cases there.[3] The single Worcester instance occurs in 1271 when, at a meeting of the Warwick chapter at Snitterfield, M. Hugh Tankard, official of Robert de Asthall, archdeacon of Worcester, and Geoffrey, dean of Warwick, rector of St Michael's church there, acted as presidents and gave judgement in a mortuary dispute "de consilio et consuetudine capituli nostri de Warwyke".[4]

Of judicial activities in rural chapters there is much evidence in thirteenth-century statutes;[5] but to whom did such jurisdiction belong? Certainly in the following century we can seldom, if ever, be sure to what extent the jurisdiction of the rural dean *ex officio* and of the ruridecanal chapter itself functioned independently of the archdeacons' officials.[6]

For the Worcester diocese a roll of corrections made in the deanery of Droitwich has survived. Its preservation may be due to the fact that

---

causa, potest semel in anno visitare . . . sed si subsit causa saepius visitandi, potest etiam saepius in anno visitare."

[1] Archbishop Romeyn ordered the archdeacons not to hold their chapters in the same week as his consistory at York "ut sic illi, qui tam in consistorio quam in capitulis forsan simul et semel utrimque habuerint facere, tam hic quam ibi absque incomodo contumacie valeant interesse". *York Reg. Romeyn* 1, pp. 83–4. For Worcester evidence see below, pp. 53, 54, n. 5.

[2] See below pp. 67 et seq. Sometimes they appear to be the same, as, for instance, in the complaint of the clergy of the deanery of Holderness in the archdeaconry of the East Riding: "Consuevit officialis archidiaconi cum decano loci et clerico suo, aliquando cum altero eorum tantum . . . ad nos et ecclesias nostras declinare, pro suis capitulis tenendis." The burden of the complaint was that whereas three or four mounted men had formerly sufficed, eight or nine had become the usual number, so that the clergy laboured under an oppression akin to that of the Israelites under Pharaoh. *York Reg. Wickwane* (1279–85), pp. 248–9.

[3] Foster, "Rural Deans", p. 145.

[4] *Monasticon* 2, p. 31; Dansey 2, p. 75n. Cf. Foster, "Rural Deans", p. 140.

[5] Foster, op. cit., pp. 66–8, 110–11. There is only one mention in Worcester statutes, those of Cantilupe: *Concilia* 1, p. 676, and see p. 70 below.

[6] See pp. 69–71 below.

somehow it found its way into the diocesan archives.[1] Because of its early date (1300) and unusual nature, this document is of exceptional interest.[2] It records the judicial proceedings of four chapters held at Dodderhill (13 May), Salwarpe (15 June), Northfield (5 July),[3] and Droitwich St Andrew (18 July),[4] which are almost entirely concerned with instances of fornication and adultery. On the dorse of the roll is a heading intended to preface an account of proceedings in Northfield church on Tuesday after the feast of SS. Peter and Paul—the same day that the chapter was held there. Beneath this is a partial entry recording the certification by the dean of Wich (Droitwich) of an inquiry into the vacancies of Hadzor and Oddingley by the rectors and vicars of the whole deanery.[5] It begins: "Cum constaret nobis per certificatorium decani de Wych", and because it was left unfinished we do not know to whom "nobis" refers. It could, of course, refer to the bishop; but if so, why did he send the mandate direct to the rural dean contrary to the usual practice? Was it another of Giffard's encroachments upon the customary rights of the archdeacon? The latter was an absentee, and a possible explanation is that his official was also away from the diocese, or merely unable to execute the mandate personally.[6] Alternatively "nobis" could refer to the archdeacon's official, in which case the entry might be interpreted as a memorandum of the report

1 It appears to be the only record of its kind at Worcester. It may be noted that Archbishop Wickwane had the rolls of the rural chapters of the York archdeaconry deposited at York "prout ab antiquo invenimus ordinatum": a measure which seems to have annoyed the archdeacon. *York Reg. Wickw.*, p. 202.

2 D. & C. MS. C. 885a. Edited by F. S. Pearson in *Collectanea* (*W.H.S.*), pp. 69–80.

3 The MS. reads "die Martis proxima post festum Sancti Petri". This must refer to the feast of SS. Peter and Paul on 29 June.

4 The intervals between these chapters were thirty-two, nineteen, and twelve days respectively. Lyndwood (p. 14 ad ver. *capitulis ruralibus* glosses: "Et horum capitulorum quaedam tenentur de tribus hebdomadis in tres, quaedam semel in quarta anni: & haec dicuntur capitula principalia, propter majorem confluentiam cleri, & quia in his de negotiis arduioribus tractari consuevit...". Foster (op. cit., p. 119) notes that thirteenth-century statutes of Winchester [Wells?], Exeter, and York urged monthly chapters. He suggests that there might be a case for monthly meetings in the Worcester diocese if the third of the Droitwich chapters could be shown to have been exceptional. His postulation of an archidiaconal synod is mistaken (see n. 5 below), but it may be that a special chapter was summoned to inquire about vacant benefices (see below). It should be remembered, however, that the date had already been settled at the previous chapter on 15 June.

5 The MS. has "decanatus" which the editor (p. 80) renders "archidiaconatus". This led Foster (op. cit., p. 95) to conclude that an archidiaconal synod was held. In fact it was a routine inquiry in the rural chapter.

6 Cf. mandates in *Linc. Rot. & Reg. Sutton* 1, pp. 150–1, addressed "officiali archidiaconi Lincoln' seu eo non existente decano de Graham", "archidiacono Lincoln' vel ejus officiali seu in eorum defectu decano de Calsewath".

sent by the rural dean as his commissary.[1] It was certainly the regular practice at Worcester for archdeacons or their officials to return such mandates to the bishop.[2] What is clear is that the rural dean held the inquiry[3] and there was no delay in sending the result to the bishop, for he instituted a clerk to Hadzor on 6 July, the day following the chapter. It is not unreasonable to suppose that he had awaited its outcome.[4]

There is no statement that the rural dean conducted the judicial business of the chapters, but his presence at one of them suggests that he may have done so. If such was the case, did he act merely as a delegate of the archdeacon's official? It would seem so. The cases dealt with are those which lay within the competence of the arch- deacon and there is no evidence that his jurisdiction was merely con- current with that of the rural deans or of the ruridecanal chapters.[5] On the contrary, the many references to the making of corrections imply that, apart from the bishop and his officers, it was confined to those who exercised exempt jurisdiction and to the archdeacons.[6]

In most dioceses the archdeacons had cognition of lesser causes, although the bishops were sometimes unwilling to admit that this belonged to them of right.[7] This jurisdiction was ordinarily concurrent with that of the bishop. For instance, the agreement in 1254 between the bishop elect of Winchester (Aymer de Lusignan) and the arch- deacon of Surrey permitted the latter to make inquiries and corrections in his archdeaconry, but the bishop and his officers could also do so when they thought fit. The archdeacon was to have jurisdiction in matrimonial cases "extra sententiam divorcii" provided that they were

1 There are instances in *York Reg. Giffard* (pp. 22, 24) of rural deans carrying out mandates directed to the archdeacon's official. Cf. *Linc. Rot. Welles* 1, p. 110.

2 See pp. 55–6 below.

3 The editor of the MS. has (p. 80): "Legitime omnibus et singulis vocatis et expectatis, infrascripti continuatim contraxerunt." The rector and vicar of Dodderhill, the rectors of Salwarpe, Upton [Warren], and Stoke [Prior], who are then mentioned, he takes to be the usual "committee" formed to discuss the matter. But the editor's "continuatim" seems to be "contumac" in the MS., and the phrase perhaps "infra- scripti contumac[iam] contraxerunt". Even if "contraho" cannot be made to bear the meaning "incur" here (though "debitum contrahere" is often found) the context suggests that this was the sense intended: after lawful summons those of the clergy who had not obeyed were declared contumacious. Cf. below pp. 56, n. 2, 73, n. 10.

4 *Reg. Giffard*, fo. 448r., p. 527. Another clerk was instituted to the chapel of Oddingley on 5 August (ibid., fo. 448v., p. 528).

5 This point is elaborated on pp. 68–70 below.

6 See, for instance, pp. 26 (and n. 9), 48, 59, n. 5, 60, n. 1.

7 For example, Aymer de Lusignan's claim: "Non ad ipsum archidiaconum sed ad se diceret jure episcopali omnia predicta spectare, negans dictum archidiaconum in eorum possessione pacifica esse vel fuisse." *Winch. Reg. Pontissara*, p. 3.

brought into his court first.[1] A later composition (1338) between the bishop of Bath and Wells, Ralph of Shrewsbury, and the archdeacon of Wells, provided that the archdeacon should have powers of correction and punishment if in his citations he anticipated the bishop and his ministers.[2] At Ely the archdeacon had concurrent jurisdiction with the bishop in lesser causes, and suits in which frivolous appeal was made to the bishop's audience were to be remitted to his court.[3] Archbishop Giffard, while acknowledging that the archdeacon of Cleveland had cognition of causes, asserted the right of his officers to rescribe in both lesser and greater causes "ne videretur negari justicia".[4]

At Worcester likewise, Bishop Giffard did not recognize any suit as belonging exclusively to the cognizance of an archdeacon in the first instance. It was urged against the bishop that his officials and commissaries had attracted to their own examination disputes and lesser causes[5] pending before the official of the (Gloucester) archdeacon in his chapters, as well as other causes which pertained to archidiaconal citation by ancient custom, and that they had inhibited the archdeacon or his official from proceeding with them. All this Giffard denied, saying that his officials and commissaries by prevention had cognizance of all causes, though allowing jurisdiction to inferiors.[6]

There is a reference in Register Cobham to the cognizance of a cause of perjury, one of the greater causes reserved to the bishop, by an inferior judge who, we are told in a marginal rubric, was the official of the (Gloucester) archdeacon.[7] Sarra, wife of William Beyonde Toune, had acted as compurgatrix for Clarence de Upcote, accused of counterfeiting a key to a rectory granary. The holder of the court had convicted the latter of perjury and, considering Sarra to be likewise perjured on that account, had imposed penance on her also. Whereupon Sarra complained to the bishop. Cobham pointed out that perjury was one

---

1 Op. cit., pp. 3 et seq.   2 *H.M.C.R.* X, App. pt. 1, pp. 538–9.

3 *Vetus Lib. Arch. Elien.*, pp. 184–6.   4 *York Reg. Giffard*, p. 96.

5 The distinction between lesser and greater causes is not always consistent. Cf., for instance, the variation between the "reserved cases" on pp. 26 and 196 of the *Vetus Lib. Arch. Elien.*

6 "Item, eiusdem domini episcopi . . . officiales suique commissarii iurgia et modicas causas coram officiali domini archidiaconi in capitulis suis pendentes et alias causas ad vocationem archidiaconalem ab antiqua consuetudine pertinentes ad suum examen traxarunt, et ne per ipsum archidiaconum seu ipsius officialem aliqualiter procedatur in causis huiusmodi inhibebant." Reg. Giffard, fo. 472v. Thomas (*App.*, p. 73) inserts "archidiaconales" after "alias causas", but this word is not in the MS.

7 This rubric is written in another hand as follows: "Ut officialis archidiaconi non cognoscat in arduis et maioribus causis." But the final sentence of the entry suggests that it may refer to the court of the jurisdiction of Withington, an exempt manor: "Et

of the causes reserved to himself.[1] Moreover, it was erroneous to conclude that if the principal defendant was convicted of perjury the
compurgators were *ipso facto* guilty as well, for they could have taken
their oaths in good faith.

It has been suggested that tithe disputes probably constituted "the
most important judicial business which the archdeacon and his official
transacted in the thirteenth century".[2] There is plenty of evidence that
the Gloucester archdeacon or his official heard such cases, claiming
the right to do so by long established custom.[3] But often—perhaps with
increasing regularity during the fourteenth century, they were decided
by the bishop or diocesan official and sometimes formal instruments
incorporating the awards were drawn up and confirmed by the Worcester prior and chapter.[4]

To sum up then, what evidence we have shows that the jurisdiction
of the episcopal and archidiaconal courts were concurrent in so far as
minor cases were concerned. Cases of incontinency occur frequently in
the only detailed record which survives of proceedings in the episcopal
court of audience;[5] similar cases occupy most of the space on what may
be the roll of an archidiaconal court. Obdurate offenders were sent to
the bishop, to whose courts appeal could be made from that of the
archdeacon. Sometimes a bishop issued a special commission for the
taking over of a case begun in the archdeacon's court.[6] In 1318 the right
to exercise jurisdiction in both archidiaconal and consistory courts
within the Gloucester archdeaconry was vested in one person, John de
Broadwas.[7] This was only a temporary arrangement during the

---

si alia subsit causa usque ad adventum nostrum apud Wythindon qui erit in proximo
differas execucionem ipsius" (*Reg. Cobham*, fo. 77v., pp. 129–30).

[1] "... cum causa periurii sit de causis maioribus et episcopo reservatis." Ibid.

[2] Foster, "Rural Deans", p. 144.

[3] "De antiqua et approbata et hactenus pacifice observata consuetudine, huiusmodi causarum cognitio in archidiaconatu suo Gloucestrie ubi decime ipse consistunt,
pertinet ..." (from bull of Boniface VIII, 1300). *Landboc Winch.* 2, pp. 81–2 *et passim*.

[4] Ibid., pp. 135–6, 268–72, 337 et seq., 554–7.

[5] Reg. Bransford 2, ff. 8r.–9r. It should be pointed out that John de Severleye, who
as the bishop's commissary presided over the court, was also the archdeacon of Worcester, and it is possible that some of the cases would ordinarily have been heard in the
archdeacon's court.

[6] See *Reg. Cobham*, fo. 6r., p. 7. Commission for the prior, subprior, and official to
continue a case begun by the official of the Worcester archdeacon.

[7] He was appointed "ad tenendum omnia consistoria et capitula tam nostra quam
archidiaconatus Gloucestrie in manibus nostris ad presens existentis, et ad exercendum
omnia et singula que ad dicta capitula et consistoria spectare noscuntur". *Reg. Cobham*, fo.
3v., p. 4. Cf. Bishop Wykeham's detailed commission (1387) to the sequestrator of Winchester archdeaconry to exercise archidiaconal functions "sinodaque et capitula
tenendum" on the death of Archdeacon Bloxham. *Winch. Reg. Wykeham* 2, p. 407.

vacancy of the archdeaconry and prior to Cobham's appointment of an official of the diocese.

At Worcester, as in other dioceses, it was customary, on receipt of the episcopal mandate for the summoning of the clergy to undergo visitation, for the archdeacon's official to desist from the holding of chapters and from the exercise of all archidiaconal jurisdiction. A formal prohibition to that effect was included by the bishop in his *premunicio visitacionis*, which remained in force until the completion of the visitation.[1]

When presentation was made to a vacant benefice, unless the full facts were already known to the bishop or those acting for him,[2] an inquiry was set on foot by an episcopal mandate directed to the official of the appropriate archdeacon.[3] Comparatively few of these mandates are recorded in the bishops' registers, though memoranda concerning the inquiries are frequently to be found.[4] The form of the mandate was well established by the fourteenth century and is too well known from published registers of other dioceses to require much comment

[1] "Et quia in diocesi nostra Wyg' de consuetudine hactenus usitata est obtentum, quod a tempore quo officiales dominorum archidiaconorum Wyg' ecclesie mandata episcopi qui pro tempore fuerit de vocando clerum et populum ad subeundum visitacionem eiusdem receperint, celebracioni capitulorum in suis archidiaconatibus eadem visitacione pendente supersedere tenentur omnino, vobis in virtute obediencie firmiter iniungendo mandamus, quatenus a tempore recepcionis presentis nostri mandati in locis predictis per vos vel per alium seu alios capitulum non teneatis quodcumque donec visitacionem nostram compleverimus in eisdem, nec correcciones aliquas faciatis, nec litteras purgacionis seu correccionis sub data visitacionem nostram precedente predictam aliqualiter concedatis." (Bishop Bransford to the official of the Worcester archdeacon, 30 September 1339, informing him of his intention to begin his primary visitation. Reg. Bransford, fo. 10r. (89).)

[2] At the time of the institution to the hospital of Longbridge in 1349 it was noted: "nulla inquisicione premissa, quia de inquirendis in hac parte constabat ad plenum". Reg. Bransford 2, fo. 17r. (1512).

[3] Practice varied in the dioceses. At Hereford mandates for inquiry were directed to the diocesan official "cui racione officii super vacacione ecclesiarum in diocesi Herefordensi hactenus scribi consuevit", for example, *Hereford Regs. Cantilupe*, pp. 153–4; *Swinfield*, pp. 521–2; at Salisbury they were often addressed to the rural deans (*V.C.H. Wilts.* 3, p. 9); and in Lincoln diocese to the officials of the archdeacons or, in their absence, to the rural deans (for example, *Rot. & Reg. Sutton* 1, *passim*). Some original returns by rural deans are preserved at Lincoln (*Linc. Archives Comm., Archivist's Rpt.*, March 1952–3, p. 43). At Worcester the person to whom the mandate was addressed (ordinarily the archdeacon's official) was responsible for its return, and this was apparently the practice in most dioceses. But at Salisbury the presentee seems to have secured the mandate from the bishop and to have brought back ("reportavit") the result of the inquiry himself. For example, *Salisb. Reg. S. de Gandavo*, pp. 562, 563, 568, 591, etc.

[4] In the list of institutions at the time of the Black Death it is noted in almost every instance that a mandate for inquiry was sent by the bishop. Reg. Bransford 2, ff. 10r. et seq.

here.[1] In the preamble the bishop stated that a presentation had been made on the grounds of vacancy. The inquiry itself was concerned with the right of patronage, whether the benefice was the subject of litigation or burdened with a pension or portion, and the suitability of the clerk presented. The archdeacon's official was instructed either to hold the inquisition at the next chapter or at one specially summoned for the purpose.[2]

Archidiaconal chapters were used to acquaint the clergy with episcopal mandates and with matters of general importance. Thus Bishop Cobham ordered the official of the Worcester archdeacon, in the chapters of his archdeaconry and in other clerical convocations, to admonish those having cure of souls to reside in their benefices.[3] When the friars of the hospital of the Holy Spirit came from Rome begging alms of the faithful, Bishop Gainsburgh directed the officials of the archdeacons to receive them in their next chapters and before any other business of a similar nature—save that of the cathedral fabric.[4] At the time of the Black Death Bishop Bransford likewise ordered the royal ordinances for the regulation of wages and prices to be published in chapters and elsewhere.[5]

---

[1] See the early fourteenth-century forms transcribed from Bodl. MS. Rawlinson D. 893, fo. 114v., in the appendix to an article by J. W. Gray on the "Ius Presentandi in England". *E.H.R.* LXVII, pp. 508–9.

[2] Either "in pleno loci capitulo secundum communem cursum celebrato", "non expectato pleno loci capitulo", or "in pleno loci capitulo ob hoc celebrato". There is ample evidence that such inquiries were held in the ruridecanal chapters. For example, in chapters at Tetbury (27 November 1343), Campden (27 April 1344), and Elmbridge (7 November 1346), inquests were held into vacancies at Brimpsfield, Aston Somerville and St Andrew's, Droitwich respectively. Reg. Bransford, ff. 59r., 72r.–v., 102v.–103r. (al. ciii–ciiii); (524, 623, 811); and see pp. 51–2 above. Cf. Gray, op. cit., pp. 492–3.

[3] *Reg. Cobham*, fo. 80v., p. 135 (1322). Though by this time the phrase "in capitulis archidiaconatus predicti et aliis cleri convocacionibus" had hardened into common form.

[4] *Reg. Gainsburgh*, fo. 23v., pp. 77–8. "Frater W. &c. Wygorn' et Glouc' archidiaconis vel eorum officialibus, salutem graciam et benediccionem. Mandamus vobis firmiter iniungentes quatinus cum fratres hospitalis Sancti Spiritus in Saxia in Urbe Romana vel eorum nuncii veri et honesti ad vos accesserint subsidium fidelium petituri et recepturi ipsos in proximis capitulis vestris celebrandis post inspeccionem presencium pre ceteris negociis consimilibus, excepto negocio fabrice ecclesie nostre cathedralis Wyg', benigne et sine difficultate admittatis . . .' (A.D. 1303).

[5] The royal writ is dated 18 June 1349 and its substance is in *Foedera* 5, pp. 693–5. Bransford sent mandates to the commissary of the Worcester archdeacon and to the official of the Gloucester archdeacon for its publication and enforcement: "Quocirca vobis committimus et mandamus . . . quatinus prefatas ordinaciones in singulis ecclesiis vobis subditis, capitulis et aliis cleri convocacionibus, ac locis aliis quibus videritis expedire, iuxta formam vim et effectum dicti brevis publice et solenniter publicetis, et faciatis per alios publicari, eciam in vulgari." Reg. Bransf. 2, ff. 2r.–3r. (1334).

From the eleventh to the fourteenth century there is intermittent evidence from a number of dioceses of the existence of archidiaconal synods.[1] The editor of the late thirteenth-century register of Bishop Oliver Sutton states that such assemblies were meeting regularly in Lincoln diocese, and that the bishop's mandates assumed this as a matter of course.[2] But there seems to be no record of the holding of a synod *eo nomine*[3] in the Worcester diocese during the fourteenth-century.[4]

Mandates for induction to those benefices subject to his jurisdiction[5] and within the territorial limits of his archdeaconry were ordinarily addressed to the archdeacon or his official.[6] A constitution ascribed to Archbishop Stratford laid down that if the archdeacon himself inducted he was to have forty pence for expenses, if his official, two shillings.[7] The Worcester records are silent on this matter of remuneration.

Archdeacon Ledbury, in 1354, was claiming the right to induct to benefices *iure archidiaconali*,[8] and administrative practice as exemplified by the diocesan registers shows that this claim was tacitly accepted in the ordinary course of events. Bishop Giffard, however, had some altercation with an earlier archdeacon of Gloucester, Walter Burdon,

---

[1] For example, Coventry and Lichfield, Ely, Lincoln, Norwich, Salisbury, and Winchester (above, p. 54, n. 7). See Foster, "Rural Deans", pp. 94–5, 102.

[2] *Rot. & Reg. Sutton* 3 (ed. Rosalind Hill), intro. pp. xxx–xxxii. She equates Pecham's "four principal rural chapters" with synods, and it would certainly be difficult to draw a distinction between them. The reference in the Longdon (Worcestershire) appropriation document to "chapters and synods" at which the church was to be represented by its vicars, could be to archidiaconal chapters.

[3] But the common term "capitula" could have included "general" or "principal" chapters which served much the same purpose. See n. 2, above and p. 68, nn. 3, 4, below.

[4] See above, p. 51, n. 5.

[5] For induction to exempt parishes see pp. 21, 24 above.

[6] Lyndwood points out that he was merely the bishop's instrument in this matter: "Nam nec archidiaconus nec quivis alius debet aliquem inducere in ecclesiam absque mandato instituentis" (p. 140 ad ver. *superioris*), "ex hoc apparet quod non sit in archidiaconi potestate inducere, vel non inducere, postquam super hoc mandatum receperit a suo superiore, quia tenetur ejus mandatis obedire" (p. 140 ad ver. *tenentur*). Archbishop Giffard made this point clear to the archdeacon of Cleveland: "Institutiones quidem rectorum quorumlibet non habetis, set eos ad mandatum nostrum, sicut et priores et abbates in possesionem inducitis corporalem". *York Reg. Giff.*, p. 96.

[7] "Item quia archidiaconi" (Lyndwood, pp. 140–1; *Const. Prov.*, p. 50). Lyndwood (p. 140 ad ver. *quantitate pecuniae*) denied the archdeacon's right to receive any money if he did not carry out the induction himself or in the person of his official: "sed quid si inducatur per alium quam per ipsum archidiaconum, vel ejus officialem, tamen de mandato ipsius archidiaconi; an tunc archidiaconus aliquid posset recipere pro tali induccione? dic quod non: sed taliter inducens habebit ab inducto expensas necessarias suo statui competentes sub moderatione quae conceditur ipsi archidiacono, vel ejus officiali".   [8] See p. 21 above.

on this subject. It was alleged that the bishop had caused inductions to be carried out by persons other than the archdeacon or his official although anciently, by approved right and custom, inductions had belonged to them. To this Giffard replied that inductions had always been made by the bishop or by someone deputed by him, just as he wished.[1] It is possible that the archdeacon was complaining more particularly about the sending to special commissaries of mandates for induction to the churches of episcopal manors. A later bishop, Cobham, certainly infringed what the archdeacons considered to be their rights of induction, for he directed many such mandates to rural deans.[2] Bransford's long register, however, shows that he conformed rigidly to the customary practice of sending them to the archdeacons' officials.

It would be tedious to enumerate the many other classes of episcopal mandate which were from time to time sent to the archdeacons' officials. Among them were mandates for the publication of excommunication—though these were often sent to the rural deans, for the imposition of sequestration, for the collection of arrears of tenths, and for the execution of royal writs, particularly those of *levari facias* which necessitated the sale of the goods of indebted clerks who had no lay fee.

The profits of jurisdiction did not go entirely to the archdeacons. We have seen that Giffard wished inquiry to be made as to whether they had rendered a proportion of certain receipts in their general account.[3] This must refer to the bishop's portion, which in the case of profits of visitation was two thirds of the total—or so Giffard claimed.[4] There were both winter and summer accounts. Bishop Maidstone, for instance, gave an acquittance under his private seal to his sequestrator, Stephen de Northeye, for the sum of £53 "de perquisitis compoti yemalis archidiaconatuum Glouc' et Wyg' de anno domini M°CCC°XV°".[5] Of this sum £28 10s. 7½d. came from the collection of Peter's Pence, the remaining £24 9s. 4½d. from unspecified sources.

---

[1] "Item, dominus Wygorn' episcopus induci facit in corporalem possessionem ecclesiarum archidiaconatus Glouc' rectores institutos per alium seu alios quam per ipsum archidiaconum Glouc' seu eius . . . officialem, licet ab antiquo de iure et consuetudine approbata huiusmodi inducciones ad ipsos pertinea[n]t.

"Ad tricesimum secundum [articulum] respondet episcopus, quod inducciones huiusmodi semper consueverunt fieri per episcopum, vel aliquem per eum deputandum, pro sue libito voluntatis." Reg. Giffard, fo. 472v. (printed in Thomas, *App.*, pp. 71–2).

[2] See the edition of Cobham's register, App. 1, pp. 228 et seq.

[3] See p. 49 above.

[4] See pp. 49, 60, and for the Worcester archdeaconry, p. 27.

[5] Reg. Maidstone, fo. 41r. In 1337 the appointment of penitentiaries apparently took place at the time when the accounts for the archdeaconries were rendered. Reg. Montacute 1, fo. 30v.; 2, fo. 21v.; also p. 177 below.

Doubtless Pentecostals—from the Gloucester archdeaconry only[1]—
and Synodals made up the bulk of the latter sum. There is no mention
of the bishop's portion of archidiaconal profits and it may be that this
account comprises only those sums collected by the archdeacon on the
bishop's behalf.[2]

We learn much about the prescriptive rights of the archdeacons from
articles 32 to 36 of Archbishop Winchelsey's indictment of Giffard
drawn up after his metropolitan visitation in 1301.[3] A number of them
have already been mentioned. It cannot be doubted that these five
articles are a statement of Archdeacon Walter Burdon's grievances
against Giffard, but it should not be assumed on that account that the
rights of the Worcester archdeacon were fundamentally different.

Article 32, concerning mandates for induction, has been discussed
above.[4] In the next article complaint is made that the appropriation of
the church of Ampney St Mary to the abbey of Cirencester had been
prejudicial to the archdeacon of Gloucester and his archdeaconry
because of the deprivation of inductions, canonical obediences, rights
of citation, corrections, and the office of the rural deanery.[5] This was
more especially the case because no vicarage had been ordained, and
the religious claimed to be exempt because they could not be cited
outside the town of Cirencester by ordinary authority.[6] The bishop
replied that he had only restored the church, which had been appropriated long before. The rest he denied.

It may be noted at this point that when Bishop Gainsburgh ordained
the vicarage of the church of Wickham—appropriated by Giffard to
the Cistercian abbey of Bordesley, the rights of the archdeacon of

---

[1] Those from the Worcester archdeaconry were paid to the sacrist. In 1329 Orleton
ordered the deans of the archdeaconry to admonish all those who had not paid their
Pentecostals to the sacrist, Robert de Clifton, to do so within a month. Reg. Orleton 2,
fo. 11v. [2] See pp. 71–2 below.

[3] See Rose Graham's article on this visitation in *English Eccles. Studies*, pp. 330–59.
She would seem not to have been aware of the copy of Winchelsey's injunctions to
Worcester Priory in Reg. Montacute 2, ff. 44r.–45r.

[4] Pp. 57–8 above.

[5] "... quia ab illis rectoribus ipsius ecclesie de Ameneye sicut de aliis ecclesiarum
rectoribus predicti archidiaconatus consueverunt archidiaconi Glouc' habere primas
inducciones, obediencias canonicas, *vocaciones, correcciones, et officium decanatus
ruralis &c., de quibus spoliatur archidiaconatus predictus per ipsam appropria-
cionem ..." (Reg. Giffard, fo. 472v.; Thomas, *App.*, p. 72). *Thomas could not read
this word and left a blank.

[6] Unless custom ran to the contrary an archdeacon could have no jurisdiction over
the religious themselves (*Extra.* 1, 23, c.10). Archbishop Romeyn rebuked the official
of the archdeacon of York for citing a canon of Drax to appear "in archidiaconali
capitulo" and quashed his excommunication of a servant of the Cistercian priory of
Nun Appleton. *York Reg. Romeyn* 1, pp. 126–7, 103.

Gloucester were specifically reserved by a special clause added to the ordination document.[1]

The thirty-fourth article reveals that Giffard had been in the habit of exacting two-thirds of the archdeacon's profits when the latter made personal visitation.[2] He claimed that his predecessors had done the same time out of mind, and that such portion belonged to his church by long observed custom.

In the next article it is alleged that Giffard had inhibited the archdeacon, his official or commissary, from dealing with crimes or faults committed by religious persons outside their monasteries, and with defects of chancels, the repair of which pertained to such religious. To this Giffard replied that the correction of the excesses of the religious within his diocese had belonged, and still belonged, to the bishop and his official.[3] As to the defects of chancels,[4] he had not interfered except at times of visitation.[5]

---

[1] "Huic eciam ordinacioni adicimus per presentes quod archidiaconi loci et ipsorum officiales qui pro tempore fuerint excessus et peccata parochianorum ecclesie supradicte, necnon ministrorum et serviencium dictorum abbatis et conventus si in dicta parochia deliquerint, et aliorum quorumcumque in ipsa parochia seu in manso rectorie delinquencium cuiuscumque status aut condicionis existant, corrigendi et puniendi ac alias iura archidiaconalia excercendi sicut tempore suo et predecessorum suorum excerceri consueverant, non obstante quocumque privilegio per dictos abbatem et conventum seu eorum successores impetrato seu impetrando, liberam habeant potestatem." (*Reg. Gainsburgh*, fo. 1r., pp. 1–2). Athon has a lengthy gloss on the subject of the archdeacon's rights over appropriated churches (p. 53 ad ver. *visitent*), which he begins: "Quaero unum quod est facti, an contra archidiaconum loci per religiosos habentes parochialem ecclesiam appropriatam possit contra visitationem, seu prestationem obedientiae praescribi? Videtur quod non: cum ejus superioritas, sicut episcopi, sit juris communis." He then examines the contrary view. ". . . qui habet distinctam limitationem sui archidiaconatus: tunc enim habet jurisdictionem separatam ab Episcopo, quae cum sit consuetudinaria, potest praescribi." He concludes: "Prima opinio verior est".   [2] See p. 49 above.

[3] Regular houses were not subject to the archdeacon (see p. 59, n. 6) as Lyndwood points out (p. 220, ad ver. *ecclesiis sibi subjectis*): "Sunt enim quaedam ecclesiae, licet infra ambitum alicujus archidiaconatus constitutae, quae tamen ipsi archidiacono non sunt subjectae, utputa, ecclesiae regulares, quales sunt monasteria monachorum, canonicorum regularium, & monialium." The rights of archdeacons in appropriated churches are discussed above (n. 1).

[4] For the obligation of the archdeacon to ensure the repair of the church fabric, especially the chancel, see Lyndwood, p. 53. John de Athon tells us that the rector's obligation to repair the chancel derived from the common custom of England ("communis consuetudo Anglicana") and adds an exhaustive gloss on the subject (p. 113, ad ver. *cancellos etiam ecclesiae* and *ad hoc tenentur*: Cf. Lyndwood, p. 53 ad ver. *reparatione*).

[5] "Idem [*sic*], idem episcopus inhibet, et inhiberi facit, ne de criminibus seu delictis religiosorum in archidiaconatu suo Glouc' perpetratis seu commissis et extra loca religiosa, ac eciam de defectibus cancellorum ad religiosos spectantibus reparandis, idem archidiaconus per se vel . . . officialem seu commissarium aliqualiter intromittat.

Finally, in article 36, the bishop is stated to have encroached upon the jurisdiction of the archdeacon in lesser causes.[1]

The archdeacon, like the bishop himself, derived his authority from the common law of the church. By long approved custom he also claimed that certain functions belonged to him *iure archidiaconali*. It was the latter which were challenged by Giffard. He would admit no custom that mandates for induction should be directed to the archdeacon by right, nor would he allow that the archdeacon had other than a concurrent jurisdiction in lesser causes. It is doubtful whether Giffard was correct in his assertion that he had only restored the church of Ampney St Mary to Cirencester Abbey, and that it had been appropriated at the time of the latter's foundation.[2] According to the *inspeximus* and confirmation by Edward III of the abbey's charter of foundation (1133) Henry I had included among his benefactions: "In Amenel [Ampney] iiii hidas et i virgatam et ecclesiam villae".[3] But this is no evidence of formal appropriation.[4] In the absence of any earlier information we cannot assess Giffard's right to two thirds of the profits of archidiaconal visitation which he, in his turn, had claimed by approved custom. His contention that the correction of religious persons belonged to the diocesan was a sound one, and it is doubtful whether in practice the archdeacon could have maintained his claim to such jurisdiction. As to interference in the matter of church chancels, it was his undoubted right—if the archdeacon proved negligent, though he admitted to having done so only at times of visitation.

The natural ebullience, not to say bellicosity, of Bishop Giffard undoubtedly played a part in these disputes, but there were also deeper causes. If one can risk a broad generalization, there was little chance after the thirteenth century of an archdeacon extending his powers at the expense of his diocesan: that he tended to encroach upon those of the rural dean is well known.[5] In many dioceses, as we have seen,[6]

"Ad tricesimum quintum [articulum] respondet episcopus quod ab antiquo correccio excessuum religiosorum in sua dyocesi semper pertinuit et pertinet ad episcopum et eius officialem et non ad inferiorem prelatum. De defectibus vero cancellorum dicit se non intromittere nisi tempore visitacionis." Reg. Giffard, fo. 472v. A slightly incorrect version is given by Thomas, *App.*, p. 72. [1] See p. 53 above.

[2] *Reg. Giffard*, fo. 436r. al. ccccxlii, p. 508. The editor supplies "Emley" instead of "Ampney" for the MS. "Amenel". [3] *Monasticon* 6, p. 177.

[4] Such was the view of the royal chancery. In 1314 a fine of £20 was imposed on the monastery for not having secured a mortmain licence (*C.P.R.* 1313–17, p. 103).

[5] As Barlow points out, he might also turn his attention to the exempt jurisdictions within his borders. *Durham Jurisd. Peculiars*, intro. p. xvi. For disputes in the Worcester diocese about the right to exercise archidiaconal jurisdiction see pp. 21, 26, 27–8 above. [6] P. 44 above.

the position was stabilized by compositions, probably concluded only after years of friction. At Worcester there is unfortunately no composition, but the matters in dispute are similar to those found elsewhere; that they were confined to the southern archdeaconry may perhaps be explained by the fact that since the death of Cardinal Hugh of Evesham in 1287 the Worcester archdeaconry had been held by non-resident foreigners. After Giffard's death there is no trace during our period of any further dispute of this kind. The friction between archdeacon and bishop which is so common in the thirteenth century would appear to have resulted largely from the development of an increasingly centralized diocesan administration. The Worcester statutes serve to emphasize the important position attained by the diocesan official, and his court, the bishop's consistory, obviously detracted from the importance of that of the archdeacon. There is no evidence that the bishop was making less use of the local machinery of archdeaconry and rural deanery: in at least one sphere there was a contrary tendency.[1] On the other hand, the growing complexity of diocesan administration had forced him to delegate more of his powers to specific officers, and he came to rely to an increasing extent on a specialized staff of clerks who were ready at all times to deal with his business in any part of the diocese.

THE RURAL DEANERIES[2]

Like archdeaconries, rural deaneries formed useful sub-divisions which enabled inquiries to be conducted and the substance of episcopal mandates made known within a strictly limited area. Episcopal registers show that a large number of mandates were directed to rural deans on the basis of the territorial limits of their deaneries.[3] They did not receive such mandates as of decanal right but because it was administratively convenient. Moreover, the bishop sometimes went over the

[1] See p. 89 below.

[2] For an account of rural deans based on the printed sources of his time see William Dansey, *Horae Decanicae Rurales* (2nd ed. 1844, 2 vols.). A modern account is given by A. Hamilton Thompson in *English Clergy*, pp. 63–70, and in *Diocesan Organization* (*P.B.A.*), pp. 17 et seq. "The activities of Rural Deans in the 12th and 13th centuries", a thesis submitted by J. Foster in 1955 for the M.A. degree of Manchester, is a comprehensive account from printed sources and Professor Cheney's transcripts of episcopal statutes.

[3] But see *Dioc. Organization*, p. 36: "Nor were such mandates, involving commissions of enquiry, necessarily issued to the rural dean in whose province lay the places and persons mentioned: he was merely on a level with any commissary whom a bishop might choose to appoint *ad hoc*." In the Worcester diocese it can be said that such mandates were normally, though not exclusively, sent to the rural dean. We learn nothing of a *ius decanale*.

head of the rural dean by appointing his official, the archdeacon's official, or some other special commissary to deal with a matter even though it concerned one particular deanery. None the less, the importance of the rural dean as a local officer with a special oversight of the clergy within his deanery, and one to whom episcopal instructions with reference to places or persons within such an area were ordinarily sent, is amply demonstrated by the records of the thirteenth and fourteenth centuries.[1]

At Worcester Giffard's register (1268–1302) contains many mandates addressed to rural deans,[2] and their number does not decline noticeably during the first half of the fourteenth century. A few examples may serve to illustrate the usual practice in the diocese.

During his visitation in 1301 Archbishop Winchelsey had discovered much that was amiss in the deanery of Bristol. For the publication of his inhibitions and ordinances he wrote, not to the official of the diocese, nor yet to the archdeacon's official, but to the dean of Bristol.[3] Similarly Bishop Gainsburgh, on learning that certain priests in the city and suburb of Worcester had granted absolution in reserved cases without his licence, ordered the dean of Worcester to put a stop to such abuses by publishing his prohibition in the churches of the area.[4] In 1309, however, Bishop Reynolds instructed the official of the Worcester archdeacon—not the dean of the Christianity of Warwick—to hold an inquiry to ascertain the names of those beneficed in the deanery of Warwick who had not proceeded within a year to the priesthood, as ordered by the general council.[5] But it was the dean of Bristol whom Cobham instructed to discover the names of those who had damaged the fabric of the chancel of St Giles, Bristol, and despoiled it, and to cite them to appear before him on the eighth law day after the inquiry.[6] In 1339 the dean of Winchcomb was ordered to make known in every

1 Foster (op. cit., p. 6) poses the question "whether the emergence of the episcopal register coincided with the period of greatest ruridecanal activity or whether the registers give us a greater insight into activities which were previously performed but not recorded".

2 Foster (op. cit., p. 11) calculates from the printed register that there are 150, or rather less than five a year.

3 *Reg. Gainsburgh*, fo. 3r., pp. 7–8: Cirencester, 18 May 1301. The printed edition has "15 Kal. Jun. 1303, second year of consecration". The MS. reads "xv Kalen' Junii anno domini MoCCCmoprimo, consecracionis nostre septimo". The date of consecration is that of Archbishop Winchelsey and not that of Gainsburgh as the editor assumed. See App. D, p. 354 below.

4 Ibid., fo. 2v., p. 6, 10 February 1304. See App. D, p. 355 below.

5 *Reg. Reynolds*, fo. 6v., pp. 4–5, 30 January (1309). See App. D, p. 356 below. The regulation was laid down at the Council of Lyons (1274) and incorporated in *Sext* 1, 6, c.14 ("Licet canon"). 6 *Reg. Cobham*, fo. 38r., p. 35 (undated).

6

church of his deanery that any who wished to oppose the purgation of John de Abbotesbury and John de Felipeston, apprehended on a charge of robbing the cellarer of Winchcomb, were to appear in the cathedral church on a stated day to show reasonable cause why such purgation should not be proceeded with.[1] In fact mandates of this kind were invariably addressed to the rural dean of the locality in which the offence had been committed.

We have seen that at Worcester inquiries into vacancies were held by the appropriate archdeacon's official on receipt of an episcopal mandate *ad hoc*.[2] Other inquiries about benefices were commonly entrusted to the official of the archdeacon, or to special commissaries, rather than to the rural dean as such. The right to induct to benefices was considered by the archdeacons to belong to them, though Cobham at least addressed many mandates for induction to rural deans.[3]

However, certain mandates were usually addressed to rural deans. Such include citations of persons to appear before the bishop or his commissary, both in the ordinary course of judicial business and after episcopal visitation, and instructions for the publication of sentences of excommunication for offences committed within their territory. Undoubtedly the business of citation was prominent among the activities of rural deans at this time.[4] Though the rural dean might serve citations himself,[5] this was the regular function of the apparitor, the bishop normally appointing one for each deanery.[6] During a case heard in 1312 before Reynolds' auditor, William de Birston, archdeacon of Gloucester, one of the parties alleged that no citation had reached him. In consequence the dean of Hawkesbury was summoned to answer

---

[1] Reg. Bransford, fo. 11v. (100).   [2] See p. 55 above.

[3] See pp. 57–8 above. In Cantilupe's statutes deans are forbidden to receive anything "pro missionibus clericorum in possessionem ecclesiarum" (*Concilia* 1, p. 671). Foster ("Rural Deans", p. 24) remarks: "A rapid perusal of a number of thirteenth-century episcopal registers reveals that one of the duties which was most often deputed to the rural dean was that of inducting a clerk into his living." The present writer's impression from those fourteenth-century registers which have been printed is that in most dioceses the archdeacons claimed the right to induct, and that by and large this was conceded in practice. In such dioceses, it is true, many mandates were addressed to rural deans, but some of these can be explained by the special privilege of exempt jurisdiction (see above, p. 18, n. 1). In at least one diocese, Hereford, the mandates seem to have been regularly sent to rural deans. All this would suggest that the archdeacon had in some dioceses established his right to inductions at the expense of the rural dean, but the matter requires closer investigation.

[4] Lyndwood glosses *decani ruralis* (p. 81): "Cujus officium est, in causis ecclesiasticis, citaciones et transmissas exequi. . . ." Cf. Foster, "Rural Deans", pp. 70 et seq.

[5] See Lyndwood, pp. 225–6, ad ver. *duntaxat* and *non equitem*.

[6] See pp. 137–40 below.

for his disobedience and contempt in failing to certify what he had done about the citation.[1]

Rural deans figure prominently among those appointed to secure criminous clerks from the secular authorities,[2] a function assigned to them by Bishop Blois in his statutes.[3] They frequently exercised the office of penitentiary, sometimes in their own deaneries, often in a much wider area. There is record of their having attested the validity of ordinands' titles[4] and very occasionally they are named in commissions for the holding of purgation.[5] There is also an instance of a rural dean granting probate of a will, but only as the special commissary of the diocesan sequestrator.[6]

The thirteenth-century statutes tell us something about those of the rural deans' activities which are not initiated by episcopal mandates. They were to denounce to the bishop or his official those who had dealings with excommunicates, and their importance as overseers of the moral welfare of their deaneries is implied by the threat of deprivation and heavy punishment for the concealment of crimes.[7] When a rector or vicar died it was the rural dean's business to look after his goods until it was clear whether he had left a will or not.[8] He had also to cultivate the lands of vacant churches, on the understanding that his expenses were to be refunded by the next incumbent. Alternatively he could farm them out for a portion of the profits.[9] His standing in

---

[1] *Reg. Reynolds*, fo. 56v., pp. 49–50.

[2] Particularly the rural deans of Gloucester, Warwick, and Worcester, at times when the justices were visiting those places.

[3] *Concilia* 1, p. 571 (1219); ibid., p. 626 (1229).   [4] See p. 168 below.

[5] In 1339 the dean of Kineton was appointed to admit the purgation of the rector of Dry Marston. Reg. Bransford, fo. 7v. (64).

[6] Bodl. MS. Glouc. Ch. 2 [1350]. The dean of Winchcomb was acting for Henry de Neubold, Bishop Thoresby's sequestrator. A *sede vacante* formula (R.S.V. fo. 134r.) directs the rural dean to render account before the prior or his vice-gerent of the sums received from vacant benefices and the insinuation of testaments "occasione nostre iurisdiccionis ecclesiastice". But it is probable that he performed these functions as an agent (see below, pp. 116 et seq.). Instances of testamentary activity by rural deans in the fourteenth century are comparatively rare. Archbishop Wickwane delegated powers of probate to the dean of Holderness with the warning that he was not to act in ignorance of the law. *York Reg. Wickw.*, p. 113. In Lincoln diocese rural deans are known to have exercised such jurisdiction despite episcopal efforts at restriction. See C. Morris in *J.E.H.* Vol. 10, no. 1, pp. 56–7. In Norwich diocese they retained the right to grant probate of lesser wills. Blomefield, *Norfolk* 4, pp. 63, 554; cf. pp. 121–2 below. See also Dansey, op. cit. 2, pp. 79–84.

[7] *Concilia* 1, pp. 625 (Blois, 1229), 671 (Cantilupe). See below, p. 67, n. 5.

[8] Ibid., pp. 571 (Blois, 1219), 626 (Blois, 1229).

[9] Ibid., pp. 627 (Blois, 1229), 675 (Cantilupe). The synodal statutes of York (?1259) and Exeter (1287) made similar provision for the safeguarding of vacant benefices. See Foster, op. cit., pp. 43–4.

the deanery is emphasized by the special commemoration of his death prescribed by Bishop Blois.[1] Over the clergy he would seem to have had considerable power of coercion and in the last resort that of suspension.[2]

There is apparently no corroborative evidence in the episcopal registers of the performance of these functions, except in the case of sequestration. As custodians of sequestrated property, rural deans continued to play an important rôle throughout the first half of the fourteenth century.[3]

Innocent III had laid down the rule that the bishop and archdeacon were to appoint and dismiss rural deans jointly.[4] John de Athon agreed that this was the lawful procedure—saving local custom.[5] In practice there was much variation, and Foster, after reviewing the evidence, concluded that in England either bishop or archdeacon, or the two together, made the appointments.[6] So far as the Worcester diocese is concerned, it is clear that the archdeacons acted, if at all, in no more than an advisory capacity. Indeed, Bishop Montacute empowered his official both to amove deans and their apparitors throughout the diocese and to appoint others in their place as he thought fit.[7] So that it would seem that the appointment and dismissal of rural deans belonged solely to the bishop and to the prior *sede vacante*.[8]

Lyndwood wrote that rural deans were appointed for a period of time only.[9] Pecham's constitution "Quidam Ruralium" provided

1 *Concilia* 1, p. 570 (Blois, 1219).

2 Ibid., p. 673. Rectors and vicars were not to be suspended by archdeacons or rural deans "dum tamen per bona sua, vel personas coerceri poterint competenter". But did deans have this power of suspension in the fourteenth century? Athon (p. 15, ad ver. *erubescunt*) thought not: "Decanus saltem de consuetudine vice archidiaconi jurisdictionem habet cognitialem quoad effectum corrigendi . . . licet non quoad effectum removendi tales [clericos] a villicatione, & suspendendo eos ab officio."

3 See pp. 71–2 below.

4 *Extra* 1, 23, c. 7. See also Lyndwood ad ver. *decani rurales* (p. 79).

5 "Non ar. quod decanatus rurales, & per consequens decani ibi, praefecti sunt ipsorum archidiaconorum: sed certe salva consuetudine locorum tam praefici debent decani tales, quam etiam amoveri per episcopum & archidiaconum simul de iure" (ad ver. *decanatuum suorum*, p. 10).

6 "Rural Deans", pp. 18–21.

7 ". . . necnon ad amovendum decanos et apparitores eiusdem nostre diocesis et loco amotorum alios subrogandum prout vestre circumspeccioni faciendum esse videbitur . . ." Reg. Montacute 2, fo. 2v: 25 July 1334.

8 For an appointment *sede vacante* of a dean of Powick see *R.S.V.*, fo. 134v., p. 244. On the other hand, the Gloucester archdeacon complained that by appropriation he lost the "officium decanatus ruralis" due from rectors of his archdeaconry. Can this mean the obligation to serve as rural dean? See pp. 59, n. 5, 73.

9 ". . . & eorum officium est temporale, & non perpetuum" (p. 79 ad ver. *decani rurales*): "et sunt hi decani temporales ad aliquod ministerium sub episcopo vel archiepiscopo exercendum constituti . . ." (pp. 14–15 ad ver. *decanos rurales*).

that they should take a yearly oath in the episcopal synod, and Lynd-wood in his gloss suggests that this was very probably because they were changed every year and new ones appointed.[1] In the Worcester registers of our period there is no mention either of the appointment of a rural dean by the bishop[2] or of the holding of a diocesan synod,[3] but it is clear that rural deans enjoyed a longer tenure of office than Lynd-wood would have us believe. Whether this was the result of annual reappointment cannot be determined, though Montacute's commission seems to imply that they held office during good behaviour.[4]

The position of the rural dean *vis-à-vis* the archdeacon is not easy to discover. Archidiaconal instructions to rural deans, apart from those which had their origin in episcopal or *sede vacante* prioral mandates, obviously found no place in the registers. A passage in Cantilupe's statutes might be taken to mean that rural deans were accounted *ministri* of the archdeacons, but this interpretation is doubtful.[5] More-over, the probability that they were appointed by the bishops in the fourteenth century makes it unlikely that their status was such at that time. The rural dean certainly owed obedience to the archdeacon,[6] but how far he acted *motu proprio* rather than at the behest of arch-deacon or bishop it is impossible to say. In particular we have no means of telling what the rural dean did, or was permitted to do, in the rural chapter.

The whole question of the rural chapter is a difficult one. Dansey contended[7] that the rural dean originally monopolized the presidency, and that it was the "archidiaconal intrusion" as a consequence of Otto's constitution "De Archidiaconis"[8] that delivered the "death-

---

[1] "Hoc ideo dicit fortassis, quia quolibet anno mutantur decani, & fiunt novi . . ." (p. 85 ad ver. *omni anno*). In Bath archdeaconry rural deans were said (1319) to be elected yearly by the incumbents of each deanery. They took an oath of fidelity to the archdeacon. This may have been true of the whole diocese of Bath and Wells. *B. & W. Reg. Drokensford*, p. 286. See p. 73 below.   [2] But see p. 66, n. 8 above.

[3] The last recorded synod was held in 1252. See below, pp. 87 et seq.

[4] Above, p. 66, n. 7.

[5] "Nec archidiaconi nec eorum ministri officiales videlicet aut decani vel etiam sacerdotes in parochiis suis pecuniam recipiant pro criminibus celandis." Similarly by implication it would seem that deans guilty of such offence were to be punished by someone other than the bishop. Could the archdeacon have been intended, or merely the bishop's official? "Quod si decani vel sacerdotes fecerint ab officiis amoti gravius puniantur. Archidiaconi vero et rectores ecclesiarum et vicarii perpetui relinquantur episcopo puniendi." *Concilia* 1, p. 671.

[6] As laid down in *Extra* 1, 23, c. 7 para. 2: "Archipresbyteri autem, qui a pluribus decani nuncupantur, eius iurisdictioni se noverint subiacere."

[7] Op. cit. 2, p. 110.

[8] Athon, p. 54: "Sint autem solliciti frequenter interesse capitulis per singulos Decanatus."

blow" to the rights of the chapters. Foster challenges this view by pointing out that twelfth-century evidence shows the archdeacon acting as president more often than the rural dean.[1] In the following century the archdeacon, his official, the rural dean, and even the diocesan official, occur as presidents.[2] From Pecham's constitution "Quia Incontinentiae"[3] Foster argues that it was the archdeacon's prerogative to preside over the rural chapters, but that circumstances forced him to delegate this duty to his official or to the rural deans.[4] This coincides with Gibson's interpretation of Athon's statement, written while Stratford was archbishop of Canterbury (1333–48),[5] that in his day such chapters were held by the archdeacons' officials and sometimes by the rural deans.[6] Gibson understood this to mean that they were presided over "by the officials, in the absence of the archdeacon, and by the rural dean only in the absence of both".[7]

In the light of the evidence it would not be unreasonable to identify the fourteenth-century "archidiaconal chapters" of the Worcester diocese with "rural chapters", which as late as Lyndwood's time were said to be meeting at three-weekly intervals and quarterly, under the title of "principal chapters", for more important business.[8] If this is a valid conclusion it was in rural chapters that the archdeacons' officials were instructed to make known episcopal mandates of general concern and in which they conducted at least some of their judicial business.[9] This seems to make sense of the available material. There is no mandate in the registers of our period ordering a rural dean to take any action

[1] Op. cit., p. 108.   [2] Foster, op. cit., pp. 108, 111.

[3] *Const. Prov.*, p. 24: "... praecipimus archidiaconis universis ... quatenus constitutionem supradictam faciant in quatuor anni principalibus capitulis ruralibus per se, vel per eorum officiales, vel saltem per decanos rurales, seu gerentes vices eorum ... coram toto capitulo ... recitari."

[4] Op. cit., p. 111. He supports this conclusion by showing (ibid., pp. 97–8) that the "capitula archidiaconorum" which various ecclesiastical statutes decreed should be held were in fact rural chapters. Significantly the statutes of Peter des Roches (1224?) and Walter Kirkham (?) include the rural dean among the possible presidents (Bodl. MS. Hatton 92, fo. 156r.; *Concilia* 1, p. 706); so too does Pecham's constitution (n. 3 above).

[5] Whom he describes as "doctorem meum" (p. 129 ad ver. *quod habita possessione*).

[6] P. 54 ad ver. *capitulis*: "Ruralibus, quae hodie tenentur per officiales archidiaconorum, & quandoque per decanos rurales. ..."

[7] *Codex* (1713) 2, p. 1013.

[8] See above, p. 51, n. 4, and cf. p. 57, nn. 2, 3.

[9] For mention of the activities of archdeacons in chapters see above, pp. 50, 53, n. 6, 54, n. 7, 55, n. 1, 56–7, 56, nn. 1 and 2. It is not suggested that all archidiaconal cases were conducted in local chapters, but that some of them were, as the Droitwich roll can be taken to show (see pp. 50–2). John de Wakerley, Archdeacon Burdon's official (see p. 42) and commissary *ad hoc*, conducted a tithe case in the parish church of St John, Gloucester (*Landboc Winch.* 2, p. 344), but we learn nothing of a fixed place

in a chapter. It was in the parish churches of his deanery that he was instructed to publish, or to have published, the contents of the bishop's mandates. At least by the late thirteenth century the holding of chapters and the making of corrections there was considered to pertain to the *ius archidiaconale*[1] although Giffard's provision for inquiry as to whether deans were holding adulterine chapters may indicate a survival of independent decanal action.[2]

There would appear to be only two recorded instances of rural deans acting in chapters within the bishop of Worcester's jurisdiction.[3] The dean of the Christianity of Warwick was joint president with the Worcester archdeacon's official of a chapter which met at Snitterfield in 1271, and the dean of Droitwich conducted an inquiry into a vacant benefice in a chapter assembled at Northfield in 1300,[4] and perhaps presided over judicial proceedings there.[5] Slight though the positive evidence is, it seems likely that the rural dean often acted as president of the ruridecanal chapter and heard cases there as the delegate of the archdeacon's official.[6] If the chapters were held as often as the Droit-wich roll of 1300 indicates,[7] the archdeacon's official could hardly have presided at all of them and the local rural dean was probably recognized as the person who ordinarily acted for him.

It is now possible to say something of the business of the rural chapters so far as this can be ascertained from the Worcester records.[8] Bishop Blois laid down that two priests were to be appointed in every deanery by the chapter to hear the confession of priests, although in the fourteenth century this function would appear to have been carried

---

where sessions were regularly held. In the late fifteenth and early sixteenth century the archdeacon of Canterbury's court had sessions at Canterbury and in the deanery of Sandwich and went on circuit through the rural deaneries in the west of the diocese. Woodcock, *Eccles. Cts.*, pp. 34–6.

[1] See above, p. 26, n. 9.

[2] "Item, an . . . decani locorum capitula teneant adulterina. Et utrum huiusmodi capitulis aliquid duxerint explicandum, a quibus et ex qua causa, et utrum quesita huiusmodi inter cetera generaliter computentur." Reg. Giffard, fo. 67v. This is the fourth of a series of articles dated 1276. See above, pp. 48 et seq.

[3] There is also record of a mortuary dispute decided in an Evesham rural chapter of 1271, presided over by the abbot of Evesham and the rural dean of the place. *Monasticon* 2, p. 31; Dansey 2, p. 75n. See p. 70 below.

[4] See pp. 50–1 above.   [5] See p. 52 above.

[6] It is probably in this sense that we should interpret the twentieth of Cobham's visitation articles: "An archidiaconus vel suus officialis seu decani . . . dimittant peccata subditorum incorrecta." See above, p. 49, n. 2; cf. p. 66, n. 2.

[7] See p. 51, n. 4.

[8] It is not worth while to re-examine the general evidence which has been fully discussed by Foster ("Rural Deans", chap. 5, pp. 121 et seq.) and by Dansey (Vol. 2, pp. 22–105).

out by the bishop.[1] Cantilupe ordered portions of his penitential and of his constitutions to be read aloud in every chapter and difficult passages explained. Those who abused feast days by trading or who held pleas in sacred places,[2] were to be brought before the chapter and heavily punished there.[3] It is impossible to say to what extent these provisions were observed. In the fourteenth century inquisitions into vacant benefices and the publication of the bishop's instructions—both initiated by mandates directed to the archdeacon's official—were regularly carried out in rural chapters, but of other, apart from judicial business, there is no trace in the records.

The judicial activities of the ruridecanal chapter present difficulties. There are three possible elements: judicial action by the dean *ex officio*, that of the chapter itself, and that of the archdeacon, his official, or some delegate acting in the chapter.[4] Foster concludes that the evidence (before 1300) for the rural dean's exercise of jurisdiction by virtue of his office is slight, but should not on that account be disregarded. He points out the difficulty of deciding when a dean was acting in a personal capacity and when as capitular president.[5] The chapters of Warwick and Evesham, which met in December 1271, each dealt with a question about the payment of mortuary and heriot.[6] The rural dean sat as joint president on both occasions—the dean of Warwick with the Worcester archdeacon's official, but the judgements were pronounced "de consilio et consuetudine capituli nostri de Warwyke" and "de consilio virorum prudentium presentis capituli".[7] Yet forty years later we are told plainly in the Liber Albus that the Warwick chapters had belonged to the archdeacon time out of mind, and that it was his jurisdiction that was ordinarily exercised within them.[8] As has been argued above,[9] the cases heard in the Droitwich chapter of 1300 pertained likewise to the archdeacon's jurisdiction. It seems then, that the jurisdiction of the archdeacon had come to overlay that which at one time may have been exercised by dean or rural chapter. We know nothing of the details of the process and far too little about the relationship between chapter, rural dean, and arch-

---

[1] See chap. 4 below under "Penitentiaries".

[2] Cf. no. 19 of Cobham's visitation articles: "An mercata, ludi seu placita teneantur alicubi in locis sacris." *Reg. Cobham*, fo. 126v., p. 226.

[3] *Concilia* 1, p. 676.   [4] See above, pp. 50, 52.

[5] "Rural Deans", pp. 66–8.

[6] *Monasticon* 2, p. 31; Dansey 2, p. 75n. See above, pp. 50, 69. Evesham Abbey was an interested party in both cases.

[7] See above, pp. 52, 69.

[8] See p. 27 above. It was sometimes contested by the deans of the collegiate church.

[9] Pp. 50–2.

deacon. But it does seem reasonable to conclude that there is no necessity to postulate archidiaconal chapters distinct from those of the rural deaneries, and that neither rural dean nor ruridecanal chapter was exercising rights of correction concurrent with those of the archdeacon in the fourteenth-century Worcester diocese.

The rural deans were important as financial agents of the bishop and had to render account of the money received on his behalf. Of their own perquisites we have little definite knowledge. In 1317 John de Broadwas[1] was empowered by Bishop Cobham to seek out, exact, and receive from the deans of the Gloucester archdeaconry, all the money received and still held by them, which he had sequestrated both during the bishop's own time and that of his predecessor Maidstone.[2] There are many instances in the registers of the custody by rural deans of sequestrations[3] imposed either by the diocesan sequestrator or by the bishop, and doubtless the income from these figured in their accounts.[4] In 1334 Bishop Montacute empowered his official, M. John de Clipston, to audit the accounts of every deanery in the diocese, to issue letters of acquittance, and to appoint deans and apparitors.[5]

To what extent rural deans rendered accounts which were separate from those of the archdeacons' officials is by no means clear. Peter's Pence was collected by deaneries[6] but included in the accounts for the

[1] See above, pp. 38, n. 6, 54, n. 7.

[2] "Tercio Kal' Januarii [30 December 1317] anno et loco supradictis idem pater magistro Johanni de Bradewas vices suas cum cohercionis canonice potestate commisit, ad petendum exigendum et recipiendum a decanis archidiaconatus Gloucestrie omnem pecuniam per eosdem quoquomodo collectam et in manibus eorum existentem ac per ipsum tam de tempore bone memorie W. predecessoris sui quam suo sequestratam et acquietancias faciendum &c." *Reg. Cobham*, fo. 3v., p. 4. Broadwas held the office of sequestrator under both Maidstone and Cobham.

[3] For their duties under thirteenth-century statutes, see p. 65 above. Foster ("Rural Deans", pp. 37 et seq.) examines the twelfth/thirteenth-century evidence and shows that in a number of dioceses rural deans played a part in sequestration. See below, chap. 3 under "Sequestrators", for Worcester practice.

[4] The rural dean himself sometimes imposed sequestration on the authority of an episcopal mandate. Thus, in 1339 Bransford ordered the dean of Campden to relax the sequestration he had imposed on the goods of the rector of Dry Marston until such time as he should be otherwise instructed. Reg. Bransford, fo. 28v. (203).

[5] "...ad audiendum raciocinium singulorum decanorum omnium decanatuum nostre diocesis de quibuscumque proventibus nos in dicta diocesi concernentibus quovismodo, ac ad allocandum seu disallocandum allocanda vel disallocanda prout raciocinii huiusmodi exitus ex hoc requirit, et ad faciendum acquietancie litteras in hac parte, necnon ad amovendum decanos" (etc., see above, p. 66, n. 7). Reg. Montacute 2, fo. 2v. The authority given to Clipston for the direct audit of ruridecanal accounts can be paralleled *sede vacante* by a formula ordering their presentation before the prior or his vice-gerent (see p. 65, n. 6).

[6] Bishop Simon (1125-50) had granted to the Worcester monks "denarios Sancti

archdeaconries,[1] which was the custom in English dioceses.[2] The priors' accounts *sede vacante*—the only detailed ones that we have, consist almost entirely of the accounts of the archdeacons' officials made up of totals for each deanery subject to them.[3] Such totals may well have been the outcome of individual accounts rendered to the archdeacons' officials by the rural deans.

It is even more difficult to lift the cloak of anonymity from rural deans than from the archdeacons' officials. Richard de Beverborn[4] appears to have been the dean of the Christianity[5] of Worcester for most of Gainsburgh's episcopate. He is specifically mentioned as dean in 1305, 1306, and 1307, when he was among those appointed to receive criminous clerks from the justices at Worcester.[6] In 1306, the dean of Worcester, doubtless the same Beverborn, was joined with others in a commission for the admission to purgation of Ralph le White, rector of Colesborne, imprisoned for the homicide of Gainsburgh's former chancellor and vicar-general.[7] Three years later, at the beginning of Reynolds' episcopate, he was again appointed to receive criminous clerks, though this time he is not given the title of dean.[8] We can trace him back to Giffard's register, for in 1299 his name came before the bishop's council. He was then rector of Spetchley[9] but living permanently at the chantry of the Carnary at Worcester.[10] Apparently he re-

---

Petri, quod decani nostri de terris eorum exigere solebant, quorum summa usque ad viginti solidos estimabatur". Thomas, *App.*, p. 7; *Reg. Prioratus*, fo. 98a and b.

[1] See p. 58 above.

[2] For instance, there is a list of the sums from the various rural deaneries of Canterbury diocese in the Black Book of the Archdeacon (*H.M.C.R.* VI, App. p. 498). The same method was used in the diocese of Bath and Wells, and the official of the archdeacon of Wells appealed to Canterbury when Bishop Ralph of Shrewsbury forbade the rural deans of his archdeaconry to surrender the money they had collected. *B. & W. Reg. Shrewsb.*, p. 310; cf. *Reg. Drokensford*, pp. 285–6. See also *Winch. Reg. Woodlock*, p. 131, and the early fifteenth-century lists for the ten deaneries of Chichester diocese in *Chich. Reg. Rede*, p. 415. Only a part of the amount collected was actually paid to the pope: see p. 123, n. 6 below.

[3] See below, pp. 311 et seq.

[4] Barbourne in Claines, near Worcester.

[5] For this title see *English Clergy*, p. 64. In the Worcester diocese it was used of the deans of Worcester, Warwick, Gloucester, and Bristol.

[6] *Reg. Gainsburgh*, ff. 8v., 10r., 11r. (*bis*); pp. 23, 27, 29 and 30.

[7] Ibid., fo. 10v., p. 28: 13 May 1306.

[8] *Reg. Reynolds*, fo. 12r., p. 11: 1309.

[9] Which is a few miles from Worcester on the Alcester road.

[10] *Reg. Giffard*, fo. 442r. and attached MS., pp. 515, 517. "Item, queratur si iuste dominus episcopus poterit permittere dominum Ricardum de Beverborn rector capelle de Spechesl' morari perpetuo apud cantariam carnarie Wyg' nichilominus deputari ut prius, cum sint tales presbiteri ipsius carnarie stipendiarii et quasi ad voluntatem magistri loci ipsius annis singulis amovendi."

tained Spetchley until 1325 when he resigned and was instituted to the Spagard chantry in St Helen's, Worcester.[1]

In 1339, during Bransford's episcopate, Walter Marny is twice mentioned as dean of Gloucester. He was rector of St John's church there, and received commissions for the securing of criminous clerks and for the exercise of the office of penitentiary.[2] One Richard was dean of Bristol in 1308, when he took some part in the proceedings against St Augustine's abbey.[3] In 1334 Roger, perpetual vicar of St Nicholas', Bristol, is described as dean of the place at the time of his appointment as penitentiary.[4] From the register of Ralph of Shrewsbury, bishop of Bath and Wells, it appears that Richard le White was dean of Bristol in 1343. He can probably be identified with the clerk of that name instituted to the vicarage of All Saints, Bristol, in 1326.[5] Thomas, rector of Little Rissington,[6] is mentioned in 1347 as dean of Stow. In that year, together with the rector of Yeovil, he certified that on the bishop's mandate he had admitted the vow of chastity taken by Alice Maidegod of Stow and had given the usual benediction.[7]

Where we can put a name to a rural dean we find invariably that he was beneficed locally.[8] This was essential if he was to carry out his duties effectively. Moreover, he often held office for a number of years, possibly during good behaviour.[9] It is probable that the beneficed clergy were under obligation to serve as rural deans if called upon, and this could be an explanation of the Gloucester archdeacon's complaint that an appropriation deprived him of the "officium decanatus ruralis" which, among other things, he was accustomed to receive from all the rectors of his archdeaconry.[10]

[1] *Reg. Cobham*, ff. 104v., 106v., p. 244.
[2] Reg. Bransford, ff. 6v., 9r., 20v. (*bis*) (53, 81, 150, 152).
[3] *R.S.V.*, ff. 61v.–64r., pp. 117–20. See p. 305 below.
[4] Reg. Montacute 1, fo. 7v.
[5] *B. & W. Reg. Shrewsb.*, p. 460; *Reg. Cobham* fo. 112v., p. 246. Bishop Montacute licensed a Richard le Wyt of Bristol to have Mass celebrated in his oratory for two years (Reg. Montacute 2, fo. 5r.). [6] Which lay in Stow deanery.
[7] Reg. Bransford, fo. 103v. al. ciiii (817).
[8] Bishop Blois laid down: "Nullus fiat decanus, nisi habeat beneficium." *Concilia* 1, pp. 570 (1219), 625 (1229). [9] See p. 66 above.
[10] See above, pp. 59 (and n. 5), 66, n. 8, 67, n. 1. The beneficed clergy of Bath and Wells diocese held the office in turn as is suggested by the ordination of the vicarage of Keynsham (1404). *V.C.H. Som.* 2, p. 67; *Som. R. S.* XIII, p. 47. But another possible explanation is that the phrase refers to the obligation of incumbents to attend chapters. Foster ("Rural Deans", p. 116) regards the evidence for some form of compulsory attendance as "overwhelming". At Worcester those who could not attend inquests into vacancies—which were held in chapters (see above, p. 56, n. 2)—sent proctors. When Longdon was appropriated Montacute laid the vicar under obligation

Of the rural deans themselves, as of their deaneries, we would gladly know more than the few meagre facts which can be gleaned mainly from the folios of the episcopal registers. Even in the first half of the thirteenth century the diocesan statutes show that they were overshadowed in local matters by the archdeacons, and to a lesser degree by the diocesan official.[1] During the fourteenth century mandates were still directed to them in considerable numbers, but for the most part these tended to fall readily into well-defined categories.[2] For less stereotyped business the bishop relied to a growing extent on commissaries *ad hoc* who were drawn in the main from a small group of familiar clerks, the more important of whom held administrative or judicial office.

---

to represent the church at "chapters and synods" (other than those summoned by himself), and these could have been archidiaconal. See pp. 87-8 below.

[1] Cf. pp. 46-8 and 65-6.   [2] See pp. 64-5, 89.

3

CENTRAL ADMINISTRATION:
THE BISHOP AND HIS STAFF

THE EPISCOPATE

At the hub of diocesan affairs was the bishop himself. It is sometimes too readily assumed that his personality had little or no effect on the diocese as a whole. It is true that whether a bishop was absent or present the day-to-day work of administration continued unabated. If he were absent his vicar-general could exercise by commission all episcopal powers, save those sacramental ones for the performance of which the services of a neighbouring or of an Irish bishop could be secured. But this was no adequate substitute for a resident bishop with an awareness of his pastoral office.

It is also true that even what a resident bishop saw of his diocese was to a great extent determined by the number and position of its manors. This was not entirely so, for their produce could be moved to his favourite residences, and some bishops were far more peripatetic than others. In any case, the distribution of the manors of the Worcester bishops was eminently suitable for diocesan activities. In the far south, within easy reach of Bristol, was Henbury in Salt Marsh. Roughly in the middle of the diocese was Withington, with Cleeve a near-by alternative. In Warwickshire the bishops often stayed at Hampton, and in Worcestershire, Hartlebury and Alvechurch were conveniently situated on opposite sides of the county, with Ripple and Kempsey in the south. On the eastern border of the diocese were Tredington, Blockley, and Bibury, while bishops who wished to make the journey to London for business or a change of scene had the advantage of a house in the Strand and a manor at nearby Hillingdon in Middlesex. Study of episcopal itineraries suggests that the bishops' movements were by no means controlled by the economic reasons for moving from manor to manor. There were pastoral, personal, and doubtless other considerations as well.

The registers, on which we have to rely for our knowledge of bishops' activities, are impersonal. They record episcopal acts—or some of them, and the common form of the entries and their often stylistic and sonorous phrasing tend to conceal what is individual and particular. Even so, the careful searcher will find many clues to the attitude of the individual bishop to the responsibilities of his office.

The bishops who occupied the see during our period varied considerably in their origin and character.[1] Royal clerks predominated, and Worcester, like neighbouring Hereford, tended to provide a useful jumping-off ground for those who anticipated more lucrative preferment. Gainsburgh was a Franciscan friar; Bransford and Hemenhale were Benedictine monks. The remainder, the secular clerks, were *literati*, or in the case of Cobham and Montacute *sublimes*, men of noble birth who showed aptitude for a clerical career.[2]

Gainsburgh,[3] a former divinity lecturer of the Franciscans at Oxford, had often been sent by Edward I on embassies to France and in 1300 went with the bishop of Winchester (Pontissara) to Pope Boniface VIII, who was acting as arbitrator between the kings of England and France. He is said to have "commended himself to the Pope by his uncompromising adherence to the claims of spiritual suzerainty".[4] Boniface made him a reader in theology in his palace, and in October 1302 provided him to the see of Worcester, vacant since Giffard's death on 26 January. The following February Gainsburgh swore fealty to the king, renounced that part of his provisory bull which claimed to grant the temporalities of the bishopric,[5] and stood condemned to pay a thousand marks for his trespass in admitting it. He received a pardon for this sum three years later.[6]

---

[1] Surveys of the occupants of English sees in the fourteenth century are made by K. Edwards, "Bishops and learning in the reign of Edward II" (*C.Q.R.* CXXXVIII, 1944); "The social origins and provenance of the English bishops during the reign of Edward II" (*R.H.S.T.* 5th ser. Vol. 9, pp. 51–79); and (for the whole period) by W. A. Pantin, *English Church*, pp. 9–26. J. R. L. Highfield extends Miss Edwards' studies into the following reign, with some modification of Mr Pantin's analysis: "The English hierarchy in the reign of Edward III" (*R.H.S.T.* 5th ser. vol. 6, pp. 115–38).

[2] The distinction is first drawn in the decretal "De Multa" (*Extra*, 3, 5, c. 28). The author of the "Vita Edwardi II" comments caustically on its operation after comparing the merits of Cobham, "ipse flos Cantie, nobilis generis" and Reynolds, at the time of the latter's provision to Canterbury in 1313. *Vita Edw. II*, ed. Denholm-Young, p. 45. Possibly the most notorious example of a *vir sublimis* is Bogo de Clare, second son of Richard, earl of Gloucester (*ob.* 1262). See A. H. Thompson in *A.A.S.R.P.* XXXIII, pp. 53–7: *G.E.C.* 5, p. 701n.

[3] There is an account of his life by Mandell Creighton in *D.N.B.* See also R. A. Wilson's introduction to the edition of his register (*W.H.S.* 1929).

[4] Creighton, loc. cit.

[5] From this time forward bishops regularly renounced those clauses of their provisory bulls which might be prejudicial to the king.

[6] *C.P.L.* 1198–1304, p. 604; *C.P.R.* 1301–7, pp. 110, 421; *C.F.R.* 1272–1307, p. 449.

After his promotion Gainsburgh continued in the king's service, and this may partly explain why his register shows fewer signs of personal diligence than might have been expected. In 1305 he was sent on an embassy to the newly elected pope, Clement V, and was absent from the diocese for some five months, returning towards the middle of March in the following year.[1] He was away again from Christmas 1306 until the ensuing Easter, attending the parliament which assembled at Carlisle in January 1307 to discuss Scottish affairs.[2] In July he left on a further embassy to the pope, but died at Beauvais on the return journey.[3]

Reynolds[4] was provided to Worcester in February 1308, though earlier he had been elected by the chapter in accordance with a royal letter of recommendation.[5] Neither contemporary writers nor subsequent historians have had a good word to say for his character. "Reynolds", wrote Tout,[6] "seems to have been one of those evil-living, secular-minded clerks whom Edward I did not scruple to use in his rougher business, and did not hesitate to add to the household of Edward, his young son." Stubbs described him as "a mere creature of court favour",[7] and the author of the *Vita Edwardi II* wrote of him at the time of his promotion to Canterbury in 1313: "Dictus vero episcopus nuper erat simplex clericus et minus competenter litteratus, sed in ludis theatralibus principatum tenuit, et per hoc regis favorem optinuit."[8]

Whatever his personal character may have been, he certainly bothered little with his diocese. He was within its confines for less than eight months of his five years' episcopate, though this is hardly surprising in view of the fact that he was treasurer of the Exchequer from 1307 until 1310, and chancellor from that year until 1314.[9] At the king's request, and on account of his occupation with state affairs, the

---

[1] *C.P.R.* 1301, pp. 384, 387; Rymer & Sanderson, *Foedera* 1, ii, p. 974; *C.C.R.* 1302–7, p. 351; Reg. Gainsburgh, ff. 37r., 38v.

[2] Reg. Gainsburgh, fo. 43v. See below, p. 102, n. 2.

[3] *C.P.R.* 1301–7, pp. 529, 533; *C.C.R.* 1302–7, p. 508; Reg. Gainsburgh, fo. 46v.; R.S.V. fo. 50v.

[4] T. F. Tout summarized his life in *D.N.B.* His administrative career can be pieced together from the many references in the same author's *Chapters* (see Vol. 6, index sub nom.). For his part in the deposition of Edward II, see the essay by M. V. Clarke in *Historical Essays in honour of James Tait*, pp. 27–45.

[5] Thomas, *Account*, pp. 158–9; *R.S.V.*, introduction to pt. 2, pp. viii et seq.

[6] *D.N.B.*   [7] Stubbs, *Const. Hist.* 2 (1875), p. 335.

[8] Ed. Denholm-Young, p. 45.

[9] *Chapters* 6, pp. 7, 20. Of his activities as chancellor Tout remarks (ibid. 2, p. 215): "From 1310 to 1312 his own idleness and slackness, and from 1312 to 1314 the ill-will of the ordainers, made it the exception rather than the rule for him to be in personal charge of the seal."

pope permitted him to put off his consecration until the feast of St Andrew (30 November) 1308.[1] In fact, he was consecrated at Canterbury on 13 October, nearly a year after his election and eight months from the time of his provision.[2] He did not undertake a personal visitation of the diocese and his register provides no evidence of his appointment of commissaries for this purpose, though in 1309 a papal indult enabled him to visit by deputy.[3] In the same year he was granted papal faculties to license six clerks to hold two benefices each, a further six to hold one each though of less than canonical age, and to reconcile polluted churches and churchyards by deputy.[4] At the same time, at the king's request, the pope confirmed the collation to him of the wardenship of St Leonard's hospital at York. He then held, apart from his bishopric, the churches of Wimbledon, Sawbridgeworth, and Snitterley (Norfolk), as well as a canonry of St Paul's.[5] Furthermore, on account of his debts to the Holy See, he was permitted to hold for two years the benefices in the hands of William Testa, the papal sequestrator.[6] At Worcester he followed Gainsburgh's practice of granting benefices *in commendam*, a system which he later found useful at Canterbury.[7] Stubbs' assertion that he strove to limit the abuses of pluralities and the ordination of unsuitable candidates[8] derives from Lyndwood's erroneous attribution to him of certain canons allegedly promulgated at a Council of Oxford in 1322.[9] In his own person he epitomized those very abuses, the fruits of which he enjoyed by virtue of his slavish dependence upon the dispensatory powers of the pope.

There is a close resemblance between Reynolds and his successor at Worcester, Walter Maidstone. Like Reynolds Maidstone was a pluralist.[10] He too found employment in the king's service, and showed a corresponding dependence on papal favours. While at the Curia, urging the royal wish for Reynolds' translation to Canterbury, he secured for himself the vacated see of Worcester. After his consecration he returned to England in February 1314, bearing with him the archbishop's pallium.[11] Murimuth says that the pope gave the bishopric

---

[1] *C.P.L.* 1305–42, p. 41. See also ibid., p. 37.   [2] *Anglia Sacra* 1, p. 532.

[3] *C.P.L.* 1305–42, p. 52: 21 May 1309.   [4] Ibid.

[5] Ibid.   [6] Ibid.   [7] See Churchill 1, p. 114.

[8] Stubbs, *Const. Hist.* 2 (1875), pp. 418–19. Tout adopts the same view in his *D.N.B.* article.

[9] See Professor Cheney's examination of this and other attributions in *E.H.R.* L, pp. 414–15; LXXV, p. 21.

[10] But on a smaller scale. In 1308, when a canon of York, he had received papal dispensation to accept additional benefices worth £50. *C.P.L.* 1305–42, p. 37.

[11] *C.P.L.* 1305–42, pp. 113, 115; Cant. Reg. Reynolds, fo. 4r.; *Anglia Sacra* 1, p. 532. Cobham's election to Canterbury was disallowed by the pope.

"domino Waltero de Maneston, viro utique diffamato in Anglia de inhonesta conversatione et vita".[1] The new bishop took the opportunity before leaving the Curia of obtaining a licence to raise a loan of three thousand florins, and an indult to visit his diocese by deputy for three years.[2] Throughout his episcopate he was in dire financial straits, and there are many references in his register to the loans which he was forced to contract.[3] He did make some effort to deal personally with diocesan business though he was twice sent abroad by the king. On the first occasion, in 1314, he had to leave his inchoate primary visitation in the hands of commissaries.[4] While abroad on his second mission he died on 28 March 1317.[5]

Maidstone's successor, Cobham,[6] was a man of an entirely different stamp. A member of the well-known Kentish family of Cobham, he had been regent in Arts at Paris, in Canon Law at Oxford, and in Theology at Cambridge.[7] He had been employed in Court business at Rome, and in 1313 the Canterbury chapter chose him as archbishop. Edward II had other ideas for Canterbury and at his persuasion the pope translated Reynolds from Worcester.[8] Cobham had to wait another four years before he was partly compensated by his provision to the comparatively minor see of Worcester.[9] He was a notable pluralist,[10] though in accordance with current practice he had not advanced beyond sub-deacon's orders at the time of his election to Canterbury. After Cobham's promotion Pope John XXII treated his benefices as vacant in the Curia and disposed of them by provision.[11]

Cobham, who was deeply involved in political affairs,[12] did not reach his diocese until March 1319—two years after his provision. It was November before he began his primary visitation. The process was a

---

[1] *Continuatio Chronicorum (R.S.)*, p. 19. Cf. *Flores Hist.* 3, p. 177. Maidstone gave an annual pension to an Adam Murimuth, apparently the chronicler. See Thomas, *Account*, pp. 164–5; *App.*, p. 98, no. 82; Emden, sub nom.; and below p. 94, n. 7.

[2] *C.P.L.* 1305–42, p. 119.

[3] Thomas, *Account*, pp. 164–5; *C.C.R.* 1313–18, pp. 191, 213.

[4] *C.C.R.* 1313–18, p. 101; Reg. Maidstone, fo. 15r.

[5] *C.P.R.* 1313–17, p. 610; R.S.V., fo. 99v.

[6] R. L. Poole gives an account of him in *D.N.B.* Bishop Pearce in his *Thomas de Cobham* (S.P.C.K. 1923) deals particularly with his activities as diocesan, but this is by no means a critical study and at times is merely a panegyric. See also Emden, *Biographical Reg.*, sub nom.

[7] *Vita Edwardi II*, p. 45.   [8] Cant. Reg. Reyn., ff. 1r., 2v.–3r.

[9] *C.P.L.* 1305–42, p. 140: 31 March 1317. Wharton (*A.S.* 1, p. 533) suggests that Cobham was offered Worcester in 1313. Pearce (op. cit., p. 29) calls the statement "unsubstantiated".

[10] Pearce (p. 14, n. 3) estimated the total income from his benefices as £234.

[11] *C.P.L.* 1305–42, pp. 151, 155, 156. But cf. Pearce, pp. 34–5.

[12] See J. Conway Davies, *The Baronial Opposition to Edw. II*, pp. 448–51 *passim*.

7

protracted one, even though most of it was hurried through by commissaries, while the bishop personally visited the monasteries to collect
his procuration. It was still incomplete in January 1321 when Cobham
was called away to the north to take part in negotiations with the
Scots.[1] On the whole, however, he was a diligent bishop who, apart
from regular brief visits to London, was actively engaged in diocesan
affairs until his death in 1327.

Very different was his successor, Orleton,[2] who was translated from
Hereford against the wishes of the Worcester chapter which had
elected Wolstan de Bransford, the prior.[3] It is not necessary to trace
here the political career of this crafty and ambitious clerk who played
such an important part in the deposition of Edward II and who,
during the minority of Edward III, was for a brief while treasurer of
the Exchequer before he retired to influence the course of events from
the background.[4]

The most generous interpreter of his register cannot but assume that
his heart, as well as his person, was often elsewhere than in his diocese.
He was frequently absent on official business, both in England and
abroad,[5] and also at his favourite manor of Beaumes in the diocese of
Salisbury. He held three ordinations there and another three in France.
From Hereford he brought a number of clerks whom he appointed to
the important offices and provided with benefices, permitting some of
them to hold in plurality by the title of commend. He attempted to
raise a subsidy—euphemistically described as a spontaneous gift—

---

[1] *Reg. Cobham*, fo. 63r., p. 99.

[2] There is a useful account of him by Bannister in his introduction to *Heref. Reg.
Orleton* (1317–27). For his political and administrative career see Tout, *Chapters* 6,
index sub nom. See also M. V. Clarke in *Hist. Essays in honour of J. Tait*, pp. 27–45.

[3] An account of Orleton's struggle to secure the bishopric is given in the author's
"Bishop Bransford", pp. xvii–xx. After his appointment he promised 2,357 florins
2s. 1d. to the Curia. *Heref. Reg. Orleton*, p. 381.

[4] See Tout, *Chapters* 3, sect. 1; Stubbs, *Const. Hist.* 2 (1875), pp. 366–73.

[5] In 1328 he was appointed with the bishop of Chester to demand Edward III's
rights as heir to the Crown of France (*C.P.R.* 1327–30, p. 271). In 1330 he was one of
the proctors sent to arrange a marriage between Philip's eldest son, John, and
Edward's sister, Eleanor (ibid., pp. 482, 483). A month later (28 February) he was
also appointed to resume negotiations for peace with France and to discuss the homage
due for Aquitaine. In April he was granted an extension of protection from Whitsun
until midsummer (ibid., pp. 491, 509, 513). On 8 May the preliminary treaty of
Vincennes was concluded (ibid., p. 534). In January 1331 Orleton was sent to resume
negotiations, with protection until Whitsun (*C.P.R.* 1330–4, pp. 41, 42, 48). The
convention of St Germain-en-Laye was drawn up on 9 March (see Tout, *P.H.E.* 3,
p. 328). In 1332 and 1333 he was negotiating with Philip mainly about the proposed
Crusade and the marriage projected between Edward, earl of Chester, and Joan,
daughter of the count of Eu (*C.P.R.* 1330–4, pp. 273, 277, 359, 361, 373, 413, 466,
467, 472).

from each archdeaconry,[1] though how successful the attempt we do not know. There does not appear to have been any systematic visitation though Orleton is known to have visited at least one monastery himself. In 1333 John XXII translated him to the richer prize of Winchester,[2] which he secured despite the opposition of Edward III.

Simon de Montacute, his successor, was a kinsman of William de Montacute, the boon companion of Edward III and prime mover in the overthrow of Mortimer, who in 1337 was rewarded with the earldom of Salisbury. Both by birth and the certainty of royal favour he was marked out for rapid promotion.[3] In 1329 he was laying claim to the archdeaconry of Wells[4] while holding canonries both there and at York.[5] The following year he was made a papal chaplain.[6] In 1332, at the king's urgent request, he was provided to the archdeaconry of Canterbury.[7] Edward's attempt to secure the bishopric of Winchester for him in 1333 was only foiled by Orleton's opportunism. Instead, Montacute was appointed to Orleton's vacated see of Worcester by a bull of 4 December 1333.[8] He was in subdeacon's orders at the time and was granted a faculty to receive those of deacon and priest from any catholic bishop.[9]

During his short stay at Worcester he busied himself with diocesan matters. His primary visitation was thorough and he preached frequently on a variety of texts.[10] He won the gratitude of the prior and

---

1 *Reg. Orleton* 2, fo. 11r. The bishop promised that the grant would not prejudice the clergy's future position. For levies of this kind see F. R. H. Du Boulay, "Charitable Subsidies granted to the Archbishop of Canterbury, 1300–1489" (*B.I.H.R.* Vol. XXIII, no. 68, pp. 147–64).

2 *C.P.L.* 1305–42, pp. 397, 512. Of Orleton Wharton quotes "Ex archivis castri de Belvoir" (*A.S.* 1, pp. 533–4):

　　　　　　Trinus erat Adam; talem suspendere vadam
　　　　　　Thomas despexit, Wlstanus non bene rexit.
　　　　　　Swithinum maluit. Cur? quia plus valuit.

3 In a letter of 1329 to the pope Edward wrote: "Laudanda virtutum merita, dilecti clerici nostri, magistri Simonis de Monte Acuto qui, claris ortus natalibus, generis sui nobilitatem morum et conversationis venustate studuit decorare..." (Rymer, *Foedera* 4, p. 379).

4 He claimed by royal presentation on account of a vacancy *temp.* Edward I, possibly that of 1292, but it seems that he never secured possession. Robert de Wambergh had held the archdeaconry since 1326 (by exchange) and won his appeal at the Curia. *B. & W. Reg. Shrewsb.*, intro. pp. xxxviii–xl, and pp. 8, 25, 33 et seq., 49, 132 et seq., 135, 139.

5 *C.P.L.* 1305–42, p. 314.　　　　6 Ibid., p. 315.

7 Ibid., p. 357.

8 Ibid., p. 405, cf. p. 512; Reg. Montacute, 1, fo. 11r. The bull is printed by Thomas, *App.* 95, pp. 109–10.

9 *C.P.L.* 1305–42, p. 397.

10 Sermon texts are not often recorded in Worcester visitation itineraries.

convent by restoring to them the manor of Crowle, and they inserted his name in their martyrology.[1] However, in 1337, he was translated to the greater eminence of Ely—again on the urgent representation of the king.[2]

He was succeeded by Hemenhale, a monk of Norwich, about whom little is known. In 1336 he had been elected to the see of Norwich and without royal consent had gone post-haste to the Curia to secure papal confirmation.[3] Benedict XII forced him to resign and provided Antony Bek, dean of Lincoln, in his stead. But the Ely vacancy gave him the opportunity of translating Montacute thither and of simultaneously providing Hemenhale to the vacated Worcester.[4]

On reaching England in July 1337 Hemenhale renounced, in a chamber within the Tower, any words in his bull which might be prejudicial to the king.[5] But his temerity cost him a fine of a thousand marks which he proceeded to pay in instalments of £100.[6] He did not reach his diocese until September. The earlier part of his register, probably the smallest at Worcester,[7] is occupied by the doings of his vicars-general, whom he had appointed while still at Avignon. The later portion is mainly concerned with routine matters. So far as we can judge, he showed promise of becoming a good diocesan personally attentive to his duties, but fifteen months after his arrival, on the feast of St Thomas the apostle (21 December) 1338, he died.

The Worcester monks must have assembled in their chapter house on the feast of the Circumcision (3 January 1339) with some misgivings. They had not succeeded in electing a bishop of their own choice within living memory.[8] Their election of John of St Germans in 1302 had been frustrated by archbishop and pope. In 1307 they had elected Reynolds at the king's command, but even that election was superseded by a later bull of provision. They had elected their prior, Bransford, in 1327, but he had been ousted—despite governmental support and the confirmation of his election by king and archbishop—by the influential Orleton. This time, however, there was no difficulty, and at last, after a succession of seven provided bishops they success-

---

1 Reg. Montacute 2, ff. 19, 20.

2 *C.P.L.* 1305–42, p. 540; *Foedera* 4, pp. 733, 744.

3 *Foedera* 4, p. 714.

4 *C.P.L.* 1305–42, pp. 540, 541, 542; *Foedera* 4, pp. 732, 733.

5 *P.R.O. Lists & Indexes* XLIX, *Papal Bulls*.

6 *C.C.R.* 1337–9, p. 276; *C.P.R.* 1338–40, pp. 52, 163.

7 There are thirty-six folios.

8 Since at least 1268. Even then both Giffard and his predecessor, Nicholas of Ely, had been royal chancellors.

fully exercised their right of election. Their choice fell for the second time[1] upon their prior, Bransford.

Wolstan de Bransford may well have been born in the hamlet of that name some few miles from the cathedral city. At any rate he was a local man for his father was a citizen of Worcester.[2] Very little is known of his early life. Bishop Reynolds admitted his profession as a monk of the cathedral priory on 21 September 1310, at the time of his tardy enthronement.[3] In 1317, on the death of Prior John de Wyke, he was one of the seven monks nominated by the convent for presentation to the bishop. From among them Cobham's commissary, James de Cobham, chose him as prior. Much can be learnt of his twenty-one years of office from the pages of the Liber Albus—the prior's register. As a capable administrator he soon made his mark, but he did not look ambitiously for promotion. Though for some months in 1327–8 he administered the diocese as bishop elect and confirmed, he retired again to the priory without protest to make way for Orleton who was in every respect his inferior. Both in 1327 and 1338 he acted, by reason of his office, as official *sede vacante*. In 1334 he was Montacute's vicar-general for a short space, and three years later acted for Hemenhale in the same capacity, so that by the time he became bishop he was well versed in diocesan affairs.

Of the bishops with whom we are at present concerned Bransford was the only one whose interest lay solely within the confines of the diocese, which he did not leave for more than a few weeks during the ten years of his episcopate.[4] His register, by far the largest of our period, bears ample witness to his zeal in diocesan affairs. His primary visitation, which he conducted personally, included every deanery in both archdeaconries, and was the most thorough of which we have record.[5] Moreover, he attempted to maintain the rule of triennial visitation. He was careful to see that not one of his regular clerks was a pluralist, and the comparatively moderate number of licences of absence granted to

1 There is no evidence that Bransford was elected more than twice, despite many statements to the contrary. For example, Willis Bund in *V.C.H. Worcs.* 2, p. 31 writes of "his fourth election". Cf. Harvey Bloom, *Liber Ecclesie Wyg.*, intro. p. x; Wilson, *Calendar of the Liber Albus*, intro. p. xv.

2 *R.S.V.*, fo. 39r., p. 88.

3 "Deinde multos pueros confirmavit et magnam missam celebravit, ad quam ante evangelium professionem duorum monachorum fratrum Wlstani et Symonis de Wygorn' admisit in forma consueta." Liber Albus, fo. xlv v.

4 Apparently he attended Archbishop Stratford's council at St Paul's in 1342, but dates in his register show that he could not have remained long in London. *Const. Prov.*, p. 43; Reg. Bransf., ff. 66v.–67r. (581); and see below, pp. 187, 213, n. 10.

5 What little we know of Montacute's primary visitation suggests that it might well have borne comparison with Bransford's.

rectors may have been the outcome of deliberate policy.[1] In particular
he conceded very few for study. This may have been because he was
not a university man himself, or perhaps he doubted whether the profit
derived from absence at the Schools compensated for the lack of personal
residence in the parish.[2] He regularly paid visits to the southernmost
part of his diocese, and right up to the very last day of his life he was
personally instituting clerks to benefices.[3] Despite his extremely active
life we learn that from the early days of his episcopate he suffered from
ill health.[4] It was, indeed, a misfortune for the diocese that he had not
become bishop at the time of his first election in 1327 when he was in
the prime of life.[5]

After Bransford's death the series of royal clerks promoted with
papal connivance was resumed with the translation of John Thoresby
from St David's (4 September 1349).[6] Thoresby had been keeper of the
privy seal, and shortly before his translation was made chancellor.[7]
As was to be expected, he could spare little time for his new diocese.
He did not arrive there until 1351 and was not enthroned until 12
September in that year.[8] In the meantime he secured a papal indult
which enabled him to raise a subsidy from the clergy, both secular and
regular,[9] as Orleton had done. He was translated to York in 1352,[10] a
see more in keeping with his importance in affairs of state.

At York (1352–73) he was an active diocesan. As Hamilton Thompson wrote: "Zealously earnest for the good of his much-tried people,
Thoresby assiduously held visitations, and provided his clergy with an
epitome of the religious teaching which he desired them to give."[11]
This treatise, the so-called "Lay-Folk's Catechism", was in English

[1] See below pp. 206 et seq., 209, n. 1.

[2] Cobham, who granted more licences for study than any other Worcester bishop
in the period under review, came to admit that they were often abused. *Reg. Cobham*,
ff. 8ov.–81r., p. 135; and see below, pp. 207, n. 5, 208.

[3] He died in Hartlebury Castle 6 August 1349 at the height of the Black Death in
the diocese. He instituted clerks to Naunton and Withington "statim post ortum solis
eiusdem diei". Reg. Bransford 2, fo. 19v. (1566–8).

[4] In 1340 he was excused from attending parliaments and councils: "Tanta debili-
tate & infirmitate corporis sui detinetur, quod absque gravi dampno & corporis sui
periculo non potest commode laborare, ut accepimus." *Foedera* 5, p. 191. G. G.
Coulton's implied stricture on Bransford's conduct at the time of the Black Death
ignores this fact and also the bishop's continued activity at Hartlebury. See *Medieval
Panorama*, p. 748, nn. to chap. 38.

[5] Probably about forty-five years old.   [6] Cant. Reg. Islep, fo. 7v.

[7] He held the office from 16 June 1349 until 27 November 1356. Tout, *Chapters* 6,
p. 14.

[8] Reg. Thoresby, fo. 26r.

[9] *C.P.L.* 1342–62, p. 331: 17 October 1349. Cf. *C.P.P.*, p. 180.

[10] Thomas, *Account*, p. 180; ibid. *App.*, pp. 116–19.

[11] *V.C.H. Yorks.* 3, pp. 39–40.

verse form, and was intended to be learnt by heart. Derived from Pecham's constitution (1281) "Ignorantia Sacerdotum", it provided a popular summary of religious belief.[1]

It was unfortunate that Thoresby's tenure of the Worcester bishopric was too short for him to give proof of the pastoral ability he was to show at York.

THE BISHOP IN HIS DIOCESE

The functions of a bishop were pastoral, judicial, and administrative in character, and his activities were often a combination of all three. Pious preambles tell at length of his pastoral duties. It was for the bishop to plant holy religion, to foster it when planted, to nourish things that are right, and to pluck out such as impede the growth of virtue.[2] Or again, the Holy Church of God was likened to a garden of delights which from the beginning was without thorns, brambles, nettles, or any plant which did not produce fruit in due season. Not least among which plants was the church of Worcester which the bishop hoped to preserve unblemished.[3] It was with such picturesque and disarming phraseology that the diocesan sometimes masked the stern duties of inquiry, correction, and punishment.

Then too, it was the bishop's special charge to foster an increase in the orthodox faith, especially by the celebration of Masses, as we learn from the preamble of many a chantry ordination.[4]

[1] Pantin, *English Church in the XIVth Cent.*, pp. 211–12; T. F. Simmons and H. E. Nolloth, *E.E.T.S.* orig. ser. 118 (1891).

[2] Preamble to Bishop Bransford's warning of his intended visitation of the Worcester chapter, 22 September 1339. Reg. Bransford, fo. 9v. (85).

[3] "Ortus deliciarum ecclesia sancta dei sic fuit a principio stabilata, ut non erant in ea spine que pungerent pedes rectos, non vepres que lederent incedentes, non urtice rosas in vicino perurentes, planta nulla que fructum non faceret tempore suo. Cuius orti planta non minima ecclesia nostra Wygorn' ut pars congruens suo toti ipsius condiciones a diu est sequuta quod suorum patronorum merita luce clarius manifestant. Verum quamquam firmiter speremus istam plantulam sponsam nostram nullam maculam contraxisse, per quam a perfeccione declinaret primeva, nos qui summis desideriis affectamus omnes et singulos nostri [*sic*] iurisdiccioni subiectos, et maxime in dicta nostra ecclesia conversantes, bonos esse, ac ipsos tales recipere et fovere, cum non solum debeat prelatus ad corrigendos subditorum excessus assurgere, verum eciam religionem sanctam plantare sicque plantatam servare, et que sunt recta nutrire ac toto conamine custodire, ad nostre serenacionem consciencie et officii nostri pastoralis debitum exequendum ad vos iuxta modulum nostrum reficiendos pabulo verbi dei necnon ad nos mutuo consolandos, disposuimus deo duce noviter vos videre." (Bishop Bransford warns the Worcester chapter of his intention to visit them for the second time: fo. 6or. (530): 3 October 1342. Cf. the variation of this preamble in *Reg. Cobham*, ff. 41v.–42r., pp. 43–4.)

[4] For example, that of Adam de Herwynton in Pershore Abbey, 27 February 1346: "Inter omnia que curam nostram cotidiana meditacione solicitant precipuum habemus in votis ut in diocesi quam deus nobis credidit gubernandum ortodoxe fidei cultus

The bishop was also the *judex ordinarius* of the diocese—saving the exempt areas of Churchdown and the Vale of Evesham—within which there was no appeal from his courts. These were two in number: his consistory, presided over by the diocesan official or his commissary; and his court of audience, which went with him round the diocese and in which cases were heard either *coram episcopo*[1] or by his auditors or commissaries, amongst whom the diocesan chancellor sometimes figured.

As one of the king's great tenants-in-chief,[2] the bishop did homage in the usual way and was under obligation to provide service and counsel. His fief included extensive manors—all, save Hillingdon (Middlesex), within the confines of the diocese. Details of their administration do not concern us here,[3] but because appointments of temporal officers are regularly entered in the registers, some account of them is given below.[4]

The many royal writs addressed to the diocesan attest his importance as an agent of the king's government. Among other things, he saw to the collection of tenths and other taxes,[5] the sequestration and sale of the goods and chattels of clerks, served summonses on them to appear before the royal justices, and gave information on matters which came within the scope of ecclesiastical jurisdiction.[6]

The bishop's powers over his subjects, which in some cases were limited by custom or composition, rested ultimately on canonical sanction. Ecclesiastical persons, both secular and regular, took an oath of obedience to him, and were bound to obey his lawful mandates.

---

nostris temporibus augeatur et precipue in missarum celebracionibus in quibus venerabile sacramentum corporis Christi salvatoris nostri deo patri tam pro vivis quam pro mortuis immolatur, in quo vite suffragium consequimur et salutis." Reg. Bransford, fo. 121v., al. cxxii (906).

1 The term *coram episcopo* (or *coram nostro*) may not always have been used in a literal sense.

2 The churches of the bishopric (i.e. the advowsons) were also considered to form part of the barony as Gilbert de Clare, earl of Gloucester, pointed out in the king's Council (1290) at the time of Giffard's attempt to make some of them prebendal to Westbury. *Ann. Wigorn.*, p. 502.

3 *The Red Book of Worcester*, ed. M. Hollings (*W.H.S.* 1934–50), contains surveys of the episcopal manors. For a study of the administration of a bishop's secular estates, see E. Miller, *The Abbey & Bishopric of Ely* (Camb. 1951).

4 See under "Temporal officers".

5 On receipt of a royal mandate *ad hoc* the bishop commonly appointed a collector for each archdeaconry from among the heads of religious houses. To collect arrears he usually employed his official, his sequestrator, or the official of the appropriate archdeacon.

6 Writs of *quod distringas, levari facias, fieri facias, venire facias,* and *certiorari*. See p. 7 above.

If they did not do so they could be cited to appear in the episcopal court for contempt,[1] so that in the last resort episcopal mandates were enforced by judicial action.[2]

During the thirteenth century bishops must have conducted much business of general concern to their dioceses in synods. Professor Cheney has shown that the synod's functions were administrative, judicial, legislative, and pastoral.[3] In the Worcester diocese six synods, ranging in date from 1219 to 1252, are known to have been held.[4] Three of them met on 24 September, two in May, and one in July; from which it has been inferred that summer and autumn synods were held annually.[5] But if synods met so regularly in the time of Bishops Blois and Cantilupe, it seems strange that there appears to be no record of a specific assembly of this kind either in Giffard's bulky register (1268–1302)[6] or in those of our period.[7]

That diocesan synods were summoned in the fourteenth century would seem to be implied by an entry in Register Montacute. At the time of the appropriation of Longdon to Westminster Abbey the bishop, acknowledging the monks' papal privilege which exempted them from compulsory attendance at chapters and synods on behalf of their appropriated churches, permitted the church of Longdon to be represented by its vicars at such assemblies. On the other hand, when he or his successors should happen to hold a synod, or general

---

[1] Because the dean of Campden had failed to execute an episcopal mandate he was summoned before the bishop's commissary "pro dictis contemptu et inobediencia penam debitam recepturus". Reg. Bransford, fo. 4r. (29).

[2] Professor Barraclough (*Papal Provisions*, pp. 138, 140) stresses the legal aspect of episcopal actions, declaring that bishops, in the same way as the pope, might follow up their *littere rogatorie* with *littere monitorie, preceptorie*, and *executorie*, but there is nothing to suggest that such forms were in regular use at Worcester during our period.

[3] *English Synodalia*, chap. 1.

[4]

DATE OF SYNOD	BISHOP	REFS.
1219 24 Sept.	William of Blois	*Ann. Mon.* 4, 411.
1220 24 Sept.	,, ,,	*Ibid.* 1, 65.
1229 8 May	,, ,,	*Ibid.* 1, 73.
1233 17 May	,, ,,	*Ibid.* 1, 90; 4, 425.
1240 26 July	Walter Cantilupe	*Ibid.* 4, 432; *Concilia* 1, 665.
1252 24 Sept.	,, ,,	*Ann. Mon.* 1, 150.

For synods held in other dioceses see Cheney, *English Synodalia*, p. 17.

[5] Cheney, loc. cit. Frequent synods were obviously envisaged by Bishop Blois in his 1229 statutes: *Concilia* 1, pp. 625, 626.

[6] The editor, Willis Bund, called the council which met in 1300/1 a synod (intro. p. lxi), and although it has been pointed out that the words were sometimes synonomous (Cheney, *E.H.R.* L, 1935, p. 196), there seems to be no doubt that this was not a diocesan synod but a meeting of the bishop's counsellors. See below, p. 97, n. 4.

[7] The right to convoke and celebrate synods was also included among the prior's powers *sede vacante*, but there is no evidence of its exercise. App. C, p. 342 below.

assembly of the clergy, the religious were to be present or to send a suitable proctor.[1] But clauses of this kind are exceptional in appropriation documents, and this one was certainly prompted by Westminster's known privilege. Hence it may well be a declaration of abstract right and not, by itself, reliable evidence for the regular meeting of diocesan synods.

The assembly which Bransford called in 1339 was clearly unusual. The archdeacons were instructed to summon the clergy to appear before them at Winchcomb—considered to be roughly the centre of the diocese—so that they could make known the contents of the king's writ asking for help against the French.[2]

Despite the relative abundance of fourteenth-century records, the lack of any positive evidence to the contrary suggests that synods, or closely related general assemblies of the clergy, had become an exceptional rather than a regular feature of diocesan administration at Worcester.[3]

The course of the synod's decline, even if this could be accurately traced, need not concern us here, but a number of changes which were roughly concurrent with it, and which perhaps helped to deprive the synod of its *raison d'être*, may be noted. The growth of the bishop's courts, in particular of the consistory with its regular sessions in various parts of the diocese, made the judicial activity of the synod less necessary.[4] Administratively the improved machinery of archdeaconry and rural deanery provided an alternative and all-the-year-round medium for the publication of episcopal mandates:[5] the establishment of the office of the archdeacon's official, the ready availability of rural deans, and the expansion of the bishop's chancery may all have contributed to this development. The growth of centralized diocesan government with specialized *officia* and trained clerks meant that business could be dealt with as it arose instead of at periodical synods.

In the thirteenth century a diocesan's instructions to the clergy and

---

[1] "... quod quando nos vel successores nostros synodos celebrare contigerit, vel clerum nostrum generaliter convocare, religiosi predicti teneantur in huiusmodi synodis et congregacionibus nomine predicte ecclesie appropriate eisdem per se vel per procuratorem ydoneum comparere..." Reg. Montacute 1, fo. 18r. For other examples of limitation of this monastic privilege see Cheney, *Synodalia*, pp. 22–4.

[2] Reg. Bransford, fo. 2r. (18). Cf. *Concilia* 2, pp. 754–5.

[3] In some dioceses however, for example, Durham, Ely, and York, synods would appear to have been regularly held in the fourteenth century. See Cheney, op. cit., p. 17.

[4] See Cheney, *Becket to Langton*, p. 144; *Synodalia*, p. 33.

[5] See above, pp. 56–7, 63–4.

his formal statutes had often been issued in synods;[1] in the fourteenth a "mandatory system" served much the same purpose.[2] Episcopal mandates of widespread application, some of which quoted from or even added to existing statutes,[3] might be sent for publication to the official or, as was common in the Worcester diocese, to the archdeacon's official, who used the archidiaconal chapters for this purpose. Matters of more local import could be made known in the churches of an individual rural deanery.

Similarities between the diocesan synod and episcopal visitation have often been pointed out: "At the former the clergy gathered to meet their bishop, at the latter the bishop went round to interview his clergy."[4] Formal synodal legislation may sometimes have followed visitation and conversely a synod might be held to discover *reformanda*.[5] Regular visitation had become common in English dioceses by the late thirteenth century[6] and the synod may have suffered as a result, although the relationship between the decline of the synod and the growth of episcopal visitation has not been established.

As we have seen, the synod, so far as is known, played little or no part in fourteenth-century Worcester administration. None the less, a useful purpose has been served by some mention of its earlier importance in the diocese and the changes which accompanied and possibly contributed to its decline, if only because of the light thrown on the methods and machinery in use during our period. The local administration of exempt jurisdiction, archdeaconry, and rural deanery, has been surveyed above: such divisions were already old by the beginning of the thirteenth century. Comparatively new was the

---

1 Bishop Blois' 1229 statutes required the presence in synod of all priests with cure of souls. Cantilupe reserves matters touching the religious to their own chapters. *Concilia* 1, pp. 626, 676.

2 Canon Kemp has listed 121 of these mandates issued between 1313 and 1378 by English bishops (typescript). Even so, his list is not exhaustive and includes no Worcester mandates. Pantin, *English Church in the XIVth Cent.*, p. 100n., states that Grandisson of Exeter issued about thirty-five between 1328 and 1361. Cf. Cheney, *Synodalia*, pp. 43–4, and see below, App. D, pp. 354 et seq.

3 The writer does not know of any Worcester mandate which quotes a thirteenth-century diocesan statute, although quotations from provincial statutes are sometimes found.

4 Frere, *Visit. Articles* 1, p. 49. White Kennett, *Paroch. Antiqu.* 2, p. 363, says that the synod was "in effect a bishop's general visitation of his whole diocese".

5 See, for instance, the letter sent to an English bishop by Cardinal Ottobon sometime in 1268: "Mandamus quatinus . . . synodum convocetis in defectus et errores tam rebus quam personis ecclesiasticis imminentes et alia que correccione aut legis sanccione inveneritis indigere sollicite perquirentes. . . ." *E.H.R.* XV (1900), pp. 119–120, ed. Rose Graham. See also Cheney, *E.H.R.* L (1935), pp. 206–7.

6 Cheney, *Becket to Langton*, pp. 139–41.

"central administration"—if it can be called such—of specialized clerks and offices with recognized duties, which were to some extent defined in written commissions. The system was a flexible one. At any time the bishop's will could be implemented by *ad hoc* mandates, in the main directed for important business to members of this group of clerks. The rest of the present chapter will be chiefly devoted to them and to their functions.

THE BISHOP'S CLERKS

Each bishop gathered round him an intimate circle of clerks, whose help made possible the administration of the diocese. They took an oath of fidelity and promised to give help and counsel and not to reveal the bishop's affairs.[1] They are variously described as "clerici familiares" or "clerici commensales", and those of more exalted status "clerici maiores". The importance of these greater clerks, as well as the ample provision made for them, can be gathered from the grant by Bishop Maidstone to Richard de Chaddesley whom he later appointed joint vicar-general during his absence abroad in 1317. Together with the sum of one hundred shillings, payable in two instalments, Richard was to receive robes and furs of the sort worn by the bishop's greater clerks, to have his keep with the bishop, as well as three horses, three grooms, and other necessaries for the same, such as the other greater clerks were wont to receive. Whenever he stayed in or outside the diocese on episcopal business he was to be paid necessary expenses.[2]

Episcopal clerks, as a class, have received far too little attention from

---

[1] In Register Giffard (fo. 448r.) there is an interesting entry which records the admission of John de Broadwas *tabellio* to the domestic service and *familia* of the bishop on 3 August 1300. "Memorandum quod iii° Non. Augusti apud Alvech' anno domini M°CCC°, consecracionis domini episcopi xxxii°, idem dominus episcopus admisit ad suum servicium domesticum et familiaritatem magistrum Johannem de Bradewas clericum tabellionem condicionibus quibus stetit secum aliquando Magister Henricus de Lich', videlicet cum uno equo et uno puero et duabus robis per annum, a quo magistro J[ohanne] recepit episcopus supradictus sacramentum fidelem quod bene pro posse et fideliter deserviret, suum consilium non revelans, nec suum dampnum seu scandalum sciens nisi ipsum super hoc statim premuniret et defenderet iuxta posse."

[2] "Pateat universis per presentes quod nos Walterus permissione divina Wyg' episcopus dedisse concessisse dilecto nobis in Christo magistro R. de Chaddesley clerico nostro pro fideli servicio suo nobis impenso et in posterum impendendo, centum solidos annue pensionis solvendos eidem ad duos anni terminos, videlicet medietatem in festo Sancti Michaelis et aliam medietatem in festo Annunciacionis Dominice, cum robis et pelluris de secta clericorum nostrorum maiorum, una cum mora sua nobiscum faciend'*, cum tribus equis et tribus garcionibus et aliis necessariis ad eosdem, sicut alii clerici nostri maiores in premissis percipere consueverunt, quousque per nos de competenti beneficio ecclesiastico dicto magistro Ricardo fuerit provisum quod

ecclesiastical historians.[1] Like royal clerks they were not expected to be resident in their benefices[2] which they regarded primarily as a source of income. The statutes of secular cathedrals permitted the diocesan to claim exemption from non-residence fines for two or three canons in his employ. At Lincoln the fourteenth-century lists of *nullo modo residentes* show that in each year between five and eight non-resident canons were ordinarily exempted from payment of their "seventh" because they were with the bishop.[3]

If a clerk was in the service of one bishop, though beneficed in the diocese of another, it was usual for the latter to license him to be absent for the period of such service.[4] Bishop Cobham asserted that by the custom and agreement of the bishops of the province of Canterbury he could lawfully retain the services of a clerk from another diocese in such a way that he would be accounted resident, just as if his own diocesan had kept him by his side.[5] Sometimes a clerk

---

duxerit acceptandum. Pro quibus omnibus promisit magister Ricardus supradictus iuramento corporali prestito in nostris agendis auxilium consilium fideliter impendere contra quoscumque, dominis suis preiuratis dumtaxat exceptis. Ita tamen quod si pro negociis nostris alicubi in nostra dyocesi vel extra dictum Ricardum declinare contigerit eidem necessarias expensas ministrari faciemus. In cuius rei testimonium &c. Dat' [&c.]." Reg. Maidstone, fo. 35v: 20 May 1315.

(* Part of this phrase seems to have slipped out.)

1 With the publication of A. B. Emden's *Biographical Register of the University of Oxford*, the task of tracing many of their careers has been greatly simplified. This has now been supplemented by the same author's *Biographical Register of the University of Cambridge* (1963), and the new edition (in progress) of Le Neve's *Fasti Ecclesiae Anglicanae (1300–1541)*.

2 The claim that royal clerks had been exempt from the obligation to reside from time immemorial is made in the response to art. 8 of the *Articuli Cleri*. Statutes 1, p. 171: 24 November 1316, York.

3 Edwards, *Secular Cathedrals*, p. 91 and ibid. App. 1.

4 Many Worcester examples of licences to attend a bishop "pro suo bene placito" could be cited (see the edition of Reg. Reynolds, Leave of Absence, pp. 85 et seq.). There are also others for a term of years. According to the decretal "Licet Canon" (*Sext*, 1, 6, c.14) the ordinary could dispense from the obligation of residence *ad tempus*.

5 He wrote to the *custos* of the spiritualities of the vacant see of Lichfield on behalf of his clerk R. de S. in the following terms: "Quia dominus R. de S. rector ecclesie de Birton diocesis antedicte locum maximum nobis tenet, cuius presencia carere non possemus absque magno incommodo domus nostre, quem quia licet de consuetudine et consensu episcoporum Cant' provincie possemus nobiscum licite retinere ita quod pro residente in omnibus haberetur, ac si suus diocesanus episcopus iuxta latus suum retineret eundem; bone tamen memorie Walterus nuper ibidem episcopus ipsum nobis specialiter exhabundanti concessit: vestramque igitur amiciciam toto cordis affectu requiramus et rogamus, quatenus pro tempore vacacionis instantis velitis graciose permittere quod ipse nobis inpune deserviat prout antea deservivit." *Reg. Cobham*, fo. 74v., p. 122; cf. fo. 89r., p. 156. See also the formal "Littera pro clerico morante in obsequiis domini" in Reg. Maidstone, fo. 26r.

would be engaged in the service of more than one bishop at the same time.[1]

On occasion the archbishops of Canterbury demanded the services of clerks employed by their suffragans.[2] In 1320 Reynolds was claiming that in accordance with his prerogative dignity he was entitled to call any clerks within his province to his household, even if they were bound to reside elsewhere. On these grounds he demanded the assent of the chapter of Wells to the licence of absence granted by Bishop Drokensford to M. John de Bruton,[3] chancellor of Canterbury and treasurer of Wells.[4]

The various migrations of episcopal clerks would make an interesting study. A great number of those who found service with the Worcester bishops were born and beneficed in the diocese, but many, particularly those who were appointed to the important offices, came from other dioceses. This was mainly because a new bishop tended to introduce clerks who had already served him elsewhere.

Gainsburgh introduced Benedict de Feriby and Walter de Wotton, both clerks from his native diocese of Lincoln and who had had administrative experience there.[5] Cobham too employed men whom he had known before his elevation.[6] But the most conspicuous example of a wholesale importation of clerks occurred with the translation of Orleton from Hereford to Worcester in 1327. Though he himself saw little of his new diocese he made sure that it was administered by those whom he had formerly entrusted with similar functions at Hereford. Of the men who filled the office of vicar-general, Adam de Herwynton,[7]

1 Thus Thomas de Teffunte was the clerk both of Archbishop Reynolds and of Bishop Maidstone who described him as "clericum ipsius patris et nostrum" (*Reg. Maidst.*, fo. 7r.). Likewise Cobham in a letter to Stephen Gravesend, bishop of London, spoke of Richard Dunstan as "clericus noster communis" (Reg. Cobham, fo. 75v.).

2 For some examples see Churchill 1, p. 350, n. 3. The supposed instances in Reg. Cobham do not refer to the archbishop's claim, but to that of any bishop to have his clerks counted as resident when beneficed in another diocese of the province (see above, p. 91, n. 5).

3 See Churchill, index sub nom. He was acting as Reynolds' chancellor in 1316 and became archdeacon of Canterbury in 1323 (op. cit. 1, pp. 17, 46–7; 2, p. 244).

4 *H.M.C.R.* X, App. pt. 1, p. 190. Bruton exchanged the treasurership the same year with M. William de Clopcote who was later cited by Bishop Cobham for not residing in his church of Olveston. The dean and chapter pointed out that as he was performing his residence at Wells he should be excused. Ibid., pp. 190–1, 216.

5 See *Rot. & Reg. Sutton* 3, index sub nom.

6 Pearce (*Thomas de Cobham*, chap. 2) discusses their origins.

7 In 1327 Orleton had appointed him vicar-general at Hereford, jointly with Fownhope. By a separate commission he was empowered to confer benefices in the bishop's collation (*Heref. Reg. Orleton*, pp. 209, 374, 375). Michael Hodgetts has written a short biography of him: "Adam of Harvington, Prelate and Politician"

William de Fownhope,[1] and Roger de Breynton[2] were all canons of Hereford. Fownhope also acted as official during the early years of the episcopate.[3] A later official, Robert de Worth,[4] was a canon of Salisbury, a diocese with which Orleton had some connection on account of his manor of Beaumes. A third, John de Kareslegh (sometimes "Cassele"), was rector of Kidderminster,[5] and the only clerk initially beneficed in the Worcester diocese to hold important office under Orleton. The diocesan sequestrator, Nicholas de Kaerwent, again one of Orleton's Hereford clerks had been rewarded with the rectory of Kinnersley in that diocese.[6] Others, who likewise figure prominently in Orleton's Worcester register, were Walter Carles,[7] Adam de Aylton,[8] and John de Radenhale,[9] and they by no means exhaust the list.

It was not to be expected, what with the preference of individual bishops for their own men, and the limited prospects of advancement, that the more ambitious clerks would stay for long periods. It is hardly surprising to find that a number of them used Worcester merely as a spring-board to further promotion. Benedict de Paston, Reynolds'

(*Trans. Worc. Arch. Soc.* XXXVI, pp. 33–41). Herwynton died in 1344 and his executors carried out his plans for the foundation of a chantry in the nave of Pershore Abbey where he was buried. Reg. Bransf., fo. 72r. (621) and fo. 94r. (772) et seq.

[1] William Russell of Fownhope had been one of the most prominent of Orleton's clerks at Hereford. See *Heref. Reg. Orleton*, index sub nom., for a long list of references to his activities. In 1328, when he was official of Worcester, Orleton granted him an acquittance "de omnibus denariis qui ad manus suas nostro nomine devenerunt de toto tempore quo idem magister Willelmus nobis in episcopatu seu diocesi Hereford' deservivit . . ." Reg. Orleton 2, fo. 11r.

[2] In 1318 he had been appointed one of Orleton's proctors at the Curia with power to take the oath of fealty to the pope on his behalf. *Heref. Reg. Orleton*, pp. 77–8. In 1331 he became archdeacon of Gloucester (p. 39 above).

[3] All three were later prominent in the administration of Orleton's nephew, John Trilleck, bishop of Hereford (1344–60).

[4] In 1331 he was joint vicar-general with Herwynton. For his earlier career see *Salisb. Reg. S. de Gandavo*, index sub nom.

[5] Inst. 24 June 1312: Reg. Reynolds, fo. 54r.

[6] In 1326 he had acted at Hereford in the absence of the diocesan official. One of Orleton's most faithful clerks, he was at his death-bed in Farnham Castle in 1345—as was Adam de Aylton. *Heref. Regs. Orleton*, pp. xlvii n., 263, 361, 389; *Trilleck*, p. 55. A clerk of this name was serving the bishop of Winchester in 1366 and held the wealthy living of Crundale with the prebend of Hinton in the church of Hereford. *Cant. Reg. Langham*, pp. 13–14.

[7] Rector of Cradley and canon of Hereford. He had been Orleton's receiver. In his will the bishop appointed him one of his executors; Roger de Breynton was another. *Heref. Reg. Orleton*, pp. xlvii n., 178, 247, 387, 388.

[8] See *Heref. Reg. Orleton*, index sub nom. He secured the deanery of Westbury in 1333 while at the Curia. A papal bull dispensed him from residence while in Orleton's service (pp. 28–9 above).

[9] *Heref. Reg. Orleton*, p. 353. He was a notary public.

vicar-general and official, was fortunate in that his patron was translated to Canterbury. He followed at once and was made an auditor of causes.[1] John Bloyou acted as Maidstone's official and was reappointed in 1318 by Cobham. Three years later he exchanged his Westbury prebend for another at Exeter.[2] He became Bishop Grandisson's official and, in 1328, official of the Court of Canterbury.[3] The interesting career of John de Severleye, archdeacon of Worcester and Bransford's chancellor, who became auditor and commissary of causes at Canterbury, has been sketched above.[4] But clerks of such merit and ambition were somewhat exceptional at Worcester.

It was no easy task for a bishop to provide for the band of clerks which went with him about the diocese, for his officers, and for the necessary proctors at Canterbury, the Curia, Parliament, and elsewhere. For those who were with him as he travelled from manor to manor there was a certain amount of payment in kind,[5] but for the most part the bishop had to rely on the benefices in his collation,[6] eked out by pensions which were usually granted until such time as an acceptable benefice should become available.[7]

The extent of episcopal patronage was seriously curtailed in a number of ways. Whenever a see fell vacant the king claimed the right to

---

[1] Churchill 2, p. 211: 17 April 1314. See also ibid. 1, p. 138.

[2] *Reg. Cobham*, fo. 26v., p. 236.

[3] *Exeter Reg. Grandisson*, pp. 207, 420; Churchill 1, p. 437. It is possible to answer Churchill's query (loc. cit., n. 4) in the affirmative. The Bloyou of Cobham's register (wrongly termed "Bloyon" by the editor) is the same man as the one in Reg. Grandisson.

[4] Pp. 36–7 above.   [5] Pp. 90–1 above.

[6] Supplemented by those which fell to his presentation by lapse.

[7] Reynolds granted a pension of £5 to M. Andrew Sapity "pro bono et laudabili servicio nobis impenso et impendendo"—the usual formula in the case of legal proctors (*Reg. Reyn.* fo. 6r.). Sapity—probably an English-speaking Italian, was for many years a permanent royal proctor at the Curia. He seems to have been proctor for a number of bishops and for the monks of Westminster who paid him a pension (*H.M.C.R.* IV, p. 175). For an account of him see J. B. Kirsch, "Andreas Sapiti, Englischer Prokurator an der Kurie im 14 Jahrhundert", in *Historisches Jahrbuch* XIV (1893), pp. 582–95; see also P.R.O. Roman Transcripts, 31/9/17A. Maidstone granted several pensions in 1315. Five marks a year were promised to Adam Murimuth, professor of civil law, and a similar sum to Masters Andrew de Brugg, John de Stratford, and Richard de Gloucester, the bishop's advocates in the Court of Canterbury. Each advocate was to receive his money "quamdiu in officio postulandi steterit in curia memorata". M. Thomas de Teffunte (see above, p. 92, n. 1) was promised the smaller sum of forty shillings annually as "procurator domini" (Reg. Maidst., ff. 29r., 37r.). Montacute conceded an annual pension of four marks to M. Stephen de Kettlebury, his advocate in the Court of Arches, "pro quibus promisit magister Stephanus corporali prestito iuramento in nostris agendis auxilium et consilium fideliter impendere contra quoscumque, dominis suis preiuratis dumtaxat exceptis" (Reg. Montacute 1, fo. 6v.).

present to those benefices which *sede plena* were in episcopal collation.[1] Moreover, at the time of a bishop's promotion both the king[2] and the archbishop[3] claimed a benefice for one of their clerks, or a pension in lieu. Furthermore the papal practice of providing to benefices which fell vacant in the Curia meant that once such provision had been made it proved extremely difficult to recover the right of collation at subsequent vacancies.[4] Further difficulties were created by the bishops themselves. As soon as benefices became vacant they filled them, naturally enough, with their own familiar clerks, sometimes too, and less commendably, with their relatives and friends.[5] Reynolds, for instance, secured Tredington for his youthful kinsman, Ralph of

---

[1] In 1321 Edward II presented to the Worcester archdeaconry, "vacantem et ad ipsius donacionem hac vice spectantem racione episcopatus Wygorniensis dudum vacantis" (*Reg. Cobham*, fo. 66v., p. 106), although this was apparently done with the bishop's connivance (see pp. 34–5 above). In 1317 and 1318 he presented to the Gloucester archdeaconry (see p. 38). Royal presentations were made on this pretext to Tredington, an episcopal benefice taxed at £26 13s. 4d., in 1327, 1328, 1339, and 1344 (*C.P.R.* 1327–30, pp. 205, 232, 347; ibid. 1338–40, p. 175; ibid. 1343–5, p. 349). Bransford contested the king's right to present, but the Court of King's Bench decided against him (*C.P.R.* 1343–5, p. 419). Meanwhile the pope had provided another clerk and a dispute ensued—which was sometimes violent—between the royal and papal nominees until in 1348 the king withdrew his presentation (*C.P.R.* 1343–5, pp. 419, 589; 1345–8, pp. 171, 313, 322, 383, 447: 1348–50, p. 220). The papal provisor, Dunclent, was in possession at the time of the 1366 plurality return (*Cant. Reg. Langham*, p. 37). If Nash's list of institutions is complete, the bishops did not recover their right of collation until 1436 (Nash 2, p. 431; Reg. Bourchier, fo. 33r.). For a general view of this right of *regale* see Deeley, "Papal Provisions", pp. 507 et seq. At Lichfield thirty—roughly a tenth—of those who became canons in the fourteenth century did so as a result of royal presentation, mainly on account of the bishopric's vacancy (Jenkins, "Lich. Cath.", p. 179).

[2] In 1339, for instance, Bransford acknowledged his obligation "racione nove creacionis nostre" to pay one hundred shillings a year "Roberto de Kyngestone ipsius domini regis clerico per eumque nobis per breve suum de cancellario nominato" until he should be provided with a competent benefice. Reg. Bransf., fo. 6v. (56).

[3] See the formal claim in *Lit. Cant.* 1, p. 33, no. 40; cf. Churchill 1, p. 350 and n. 1. The same custom seems to have obtained in the northern province, although Bishop Kellawe professed ignorance of it. *Reg. Palat. Dunelm.* 1, pp. 23–5.

[4] Papal provision to the archdeaconry of Worcester (pp. 32–4 above) is a case in point. Cobham complained to John XXII about papal encroachment on his right of collation: "Quia sic sum oneratus multitudine expectancium de gracia sedis apostolice, quod in beneficiis ad meam collacionem spectantibus nullum valeo promovere" (*Reg. Cobh.*, fo. 67r., p. 107). A similar complaint was made in 1342 by Bishop Bury of Durham who asked permission of Clement VI to provide his familiar clerks with benefices in his collation notwithstanding papal graces. *Letters from Northern Regs.*, p. 383; *Reg. Palat. Dunelm.* 3, p. 506.

[5] Even Bishop Oliver Sutton of Lincoln, a commendable diocesan, caused considerable disturbance by collating the prebend of Thame, which was to be held in plurality, to his relative, M. Thomas de Sutton (*Rot. & Reg. Sutton* 3, pp. xl–xli). Grandisson frankly acknowledged the practice: "Per multos annos non potui familiaribus meis aut nepotibus providere" (*Exeter Reg. Grand.*, p. 182, n. 2).

8

Windsor,[1] while Orleton provided for his brother John[2] and his nephews, the brothers John[3] and Thomas Trilleck.[4] But, whether merely relatives or active diocesan officers, such clerks tended to follow the bishop to whom they owed their promotion or, on his death, to look for employment elsewhere. The result was that some time elapsed before the succeeding bishop had a sufficient fund of patronage to provide for all his clerks.[5] If a clerk already had a benefice, but outside the diocese, he tended to exchange it for one within its confines. If, on the other hand, he had a benefice within the diocese he might attempt to secure promotion to a more lucrative one which happened to fall vacant, and in this way he could gradually increase his income. Some bishops, notably Orleton, allowed a certain amount of plurality among their clerks,[6] but Bransford permitted none, and though his clerks

1 In 1310 it was granted to him *in commendam* (*Reg. Reynolds*, fo. 25r., p. 151). Ralph was then only fifteen. Four years later he received dispensation, at the instance of Reynolds, by then archbishop, to retain Tredington as well as two canonries (*C.P.L.* 1305–42, pp. 121–2). In 1328 Orleton was ordered by the official of the Court of Canterbury to cite Henry de Clifton who claimed that Tredington was vacant and that he had been presented to it. Doubtless he can be identified with the Henry "de Clyf" who received the royal presentation *racione vacacionis* in 1327 (*C.P.R.* 1327–1330, p. 232; cf. p. 95, n. 1 above). Windsor's appeal was dismissed and he lost the benefice (*Heref. Reg. Orleton*, pp. 376–7, 378–81; the entries properly belong to Orleton's Worcester register). The editor of Heref. Reg. Orleton is mistaken in assuming that John de Orleton was ever rector of Tredington. He held the rectory of Tytherington, Gloucestershire.

2 See p. 34 above.

3 He received the prebend of Aust in the church of Westbury in 1329 and the following year the rectory of Bredon. Both were in the bishop's collation. He was licensed to leave Bredon for seven years for purposes of study (Reg. Orleton 1, ff. 20r., 21r.; 2, ff. 34r., 35v.). He was also a canon of Hereford, having secured the prebend of Wellington by papal provision in 1327 (*Heref. Reg. Orleton*, p. 389). In 1344 he became bishop of Hereford.

4 Already a canon of Wells and of Hereford, holding the prebend of Yatton in the former and that of Moreton in the latter, he received the collation of Ripple in 1331. *Heref. Reg. Orleton*, pp. xli, n. 3, 381, 389; Reg. Orleton 1, fo. 24r.; 2, fo. 46v.; and see intro. to *Heref. Reg. Trilleck*, pp. 1 et seq.

5 Pontissara, writing from France in 1289 to Archbishop Pecham, stated that since his departure only three slender (*exilia*) benefices had fallen vacant. These he had collated to his official, the steward of his household, and to his chaplain—all familiar clerks of his. *Winch. Reg. Pontiss.*, p. 185.

6 It is necessary to mention only two in addition to John Orleton and the brothers Trilleck (see above). Roger de Breynton, canon of Hereford, received Hanbury in 1329 and Alvechurch *in commendam* the following year. Both were episcopal churches (Reg. Orleton 1, fo. 20r.; 2, ff. 34r., 36r.). In 1331 he exchanged Hanbury with John de Usk, another of Orleton's clerks, for the archdeaconry of Gloucester (see p. 39 above). Adam de Aylton, non-resident dean of Westbury (see pp. 28–9 above), was also rector of Rock, Hereford diocese. In 1328 he was granted Bredicot *in commendam*, but resigned it after a fortnight (Reg. Orleton 1, fo. 17v.). For further details of Orleton's clerks see pp. 92–3 above.

sometimes changed benefices, at no time did any of his *familiares* hold more than one at a time.

By the fourteenth century the bishops *vis à vis* their dioceses were in a position which corresponded to that of the popes with regard to the Church as a whole: unable or unwilling to provide for their administrative staff from ordinary revenues they looked on benefices as an essential means of making such provision.[1] The foundation of certain collegiate churches was closely connected with the growing need for a larger fund of patronage,[2] although as canonries became the "staple commodity of the papal market"[3] this may not have proved a successful policy in the long run. In any case, partly because of outside demands, partly because of the increased complexity of administration, the problem of the remuneration of episcopal clerks was a very real one at this time.

THE BISHOP'S COUNCIL

It is probable that only the greater clerks took a prominent part in the deliberations of the bishop's council. How far such a council was an established administrative organ, and how far an informal meeting of clerks called together for the occasion to give advice, it is difficult to determine. When we read that a bishop acted "de consilio iuris peritorum" we should probably be wise to assume that he had merely been guided by the opinion of his legal advisors, and not that the matter had necessarily been laid before a formal council. But that such an institution did exist in the Worcester diocese is shown by a number of entries in the registers.

A council may well have been a regular feature of Bishop Giffard's administration, for in his register are some council agenda though these, it is true, date from the last years of his episcopate.[4] Then too, during

---

1 See Barraclough, *Papal Provisions*, pp. 71–2. He regards the use made by the bishops of their patronage as a narrow one. They were, he writes, "too prone to regard personal service and personal connection as the foremost qualification" (ibid., p. 160).

2 One of the reasons given by Bishop Bek of Durham when he made three of his churches collegiate was that there were not enough lawyers and counsellors to aid the diocesan in the arduous affairs of his church (*Records of Bek*, pp. 3, 7; and see p. 28 above). Pecham used his newly founded college at Wingham to provide for "his most faithful clerks and chaplains" (Douie, p. 150).

3 Maitland, *Canon Law*, p. 67n. In 1290, at the time of Giffard's attempt to make episcopal churches prebendal to Westbury, the king's council pointed out that all but five of the Lincoln prebends, as well as the Worcester archdeaconry, were "in manibus Romanorum" (*Ann. Wigorn.*, pp. 501–2).

4 *Reg. Giffard*, ff. 441v., 442r. al. ccccxlviii r., and fragments attached to the latter, pp. 514–17. The earlier of these agenda (fo. 442r.) is headed: "Tractatus domini . . . Wyg' episcopi habitus cum suo consilio apud Hertlebur' die Beati Stephani anno

the first year of Bishop Gainsburgh's rule (1303) we learn that the subject of the appropriation of the church of Dodderhill came before the "consilium clericorum episcopi Wygorn.".[1] At the end of Bishop Maidstone's register has been written a form suitable for use when the bishop sought the consent of the cathedral chapter to the farming of an episcopal manor, which suggests that the council may have taken a prominent part in a transaction of this kind.[2] The formula runs as follows: In the presence of the bishop's council and the auditors of his accounts it was found that the manor of A. had shown a profit at the end of the year. For the benefit of himself and his successors the bishop proposed to let it out to farm for the term of his life at £100 a year. The chapter might therefore be willing to approve the farm and to confirm it with their common seal, in the knowledge that the approval of the whole of the bishop's council had been given to the transaction.[3] There is also mention of such a council in Bransford's register.[4]

Yet, though there is some tantalizing evidence of the existence of an episcopal council at Worcester, to what extent it was a permanent body or prominent in diocesan affairs during our period we can only surmise. It is likely that councils existed in other dioceses, though they are rarely mentioned in the registers. Ralph of Shrewsbury, bishop of Bath and Wells, adjourned a case against those who had violated the liberties of his manors of Axbridge and Cheddar "quia . . . non habuit consilium suum ibidem",[5] while at Salisbury there is mention of the clerks of Bishop Simon of Ghent's council.[6] Churchill suggests that Reynolds' experience of a council at Worcester may have been responsible for some of the developments of the system at Canterbury.[7]

---

pontificatus eiusdem xxxii⁰" (26 December 1299); the later (fo. 441v.): "Tractatus habendus coram domino episcopo et suis cons' apud Hertl' anno xxxiii⁰" (23 September 1300/23 September 1301).

1 R.S.V., fo. 20r. As Churchill notes (1, p. 16, n. 1) there is no mention of a "writ of the council of clerks" as stated by Willis Bund in his edition of the register (p. 57). There is mention of Bishop Reynolds' council in 1312. In response to a petition of the burgesses of Bristol he wrote that he would have to discuss the matter with his chapter and council. *Reg. Reynolds*, fo. 42r., p. 33; and see p. 107 below.

2 Although an alternative formula makes no mention of the council.

3 *Reg. Maidstone*, fo. 56v.

4 ". . . si eidem domino episcopo et eius consilio videatur quod alio modo prefatus episcopus servari non possit indempnis (&c.) . . ." *Reg. Bransford*, fo. 58v. (521).

5 *B. & W. Reg. Shrewsb.* p. 123: 1332.

6 *Salisb. Reg. S. de Gandavo*, intro. p. xv, 862.

7 *Cant. Admin.* 1, p. 16. For the council at Canterbury see ibid., pp. 11 et seq. and Douie, *Abp. Pecham*, p. 59. There is much information in the Durham records about the bishop's council, but this seems to have been mainly occupied with the affairs of the franchise.

VICARS-GENERAL

As is well known, the vicar-general was the deputy of an absent bishop who by virtue of his commission could carry out the day-to-day administration of the diocese and proceed with all matters for which episcopal orders were not required. Within the limitations imposed by such a commission the vicar-general was entitled to exercise the same powers as the bishop himself, had he been present.[1] If his commission was not explicit the powers of the vicar-general were governed by the custom prevailing in the diocese.[2]

The practice followed in most English dioceses at this time was for the bishop to appoint a vicar-general when he went abroad: if he left the diocese temporarily, but remained in the country, he did not necessarily do so. Stephen de Mauley, dean of Auckland, was acting as vicar-general of the bishop of Durham in 1309-10 although Bek was in the diocese and later in London, where he was engaged as a papal commissary in the proceedings against the Templars.[3] But this was comparatively unusual. In most cases of temporary absence it was enough for the bishop to extend the powers of one or other of his clerks, usually his official.[4] At Worcester Walter Reynolds, during an episcopate of five years, stayed in the diocese for less than eight months— three weeks in 1310 and seven months in 1312.[5] He visited places as far apart as Oxford, Newcastle, St Albans, and Rochester, but none the less exercised personally many of the administrative powers of a diocesan, issued commissions, and received writs.[6] He did appoint a vicar-general in 1309, but only because he was about to leave England for

---

[1] In 1337 Hemenhale empowered his joint vicars-general to do all such things "que nosmet possumus facere si personaliter presentes essemus" (Reg. Hemen., fo. 6r.).

[2] Thus the first of Orleton's 1328 commissions granted powers "in hiis que ad officium vicarii pertinent" (Reg. Orleton 2, fo. 3v.): the second, "ad omnia et singula faciend[um] et excercend[um] que vicariatus concernunt officium" (ibid., fo. 6v.). Bishop Montacute empowered his vicar-general "ad faciendum excercendum et expediendum omnia et singula que ad huiusmodi officium de iure vel consuetudine pertinere noscuntur" (Reg. Montacute 1, fo. 1r.).

[3] Records of Bek, pp. 137 (bis), 151, 153. Cf. Reg. Palat. Dunelm. 3, pp. 208, 286 Halton was forced to appoint a vicar-general in 1313 when Scottish incursions made it impossible for him to live within his diocese of Carlisle. Carlisle Reg. Halton 2, pp. 99–100, and cf. ibid., p. 200.

[4] For example, when Sandale, bishop of Winchester, attended the York parliament of 1318 he merely appointed two clerks to fill vacant benefices. Winch. Reg. Sandale, p. 104.

[5] See his itinerary in the edition of Register Reynolds, pp. 181–3.

[6] One such writ overtook him on the road near Uxbridge: "Istud breve venit iii Kalend' Januarii (30 December) in via regia iuxta Woxebrugg". Reg. Reyn., fo. 107v., p. 173.

the Curia on royal business.[1] As soon as he returned, he resumed the custody of his registers, and his vicar-general's powers came to an end.[2] Again, Maidstone, despite his absences, did not appoint a vicar-general until 1317 when he finally went abroad. It is clear then that vicars-general were appointed at Worcester on a temporary basis only and, so far as can be judged from those registers of other dioceses which have been printed, the same was true elsewhere.[3]

Of the ten commissions of this type recorded in the Worcester registers between 1300 and 1350, seven were issued because of episcopal absence from the realm. The remaining three were issued at the beginning of episcopates before the respective bishops had had time personally to assume the administrative reins.[4] Though James de Cobham's commission is not recorded in the registers, he too was acting as the vicar-general of his brother, Thomas de Cobham, prior to the latter's arrival in the diocese.[5]

Bishop Gainsburgh during his absence abroad in 1307 did not appoint a vicar-general, but issued instead a commission empowering his official, John de Rodberrow, to admit, institute, and induct suitable clerks to benefices, to return writs, and to issue letters dimissory.[6] Similarly, Bishop Maidstone, when detained outside the diocese by pressure of business, empowered certain of his clerks to carry out institutions.[7]

In only one instance has the revocation of a vicar-general's commission been entered in the registers of our period. This was in 1334[8] when Bishop Montacute withdrew the powers which he had conferred on Wolstan de Bransford in March of the same year. At the time the bishop was at Crookham in Berkshire.[9] In the ordinary course of events

---

[1] "Cum pro diversis et arduis negociis, serenissimum principem dominum E[dwardum] dei gracia regem Anglie illustrem et regnum Anglie contingentibus, in curia Romana et alibi procurandis, nedum a nostra diocesi sed eciam a regno Anglie ad tempus aliquod oporteat nos abesse..." (*Reg. Reynolds*, fo. 9r., p. 7 : 16 March 1309).

[2] *Reg. Reynolds*, fo. 12r., pp. 10–11.

[3] Cf. Hamilton Thompson, *English Clergy*, pp. 46–7.

[4] Two by Orleton dated 29 February and 15 May 1328, from York and Northampton respectively, the bishop describing himself as *in remotis* (Reg. Orleton 2, ff. 3v., 6v.). He was not enthroned until 19 June (ibid. fo. 6v.). Montacute issued the third, dated 11 March 1334, from Oxford (Reg. Montacute 1, fo. 1r.). He was not consecrated until 8 May 1334 (ibid., ff. 6v., 11r., 13r.).

[5] Reg. Maidstone, ff. 52 et seq.   [6] *Reg. Gainsburgh*, fo. 11r., p. 30.

[7] Reg. Maidstone, ff. 2v., 20v.

[8] Though this entry is undated the previous one is dated XI Kal' Junii (21 June) from the same place (Crookham). Reg. Montacute 1, fo. 8r.

[9] Ibid., ff. 1r. and 8r. "... Nos tamen ad presens certis et legitimis de causis nos moventibus nostrum propositum mutare volentes ipsam commissionem nostram

the vicar-general's powers lapsed as soon as the bishop returned to his diocese, and the first evidence in the registers of his supersession is provided by the record of the bishop's presence or his performance of some administrative act.

The first commission for the appointment of a vicar-general recorded in the Worcester registers[1] was issued by Bishop Gainsburgh on 17 October 1305.[2] It enabled M. Walter de Wotton, archdeacon of Huntingdon and canon of Westbury, to act on the bishop's behalf during his absence at the Curia.

The commission is a detailed one. The vicar-general was empowered to examine both the elections to religious houses and the persons elected, to confirm them, and to grant licence for the elect to receive benediction from any bishop of the Canterbury province; to receive clerks presented to benefices and to institute and induct them, as well as to appoint to monasteries and churches, where this belonged to the bishop by right or custom; to choose a prior of Worcester, in the event of a vacancy, in accordance with the composition agreed between Bishop William of Blois and the then prior and chapter; to remove, after legal process, those wrongfully detaining ecclesiastical benefices etc., to deprive at will ("pro tue libito voluntatis") the bishop's servants, both spiritual and temporal, of their administrations, offices, and bailiffships, and to substitute others; to confer benefices except those of the bishop's own personal collation;[3] and to appoint a substitute and to revoke such appointment whenever he thought fit. In general terms he was to act in all matters relating to the administration of the bishop's spiritualities and temporalities; to perform everything pertaining to the office of vicar-general; and to exercise the plenitude of episcopal jurisdiction.

There is a special "Register of the time of Master Walter de Wotton" which commences on 21 October 1305.[4] It has no formal termination

---

vobis concessam revocamus. Mandantes quatinus dicta commissio et potestas sic ut premittitur vobis facte ultra diem confeccionis presencium nullatenus durare valeant, nec robur aliquod habeant firmitatis" (fo. 8r.).

1 Giffard is not recorded to have appointed a vicar-general. Thomas (*Account*, p. 156) states that John de Rodberrow and Robert de Sutton, rectors of Hartlebury and Dursley respectively, were appointed vicars-general by Gainsburgh in a commission of 8 February 1303. This is based on a misreading of an entry in the *R.S.V.* (fo. 15v., p. 38). In fact they were appointed to receive the canonical obedience of the clergy.

2 *Reg. Gainsburgh*, fo. 9v., p. 26. See App B, p. 326 below.

3 The vicar-general could dispose of those benefices the right of presentation to which had lapsed to the bishop because of uncanonical delay or for some other reason.

4 "Registrum temporis magistri W[alteri] de Wotton archidiaconi Hunt' venerabilis patris domini W[illelmi] dei gracia Wygorn' episcopi vicarii generalis a die

but the bishop was back in the diocese by 16 March of the following year.[1]

Bishop Gainsburgh did not appoint another vicar-general even though he was absent at the Carlisle parliament from Christmas 1306 to the following Easter[2] and left the country altogether in July.[3] Instead he gave additional powers to his official, John de Rodberrow.[4]

In 1309 Bishop Reynolds appointed as vicar-general his official, M. Benedict de Paston.[5] The commission of appointment is virtually identical with that of M. Walter de Wotton. The only significant alteration occurs in the clause empowering the vicar-general to remove the bishop's spiritual and temporal officers. These were not to be deprived merely at the vicar-general's whim ("pro tue libito voluntatis"), but only if he found them unsuitable ("si eos minus idoneos repereris").

Paston's register[6] runs from 23 March 1309 and his authority had been terminated by July. On the 22nd of that month at Sawbridgeworth (Hertfordshire) Reynolds received at the hands of William de Drax, his clerk, not only his own register, but also those of his immediate predecessors William Gainsburgh and Godfrey Giffard.[7] They had been sent to him by M. Benedict de Paston, his official, and during his absence from England, vicar-general.[8]

By Maidstone's commission of 1317 Masters Richard de Clara and Richard de Chaddesleye were appointed jointly and severally to exercise the office of vicar-general. The commission differs in some important respects from those of Gainsburgh and Reynolds. It conferred the additional power of correction and punishment of the excesses of

---

Jovis proxima post festum Sancti Luce Ewangeliste, videlicet XII Kalen' Novembris anno domini MᵒCCCᵒ quinto, consecracionis vero dicti patris tercio. Quo die transfretavit versus curiam Romanam dictus pater." *Reg. Gainsburgh*, fo. 37r., p. 142. Rubric.

[1] See *Reg. Gainsburgh*, ff. 11 r., 38v.; pp. 29, 148.

[2] "Ipso [Willelmo] existente apud Karliolen' in parliamento a Nativitate usque Pascham anno supradicto" (*Reg. Gainsburgh*, fo. 43v., p. 177).

[3] ". . . in absencia domini episcopi existentis ultra mare versus Pictaviam" (ibid., fo. 46v., p. 181).

[4] Ibid., fo. 11r., p. 30. See also the rubrics on ff. 43v. and 46v., pp. 177, 181.

[5] *Reg. Reynolds*, fo. 9r., p. 7.

[6] "Registrum temporis magistri Benedicti de Paston venerabilis patris domini W[alteri] dei gracia Wygorn' episcopi vicarii generalis a die Dominica in Ramis Palmarum anno domini MᵒCCC VIIIᵒ, quo die dictus pater transfretavit versus curiam Romanam". *Reg. Reynolds*, fo. 9v., p. 7.

[7] It is interesting to note that there is no mention of a register earlier than Giffard's (1268–1302) which is now the first in the Worcester series.

[8] See p. 4, n. 3 above.

the bishop's subjects[1]— a function usually delegated to the official.[2] The proviso "si ipsos minus idoneos esse", which had qualified the right to remove episcopal officers in Reynolds' commission, is retained. There is no mention of the right to appoint the Worcester prior, but the vicars-general were specifically inhibited from making presentation to benefices in the bishop's collation.[3] The clause permitting the appointment and removal of substitutes is omitted, though it must be remembered that the commission was a joint one.

The next six commissions do not give details of the powers which they conferred. There is no reference to the temporalities of the bishopric, and those appointed were designated vicars in spirituals only.[4] They are all couched in similar general terms though the wording varies. The first five were issued by Orleton,[5] the sixth by Montacute in 1334. Montacute appointed Prior Bransford but revoked the commission three months later.[6]

[1] "Ad ... excessusque subditorum nostrorum quorumcumque corrigend[um] et puniend[um] ..." Reg. Maidstone, fo. 50r.

[2] But only as a *specialis potestas*. See pp. 109–10 below.

[3] "... presentacionibus et collacionibus beneficiorum nostri patronatus seu aliorum quorumcumque vacancium dumtaxat exceptis ..." Reg. Maidstone, fo. 50r.

[4] As in the rubric of Orleton's commission of 1331: "Vicaria commissa in spiritualibus in absencia domini" (Reg. Orleton 2, fo. 39r.). The commissions of Bishops Gainsburgh and Reynolds empowered the vicars-general to act in all things "que ad administracionem spiritualium et temporalium nostrorum pertinere noscuntur" (*Regs. Gainsburgh*, fo. 10r., p. 26; *Reynolds*, fo. 9r., p. 7).

[5]
(i)	Adam de Herwynton	29 Feb. 1328 York	Reg. Orleton 2, fo. 3v.
(ii)	Adam de Herwynton William de Fowehope	15 May 1328 Northampton	Ibid. fo. 6r.
(iii)	Robert de Worth, official. Roger de Breynton	18 Jan. 1331 London	Ibid. fo. 39r.
(iv)	Adam de Herwynton	20 April 1332 Withington	Ibid. 1, fo. 40r.
(v)	Adam de Herwynton Roger de Breynton	9 Nov. 1332 London	Ibid. 1, fo. 27r. 2, fo. 53r.

(There is a transcript of this commission in the printed edition of *Heref. Reg. Charlton* (p. 25), where it is dated 20 November 1332. From *B. & W. Reg. Shrewsb.* (p. 151) we learn that Breynton wrote from Hereford on 28 August 1333 to ask Bishop Ralph to reconcile the cathedral church at Worcester, which had been polluted by the shedding of blood.)

In 1331 Worth and Breynton were appointed *vicarios* with the omission of the qualifying *generales*, and this wording was followed in the 1332 commissions. The word "generalis" is also omitted from the body, though not from the rubric, of Orleton's second commission of 1328. None the less, in a memorandum of institutions carried out in the bishop's absence by virtue of this commission William de Fowehope is described as "vicarius domini in ipsius absencia in spiritualibus generalis" (Reg. Orleton 2, fo. 24r.). In the first of the 1328 commissions Orleton appointed Herwynton "nostrum vicarium generalem".

[6] Reg. Montacute 1, ff. 1r., 8r. See p. 100 above.

The very full commission whereby Bishop Hemenhale appointed Prior Bransford, Stephen de Kettlebury, and Andrew Offord to act as his vicars-general[1] differs both in form and content from the detailed commissions of Bishops Gainsburgh and Reynolds which have been examined above. It was drawn up as a public instrument and notarially attested by Nicholas North, a clerk of the diocese. After a somewhat lengthy preamble come the actual words of appointment[2] which, for the first time, precede the detailed enumeration of powers. The vicars-general were granted full administrative authority and every faculty to make decisions (or appointments) in the bishop's name ("statuendi nostro nomine"), to reform, inquire into, and make visitation of ecclesiastical persons and religious houses, to punish excesses, to impose sentences of interdict, suspension, or excommunication, and to remove from their benefices, either permanently or for a time, those whose faults merited it; to examine elections to monasteries, churches, or other benefices in the diocese, to inquire about the life and conversation of those elected, to confirm or annul such elections, and to make provision for abbots to receive episcopal benediction; to present boys and clerks for the sacrament of chrism,[3] for the first tonsure, and all minor and holy orders, and to grant them letters *ad hoc*. The bishop specially reserved his rights of collation to benefices, but the vicars-general were given authority and special mandate to secure or recover all rights, income, jurisdiction, or first fruits which belonged to the bishopric. Finally, they were empowered to do anything which true and lawful vicars-general were entitled to do, or which the bishop himself could have done had he been in the diocese, with the promise that their acts, whether performed in person or by proxy, would be upheld by the bishop.

Comparing this commission with those of Gainsburgh and Reynolds we find that, unlike them, it contains no specific provision for the appointment of a Worcester prior, and reserves to the diocesan all institutions whether belonging to him by right of collation or by devolution. On the other hand, it did confer the power to make visitation, enforceable by interdict and excommunication, to present clerks for ordination, and to secure the bishop's rights and jurisdiction— a natural corollary of Hemenhale's recent elevation to the episcopate.

[1] Reg. Hemenhale, fo. 6r.–v.: 3 April, Avignon.
[2] ". . . ideoque vos et vestrum quemlibet in solidum nostros et dicti episcopatus nostri Wygorn' in spiritualibus generales vicarios facimus constituimus ac ordinamus."
[3] "Ad sacramentum chrismatis". Cf. Lyndwood, p. 36 ad ver. *chrismatis*: "Et quandoque dicitur sacramentum, in quantum viz. adjungitur corpori, puta in confirmatione."

In common with all the other commissions from 1328 onwards there is no mention of the temporalities of the see, and those appointed were vicars-general in spirituals only.[1]

OFFICIALS[2]

With the exception of the vicar-general, whose appointment was in any case occasional and limited by the period of the bishop's absence, the official was the most important episcopal officer. According to Peter of Blois the office had been introduced into England by Richard of Ilchester, bishop of Winchester (1174–88).[3] The earliest mention of an official at Worcester is during Baldwin's episcopate (1180–4),[4] and by 1219 Bishop Blois' arrangements for the commemoration of his death bear witness to his pre-eminent position in the administrative hierarchy.[5]

The official was the bishop's deputy. Although in the fourteenth century the commissions for his appointment mention only his work in the judicial sphere, the registers as a whole tell a very different story. They show that he was intimately connected with almost every facet of diocesan administration. He was the obvious person to be entrusted with special responsibility. All this will appear as the various aspects of

1 The acts of the vicars-general, mostly those of Prior Bransford, are contained in the first five folios of Reg. Hemenhale (numbered 6 to 10). This register was begun "mense Maii" and the earliest entry (the fifth) is dated 27 May [1337]. The bishop was issuing commissions from London as early as 10 July. Bransford, however, was still acting as vicar on 21 July when, in the chapel of St Nicholas, called the prior's chapel, he absolved John of Northampton from the sentence of greater excommunication. It is interesting to note that the document recording the proceedings was drawn up by the same Nicholas North who had attested the commission at Avignon. D. & C. MS. B. 1637; Reg. Hemenhale, fo. 10r. Hemenhale was in the diocese by the beginning of September when the commission to his vicars-general must have lapsed automatically.

2 The usual designation in the Worcester registers, although John de la Lowe is described by Bishop Bransford in July 1349 as "officialem nostrum principalem" (Reg. Bransf. 2, fo. 15r. (1484)). There is no evidence that there was another official at the time. Cobham on one occasion (September 1320?) did appoint two clerks jointly to hear those causes pertaining to the officiality—the only instance of such a joint appointment, Reg. Cobh., fo. 22v., p. 27. There is no indication that there were any of Lyndwood's "officiales foranei", who might be deputed to hear causes in part of a diocese only and from whom appeal lay to the bishop. See Lyndwood ad ver. officiales principales, p. 105.

3 See Cheney, Becket to Langton, p. 147 and ibid., n. 2. Colin Morris has contributed a useful introduction to the official in his article "A Consistory Court in the Middle Ages", J.E.H. Vol. 14, no. 2, pp. 150–9.

4 Landboc Winch. 1, pp. 70–1.

5 Concilia 1, p. 570: "Mortuo autem officiali episcopi per totum episcopatum predictum servicium pro anima ipsius fiat semel in qualibet ecclesia."

episcopal activity are reviewed in the next chapter. For the present we will examine the recorded appointments and the official's judicial functions.

The official was appointed by written commission and probably received the seal of the officiality at the same time. He presided over the consistory courts of the diocese either in person or by commissary. There could be no appeal from his court to the bishop, for the auditory of the one was the same as that of the other.[1]

At least four consistory courts were regularly held in the Worcester diocese:[2] at Worcester, Gloucester,[3] Warwick, and Bristol, the most important towns.[4] Few details of their proceedings are to be found in the episcopal registers because they possessed their own muniments and rolls which, in 1313, were said to be in the charge of a clerk of the consistories[5] and kept in chests, the keys of which were in his possession.[6] A form of citation has been recorded in which the prior *sede vacante* orders the register of causes[7] of the Gloucester and Bristol consistories to be produced before himself or some other president of the Ciren-

---

[1] "Non putamus illam consuetudinem ... consonam rationi, quod ab officiali episcopi ad eundem episcopum valeat appellari: ne ab eodem ad se ipsum, quum sit idem auditorium utriusque, appellatio interposita videatur" (*Sext* 1, 4, c. 2). Cf. Lyndwood (p. 105) ad ver. *officiales principales*: "Ipsorum auditorium est idem cum auditorio ipsorum episcoporum". It is not always recognized that all cases (within his jurisdiction) pertained to the bishop's audience, though some were heard in his consistory and others outside it. The extra-consistorial court monopolized the term "audience court".

[2] Pecham in 1283 restricted the holding of consistories within Hereford diocese to Hereford, Ludlow, Monmouth, and Ross, although Winchelsey's mandate reaffirming this (1299) mentions only Hereford and Ludlow. Churchill 1, p. 351, n. 1; Douie, p. 144.

[3] The Gloucester consistory was held in the church of St Nicholas there (for example, in 1313: *Landboc Winch.* 2, p. 342).

[4] They are thus enumerated in *R.S.V.* fo. 8ov., p. 138: but there were others. In 1266 an appeal of the Worcester chapter was published in Winchcomb church "in publico loco consistorii" (D. & C. MS. B. 1612). The Cirencester consistory is twice mentioned on fo. 135v. of the R.S.V.

[5] There was a comparable officer in the dioceses of Bath and Wells, and Exeter. In 1330 Bishop Ralph of Shrewsbury committed the custody of the consistory registers to Walter de Banewell "quamdiu nobis placuerit et se laudabiliter gesserit in eodem". He ordered the admission of Walter as registrar of the consistories. *B. & W. Reg. Shrewsb.* pp. 40–1, nos. 149, 150: for Exeter see n. 6 below.

[6] On being asked by the Worcester prior, in his capacity of official *sede vacante*, to deliver up the "rotulos et registra consistoriorum una cum clavibus scriniorum et litteris certificatoriis aliisque munimentis et instrumentis consistoria concernentibus", Benedict de Paston, who had been Reynolds' official, replied: "Magister R. clericus consistoriorum penes se habet hec omnia". R.S.V., fo. 8ov. The Exeter consistory (*c.* 1390) was kept locked, for among the expenses of the registrar is the item: "In i clave pro ostio consistorii". *Exeter Reg. Brantyngham* 1, p. 219.

[7] "Causarum" in the marginal rubric but "animarum" in the entry itself.

cester consistory.[1] In 1309 William de Notgrove, who by the adoption of their habit pretended to be one of the brothers of the hospital of St Margaret outside Gloucester, was summoned before two consecutive sessions of the Gloucester consistory on 4 and 26 June.[2] In 1349 we hear of a matrimonial cause pending in the same consistory.[3] But such fragmentary details would seem to have found their way into the registers only by chance.

The mayor and commonality of Bristol claimed that all cases involving their burgesses should be decided by the official or his commissary within the liberty of the town and not elsewhere.[4] They petitioned Bishop Reynolds to that effect, but he replied that the matter required greater deliberation and that on his return to the diocese he would discuss it with his council and the chapter.[5] Unfortunately the outcome is not recorded, but a memorandum of 1317 in the Little Red Book of Bristol asserts the immunity of burgesses from citation outside the deanery—a privilege which Archbishop Winchelsey had merely confirmed.[6]

---

[1] R.S.V., fo. 135v.   [2] Reg. Reynolds, fo. 10r.   [3] Reg. Bransford 2, fo. 2r. (1329).

[4] *Reg. Reynolds*, fo. 42r., p. 33. "... Cum venerabiles patres omnes predecessores vestri Wygorn' episcopi de sua gracia speciali concesserint ac permiserint progenitoribus nostris et nobis burgensibus ville predicte a tempore cuius memoria non existit, quod omnes cause et negocia ecclesiastica progenitores nostros vel nos quomodolibet contingencia per officialem Wygorn' aut ipsius commissarium infra libertatem ville Bristoll' supradicte et non alibi infra diocesem ventilarentur et ibidem fine debito deciderentur ..." This "Supplicacio maioris et communitatis ville Bristoll" (marginal rubric) is undated, but the bishop's reply, which immediately follows it, is dated 29 January (1312). Cf. Archbishop Winchelsey's injunction to the ordinaries of the Bristol deanery (see p. 63 above): "Ordinariis eciam publice inhibuimus ne pro testamentorum probacionibus [&c.] ... quicquam extorqueatur aliqualiter inposterum ab invitis, nec ea occasione municipes et habitores eiusdem municipii extra ipsum municipium ad loca remota sint maliciose pro aliquorum vexacionibus nimis voluntariis et iniustis [sicut] hactenus factum fuisse comperimus trahantur inviti ..." Reg. Gainsburgh, fo. 3r. Winchelsey instructed the rural dean to let the mayor and commonality have a copy of his mandate under seal, if they asked for one. This is apparently the document later referred to as being in the commonality's coffers. See *Bristol Charters* (*B.R.S.* XI), p. 59; *Great Red Book of Bristol* (*B.R.S.* IV), pp. 91–3 (transcript of the mandate).

[5] *Reg. Reynolds*, fo. 42r., p. 33. "Verum quia peticio huiusmodi maiorem exposcit deliberacionem, nec aliquos de consilio nostro sciverunt aliqualiter informare, nos deo propicio ad nostram diocesem nostramque cathedralem ecclesiam visitacionis causa sumus in brevi reversuri, in huiusmodi regressu nostro cum capitulo et consilio nostro, tractatu super hoc habito prout decet, quatenus absque preiudicio ecclesie nostre poterimus super huiusmodi peticione vestra intendimus facere et concedere quod merito concentari debetis."

[6] *Bristol Charters* (*B.R.S.* XI), p. 59; cf. n. 4 above. According to the custumals no burgess was to swear before the ordinaries for sins committed, or any other cause, except testamentary and matrimonial causes. *Great Red Book of Bristol* I (*B.R.S.* IV), intro. p. 24 (A.D. 1372).

Making the circuit of the consistory courts was an expensive business.[1] In 1301 Winchelsey found that the hospitality shown to the Worcester bishops by the monasteries of Worcester, Gloucester, Llanthony-by-Gloucester, Bristol, and Cirencester, had come to be claimed as of right by Giffard's officials. At the times of the consistory courts held in those places, or nearby, the officials had remained for three, four, or even eight days at the monasteries' cost, to their great injury. The archbishop commissioned the abbots of Winchcomb and Pershore, and the rector of Cleeve, to prevent a recurrence of this evil, while the religious themselves were forbidden to receive such officials or ministers of the bishop at their expense.[2] Pope Clement V reversed this decision in 1307 when he confirmed the bishop's right to have his official and servants lodged as they went about the diocese on business.[3] But in 1315 the houses of Worcester, Gloucester, Llanthony, and Cirencester entered into an agreement to resist the officials' claim, whether by right or grace, to receive hospitality or procuration when celebrating near-by consistories. They created a common fund and each appointed a proctor to implement the agreement.[4]

Other religious houses may also have been burdened in this way. In 1313 Bishop Reynolds promised that the hospitality given to his official at the time of the recent consistory by the brethren of the hospital of St Wulstan at Worcester should not prejudice them in future.[5] But that this was not the only means whereby the official defrayed his expenses is shown by a mandate sent in 1334 by Bishop Montacute to his sequestrator, John de Stanford. Stanford was instructed to pay out of the perquisites of his office the necessary expenses of the official or his commissary, at least for the days of the consistory, as had been customary in the time of the bishop's predecessors.[6]

---

[1] Stratford's constitution "Excussis" provided that the costs were to be defrayed by the principals (domini)—the bishops in this case (Lyndwood, p. 99).

[2] L.A., fo. 5v. See Wilson's summary in Worc. Liber Albus, no. 53, pp. 16–17.

[3] C.P.L. 1305–42, p. 26.

[4] Cart. S. Petri Glouc. 1, pp. 140–6. There is a mutilated copy of this agreement at Worcester (D. & C. MS. B. 1633). The Worcester proctor was Wolstan de Bransford, the future prior and bishop.

[5] Reg. Reynolds, fo. 95v., p. 74.

[6] Reg. Montacute 1, fo. 5r.: 5 April 1334: "LITTERA DIRECTA SEQUESTRA-TORI WYG' PRO EXPENSIS LIBERANDIS OFFICIALI EIUSDEM VEL EIUS COMMISSARIO. Symon dei et apostolice sedis gracia Wyg' ecclesie electus confirmatus, domino Johanni de Stannford clerico et sequestratori nostro generali, salutem in domino. Vobis iniungimus et mandamus, quatinus de perquisitis officii vestri officiali nostro Wygorn' vel eius commissario cuicumque et familiaribus suis expensas necessarias prout [tempore] precessoris et predecessorum nostrorum exstiterat consuetum, saltim diebus consistorii, ministretis seu faciatis congrue ministrari. Dat' die loco et anno supradictis."

There are no details in the Worcester records of the internal workings of the consistory courts. For Durham there is a series of regulations
governing their conduct in Bishop Kellawe's statutes.[1] The official,
his commissary-general, and other ministers of the court of Durham,
had to swear to eschew fraud and malice, to act without motives of
animosity, favour, or gain, and to observe the customs of the court.
The oaths to be sworn by advocates and proctors are given in full.
The official, his commissary-general, and the clerk of the registry,[2]
were all bound to reside in Durham. The poor were to have the services
of advocates and proctors free, while to prevent fraud no official in
the courts of the archdeacons of Durham or Northumberland was to
hold office in the Durham consistory. An advocate or proctor acting
against the jurisdiction of the church of Durham was to be removed
"cum nota infamiae". Corresponding regulations were issued for the
Lincoln consistory in 1334. Here too the focus is on the functions and
qualifications of advocates and proctors.[3] For Exeter some late fourteenth-century accounts of the consistory have been printed from
Register Brantyngham. There the president received a salary of 13s. 4d.
a month which was to be paid by the registrar of the consistory.[4]

In the Worcester registers of the first half of the fourteenth century
there are eight commissions for the appointment of officials. In general
terms they permitted the exercise of those of the bishop's powers which
pertained to the office of the officiality of the diocese.[5] They usually
provided for the exercise of an additional *specialis potestas* which enabled the official to conduct the preliminary inquiries into offences and
to correct and punish the offenders.[6] Bishop Gainsburgh, in addition,
empowered his official to remove from their benefices and administrations such clerks as were to be lawfully deprived.[7]

[1] *Reg. Palat Dunelm.* 3, pp. 578–81.
[2] The same officers are found in the Hereford consistory during Trilleck's episcopate
(1344–60). In the absence of the official and commissary-general, the registrar was
on one occasion commissioned to grant probate of wills. *Heref. Reg. Trilleck*, p. 130.
[3] *Concilia* 2, p. 571. These are discussed by C. Morris, op. cit., pp. 156–7.
[4] *Exeter Reg. Brant.* 1, pp. 214–19. There is also an account for the period November
1393 to October 1394 of the sums spent on parchment, wax, and ink. For licences
permitting advocates to postulate in the Winchester consistory, see *Reg. Wykeham* 2,
pp. 162, 268; and for suspension of a proctor for professional misconduct, *Reg. Woodlock*, pp. 379–80.
[5] "In hiis omnibus et singulis que ad officialitatis officium in nostra Wygorn'
diocesi pertinent, vobis vices nostras . . . committimus [&c.]". Reg. Gainsburgh,
fo. 11r. *inter alia.*
[6] ". . . necnon specialem potestatem inquirendi corrigendi puniendique subditorum
nostrorum . . . excessus" loc. cit. This clause is not in either of Cobham's commissions.
[7] ". . . ac eciam clericos de iure privandos a suis beneficiis et administracionbius
amovendi, committimus per presentes cum cohercionis canonice potestate." Ibid.

Technically the official's powers were restricted to the hearing and determining of causes. He had no right *ex officio* either to hold any preliminary inquiry or to follow up sentence with correction and punishment. This coincides with Lyndwood's dictum,[1] derived from Sext (1, 13 cc. 2, 3), that officials could not proceed to the correction of crimes, the punishment of excesses, or the amoval from benefices without an *ad hoc* commission.[2]

In origin the official was the minister specially charged with the exercise of the bishop's contentious jurisdiction[3]—that which arose from suits brought either *ex officio* or at the instance of parties; our distinction between "criminal" and "civil" cases. By itself this is too limited a description of the thirteenth/fourteenth-century official. Likewise open to criticism is the view that at this time he was concerned basically with instance rather than *ex officio* business. Other officers, it is true, were being used extensively for correction, but the scope of their activities was not in this respect wider than that of the official, and their commissions often included a clause safeguarding his collateral powers.[4] It has been remarked[5] that specific mention of correction in commissions issued to officials stems from Pope Boniface's ruling incorporated in Sext, but it does not follow that the appearance of clauses of this kind in the early fourteenth century indicates an advance by the official into a new sphere. Officials seemingly had been exercising such powers long before, and the position was merely regularized in the light of the new legislation.

At Worcester the first recorded fourteenth-century commission was issued by Bishop Gainsburgh in 1306.[6] It empowered John de Rodberrow to exercise the office of the officiality with the special additional powers of inquiry, correction, and punishment, and of removing from benefices and administrations those clerks to be lawfully deprived, together with the right of canonical coercion.[7] No other official

---

[1] In Maitland's view (*Roman Canon Law in the Church of England*, pp. 4–5) Lyndwood, who finished his gloss on the provincial constitutions of Canterbury in 1430, was, as the archbishop's principal official, "the first man in England whose opinion we would wish to have about any question touching the ecclesiastical law that was being administered in England". See also the "Domini Gulielmi Lindwood . . . Praefatio" in the Oxford (1679) edition of the *Provinciale*.

[2] Ad ver. *officiales principales* (p. 105).

[3] The bishop's "gracious" jurisdiction was concerned with the conferment of benefits and the initiation of procedures such as visitation. *English Clergy*, p. 51; and see pp. 318–20 below.

[4] See below, pp. 131 et seq.   [5] Morris, op. cit., p. 152.

[6] *Reg. Gainsburgh*, fo. 11r., p. 29 (where it is incorrectly ascribed to the year 1307): 27 December 1306. See App. B, p. 331 below.

[7] See p. 109, nn. 5–7.

during this period was appointed with specific authority to remove clerks.

The two commissions in the register of Bishop Reynolds are similar in form,[1] and follow the Gainsburgh commission with slight modification, save for the clause about the removal of clerks, which is omitted.

There is no commission for the appointment of an official in Maidstone's register, but the earlier of the two in Register Cobham is unusual in some respects. M. John Bloyou was empowered to act in matters pertaining to the officiality in the usual way. In addition, however, there is mention of the livery to him of the seal of the officiality and a reservation of matters touching the episcopal dignity.[2] The clause permitting inquiry, correction, and punishment, is omitted in both this and the next commission.[3]

Cobham's second commission empowered M. Nicholas de Gore and M. John de Broadwas, jointly and singly, to take cognizance of and to proceed with all causes, moved or to be moved, which were known to pertain to the officiality, and to terminate them, with power of canonical coercion.[4] This was the only occasion on which joint officials are known to have been appointed. But though Nicholas de Gore is subsequently mentioned as official,[5] John de Broadwas is never given the title.

The next recorded commission was issued by Orleton in 1330. Robert de Worth, canon of Salisbury, addressed as the bishop's official,[6] was empowered to hear and determine causes and suits in the consistory courts and to inquire into, correct, and punish the excesses of the bishop's subjects, with power of canonical coercion.[7] There is no

---

[1] *Reg. Reynolds*, fo. 1r. and 3v. (pp. 2, 4): 20 October 1308 and 1 January 1309. By the first, M. John de Rodberrow was appointed; by the second, M. Benedict de Paston, professor of civil law. After the address the earlier commission begins: "In hiis omnibus et singulis que ad officialitatis officium in nostra Wygorn' diocesi pertinent"; the later one: "In omnibus et singulis que ad officialitatis officium in nostra Wygorn' diocesi de iure vel consuetudine pertinere noscuntur." Otherwise they are *mutatis mutandis* the same.

[2] "... tibi in hiis [&c.] ... pertinere noscuntur, cum cohercionis canonice potestate, ac sigilli officialitatis tradicione, que ad episcopalem pertinent dignitatem nobis reservantes, vices nostras committimus per presentes." *Reg. Cobham*, fo. 4v., p. 5: 31 January 1318.

[3] This would not in itself entitle us to assume that Cobham's officials did not exercise such powers.

[4] *Reg. Cobham*, fo. 22v., p. 27. Undated (September 1320?).

[5] And also as commissary-general.

[6] Rodberrow is similarly addressed in Gainsburgh's commission of 1306. See App. B, p. 331 below.

[7] Reg. Orleton 2, fo. 12r.: 1(?) September 1330.

9

specific mention in the body of the commission[1] of the conferring of the office of the officiality, but that this was intended is obvious from Orleton's concurrent mandate to the clergy and people of the diocese enjoining obedience to Robert de Worth "sicut officiali".[2]

This mandate is of particular interest both as an illustration of the official's theoretical position and because the formula, which is not found elsewhere in the Worcester registers, was copied from Woodlock's commission (1312) appointing Orleton as official of Winchester.[3] In the preamble the bishop likens himself to Moses, who, because of the number of those seeking judgement, and to prevent his being worn out with excessive labour, appointed others as helpers; and so the burden when distributed among many was borne lightly.[4] In this way, Orleton continues, example was left to himself—as to others exercising the cure of pastoral office, that whenever he could not be present he might share the burdens incumbent upon him with suitable men competent to represent his authority.

Montacute's commission of 1334 is once again in a different form. After a brief preamble John de Hildesle was appointed official with the power of inquiring into, correcting, and punishing the excesses of the bishop's subjects,[5] and of exercising his ordinary and spiritual juris-diction, with canonical coercion. He was enjoined to deliver justice with balanced fairness according to God's inspiration. Any earlier commissions issued in favour of M. Thomas de Wyche were revoked, though of them there is no trace in the register.[6]

The last commission entered in the registers during our period is dated 19 September 1339. It approximates closely to the commissions of Gainsburgh and Reynolds, and simply empowered John de la Lowe to act in all matters concerning the office of the officiality, with the special power of inquiry, correction, and punishment.[7]

The eight commissions which survive were by no means the only ones issued, nor indeed are they indicative of the number of those who were accorded the title of official.[8] John Bloyou, for instance, was Maidstone's official, but his commission is not to be found in that bishop's register. On 12 June 1314 he was given wide powers of inquiry, correction, and punishment, as well as of imposing suspension from

---

1 The marginal rubric is: "Commissio officialitatis".
2 Reg. Orleton 2, fo. 12v.   3 *Winch. Reg. Woodlock*, p. 584.
4 Ex. 18. 13 et seq.
5 Obviously an addition to the powers exercised *qua* official.
6 Reg. Montacute 1, fo. 4v.: 3 April 1334. See App. B, p. 332 below.
7 Reg. Bransford, fo. 3r. (23).
8 A list of officials is given in App. A.

spiritual administration and of dealing with testamentary matters.[1]
None the less, there is no mention of the officiality or of the consistory
courts.

In some instances persons were appointed to exercise the powers
ordinarily conferred on the official though they may not have enjoyed
that office and title. In 1305 M. John de Rodberrow was empowered
to act in all causes and legal business moved, or to be moved in the
consistory courts, or which concerned them in any way, and was also
granted the special power of inquiry, correction, and punishment of
the bishop's subjects, with the right of canonical coercion. But the
commission was only to remain in force until Christmas, a period of
little more than two months.[2] Another interim commission was issued
by Bransford prior to his consecration. He empowered M. William de
Abergavenny[3] to take cognizance of, and to terminate, all suits and
causes in the consistory courts of the city and diocese of Worcester, and
to exercise full episcopal jurisdiction, with powers of coercion.[4] It is
clear that William de Abergavenny was never official and that this was
merely a temporary commission pending Bransford's arrival in the
diocese and the making of a permanent appointment.

Sometimes, when the official had to be absent from the diocese, a
deputy was appointed. Two appointments of this kind were made
during the absence of John Bloyou who probably acted as official
throughout Maidstone's episcopate. In 1315 M. Richard Mahel (or
Maiel[5]) was appointed to act for Bishop Maidstone in matters pertaining to the office of the officiality during the official's absence, with
power of canonical coercion.[6] The following year M. Nicholas de
Gore was authorized, again for the period of the official's absence, to
take cognizance of, proceed with, terminate, and to pronounce definitive sentence in all causes, moved or to be moved, which were known to
appertain to the office of the officiality, as well as to inquire into,
correct, and punish the excesses of the bishop's subjects, with the usual
right of canonical coercion.[7]

[1] Reg. Maidstone, fo. 12v.

[2] *Reg. Gainsburgh*, fo. 9r., p. 25: 10 October 1305. Rodberrow was appointed
official in December 1306 (see p. 110). Lyndwood warns us (ad ver. *officiales principales*,
p. 105): "... sola commissio generalis cognoscendi in causis non sufficit ad constituen-
dum aliquem officialem principalem", and "cum etiam non omnes deputati ad
universitatem causarum sint officiales ..." We might add that not all of those deputed
to hear causes in the consistory courts were officials.

[3] For him, see p. 129, n. 4 below.

[4] Reg. Bransford, fo. 1r. (7): 16 February 1339.   [5] See pp. 41–2 above.

[6] Reg. Maidstone, fo. 36v.: 20 September 1315.

[7] Ibid., fo. 45r.: 8 June 1316.

Occasionally special commissions are to be found for the holding of consistory courts, either because the official was away, or because no-one had been appointed to exercise the office. In December 1317, prior to the appointment of his official, Bishop Cobham deputed John de Broadwas to hold the consistory courts in the Gloucester archdeaconry.[1] Orleton empowered the dean of Worcester to hold a session of the consistory court in the cathedral church[2] and to appoint days for the hearing of causes in the usual way, owing to the official's occupation with other business.[3] At about the same time John of Usk is described as the bishop's commissary in the absence of his official.[4] In the above cases it was the bishop who appointed the official's deputy, but John de Clipston, Montacute's official, himself appointed William de Bosco to act for him in all causes and legal business.[5] This is the only occasion on which an official is recorded to have delegated his powers.

SEQUESTRATORS

The office of sequestrator probably came into being during the thirteenth century:[6] in the fourteenth it is widely found. In a few dioceses there seems to have been a sequestrator for each archdeaconry,[7]

---

[1] *Reg. Cobham*, fo. 3v., p. 4 (see above, p. 54, n. 3). John Bloyou was appointed official 31 January 1318 (see p. 111 above).

[2] In medieval times the consistory was held "in maiori ecclesia Wygorn"—the cathedral nave (D. & C. MS. B. 1618 *inter alia*). Green writes that after the repairs of 1748–56 the court, which had formerly occupied the west end of the south aisle of the nave, was removed, and its sittings were subsequently held in the east end of the same aisle in the Lady Chapel (*Antiquities of Worcester* 1, pp. 140–1). At York in post-Reformation times, the archbishop's consistory was in the west aisle of the north transept (A. H. Thompson, *Cath. Churches*, plate XIV), that of Norwich in the Lady Chapel off the south ambulatory of the choir (Blomefield, *Norfolk* 4, map facing p. 6). The medieval consistory at Durham would appear to have been celebrated in the Galilee Chapel, to the west of the nave (for example, *Reg. Palat. Dunelm.* 1, p. 13). See also R. S. Ferguson, "Consistory Courts & Consistory Places", *Arch. Jnl.* LVI (1899), pp. 85–122.

[3] Reg. Orleton 2, fo. 12r.: 7 January 1330.

[4] Ibid. ff. 37v.–38r.: 18 October (1330): "...Johanni de Usk nostro in officialis nostri absencia commissario."

[5] Reg. Montacute 1, fo. 9r.: 25 May 1334. See p. 43, n. 3 above.

[6] Foster ("Rural Deans", pp. 48–53) gives some account of the office before 1300. See also C. Morris, "The Commissary of the Bishop in the Diocese of Lincoln", *J.E.H.* Vol. 10, no. 1, pp. 50–65. At Lincoln the title "commissary" or "commissary-general" began to be used instead of "sequestrator" from about 1350 (op. cit., p. 55).

[7] For example, Chichester, *Reg. Rede*, pp. 128, 237; Winchester, *Reg. Wykeham* 2, pp. 8–9, but cf. ibid. 1, p. 305 (groups of deaneries); York, *Regs. Romeyn* 1, pp. 286, 389 and *Newark*, p. 260. "General" or "principal" sequestrators, acting in the diocese as a whole, are sometimes to be found in conjunction with these local officers, for example, at York (*Reg. Romeyn* 1, p. 303).

and sometimes archdeaconries were grouped together.[1] At Worcester there was only one sequestrator for the whole diocese.

The origin of the office is undoubtedly bound up with the diocesan's claim to the fruits of vacant benefices within his jurisdiction, which is clearly enunciated in a number of fourteenth-century registers.[2] It will usually be found, however, that sequestrators were also important legal officers, often exercising probate jurisdiction,[3] and sometimes closely connected with the consistory court.[4] In certain dioceses the archdeacon received a portion—generally a third—of the profits of sequestrated benefices.[5] This was so, for example, at Bath and Wells,[6] Lincoln[7] (save for the archdeaconry of Buckingham),[8] and Salisbury,[9] but not at Worcester. The existence of the archdeacon's right can often be traced by the compensation provided at times of appropriation for his loss of emoluments.[10] In Bath and Wells diocese, although the ancient prerogative of the bishop to receive two-thirds of the sequestrations was acknowledged throughout the thirteenth and fourteenth centuries, the dean and chapter regularly enjoyed them, not without

[1] At Lincoln there were sometimes sequestrators for individual archdeaconries (for example, *Rot. & Reg. Sutton* 3, pp. 3, 66, *et passim*), at other times for more than one (for example, *Eynsham Cart.* 2, p. 181; Morris, op. cit., p. 54, n. 1). During Sutton's episcopate sub-sequestrators of Holland and Peterborough are also recorded (op. cit., pp. 11 (cf. 101), 119) and the bishop may have had one in every deanery (Morris, p. 53).

[2] For example, Durham, *Reg. Palat. Dunelm.* 3, p. 306; Lincoln, *Rot. & Reg. Sutton* 3, pp. 32, 73, 75; Winchester, *Reg. Sandale*, pp. 123–4. For Worcester, see p. 116 below. Ottobon specifically inhibited bishops from receiving such fruits (Athon, p. 110): "Nisi forte iidem praelati jus huiusmodi sibi ex speciali privilegio vel ex consuetudine ab antiquo valeant vendicare." Athon glosses ad ver. *vel ex consuetudine*: "Cui consuetudini innituntur plures praelati in regno Angliae."

[3] For example, (Lincoln) Morris, op. cit., pp. 56 et seq.; *Winch. Reg. Wykeham* 2. pp. 8–9; *York Reg. Newark*, p. 260.

[4] Kellawe appointed his sequestrator as receiver of the consistory (*Reg. Palat. Dunelm.* 1, p. 254), while at Bath and Wells and Salisbury the office is to be found combined with that of the registrar or clerk of the consistory (*Regs. Shrewsb.*, pp. 323–4; *S. de Gandavo*, p. 794).

[5] Broadly speaking, episcopal sequestrations were of three kinds: those of benefices on account of vacancy, of benefices for punitive reasons, and those of the goods of intestates. It was the proceeds of the first category which were ordinarily shared with the archdeacons, although it was agreed in 1254 between the archdeacon of Surrey and the bishop-elect of Winchester that both profits of vacant churches and the goods of intestates were to be divided equally between them. *Winch. Reg. Pontissara*, pp. 2–3.

[6] See for instance, the acquittance by the dean of Wells to the archdeacon of Bath dated 17 December 1321. *H.M.C.R.* X, App. pt. 1, p. 194.

[7] For example, *Rot. & Reg. Sutton* 3, p. 73.

[8] Churchill 2, pp. 45–6.

[9] *Reg. S. Osmundi (R.S.)* 2, p. 20.

[10] For example, Bath and Wells, *H.M.C.R.* X, App. pt. 1, pp. 164–5, 185, 521; Lincoln, *Rot. & Reg. Sutton* 2, p. 90 and *Eynsham Cart.* 2, p. lxxvii.

occasional dispute—by virtue of long-standing episcopal concession.[1]

At Worcester the diocesan sequestrator or, as he was frequently termed, the sequestrator-general, was an administrative officer who in normal times was second only to the official in importance. He exercised his office by virtue of the bishop's written commission of appointment, of which a number of examples are to be found in the registers with which we are particularly concerned.

The earliest of these recorded commissions was issued by Gainsburgh in 1305. He appointed M. R[obert] de Sutton his sequestrator-general, committing to him the powers necessary for the exercise of the office and everything belonging to it throughout the diocese and in every part of it,[2] with the right of canonical coercion.[3]

There are two commissions in Reynolds' register, both for the appointment of M. John de Broadwas. By the first he was made sequestrator-general, with the power to exercise that office and to correct and punish the excesses of the bishop's subjects.[4] The second has a preamble in which the bishop sets out his claim to all fruits and obventions of vacant churches by the right and custom of the church of Worcester, with the assertion that such had likewise belonged to his predecessors. He therefore gave special authority to John de Broadwas to collect and receive them throughout the diocese and to exercise the office (of sequestrator) with power of canonical coercion.[5]

The form of Bishop Maidstone's commission for the joint appointment of John de Broadwas and Stephen de Northeye is the same as that of the earlier of Reynolds' commissions.[6] In Cobham's register, however, there is no record of the appointment of a sequestrator, though John de Broadwas was acting in that capacity at the beginning of the episcopate.[7]

In 1328 Bishop Orleton deputed Nicholas de Kaerwent to act as his sequestrator in the city and diocese of Worcester. There is no mention

---

[1] H.M.C.R. X, App. pt. 1, pp. 5, 67, 191, 193–5, 248–50, 308, 530.

[2] In practice his authority did not run in the episcopal manors or in other areas of exempt jurisdiction.

[3] Reg. Gainsburgh, fo. 9r.: 8 October 1305. See App. B, p. 335 below. Sutton had been acting as sequestrator as early as 1303 (ibid., fo. 23r.). The sequestrator for the last twenty years of Giffard's episcopate was M. Richard de Stanford (appointed 1283: Reg. Giff., fo. 191v., p. 217).

[4] Reg. Reynolds, fo. 1r.: 20 October 1308.

[5] Ibid., fo. 12v.: 18 August 1309. See App. B, p. 335 below.

[6] Reg. Maidstone, fo. 36v.: 21 September 1315. See App. B, p. 336 below.

[7] For example, in 1317 and 1319 (Reg. Cobham, ff. 4r., 42v.; pp. 4, 44). There is no mention of any other sequestrator.

of any power of correction and punishment, such as we have found in Reynolds' second commission and that of Maidstone.[1]

Two commissions bearing the same date, 7 December 1335, were issued to M. Henry de Neubold by Bishop Montacute. By the first he was appointed commissary-general and sequestrator.[2] The second is in the same form as Reynolds' later commission. By the terms of the former, Neubold was empowered to exercise the office (of commissary-general and sequestrator) and to correct and punish the excesses of the bishop's subjects; to receive probate of, to register, and to declare valid the wills of those dying in the diocese or, if they died elsewhere, to secure those of their goods which lay within it, to commit the administration of such goods (to executors), to audit the accounts of their administration, and to grant letters of acquittance; to appoint administrators or guardians of vacant churches, to dismiss them as often as necessary, and to put others in their place; and to do all other things necessary for the above, with the power of canonical coercion and of the imposition of sequestration.

Bishop Bransford issued two commissions in the same form to M. Henry de Neubold, one while bishop elect and confirmed, the other after his consecration.[3] Neubold was empowered to seek out and receive proofs of wills of those dying in the city and diocese, to declare their validity and to register them, to commit to executors the administration of the goods of the deceased, whether they left a will or died intestate, and to perform every function known to belong by right or custom to the office of sequestrator in the city or diocese of Worcester with power of canonical coercion.

That the goods of intestates belonged to their disposition was often asserted by English bishops.[4] Ottobon's constitution "Cum mortis

---

1 Reg. Orleton 2, fo. 4r.: 29 February 1328. A blank has been left in the MS. for his name and another for that of his benefice, but the commission was obviously intended for Kaerwent.

2 Reg. Montacute 2, fo. 17r.; App. B, p. 356 below. At Lincoln the first commission to a sequestrator-commissary is dated 1354. There the old office of sequestrator was gradually turned into the new one of commissary or commissary-general. Morris, pp. 55 et seq. For the use of the titles "commissary" and "commissary-general" at Worcester see below, pp. 128 et seq.

3 Reg. Bransford, ff. 1r., 3v. (8, 26): 16 February and 30 March 1339. After Bransford's death Neubold must have been reappointed by his successor, Thoresby. There exists an original will proved by Neubold's commissary on 30 December 1350 Bodl. MS. Glouc. ch. 2.

4 For example, B. & W. Reg. Drokensford, p. 208; Salisb. Reg. S. de Gandavo, p. 94; Winch. Regs. Pontissara, pp. 236–7 (Consts. of Bishop Gervais) "que ad episcopalem disposicionem secundum ecclesie Anglicane consuetudinem pertinere noscuntur"; and Woodlock, p. 619.

incerta" inhibited prelates from treating such goods as their own,[1] and there is an interesting example from Durham diocese of what may have been the usual method employed for their disposal. This was in 1313 when Bishop Kellawe appointed the widow and two others to act as administrators of the goods of Robert Haunsard, knight, who had died intestate. After satisfying creditors[2] the residue of the goods was to be assigned in equal parts to the dead man, his widow,[3] and to his children, in accordance with the custom of the realm of England. The dead man's portion was to be expended in pious works for the good of his soul.[4] Although it is clear from various commissions that the bishops of Worcester exercised their right to dispose of the goods of intestates, there are no details of how this was done.

It is not easy to determine exactly what duties belonged to the sequestrator's office as such—whether at Worcester or elsewhere. From the preambles to Reynolds' 1309 commission and the corresponding one issued by Montacute in 1335, it would seem that the sequestrator's functions stemmed primarily from the diocesan's claim to the fruits of vacant benefices. In practice, however, it was not uncommon for powers of correction and punishment to be added, as in the commissions of 1308, 1315, and Montacute's longer one of 1335. Then again, in the last mentioned commission, as in that issued by Bransford, powers were specifically granted for dealing with testamentary matters. Montacute's commission was for the appointment of a sequestrator and commissary-general, so that we may well ask which of the powers enumerated were proper to the former officer, and which to the latter. It would certainly be unwise to assume that any particular sequestrator did not exercise testamentary powers merely because these were not specified in his commission of appointment. In neither of Reynolds' commissions is there any mention of such powers, yet it is obvious from the dispute with the official of the Court of Canterbury, which is discussed below, that the bishop's sequestrator was in fact exercising them by virtue of his office.[5] Giffard's sequestrator, M. Richard de Stanford, was not only himself engaged in the business of probate but

[1] Athon, pp. 121–2. In 1270 Archbishop Giffard authorized his sequestrator to pay out 100s. from the goods of intestates for household expenses. *York Reg. Giffard*, p. 115.

[2] Cf. Wykeham's mandate on this subject to the sequestrator of the archdeaconry of Surrey. *Winch. Reg. Wykeham* 2, pp. 228–9.

[3] Cf. Bishop Drokensford's mandate (1315) for the dean of Axbridge to restore the widow's third to Petronilla Cogan—a right which "our synodal constitution" had made known to the whole diocese. *B. & W. Reg. Drokensf.*, p. 98.

[4] *Reg. Palat. Dunelm.* 1, p. 369. For a general account of the law relating to intestacy, see *Pollock and Maitland* 2, pp. 356–63.

[5] *Reg. Reynolds*, ff. 46r.–v., 86r.; pp. 36–7, 67.

also had a number of assistants.[1] We know that Montacute's sequestrator-general, John de Stanford, proved and registered the will of a certain Richard Aston, although, it is true, such probate and registration were later approved by the bishop himself.[2] There is similar evidence of probate by Thoresby's sequestrator, Henry de Neubold.[3] In short, it might be suggested that testamentary jurisdiction belonged to the sequestrator *ex officio*.

Evidence from other dioceses indicates that the duties of sequestrators were not dissimilar there. We have already noticed instances of sequestrators able to grant probate or who held office in the consistory court.[4] At Lincoln the scope of the sequestrators' authority was enlarged in the first half of the fourteenth century to include powers of proceeding against incumbents responsible for dilapidations, of granting probate, and of administering corrections.[5] In Winchester diocese Bishop Wykeham empowered his sequestrator-general in the archdeaconry of Surrey, among other things, to collect the fruits of vacant benefices, to take charge of the goods of intestates, and to grant probate.[6] At Durham testamentary jurisdiction was sometimes specifically conceded to sequestrators, and at Bath and Wells the right to punish offences.[7] The only extant commission of this kind for Canterbury diocese was issued by Archbishop Reynolds in 1325. He appointed a sequestrator-general with powers of inquiry, though not of punishment.[8]

At this point it may be useful to return to the testamentary jurisdiction of the Worcester sequestrators, and to examine it against the background of an appeal made by Reynolds to the Holy See against

---

1 At Giffard's Hartlebury council of 1300 or 1301 (see above, p. 97, n. 4) there was mention of those who granted probate under his seal: "Item de numero apparitorum equitum per diocesem et illorum qui habent probaciones testamentorum sub suo sigillo nomine magistri Ricardi de Stanford." *Reg. Giff.*, fo. 441v., p. 514.

2 *Reg. Montacute* 2, fo. 23r. The will itself is on ff. 22r.–23r. The right to approve or declare the validity of a will usually lay within the sequestrator's province as the commissions show. For these terms see p. 23, n. 6 above. There is no record of Stanford's appointment.

3 Bodl. MS. Glouc. ch. 2. See above, p. 117, n. 3.

4 See pp. 115–17 above.

5 Morris, pp. 53 et seq.; above, p. 114, n. 6.

6 *Winch. Reg. Wykeham* 2, pp. 8–9 (?1367). A similar appointment was made for the Winchester archdeaconry (ibid., p. 9).

7 *Reg. Palat. Dunelm.* 1, p. 44 (1311), but cf. ibid., p. 152; *B. & W. Reg. Shrewsb.*, pp. 323–4, 494.

8 Churchill 1, p. 61, n. 1. There is a possibility that Reynolds, who must have known all about the office at Worcester, introduced it to Canterbury. If so, the experiment was short-lived.

the action of the official of the Court of Canterbury. The official, it was alleged, had presumed to take cognizance of a direct appeal from the jurisdiction of the Worcester sequestrator, thereby ignoring the intermediate jurisdiction of the diocesan.[1] In the preamble Reynolds claimed that both by right and ancient custom, which had formerly been peacefully observed, it belonged to the bishop to admit the registration and declaration of validity of the wills of those deceased persons, both laymen and clerks, who in their lifetime had held goods in the Worcester diocese, even if they had possessed similar goods in other dioceses;[2] to commit the administration of such wills to executors, and to appoint others should they prove deficient; to exact and receive executors' accounts, as well as to impose sequestration, prior to registration and declaration of validity, on the goods of the deceased, as upon churches and benefices in the diocese, together with the ecclesiastical effects pertaining to such; and that appeals and complaints of subjects of the Worcester diocese from lesser judges ("prelati") or other subjects of the bishop of Worcester should be brought to the audience of the bishop, the immediate judge, for decision, and not "omisso medio" to the Court of Canterbury or the metropolitan. The inhibition of the Court of Canterbury then follows. It is addressed to John de Broadwas who, claiming to be the bishop of Worcester's sequestrator-general, had allegedly summoned the executors of John de Kerdyf to appear before him to render account, but assigned them too brief a term. They had duly appeared and produced the original will of the deceased, but though the sequestrator had long held a copy of the will he had failed to restore the original, despite repeated requests, to the great prejudice and damage of the executors. Therefore, an appeal had been lodged on their behalf and the official meanwhile inhibited the sequestrator from proceeding with the case, citing him to appear before him. The bishop, however, since Broadwas was his immediate subject, born in the diocese, beneficed and living there,

---

[1] According to an entry in *Heref. Reg. Swinfield* (p. 32) it was determined at a meeting of bishops held at London in 1282 that the Canterbury official should not rescribe *omisso medio* on the plea of any subject of a suffragan bishop, except in the case of a testator who had *beneficia* in more than one diocese and had appointed many executors. Swinfield was obviously continuing Cantilupe's dispute on this subject with Archbishop Pecham. See Churchill 1, pp. 428–9, 472–5; Douie, pp. 197 et seq.; *Heref. Reg. Swinfield*, pp. 33 et seq.

[2] Reynolds thus rejects the metropolitan's claim to grant probate when the goods of the testator lay in more than one diocese and also ignores his alleged "ius recipiendi probaciones testamentorum personarum nobilium" (for example, Reg. Bransford 2, fo. 3r.–v.). See p. 122 below and, for a full discussion of the evolution of these claims, Churchill 1, pp. 380–423.

from whom appeal lay to his audience and not to the metropolitan or the Court of Canterbury,[1] appealed to the Holy See by reason of this *gravamen*, and published an appeal and provocation against any further action prejudicial to himself or his see of Worcester.[2] Later, Nicholas de Gore, the examiner-general of the Court of Canterbury and commissary of the official, remitted the case to the Worcester official and to John de Broadwas, and condemned the executors to pay forty shillings costs to the latter.[3] The case is of interest, not only because it gives details of the exercise of the sequestrator's office at Worcester, but also because it provides another instance of the interference of the Court of Canterbury with the rights of a diocesan bishop in an appeal from one of his officers.[4]

At Worcester, if we except the areas of exempt jurisdiction[5] and the archbishop's claims, the diocesan alone had powers of testamentary jurisdiction,[6] which he regularly delegated to the sequestrator. This ensured a more centralized system for the granting of probate than is to be found in many other dioceses where lesser ordinaries claimed a share in such jurisdiction. In Norwich diocese the rural deans could have probate of lesser wills[7] where the deceased had goods in a single deanery, the archdeacon if in several deaneries. If the goods lay in more than one archdeaconry, the bishop granted probate. In Lincoln diocese the archdeacon of Lincoln, and probably other archdeacons

---

1 In Archbishop Pecham's time a commission had ruled that as the pope's representative the archbishop could himself hear appeals from any ecclesiastical court, but that his power was not vested in his official who represented him in his capacity as metropolitan. Douie, p. 197.

2 *Reg. Reynolds*, fo. 46r.–v., pp. 36–7. The appeal is dated 29 March (1312).

3 *Reg. Reynolds*, fo. 86r., p. 67: "Remissio negocii cuiusdam agitati in Curia Cant' pro sequestratore domini" (marginal rubric). The *remissio*, addressed to the Worcester official, is dated 5 July 1313 from London.

4 For two other encroachments during Giffard's episcopate, see Douie, p. 202.

5 But see pp. 22, 23–4 above.

6 Although these did not extend to the devise of burgage tenements in Bristol, Gloucester, and possibly elsewhere. It has been shown (*Pollock and Maitland* 2, pp. 330–1) that boroughs eventually established the principle that such tenements had nothing to do with the bishop, and in the fourteenth century separate documents were sometimes drawn up for the devise of chattels and tenements. At Bristol the custom was said to be (1334): "Quod omnia testamenta burgensium ville in quibus terre, tenementa vel redditus legantur, probentur in pleno hundredo coram maiore et duobus probis hominibus cum eo assidentibus." *Little Red Book of Bristol* 1, pp. 32–3; cf. *Great Red Book* (*B.R.S.* ii), intro. pp. 66 et seq.; p. 107, n. 6 above; *Records of Gloucester*, ed. Stevenson, pp. 337, 339.

7 The bishop had probate in the case of the clergy, and wills not involving *bona notabilia* could be proved in his court if desired. The wills of those who had *bona notabilia*, or goods of over £5 in different dioceses, were regularly proved in the archbishop's prerogative court. Blomefield, *Norfolk* 4, pp. 63–4, 554–5.

too, claimed probate of the wills of those dying within his archdeaconry,[1] and some rural deans are known to have exercised similar powers.[2] Bishop Bek deputed five sequestrators—with powers of probate—in 1347, and five or six was the usual number for a century afterwards.[3]

An indication of the variations in practice is given by the endorsements on the will of Sir John Botynton, who died in 1350. Probate was granted for those of his goods in Worcester diocese by the dean of Winchcomb, commissary of the sequestrator-general, Henry de Neubold; for those in Hereford diocese by the dean of the Forest, acting as Bishop Trilleck's commissary; and for those within the archdeaconry of Wells by the commissary of the archdeacon's official.[4] The archbishop's claim to superior jurisdiction where goods lay in more than one diocese seems to have been ignored.[5]

Episcopal mandates directed to sequestrators in the ordinary course of their duties throw further light on their activities. In 1303 Gainsburgh ordered his sequestrator, M. R[obert] de Sutton, together with the dean of Stonehouse, to hold an inquiry into the reported wastage of the goods of Tetbury church by the rector.[6] In 1313 Reynolds instructed his sequestrator to ascertain the quantity and value of the goods of Doso, son of William Marquess, who had died intestate, and to discover the names of those detaining, concealing, or occupying them.[7] John de Broadwas, Maidstone's sequestrator, was ordered to sequestrate the goods of the former rector of Badminton, and to prevent his executors from laying their hands on them, until satisfaction had been made for such defects in the houses, chancel, and ornaments of the church as should be brought to light by an inquiry to be held by him with the aid of local rectors and vicars.[8] Again, when it came to Orleton's notice that the hospital of Blessed Mary at Droitwich, because it had been without a lawful head for a long time, had suffered heavily in spirituals and temporals, he directed his sequestrator, Nicholas de Kaerwent, to collect such goods as there were to be collected and to sequestrate those which had been carried off or stolen.[9]

---

[1] See *Arch. Jnl.* 72, p. 242, n. 2, for the transcription of an entry from a MS. volume (at one time in the diocesan registry at Peterborough) which gives full details of the archdeacon's powers.

[2] See p. 65, n. 6 above.   [3] Morris, p. 55; cf. p. 119 above.

[4] Bodl. MS. Glouc. ch. 2.

[5] Churchill notes (1, p. 385, n. 1) a number of instances in which the archbishop's claims were ignored, and suggests that this was through oversight or ignorance.

[6] *Reg. Gainsburgh*, fo. 23r., pp. 76–7: 14 October 1303.

[7] *Reg. Reynolds*, fo. 83r., p. 65: 10 May 1313.

[8] Reg. Maidstone, fo. 26v.: (26 May) 1315.

[9] Reg. Orleton 2, fo. 8v.: 29 July 1328.

The sequestrator received considerable sums of money on behalf of the bishop by virtue of his office. Sometimes he accounted for other receipts as well. In the presence of Reynolds' auditors John de Broad- was rendered account of all the income and expenditure connected with his office from the time of his appointment[1] until Michaelmas 5 Ed- ward II (1311), except for the money from vacant churches which he had not fully computed.[2] Orleton's sequestrator, Kaerwent, delivered twenty marks to the bishop at Henbury by the hand of John de Loute- burgh. Shortly afterwards, a further £58 from the perquisites of the jurisdiction and office of sequestrator was sent to Orleton at Wick- next-Worcester by the agency of William de Breynton.[3] Maidstone's sequestrator, Stephen de Northeye,[4] sent £53 for the winter account of the archdeaconries of Gloucester and Worcester,[5] some £28 of which came from the return of Peter's Pence.[6] A separate sum of £5 10s. was sent on Northeye's behalf by the bishop's notary, M. William de Mees. The whole amount was delivered to Maidstone at Hartlebury by his specially deputed clerks, John Poget and Thomas Maidstone, and letters of acquittance for the sequestrator were made out under the bishop's private seal.[7] In this case it is obvious that the sequestrator was acting as the bishop's general receiver.

The sequestrator, as we have seen, was empowered to take charge of benefices as they fell vacant, but sometimes he acted on the authority of an episcopal mandate *ad hoc* in conjunction with the rural dean.[8] The latter's position with regard to the sequestrator needs clarifica- tion. Statutes of the thirteenth century imply that the rural dean could

[1] In 1308. See p. 116 above.

[2] Reg. Reynolds, fo. 42v.: 30 January 1312.

[3] Reg. Orleton 2, fo. 9r.: 6 July and 1 August 1328.

[4] See p. 116 above for his appointment.

[5] The *sede vacante* account of 1302/3 was so divided. At that time the total of the winter account for the archdeaconries amounted to £32 18s. 2d., but whether this included Peter's Pence is uncertain. See pp. 71–2 above. and chap. 5 below.

[6] To be exact, £28 10s. 7½d. In the R.S.V. the annual total of Peter's Pence is given as £34 2s. 7½d., of which £10 5s. was sent to Rome and the remaining £24 7s. 7½d. [*sic*] retained by the bishop (fo. 14r., pp. 33–4). John XXII's bull of 1316 (*Heref. Reg. Orleton*, pp. 49–50) was intended to prevent the appropriation of Peter's Pence by the various collectors. On the dorse of the front cover of Reg. Orleton 2 is a copy of Gregory X's letter of 22 April 1273 (printed *York Reg. Romeyn* 2, p. 177), which details the sums due from fifteen English dioceses (excluding Durham and Carlisle). The total for Worcester is £10 5s.: i.e. the net amount paid in the fourteenth century. See p. 71 above.

[7] Reg. Maidstone, fo. 41r.: 23 December 1315.

[8] For example, the church of Aston Cantlow was entrusted by Bransford in August 1345 to his sequestrator, Neubold, and to the dean of the Christianity of Warwick. Reg. Bransf., fo. 91r. al. lxxxxii (749).

exercise control over vacant benefices *motu proprio*,[1] but from some of the commissions which have just been reviewed it is plain that the right to appoint and remove all such administrators lay with the sequestrator. On the other hand, a commission issued in 1317 to M. John de Broadwas indicates that the persons ordinarily entrusted with the collection of the revenues of vacant benefices were the rural deans.[2] The deans would seem to have largely lost the initiative in this matter by the fourteenth century, although they probably performed much the same functions as formerly.[3]

It has been shown that the *ex officio* functions of the sequestrator were many. Vacant benefices may have been his chief concern, but powers of correction and punishment were often included in his commission, and he was the officer entrusted with the exercise of the bishop's testamentary jurisdiction. The fiscal duties of his office were capable of expansion, and he may sometimes have acted as episcopal receiver. All this, however, gives only a partial indication of his activities within the diocese. Mandates for induction to benefices in episcopal collation were frequently sent to him, as to other diocesan officers. Moreover, when a bishop granted the *custodia sequestri* of a benefice, the mandate *de sequestro liberando* was regularly directed to the sequestrator because he was in possession of the fruits and profits.[4] He was frequently appointed to carry out all kinds of judicial and administrative business, to exercise the office of visitation on the bishop's behalf and to correct those faults which were brought to light, to examine the reasons for the proposed appropriations of churches, and to perform various other tasks as occasion demanded. In short, like the official, he played an extremely active part in almost every sphere of diocesan business.

CHANCELLORS

Little can be gleaned from episcopal registers about the functions of bishops' chancellors at this time. The essential fact about the chancellor, as we might expect, was that he had the custody of the bishop's seals. At

---

1 See pp. 65–6 above.

2 See above, p. 71, n. 3 and cf. p. 65, n. 6.

3 Some evidence from other dioceses (before 1300) has been sifted by Foster ("Rural Deans", pp. 43 et seq.). According to a York statute of ?1259 (B.M. MS. Lansdowne 397, fo. 250v.) whoever implemented the mandate for sequestration, the archdeacon, his official, or the rural dean, was to receive one-third of the profits, and Foster concludes that these officers probably performed identical duties in some dioceses (op. cit., pp. 53–4, 61). Archbishop Wickwane considered that the rural dean could be sequestrator in his deanery "sine quavis injusta servicia" (*York Reg. Wickw.*, p. 215). On the whole, it can be said that a more regular system emerges from the Worcester records.

4 See chap. 4 below under "Custodia sequestri".

Worcester these seem to have been three in number, the great seal, the small or private seal, and the seal *ad causas*.[1] It would appear that the chancellor was appointed simply by the transference to him of the seals proper to his office. In Gainsburgh's register a memorandum records that on 30 September 1303, at Kempsey, at the hour of Vespers, M. Walter de Wotton, archdeacon of Huntingdon, received the seals of the bishop as his chancellor.[2] It is very probable that an inchoate entry in Montacute's register would have recorded a similar transfer of that bishop's seals to Robert de Worth, who later appears as chancellor.[3]

At the time of the 1338/9 vacancy Prior Wolstan, the official *sede vacante*, in his reply to a mandate of the vicar-general of the archbishop of Canterbury for the sequestration of the late Bishop Hemenhale's goods, tells of his difficulty in discovering the whereabouts of the latter's seals. He had been unable to get precise information as to their custody, though it was said by some who had served the late bishop that the two seals[4] which his chancellor had been accustomed to carry about were still in the possession of M. Andrew Offord, Hemenhale's chancellor. He had not cited him because Offord had lived outside the diocese since the bishop's death and so could not be apprehended.[5]

For the Worcester diocese nothing can be said of the chancellor's connection with the episcopal chancery, for the registers are completely silent on the subject. The very word "cancellaria" is seldom to be found, though on one occasion Maidstone wrote of letters of institution which had emanated from his chancery.[6] Much the same is true of

---

1 See pp. 10–11 above.

2 *Reg. Gainsb.*, fo. 22v., p. 75: 30 September 1303. "DE CANCELLAR' EPISCOPI. Memorandum quod ii Kalen' Octobris anno domini MᵒCCCᵒ tercio apud Kemes' hora diei vesperarum recepit magister Walterus de Wotton archidiaconus Hunt' sigilla domini Wyg' episcopi tanquam cancellarius eiusdem." Cf. Drokensford's handing of his seals to John Martel at the time of the latter's admission as chancellor (22 August 1311). *B. & W. Reg. Drokensf.*, p. 42.

3 Reg. Montacute 1, foot of fo. 9r. On Sunday the feast of St Boniface (5 June) 1334 "magister Robertus de Worthe venit ad dominum Wygorn' apud Crokham et".

4 Doubtless one of them was the great seal, the other may have been the judicial seal *ad causas*. At Canterbury Reynolds' chancellor, John de Bruton, carried about the archbishop's great and small seals. The private round seal remained in Reynolds' own custody (Churchill 1, p. 17, n. 2). At Durham the seals of each bishop were broken on the day of his burial and offered at St Cuthbert's shrine (*Archaeologia* 72, pp. 3–4).

5 *R.S.V.*, fo. 147v., p. 259. "... et inquiri fecimus penes quem vel quos prefati episcopi sigilla obitus sui tempore residebant seu resident, super hoc tamen nequivimus nec adhuc poterimus veraciter certificari, dicitur tamen ab aliquibus dicti episcopi famularibus dum vixit duo sigilla que suus cancellarius deferre solebat penes magistrum Andream de Offord ipsius cancellarium, qui extra diocesim Wygorn' a tempore obitus predicti episcopi semper conversatus est, resident in presenti, et ideo ipsum non citavimus quem apprehendere non potuimus quovismodo."

6 Reg. Maidstone, fo. 2v.

other dioceses. Bishop Drokensford is recorded to have granted a salary of ten marks to one of his clerks while he served "in officio nostrae cancellariae",[1] and there are occasional references to letters emanating from diocesan chanceries,[2] but little more.[3]

It should not be assumed that the chancellor was necessarily an eminent lawyer detached from all diocesan business, though this may have been so in some cases. Gainsburgh's chancellor, M. Walter de Wotton, also acted as vicar-general and was prominent in the bishop's service until his death in 1306.[4] M. John Renham, who is mentioned as Cobham's chancellor in 1326 was one of the most active of that bishop's clerks.[5] M. Robert de Worth likewise took part in Montacute's administration,[6] while M. Andrew Offord had been one of Hemenhale's vicars-general.[7] About Bransford's chancellor, John de Severleye, enough has already been written. Though first mentioned as chancellor in 1342 Severleye was seldom in the diocese until 1349, when he played a leading part in affairs until the bishop's death on 6 August.[8]

In some other dioceses, too, the chancellorship was held by men active in the administration. At Bath and Wells, Bishop Drokensford's chancellor, John Martel, was often engaged in episcopal business.[9] M. John de Esse, chancellor of Walter Bronescombe, bishop of Exeter, combined the office with that of official principal.[10] But on the whole the trend was possibly towards absentee chancellors who did not participate in the day-to-day work of diocesan administration.[11]

We have seen that the consistory court was the diocesan official's judicial sphere, and it is sometimes suggested that the audience court was likewise that of the chancellor.[12] From time to time individual cases

---

1 *B. & W. Reg. Drokensf.*, p. 42.

2 For example, *Salisb. Reg. S. de Gandavo*, pp. 41, 59. At York some letters of institution were duplicated "ad preceptum cancellarii" (*Reg. Romeyn* i, p. 311).

3 Cf. Cheney, *Bishops' Chanceries*, pp. 38 et seq.

4 See pp. 101–2 above. There was some occupational risk in episcopal service. Wotton was killed by the rector of Colesborne in a fracas, or so it was said, for the latter successfully proceeded to purgation. *Reg. Gainsburgh*, ff. 9r., 10v., 40v.; pp. 25, 28, 162.

5 *Reg. Cobham*, fo. 110r., p. 196. See also the index to the printed edition sub nom.

6 He had been official and vicar-general during Orleton's episcopate. See pp. 93, 111 above.

7 See p. 104 above.   8 See pp. 36–7 above.

9 See for instance, *B. & W. Reg. Drokensf.*, pp. 19, 42, 51, 115, 142 etc. By 1331 he was acting as official of the bishop's successor, Ralph of Shrewsbury, and in 1332 was vicar-general (*Reg. Shrewsb.*, pp. 88, 93, 96, 116–17, 122 etc.).

10 *Exeter Reg. Bronescombe*, pp. 12, 15.

11 See the instances advanced by Cheney, *Bishops' Chanceries*, pp. 41 et seq.

12 Professor Hamilton Thompson (*English Clergy*, p. 54) wrote of "the court held *coram episcopo* by his household chancellor and clerks".

heard in the audience court[1] by the bishop, his commissary, or auditor, are to be found in the registers.[2] But the only considerable record of proceedings is entered in the second volume of Bransford's register.[3]

The rubric which prefaces this register of causes suggests that business was usually conducted by the bishop in person or by his commissaries,[4] though in the event John de Severleye acted exclusively. Whatever he may ordinarily have done, Bransford was at that time too ill to cope with judicial business. Severleye, however, presided over the court not *qua* chancellor but as the bishop's commissary.[5] Before the record of proceedings is the commission by virtue of which he acted: a "Commissio ad causas et negocia" dated 4 October 1342,[6] which had already been written out on an earlier folio of the register.[7] It empowered him to inquire into, correct, and punish the crimes and excesses of the bishop's subjects, to take cognizance of causes belonging to his jurisdiction, both matrimonial and others, whether moved or to be moved, and to discuss and terminate such causes, with the power of coercion.[8]

It must be admitted that it is impossible to be precise about the functions of the Worcester chancellors. For long periods we do not even know their names and can only presume that appointments were made. When they took part in diocesan affairs it was not, so it would seem, primarily by reason of their chancellorship. Those, like Severleye,

[1] Such judicial proceedings are regularly indicated by a marginal *Acta*.

[2] For example, *Reg. Reynolds*, ff. 54r.–56v., pp. 46–50. Proceedings were brought by Reynolds against Robert Allot of Wych, rector of Alvechurch and Tytherington, on a number of counts, including incontinency, non-residence, and the abuse of his exempt jurisdiction at Alvechurch. They were conducted by Benedict de Paston, the official, and by William de Birston, archdeacon of Gloucester, the bishop's auditor and commissary-general.

[3] Ff. 8r.–9r.

[4] Reg. Bransford 2, fo. 8r. "Registrum causarum et negociorum in audiencia curia venerabilis patris domini Wolstani dei gracia Wygorn' episcopi tam coram ipso domino episcopo quam commissariis suis motorum a terciodecimo die mensis Junii anno domini millesimo CCC^{mo}XLIX^{no} [&c.]." The cases begin on 18 June and continue until 31 July.

[5] In the rubrics preceding each set of *Acta* he is termed "commissary" but, on one occasion, he describes himself as the bishop's "commissary-general". Reg. Bransford 2, fo. 8r. (1366).

[6] By another later commission (10 December 1342) Bransford empowered him to hear and terminate causes "ad audienciam nostram extra consistorium nostrum". Reg. Bransford, fo. 64r. (566).

[7] Reg. Bransford 2, fo. 2r. (1330). The marginal rubric is: "Commissio generalis in omnibus causis et negociis."

[8] Commissions to chancellors for the hearing of causes are seldom recorded, but Bishop Wykeham appointed his chancellors John de Sheppeye, doctor of laws, and William Loryng, canon of Salisbury, to exercise judicial powers. *Winch. Reg. Wykeham* 2, pp. 24, 211–12: 1368 and 1374.

who were away from the diocese for long periods, could seldom have had the seals in their possession,[1] while even in the audience court the chancellor's status was the same as that of other commissaries appointed to hear causes. In comparison with the official and sequestrator the chancellor played a minor rôle in diocesan business, so far as can be determined from the available evidence.

COMMISSARIES-GENERAL, COMMISSARIES, AUDITORS, ADJUTORS

The term "commissary" is often used in the registers to indicate a person deputed by the bishop, or even by his vicar-general, official, or some other officer, to carry out a particular task. In such cases the person so deputed is commonly termed a commissary *ad hoc, specialis*, or *specialiter deputatus*. If the work was of a continuous nature then the commissary might be *generaliter deputatus*. But we are concerned with the title "commissary" or "commissary-general" in a more specific sense, as applied to a clerk deputed by the bishop to exercise judicial functions.

It has been shown that vicars-general, officials, and sequestrators were empowered to do everything which appertained to their respective offices—"ad faciendum omnia que ad officium . . . pertinere dinoscuntur", or some similar phrase. Though this is common form, there can be no doubt that the powers proper to the various offices were well established by the fourteenth century and were understood even when not exemplified in the appropriate commissions. Nowhere in the registers, however, is there any mention at this time of the "office" of commissary-general.[2]

It would not be correct to assume that the commissary-general was merely a clerk deputed to hear causes. By no means all those so deputed are given such a title. There are only two instances of the appointment of a commissary-general as such. In 1312 Reynolds appointed William de Birston "auditorem seu commissarium nostrum . . . generalem"[3] and, in 1335, Montacute made Henry de Neubold "commissarium nostrum generalem . . . et sequestratorem".[4]

It is noteworthy that there is occasional mention of a commissary-general at the very beginning of an episcopate, shortly after the

[1] Perhaps there were temporary "keepers". M. Jocelyn of Kirmington, who was in possession of Bishop Oliver Sutton's seals at Lincoln, frequently witnessed official documents, but is not given the title of chancellor. *Rot. & Reg. Sutton* 3, p. xxvi.

[2] Though M. Henry de Neubold was appointed commissary-general and sequestrator and entrusted with the exercise of "this" office. See pp. 117, 118 above.

[3] Reg. Reynolds, fo. 56r.   [4] See p. 117 above.

assumption of jurisdiction on the bishop's behalf. John de Rodberrow appears as Gainsburgh's commissary-general in 1304,[1] and we know that in the previous year he had been commissioned, jointly with Robert de Sutton, to take cognizance of causes, to receive the canonical obedience of the bishop's subjects, and to correct their excesses.[2] Similarly, though Orleton's register does not begin until February 1328, it is in that month that William de Fowehope is first mentioned as his commissary-general.[3] In 1339, Bransford, while still only bishop elect and confirmed, deputed M. William de Abergavenny[4] to hear and determine suits in the consistory courts and to exercise all episcopal jurisdiction in the city and diocese either in person or by proxy.[5] He was not entitled commissary-general, so far as we know, but his position would seem to have been analogous to that of John de Rodberrow and William de Fowehope.

Commissions of this kind were sometimes issued in other dioceses. At Durham, in 1311, Bishop Kellawe appointed William de Gyseburn, a monk of the cathedral priory, his commissary-general. He was granted judicial powers, as well as those of inquiry and correction, of receiving canonical obedience, instituting to benefices, exercising testamentary jurisdiction, and of imposing or removing sequestrations. This was clearly a temporary measure pending the bishop's arrival in his diocese.[6]

Professor Hamilton Thompson concluded from the evidence of the Hereford episcopal registers of the fifteenth century that the commissary-general in that diocese was merely the official's assessor.[7] It is apparent that this was also the case there in the preceding century. In Orleton's register, for example, Richard de Sydenhale describes himself as the bishop's commissary-general in the absence of his official, and Bishop Swinfield refers to Adam Carbonel, whom he had authorized to hear causes for the same reason, as his "commissary".[8] In the

---

[1] *Reg. Gainsburgh*, fo. 4v., p. 12.   [2] R.S.V., fo. 15v. See chap. 5 below.

[3] Reg. Orleton 2, fo. 13r. He also occurs as commissary-general in March 1328 (ibid. fo. 13r.–v.).

[4] A clerk of the cathedral priory and one of those who carried the news of Hemenhale's death (1338) to the king (*R.S.V.* fo 145r., p. 257). In May 1341 he was regent doctor in Theology and was elected chancellor of Oxford in that year and again in 1343 (*Snappe's Form.*, pp. 80, 81, 325). See Emden, *s.v.* "Burgevenny", for other details of his career; the 1339 commission is not mentioned.

[5] Reg. Bransford, fo. 1r. (7): 16 February 1339. He was also one of those ordered to receive the canonical obedience of the clergy (ibid., 1r. (8)). See p. 113 above.

[6] *Reg. Palat. Dunelm.* 1, pp. 10–11. For his activities by virtue of the commission, see ibid., pp. 11–13.

[7] *English Clergy*, p. 52, n. 1.

[8] *Heref. Regs. Orleton*, p. 85; *Swinf.*, pp. 442, 450.

ordinary course the commissary-general at Hereford was a regular officer of the consistory court.[1] In Winchester diocese, M. Michael de Hellestone, Pontissara's commissary-general while his official was away (1299), was empowered to deal with cases in or outside the consistory.[2] At Lincoln, on the other hand, the office of commissary or commissary-general developed from that of sequestrator. The commissaries acted in individual archdeaconries (or groups of archdeaconries) and, unlike the diocesan official, could not hear instance cases.[3]

At Worcester the title "commissary", rarely if ever that of "commissary-general",[4] was regularly given to a clerk exercising the official's powers for a time.[5] But the commissions *in omnibus causis et negociis* to be found in the Worcester registers at this period make no mention of the consistory court. On the contrary, they make provision for the hearing of causes *coram episcopo*, that is, in the court of audience. The marginal rubric is usually "Commissio pro . . ."—the names of those appointed being added. At other times it is simply "Commissio generalis". We do not know how many of those who exercised such commissions were called commissary-general.

It is probable that the commissary-general who is to be found at the beginning of an episcopate was empowered to act in the consistory courts, as in the case of William de Abergavenny. Certainly it must have been the new bishop's immediate concern to depute a clerk for the holding of such courts, and the appointment of an official was seldom made until much later. At other times the commissary-general's sphere of action was the audience court. It was over a session of this court held at the episcopal manor of Bredon that William de Birston, auditor or commissary-general, presided in 1312. The commission which authorized him to act is at the foot of the folio recording the proceedings.[6] Similarly, John de Severleye, Bransford's commissary-general, heard cases in the audience court which was held variously in

---

1 See above, p. 109, n. 2. This was also the case in Durham diocese, although there, what appears to be the same officer is termed commissary-general of the bishop's official. For example, *Reg. Palat. Dunelm.* 1, pp. 120, 185, 336; cf. ibid. 3, p. 578; and see p. 109 above.

2 *Winch. Reg. Pontissara*, p. 88. William de Wamberge was commissary of the Winchester official during Sandale's episcopate. *Winch. Reg. Sand.*, pref. p. lxii and index sub nom.

3 Morris, pp. 54 et seq.; cf. pp. 114, n. 6, 119 above.

4 In 1331 M. William de Bosco occurs as Orleton's commissary-general in the vacant archdeaconry of Gloucester. But he was exercising the archdeacon's and not the official's powers. See p. 40 above.

5 See pp. 113–14 above.

6 Reg. Reynolds, fo. 56r. It is marked with a marginal "A" to indicate that it should precede the *acta* which are similarly indicated by a marginal "B".

the church, churchyard, and castle of Hartlebury during the months of June and July 1349.[1] The official might also act in the court with the bishop's commission. Benedict de Paston, Reynolds' official, was appointed special auditor to continue the case against Robert de Wych, the rector of Alvechurch.[2]

Three commissions *in omnibus causis et negociis* are to be found in Gainsburgh's register: the first for M. Walter de Wotton and M. Benedict de Feriby; the second for M. Benedict de Feriby and M. Thomas de Stratton; and the third for M. John de Rodberrow, M. Benedict de Feriby, and M. Thomas de Stratton.[3] All these men were important members of the bishop's *familia*.[4] The wording of the first two of these commissions differs slightly but the powers conferred are identical. Those named were to act for the bishop in all causes and legal business, moved or to be moved *coram episcopo* ("coram nobis"), whether *ex officio* or at the instance of parties, and to inquire into, correct, and punish the excesses of his subjects, with power of canonical coercion. The third commission in addition conferred the special power of removing the bishop's subjects from their benefices, and was granted until revoked.

Bishop Reynolds appointed William de Birston, archdeacon of Gloucester, his auditor or commissary-general, with cognizance of all causes, and powers of inquiry, correction, and punishment.[5] There is an additional clause "nolentes" whereby the bishop stated that he did not wish by this commission to derogate from the jurisdiction or cognizance of the official.[6] Exactly the same powers were conferred on M. Simon de Walpole, M. Richard de Chaddesleye, and M. Gilbert de Kyrkeby, by Maidstone's commission of 1315. The clause "nolentes"

---

1 See p. 127 above.

2 *Reg. Reynolds*, ff. 54r., 55r.; p. 47. See above, p. 127, n. 2. "... vos in premissis auditorem nostrum constituentes tenore presencium specialem" (Hartlebury, 18 April 1312).

3 Reg. Gainsburgh, ff. 4v. (*bis*), 11r. Dated respectively 20 September 1303, 16 January 1304, 16 March 1306.

4 Rodberrow was made official in 1306 (pp. 110-11 above), Wotton chancellor in 1303 and vicar-general in 1305 (pp. 101-2, 125).

5 *Reg. Reynolds*, fo. 56r., p. 49. There is also a memorandum of this commission on fo. 52v.: "COMMISSIO GENERALIS. Id[ibu]s Junii anno et loco predictis dominus episcopus deputavit et assignavit magistrum Willelmum de Byrston archidiaconum Glouc' auditorem seu commissarium suum in omnibus causis et negociis quibuscumque coram ipso in diocesi sua auctoritate ordinaria motis et movendis de iure vel consuetudine coram ipso ventilandis cum cohercionis canonice potestate" (Bredon, 13 June 1312).

6 "Nolentes per commissionem seu deputacionem huiusmodi iurisdiccioni seu nocioni officialis nostri in aliquo derogari."

is also repeated.[1] Orleton deputed William de Fowehope, who is mentioned a little before as his commissary-general, to hear and determine causes, with powers of inquiry, correction, and punishment. The words "coram nobis" are omitted and the form "Ad audiendum et fine debito terminandum causas et lites" is reminiscent of certain commissions to officials or those appointed temporarily to hear causes in the consistory courts.[2]

In 1339 Bishop Bransford appointed Hugh de Penebrugg his adjutor or special commissary to act in all causes "coram nobis", with powers of correction, inquiry and punishment—in the usual form.[3] The clause "nolentes" has the words "seu commissarii generalis" added after "officialis nostri".[4] This suggests that the commissary-general was a recognized judicial officer and that the adjutor or special commissary was merely an additional auditor in the bishop's audience court.[5] At this date, however, there is no mention in Register Bransford of a commissary-general whose assessor the adjutor might have been.

It is clear that the title "commissary-general" was occasionally used somewhat loosely. Sometimes it was a synonym for auditor of causes in the audience court, at other times it was used of clerks who were given wide judicial powers at the beginning of an episcopate, and who probably held sessions of the consistory. It is possible that some commissaries-general acted as assessors to the official, though such assessors were usually termed commissaries. The sequestrator/commissary-general was not authorized to hear instance cases, and his judicial activities in matters of probate and correction probably took place outside both consistory and audience courts. There can be no doubt that the commissary-general proper was at this time an officer whose primary function was to hear causes in the audience court, with the same additional powers of inquiry, correction, and punishment as were enjoyed by the official.

Like other episcopal officers the commissary-general had his duties considerably extended by various commissions. Thus Nicholas de Gore, Cobham's commissary-general, was empowered to admit, institute, and induct to benefices during the bishop's absence. He was later appointed coadjutor to the rector of Winterbourne, and a mandate

---

1 Reg. Maidstone, fo. 25v.: 11 April 1315.
2 Reg. Orleton 2, fo. 4r.: 29 February 1328. The marginal rubric "COMMISSIO PRO COMMISSAR' IURISDIC' SUBSTITUEND'" implies that this was a commission for the taking over of jurisdiction from the official "sede vacante".
3 Reg. Bransford, fo. 7v. (65): 1 July 1339.
4 See p. 131, n. 6.
5 Cf. Birston's commission (p. 131, n. 5).

for induction to the church of Snitterfield was directed to him.[1] In each instance he is specifically addressed as commissary-general.

LESSER OFFICERS:
REGISTRARS, SCRIBES AND NOTARIES; RECEIVERS, APPARITORS, MESSENGERS, AND OTHERS

So far we have studied the commissions and some of the activities of the most important of the episcopal officers—important, that is, not only on account of the powers they exercised by virtue of their respective offices, but also because of the large number of additional *ad hoc* commissions and mandates addressed to them. Yet, while they formed the nucleus of the bishops' administrative and judicial staff, there were other clerks who had specific and only less important offices and duties.

The office of registrar does not emerge from obscurity until the second half of the fifteenth century during Carpenter's episcopate (1444–76). In his time there were separate appointments to the office of scribe and registrar of the consistory and of the commissaryship[2] and to that of principal and general registrar in the city and diocese of Worcester.[3]

In Lincoln diocese during the last two decades of the thirteenth century John de Schalby (or Scalby) acted as Bishop Sutton's registrar, and was in regular attendance upon him together with two or more scribes.[4] Yet at Worcester the appellation "registrarius" is rarely found during the fourteenth century. It occurs once in Register Cobham, when M. John of Barnby is given the title.[5] In view of this, it is highly probable that the "scribae" of Bishops Reynolds, Orleton, Hemenhale, and Bransford performed functions identical with those of Cobham's registrar. Moreover, when a bishop seems to have had neither registrar nor scribe, the same work may have been performed

---

[1] *Reg. Cobham*, ff. 24r., 26v., 117v.; pp. 28, 31, 207. For his manifold activities see the index to the printed edition sub nom.

[2] At Exeter in the late fourteenth century there was a "registrarius et actorum scriba consistorii episcopalis". He is also termed "registrarius et receptor consistorii" and was responsible for paying the president's salary. *Exeter Reg. Brantyngham* 1, pp. 214–219; see also p. 109 above.

[3] See the lists in Price, Notitia, pp. 132–3. Churchill (1, p. 21) makes a corresponding distinction between the registrar or scribe of the archbishop and the registrar or scribe of the acts of the Court of Canterbury.

[4] *Rot. & Reg. Sutton* 3, p. xxvi; J.H. Srawley, *The Book of John de Schalby* (*Linc. Minister Pamphlets* no. 2).

[5] Fo. 110 r., p. 196.

by a clerk without specific title. But though such officers are often mentioned in the registers there are no commissions of appointment, and it is probable that these were verbal.

Quite often those who exercised the functions of registrar also enjoyed the status of notary public, as was the case with John of Barnby[1] and Henry de Playforde, Hemenhale's scribe.[2] Other notaries may have acted as registrars, or perhaps as their assistants. In 1303, on the authority of a faculty granted to him by Boniface VIII, Gainsburgh appointed John, called Caleys, to exercise the office of "tabellio".[3] Thereafter Caleys appears frequently as the bishop's notary[4] and clerk.[5] Richard de Ledbury occupied a corresponding position during Montacute's episcopate.[6] Another *tabellio*, John de Broadwas, may have served Giffard in the same way, and there is record of his formal admission to that bishop's *familia*.[7] Though comparatively few of the many notaries whose names appear in the registers were directly concerned with episcopal business, every bishop had one or more in his regular service.[8]

As we might expect, the bishop's scribe had custody of his register and those of his predecessors. On this point there is an illuminating entry on the dorse of the inside cover of Bishop Morgan's register (1419–26) which must have been removed from that of Bishop Hemenhale. It is a memorandum of certain proceedings in Hemenhale's principal chamber at Hartlebury on 22 August 1338. The bishop, in the presence of

1 *Reg. Cobham*, fo. 117v., p. 208. So too at Bath and Wells, where Bishop Ralph of Shrewsbury's scribe, Robert de Chigwell, is so described. *Reg. Shrewsb.*, p. 139 et ibid., index sub nom. When commissions of appointment appear in the Worcester registers during the latter half of the fifteenth century the registrar is invariably a notary public.

2 See p. 135 below.

3 *Reg. Gainsburgh*, fo. 5v., p. 14: 22 April 1303. The faculty is dated 24 November 1302.

4 Whatever the technical distinction between notary and *tabellio* (see R. L. Poole, *Lectures in the history of the Papal Chancery*, pp. 52 et seq.), in the fourteenth century those appointed to the latter office regularly described themselves as notaries public and were so addressed. The rubric against Caleys' admission is illustrative of this practice: "Constitucio notarii publici auctoritate domini Bonifacii pape VIII."

5 For example, *Reg. Gainsburgh*, fo. 25r., p. 83: "...Johannem dictum Caleys clericum dicti patris."

6 See p. 10, n. 4 above.   7 See p. 90, n. 1 above.

8 Cobham (in 1321?) wrote to the bishop of Winchester, to whom the pope had granted the faculty "concedendi tabellionatus officium singulis personis quas singuli diocesani regni Anglie...duxerint nominandas", on behalf of his clerk, John Thomas of Barnby (see p. 133 above): "Nos laboriosam circumspeccionem grataque obsequia dilecti clerici nostri Johannis Thome de Barneby super Don Eboracensis diocesis que nobis in nostris et ecclesie nostre negociis sollicite in futurum impendet provide attendentes, ipsum vobis ad tabellionatus officium assumendum tam nostro nomine quam ecclesie nostre Wygorniensis predicte nominamus et presentamus [&c.]." *Reg. Cobham*, fo. 68r., p. 109.

M. Andrew Offord and M. John Botoner, of M. John de Redyng and many others, produced a register sealed with the impression of a certain great seal with the circumscription "Sigillum Symonis dei gracia episcopi Wygorniensis",[1] and handed it to his scribe Henry, called "de Playforde", a clerk of Blofield in Norwich diocese and a notary public.[2] At the same time he declared that there on that very day the register had been handed to him for the first time and had come to his notice in the presence of M. Andrew aforesaid and Richard Trappe, who gave testimony to that effect.[3]

This entry must have been written by Playforde himself for, though it is only a memorandum and not a copy of a formal document, it refers to him in the first person and "Playforde" is added at the foot together with his sign

Now this is the same sign or mark[4] which occurs on folios 17r., 18r., and 18v. of Hemenhale's register in conjunction with a distinctive hand identical with that of the entry in Register Morgan.[5] In other words, it seems that Playforde, as Hemenhale's scribe, personally wrote part of the register.

The other hand in Hemenhale's register is that of Nicholas North, the bishop's notary.[6] His marks

sometimes with his surname between them appear on many folios.[7] He was responsible for the greater part of the register.[8]

1 The register and seal of Simon de Montacute (1334–7), the bishop's predecessor.

2 A marginal note in Reg. Cobham (fo. 52r., p. 72) records the collation by Henry Playforde of a copy of a papal bull with the original.

3 Reg. Morgan, dorse of inside cover. The medieval covers of the Worcester registers are in many cases bound within the early nineteenth-century bindings of boards covered with white vellum.

4 It is not the proper notarial mark which was a far larger and more elaborate affair.

5 In this hand are written the ordination lists on ff. 27r.–36r. Of course, writers of registers frequently copied signs which they found on their originals, but the marks in question are against a number of entries which were certainly not derived from notarially attested documents. Moreover they are only to be found in conjunction with one particular hand.

6 Reg. Hemenhale, fo. 6v.: "Notarium nostrum".

7 For example, ff. 6r.–v., 7r., 9v., 10r.–v., 11v., 12r.–v. (with "North"), 14r. (with "North"), 38r.–v., 43r. They also occur twice in a copy of a public instrument drawn up by him and which is in the same handwriting as the entries in the register. (D. & C. MS. B. 1637. Cf. Reg. Hemenhale, fo. 10r.).

8 If these conclusions are correct the Hemenhale register was not started until North's return from Avignon. See above, p. 105, n. 1.

The registers of other bishops may likewise have been written by their respective scribes and notaries. Robert Marny, for instance, was a notary who certainly wrote part of Bransford's register.

The bishop's receiver ("receptor denariorum") occurs not infrequently in the registers. The sacrist of the cathedral priory was often entrusted with this duty, doubtless because his appointment lay with the bishop, who found it most convenient to make use of his nominee in an administrative capacity. Thus Bishop Reynolds appointed John de St Briavels, the Worcester sacrist, receiver of all the money from the issues of his bishopric, whether from the spiritualities or the temporalities. He was to give acquittances by means of tallies, or in some other way, and to render true account of his receipts if required to do so by the bishop or his deputies.[1]

John de St Briavels was reappointed sacrist by Reynolds' successor, Maidstone,[2] who also made him receiver. He was empowered to receive from the episcopal bailiffs, reeves, and ministers all sums of money due for whatsoever reason, as well as those from the issues of the spirituality and from debtors willing to discharge their debts to the bishop; to grant acquittances and tallies in the bishop's name, and to safeguard for his use the sums received.[3] There is a memorandum in Montacute's register of a similar commission to his sacrist.[4]

However, the sacrist was not invariably chosen as the episcopal receiver. Bransford appointed one of his secular clerks, M. John le Botoner, to act for him in that capacity. The commission was not copied into the register but, in September 1342, Botoner received an acquittance for all the sums for which he had rendered account and which had been paid to him in the bishop's name "a principio mundi usque ad diem confeccionis presencium".[5] Another acquittance was granted in the following year for the sum of £100 which Botoner had sent by the hand of the bishop's servant, John de Wych.[6]

---

[1] *Reg. Reynolds*, fo. 20r., p. 14: 24 February 1309. There is a later commission on fo. 32v., p. 25, dated 27 August 1311. There are a number of acquittances for money paid by him (see index to printed edition of the register under "Brevel"). Reynolds had appointed him sacrist from London, 27 October 1308 (fo. 1r., p. 2).

[2] Reg. Maidstone, fo. 2r.: London, 29 March 1314.

[3] Reg. Maidstone, fo. 20r.: 23 December 1314. Cf. p. 146 below.

[4] Reg. Montacute 1, fo. 9r.: 25 May 1334. "COMMISSIO SACRISTE WYG'. Item, memorandum quod VIII Kalen' Junii anno domini MoCCCmoXXXIIIIto apud Crokham dominus commisit vices sua[s] sacriste ecclesie Wygorn' ad exigendum colligendum et recipiendum pecunias ballivorum et prepositorum sue diocesis et ad reddendum compotum de perceptis donec eas &c."

[5] Reg. Bransford, fo. 62v. (541): 29 September 1342.

[6] Ibid., fo. 63r. (555): 17 January 1343.

We know that the sequestrator also took part in the collection of money due to the bishop quite apart, that is, from the sums which were paid to him by reason of his office. Maidstone's sequestrator, Stephen de Northeye, rendered an account for the archdeaconries;[1] while Bransford's sequestrator, Henry de Neubold, was specially deputed to levy, collect, and receive all pensions and procurations due to the bishop throughout the diocese.[2]

Doubtless the receiver of the bishop's wardrobe ("garderobe receptor") dealt with income and expenditure of a more personal kind. Gainsburgh acknowledged his obligation to repay £94 16s. 5d. to Elias Russel, a citizen of London, for divers purchases made on his behalf from the feast of the Purification 1303 until the time of his enthronement,[3] particulars of which, under the seal of Elias, were kept in three schedules in his wardrobe.[4] John de Stanway, we learn from a later entry, was the receiver of the wardrobe. His accounts were audited in 1303 by Simon de Grenehull and Roger le Mareschall and were found to be £9 9s. 8d. in arrears. This sum was immediately paid by Stanway who thereupon received the bishop's full acquittance.[5]

The apparitor was essentially an officer of a court, whose duty lay in the serving of citations.[6] Broadly speaking apparitors were of two kinds: episcopal and archidiaconal.[7] But sometimes the same apparitors seem to have acted both for bishop and archdeacon,[8] as did the rural dean, himself an officer much concerned with the business of citation.[9] From time to time there occurs in some dioceses a more important officer, the apparitor-general,[10] who was appointed by the bishop to

1 See p. 123 above.
2 Reg. Bransford, fo. 126v. al. cxxvii (913). "... ad levandum colligendum et recipiendum quascumque pensiones et procuraciones in dicta nostra diocesi nobis quomodolibet debitas collector specialiter deputatus ..."
3 He was enthroned on 9 June.   4 Reg. Gainsburgh, fo. 16r.
5 Reg. Gainsburgh, fo. 24v.: 20 November 1303.
6 Cf. Lyndwood, p. 91 ad ver. *apparitores*: "Sic dictos quia faciunt reos apparere in conspectu judicum."
7 The archdeacon of Ely was allowed three apparitors by Archbishop Arundel's award (see p. 44, n. 7 above) and the same rule obtained in Hereford diocese. *Vetus Lib. Arch. Elien.*, p. 187; *Heref. Reg. Trilleck*, p. 187.
8 Lyndwood allows this (p. 226 ad ver. *duntaxat*): "Apparitores in singulis decanatibus constituti essent etiam apparitores episcopi, sicut alias solet dici de decanis ruralibus."
9 See p. 64 above.
10 In 1330 Ralph of Shrewsbury appointed during pleasure Richard de Derby, clerk, to be apparitor in the whole diocese. His attachment to the consistory court is shown by the fact that the official and commissary–general were ordered to admit him (*B. & W. Reg. Shrewsb.*, p. 45). At Winchester Bishop Wykeham appointed (1368) John de Molyngtone, *literatus*, to the "officium apparitoris nostri principalis"

exercise powers throughout the diocese. It is possible that he can be equated with the single mounted apparitor permitted to each bishop of the Canterbury province by Stratford's constitution "Cum Apparitorum".[1]

In Bath and Wells diocese the agreement (1338) between Ralph of Shrewsbury and the archdeacon of Wells[2] stipulated that the bishop was not to have an apparitor on foot within the archdeaconry, but was to be content with his apparitor-general, the archdeacon being allowed only one unmounted apparitor.[3] Bishop Kellawe laid down in his Durham statutes that there were to be two episcopal apparitors, one in each archdeaconry, who because of the honour and respect due to the bishop were to travel on horseback. The archdeacons were to have an apparitor in each deanery, or one for two or more deaneries grouped together.[4] At Winchester, by contrast, the statutes of Bishop Gervais (1262–8) seem to have envisaged a system in which the decanal apparitors did service for both the diocesan official and the archdeacons.[5] There was to be one unmounted apparitor in each deanery, except in the more scattered deaneries where mounted apparitors were permitted.[6]

Archbishop Wickwane (1279–85) took action against the abuses of the system which he found at York. He removed the apparitor of the Christianity of York for extortion and ordered the official to dispense with his apparitor "preparatus ad predam", giving instructions that the rural deans were to fulfil the office as they had formerly done.[7] The archbishop and his chapter then ordained that for the relief of the rural deans and parish priests[8] common serjeants ("communes servientes") were to be assigned to each archdeaconry. These were appointed by

---

Elsewhere in that bishop's register he appears as "nuncium nostrum et apparitorem generalem". Molyngtone, a married clerk, was later killed in the course of his duties (*Winch. Reg. Wykeham* 2, pp. 9–10, 186–7). At Canterbury there were apparitors or apparitors–general of the Prerogative, of the Court of Canterbury, and of the Court of Audience (Churchill 1, pp. 417–19, 456–7, 480–1).

[1] *Const. Prov.*, p. 52.
[2] See p. 44, n.7 above.
[3] *H.M.C.R.* App. pt. 1, pp. 538–9. The bishop forbade his subjects in the archdeaconry to admit any mounted apparitor other than his own apparitor-general (*B. & W. Reg. Shrewsb.*, p. 343). For his dispute with the archdeacon of Taunton whose officers, including apparitors, he was alleged to have appointed, see ibid., p. 372.
[4] *Reg. Palat. Dunelm.* 3, p. 575.
[5] They were to be appointed jointly by the bishop or his official and the archdeacon.
[6] *Winch. Reg. Pontissara*, p. 236.
[7] *York Reg. Wickwane*, pp. 211, 214–15.
[8] Stratford's constitution "Excussis" was to forbid citation except by officials (of bishops and archdeacons), deans, apparitors, or their ministers. *Const. Prov.*, p. 52.

the official and were under obligation to attend every consistory of the Court of York.[1]

The excessive increase in the number of apparitors and the abuses of their office are inveighed against in the preamble to Stratford's constitution "Cum Apparitorum". This limited the bishops of the province to a single mounted apparitor,[2] while each archdeacon was allowed to have only one on foot in each deanery.[3]

In the first half of the thirteenth century the arrangements at Worcester, so far as they can be determined from the diocesan statutes, approximated to those prescribed for Winchester diocese by Bishop Gervais. The apparitors were attached to the deaneries and regularly described as "apparitores decanorum". Bishop Cantilupe decreed that they were to be elected jointly by the diocesan official and the archdeacon:[4] almost certainly an indication that they acted in matters of citation for both parties. Bishop Blois had earlier laid down that no dean was to have an apparitor unless he was a clerk in acolyte's orders at least.[5]

By the fourteenth century it is clear that the appointment of apparitors lay with the bishop alone, and *sede vacante* the prior. Bishop Montacute even empowered his official to appoint and remove them as he thought necessary.[6] Appointments are recorded every now and then in the registers but nowhere are the powers and duties of the office exemplified. Almost invariably an apparitor was appointed for a single deanery only.[7] Cobham's grant of the office in the deaneries of (Droit)wich and Kidderminster, for the duration of his episcopate and subject to the satisfactory execution of its duties, is exceptional.[8] That the office was not without financial attraction is suggested by the *sede vacante* appointment of Hugh de Grete as apparitor of Pershore deanery. This was made, Prior Bransford explained in his mandate to the dean, at the instance of Peter de Grete "amicus noster specialissimus".[9]

---

1 *York Reg. Wickwane*, p. 215.

2 Although Lyndwood saw a loophole here: "Per hoc intellige sic, quod episcopus non habeat plures apparitores equites; per hoc tamen non prohibetur episcopo quin plures habeat pedites; maxime ubi inter ipsum & archidiaconum est dare praeventionem" (p. 225 ad ver. *duntaxat*).

3 *Const. Prov.*, p. 52.   4 *Concilia* 1, p. 671.

5 *Concilia* 1, p. 571 (1219); ibid., pp. 625–6 (1229).

6 See p. 66 above.

7 Cf. p. 64 above.

8 *Reg. Cobham*, fo. 106r., p. 204: "Per totum tempus dicti patris pacifice optinend[um], dumtamen sicut retroactis temporibus fecerit laudabiliter se habeat in futurum."

9 *R.S.V.*, fo. cxlv r., p. 257. The Grete family had an estate in Pirton near Pershore. The name Peter de Grete appears both among the knights of the shire and the members for Worcester city during the early years of Edward III. *V.C.H. Worcs.* IV, p. 182; Nash 1, pp. xxvi, xxix.

There is no trace at Worcester during this time of an office of apparitor-general. As so many other commissions of varying types were entered in the registers it may be suspected that no appointment of this kind was made. The only mention of riding apparitors is in 1300/1 when the question of their number was to be raised at Giffard's Hartlebury council.[1] We are not told whether they were acting for the bishop or the archdeacon. The records are equally silent on the subject of separate archidiaconal apparitors, and this despite the fact that bishop and archdeacon had concurrent jurisdiction in lesser causes, which might well have given rise to dispute. There is no evidence that mandates for citation were sent other than to the rural dean, although in the virtual absence of court records this is not conclusive. The rural dean could execute mandates himself or in the person of his apparitor. In the event of negligence he would be summoned by the judicial officer concerned to show cause why he had not made citation.[2] The apparitor then, appears as an officer immediately subordinate to the rural dean, whose instructions he carried out.[3]

The duties of episcopal courier were in some respects not unlike those of an apparitor-general, and at Winchester John de Molyngtone combined both offices during Wykeham's episcopate.[4] Every bishop must have employed many persons to carry letters and mandates of all kinds, both to places within his diocese and to others beyond its borders. Bishop Sutton of Lincoln had two *cursores*, John of Stow and Stephen, whose activities can occasionally be traced in his register.[5] Roger de Clehonger, the *nuncius* of Richard Swinfield, bishop of Hereford, swore in 1291 to serve his lord faithfully "in officio nuncii" and produced two sureties.[6] At Worcester, Bishop Gainsburgh appointed John de Saxeby as his messenger and courier ("nuncius et cursor") for the carrying of letters to the Holy See as well as to other persons and places.[7] John de Molyns likewise appears as Montacute's *nuncius* on several occasions. He carried some £15 to London as procuration for the papal nuncios and returned with letters of acquittance which he handed to the bishop's chamberlain at Bredon.[8] He also

---

1 See above, p. 119, n. 1.

2 For an instance of this, see pp. 64–5 above.

3 This is emphasized by Prior Bransford's mandate to the dean of Pershore at the time of Grete's appointment: "Ipsum Hugonem pro apparitore dicti decanatus habeatis ... consilium et auxilium vestrum quatenus ad dictum officium pertinet cum ad vos venerit impendentes eidem.".

4 See above, p. 137, n. 10.   5 *Rot. & Reg. Sutton* 3, pp. xxvi, 42–3, 63, 153, 178–9.

6 *Heref. Reg. Swinfield*, p. 276.

7 Reg. Gainsburgh, fo. 23r.: 8 October 1303.

8 Reg. Montacute 2, fo. 19r.

carried to the Exchequer the money raised in response to writs of *levari facias*.[1]

TEMPORAL OFFICERS[2]

Though it is not intended to give any detailed analysis of the administration of the bishops' temporalities, the number of commissions concerning temporal officers to be found in the registers demands at least a cursory treatment of this subject.

It is probable that the bishops appointed persons to receive seisin of their temporalities when these had been released by the royal escheator on receipt of the usual mandate for livery. Montacute, for instance, gave to all his knights, free tenants, and others, notice of his appointment of Thomas de Brayles, clerk, and of Adam de Wiluby to receive and retain corporal possession of all manors, temporalities, rights, liberties, and appurtenances belonging to the bishopric, to admit the oaths of fidelity from his vassals and subjects, and to receive the stock "et quascumque res nobiles"[3] which belonged to him by reason of the bishopric.[4]

Most important of the temporal officers was the bishop's steward ("senescallus"), commissions for whose appointment appear regularly in the registers. Bishop Gainsburgh informed all his bailiffs, free tenants, bondmen, customary tenants, reeves, and all others whom it concerned, that he had appointed Simon de Grenehull steward and warden ("custos") of all the lands, tenements, and liberties which belonged to him by virtue of his church of Worcester, and ordered them to be intendant to him in all things pertaining to the office of steward until such power should be revoked.[5]

Sometimes two stewards were appointed. Bishop Bransford made Peter de Grete (Groete) steward of all his temporalities in the counties of Worcester and Warwick with the power of doing everything known to belong to that office. Every year during the bishop's lifetime and his own good behaviour ("dum se bene gesserit in dicto officio"), he was to take from the manor of Whitstones clothes and sustenance for himself and his horses, as well as £8 by equal portions at the terms of

---

[1] Ibid., fo. 32v.
[2] Broadly speaking the officers in the Worcester diocese correspond to those found in that of Ely at this time. See E. Miller, *The Abbey and Bishopric of Ely*, chap. 8.
[3] Error for "*mobiles*"?
[4] Reg. Montacute 1, fo. 2r.: 16 March(?) 1334.
[5] Reg. Gainsburgh, fo. 20v.: 15 September 1303.

Michaelmas and the Annunciation.[1] Shortly afterwards, William of Cheltenham was appointed in the same form as steward of the Gloucestershire temporalities. In addition to clothes and sustenance he was to receive 10 marks (£6 13s. 4d.) to be paid quarterly on the feasts of the Nativity of St John the Baptist, St Michael, the Lord's Nativity, and the Annunciation, by the reeve of the bishop's manor of Henbury in Salt Marsh.[2]

One of the steward's principal duties was the holding of manorial courts.[3] It was not uncommon for a layman of his consequence to be absent from the diocese, so there are a number of commissions for the holding of such courts by deputies. In 1303 and 1307 John de Feckenham was empowered to hold the courts of a number of manors in Worcestershire and Warwickshire and in Oswaldslow hundred.[4] Similarly, in 1328, Bishop Orleton informed his tenants that in the absence of the steward he had deputed John de Stone to hold the courts of his manors throughout the bishopric.[5]

Bailiffs might have charge of a single manor or of a group of manors. At the very beginning of his episcopate Gainsburgh appointed Geoffrey of Hanbury bailiff of his Worcestershire manors, Walter de Beruthorp of his Warwickshire manors with Blockley, Tredington, Hampton, and Stratford, and Simon Revel of the episcopal lands and manors in the county of Gloucester.[6] This could have been a temporary arrangement, for the following year Ralph de Geveldale was granted custody of Stratford and Hampton manors with power to hold their courts and that of Gilput hundred[7] during the steward's absence.[8] Shortly afterwards he received custody "sub tenore predicto" of the manors of Tredington and Blockley.[9] Unusual—in fact unique during our period

1 Reg. Bransford, fo. 4v. (33): 6 April 1339.

2 Ibid., fo. 8r. (67): 29 April 1339.

3 Cf. Miller (op. cit., pp. 260–1) who comments that it is "as a holder of courts that the seneschal figures most prominently in the [Ely] records".

4 Reg. Gainsburgh, ff. 11r., 22v., pp. 30, 76. For the later of these commissions (though the first recorded in the register) the word "Senescall" has been added in a contemporary hand to the marginal rubric "Commissio J. de Feckenham", but it was obviously only a temporary commission.

5 Reg. Orleton 2, fo. 6r.: 14 April 1328. He was bailiff of Oswaldslow, see p. 145 below.

6 Reg. Gainsburgh, fo. 13r., p. 32: 27 March 1303.

7 According to Dugdale a court of this name was held every three weeks in the hundred of Pathlow. Warwickshire, 1765 ed., p. 448.

8 Reg. Gainsburgh, fo. 2r., p. 4. He is not, however, termed "bailiff". Bransford in 1339 appointed Adam de Styventon bailiff of the manors of Old Stratford, Hampton on Avon, and the town of Stratford, with the power to hold "parvas curias nostras simul cum hundred' de Path' et Gilpuc in comitatu predicto [i.e. Warwick]." Reg. Bransford, fo. 4r. (31).

9 Reg. Gainsburgh, fo. 2r., p. 4.

—was Orleton's appointment of Osbert Spelly[1] to supervise the five manors of Wick, Whitstones, Hartlebury, Alvechurch, and Hanbury—all in Worcestershire.[2]

The bishop also held certain lands in London and its neighbourhood. Bishop Mauger (1200–12) had purchased a number of houses in the Strand for the sum of 50 marks of silver from John de Lucy whose father, Godfrey, had bought the land and had them built before he became bishop of Winchester.[3] Hillingdon church had been conceded to the Worcester bishops in 1248 as compensation for the loss of jurisdiction in the Vale of Evesham.[4] In the registers we find appointments of proctors for the church and of guardians of the "manors" of Hillingdon and London. In 1303, for example, Bishop Gainsburgh ordered all his tenants in the city of London to be intendant to William de Morton, his proctor for Hillingdon church,[5] whom he had appointed during pleasure as custodian of his manor of London, to answer for its issues.[6] A letter of the same date was sent to Adam le Taverner with instructions to deliver up the guardianship of the manor or house ("manerium seu hospicium").[7] In 1340 Bishop Bransford appointed William de Netherton guardian of his house and dwellings in the parish of Blessed Mary in the Strand, and receiver of all his rents in the city and in the said suburb of London, with powers of distraint.[8] He was to receive, during good behaviour, whatever his predecessors in the office had been accustomed to receive.[9]

Chief among the episcopal bailiffs was that of the hundred of Oswaldslow. King Edgar is said to have formed Oswaldslow from three separate hundreds, and to have given it to Bishop Oswald and the Worcester monks in 964. In 1244 Bishop Cantilupe agreed with the

---

[1] Nash states (1, p. 205) that a person of this name, son of Richard Spelly, was granted land at Claines by Bishop Cobham "for having discharged the office of bailiff of Whiston with singular industry and fidelity".

[2] Reg. Orleton 2, fo. 6r.: 14 April 1328. ". . . ad superintendendum negociis nostris in maneriis predictis prout nobis et commodo nostro melius viderit expedire . . ."

[3] Diocesan Registry MS. F. 2. 210 (in box of miscellaneous charters). Godfrey Lucy was bishop of Winchester 1189–1204.

[4] See p. 17, n. 1 above.

[5] In this he had been joined with William, perpetual vicar of the place. Reg. Gainsburgh, fo. 2r.

[6] *Reg. Gainsburgh*, fo. 2r., p. 4.

[7] Ibid.

[8] The MS. reads: "Dantes eidem Willelmo plenam potestatem dicta redditus et arreragia nomine nostro petendi, et pro eisdem quociens opus fuerit distribuendi et distribuciones retinendi quousque de eisdem nobis fuerit satisfactum." No doubt "distringendi et districciones retinendi" was intended.

[9] Reg. Bransford, fo. 19v. (140): 1 September 1340.

monks that the bailiff should be presented to them, and if they produced good reasons within eight days why he should not be elected
then the bishop was to choose someone else.[1] We do not know whether
this arrangement was adhered to in the fourteenth century, but there
is evidence that the prior and chapter occasionally proffered advice
and that sometimes they confirmed the appointments.[2]

Within the hundred the bishop had the right to the return of all
writs and the sheriff could not hold courts there. These privileges had
caused disputes between Bishops Cantilupe and Giffard and the
hereditary sheriffs of Worcestershire, the Beauchamp earls of Warwick,
which were resolved by composition in 1279.[3] There is at least one
instance of governmental interference in the bishop's jurisdiction there
—a writ copied into Bransford's register, which instructed the sheriff
not to refrain from carrying out distraints at Wast Hills by reason of
its being within the bishop's liberty.[4]

In 1312 Bishop Reynolds appointed John de Feckenham to hold the
"hundreds" of Oswaldslow,[5] to have the return of royal writs, and
to do all other things incumbent on the office, in accordance with the
fine or composition between the bishop's predecessors and those of the
earl of Warwick.[6] Feckenham also enjoyed the office under Maidstone
who, in 1314, notified his knights and free tenants within the liberty
that he had appointed him bailiff and custodian with power to do
whatever was in the bishop's best interests.[7] On the same day Maidstone
wrote to the sheriff of Worcestershire, informing him of the appointment and presenting the new bailiff to him for admission in accordance
with the composition.[8] During Cobham's episcopate Richard Hawkslow
claimed the bailiffship, and appealed to the Court of Canterbury
against an unlawful excommunication which he alleged had been

---

1 Nash 1, pp. lx–lxi; *V.C.H. Worcs.* 1, pp. 246 et seq. The most recent discussion of
the origin of the Oswaldslow liberty is by Eric John, *Land Tenure in Early England*
(1960), chaps. v–viii. He appends (ibid., pp. 162–7) a text of the *Altitonantis* charter
(28 December 964).

2 *Reg. Cobham*, fo. 74r., p. 121; L.A., fo. cx r.; *C.P.R.* 1338–40, p. 90.

3 Nash, loc. cit.; Thomas, *Account*, p. 136 and *App.*, 47, pp. 30–2.

4 Reg. Bransford, fo. ccxx al. 150r.–v. (1124): 4 May 1339. "Precipimus . . . quod
non omittas propter libertatem episcopi Wyg' de Oswaldeslowe quin eam ingrediaris
et distringas tenentes quedam tenementa apud Wasthull. . . ." Writs of *non omittas*
were issued in cases of default. See *Pollock and Maitland* 1, p. 583.

5 In 1303 he was termed "hundredarius de Oswaldeslowe" (*Reg. Gainsb.*, fo. 13r.,
p. 32) and in that year and in 1307 Gainsburgh commissioned him to hold courts in
certain named manors and in Oswaldslow hundred (ibid., ff. 11r., 22v., pp. 30, 76).
See also p. 142 above.

6 *Reg. Reynolds*, fo. 43r., p. 34: 2 February 1312.

7 Reg. Maidstone, fo. 2r.: 24 February 1314.

8 Ibid.

pronounced against him by the bishop. Cobham eventually secured his removal from the office, but only at the price of an annual pension of forty shillings.[1] Hemenhale granted it for life to Thomas de Somery of Bishampton, as a reward for services rendered to himself and his predecessors.[2] Somery must have been dispossessed, for in 1343 he was reappointed by Bishop Bransford.[3] For some unknown reason two appointments were made in 1349, the first on 27 June of Richard de Bromwich, the second, three days later, of Thomas atte Mulle.[4]

Some details of the conditions under which the office was held are given in Bishop Orleton's letters patent of 1328. These set forth his grant during pleasure of the bailiffship of Oswaldslow to John de Stone,[5] to be held with all profits of justice, saving the chattels of felons and fugitives and the fines and amercements imposed in the king's court and by summons of the Exchequer, which belonged to the bishop.[6] He was to render to Orleton and his successors the sum of ten marks a year in four terminal payments.[7]

Some of the episcopal manors were farmed out, and formulas for the securing of capitular assent to this step are to be found at the end of Maidstone's register.[8] Cobham farmed out the manor of Knightwick in 1318 for nine years at a rent of £10 a year, and that of Aston in 1324 for a term of two lives at ten marks' rent.[9] Bishop Bransford granted Stratford manor to John de Peyto for life at an annual rent of £60, saving the knights' fees and the advowsons of churches and of the newly founded chantry in Stratford church. Peyto was also to hold all

---

1 *Reg. Cobham*, ff. 74r.–v., 98v.–99r., pp. 121, 180–1; L.A., fo. cxiii v; *Thomas de Cobham*, pp. 214–17.

2 *C.P.R.* 1338–40, p. 90: 14 June 1338. *Inspeximus* and confirmation of letters of the prior and chapter dated 21 March.

3 *C.C.R.* 1343–46, p. 202; Reg. Bransford, fo. 64r. (565): 1 October 1343(?). The Somerys were a prominent Worcestershire family, with a seat at Dudley Castle. *V.C.H. Worcs.*, index sub nom.; Nash 1, pp. 88, 358.

4 Reg. Bransford 2, fo. 2r. (1331, 1332). Both were later to act as executors of Bransford's will. See Thomas, *Account*, p. 179.

5 See p. 142 above for his appointment to hold the manor courts in the steward's absence.

6 "... tenendam dictam balliviam cum omnibus finibus et amerciamentis de predicta libertate qualitercumque provenientibus cum omnibus suis pertinenciis quamdiu nobis placuerit; salvis nobis catallis felonum et fugitivorum finibus et amerciamentis in curia domini regis et per summonitionem scaccarii eiusdem regis nobis quoquomodo debitis. . . ." For these aspects of seignorial jurisdiction, see *Pollock and Maitland* 1, pp. 583 et seq.

7 Reg. Orleton 2, fo. 5v.: 13 April 1328. William Broumon, whose appointment was confirmed by the prior after Maidstone's death, also paid ten marks a year for the bailiffship. L.A., fo. lxxx r., 1317.

8 See p. 98 above.

9 *Reg. Cobham*, ff. 54r., 98v. et seq., pp. 75, 180 et seq.

the bishop's hundreds and liberties in the county of Warwick with their profits, excepting the liberty of Hampton manor.[1]

Something has already been said about the receivers of the bishops' temporalities, who were empowered to issue acquittances and tallies for the sums which they had collected from the various manors.[2] The accounts were also subject to the inspection and supervision of officers specially appointed for that purpose. Gainsburgh ordered his sub-bailiffs and reeves to be intendant to John Salemon, clerk, whom he had deputed "ad supervidendum vis[um] compot[i] maneriorum nostrorum et ad faciendum eundem compotum".[3] Bishop Reynolds seems to have contemplated a more thorough overhaul of manorial finances. He ordered the bailiffs and faithful men of the bishopric to be intendant to William Merre whom he had appointed to ascertain the state of the manors and liberties of the bishopric, and of their goods and chattels, and to supervise and examine the manorial accounts.[4] In 1312 he gave instructions to Robert de Clyderhowe, his steward, for the improvement and letting of the waste and for the commutation of labour services for fixed rents.[5] The Black Death severely damaged the economy of the episcopal manors. Thoresby recovered a thousand marks for dilapidations and £100 for stock from the executors of Bishop Bransford, who died on 6 August 1349 when the plague was at its most virulent in the diocese.[6]

The bishops appointed a constable of their castle of Hartlebury, though only a few of the commissions are recorded in the registers.[7] Then there were keepers of the palace of Worcester and of the episcopal gaol attached to it.[8] The office of woodward at Stock and

1 Reg. Bransford, fo. 9r. (80) : 12 August 1339. He received pardon on fine of 5 marks for accepting this grant without royal licence. *C.P.R.* 1338–40, p. 329: 28 October 1339.

2 Above, pp. 136 et seq.

3 *Reg. Gainsburgh*, fo. 7v., p. 20: 4 May 1305.

4 *Reg. Reynolds*, fo. 8v., p. 6: 18 March 1309.

5 *Reg. Reynolds*, fo. 43r., p. 34. Robert de Clyderhowe was appointed steward with the power to audit accounts in 1311 (ibid., fo. 27r., p. 20). He was a clerk and is often mentioned in Reg. Reynolds in connection with the bishop's temporalities. See index to printed edition sub nom.

6 Reg. Thoresby, ff. 4r., 8v., 16v.; Thomas, *Account*, p. 179. The numbers of institutions to benefices in May, June, July, and the first week of August (1349) were 39, 45, 67, and 13 respectively. The corresponding figures for known deaths of incumbents are 30, 36, 52 and 8.

7 Bransford appointed Peter de Penebrugg constable, 4 April 1339: "Capiendo de nobis sicut consimiles constabularii eiusdem loci temporibus predecessorum nostrorum pro illo officio capere consueverunt". Reg. Bransf., fo. 4v. (32).

8 In 1334 John de Bolehull, Henry de Bolehull, Nicholas de Bolehull, and Thomas Molendinarius by letters patent declared that they had received the custody of the

Bradley (Worcestershire) was hereditary, as appears in 1312 when Reynolds extended the area under the wardenship of Ralph Pauncefoot to include the near-by woods at Hanbury and Goose Hill.[1] There is also a solitary commission for the appointment of a woodward at Malvern, who was to receive during Montacute's good pleasure what was customary.[2] The hereditary nature of such appointments may account for their rare occurrence in the registers.

---

palace, the prison, and of the prisoners, and acknowledged their obligation to keep the prisoners securely: "Ad que omnia et singula bene et fideliter facienda obligamus nos et omnia bona nostra, terras et tenementa . . ." Reg. Montacute 1, fo. 5v.

[1] *Reg. Reynolds*, fo. 41v., p. 33.
[2] Reg. Montacute 1, fo. 5r.: 5 April 1334 [?].

4

SOME ASPECTS OF EPISCOPAL WORK
AND ADMINISTRATION

VISITATION[1]

Seldom is it possible to give more than a fragmentary account of the visitatorial activity of a fourteenth-century bishop. Visitation rolls were of somewhat transitory importance, and this may be why they have not often survived.[2] In most episcopal registers visitation details are only perfunctorily recorded and rarely is anything like a full itinerary given. A search of the Worcester records is comparatively rewarding in this respect, and a fairly satisfactory account of episcopal visitation can be built up.

A visitation was both pastoral and judicial. The duty of inquiry, correction, and punishment loomed large,[3] but the bishop also preached, held ordinations, confirmed children, dedicated churches, consecrated altars, and reconciled burial grounds, as well as attending to a great variety of everyday business. A primary visitation was in the nature of a formal progress through the diocese.

The usual routine of visitation in the Worcester diocese is easy to establish, though seldom are all the relevant documents entered in any one register and the form of some of them varies considerably. The bishop first sent a formal intimation ("premunicio visitacionis") to the monks of the cathedral priory of his intention to conduct a visitation in their chapter house on a stated day.[4] He also wrote to the archdeacons' officials, sometimes with an outline of his proposed itinerary, ordering

---

[1] For a general introduction to the subject see Frere, *Visitation Articles and Injunctions* 1, intro. pp. 1–117. The process of monastic visitation can be studied in *Visitations of Religious Houses in the Diocese of Lincoln (1420–49)*, ed. Hamilton Thompson. See also Cheney, *Episcopal Visitation of Monasteries in the 13th century*.

[2] Cf. *Rot. & Reg. Sutton* 3, intro. pp. xxviii–xxix, xlii.

[3] Bransford in his primary visitation set out "de commissis excessibus criminibus et defectibus inquirere et errata corrigere et reformare prout decet et ad nos pertinet ex debito assumpti officii pastoralis". Reg. Bransford, fo. 10r. (89).

[4] Innocent IV had made the regulation that a bishop must first of all visit his chapter. *Sext.* 3, 20, c. 1.

them to summon the clergy and representatives of the laity[1] to undergo visitation, and suspending their archidiaconal jurisdiction for the period of such visitation.[2] Separate warnings were sent to the religious houses which the bishop planned to visit, and sometimes also to individual rural deans and to deans of exempt jurisdiction.[3]

After his visitation of the priory the bishop proceeded to visit and correct the clergy and people of the churches of the city and neighbourhood assembled in the cathedral nave. In the ordinary course the remainder of the Worcester archdeaconry was then visited, and subsequently, usually after an interval of some months, the Gloucester archdeaconry. There was considerable variation in the thoroughness of visitation, though it is difficult to make exact comparisons owing to the partial nature of the records. The process was rounded off by the appointment of commissaries to deal with the *comperta* which had been brought to light.

The Worcester records provide few details of the actual process of visitation. The bishop must have travelled on horseback, with a retinue restricted by Alexander III to thirty,[4] a number which may have been substantially exceeded by individual bishops.[5] The necessary records and impedimenta were probably carried on packhorses.[6] A pronounced feature of most if not all visitations was the inspection of documents relating to benefices and their incumbents.[7] So great was the expense

---

[1] "... de cuiuslibet parochialis ecclesie parochia quatuor et de singulis capellis tres parochianos fidedignos et meliores, non quos singuli rectores et vicarii duxerint eligendos sed quos vos ipsi eligeritis...": Reg. Bransford, fo. 10r. (89); primary visitation, 1339. "... et de qualibet parochia supradicta quatuor vel sex viros de fidedignioribus secundum parvitatem vel amplitudinem parochiarum pro vestro arbitrio assumendos" ibid., fo. 60v. (531); second visitation, 1342.

[2] The *laudum* (1401) of Archbishop Arundel laid down that the bishop of Ely was to complete his visitation in the archdeacon of Ely's jurisdiction within fourteen weeks (*Vetus Lib. Arch. Elien.*, p. 184). Blomefield states that at Norwich "all other spiritual jurisdiction ... ceased for a whole year from the date of the inhibition; if the bishop did not like of his own will to relax part of that time by formal letters of revocation of his inhibition" (*Norfolk* 4, p. 554). Bishop Ralph of Shrewsbury admonished the archdeacon of Taunton's official for acting against his visitation by holding chapters and making corrections (*B. & W. Reg. Shrewsb.*, pp. 176–7, and cf. ibid., p. 315).

[3] See above, p. 20, n. 3.

[4] *Extra* 3, 39, c. 6: "xx vel xxx".

[5] If the allegation is true Giffard on one occasion arrived at the cathedral priory with numerous relations and a hundred horses (Thomas, *App.*, p. 71). This probably refers to 1290 when the Worcester annalist states that he came with 140 horses "et per tres dies visitavit cum magna multitudine" (*Ann Wigorn.*, pp. 503–4).

[6] Cf. *Rot. & Reg. Sutton* 3, intro. p. xxvii.

[7] For example, Reg. Bransford, fo. 10r. (89): "Coram nobis mane compareant, titulos, privilegia, munimenta, dispensaciones, et litteras si quas habent super appropriacione percepcione seu detencione dictorum beneficiorum...." When the dean

and risk involved in the frequent production of its charters, that Winchcomb Abbey eventually found it worth while to secure a papal bull which was to be accounted sufficient evidence in the future.[1] It is likely that a series of articles, such as those to be found in the registers of Giffard and Cobham,[2] formed the basis of inquiry in the rural deaneries. The normal procedure was for bishops to visit a deanery in a single church.[3] The visitation might take longer than one day, but there is no Worcester evidence that it ever occupied more than two. In view of this, it is noteworthy that both Montacute and Bransford, at the time of their primary visitations, visited a number of deaneries in three or more churches.[4] This would seem to argue a greater degree of diligence.[5] It is true that more time was spent in travelling from place to place, but the whole visitation occupied a much longer period. It could even be contended that the actual time available for visitation on a single day was in many instances not greatly different under the two systems. A start was usually made in the morning[6] and we can surmise that if necessary the visitation might continue well into the afternoon. If, however, the bishop was moving on to another part of the deanery, he would not have to allow more than two hours or so to cover the few miles to his next stopping place, where it is often recorded that he had a meal and spent the night. This was either at or within easy distance of the place he intended to visit on the morrow. Naturally, the bishop did not always follow this routine, nor did he conduct visitation every day.

and his assistants visited (1297) certain parishes within the jurisdiction of St Paul's, they must have carried with them an inventory of all the books and muniments formerly in the chancels (*Camd. Soc.* N.S., vol. 55, 1895). Defects of chancels were the regular concern of archdeacons, and ordinarily the bishop concerned himself with them only at times of visitation. See p. 60 above.

[1] *Landboc. Winch.* 2, pp. 8 et seq.: "Nota quod ista bulla debet exhiberi in visitacione episcoporum et non alia." The bull was issued in 1410 by John XXIII, who was later deposed.

[2] See pp. 48–9 above.

[3] This is expressly stated to have been the custom at York: "Et ibidem in uno loco...visitabuntur clerus et populus, prout moris est, decanatus ipsius." *Reg. Wickwane,* p. 174.

[4] Details are given below.

[5] It is difficult to find a contemporary statement to support this view, though at Winchester Bishop Gervais had laid down that archdeacons were not to visit many churches in one day (*Reg. Pontissara,* p. 234). It could be argued that there was pecuniary advantage in thus prolonging visitation, for the bishop was entitled to one procuration a day, whether he visited one place or many. This could be paid in money. Four marks (£2 13s. 4d.) seems to have been the normal daily procuration. Boniface VIII's regulations on these matters are incorporated in *Sext.* 3, 20, c. 3. Cf. Benedict XII's constitution "Vas electionis" (*Extrav. Commun.* 3, 10, c. 1) which (in 1336) set upper limits to the amount of procuration.

[6] See above, p. 149, n. 7.

Sometimes he rested, occupied himself with the dedication or reconciliation of a church which lay on or near his route, or perhaps did other things of which the records tell us nothing.

Two days were sometimes allotted for the visitation of the greater monasteries. The bishop apparently made his inquiries on the first day, the depositions of the inmates forming the *detecta* from which he and his clerks deduced their findings or *comperta*.[1] For this purpose formal articles of inquiry may have been used, comparable to those drawn up for the secular clergy.[2] On the second day the bishop administered corrections. If he found it necessary to issue injunctions, which had statutory force, these were usually sent on after a short interval.[3]

Bishop Gainsburgh visited the cathedral priory for the first time on 26/27 September 1303,[4] and issued a series of injunctions.[5] The most interesting aspect of this visitation is the influence exercised by Boniface VIII's new ordinance "Debent".[6] This had its origin in the dispute between Antony Bek, bishop of Durham, and Prior Hoton and the monks of the cathedral church.[7] The Durham monks claimed that the bishop should visit them unaccompanied, making use of one or more of their number as notaries, and that no outsider should enter the chapter house. Boniface would not allow an arrangement which so detracted from the bishop's dignity and ruled that in future he was to conduct his visitation with two or three clerks, at least one of whom was to be a Benedictine monk, together with a single notary. The discussion which preceded visitation at Worcester turned on the point whether the decretal was of general or merely local application. According to

---

[1] Although these terms are found occasionally in Worcester documents, actual details of the visitation process have not been recorded.

[2] The schedule of sixty-six questions put to the Durham monks by Bishop Langley at his visitation in 1408 is printed by Hamilton Thompson, *English Clergy*, App. vii (pp. 293–9).

[3] Miss Edwards comments (*Eng. Secular Caths.*, p. 116) that although in regular houses these were commonly regarded as judicial mandates and admitted on episcopal authority alone, at the secular cathedrals it was usual for them to be formally accepted and confirmed by the dean and chapter. In 1291 Giffard, on the mediation of Robert Burnell, bishop of Bath and Wells and royal Chancellor, revoked the statutes which he had ordered the Worcester monks to obey on pain of excommunication (*Ann. Wigorn.*, p. 505).

[4] *Reg. Gainsburgh*, fo. 20r., p. 65; L.A., fo. 16r.–v.

[5] Reg. Montacute 2, fo. 42v.

[6] Anagni, 23 July 1302. *Records of Antony Bek* (Surt. Soc. CLXII, 1947), pp. 86–7. Later incorporated in *Extrav. Commun.* 1, 7, c. 1.

[7] See C. M. Fraser, *History of Antony Bek*, chaps. 7 & 8; *Records of Antony Bek*, pp. 57 et seq., 113–18, 191, App. B. Gainsburgh was one of those appointed in 1304 by Benedict XI to investigate Hoton's administration of the monastery (*Hist. of A. Bek*, p. 163).

the 1224 composition between Bishop Blois and the chapter, the bishop had to state beforehand whether he wished to discuss spiritual or temporal matters. In the former case he was to enter the chapter house alone, but in the latter he could bring his secular clerks with him.[1] The new decretal clearly affected this arrangement and the prior eventually agreed, under protest and saving the composition, to admit the bishop with two clerks and a notary, as though the ruling were of general application. Gainsburgh after a similar *protestacio* entered with M. Walter de Wotton, M. John de Rodberrow, and his notary, M. John Caleys.[2] His visitation lasted until the ninth hour of the second day (the 27th).[3] We hear no more about "Debent" at Worcester, but as late as 1325 there was uncertainty at Canterbury as to whether it was intended to form part of the Common Law of the Church.[4]

On 3 September 1303—the same day that he had given warning to the prior—Gainsburgh wrote to the official of the Worcester archdeacon, announcing his intention to visit that archdeaconry.[5] Later he appointed days for the visitation of Worcester and Powick deaneries.[6] He told the prior of Little Malvern to expect him on 5 October and in May 1304 appointed Benedict de Feriby to visit Beckford priory.[7] Little more can be discovered about this visitation, but a study of the bishop's itinerary suggests that he may have visited parts of the southern archdeaconry during 1304.[8] In the Liber Albus is Gainsburgh's warning of his intention to visit the cathedral priory again on 25 September 1306,[9] but his register has no reference to any second

[1] Thomas, *App.*, p. 76. In 1300 the priory refused to admit Giffard's official and John de Rodberrow because of the composition, so the bishop, who was ill, appointed the Worcester sacristan to carry out the visitation alone "quatenus contingit spiritualia", and with the official "quoad temporalia". *Ann. Wigorn.*, pp. 545, 546–7.

[2] See p. 134 above.

[3] There is a summary of the proceedings in J. M. Wilson's *Worc. Liber Albus* (pp. 36–7). On the advice of A. L. Poole the editor mistakenly assumed (p. 37, n. 2) that the dispute was about procuration and the new constitution on that subject incorporated in *Sext* 3, 20, c. 3.

[4] *Lit. Cant.* 1, p. 164 (cf. *ibid.*, pp. 301–2): "Et quidam dicunt quod jus speciale est et locale, et dumtaxat se extendit ad episcopum et capitulum Dunolmensem tempore visitacionis, pro quibus specialiter edita fuit. Alii dicunt quod jus commune est, et se extendit ad omnes cathedrales conventuales et collegiatas. . . ."

[5] *Reg. Gainsburgh*, fo. 20r., p. 65.

[6] Ibid., fo. 21r., p. 67. Worcester deanery in the cathedral church on 7 and 8 October, Powick in the parish church on 10 October.

[7] Ibid., fo. 21r., pp. 67–8; fo. 4r., p. 10.

[8] See R. A. Wilson's introduction to *Reg. Gainsburgh* (*W.H.S.* 1929), pp. xii–xiii.

[9] L.A., fo. 26v. The bishop also issued injunctions on this occasion. See Reg. Montacute 2, ff. 42v.–43r.

visitation. It could not have been extensive, for the bishop left the diocese at Christmas and did not return until the following Easter.[1]

Reynolds, who was but seldom in the diocese, does not appear to have carried out a visitation at all, though in 1312 he expressed a wish to do so in the near future.[2]

Maidstone seems to have visited the diocese partly in person and partly by commissaries during the years 1314 and 1315, but it is difficult to estimate the extent of his visitation or to discover the order in which it was carried out.[3] On 1 September 1314 the bishop, prevented by the pressure of state affairs from proceeding further with his inchoate visitation, empowered M. John Bloyou, his official, and Gilbert de Kirkeby, one of his clerks, to continue it on his behalf.[4] After his return to the diocese he issued a further commission, dated 20 October, to Simon de Walpole, John Bloyou, John de Broadwas, and Gilbert de Kirkeby.[5]

Maidstone's register tells us nothing about the activities of these commissaries, and it would seem that the bishop himself took little part in the work of visitation until the spring and summer of 1315 when he made a double circuit of the diocese. He began by visiting Pershore Abbey on 14 April. As he travelled south he held further

---

1 See intro. to *Reg. Gainsburgh*, p. xv.

2 Reg. Reynolds, fo. 42r.: "Nos deo propicio ad nostram diocesem nostramque cathedralem ecclesiam visitacionis causa sumus in brevi reversuri . . ." (Alvechurch, 29 January 1312). In 1309 he had secured a papal indult which enabled him to visit the diocese by deputy (see p. 78 above). There is no evidence that he took advantage of it.

3 Thomas in his *Account* (p. 161) states that Maidstone visited the Gloucester archdeaconry after 22 May 1314 and the Worcester archdeaconry in August. It would have been uncanonical not to have visited the cathedral priory first of all (see p. 148, n. 4 above), but in any case there is no evidence in the register to support Thomas' interpretation. Maidstone was certainly in the Gloucester archdeaconry in May and he held a large ordination at Cirencester on 1 June, but there is no indication that he was conducting his primary visitation at the time.

4 Reg. Maidstone, fo. 15r.: "Cum nos disponente domino visitacionis nostre officium in ecclesia nostra Wygorn' et in personis et rebus eiusdem excercuerimus ac intenderimus ipso mediante ulterius in nostra diocesi idem nostre visitacionis officium in forma iuris continuasse, nos certis arduis et legitimis de causis statum regni et domini nostri regis Anglie ac rei publice contingentibus ad ipsius domini regis mandatum multipliciter occupati, ad continuandam eandem visitacionem personaliter de quo non modicum dolemus interesse non valentes, de vestris circumspeccione et industria confisi, ad excercendum in eadem nostra diocesi nostram visitacionem huiusmodi [&c.]. . . ." If this preamble is to be taken literally, the bishop must already have visited the cathedral priory. He had given notice of his intention to visit Studley priory on Thursday 9 May 1314, on account of serious wastage of the temporalities and neglect of religion, "Licet ad ecclesiam nostram cathedralem nondum accesserimus nec ibidem aut alibi officium visitacionis hucusque excercuerimus" (ibid., fo. 6r.).

5 Ibid., fo. 18r.

visitations at the abbeys of Winchcomb (17 April), Cirencester (21st), and St Augustine's, Bristol (26th). After visiting other religious houses in Bristol "per se et suos commissarios", as well as the neighbouring collegiate church of Westbury, he returned northwards. On the way he continued his visitation of monasteries at Stanley (5 May), St Peter's Gloucester (7th) and Llanthony (8th). He was at Tewkesbury on 9 May and, after visiting the abbey, he dined at his near-by manor of Bredon and spent the night there.[1] On the 20th, by which time he had reached Hartlebury, Maidstone wrote to the abbot and convent of St Peter's, Gloucester. During his visitation, he told them, he had discovered that certain observances, which were required by their Rule and other lawful sanctions, had been neglected. Because of this, he was sending his official, John Bloyou, to do what was proper to the episcopal office and that which pastoral care demanded.[2] On the same day he empowered John de Wyke, the Worcester prior, to correct and punish the excesses of his fellow monks which had been brought to light at the recent visitation, except those of the officers appointed by the bishop himself.[3]

Maidstone consecrated the high altar of Kidderminster church on 13 June, and for the rest of that month he wandered about Warwickshire dedicating churches and consecrating altars. Throughout July, September, and October he was doing similar work, mainly in Gloucestershire, and he again went as far south as Bristol. We do not know for certain that he was conducting a formal visitation during this period.[4]

More than two years had elapsed since his consecration before Cobham began his primary visitation. He gave notice that he intended to visit the cathedral priory on 26 November 1319.[5] This was to be followed by a visitation of the deaneries of Worcester and Powick on 3 and 10 December respectively.[6] Nothing further seems to have been

---

[1] Reg. Maidstone, ff. 23v.–25r. It will be observed that Maidstone seems to have allowed only one day for each religious house.

[2] Ibid., fo. 25v.: ". . . in premissis et circa ea facturum et ordinaturum quod officio nostro convenit et pastoralis cura exigit."

[3] Ibid., fo. 26r. The bishop was entitled to appoint one of the two tumbaries who guarded the shrine and also the sacrist.

[4] Ibid., ff. 29r.–v., 37r. In view of the bad character given to him by some chroniclers (see pp. 78–9 above) the bishop showed commendable diligence.

[5] Reg. Cobham, ff. 41v.–42r.: 8 November 1319. Some undated injunctions issued by Cobham are in Reg. Montacute 2, ff. 43r.–44r. Mention of the Broadwas corrody on fo. 44r. points to a date later than that of its grant—July 1322 (L.A., fo. 106r.), but the injunctions may comprise two separate sets, viz. fo. 43r.–v., and ff. 43v.–44r. If this is so, the first could refer to the 1319 visitation and the second to one which may have been held in 1326 (see p. 155 below).

[6] *Reg. Cobham*, fo. 42r.–v., pp. 44–5.

attempted until the following year when, in February, Cobham appointed M. John de Broadwas and M. Adam de Sandwich to take cognizance of, proceed with, and correct the excesses and defects discovered in the two deaneries.[1] By 3 July the remaining deaneries of the Worcester archdeaconry, excepting Blockley, had been visited.[2] The bishop seems to have adopted the plan of visiting the monastic houses himself, leaving the secular clergy to be dealt with by his clerks, probably on account of the procuration due at times of personal visitation.[3] The deanery of Bristol was visited on 17 September,[4] but there is no mention of the other deaneries in the southern archdeaconry. Apparently something still remained to be done in this protracted visitation when on 2 January 1321 Cobham, who had been called away to the north of England,[5] appointed M. Nicholas de Gore and M. John de Broadwas to continue it.[6] A later commission empowered the same two clerks to visit the diocese, excepting monasteries and places from which the bishop was accustomed to receive procuration in money. It is dated simply 28 February, but may belong to the year 1326.[7] If so, there are no other traces of a visitation at that time.

The usual warnings of impending visitation are not to be found in Orleton's register, but that he did conduct some sort of primary visitation is evident from a number of entries. In July 1329 lengthy constitutions embodying corrections which the bishop had made at the time of his visitation of Winchcomb Abbey were drawn up in the form of a public instrument.[8] In November there is mention of his having

---

[1] Ibid., fo. 18v., p. 22 (undated). Cf. fo. 44r., p. 48.

[2] 21 April, Warwick; 23rd, Kineton (ibid., fo. 20r., p. 24); 14 May, Pershore (ibid., fo. 20r., p. 25); 30 June, Kidderminster (ibid., fo. 21v., p. 26); 3 July, (Droit)-wich (ibid.).

[3] This would seem to be confirmed by the commission of ?1326 mentioned below. The Canon Law ruling was: "Procurationes, quae ratione visitationis debentur episcopis . . . absque manifesta et necessaria causa nullatenus exigantur, nisi quando personaliter officium visitationis impendunt" (*Extra* 3, 39, c. 23: Fourth Lateran 1215, c. 33). Gregory X at the Council of Lyons II (1274, c. 24) had forbidden the exaction of pecuniary procuration, but Boniface VIII modified this by permitting those who so wished to pay in money, provided visitation was made personally (*Sext* 3, 20, cc. 2, 3). For a contemporary review of this legislation, see *Hereford Reg. Swinfield*, p. 349 (1298), and cf. the constitution "Quamvis lex naturae" attributed to Stratford (*Const. Prov.* pp. 51–2).

[4] *Reg. Cobham*, fo. 22v., p. 27.

[5] See p. 80 above.   [6] *Reg. Cobham*, fo. 63r., p. 99.

[7] Ibid., fo. 110v., p. 196. Pearce (*Thomas de Cobham*, chap. 8) gives an uncritical account of the bishop's activities as a monastic visitor.

[8] Reg. Orleton 2, ff. 31r.–32v. "Ordinaciones seu constituciones edite per venerabilem patrem dominum Adam dei gracia Wig' episcopum super correccionibus factis in visitacione monasterii Wynchecumbe in publica forma redacte."

visited the college of Westbury,[1] and in January 1330 William de
Fowehope, Nicholas de Kaerwent, and John de Usk were appointed to
proceed against the vicar of the church of St Nicholas, Bristol, as a
result of the visitation held in that town.[2]

Orleton seems to have left the Worcester archdeaconry until later.
On 15 September 1331 he dedicated the high altar of Alcester parish
church, celebrated Mass there in pontificals, and preached to the
people in the mother tongue.[3] The following day, at the instance of
Thomas de Evesham, he dedicated the church of Sedgeberrow and
three altars there. He again celebrated Mass and preached.[4] On the
23rd, the feast of St Clement, he visited half of the (Droit)wich deanery
in the church of Tardebigge.[5] Here the record of his activities peters
out. There is no trace of a second visitation. Indeed, there would
hardly have been time for one since Orleton was translated to Winchester in 1333.

By chance, or so it seems, we can follow at least part of Montacute's
primary visitation in some detail, for several relevant documents,
together with a portion of his itinerary, were copied out on a loose
quire and subsequently added to the second volume of his register.[6]
On 13 October 1335[7] the bishop made known to the prior and convent
his intention to visit them on the Monday after All Saints Day (i.e.
6 November).[8] On that day the convent expressed their willingness to
admit him, and he duly held the visitation, administering corrections
on the morrow. On the 9th he appointed John de Clipston, his official,
and Henry de Neubold, his auditor of causes, to publish the faults

[1] Reg. Orleton 2, fo. 16r.

[2] Ibid., fo. 34v. "Ad cognoscendum et procedendum in negocio correccionis super
diversis criminibus sive excessibus per nos clerum et populum ville Bristoll' nostre
diocesis canonice visitantes contra Walterum qui se gerit pro perpetuo vicario ecclesie
Sancti Nicholai eiusdem ville clamosa et frequenti insinuacione compertis. . . ."

[3] Ibid. 1, fo. 37v.

[4] Idem. This church, a simple rectangular building with no structural division between nave and chancel, has remained largely unaltered since its dedication.

[5] Ibid. 1, fo. 38r.

[6] The folios are of a smaller size than those of the register proper and contain a
valuable series of injunctions to the priory issued by Archbishop Winchelsey and by
Bishops Giffard, Gainsburgh (2 sets), and Cobham (? 2 sets). The folios were numbered
42 to 48, but now the next folio after 45 is 48.

[7] The writer of V.C.H. Worcs. 2, pp. 105–6, has completely misinterpreted the
entries in Reg. Montacute. He dates the visitation Monday before (sic) the feast of
All Saints 1333 (i.e. prior to the time of Montacute's provision to the see) and ascribes
to Montacute injunctions which are a mixture of those issued by Gainsburgh and
Cobham, and this despite the marginal rubrics.

[8] Reg. Montacute 2, fo. 42r. There is a further undated letter from the bishop
regarding his intentions for the visitation.

discovered, to make inquiries, and to proceed to correction and punishment.[1] It appears that these commissaries put a number of questions to the prior, Wolstan de Bransford, and a letter from the convent declared confidence in the validity of his replies.[2]

Meanwhile, Montacute had ordered the dean of Worcester to summon the clergy and laity of the city to undergo visitation on 9 December.[3] He wrote to the archdeacons or their officials, announcing his intention of visiting the diocese in person, and ordering them to warn both the religious and others to prepare themselves.[4] An unusual entry is that of the bishop's warning of impending visitation directed to the dean of the jurisdiction of Cleeve or, in his absence, the rector of the church.[5]

The bishop resumed his visitation early in the following year (1336). On 22 January he visited the abbey at Alcester and for the rest of the month and during the early part of February he was busily visiting the churches and religious houses of Warwickshire.[6] Between 19 and 21 February he held a visitation of the deanery of (Droit)wich, while during the months of April and May, and in the first week of June, he is recorded to have visited the clergy of the southern archdeaconry in the deaneries of Stow, Fairford, Cirencester, Hawkesbury, Bitton, and Bristol, as well as the hospital of St John at Lechlade and the religious houses of Bristol.[7] It is clear that we have only a part of the bishop's itinerary, but what there is of it shows that he visited personally and with great diligence.

There is nothing in Hemenhale's register to suggest that during his brief episcopate he made any attempt to visit the diocese in person or by deputy.[8] By contrast, much information about visitations during the last decade of the half century is to be found in Register Bransford.

Bishop Bransford began his primary visitation on 14 October 1339,

1 Ibid. and L.A., fo. 143: 6 April 1336 (not 1334 as given by Wilson in his calendar of the L.A.).

2 Ibid., fo. 48r.; L.A., fo. 143: 10 April 1336.

3 Reg. Montacute 2, fo. 45r.: 28 November 1335.

4 *Idem.* 1 December 1335. The more usual procedure was for the bishop to send warnings to the religious houses individually.

5 *Idem.* Dated 15 November 1335. Montacute visited the clergy and people of the jurisdiction on the following Monday (20th) and preached on the text "Pastor bonus animam suam ponit pro ovibus suis" (John 10. 11). Why he visited Cleeve first of all is not clear, unless it was because he seized the opportunity on account of his stay at the near-by manor of Bredon. On the subject of the visitation of such exempt juris-dictions (Cleeve was an episcopal manor) see above, p. 20, n. 3.

6 Reg. Montacute 2, fo. 45v. He preached frequently and the texts of his sermons are given in the register.

7 Ibid., fo. 48r. (which follows fo. 45).

8 Though the right to carry out visitation was included in the commission to his vicars-general. See p. 140 above.

some seven months after his consecration.[1] By 19 November he had completed a personal visitation of the archdeaconry of Worcester, including many religious houses. 25 November found him back at Hartlebury where he spent Christmas. At the beginning of February he journeyed to Sedgeberrow, just beyond Evesham, which he reached on the 6th. The next day he began his visitation of the Gloucester arch-deaconry at Beckford in Campden deanery. On 13 March he was at his manor of Cleeve, having completed the greater and more arduous part of his work in the archdeaconry.[2] He returned to Hartlebury for a short time and then, making his way south again, he visited the churches of Tewkesbury and Deerhurst on 18 May from his manor of Bredon. On the 22nd he set out in earnest to complete his visitation. This part was to prove far less strenuous, interrupted as it was by several days spent at his manor of Henbury in Salt Marsh within convenient reach of Bristol. Returning northwards, he reached Eastington where he dedicated the church on 29 June, and there his itinerary ends.

Meanwhile the machinery of correction had been set in motion. The bishop appointed his official, John de la Lowe, and his sequestrator, Henry de Neubold, to take cognizance of and to proceed with all the *comperta* of his recent visitation in the Worcester archdeaconry, as well as to make inquiries about them and to see to their correction and due punishment.[3] He ordered the dean of Pershore to cite certain persons whose names were listed in an attached schedule to appear before him or his commissaries on 14 December in the church of St Andrew, Pershore, to receive corrections and to answer questions put to them. Certain matters were reserved for correction at a later date.[4] Detailed injunctions were drawn up for the Augustinian house at Bristol though, "laudato altissimo", the bishop declared that he had found more things deserving of praise than of censure.[5] On the other hand, the temporal affairs of the priory of the Holy Sepulchre at Warwick[6] were found to be in a bad state. The sequestrator was ordered to go there in

[1] The bishop's itinerary for the Worcester archdeaconry is in Reg. Bransford, fo. 12r.–v. (102). See map opposite.

[2] For the itinerary of the Gloucester archdeaconry see Reg. Bransford, ff. 15v.–16v. (117), and map p. 161 below.

[3] Reg. Bransford, fo. 12v. (104). ". . . ad cognoscendum et procedendum in omnibus et singulis in dicta visitacione nostra compertis, inquirendum eciam super eisdem, necnon huiusmodi comperta corrigendum et in modo debito puniendum. . . . committimus vices nostras cum cohercionis canonice potestate" (26 November 1339).

[4] Ibid., fo. 12v. (103). 6 December 1339.

[5] Ibid., ff. 14v.–15r. (116). These injunctions are undated but were probably issued in 1340. The bishop had visited the monastery 19–20 June 1340.

[6] Visited by Bransford on Friday 12 November 1339.

Bishop Bransford's Primary Visitation in the Worcester archdeaconry (1339)

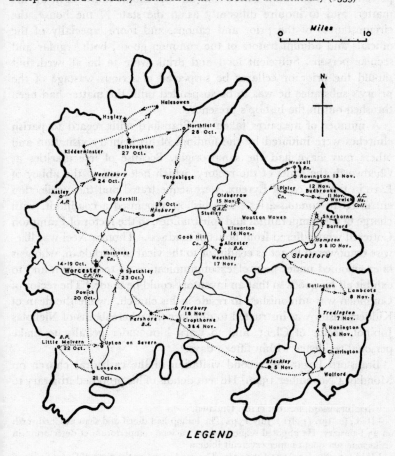

Miles

0 _____ 10

N.

Halesowen

Hagley

Northfield
28 Oct.

Kidderminster

Belbroughton
27 Oct.

Hartlebury
24 Oct.

Tardebigge

Wroxall
Bn.

Astley
A.P.

Dodderhill

29 Oct.
Hanbury

Oldberrow
15 Nov.
A.C.
Studley

Rowington 13 Nov.

12 Nov.
Pinley   Budbrooke
Cn.   11 Nov.   A.C.
Warwick   H.s.
Coll.

Sherborne

Wootton Wawen

Barford

Kinwarton
16 Nov.

Cook Hill
Cn.

Alcester
B.A.

Hampton
9 & 10 Nov.

14-19 Oct.
Worcester
C.P. H.s.

Whistones
Cn.

Spetchley
23 Oct.

Weethley
17 Nov.

Stratford

Powick
20 Oct.

Eatington

Lambcote
8 Nov.

Fledbury
18 Nov.
Cropthorne
3 & 4 Nov.

Tredington
7 Nov.

B.P.
Little Malvern
22 Oct.

Pershore
B.A.

Upton on Severn

Honington
6 Nov.

Cherrington

London
21 Oct.

Blackley
5 Nov.

Walford

LEGEND

Symbols		Religious Houses	
O Oldbury :	bp passed through	A.C. :	house of Augustinian Canons
● Stow :	visited part deanery	A.P. :	alien priory
Ŏ Nibley :	dedication of altar	Bn :	Benedictine nunnery
O Albury :	episcopal manor	B.A. :	Benedictine abbey
O. :	ordination held	C.P. :	Cathedral Priory
Coll. :	Collegiate Church visited	Cn. :	Cistercian nunnery
Ex. :	exempt church visited	H. Hs. :	hospital (s)
● Longdon 21 Oct. :	bp stayed the night		

person and to summon before him all who might throw light on the matter, and to inquire diligently as to the state of the house, the circumstances of the prior and canons, and more especially of the officials and administrators of the common goods, both regular and secular persons. Sufficient food and drink were to be allowed, but should the prior or cellarer be suspected of serious wastage of the priory's substance he was to be suspended until the matter had been thrashed out in the bishop's presence.[1]

A number of measures taken by Bransford with regard to parish churches were initiated by the findings of his primary visitation and others may have had the same origin. Because of irregularities at Chedworth the fruits of the rectory, which belonged to the abbey of Lyre in the diocese of Évreux, were sequestrated and their collection entrusted to commissaries.[2] The bishop appointed a coadjutor, with charge of the temporalities and spiritualities, to the rector of Frampton Cotterell who suffered from bouts of madness.[3] Thomas Neel was likewise empowered to act as coadjutor to the vicar of Turkdean, who was later enjoined under pain of excommunication to receive him and to exhibit all his goods so that an inventory could be made.[4] The rector of Campden was admonished to reside in his church,[5] while the dean of Kidderminster was instructed to discover the whereabouts of Nicholas Jobinol, rector of Clent, and to warn him under penalty to make personal residence within fifteen days.[6]

Bransford began his second visitation in the cathedral church on Monday 4 November 1342.[7] He sent details of his proposed itinerary to

---

[1] Reg. Bransford, fo. 16v. (118). Undated.

[2] Ibid., fo. 19r. (138): 1 July 1340. The bishop had dined and slept at Chedworth on 25 February. He imposed sequestration "racione compertorum et detectorum in visitacione sua quam nuper excercuit ibidem".

[3] Ibid., fo. 18v. (132): 24 June 1340. The coadjutor was the vicar of Great Sodbury with whom the bishop had dined on 30 May during his visitation of Hawkesbury and Bitton deaneries. For an earlier appointment, see ff. 5v.–6r. (45): 4 May 1339.

[4] Ibid., fo. 18v. (131, 133): 20 June and 1 July 1340. An inventory was regularly made in such cases as a check on the coadjutor's administration.

[5] Ibid., fo. 18r. (123): 9 April 1340: "Dictus venerabilis pater monuit rectorem ecclesie de Campedene in personam Roberti de Campeden procuratoris sui quod a tempore huiusmodi monicionis in dicta ecclesia personalem faceret residenciam sub pena iuris." Campden had been visited 14 February, so that the interval is rather long.

[6] Ibid., fo. 19r. (135): 3 July 1340: "Moneas vice et auctoritate nostra quod infra xv dies a tempore monicionis huiusmodi in dicta ecclesia personaliter resideat et eidem deserviat ut tenetur sub pena iuris." Clent had been visited 26 October 1340. In this case the interval is possibly too great, unless there was an earlier monition of which we have no record.

[7] Ibid., fo. 60r. (530). "Littera muniendi capitulum de visitacione" (3 October 1342).

Bishop Bransford's Primary Visitation in the Gloucester archdeaconry (1340)

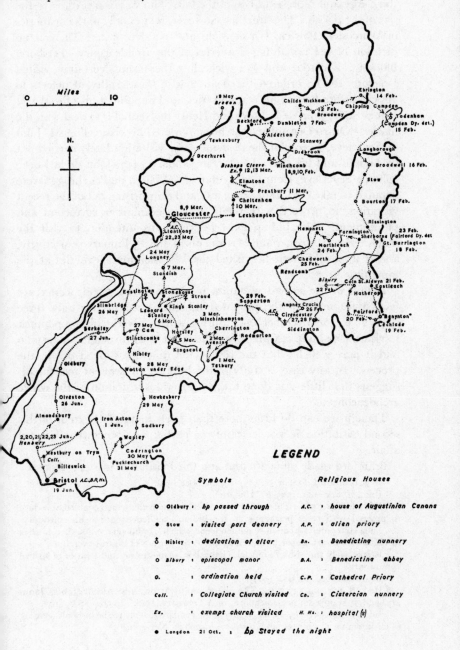

the official of the Worcester archdeacon and ordered him to summon the clergy and representatives of the laity, four or six according to the size of the parish.[1] The itinerary, however, relates only to the deaneries of Worcester, Powick, (Droit)wich, and Kidderminster. There is no mention of the remaining deaneries of the archdeaconry—Pershore, Blockley, Kineton, and Warwick. But the bishop certainly visited Pershore, for he ordered the dean to cite those guilty of defects to appear before him or his commissaries, and appointed his official and sequestrator, John de la Lowe and Henry de Neubold, to deal with the matter.[2] On 10 December 1342 he empowered his chancellor, M. John de Severleye, to correct the *comperta* of the visitation lately carried out by himself and his clerks.[3] Later, in January 1343, John de la Lowe, John de Severleye, Henry de Neubold, and Hugh de Penebrugg[4] were deputed to take cognizance of causes and suits arising out of the recent visitation, to proceed with them, and to administer correction and punishment.[5] The bishop gave notice of his intention to visit the monasteries at Alcester and Wroxall on 22 and 25 January respectively, and it is possible that he visited the Warwickshire deaneries at the same time.[6]

Details of the second visitation in the southern archdeaconry are few. A fragment of the proposed itinerary accounts for only three days, 28 to 30 November 1342, during which time the bishop planned to visit the deanery of Campden. The scribe then turned to a new folio and it may well be that the rest of the itinerary slipped out in the process.[7] In any case, a study of the bishop's subsequent movements suggests that little was done towards a serious visitation of the whole archdeaconry.

Though we can do little more than guess at the full extent of this second visitation it was certainly a partial and somewhat cursory affair.

Bransford made some attempt at a third visitation in 1345, though a

---

[1] Reg. Bransford, fo. 60r.–v. (531): 3 October 1342.

[2] Ibid., ff. 61v.–62r. (535–6). Undated.

[3] Ibid., fo. 64r. (566). This was embodied in a commission which enabled Severleye to proceed with cases pertaining to the bishop's audience outside his consistory: ". . . una cum potestate canonice puniendi et corrigendi omnia et omnimoda comperta in visitacione nostra nuper in diocesi nostra Wyg' per nos et nostros exercitata."

[4] Respectively the bishop's official, chancellor, sequestrator, and adjutor or special commissary.

[5] Reg. Bransford, fo. 64r. (567).

[6] Ibid., ff. 61r.–v. (533, 534). The bishop was at Arrow, near Alcester, on 21 January, and at Hampton, near Stratford, on 1 February. Ibid., fo. 56v. (496, 494).

[7] Ibid., ff. 60v.–61r. (532). This entry is the (undated) reply to the bishop's warning of his intention to visit the archdeaconry (dated 15 November).

mere scored out fragment of his *progressus* has survived.[1] He began proceedings with a visitation of the cathedral priory on 7 November. His commissaries are said to have visited the churches of the city and neighbourhood of Worcester, while he held a visitation of some parishes in the west of the county at Astley—an unusual division of labour.[2] There is record of the receipt of procuration from the abbey of Halesowen on account of their church of Clent, and later mention of a recent visitation of Cirencester Abbey.[3] No further information is vouchsafed to us, but we may suspect that this third visitation was even less complete than the second.

The general impression derived from a study of visitations during this period is that a definite attempt was made to conduct a primary visitation at the earliest convenient moment, the thoroughness of which depended upon the time which an individual bishop could, or was willing, to devote to the task. Reynolds, much occupied with state affairs, does not seem to have attempted a visitation at all, and Hemenhale may not have had time to do so. It was also occupation with extra-diocesan business that made the visitations of Maidstone, Cobham, and Orleton somewhat formal and partial affairs, conducted largely by deputies. Montacute, on the other hand, was a diligent visitor as the partial record of his primary progress shows. It was usual for him to take two days over the visitation of a monastery. He preached and made inquiries on the first, administering corrections on the second. He visited the deanery of (Droit)wich in three churches, and spent three, four, or even five days in those deaneries of the Gloucester archdeaconry which he is recorded to have visited. Cobham's commissaries generally found one day, or occasionally two, sufficient for the visitation of a deanery, which was invariably conducted in a single church.[4]

---

[1] Ibid., fo. 92r. al. lxxxiii (751). The itinerary covers only the days from 7 to 10 November.

[2] It is possible that the scribe made an error. The record of the commissaries' visitation of the city and other churches in St Helen's is inconsistent, ending "et prandit et pernoctavit in manerio suo de Hertlebur.". On the other hand, it is specifically stated that the bishop had stayed the previous night at Hartlebury, the commissaries in Worcester priory. Bransford would hardly have done this had he intended to conduct visitation in Worcester on the morrow.

[3] Reg. Bransford fo. 92v., lxxxxiii (753); fo. 109v., cx (835).

[4] This is not to disparage Cobham's commissaries, who acted as was customary. In the writer's view it points to the particular diligence of Montacute and Bransford, both of whom often visited the secular clergy of a deanery in several churches and on as many different days. By this method they dealt with comparatively few churches at any one time. Is it too much to argue that in consequence they were likely to become better acquainted with both the clergy and the parishes of the diocese? (see p. 150

Only Bishops Gainsburgh and Bransford, and perhaps Cobham, seem to have attempted a second visitation. Few details survive, though we know enough of Bransford's second visitation to conclude that it was on a relatively small scale.

Bransford was the most industrious of all episcopal visitors during this period. His primary progress was a monument of endurance and hard work. He did not enjoy good health and must have been close on sixty years of age. Despite this, in the first seventeen days he visited personally four deaneries, two hospitals, and four other religious houses, journeying some 120 miles through the Worcester archdeaconry. After a short interval he covered the rest of the archdeaconry in sixteen days, visiting four deaneries, the episcopal churches of Hampton and Stratford, nine religious houses, and traversing about the same number of miles as before. During the inclement months of February and March (1340) he was almost continuously on the move for five weeks. In thirty-six days he slept at no fewer than twenty-nine different places and covered about 150 miles, many of them in the hilly country of the lower slopes of the Cotswolds. The bishop's total mileage during the whole visitation could hardly have fallen short of 500 miles, not including an intervening trip to and from Hartlebury. The visitation of the more remote Gloucester archdeaconry was particularly thorough. Only two deaneries (Dursley and Gloucester) were visited in fewer than three churches, while two days were spent at each of the larger monasteries of Winchcomb, Cirencester, Gloucester, Llanthony, and Bristol. Though his two later visitations were undoubtedly somewhat sketchy by comparison there was at least an attempt to observe the rule of triennial visitation. Moreover, so far as we know, the bishop always visited in person except during part of his third visitation.

ORDINATIONS

Comparatively full records of ordinations are to be found in the episcopal registers of this period, and from Register Orleton onwards they occupy a separate section.[1] It was important to have accurate ordination lists so that former promotions could be verified, and not infre-

---

above). This suggestion of diligence accords with what we know of other aspects of their respective visitations. A bishop's primary progress afforded a unique opportunity for him to get to know his diocese. At other times it was often the case that his subjects saw little of him, save in his manor houses or cathedral city and along the routes connecting them. Cf. *English Clergy*, p. 45.

[1] They are scattered throughout the registers of Gainsburgh, Reynolds, Maidstone, and Cobham. See p. 7 above.

quently it is stated that the registers had been searched for this purpose. Ordinations *ad primam tonsuram* were held separately from ordinations to holy orders[1] and lists of those so ordained are only occasionally recorded in the registers.[2]

According to the Canon Law orders were to be conferred at the "Quatuor Tempora",[3] though it was lawful for a bishop to promote one or two persons to lesser orders[4] on Sundays and other feast days. But only the pope could lawfully ordain to the subdiaconate and higher orders at times other than the Quatuor Tempora, Holy Saturday, and the Saturday before Passion Sunday[5]—commonly called "Sitientes".[6]

The practice in the Worcester diocese at this time can be conveniently illustrated from Register Bransford which, despite some losses, contains a large quire of ordination lists. In 1343, to take the first year for which the record is almost complete, Bishop Bransford held seven ordinations. At the Quatuor Tempora[7] he ordained 104, 63, 114, and 16+ persons respectively. In addition, he held ordinations on the second Sunday in Lent, the Saturday before Passion Sunday, and Holy Saturday. On the first of these occasions he promoted two clerks to the order of acolyte; on the second, twenty-five men, of whom six were made acolytes, eight subdeacons, nine deacons, and two priests; on Holy Saturday, eleven men, of whom three were made subdeacons, four deacons, and four priests.[8] In 1345 he held no fewer than nine ordinations. The two additional ones were celebrated in his chapel at Hartlebury on Quinquagesima Sunday and Easter Day, and on each occasion three clerks were made acolytes.[9] In 1349 the bishop held eight ordinations prior to his death on 6 August. Apart

---

[1] Strictly speaking, those of subdeacon, deacon, and priest—in this context. Cf. Lyndwood, p. 17 ad ver. *sacros ordines.* Ordination lists also contained the names of those ordained to the lesser order of acolyte.

[2] But there are lengthy lists in Reg. Hemenhale, ff. 25r.–v., 27r., 33v.–34v.; and in Reg. Bransford, ff. clxxxxvii r. al. 73 to clxxxxviii v. al. 74 (1074–1107).

[3] The Ember days at the four seasons. That is, the Wednesday, Friday, and Saturday after the first Sunday in Lent, Whitsunday, Holy Rood Day, and the feast of St Lucy respectively. If either of the last two fall on a Wednesday, the first Ember day falls on the following Wednesday. Ordinations were held on the Saturdays in Embertide.

[4] I.e. to that of acolyte and below.

[5] *Extra* 1, 11, cc. 1–3.

[6] In 1349, on account of the dearth of priests, Clement VI authorized William Zouche, Archbishop of York, to hold additional ordinations. *Letts. from Northern Regs.*, pp. 401–2.

[7] The Saturdays which fell on 8 March, 7 June, 20 September, and 20 December.

[8] Reg. Bransford ff. clxxvi v. al. 17 to clxxix r. (out of order) (1050–5), clxxxx v. al. 65 (1068).

[9] Ibid., ff. 86r. al. lxxxvii (692), 86v. lxxxvii (701), clxxxvi v. 82 (out of order) to clxxxx r. 65 (1060–7 excepting 1065).

from the Ember Saturdays at Lent and Trinity, he ordained on the eve of Passion Sunday ("Sitientes"), Passion Sunday, and the feast of St Mary Magdalene (22 July).[1] But on neither Sunday, nor on the feast of St Mary Magdalene, did he ordain to an order above that of acolyte. In short, we see that there was strict adherence to the letter of the canons. Large-scale ordinations were celebrated only on Saturdays at the Quatuor Tempora, lesser ordinations on the Saturday before Passion Sunday and on Holy Saturday, while on Sundays and other feast days a few clerks might be made acolytes.

So far as we know, Bishop Gainsburgh held seventeen ordinations during the three and three-quarter years of his episcopate, eleven of them on Saturdays at the Quatuor Tempora.[2]

Ten ordinations are all that are recorded for the five years of Reynolds' episcopate, and three of them have nothing to do with the Worcester diocese. Of the latter, one was celebrated by the bishop at Fulham and the other two in St Paul's, by licence of the bishop of London, at which a very few clerks from the Worcester diocese received orders. Reynolds held only one ordination in his own diocese— on 19 September 1310, at Tewkesbury. The remainder were carried out by the bishops of Llandaff, Hereford, Bangor (on two occasions), Annaghdown, and by Roland, archbishop of Armagh. Ordinations within the diocese were celebrated at the Quatuor Tempora on five occasions, outside it on three. The remaining two ordinations were held by the bishop of Bangor on the Saturday before Passion Sunday 1312, and on Holy Saturday 1313.[3]

Maidstone's episcopate, calculated from the time of his arrival in England, lasted for rather more than three years. During this time he held seven ordinations, four of them at the Quatuor Tempora.

During Cobham's episcopate of ten years thirty-seven ordinations are recorded to have been celebrated, two of them by the bishop of Clonfert, and no fewer than twenty-two at the Quatuor Tempora.[4] However, the number of those ordained was often small, sometimes two or three, or even only one. The bishop twice celebrated orders in the chapel of his London house, and at the Lenten ordination of 1326

---

[1] Reg. Bransford, ff. ccxii v. al. 77 to ccxv v. al. 80 (1109–12) and vol. 2, ff. 4r.–5r. (1339–42).

[2] They are listed by R. A. Wilson in his introduction to Reg. Gainsburgh (p. xx). Some of his dates need correction: 2 June (1303) should be 1 June; 21 February (1304), 22 February; 24 May, 23 May; 13 June (1305), 12 June; 29 May (1306), 28 May.

[3] There is a rough list in the introduction to Register Reynolds, p. xviii.

[4] On 17 December 1323 Cobham ordained one subdeacon and one priest at Hartlebury, while on the same day the bishop of Clonfert held a large ordination on his behalf at Cropthorne. Reg. Cobham, ff. 92v.–94r., pp. 164–8.

he promoted a number of men to the diaconate and priesthood on the same day, contrary to the Canon Law.[1]

Between March 1328 and the same month in 1333 Orleton would seem to have held seventeen ordinations, including three at his manor of Beaumes in Salisbury diocese, one in Paris,[2] and two at the house of the sisters of St Clare at Nogent-sur-Seine in the diocese of Soissons.[3] Eight, including two of those held abroad, were celebrated at the Quatuor Tempora.

Ten ordinations are recorded for Montacute's episcopate. The first was celebrated at Crookham (Berkshire) on the eve of Trinity 1334, when the bishop ordained two persons; the last on the Saturday before Passion Sunday (5 April) 1337. Seven took place at the Quatuor Tempora.

Between 20 September 1337, the first Saturday in Embertide after his arrival in the diocese, and 19 September 1338, three months before his death, Bishop Hemenhale held six ordinations, four of them at the Quatuor Tempora.[4]

In Register Bransford details are given of forty-one ordinations during the ten years from 1339 to 1349, even though the records are defective for the years 1339–42, part of 1344, and for 1347 and 1348. In addition, we know from his visitation itinerary that the bishop held an ordination at Cheltenham on 11 March 1340—Saturday in the first week of Lent, though the lists of those ordained have been lost. Seventeen of the ordinations were held at the Quatuor Tempora. All of them were celebrated within the diocese and by the bishop himself.

There is some variation in the manner of recording the ordination lists in the registers. Sometimes those ordained are classified simply as acolytes, subdeacons, deacons, and priests,[5] according to the order to which they had been promoted. At other times each of those categories is subdivided to distinguish the religious from the secular

1 *Extra.* I, 11, cc. 13 and 15. *Reg. Cobham,* fo. 109r.–v., pp. 194–5.

2 He received two licences, dated 17 December 1332, from the bishop-elect of Paris, William de Chanac (1332–42), permitting him to ordain four named clerks on the following Saturday (19 December) in the oratory of his house in Paris. *Reg. Orleton* 1, fo. 14r.

3 On 27 February (Saturday in the first week of Lent) and 20 March 1332 (Saturday before Passion Sunday), respectively. He was licensed by the bishop of Soissons, Peter de Chappes (1331–49), to ordain clerks of his diocese and those from other dioceses who had letters dimissory. *Reg. Orleton* 1, ff. 14r.–15r.

4 *Reg. Hemenhale* ff. 21r.–33v., 35r.–36r.

5 "Acoliti", "subdiaconi", "diaconi", "presbiteri" with "sacerdotes" and "capellani" as variants, especially in *Reg. Cobham.*

clergy.[1] Occasionally the seculars are again subdivided into classes of beneficed and unbeneficed.[2]

The titles of subdeacons and of those who proceeded to higher orders are carefully noted.[3] In some of the registers these are said to have been proved, approved, or attested under the seal of the official of one of the archdeacons or that of a rural dean.[4] Usually we learn that the aspirant to orders declared that he was content with his title and swore that it was valid.[5] Clerks were ordained to various titles: to that of a benefice or of some religious house, to that of provision, or merely to the title of patrimony—an annual rent or pension the amount of which is often stated. A few were ordained without title *sub gracia domini* or *ad mandatum domini* and on occasions are recorded to have taken an oath not to trouble the bishop or his successors on that account.[6] Those considered insufficiently literate promised to stay in some place of learning for a year or more and not to proceed to further orders meanwhile. A title did not necessarily enable a clerk to proceed to all orders, sometimes it was specifically for one order only. In such cases he would have to seek an additional or a more substantial title before presenting himself for further promotion.

It is not clear whether letters of orders were regularly given or not,

[1] "Religiosi", "seculares" or "non religiosi". In any case the religious are ordinarily placed first and differentiated by the title "frater". R. A. Wilson in his introduction to *Reg. Gainsburgh* (p. xviii) calculates that only fifteen religious were made subdeacons, fourteen deacons, and eight priests, between 1303 and 1307—according to the ordination lists. He suggests that Gainsburgh may have ordained the religious in their own churches. Though this seems unlikely, the alternative is to assume that the lists are defective. There is a similar lack of regulars in some Hereford lists, e.g. *Reg. Cantilupe* (1275–82).

[2] "Beneficiati", "non beneficiati"; or "promoti", "non promoti".

[3] Though sometimes reference is merely made to an earlier ordination list in which the title is given. In 1303 William de Bolney was ordained to the title of patrimony "in registro ut dicit et jurat" (*Reg. Gainsburgh*, fo. 21v., p. 70), and there are other examples of this oath.

[4] See particularly Regs. Gainsburgh and Reynolds. No hint of such practice is given in Reg. Bransford.

[5] The regular phrases, often heavily abbreviated, are: "de quo reputavit se esse contentum" and "quem esse verum docuit".

[6] See, for instance, the oath sworn by Walter de Dunstaple in 1345, even though he had a title of five marks of annual rent: "Nunquam contra dictum venerabilem patrem nec contra successores suos propter huiusmodi suscepcionem ordinis predicti in formam capituli CUM SECUNDUM APOSTOLUM litem movere vel ipsos illa de causa fatigare quovismodo" (Reg. Bransford, fo. 88r., lxxxix (726)). Innocent III's decretal letter, "Cum secundum apostolum", was incorporated in *Extra* 3, 5, c. 16. It laid on the bishop the obligation to provide for those clerks he ordained without title. Clement V, notwithstanding this constitution, freed Gainsburgh from the liability to make provision for "more than two thousand" clerks ordained by his predecessor, Giffard (*C.P.L.* 1305–42, p. 26).

though visitation articles of both Cobham and Bransford suggest that they were.[1] An entry in Register Bransford lends support to the suggestion. In 1349 Andrew de Fetherston was ordained subdeacon, by letters dimissory of the bishop of Lincoln, to the title of the abbot and convent of Lilleshall. But because the written evidence of his title was not authenticated by the common seal of the monastery, the letters of orders were to be withheld until he returned with the document properly sealed, and a note to that effect was entered in the register.[2] Yet a procedure for the proof of orders which is fully recorded in the somewhat earlier register of Bishop Reynolds[3] apparently shows that such letters were not granted as a matter of course in his time. John and William, both of Willersey, claimed that they had been ordained sub-deacons[4] by the bishop at Tewkesbury.[5] To support their claim they produced four witnesses, not, it will be observed, their letters of orders. Even if these had been lost they would surely not have escaped mention during the process which ensued. The witnesses were examined on oath at Bredon in the presence of the official and their depositions were taken down. John of Willersey, after being sworn, was asked whether his namesake had been ordained subdeacon. He replied in the affirmative. Asked how he knew this, he said that it was because he had seen him leave the choir of Tewkesbury Abbey and had heard him called at the beginning when the subdeacons were being called. Asked who called him, he replied that it was William, the clerk of the official,[6] and he knew nothing further. Ralph of Willersey, who was asked about both John and William, added that the reason he knew was because he had seen them vested in albs touching books and other things, just as he himself and others who had been ordained subdeacons at that time had done. About their admission and other circumstances he knew nothing.

---

1 *Reg. Cobham*, fo. 126v., p. 226; *Reg. Bransford*. fo. 10r. (89).

2 Reg. Bransford, fo. ccxiii v. al. 78: "Et quia titulus suus non habet sigillum commune dicte domus retineantur littere ordinum suorum quousque portaverit titulum sub sigillo communi."

3 Dated 24 April [1312]: *Reg. Reynolds*, fo. 48r., p. 39.

4 "Sub gracia domini sine titulo" interlineated.

5 The ordination had been celebrated 19 September 1310. *Reg. Reynolds*, fo. 16v., pp. 116 et seq.

6 Whether the official of the archdeacon or the diocesan official is meant, is not clear; probably the former. The right to call the ordinands was disputed in the late thirteenth century. The priory claimed that it belonged to the precentor "secundum antiquam consuetudinem", but in ordinations at Westbury (1288) and Bromsgrove (1289) he had been prevented from exercising the function, on the earlier occasion by force. Giffard's contention was that by right and custom the function pertained to the archdeacon, or to anyone else whom the bishop thought fit to appoint. *Ann. Wigorn.*, pp. 495, 498; Thomas, *App.*, p. 64 (art. 4).

The third witness said the same, but added that he had heard John and
William called, as in the deposition of the first witness. The statement
of the fourth witness agreed on all points with that of the third. The
following Thursday (27 April) was appointed for John and William to
see and hear the depositions. They duly appeared before the official
who decreed that the depositions and the names of John and William
should be inserted in the register, the latter among the names of those
ordained to the subdiaconate at Tewkesbury—where they can now
be seen.[1]

Quite apart from the glimpse which it gives us of an actual ordination,
this examination is of particular interest. It indicates the use made of
the ordination lists entered in the registers. The claimants' names had
not been recorded, but after proof of orders, established by the testimony of witnesses,[2] they were inserted—a necessary preliminary to
future advancement.

If letters of orders were not issued at the time of ordination, it might
be necessary for a clerk to obtain letters testimonial from the bishop,
particularly if he had moved to another diocese.[3] They were drawn up
after due inspection of the registers, or if these proved defective, on the
evidence of witnesses. Probably a small fee *pro sigillo* was charged.[4]

Where ordinations were held depended to a large extent upon the
whim of the individual bishop, or at least upon the exigencies of his
itinerary. They might take place in the chapels of his manor houses, in
some conveniently situated parish or monastic church, either within
or—very occasionally—outside the diocese. Often the candidates had to
travel long distances. Hemenhale only once celebrated orders in the
Gloucester archdeaconry—at Tewkesbury Abbey. His other ordinations took place at his manors of Bredon and Hartlebury, in the chapel
of King's Norton (Bromsgrove parish), and, on two occasions, in the
parish church of Ombersley. Maidstone also ordained only once in the
Gloucester archdeaconry—in Cirencester parish church. Orleton, on
the contrary, celebrated orders eight times in that archdeaconry and
twice in the Worcester archdeaconry—but not in the cathedral church.
Of the forty-two ordinations which Bransford is known to have cele-

---

[1] *Reg. Reynolds*, fo. 17r., p. 118.

[2] There is an instance from Durham diocese (1311) of the proof of orders "laudabili
fide dignorum testimonio". *Reg. Palat. Dunelm.* 1, p. 103. Cf. Reg. Bransford, fo. 33r.
(266).

[3] On one occasion it is recorded that orders were proved in Durham diocese by
letters testimonial of the bishops of Worcester and Salisbury. Op. cit., p. 113.

[4] Thomas, *App.*, p. 68 (arts. 19–20). Cf. the constitution, "Nova et insatiabilis
cupiditas", ascribed to Stratford (*Const. Prov.*, pp. 49–50).

brated, no fewer than twenty-five were at Hartlebury, either in the chapel of the bishop's castle-manor or in the parish church.[1]

The number of those ordained at any one time varied from one to many hundreds. Even an ordination held at one of the Quatuor Tempora might be only on a small scale, though as a general rule large numbers were ordained at such times. R. A. Wilson gives a statistical table of ordinations during Gainsburgh's episcopate. Some 1,280 orders were conferred in three and three-quarter years, the largest number at any single time being 213 (eve of Trinity 1306).[2] During the five years of Reynolds' episcopate 1,629 orders were conferred—a yearly average approximating to that of the previous episcopate. The largest ordination was in 1309 when 425 persons received orders at Cirencester on the eve of Trinity.[3] We can do little more than guess the total number of those ordained by Bransford, for only thirty-six folios of ordination lists survive from the first volume of his register out of a probable original total of seventy-one. It is possible, of course, that other material was written on at least some of the missing folios. A further two folios of ordination lists are in the second volume of the register. From these thirty-eight extant folios we learn that Bransford ordained 757 acolytes, 681 subdeacons, 713 deacons, and 680 priests during the ten years of his episcopate, a total of 2,831 orders.[4] The true figures must be well above these. The number ordained at the largest of his ordinations of which we have record was 460, including 153 acolytes, 120 subdeacons, 133 deacons, and 54+[5] priests. This is by no means a record for the period under review. Thomas calculated that Montacute ordained 849 persons in Worcester Cathedral on 9 April 1337, comprising 391 acolytes, 180 subdeacons, 154 deacons, and 124 priests.[6]

1 But this could be misleading. Between December 1348 and his death on 6 August 1349 the bishop held nine ordinations, eight of them in his chapel at Hartlebury—doubtless because of illness.

2 Introduction to *Reg. Gainsburgh*, pp. xx–xxi.   3 Intro. to *Reg. Reynolds*, p. xxi.

4 Pearce in his *Thomas de Cobham* (App. 1) gives the corresponding totals for that bishop's episcopate, which was comparable in length to Bransford's, as: 415 acolytes, 680 subdeacons, 717 deacons, 741 priests—in all, 2,553 orders.

5 The list is incomplete.

6 Thomas, *Account*, p. 175. Other details given by him (ibid., pp. 161, 162, 166, 167, 171–2, 175, 176) are as follows:

		A.	S.	D.	P.	T.
Maidstone	1 June 1314	105	140	133	85	463
	21 Dec. 1314	50	115	136	109	410
Cobham	22 Dec. 1319	—	43	96	91	230
	18 Dec. 1322	120	102*	50	60†	332
Orleton	17 June 1329	218	47	79	62	406
	25 May 1331	221	100	47	51	419
Montacute	10 June 1335	251	115	133	22	521
Hemenhale	6 June 1338	204	141	117	149	611

Recte 103   † *Recte* 62

These figures are high, although the number of men involved was obviously much less than the total number of orders conferred.[1] What is perhaps notable is the large number of those who proceeded to the priesthood.[2]

Little can be learnt from the registers about the examination of such large numbers of ordinands. That they were examined is suggested by certain chance references, but how rigorous or effective the examination we have no means of telling. A series of notes added to the names of certain priests ordained by Reynolds in 1309 appears to have been derived from some form of examination.[3] Moreover, in 1313 Reynolds appointed his official, Benedict de Paston, and his sequestrator, John de Broadwas, to examine clerks whom they considered suitable for God's ministry "super vita literatura conversacione ac titulis", to receive them, and to present them for ordination to the archbishop of Armagh or to the bishop of Bath and Wells.[4] Two of the ordination lists in Register Bransford are prefaced by memoranda to the effect that sentence of excommunication had been brought against those of the ordained who had not been examined or admitted by the examiners deputed by the bishop.[5] In some other registers it is specifically stated that no such sentence had been promulgated.[6] Reynolds commissioned the bishop of Llandaff to dispense a clerk who had furtively taken the order of deacon, but if sentence of excommunication had been promulgated the clerk was to go to the Holy See for dispensation.[7] It is hardly

[1] For some deductions from ordination figures, particularly with regard to the numbers of assistant clergy, see Moorman, *Church Life in England in the XIII*[th] *cent.* pp. 52 et seq.; Hartridge, p. 131.

[2] This is not so noticeable in the individual ordinations listed above as it is over a period of time, for example, the episcopates of Cobham and Bransford (see above p. 171 and ibid., n. 4).

[3] *Reg. Reynolds*, fo. 18v., pp. 122–3. R. A. Wilson comments on these and kindred matters in his introduction to the register, pp. xix–xxi.

[4] *Reg. Reynolds*, fo. 78r., p. 60.

[5] Reg. Bransford, ff. cxlvii v. al. 47 (1008), clv r. al. 39 (1009). "Memorandum quod sentencia excommunicacionis fuit lata contra ordinatos in istis ordinibus non examinatos nec admissos per examinatores a dicto patre deputatos". Bishop Blois ruled that the examination of ordinands was to last three days—from Wednesday to Friday preceding the ordination (*Concilia* 1, p. 627). This seems to have been the practice at York. In Archbishop Giffard's register (pp. 194–8) are lists of those said to have been examined on 20 September 1273, the Wednesday before the Autumn ordinations. Archbishop Romeyn ordered all who wished to be promoted to Holy Orders to appear on the Thursday and Friday before ordination day: "Quo die neminem examinari volumus vel admitti sine litteris decanorum suorum testimonialibus de suis moribus, condicionibus, ordinibus, et quos, a quo, vel a quibus susceperint, necnon cum titulis sufficientibus" (*York Reg. Romeyn* 1, pp. 15–16).

[6] For example, *Reg. Reynolds*, fo. 69r., p. 132.

[7] Ibid., fo. 3v., p. 81.

surprising that among such large numbers there should have been some cases of irregularity.

The services of neighbouring bishops or of those who held Irish sees were in demand from time to time for ordinations and other functions. This was particularly so during Reynolds' episcopate for he had little time to spare for the personal exercise of his pastoral office.[1] Other bishops, such as Bransford, who had no extra-diocesan commitments, did not require assistance. It seems probable that these suffragan bishops were entitled to part of the fees due for the services which they performed. The nature of the services was usually specified in their commissions of appointment. Apart from the celebration of orders they were mainly concerned with the reconciliation of polluted churches and graveyards, the consecration of altars, and the dedication of churches, for which offices the diocesan bishop regularly exacted fees.[2] Although there is no mention of pecuniary remuneration in the registers under review, an indenture drawn up in 1395 between the prior, acting as official *sede vacante*, and the bishop of "Faro", set out the fees which the latter was permitted to retain for exercising episcopal functions within the diocese.[3] It is likely that suffragan bishops also received payment in kind. Reynolds, for instance, gave orders to his bailiffs and other officers that whenever John de Monmouth, bishop of Llandaff, who was exercising episcopal functions during his absence *in remotis*, stayed at any of the episcopal manors he was to be liberally provided with rooms, hay, wood, and litter, and anything else he asked for. The various items were to be entered in the manorial accounts.[4]

[1] See p. 166 above.

[2] In 1339 Bransford ordered the dean of Cirencester to place the church of South Cerney under an interdict unless the money due to him for his personal reconciliation of the churchyard there was paid. This amounted to £3 4s. 6d. "feodis nostrorum ministrorum inclusis in eadem pecunia". Such charges were said to have been levied "iuxta laudabilem consuetudinem ecclesie nostre cathedralis Wyg' hactenus usitatam" (Reg. Bransf., ff. 10v.–11r. (94)). Maidstone seems to have charged four marks for the consecration of a high altar and five for the dedication of a church and the consecration of its altar. See, for instance, Reg. Maidstone, fo. 29r. In Bath and Wells diocese, when the bishop received 100s. or more for dedications and reconciliations, the crucifer and marshal had half a mark each, the unbeneficed chapel clerks and the bishop's receiver one mark. If the bishop received a lesser sum, then the perquisites of his ministers were likewise reduced. Those absent on episcopal business were to receive payment as though present. See *B. & W. Reg. Shrewsb.*, p. 316.

[3] *R.S.V.*, fo. cci r., pp. 356–7. The sums were: 20s. for reconciliation or dedication; 20s. for the celebration of orders (from the letters of orders); one-third of the fee for consecrating altars (this was not to be done for less than 6s. 8d.); and for minor orders. the accustomed fees.

[4] *Reg. Reynolds*, fo. 9r., p. 7.

PENITENTIARIES[1]

From the time of the Fourth Lateran Council (1215)[2] everyone who had reached the age of discretion was obliged to confess at least once a year to his or her own priest.[3] Furthermore, a bishop who could not do the work himself was to appoint suitable persons in cathedral and collegiate churches who, as his adjutors, would hear confessions and enjoin penances.[4] Cardinal Otto later decreed[5] that in every deanery prudent and faithful[6] men were to be appointed confessors by the bishop of the place,[7] to whom rectors[8] and lesser clergy, who were not parishioners in the popular estimation,[9] could have recourse. In the cathedrals general confessors were to be appointed who, Athon glosses,[10] were not only to hear the confessions of the clergy but also those of all the bishop's secular subjects.

The general outline of this system can be traced at Worcester in the fourteenth century, but with some modifications. Bishop Gainsburgh empowered the prior, subprior, and penitentiary of his cathedral church to exercise his office towards penitents who should present themselves at the cathedral on Ash Wednesday 1305.[11] It seems likely,

1 Much information on the whole subject of penance and penitentiaries is contained in Lyndwood's glosses in the *Provinciale* (Lib. V, tit. 16: "De Penitentiis et Remissionibus", and also in those of Athon (*Const. Othonis*, tit. 5: "De Confessionibus Personarum et Clericorum"; to which frequent reference will be made in the subsequent footnotes, The development of private confession is traced by H. C. Lea, *A History of Auricular Confession and Indulgence in the Latin Church.*

2 C. 21: "Omnis utriusque sexus." *Extra.* 5, 38, c. 12. This was the minimum requirement. Cantilupe advised the faithful to make confession before Christmas, Easter, and Pentecost, so that "confessione purgati digne possint suum recipere salvatorem". *Concilia* 1, p. 669.

3 See Lyndwood's glosses on the words *proprio sacerdoti* (p. 144) and *nequeunt* (p. 337).

4 C. 10: *Extra* 1, 31, c. 15.   5 Athon, pp. 13 et seq.

6 These words are glossed extensively by both Athon (p. 13) and Lyndwood (pp. 326–7).

7 It had been provided by the Council of Oxford (1222) that two priests were to be appointed in every deanery for this purpose (*Const. Prov.*, pp. 7–8). Bishop Blois included the provision in his 1229 statutes, adding that the priests were to be chosen by the chapter of each deanery (*Concilia* 1, p. 624). Cf. Cantilupe's ruling (ibid., p. 669).

8 The text (p. 14) has *personae* which Athon glosses: "Id est rectores; loquitur enim secundum vulgare Anglicorum".

9 Ibid. ad ver. *minores clerici*: "Vicarii sc. & presbyteri, ac alii quicunque, qui vulgari opinione parochiani non vocantur: nam parochiani proprio sacerdoti Communi Jure habent confiteri."

10 Ad ver. *confessiones, generales*, p. 15.

11 *Reg. Gainsburgh* fo. 6r., p. 15. There is also an earlier commission, dated 10 February 1304, issued to the prior alone: "COMMISSIO PRO PUBLICE PENITENTIBUS. Frater W. permissione divina Wy' episcopus, dilecto in Christo filio priori ecclesie cathedralis ecclesie Wyg', salutem graciam et benediccionem. Ad excercendum officium nostrum hac instanti die Mercurii in capite Quadragesime circa omnes nostre diocesis publice penitentes qui ante fores dicte ecclesie tunc se duxerint

though, that the establishment of local penitentiaries with wide powers had made the lengthy journey to and from Worcester at the penitential season less necessary than formerly.[1] Locally the priest with cure of souls had long ceased to be the only person entitled to hear the confessions of his parishioners.[2] In the fourteenth century there were many penitentiaries who were explicitly empowered to hear the confessions of all those who wished to come to them.[3] It is also probable that the distinction between special penitentiaries—those empowered to hear the confessions of the clergy only,[4] and general or common

---

presendandos [sic] prout statuunt canonice sancciones, vobis committimus vices nostras. Valete. Dat' apud Bybur' iiii Id' Februarii anno domini M⁰CCC^mo tercio, consecracionis nostre secundo." At Hereford the cathedral penitentiary was bound to reside and to exercise his office in person. He received a share of the Common Fund. See *Heref. Regs. Cantilupe*, p. 34; *Swinfield*, p. 305.

[1] Athon (p. 15 ad ver. *cathedralibus*) deprecates this development: "Credo tales confessores generales, qui vulgariter Poenitentiarii vocantur, in singularibus decanatibus vel locis aliis illius diocesis, nisi propter longam distantiam a cathedrali ecclesia, propter aliam causam perquam magnam, constitui non debere: quia per hoc detraheretur honor majoris ecclesiae".

[2] For serious offences the priest was supposed to consult the bishop or his vicar-general (Const. attributed to Walter Reynolds [see above, p. 78, n. 9], tit: "Sacerdos in Poenitentia"; *Const. Prov.*, p. 40), or other *maiores*—a word which Lyndwood elsewhere glosses (p. 329 ad ver. *majoribus*): "sc. Poenitentiariis, utputa episcopo in casibus sibi reservatis & papae etiam in casibus sibi reservatis".

[3] Both Lyndwood (for example pp. 331-2 ad ver. *vel episcopi* and p. 344 ad ver. *proprio sacerdoti*) and Athon (p. 14 ad ver. *minores clerici*) are reluctant to admit any considerable inroad upon the right of a parish priest to hear the confessions of his parishioners. Lyndwood (p. 344) poses this question: ". . . quaero nunquid parochianus alicujus possit confiteri tali fratri sive alteri privilegiato super confessionibus audiendis sine licentia proprii sacerdotis." He concludes that confession could be made to a friar admitted in accordance with the constitution "Dudum" (*Clement*. 3, 7, c.2) "quia tales fratres admissi possunt libere audire confessiones eorum qui volunt eis confiteri". But in other instances of those privileged to hear confessions the licence of the parishioner's own priest was required "nisi in eorum privilegio contineatur aliquid tale, quod talis licentiae petitionem excludat". Elsewhere (p. 330 ad ver. *non recipiantur*) Lyndwood declares that the bishop, and therefore his penitentiary too, was the *proprius sacerdos* of each one of his subjects: "cum episcopus & ejus Poenitentiarius sint proprii sacerdotes cujuslibet subditi ipsius dioeceseos [sic] & libere possit eorum uterque audire confessiones subditorum, & liberum est ipsis subditis accedere ad episcopum vel ejus poenitentiarium, etiam licentia proprii curati non obtenta".

[4] No commission of this kind is to be found in the Worcester registers. Even in Archbishop Pecham's time the making of such appointments had fallen into desuetude, and though he renewed the former ordinances he permitted the clergy, should they wish it, to confess to the common penitentiaries (*Const. Jo. Pecham*, 1281, tit: "Licet a Sanctis", *Const. Prov.*, p. 28). On the other hand, there is a mandate in *Exeter Reg. Brantyngham* (1, pp. 323-4), addressed to the Archdeacon of Cornwall, for the appointment of penitentiaries, in accordance with Canon Law, to hear the confessions of rural deans, rectors, vicars, and parish priests "salva in omnibus auctoritate penitenciarii in nostra cathedrali ecclesia generalis". The appointments were to be published in the next chapters.

13

penitentiaries, who could hear those of clergy and laity alike, had become blurred.[1] In addition there were the friars, whose activities as preachers and confessors had merely been regulated by Boniface VIII's bull "Super cathedram".[2] In 1328, at his manor of Cleeve, Bishop Orleton admitted no fewer than thirty-three friars who had been presented to him for the hearing of confessions in the diocese.[3] Licences for smaller numbers of friars or even individuals are not infrequently to be found in the Worcester registers, as in those of other dioceses.

The question of the friars' privileges merits further comment. In 1293 Archbishop Romeyn had maintained that those who made their confessions to friars were still under obligation to confess once a year to their own parish priests.[4] Likewise, in the second decade of the fourteenth century, M. J. de Polliaco S.T.D. (Jean de Pouilly) was teaching that those who confessed to licensed friars (in accordance with "Super Cathedram") had none the less to confess the same sins once more to their own parish priests. He is also said to have taught that the pope, "stante statuto OMNIS UTRIUSQUE SEXUS edito in concilio generali", could not dispense parishioners from their duty to confess "omnia peccata sua semel in anno proprio sacerdoti quem dicit esse parochialem curatum". Had this position been maintained it would have rendered nugatory the work of the friars. It was condemned in 1321 by John XXII in his bull "Vas Electionis" which sets out the "periculosos errores" which Polliaco is alleged to have taught publicly in his sermons and in the Schools.[5] A copy of the bull is entered in Orleton's register.[6]

Commissions for the appointment of penitentiaries show considerable variation. Some were issued for a stated period only; others during pleasure, good behaviour, or until revoked. The number of cases reserved to the bishop was usually, though not always, five. Occasionally any reservation at all was waived. Penitentiaries might be empowered to act in a single parish, an area exempt from archidiaconal jurisdiction,[7]

---

[1] For these distinctions see Lyndwood, pp. 341–2 ad ver. *communes poenitentiarios* and Athon, p. 15 ad ver. *generales*.

[2] Incorporated in *Clement.* 3, 7, c.2 "Dudum". See also, *Extrav. Commun.* 3, 6, c.2.

[3] Reg. Orleton 1, fo. 8v. Of these, twenty-two were Franciscans, nine from their house at Gloucester, six from Worcester, and seven from Bristol. The remainder were Carmelites; six of them from Gloucester, five from Bristol. Cf. the licences granted to fifteen friars from the houses at Winchester and Southampton by Bishop Sandale of Winchester in 1318 (*Reg. Sandale*, pp. 84–5).

[4] *Letters from Northern Regs.*, pp. 102–3.

[5] *Extrav. Commun.* 5, 3, c.2. See also Pantin, *English Church*, pp. 124–6.

[6] Reg. Orleton 1, fo. 43r.

[7] A commission of this kind was regularly granted *in forma consueta* to the *custos* of the Bibury jurisdiction.

a deanery or group of deaneries, an archdeaconry, or even throughout the diocese. Appointments might be made simultaneously or, more usually, at various times as need arose, and could be revoked in the same ways. Those appointed might be regulars or seculars: monks, friars, canons, rectors, vicars, deans—both capitular and rural—or chantry chaplains.

Though in general the appointment of penitentiaries would seem to have been a somewhat haphazard affair, on one occasion we do know that they were simultaneously appointed for most of the diocese. This was on 6 January 1337, when Bishop Montacute appointed thirteen penitentiaries at Hartlebury,[1] eight to serve in ten of the deaneries of the Gloucester archdeaconry,[2] the remainder in five deaneries of the Worcester archdeaconry.[3] A footnote explains that they were chosen or nominated[4] by the officials of the archdeacons in the presence of the diocesan official, John de Clipston,[5] "in compot[i] reddit[u] Wyg' et Glouc."—apparently a reference to the time when the accounts of the archdeaconries were presented.[6] Instances of the simultaneous appointment of penitentiaries can be traced in some other dioceses, for example Bath and Wells,[7] Exeter,[8] and Salisbury.[9]

It was not uncommon for commissions to penitentiaries to be revoked over wide areas. Orleton, for instance, appointed the prior of the Holy Sepulchre, Warwick, to exercise the office without reservation in the deaneries of Warwick and Kineton, at the same time revoking all other

1 Reg. Montacute 1, fo. 30v.; 2, fo. 21v. (duplicated). They were appointed "simpliciter cum clasula DONEC EAS DUXERIMUS REVOCANDAS, QUINQUE CASIBUS CONSUETIS EIDEM DOMINO RESERVATIS DUMTAXAT EXCEPTIS".

2 Fairford–Cirencester, Stow, Stonehouse, Dursley, Hawkesbury–Bitton, Winchcomb, Bristol, Gloucester.

3 Warwick, Pershore, [Droit]wich, Powick, Kidderminster.

4 The words "et nominati" are to be found only in the entry in volume 2 (see n. 1).

5 The appointment in each deanery of common penitentiaries, who could hear the confessions of both clerks and laymen, on the face of it rendered unnecessary Bishop Blois' injunction that two priests were to be chosen by the rural chapter to hear the confessions of the clergy. Does nomination by the archdeacons' officials indicate that they had usurped the function of the chapters? See above, pp. 69, 174, n. 7, 175–6 and, for the continued appointment (by the bishop) of special penitentiaries in Exeter diocese, p. 175, n. 4.

6 See above, p. 58, n. 5.   7 For example, Reg. Shrewsbury, pp. 493, 524, 620.

8 Bishop Brantyngham appointed penitentiaries for the deaneries of the four archdeaconries, Barnstaple, Cornwall, Exeter, and Totnes, and sent their names to the respective archdeacons with instructions to publish them in their next chapters, "proviso quod nullus ad personam alterius decanatus, vel ad casus superius exceptos, suam presumat extendere potestatem". Exeter Reg. Brant. 1, pp. 253–4, and cf. ibid., pp. 338–9, 366–8.

9 V.C.H. Wilts. 3, p. 10, n. 51 (from Salisb. Reg. Metford, fo. 133).

commissions of the kind within those deaneries.[1] In 1339 Bransford ordered the official of the Gloucester archdeacon to make it known in the archidiaconal chapters that he had rescinded all such commissions throughout the archdeaconry, and to instruct rectors, vicars, and parish priests to inhibit their parishioners from having recourse to those who were no longer empowered to absolve them.[2] In the same way Hemenhale withdrew all the commissions for the Worcester archdeaconry.[3]

Certain cases were reserved for papal consideration,[4] but a bishop was often able to grant absolution on the authority of a mandate from the papal penitentiary. Canon Law forbade a bishop to grant absolution to anyone who had seriously injured a clerk until the offender had personally presented himself as a penitent to the pope and received his mandate.[5] But there was a loophole, for the bishop could act if the penitent was in imminent danger of death.[6] John de Tyso, who had attacked Robert Janecock, a priest, and wounded him with a knife "usque ad sanguinis effusionem", was able to receive conditional absolution from Bishop Hemenhale, "iuxta formam constitucionis edite in hoc casu", by claiming that he could not reach the Holy See (on account of the hostilities with France) without manifest risk of death.[7] He was enjoined to make the journey as soon as the danger had ceased to exist.[8] Whether he ever did so we are not told.

It was usual for a diocesan to reserve certain more serious cases for his own consideration and these were excepted from his general commission.[9] At Worcester they were commonly five in number,[10] though

[1] Reg. Orleton 2, fo. 52r.: 24 October 1332.

[2] Reg. Bransford, fo. 6v. (54): 28 May 1339.

[3] Reg. Hemenhale, fo. 10r.: 10 July 1337.

[4] See Lyndwood ad ver. *solus papa* (pp. 329–30).

[5] Causa 17, Qu. 4, C. 29: "Si quis suadente diabolo." The rigour of this canon was later mitigated (*Extra* 5, 39, c.17) and the bishop permitted to absolve in cases of slight injury.

[6] ". . . et nullus episcoporum illum presumat absolvere, nisi mortis urgente periculo, donec apostolico conspectui presentetur, et eius mandatum suscipiat." *Decretum*, loc. cit.; cf. *Extra* 5, 39, c.26.

[7] ". . . petivisti quod cum propter notorium periculum maris et itinerum absque evidenti mortis periculo ad sedem apostolicam nequeas accedere hiis diebus . . ."

[8] Reg. Bransford, fo. 7v. (66). Bransford issued letters patent (21 July 1339) attesting the facts in order to safeguard Tyso's position.

[9] See the detailed glosses of Lyndwood (p. 329 ad ver. *homicidia*) and Athon (p. 15 ad ver. *confessores* and *generales*). Following the thirteenth-century canonist, Raymond de Pennefort, they both list five cases which were normally excepted: those requiring solemn penance (see Lyndwood ad ver. *solenni poenitentia* and *imponatur*, pp. 339, 340), involving excommunication, in which some irregularity had been contracted which necessitated episcopal or papal dispensation, incendiarism, and such as were by custom reserved in any particular diocese.

[10] See above, p. 177, n. 1. But a regular form of reservation clause had not been

sometimes commissions were issued without any reservation or with a clause excepting fewer than five cases. Orleton appointed the vicar of Thornbury to hear the confessions in reserved cases of all his subjects in the deanery of Dursley and its neighbourhood, to absolve them, and to enjoin suitable penance.[1] In another commission to William Foliot, prior of St. James', Bristol, for the hearing of confessions throughout the Gloucester archdeaconry, he reserved to himself, or in his absence to his vicar in spirituals, the absolution of excommunicated persons and of those whose excesses were so great that pontifical authority had to be invoked.[2] But on the same day he specifically authorized the prior to absolve the parishioners of the church of St James from any sentence of excommunication which they had incurred by withholding tithes.[3] Bishop Hemenhale issued a commission without reservation but added that if necessary the penitentiaries, at their own discretion, might send penitents to him for absolution.[4]

Licences for individuals to choose their own confessors seem to have been carefully restricted. Only nine are recorded for the ten years of Bransford's episcopate.[5] Sometimes they were granted for a limited

---

evolved and there is much variation. To quote only two such clauses from Reg. Bransford: "Corruptoribus monialium et casibus in quibus sentencia excommunicacionis incurritur ab homine vel a iure, et eciam pendentibus vel descendentibus ex iudicaria potestate, ac aliis in quibus requiritur dispensacio pontificalis exceptis" (fo. 5v. (43)): "Corruptoribus monialium, percussoribus clericorum, fractoribus parcorum suorum et casu periurii in assisis, indictamentis et exheredacionibus ubi vertitur causa sanguinis exceptis" (fo. 34v. (286)). Similar forms are to be found in registers of other dioceses, for example, Durham and Bath and Wells. "... perjurorum in curia ecclesiastica vel laicali, ubi exhaeredatio, vel grave damnum, alicujus vertitur, jura seu libertates ecclesiae nostrae Dunelmensis infringentium, frangentium dolose parcos domini, corruptorum monialium, et ipsarum corruptarum, absolutionibus nobis reservatis" (*Reg. Palat. Dunelm.* 3, p. 273: 1340 *temp.* Bishop Bury; and also ibid., pp. 279–80): "Clericorum percussores, sanctimonialium corruptores, scientes perjurii, parcorum et clausorum ad ecclesias nostras Bathonienses et Wellenses et nos pertinencium effractores, ac aliarum quarumcumque libertatum et immunitatum ecclesiasticarum violatores" (*B. & W. Reg. Shrewsb.*, p. 144: commission to the keeper of the Glastonbury jurisdiction).

1 Reg. Orleton 2, fo. 5v.

2 Reg. Orleton 2, fo. 7r.: "Absolucione excommunicatorum quorumcumpue ab homine vel a iure et aliorum quorum excessus adeo sunt graves et enormes quod super eis pontificalis auctoritas sit merito consulenda nobis vel ... vicario nostro in spiritualibus in nostra absencia specialiter reservata, quam sub hac nostra generali commissione nolumus comprehendi."

3 Ibid., fo. 8r.

4 Reg. Hemenhale, fo. 10r.: "Intencionis nostre tamen existit quod si in casibus predictis culpe gravitas vel alia causa legitima pro correccione confitencium id exposcat, ad nos iuxta discrecionem vestram huiusmodi confitentes mittantur pro absolucionibus obtinendis."

5 Among others, for Adam de Staunton, abbot of Gloucester—for two years even in reserved cases (Reg. Bransford, fo. 11r. (97); William de Syde, the chaplain of

period only—commonly two years. Frequently the confessor chosen was permitted to absolve even in reserved cases.

During his primary visitation Bishop Gainsburgh learnt that certain vicars and priests in the city and suburb of Worcester had given verbal absolution in reserved cases without his licence.[1] He instructed the dean of Worcester to inhibit the clergy from dealing with such cases, for which recourse was to be made to his penitentiaries in the cathedral church of Worcester and in the house of the Friars Minor there.[2] Gainsburgh also had occasion to demand that the Worcester prior should restrain one of his monks, John de Aston, from exceeding his powers as a penitentiary.[3] But such abuse was rare or at any rate seldom recorded.

There are other aspects of the confessional system which find no place in the Worcester registers of this time, preoccupied as they are with administrative details. The decree "Omnis utriusque sexus" gave impetus to the composition of the manuals of instruction for parish priests which form an important branch of fourteenth-century religious literature. Their forerunners were the regulations incorporated in thirteenth-century diocesan statutes and the contemporary tracts which bishops ordered their clergy to copy down and learn.[4] At Worcester Bishop Cantilupe's statutes had emphasized the close link between the obligation of confession and the priest's duty to instruct the penitent. As a practical measure he provided his clergy with a tract on confession which was to be their guide in this work.[5] We are left to wonder what provision was made by Cantilupe's fourteenth-century successors for the instruction of penitentiaries, many of whom were working in a wider field than a single parish, and with greater powers.

Thomas lord Berkeley (ibid., fo. 30v. (240)); Richard de Ledbury, archdeacon of Gloucester (ibid., fo. 139v. (946)); and to the wives of some prominent laymen: Beatrice, wife of John de Bishopesdon (ibid., fo. 6r. (50)); Katherine Sapy (ibid., 71r. (611))—for one year, her confessor being Roger de Aldryntone; and Isabella de Clare, lady of Berkeley (ibid., fo. 33v. (269)). According to the revised *G.E.C.* (2, pp. 128–9), Isabella de Clare, daughter of Gilbert de Clare, married (as his second wife) Maurice de Berkeley, second Baron Berkeley (*ob.* 1326). She is said to have been born 10 March 1263 and to have died *s.p.* in 1333. But in Bransford's register a person of this name, termed "lady of Berkeley", is mentioned in 1339 and 1340.

[1] ". . . a peccatis quorum de iure nobis absolucio reservatur verbalem impendunt absque nostra licencia speciali, et sic multorum animas dampnabiliter decipiunt quas solvere nequiunt vel ligare, in nostri iuris episcopalis preiudicium, animarum periculum, et grave scandalum plurimorum."

[2] *Reg. Gainsburgh*, fo. 2v., p. 6: 10 February 1304. The bishop was a Franciscan and the friars doubtless owed their privileged position to this fact.

[3] Ibid., fo. 2v., p. 5 (same date).   [4] Pantin, *English Church*, pp. 191 et seq.

[5] *Concilia* 1, pp. 669, 676; Cheney, *Synodalia*, pp. 42–3.

There were some interesting developments elsewhere. William de Pagula, vicar of Winkfield (Berkshire), who was acting as a penitentiary in Salisbury diocese during the 1320s, was the author not only of the "Oculus sacerdotis", which contains an important section on confession, but also of other works which show a wide knowledge of the Church's common law and of the provincial constitutions.[1] Pagula, who may have been a Doctor of Canon Law at Oxford,[2] was obviously an exceptional man, but every penitentiary ought to have aspired to some knowledge of pastoral theology and Canon Law. At Rochester the work of the penitentiaries was said (in 1346) to have been hindered by lack of books, so Bishop Hamo Hethe gave the convent a number of volumes[3] which would form the nucleus of a small reference library. The keys were to be in the possession of the sacrist and of the bishop's (cathedral) penitentiary and the books made readily available to those with cures ("curati") and to penitentiaries.[4]

CRIMINOUS CLERKS AND PURGATION

The general outline of the procedure for the securing of clerks who had been accused of crimes and consigned to secular prisons is well known,[5] but some illustrations of its workings to be found in the Worcester registers may be of interest.

Episcopal commissions *ad exigendum clericos* are numerous. They often specify the names of the royal justices and the time and place of the gaol-delivery in question. The rural dean of the place where the secular prison was situated[6] was ordinarily chosen to claim the clerks,[7] and with him might be associated one or more persons, the official of the archdeacon, the head of a local religious house, or a clerk beneficed near-by. Occasionally two deans from neighbouring deaneries were appointed.[8] A commission might be, in fact usually was, general—

[1] Pantin, *English Church*, pp. 195–202.   [2] Ibid., p. 196.

[3] Including the Decretum, Decretals, Sext., and Clementines, some glosses, and a volume of the provincial constitutions.

[4] *Reg. Roffense*, pp. 127–8: *Reg. Hamo de Hethe*, pp. 782–3.

[5] See Cheney, "The punishment of Felonous Clerks", *E.H.R.* LI, pp. 215–36; Gabel, "Benefit of Clergy in England in the Later Middle Ages"; Poole, "Outlawry as a Punishment of Criminous Clerks", *Hist. Essays in Honour of J. Tait*, pp. 239–46; Churchill 1, pp. 524 et seq.; *Pollock and Maitland* 1, pp. 439–57.

[6] Usually Worcester, Warwick, or Gloucester. In 1314 the dean of Stow was appointed to secure clerks imprisoned within the liberty of the abbey of Fécamp in Lower Slaughter. Reg. Maidstone fo. 13v: see also *Reg. Gainsburgh*, fo. 4v., p. 11. Cf. p. 65 above.

[7] There were also commissions for the claiming of clerks throughout the diocese. For example, that issued by Bransford in 1339 to the dean of Worcester and the dean of the jurisdiction of St Helen's within the city. Reg. Bransford fo. 7v. (63).

[8] For example, the deans of Winchcomb and Gloucester and the prior of Llanthony were appointed for the Gloucester gaol-delivery in 1304. *Reg. Gainsburgh*, fo. 5r., p. 12.

for the securing of all clerks, though sometimes it was particular—for the securing of certain named ones. Episcopal letters to the justices giving the names of those appointed are occasionally entered in the registers,[1] as are others requesting details of the charges preferred against clerks.[2]

Information about the recommended procedure in these matters is contained in an entry in Register Montacute deemed important enough for preservation in a later precedent book.[3] Montacute warned the deans of Kineton and Warwick, whom he had deputed to claim clerks in the county of Warwick, to take care to claim only those who ought to enjoy clerical privilege, for not all who passed themselves off as clerks had a right to it. Moreover, in the matter of privilege married clerks were to be differentiated in many ways from unmarried ones, as is expressly stated in the *Decretals* and in *Sext* concerning married clerks, and in the latter book concerning unmarried ones.[4] They were to understand that if they acted otherwise it would greatly prejudice not only themselves but the bishop as well. They were therefore to act cautiously and with diligence, having consideration for the above laws and others, from which, if they took the trouble to examine them, they could gain further information. Furthermore, when they sent clerks to his principal prison they were to write down for the guardian of the prison, or for the person to whom the clerks were delivered, their names and surnames and the causes or crimes for which they had been delivered up by the king's justices, so that if they wished to purge themselves of those crimes—and not of any future ones in evasion of his ordinary jurisdiction, as he had heard had been done at other times—they could do so. Finally, they were always to keep his mandate with them for reference.

The principal prison of the bishops was in, or attached to, their palace at Worcester. Guardians of the palace and prison were appointed

---

[1] For example, *Reg. Gainsburgh*, ff. 8v., 10r., pp. 23, 27.

[2] These seem to have been sent after the clerks had been delivered to the bishop's commissaries. See *Reg. Reynolds*, fo. 56v., p. 50.

[3] Reg. Montacute 2, fo. 2r.; Reg. Bryan 2 (so-called), fo. xliiii v. Cf. *Lond. Reg. Baldock*, p. 8.

[4] "... non omnes qui se clericos pretendunt gaudere debeant privilegio clericali quodque in huius privilegio coniugati clerici distinguendi sunt multipliciter ... a solutis sicud habetis expresse de clericis coniugatis, EXTRA; DE CLERICIS CONIU-GATIS C. UNICO LI°VI°; et de solutis in eodem libro DE SENTENCIA EX-COMMUNICACIONIS, SI IUDEX LAICUS." I.e. *Extra* 3, t. 3; *Sext* 3, 2, c.1; *Sext* 5, 11, c. 12. The bishop might also have drawn attention to "De Bigamis" (*Sext* 1, 12, c.1; Lyons II, 1274, c.16; Stat. 4 Edw. I). A bigamous clerk forfeited his right to benefit of clergy.

with a special obligation to keep the prisoners safely.[1] There the criminous clerk stayed until he escaped, died, or was able to proceed to canonical purgation.[2]

The business of purgation was usually entrusted to commissaries in a form which does not vary during our period. The persons ordinarily deputed for this task were the diocesan official, or the Worcester prior in conjunction with the official or another of the bishop's greater clerks. In 1343, for instance, Bishop Bransford appointed the prior, John of Evesham, and M. Henry de Neubold, his sequestrator, to hear and terminate all causes which had been or were to be moved—either *ex officio* or at the instance of anyone who wished to do so—against clerks indicted for felony or apprehended for any other crimes in the diocese, and delivered for judgement *in foro ecclesiastico* according to canonical sanctions; to inquire into the truth of such crimes and the reputation, character, and conversation of the clerks concerned;[3] to admit to purgation in form of law, on such days and in such places as they appointed or which had been appointed by himself, those clerks who were able to purge themselves canonically of the crimes for which they had been delivered to his prison; and to proceed with such matters and to determine what was just according to their nature and character.[4]

In addition to such general commissions others were issued for the conduct of judicial proceedings in particular cases and, though not

[1] ". . . vous maundoms et enioyngnoms que vous facietz bien et sauvement garder de nuyt et de jour nos prisons que sount en nostre prison de Wyrcestr' ensy que eux ne eschapent a graunte peril de nous, que Dieu defende . . ." (Reg. Montacute 2, fo. 2r.). John, Henry, and Nicholas de Bolehull, and Thomas Molendinarius, appointed keepers of the palace and prison by Montacute in 1334, promised to keep the prisoners safely and securely "et dominum episcopum quamdiu contigerit nos dictam custodiam possidere versus dominum regem et quoscumque alios indempnem conservare. Ad que omnia et singula bene et fideliter facienda obligamus nos et omnia bona nostra terras et tenementa ad quorumcumque manus devenerint unumquemque in solidum" (ibid. 1, fo. 5v.). There are also some episcopal mandates to the reeve of Whiston for the sending of supplies for the prisoners to the keepers. For example, Reg. Montacute 1, fo. 5r. (cf. 2, fo. 4v.): "Symond [etc.] . . . a nostre provost de Whyston. Nous vous maundoms et chargeoms que vous livrez as gardeyns de noz paleys a prison de Wyrcestr' gages pur nostre prisones illukes auxi biene pur nostre temps passe com pur nostre temps a venir en maner que home faire solait avaunt ces houres. Et voloms que cest lettre vous soit garaunt sur la counpte. . . ."

[2] Archbishop Boniface had decreed (1261) that the clerk who was an incorrigible criminal, and who under secular law would have suffered the supreme penalty, was to be permanently incarcerated. *Const. Prov.*, p. 21.

[3] There is a detailed commission for the holding of an inquiry "super fama clerici in prisona domini episcopi" in *B. & W. Reg. Shrewsb.*, pp. 470–1.

[4] Liber Albus fo. 180v. This particular commission was not entered in Bransford's register, but on fo. 11v. (101) there is an earlier one (26 November 1339) in the same form directed to his official (John de la Lowe). Cf. *Reg. Reynolds*, ff. 12r., 39r., pp. 11, 31.

invariably, for the subsequent admission to purgation of the clerks concerned.[1]

The process of purgation appears to have been set in motion by the imprisoned clerk himself, who petitioned the bishop for admission. He was not bound to do this, but the alternative, in theory if not always in fact, was lifelong imprisonment.[2] After receiving the petition, the bishop or his vicar-general ordered the dean of the locality in which the offence had taken place[3] to give notice of the intended purgation, so that all who could show reasonable cause why it should not be undertaken might appear before the bishop or his commissary in the cathedral on a stated day.[4] The keeper of the episcopal prison was instructed to produce a clerk who wished to proceed to purgation at the hour and place appointed and, should he be liberated in accordance with the law of Holy Church, to permit him to go free.[5] Whether a clerk was

---

[1] In 1305 Gainsburgh empowered M. John de Rodberrow ". . . ad audiendum omnes et singulos per pupplicas reclamaciones premunitos, si qui sint, qui Radulphum de Luttreword et Alanum Wolney clericos super quibusdam roberiis notatos et ideo captos et incarceratos, nobisque ad iudicandum in foro ecclesiastico [etc.] . . . liberatos, super premissis criminibus voluerint accusare, aut alias in forma iuris prosequi contra eos, aut si nullus talis apparuerit, ad obiciendum dictis clericis crimina huiusmodi ex officio, ipsisque et ceteris quorum interest iusticiam in uno eventu vel alio exhibendum. . . ." The next law day after the feast of St Luke (18 October) was fixed for the hearing which was to take place in the cathedral. In the following year M. John de Rodberrow and M. Benedict de Feriby, and the dean of Worcester, or any two of them, were given similar powers to deal with the case of Ralph le White, rector of Colesborne, who had been accused of the homicide of Walter de Wotton (Gainsburgh's vicar-general), of assenting to the death of William de Hembury, and of receiving Nicholas de Staunton. Their commission included the additional clause: "Necnon specialiter ad admittendum purgacionem dicti pres-biteri super criminibus pro quibus carceri nostro liberatus fuerit si de eisdem canonice purgare potuerit . . ." *Reg. Gainsburgh*, ff. 9r., 10v., pp. 25, 28.

[2] The bishop's prison was first considered to be merely a place of custody. Later its penal use was accepted as canonical. See *Sext* 5, 9, c.3.

[3] See, for instance, Cobham's letters to the deans of Gloucester and Stonehouse (*Reg. Cobham*, fo. 25v., p. 30). Stratford's constitution "Item licet" was intended to regulate this and other aspects of purgation (*Const. Prov.*, pp. 52–3).

[4] Bransford's mandate to the dean of Winchcomb about the intended purgation of two clerks who had remained in prison for three years on a charge of robbery runs as follows: "Tibi committimus et in virtute obediencie firmiter iniungendo mandamus, quatenus in singulis ecclesiis decanatus de Wy[n]ch' diebus dominicis et festivis intra missarum solempnia cum maior aderit populi multitudo publice et solempniter proclames proclamarive facias in vulgari, ut si qui [sint qui] contra purgacionem dictorum clericorum seu alterius eorundem opponere se voluerint coram nobis commissario-ve nostro in hac parte in ecclesia nostra cathedrali Wyg' ii die iuridico post festum Sancte Katerine virginis proximo futurum, quem diem pro finali eorum purgacione admittenda assignavimus in forma iuris, compareant ad proponendum et ostendendum causam racionabilem quare ad ipsorum purgacionem rite procedi non debeat in hac parte." Reg. Bransf., fo. 11v. (100).

[5] Thus Andrew Offord, Hemenhale's vicar-general, wrote "al gardeyn du paleys e de la prison de dit piere de Wircestre" in the following terms: "Pur ceo qe nous

actually admitted to final purgation depended upon the findings of the commissary appointed to deal with the case. If he was, then sentence was pronounced in accordance with the outcome of the purgation.[1] If successful he was restored to his original good fame,[2] freed from the episcopal gaol,[3] and representation was made to the secular power for the restoration of those of his goods which had been confiscated.[4]

The clerk who failed in his purgation was probably left in the episcopal gaol.[5] Bracton had taught that he ought to be deprived of his orders,[6] but it is only in the York registers that instances of degradation are to be found at this time. Professor Cheney has traced forty cases of which detailed accounts are given in the registers of Archbishops Romeyn, Corbridge, and Greenfield.[7] An earlier case (1271) in Archbishop Giffard's register belongs not to the York diocese but to that of

---

avoms done nostre commission a mestre Henr' de Neubold persone del eglise de Hethe du diocise de *Nicole* a receyvere la purgacion [de] Gilbert Prentys de BristWitz clerk solun la ley de seint eglise sicum est en nos lettres de ceo faites pluys pleynement contenuz, vous mandoms qe vous facet[z] mener le susdit Gilbert salvement devaunt le dit mestre Henr' a quele houre e qel lieu qe le dit mestre Henr' le demandera e remener en salve garde solum la ordinance du dit mestre Henr', et en cas qe le dit mestre Henr' le susdit Gilbert delivera par la ley de seynt eglise qe vous seofret le dit Gilbert franchement aler sanz destresse ou ben li serra". Reg. Hemenhale, ff. 6v.–7r.

1 Perjury was a serious offence, but compurgators could claim to have taken the oath in good faith even though the defendant were subsequently proved to be perjured. See the pertinent case of Clarence de Upcote (pp. 53–4 above).

2 Those guilty of defaming someone who had successfully proceeded to purgation were *ipso facto* excommunicate in accordance with the constitution "Item excommunicamus" of the Council of Oxford (1222). *Const. Prov.*, p. 1. For an instance of this, see Reg. Bransford fo. 8r. (72).

3 Henry de Neubold was empowered in 1337 (see above, p. 184, n. 5): "Ad cognoscendum procedendum et statuendum in negocio purgacionis Gilberti Prentys de Bristol . . . ipsiusque Gilberti purgacionem canonicam admittendum et iuxta huiusmodi purgacionem pronunciandum, eundemque, si et prout secundum comperta legitime coram eo ipsum fore liberandum compererit, sue bone fame pristine restituendum et a carcere episcopali liberandum, et omnia alia et singula statuendum exequendum et expediendum in premissis et ea qualitercumque contingentibus que in premissis et circa ea necessaria fuerint vel oportuna". Reg. Hemenhale fo. 6v.

4 See, for example, *Reg. Reynolds*, fo. 14v., p. 14. From the royal point of view this was a concession *de gracia speciali*: see Cheney, *E.H.R.* LI, p. 231. The procedure was for the bishop to inform the king of the successful purgation and to ask for appropriate instructions for livery to be sent to the sheriff concerned. For the form used, see *Carlisle Reg. Halton* 2, App., pp. 236–7.

5 It is not possible to produce any reliable Worcester statistics, but what evidence there is supports the generally accepted view (for example, Cheney, *E.H.R.* LI, p. 232 (following Gabel); *Pollock and Maitland* 1, pp. 443–4) that the majority of clerks succeeded in their purgation. Archbishop Islep in his Lambeth constitutions (1351) attempted to tighten up the whole procedure. *Const. Prov.*, pp. 54–5.

6 *De Legibus* (*R.S.*) 2, p. 298: ". . . vel in purgatione defecerit, propter quod debeat degredari."

7 *E.H.R.* LI, p. 234.

Worcester.[1] Thomas de Bisley, a subdeacon, had been convicted in the secular court[2] of stealing articles worth seven marks (£4 13s. 4d.) from Overbury church (Worcestershire). Bishop Giffard sat judicially with his brother the archbishop—"quem . . . cum canonicae cautelae studio in subsidium duximus invitandum". The accused was brought before them for examination and the article of accusation put to him verbally. He confessed, whereupon bishop and archbishop jointly declared his degradation,[3] forbidding under pain of anathema the infliction of any further penalty.[4] No similar case occurs in the Worcester registers. A possible deduction is that degradation was not regularly resorted to in the diocese and that Giffard's action was exceptional—the direct result of his brother's influence.[5]

EXCOMMUNICATION, LETTERS OF CAPTION, SANCTUARY

It is possible that sentence of excommunication, the ultimate ecclesiastical weapon, was not so indiscriminately invoked by the diocesan at this period as is sometimes supposed.[6] In the greater number of instances it was not specifically imposed by him but was incurred *ipso facto* by those who had contravened certain canons or provincial constitutions.[7] So that the people should not be ignorant of these cases

[1] *York Reg. Giffard*, pp. 242–3.

[2] For this practice see Cheney, op. cit., pp. 229–30, 236; *Pollock and Maitland* i, p. 442 (cf. Poole, "Outlawry", p. 240).

[3] The procedure for degradation was later to be regulated by Boniface VIII. See *Sext* 5, 9, c.2.

[4] The evidence for possible instances of double penalty is examined and dismissed by Cheney, op. cit., pp. 234–5; cf. *Pollock and Maitland* i, p. 455, n. 1.

[5] It may have become uncommon in the southern province. The penalty prescribed by the Lambeth Council of 1261 was perpetual imprisonment (p. 183, n. 2 above). Churchill (i, pp. 524 et seq.) gives no Canterbury examples of degradation.

[6] Remarkably few instances of its imposition are recorded during the ten years of Bransford's episcopate. Moreover, he is known to have sent only some half dozen mandates to rural deans for the threatening or pronouncement of excommunication. But it should not be assumed that the complete story is necessarily in the register. Excommunication features more prominently in Cobham's register, which also covers a decade, but perhaps even there its incidence could not be considered excessive. Miss Hill calculates that at Lincoln, between 1280 and 1299, sixty-two sentences were directed against assaulters of clergy, twenty-eight against those who seized churches by violence, thirty-two against those who otherwise infringed the rights and liberties of churches, and thirty against persons who failed to pay tithes or other dues (*Rot. & Reg. Sutton* 3, p. xlviii). Most of these must have been incurred *ipso facto*.

[7] Eleven such cases are listed in Pecham's constitution "Cum Malum" (*Const. Prov.*, pp. 23–4). Lyndwood at the end of a lengthy gloss (p. 355 ad ver. *candelis accensis*) concluded: "Et sic in toto sunt casus excommunicationum sententiae latae clxxv et amplius, praeter casus contentos in constitutionibus Othonis et Othoboni."

Archbishop Pecham had made regulations for their periodical publication.[1] There is no Worcester reference to the observance of his constitution,[2] but cases of *ipso facto* excommunication for individual offences are not uncommon.

The malefactors who on Ascension Day 1339, while the clergy and people were processing round the churchyard, sneaked into the church of Hallow and carried off a leather-bound breviary were deemed, together with their aiders and abettors, to have thereby incurred sentence of greater excommunication.[3] Similarly, those who carried off forty-nine wax candles from before the altars and statues in Ipsley church on the feast of the Purification (1344) were declared to be excommunicate by reason of a decree of the provincial council held at St Paul's in 1342.[4]

The normal procedure, once the bishop heard of some offence which merited excommunication,[5] was for a mandate to be sent to the rural dean, or the dean of jurisdiction, within whose area it had been committed.[6] He was instructed to publish the excommunication, or to have it published, at Mass on Sundays and feast days in all the churches within his province.[7] If the names of the malefactors were

[1] Reading (1279): "Cum Malum" (see p. 186, n. 7 above.).

[2] We know that publication of such *sentenciae generales* was enjoined about this time in a number of dioceses: for example, Durham, *Reg. Palat. Dunelm.* 3, p. 578; Ely, *Vetus Lib. Arch. Elien.*, p. 224, n. 27; Exeter, *Reg. Brantyngham* 1, pp. 289–91; Salisbury, *Reg. S. de Gandavo*, pp. 378–80, 412.

[3] Reg. Bransford, fo. 6r. (49). See the *Decretum*, Causa 17, Qu. 4, C. 6. But Lyndwood maintained (p. 256 ad ver. *omnibus poenis sacrilegiis*) that whereas anyone who committed sacrilege *in personam ecclesiasticam* was *excommunicatus ipso facto*, a person who committed sacrilege *in rebus ecclesiae* was only *excommunicandus*, unless the offence took place in a church and involved arson or destruction (Cf. Lyndwood, p. 258 ad ver. *excommunicati*). Excommunication was not stated to have been incurred *ipso facto* by those who pillaged the church of St. Giles, Bristol, in 1319, despite the extent of the damage (*Reg. Cobham*, fo. 38r., p. 35). But such offenders were undoubtedly *ipso facto* excommunicate by reason of Ottobon's constitution "Ad tutelam" (Athon, pp. 102 et seq.).

[4] Reg. Bransford, ff. 68v.–69r. (597). Const. John Stratford, tit. "Immoderatae temeritatis" (*Const. Prov.*, p. 45).

[5] Matters came to the bishop's notice in a variety of ways. The following have been taken at random from the Worcester registers: "Fama vehementi referente didicimus" (during visitation); "Ex relacione multorum fidedigna"; "Ex relatu plurium gravium personarum"; "Ex parte parochianorum ... nobis est gravi conquestione monstratum"; "Querelam [cuiusdam] ... recepimus"; "Ex insinuacione [cuiusdam] ... accepimus". Cf. *Rot. & Reg. Sutton* 3, p. xliii.

[6] The interval was often a short one. The candles were taken at Ipsley on 2 February; the bishop sent his mandate to the dean of Warwick from his manor at Hartlebury on the 6th. The Hallow breviary was stolen on 6 May, and the bishop's mandate to the dean of Worcester was dated 13 May from Kempsey.

[7] "... pulsatis campanis, cruce erecta, candelis quatuor cruci affixis, accensis, et in signum perdicionis eorum de cruce depositis, extinctis, et in terram proiectis." Reg. Bransford, fo. 6r. (49). This phrase regularly occurs but with slight variations.

unknown the sentence was pronounced *in genere*[1] otherwise *in specie* or *nominatim*. In the former case the rural dean was ordered to make every effort to discover the names of the offenders and their helpers and to send a list of them to the bishop or his commissary. Sometimes, in addition, he was empowered to cite them to appear before the bishop for judgement, correction, and the imposition of penance.[2]

Preliminary warning ("monitio") of excommunication had to be given,[3] except when sentence had been incurred *ipso facto*.[4] In the latter case, as soon as the names of the offenders were discovered they were cited to appear before the bishop to show cause why they should not be declared excommunicate *nominatim*.[5] Where moveables had been stolen or illegally detained it was necessary for time to be allowed for their restoration, failing which sentence would be promulgated.[6] In all

---

[1] Miss Hill commenting ("Theory and Practice of Excommunication": *History* Vol. XLII, p. 9) on the increased use of general sentences against unnamed offenders, states that such were not recognized as valid by Gratian. The new development, she suggests, was a break from primitive tradition. She distinguishes (cf. p. 186 above) between the general sentences against unknown persons who committed crimes of which the bishop remained ignorant, and the sentences (*in genere*) against unknown persons who were guilty of specified offences.

[2] In the case of those who had cut down the woods of the monastery of Alcester, the rectors of Haselor and Alcester, and the vicar of Beoley—not, it will be noted, the rural dean—were instructed to inquire: "De nominibus malefactorum, et si quos inveneritis culpabiles in hac parte citetis eosdem, seu citari faciatis peremptorie, quod compareant termino competenti per vos assignando coram nobis vel nostro commissario ubicumque tunc fuerimus in nostra diocesi super premissis audituri, facturi et recepturi quod erit iustum, necnon super certis articulis seu interrogatoriis ipsis et eorum cuilibet ex officio nostro faciendis ad forum nostrum ecclesiasticum pertinentibus et animarum suarum salutem et correccionem canonicam concernentibus personaliter responsuri et de veritate dicenda super eisdem similiter [*sic* for "simili"] modo iuraturi, penitenciamque salubrem pro eis commissis in hac parte humiliter recepturi et iuri parituri cum effectu." Reg. Bransford fo. 4r. (30): 3 April 1339.

[3] *Extra* 5, 39, c. 48. Cf. Lyndwood, p. 349 ad ver. *monitione canonica*.

[4] "Si hoc faciat pro delictis futuris non est necessaria monitio: quia tempus monet." Lyndwood, loc. cit.

[5] The dean of Warwick was instructed to discover the names of those who had taken candles from Ipsley church (see p. 187 above): "Et si quos in premissis culpabiles seu denunciacioni tue inveneris reclamantes cites seu citari facias eosdem peremptorie quod compareant coram nobis seu nostro commissario in ecclesia parochiali de Hertlebury proximo die iur[id]ico post festum Sancti Petri quod dicitur Cathedra [22 February] proximo futurum, dicti culpabiles quare in dictam excommunicacionis sentenciam incidisse nominatim minime debeant denunciari, ipsique reclamantes reclamacionis sue causas proposituri et ostensuri ulteriusque facturi et recepturi quod iusticia suadebit." Reg. Bransford, fo. 69r. (597): 6 February 1344. This was in accordance with Lyndwood's view (p. 260 ad ver. *in genere*): "In casu quo quis incurrat excommunicationem ipso facto, ante denuntiationem opus sit citatione ipsius, qui dicitur incidisse, & declaratione super ipso facto."

[6] Bishop Bransford ordered the dean of Cleeve (an exempt manor) to excommunicate those who failed to restore the goods formerly belonging to Richard le Chapman

cases it was important for the names of the excommunicated to be made public lest others should become tainted.[1]

Some general sentences of excommunication concerned offences which were outside the scope of ecclesiastical jurisdiction.[2] Mandates for the excommunication of unknown persons who had injured individual laymen were also issued, particularly in the dioceses of Lincoln and York.[3] There do not seem to be any instances in the Worcester records.

Absolution from excommunication was granted to those who sought it after taking an oath *de stando mandatis ecclesie*. In such cases absolution and the subsequent imposition of penance were reserved to the bishop or, if the offence was grave, to the pope.[4] Details of penances are seldom noted in the registers, though there are a few instances. In 1341 Bransford imposed penances on a large number of persons who had broken into his park at Penne, near Henbury in Salt Marsh, and had subsequently sought absolution from the sentence of greater excommunication.[5] Two of the malefactors were to say the Ave Maria fifty times, three were to offer their bows and an arrow on the high altar of Worcester cathedral—because they had discharged arrows in the park, while a further thirteen were to offer a wax candle of five pounds in weight on the high altar of Holy Trinity church, Bristol.[6]

---

of Cleeve, the administration of whose will had been duly committed to executors. "Quocirca tibi committimus et . . . mandamus, quatenus omnes et singulos qui bona eiusdem defuncti celant, detinent, occupant vel occultant, seu quicquam eidem defuncto tempore mortis sue debuerunt seu debeant in presenti, nisi bona huiusmodi infra xv dies tibi aut ipsius executoribus restituant ac debita huiusmodi recognoscant et de eisdem satisfaciant ut tenentur, canonica monicione premissa, in genere excommunices et eos sic excommunicatos esse per singulas ecclesias seu capellas tue iurisdiccioni subiectas . . . publice in genere denuncies seu facias denunciari." Reg. Bransf., fo. 4v. (34): 9 April 1339.

[1] As Gainsburgh expressed it: "Attendentes pium esse excommunicatorum nomina ne alios inficiant publice divulgare. . . ." (*Reg. Gainsb.*, fo. 23r., p. 77). The editor of the register has summarized this entry incorrectly. A person who had dealings with an excommunicate fell under the same sentence himself (Causa 11, Qu. 3, C. 7). Bishop Blois had laid upon the rural dean and parish priest ("capellanus") the obligation to inquire about such offenders and to report to the bishop or his official (*Concilia* I. p. 625, 1229), but of this we learn nothing in the fourteenth century.

[2] For example, murderers, robbers, and those who impugned royal justice or infringed Magna Carta. See Hill, "Theory and Practice of Excomm.", p. 9; Council of Reading (1279): "Cum Malum"; Lambeth (1281): "Temporibus eisdem" (*Const. Prov.* pp. 23–4, 30).

[3] Hill, op. cit. pp. 9–10; *Rot. & Reg. Sutton* 3, p. xlvii.   [4] See above, pp. 178 et seq.

[5] The sentence was said to have been "in eos latam per dictum patrem", though by Ottobon's constitution "Ad tutelam" (Athon, p. 105) such offenders were *ipso facto* excommunicate. For a case of excommunication by reason of "Ad tutelam" see *Winch. Reg. Wykeham* 2, p. 213.

[6] Reg. Bransford, fo. clvi r. al. 40 (1013): 26 August 1341.

If an excommunicated person remained obdurate for forty days or more, the bishop, or his vicar-general,[1] invoked the aid of the secular arm by sending a letter of caption ("littera captionis") under the episcopal great seal. A number of such letters is to be found in the Worcester registers. A writ *significavit*[2] might then be addressed to the appropriate sheriff for the apprehension of the offender and his lodgement in the secular gaol.[3] There he stayed until he showed due contrition and promised to obey the mandates of the Church.[4] Thereupon the bishop despatched a letter *pro liberacione* to the king[5] or the appropriate sheriff.[6]

The case of John Gode of Cheltenham can be used to illustrate this process. Bishop Reynolds had adjudged Juliana Scot to be Gode's wife, but he had refused to accept this decision. He was duly excommunicated and M. Benedict de Paston, Reynolds' vicar-general, sent a letter of caption to the king in July 1309.[7] A further letter was sent by the bishop himself under his great seal in January of the following year.[8] Gode was apprehended and lodged in the secular prison at Cheltenham. There he seems to have stayed for the remainder of Reynolds' episcopate. With the advent of Bishop Maidstone he became

1 Bracton (*De Legibus* 6, p. 370) states: ". . . ad mandatum episcopi vel ejus officialis capiatur excommunicatus. Sed nunquam capietur aliquis ad mandatum judicum delegatorum, vel archidiacon[orum], vel alterius judicis inferioris, quia rex in episcopos coercionem habet propter baroniam." There is no Worcester instance of the issue of such a mandate by the official.

2 The form is in Bracton, op. cit. 6, pp. 370, 372. Cf. *Carlisle Reg. Halton* 2, App. pp. 225-6, and see above, p. 10, n. 2.

3 "Secundum regni consuetudinem approbatam" (see Lyndwood, p. 351 ad ver. *dari debet*). If the writ was refused (see Bracton 6, pp. 220, 222) the bishop, according to Archbishop Boniface's constitution "Praeterea" (cf. Blois (1219): *Concilia* 1, p. 571), was to place the cities, castles etc. held by the king within the diocese under an interdict. *Const. Prov.*, p. 18.

4 If he stayed there too long he might be suspected of heresy: "Elapso anno si permanserit in sua obstinacia, potest procedi contra eum tanquam suspectum de haeresi"—Lyndwood, p. 348 ad ver. *contemnentes*; *Extra* 5, 7, c. 13. There is no evidence for this in the Worcester records even though imprisonment sometimes far exceeded one year in duration. But there is an instance (1291) in the Lincoln register of Bishop Sutton (3, p. 102): "Quas quidem sentencias non sine clavium ecclesie contemptu et suspicione heretice pravitatis hactenus parvipendet animo indurato."

5 For example, *Reg. Maidstone*, fo. 12v. A layman was involved.

6 Cobham claimed William de Mukeltone, chaplain, from the sheriff of Gloucester. The dean of Campden was instructed to receive a sufficient and suitable pledge that William would abide by the mandates and obey the sentence of the Church (*Reg. Cobham*, fo. 16r., p. 19). The whole matter of the liberation of persons imprisoned at the request of the ecclesiastical power is discussed in Lyndwood's glosses on Stratford's constitution "Saeculi Principes" (pp. 264-6). It was claimed that the lay power should not free such persons on its own initiative.

7 *Reg. Reynolds*, fo. 12r., p. 10.   8 Ibid., fo. 19v., p. 14.

penitent and was absolved from the sentence of excommunication. On 17 June 1314—almost exactly five years after the sending of the first letter of caption—the bishop wrote to the king and asked him to instruct the sheriff of Gloucester to liberate Gode from prison, so that he could give satisfaction to God and Holy Church for his offence.[1]

Two other aspects of the excommunication process should perhaps be mentioned, although they cannot be illustrated from Worcester material. It sometimes happened that an excommunicate decided to obey the Church, after the bishop had demanded a writ of caption but before it could be implemented. In such cases the bishop asked for the process to be stayed and gave instructions for the offender to be received back into the Church's fold.[2] If a person died in a state of excommunication, he could be granted absolution and his body given a Christian burial if he had shown signs of penitence.[3] Mandates for such absolution are seldom recorded in episcopal registers, but there is one, for example, in the Winchester register of Bishop Wykeham.[4]

Closely akin to the other clerical privileges already dealt with was that of sanctuary—the immunity of churches, churchyards, and religious houses from secular jurisdiction.[5] There are several instances in the Worcester registers of the violation of sanctuary,[6] although the perpetrators of such acts were *ipso facto* excommunicate.[7] If the sanctuary-seeker fled from a secular prison to a place which enjoyed immunity and was then forcibly brought back again, he had to be recovered from the secular authorities. Thomas de Powick, to take an instance from Maidstone's register, escaped from the secular prison at Worcester and took refuge in the cathedral, whence he was dragged and imprisoned again. Maidstone wrote to the king with the request

[1] LITTERA DIRECTA REGI PRO LIBERACIONE ALICUIUS PER CAPCIONEM R[EGIAM] INCARCERATI. "... Et cum sancta mater ecclesia ad se gremium claudere non debeat redeunti, idem Johannes penitens de premissis auctoritate nostra a dicta excommunicacionis sentencia absolvi meruit et absolutus existit, ac pro sic absoluto publice nunciatus, excellenciam vestram regiam humiliter requirentes, quatinus vestro vicecomiti Gloucestr' dignetur vestra regia celsitudo litteras vestras destinare ut ipsum Johannem a dicto carcere liberet seu liberari faciat, ita quod deo et ecclesie sancte de huiusmodi offensa satisfacere valeat ut tenetur." Reg. Maidstone, fo. 12v.

[2] For example, *York Reg. Wickwane*, p. 66; *Exeter Reg. Brantyngham* 1, p. 240, "Littera de non ulterius procedendo pro capcione."

[3] *Extra* 5, 39, c.28.

[4] *Winch. Reg. Wykeham* 2, pp. 69–70.

[5] The physical extent of such immunity and the persons entitled to enjoy it are discussed at some length by Lyndwood (pp. 256, 257, ad ver. *custodia* and *canones praecipiunt*).

[6] For example, *Reg. Cobham*, ff. 77v., 126r., pp. 130, 224–5.

[7] By virtue of Ottobon's constitution "Ad tutelam" (Athon, pp. 102 et seq.).

that he should order the bailiffs of the city to restore Thomas "secundum libertatem ecclesiasticam et regni consuetudinem".[1]

BENEFICES

Admission

The regular process of presentation, inquiry,[2] admission, and induction[3] to benefices is familiar and needs no further comment here.[4]

Vacancies occurred in a variety of ways which may be comprised under three main headings: death, resignation, and deprivation.[5] Bishop Blois' 1219 statutes provided that the death of an incumbent should be notified to the rural dean,[6] who in turn seems to have informed the archdeacon.[7] Ostensibly this was to make certain that the appropriate obsequies were celebrated, but it also ensured that the vacancies themselves were made known to the archdeacon, and perhaps through him to the diocesan official. But evidence for the continuance of this routine during our period has not been found.[8] In cases of death the registers suggest that the earliest intimation of vacancy was ordinarily given by a patron's letter of presentation, although the document itself is seldom recorded.[9] Resignation and deprivation involved formal processes which were in any case the bishop's concern or that of someone deputed by him.[10]

It is regularly assumed that the distinction between institution and collation was strictly observed,[11] the latter term being used of benefices in the bishop's patronage. At Worcester this was not the case. A

[1] Reg. Maidstone, fo. 4v., "Littera directa principi pro clerico extracto ab ecclesia restituendo eidem."

[2] See above, pp. 24, 55–6.

[3] See above, pp. 21–2, 57–8.

[4] Cf. Churchill 1, pp. 106 et seq.; Purvis, *Ecclesiastical Records*, pp. 16–17.

[5] Sometimes a benefice fell vacant automatically with the incumbent's institution to another. For example, in 1349 the church of St Michael, Worcester, was declared vacant: "Eo quod . . . ultimus rector eiusdem adeptus est ecclesiam parochialem de Clifford beneficium curatum incompassibilem cum dicta ecclesia." Reg. Bransford 2, fo. 16r. (1499). See below under "Plurality".

[6] See p. 65 above.   [7] *Concilia* 1, p. 570.

[8] The publication of vacancies seems to have been one of the rural dean's duties in the diocese of York, but perhaps only in response to the diocesan's mandate. *Reg Greenfield* 2, pp. 101–2, 105.

[9] But see the formal "Litterae presentationis" in *Reg. Prioratus*, p. 132b, and for example, Reg. Bransford, fo. 26v. (176). In the Liber Albus (for example, fo. clxxxxiii r.) are a number of presentations *sub forma permutacionis*.

[10] Usually the official. See above, pp. 110 et seq.

[11] Athon (p. 96 ad ver. *collatio* and *vel institutio*) distinguishes between collation by the bishop "iure proprio, vel illius cujus vice specialiter fungitur", and institution "quae sit per prelatum auctorizabiliter ad presentationem alterius".

number of instances could be cited of clerks who were "collated and instituted" to benefices of which the bishop was patron.[1]

Plurality

The requirements of Canon Law with regard to the holding in plurality of incompatible benefices were summed up at the Council of Reading (1279) in the first part of Pecham's constitution "Audistis".[2] It had been decreed by the canon "De Multa" of the Fourth Lateran Council[3] that if anyone obtained a second benefice without dispensation he was *ipso iure* deprived of the first. On the other hand, Ottobon's constitution "Christianae religionis"[4] declared void the second institution. "De Multa" was not enforced in England until Otto's legatine council, where Cantilupe opposed it,[5] and "Christianae religionis" had never been obeyed.[6] In these circumstances, Pecham, being unwilling to heap rigour upon rigour, but desiring rather to temper justice with mercy, permitted[7] the pluralist to retain only the benefice most recently acquired, unless he had papal dispensation.[8] If he attempted to keep more than one, he was to be deprived of them all. In the second part of "Audistis" it was decreed that if in future anyone were to receive more than one benefice with cure by way of institution, commend, or custody—or one by title of institution and another by that of commend or custody, except in accordance with the Gregorian constitution,[9] he was to be *ipso facto* deprived of all his benefices and under sentence of excommunication.

John XXII in his bull "Exsecrabilis" (19 November 1317)[10] went

---

1 For example, "Collacio et institucio rectoris ecclesie de Halford" (rubric): Reg. Bransford fo. 31r. (241).

2 *Const. Prov.*, pp. 22–3. The canons were copied into Giffard's register (ff. 89v.–92v.; pp. 109–10).

3 Cap. 29: *Extra* 3, 5, c.28.   4 Athon, p. 126.

5 *Chron. Maiora (R.S.)* 3, pp. 418–19.   6 Douie, *Archbishop Pecham*, pp. 98–101.

7 Lyndwood attempted to show (for example, p. 136 ad ver. *Nos misericordiam, permittimus, sit contentus*) that Pecham was acting beyond his powers and in defiance of Gregory X's decretal "Ordinarii locorum" promulgated at Lyons in 1274 (c.18: *Sext* 1, 16, c.3). But the decrees of this council were not published in England until 1279 (Reading), as contemporary chroniclers show (Douie, *Archbishop Pecham*, p. 100, n. 3). What is more, Pecham sought papal confirmation of his statutes and asked what should be done about those who claimed that they might lawfully retain a benefice by title (of institution) with another by commend because they had held both since before the Council of Lyons, which was not retrospective (*Winch. Reg. Pontissara*, pp. 201–2: wrongly ascribed to Archbishop Winchelsey). For the whole controversy see Maitland, *Canon Law*, pp. 20 et seq.; Douie, *Archbishop Pecham*, pp. 98–102.

8 Which "De Multa" had reserved for *sublimes* and *literati*. See above, p. 76, n. 2.

9 Lyons II (1274), c.14; Sext 1, 6, c.15; "Nemo deinceps".

10 *Extrav.* John XXII, t. 3, c.1; *Extrav. Commun.*, 3, 2, c.4.

much further. He ordered all those (except cardinals and kings' sons) who held benefices with cure in plurality by virtue of papal dispensation, to surrender all but one additional benefice within a month,[1] while those who held in plurality without dispensation were to surrender all but the last of their benefices.[2] A clerk who failed to do this would be *ipso iure* deprived of all his benefices and rendered unfit to hold any in the future. The bull makes no mention of *commenda* or *custodia*, and Athon contended that it applied only to benefices held by title of institution or collation.[3] In other words it remained lawful for a man to hold an additional benefice *in commendam* without dispensation.[4] Instances of this are not hard to find.[5]

By virtue of "Exsecrabilis" John XXII is said to have made not fewer than eighty provisions,[6] often of pluralists—which lends point to some contemporary assertions that his object was not so much the curtailment of plurality as the securing of a fund of patronage.[7] At Worcester the effect of the bull was not startling. In accordance with one of its clauses Cobham ordered his sequestrator, John de Broadwas, to make full inquiries about the holding of benefices in plurality.[8] Only three rectories were surrendered and Cobham was authorized to collate one of them, Cropthorne, to a clerk of his own.[9] This probably indicates

---

[1] It was understood that such benefices were to have perpetual vicars: "Ista est veritas quod papa pluralitatem omnem cassavit beneficiorum curatorum in quibus non sunt perpetui vicarii instituti ad deserviendum ecclesiis curatis" (*Carlisle Reg. Halton* 2, p. 156).

[2] This meant, as Miss Deeley pointed out ("Papal Provision", p. 503), that the lawfully dispensed pluralist could select any two of his benefices, whereas the pluralist without dispensation could keep only one—that most recently acquired. Cf. *Carlisle Reg. Halton* 2, p. 156.

[3] P. 132 ad ver. *valeant commendari*. "Dicamus ergo dictam con. Extravag. Jo. papae intelligi de beneficiis curatis in perpetuum titulum jure institutionis seu collationis obtinendis, ut ibi satis colligitur."

[4] Cf. *Extra* 1, 6, c.54.

[5] For two Worcester examples see below, pp. 198, n. 4, 199, n. 4.

[6] Deeley, p. 503; *C.P.L.* 1305–42, pp. 171 et seq.

[7] *Murimuth* (*R.S.*), pp. 28–9.

[8] *Reg. Cobham*, fo. 4r., p. 4: 4 January 1318. "... commisit et mandavit eidem Johanni de Bradewas, sequestratori suo, ut de omnibus nominibus beneficiorum cum dispensacione retentorum, retinencium et conferencium, ac eciam sine dispensacione qui plura retinent."

[9] Adam de Eglesfield surrendered Beverstone (inst. 13 May 1306 on royal presentation: *Reg. Gainsburgh*, fo. 39r., p. 151) and John XXII provided Ralph de Horncastle (*Reg. Cobham*, ff. 59r.–6ov., pp. 87–94; *Winch. Reg. Sandale*, pp. 95, 97; *C.P.L.* 1305–42, p. 172). Ralph was licensed to attend the Curia for two years (*Reg. Cobham*, fo. 9r., p. 253). Robert de Luffenham, a royal clerk, was provided to Alvechurch (*C.P.L.* 1305–42, p. 171: see also the edition of Reg. Cobham, index sub nom.). Ingelard de Warley resigned Cropthorne and Cobham collated the church to M. Nicholas de Sandwich (*C.P.L.* 1305–42, p. 180; *Lond. Reg. Newport*, p. 186; *Reg. Cobham*, fo. 11r.,

a fairly low incidence of plurality,[1] although it should be remembered that "Exsecrabilis" concerned only benefices for which papal dispensation was required—those with cure of souls and *personatus*.[2]

The actual process of provision to a benefice reserved by reason of "Exsecrabilis" can be followed in Register Cobham. The list of benefices vacated by pluralists[3] was probably despatched to the Curia sometime in January 1318. The bull for the provision of Ralph de Horncastle to Beverstone, vacated by Adam de Eglesfield,[4] is dated at Avignon 28 April 1318. It named as executors Bishop Cobham, the precentor of York,[5] and Richard de Plymstock, a canon of Lincoln. Ralph de Horncastle, who was probably already at the Curia,[6] took the bull to Plymstock who conducted the subsequent judicial process in his house at Avignon and had it attested by a notary.[7] In accordance with the recognized procedure the executor examined the details contained in the bull and inspected instruments which purported to show that Adam de Eglesfield had surrendered Beverstone and that it was therefore vacant. Satisfied with the result of the inquiry Plymstock conferred the church on Ralph, investing him with it "per birettum nostrum" and admonishing the patrons, the abbot and convent of Gloucester, as well as the parishioners of Beverstone, to admit Ralph or his proctor within six days of the presentation of the process. He appointed M. John Bloyou and M. John de Broadwas (Worcester clerks), and M. Thomas de Schulthorp as sub-executors of the bull with the obligation to carry out its provisions and his own instructions. The sub-executors, or any one of them, were to go to Gloucester Abbey and to Beverstone within three days of receiving his mandate. There they were to carry out the admission and induction of Ralph de Horncastle, who was to be allowed to retain both the formal process of

---

p. 230). The bishops of the southern province petitioned the pope for permission to fill vacant benefices in their patronage (*Lond. Reg. Newport*, pp. 182–4; *B. & W. Reg. Drokensford*, p. 15: cf. *Reg. Cobham*, fo. 67r., p. 107; *Carlisle Reg. Halton* 2, pp. 202–3).

1 Sandale's return for Winchester contained twenty-eight benefices, fifteen of which were in other dioceses—one, Beverstone, in that of Worcester (*Winch. Reg. Sandale*, pp. 94–6). For Bath and Wells diocese Bishop Drokensford certified the surrender of six benefices—one in Lincoln diocese (*B. & W. Reg. Drokensf.*, p. 15). At London Bishop Newport received resignations of nineteen benefices, fifteen—including Cropthorne, Worcestershire—in other dioceses (*Lond. Reg. Newport*, p. 186).

2 See Deeley, op. cit., p. 503.

3 The Worcester return is not registered. Other returns show a division between benefices in lay and ecclesiastical patronage. Provision seldom encroached on the former.

4 See above, p. 194, n. 9.   5 Robert de Valognes.   6 See p. 194, n. 9.

7 The document is dated 21 June 1318. John de Barneby, who in 1326 appears as Cobham's registrar (see p. 133 above), was one of the two witnesses.

provision[1] and the original papal bull. Robert de Luffenham, Ralph's proctor, brought both documents to Little Billing, by Northampton, where he read them (23 July 1318) in the presence of Bishop Cobham, to whom he handed a copy. The bishop, in so far as he legally could, admitted Ralph to Beverstone church in accordance with the papal grace. Luffenham also went to Gloucester Abbey where, in the presence of the abbot and convent, he publicly read the bull and formal process in a loud voice. He seems to have done the same at Beverstone.[2] On 1 August in the churchyard there he formally requested John de Broadwas as sub-executor to put him in possession of the church and rectory house in the name of Ralph de Horncastle. After the apostolic letters and the process of provision had been read before the church doors, Broadwas inducted Ralph in the person of his proctor, to whom he handed the keys, and admonished the parishioners to receive him as rector. The parishioners then admitted Ralph by proxy, swore obedience, and promised to pay all offerings, tithes, and other dues to him in the future. After this had been done proctor and sub-executor, followed by many parishioners, went to the rectory house where Broadwas put the proctor in possession of the rectory manor and all other rights, appurtenances, fruits, and profits. The whole process was incorporated in a public instrument at Broadwas' command.[3]

The degree of pluralism at Worcester undoubtedly varied with the predilections of individual bishops. Both Gainsburgh and Reynolds procured papal faculties for the licensing of clerks to hold an additional benefice.[4] Orleton permitted and even promoted pluralism among the clerks of his *familia*;[5] Bransford was clearly opposed to it.[6] In 1366 fourteen pluralists were returned for the diocese,[7] while ten others, though resident elsewhere, had benefices within its confines.[8] Of the fourteen resident pluralists, two were each in possession of a rectory and a poorly endowed chapel, one of a vicarage and a canonry, and most of the others combined a rectory with a single canonry. Six of them had benefices which were together taxed at more than fifty marks (£33 6s. 8d.), one had two which were rated at £4 13s. 4d. It is clear that pluralism was limited and of a moderate kind.[9]

[1] I.e. the one drawn up on Plymstock's instructions.
[2] But some phrases seem to have slipped out of the MS. account.
[3] *Reg. Cobham*, ff. 59r.–6ov., pp. 87–94.
[4] *C.P.L.* 1305–42, pp. 26, 52. See p. 78 above and p. 219 below.
[5] See pp. 95–6 above. [6] See p. 83 above.
[7] One of them, the bishop's official, had no benefice within it.
[8] *Cant. Reg. Langham*, pp. 20, 25, 27, 35–9, 45, 47, 55 (*bis*), 65 (*bis*), 92, 98.
[9] Pantin concludes (*English Church*, p. 41): "The outstanding pluralists in the 1366 returns were busy men in official positions."

Commenda[1]

Ottobon in his constitution "Miserabilis"[2] had expressly revoked all commendations of churches "nisi ex evidenti utilitate unius tantum ecclesiae commendatio facta sit" and had declared all such to be vacant. In future no church was to be conferred *in commendam* except for some just and lawful reason,[3] and no one was to hold more than one benefice by this means. This obviously left much to the discretion of the individual bishop, but the constitution "Nemo deinceps" of Gregory X[4] restricted such grants to persons of lawful age[5] who were in priest's orders. They were only to be made "evidenti necessitate vel utilitate ipsius ecclesie suadente" and were to lapse after six months. Pecham's constitution "Ut constitutio illa"[6] declared vacant all benefices held other than in accordance with the Gregorian constitution.

There was much opposition to this legislation. The laity's point of view was put by Pecham in a letter asking the pope to mitigate its force.[7] Those beneficed before the Council of Lyons claimed to be exempt from its provisions[8] and even by the fourteenth century the position of some of them had not been regularized.[9] But it was the extent of commendation which proved one of the major obstacles to the enforcement of the new regulations. This can readily be seen at Lincoln. Bishop Sutton commended over forty churches in the archdeaconry of

1 Here we are concerned only with episcopal commendation which, unlike that of the popes, observed the conciliar regulations. For papal commendation see Mollat, "La Collation des Bénéfices ecclésiastiques" (intro. to *Lettres Communes de Jean XXII*), chap. 4 "La Commende", and Hamilton Thompson, "Pluralism in the Medieval Church", *A.A.S.R.P.* XXXIII, p. 39 et seq. There is little evidence of papal commendation in the Worcester diocese at this time, but for one instance see p. 216 below.

2 Athon, p. 130 et seq.

3 "Nisi justa causa vel legitima id exposcat." Hamilton Thompson described such arrangements as "a backstairs method of obtaining pluralities without a dispensation" (op. cit., p. 46, and cf. ibid., p. 40).

4 Lyons II (1274) c.14; Sext 1, 6, c.15.

5 I.e. in their twenty-fifth year: *Sext* 1, 6, c.14 "Licet Canon".

6 Reading (1279): *Const. Prov.*, p. 23.

7 "Item cum comites barones et alii nobiles regni Anglie plures ecclesias fundaverint, dotaverint ac earum fuerint patroni, et ad eas presentaverint filios, nepotes et propinquos qui non attigerunt xxv annum et obstante constitucione Lugdunensi non valeant institui vel admitti, petit . . . istam constitucionem mitigari ne predicti nobiles a clero se retrahant et noxiis indulgeant" (*Winch. Reg. Pontissara*, pp. 201–2). Such considerations applied equally to the holding of benefices *in commendam*. For royal objections to Lyons see *Hereford Reg. Swinfield*, p. 6 (1283).

8 See above, p. 193, n. 7.

9 See, for instance, Pontissara's confirmation of a grant *in commendam* made by his predecessor, Nicholas of Ely, prior to 1274—or so it was alleged (*Winch. Reg. Pontiss.*, p. 7). Cf. *Winch. Reg. Woodlock*, p. 67.

Lincoln between 1280 and 1299, some to persons in minor orders who were later instituted on becoming subdeacons, others to men who enjoyed them until those presented came of age or secured the removal of some other canonical bar. Of those who received churches by this title comparatively few were in priest's orders, despite the law.[1]

Entries in the Worcester registers provide details of fourteenth-century practice. As Athon contended,[2] a benefice granted *in commendam* was considered to be filled and, in the normal course, it only became vacant again six months later *per lapsum commende*. Presentation, or at least the consent of the patron,[3] was necessary, and the mandate for induction was sent in the usual way. The actual grant was evidenced by the bishop's letters patent addressed to the beneficiary, concurrent letters being issued for his induction.[4] There does not seem to have been any canonical impediment to the renewal of a grant, but few examples are to be found.[5] Not infrequently the receiving of a benefice *titulo commende* was only a preliminary to institution or collation.[6]

If the list given in the edition of Giffard's register can be relied upon, only fourteen benefices were granted *in commendam* during that bishop's lengthy episcopate (1268–1302).[7] During the subsequent five years Gainsburgh provided for no fewer than ten benefices in this way, one

---

1 *Rot. & Reg. Sutton* 1, *passim*. This discrepancy between law and practice in the case of commendation contrasts with the deprivation of many benefice holders who did not take priest's orders within a year (*Sext* 1, 6, c.14). Numerous examples of subsequent representation occur (op. cit., index *s.v.* "Benefices, presentations to repeated").

2 P. 131 ad ver. *vacantes ecclesias* and p. 132 ad ver. *vacare*.

3 Thus Peter de Montfort resigned the church of Ilmington in 1320 and, as patron, consented to its assignment *in commendam* to William de Welneford (*Reg. Cobham*, fo. 20v., p. 25). Athon concedes that this was the practice in his day: "Item quaero cum consensus patroni ad hujusmodi commendam requiritur secundum omnes in dicto ca. Nemo li. 6 quod satis observant prelati, cum aliis quam presentatis per patronos commendam non committunt . . ." (p. 131 ad ver. *commendari* col. 2).

4 For the most part only memoranda are entered in the registers of which the following is an example: "COMMENDACIO ECCLESIE DE RIPPEL. Memorandum quod VI Id' Junii [8th] apud Kemeseye dictus dominus episcopus commendavit ecclesiam de Rippil, vacantem per cessionem vel resignacionem domini J. de Stanway ultimi rectoris eiusdem V Kalen' Junii [28 May] factam et ad collacionem dicti domini episcopi spectantem, magistro Waltero de Wotton archidiacono Huntingdone usque ad sex menses secundum formam ultimi concilii Lugd., et super hoc habuit litteras patentes et induccionis." *Reg. Gainsburgh*, fo. 15r., p. 42.

5 Peter de Pirton was granted the rectory of Overbury *in commendam* 29 May 1304. This was renewed on 11 November (fuit ecclesia de Overbur' commendata iterum), and Peter was finally instituted on 28 April 1305. *Reg. Gainsburgh*, ff. 7v., 27v., 36r.; pp. 20, 96, 136.

6 Later institution of the same clerk can be traced in four out of the six cases of commendation in Reg. Reynolds.

7 *Reg. Giffard* (ed. Willis Bund), App. IV, pp. cxci–ccxlv.

of them on two consecutive occasions.[1] Reynolds permitted six benefices to be held *in commendam*, and it may well be that what he had
learnt at Worcester influenced his practice in this respect at Canterbury.[2] For the ten years of Cobham's episcopate (1317–27) only two
instances of commendation are recorded.[3] A few benefices were commended by Orleton,[4] but not one by Bransford during the decade
1339–49. The canonical requirements were scrupulously observed in
most cases.[5]

If statistics were available for other dioceses they would probably
reveal a corresponding decline in the incidence of commendation
during the first half of the fourteenth century.[6] It continued as a means
whereby the bishop could confer a benefit, but the qualifications now
demanded destroyed much of its value as a stepping-stone to institution, and under the new regulations it was no longer so attractive to
pluralists, unless they were suitably dispensed.

The legal position of the holder of a benefice *in commendam* is discussed by Athon.[7] He was, we are told, more than a mere custodian,
and therefore entitled to enjoy the fruits of a benefice in the same way as
someone who had been instituted or collated, but he was not the
praelatus ecclesiae—the rector. In practice the ordinary commendatory
could be disturbed at the bishop's will, and might also be called to
account. Archbishop Giffard ordered (1275) the citation of all custodians and commendatories to render account of the fruits and other
income which they had received.[8] Revocations of grants *in commendam*
were not uncommon, and in Winchester diocese Bishop Pontissara
instructed his vicars-general (1303) to revoke all those made by himself
or by his predecessors.[9]

---

[1] Dowdeswell, Notgrove, Overbury (twice), Ripple, Salwarpe, Sapperton, Shipton
Solers, Stowell, Warwick deanery, Whittington.

[2] See Churchill 1, p. 114.

[3] Ilmington and Wotton: the latter was resigned within four months. *Reg. Cobham,*
ff. 20v., 25r.: pp. 25, 29.

[4] His letters patent commending Alvechurch, in his own collation, to Roger de
Breynton, rector of Hanbury, are given in full (7 November 1330); so too is his mandate
for Roger's induction addressed to the dean of Hanbury.

[5] For an exception during Reynolds' episcopate see above, p. 96, n. 1.

[6] But in some dioceses, notably Lincoln, there was a very much higher incidence
during the closing decades of the thirteenth century. From the appendixes to the
printed Hereford registers it appears that forty grants *in commendam* were made by
Bishop Swinfield (1283–1317), only three by Bishop Orleton (1317–27), and none by
Bishop Charlton (1327–44) or Bishop Trilleck (1344–60).

[7] P. 131 ad ver. *commendari* and *vacantes ecclesias.*

[8] *York Reg. Giffard,* p. 267.

[9] *Winch. Reg. Pontissara,* p. 154.

Custodia

Archibshop Pecham considered *custodia* to be the same as *commenda*[1] and declared that the canons regulating the latter were equally applicable to the former.[2] Lyndwood held the same view.[3] In origin, however, there were important differences which are exemplified in fourteenth-century practice. Bishops who found themselves in conflict with patrons, to whom unsuitable persons had been presented, or who for other reasons were unable to institute to churches, had been urged by Pope Alexander III (1159–81) to appoint administrators ("oeconomos") to receive their fruits and to expend them for the good of such churches or to conserve them for future rectors ("personae"). This injunction became part of the common law and seems to form the legal basis of *custodia*.[4]

Commendation and grant of custody were the same in certain respects. Presentation[5] and induction took place in both cases, but in practice, despite Pecham's declaration, it was commonly accepted that a man who held a benefice *titulo custodie* did not have to be a priest or of canonical age. An examination of many instances from different dioceses points to the conclusion that there was invariably some factor which precluded institution or commendation. But custody was not a mere alternative to commendation. It was essentially an interim arrangement and usually lasted "usque proximos ordines"[6] or for a period seldom longer than two months.[7] There was often a proviso that institution should then be procured. In the meantime canonical defects were to be remedied by dispensation, ordination, or in other lawful ways.[8] Canonically such custody was not supposed to be of financial

---

[1] "Illa quoque quae sub specie custodiae, quam summus pontifex nihil differe aestimat a commenda": cap. "Ut constitutio illa" (*Const. Prov.* p. 23; cf. p. 197 above).

[2] In particular "Nemo deinceps" (see above, p. 197, n. 4). But neither "Nemo deinceps" nor "Dudum ecclesia" (see p. 194) mention *custodia*.

[3] P. 137 ad ver. *custodiae*: "... & ista custodia idem est quod commenda."

[4] *Extra* 1, 31, c.4 "Quum vos". The decretal letter is addressed to the Archbishop of Canterbury and his suffragans.

[5] It is likely that presentation by the patron was common but not invariable. Cf. p. 198 above.

[6] At Lincoln Bishop Sutton held an ordination in 1291 "pro habentibus custodias ecclesiarum usque ad proximos ordines vel alia forma quacumque ipsos custodes ad ordinem subdiaconatus et institutionem canonicam suscipiendum artante" (*Rot. & Reg. Sutton* 3, p. 164).

[7] There was a special custody roll at Lincoln. See, for instance, *Rot. & Reg. Sutton* 2, p. 37: "Et quia dictus magister Henricus non fuit in sacris ordinibus constitutus, episcopus commisit sibi custodiam dicte ecclesie (Woodford Halse) usque ad certum tempus prout in rotulo de custodiis ecclesiarum continetur."

[8] The following entries from Reg. Gainsburgh (ff. 24v., 30r.) concerning the chapel

advantage to the presentee, for the latter had no right to receive the fruits for his own use but only "in utilitatem ecclesie". It is difficult to determine what happened in practice. Sometimes a bishop arranged for the presentee to be kept under tutelage by granting custody of both his church and person to a third party. Worcester examples of this are lacking.[1]

The incidence of custody tends to follow that of commendation.[2] In the printed Worcester registers the details are confused because the editors did not always appreciate the distinction between *custodia* and *custodia sequestri*. In some cases the editorial "custody of sequestration" is a rendering of the manuscript's *custodia*.[3] All the same, it is clear that Giffard provided for many benefices in this way and there are also a number of instances in the registers of Gainsburgh and Reynolds. None occur in those of Cobham and Bransford. The reason for this is obscure. It would be unwise to assume that it was necessarily the consequence of a stricter and more conscientious attitude on their part. It might be partly explained by the general trend towards greater stringency in the admission to benefices which stemmed from thirteenth-century legislation.[4]

---

of Bourton on the Hill and the church of Eastington will serve to illustrate the usual practice at Worcester:

"CUSTODIA CAPELLE DE BOURTON. Memorandum quod X Kalen' Decembris [22 November 1303] apud Hampton commissa fuit custodia capelle de Burton vacantis per resignacionem Roberti de Harnehull' ultimi rectoris eiusdem Simoni de Duyn clerico ad eam presentato per dominum Robertum de Harnehull militem patronum eiusdem usque ad festum Sancti Hillarii proximum [13 January 1304]. Ita quod tunc se procuret institui in eadem et interim faciat constari domino de ordinibus et conversacione et si alibi fuerit beneficiatus, alioquin extunc nichil iuris competat in eadem occasione custodie memorate. Et scriptum fuit decano de Blockele quod sub hac forma traderet sibi corporalem possessionem."

"CUSTODIA ECCLESIE DE ESTYNTON. Frater W. permissione &c. dilecto in Christo filio archidiacono Glouc' vel eius officiali, salutem graciam et benediccionem. Quoniam [?quia] custodiam ecclesie de Estynton nostre diocesis dilecto nobis in Christo Jacobo de Thyknes' clerico usque proximos ordines nostros duxerimus committendam, vobis mandamus quatinus eum dictam custodiam interim habere faciatis. Dat' apud Alvenech' [Alvechurch] VIII Id' Julii anno domini M°CCC quinto [8 July 1305]."

1 A number of grants of *custodia ecclesie et persone* (mainly thirteenth century) can be found elsewhere. At Lincoln Bishop Gravesend committed the church of Blyborough and the presentee to the custody of a nearby rector "ita quod idem ... exhibeat in grammatica et discat et moribus informet" (*Rot. Gravesend*, App. 1, p. 349). Cf. *York Reg. Giffard*, pp. 81–3; *Winch. Reg. Pontissara*, pp. 16–17; *Carlisle Reg. Halton* 1, pp. 135–6.

2 See pp. 198–9 above.

3 For example, R. A. Wilson's remarks on "Custody of Sequestration and Commendam" in his intro. to *Reg. Reynolds*, pp. xxiii–xxiv.

4 See above, pp. 197–8, 199.

Custodia sequestri

In England it was customary for bishops to retain the fruits of vacant benefices for their own use[1] and this was the primary origin of those grants of custody of sequestration which are to be found from time to time in the registers of most dioceses. We have seen that at Worcester the sequestration of vacant benefices and the collection of their fruits lay within the province of the diocesan sequestrator, and that Montacute specifically authorized his sequestrator to appoint and remove administrators and custodians of such benefices.[2] But the bishop could appoint whom he wished to receive these fruits and profits which were entirely at his disposition.[3] He did so by committing the custody of sequestration to a clerk, and directing a mandate *de sequestro liberando* to his sequestrator.[4]

The diocesan, on his own authority[5] or that of the pope,[6] could impose sequestration on a benefice as a penal measure. In 1340 Bransford did so in the case of Chedworth, held *in proprios usus* by the abbot of Lyre, on account of the *comperta* and *detecta* of his recent visitation. Its custody was committed to the chaplain of Chedworth and two other persons.[7] The penalty was often invoked against absen-

---

[1] See above, pp. 114 et seq.

[2] See p. 117 above.

[3] Bransford claimed that the custom of the Worcester diocese was: "Quod diocesanus illius loci qui pro tempore fuerit fructus et obvenciones omnes quorumcumque beneficiorum ecclesiasticorum in dicta diocesi vacancium pro tempore vacacionis ipsorum percipiat et de ipsis disponat prout secundum deum et iusticiam sibi fore videbitur disponendos . . ." Reg. Bransf. fo. 91r. al. lxxxii (749). Cf. pp. 167 et seq.

[4] Reynolds granted the *custodia sequestri* of Kempsey (7 October 1313) in the following terms: "W. permissione &c. dilecto in Christo filio Rogero de Wyngefeld presbitero, salutem graciam et benediccionem. Ne cura ecclesie de Kemeseye nostri patronatus et diocesis per mortem domini P. de Colesbourn nunc vacantis aliquatenus negligatur, custodiam sequestri dicte ecclesie de Kemeseye et omnium pertinencium ad eandem vobis tenore presencium committimus quousque de eadem aliud duxerimus ordinandum. In cuius rei &c. Dat' Lond' Non' Octobris anno domini &c. ut supra. Et habuit litteras sequestratori domini episcopi directas ad inducendum ipsum in possessionem custodie ecclesie predicte &c." (Reg. Reynolds, fo. 95v.).
The following is a memorandum of another grant of a similar kind (6 February 1311) involving Charfield church: "COMMISSIO CUSTODIE SEQUESTRI ECCLESIE DE CHARFELD. VIII° Idus Februarii ibidem [London] anno predicto commissa fuit custodia sequestri ecclesie de Charfeld Rogero Tyrel clerico per duos menses. Et habuit litteras . . . sequestratori de sequestro eidem liberando." (Reg. Reynolds, fo. 25v.)

[5] Within canonical limits, of course.

[6] In 1339 Bransford relaxed the sequestration of the fruits and profits of Tetbury vicarage imposed by his predecessor on papal authority. Mandate for their release was sent to the dean of Stonehouse. Reg. Bransf. fo. 9v. (88).

[7] "Memorandum quod primo die Julii apud Wythyndon anno supradicto [1340] dictus pater custodiam sequestri interpositi in fructibus proventibus et obvencionibus

tees. At Durham Bishop Kellawe ordered his sequestrator-general (1313) to sequestrate the fruits of all benefices with cure of souls the rectors of which were non-resident.[1]

The granting of *custodiae sequestri* was a practice which might well have lent itself to abuse, but it does not appear to have done so.[2] Technically a benefice held in this way remained vacant,[3] and if the patron failed to present a suitable clerk within six months—or four if the benefice was in lay patronage—the right to do so lapsed to the bishop. If the latter further prolonged the vacancy the archbishop as his superior was entitled to make proper provision.[4]

It is now possible to appreciate the distinction between *custodia* and *custodia sequestri*. The former was essentially a means of putting men in possession of benefices from institution to which they were debarred by Canon Law, and, strictly used, it was only a preliminary to such institution. *Custodia sequestri*, on the other hand, was an administrative convenience which sprang from the bishop's right to administer sequestrated benefices, and it had nothing whatsoever to do with the provision of a suitable clerk for subsequent institution.[5] It conveyed no title to the holder who was merely the bishop's commissary. The *custos sequestri* received for his own use, if the bishop so ordained, those

---

rectorie ecclesie de Cheddeworth, quam abbas de Lira obtinet in proprios usus, racione compertorum et detectorum in visitacione sua quam nuper excercuit ibidem, commisit domino Ricardo de Stowe capellano de Cheddeworth et Ricardo ate Stile de Cheddeworth ac Ricardo Parkar de Shyrborn [et] dedit eisdem potestatem dictos fructus colligendi et sub arto sequestri &c." Reg. Bransf., fo. 19r. (138).

[1] *Reg. Palat. Dunelm.* 1, pp. 466–7.

[2] At Worcester its incidence would seem to have been highest during Gainsburgh's episcopate when seven such grants were made. Exceptionally a benefice would be kept vacant for some time by this means. On 20 July 1304 William de Apperley resigned the deanery of Warwick. Gainsburgh granted it *in commendam* to Robert Tankard on 17 September. The day after the canonical lapse of commend—18 March 1305—the bishop granted the custody of sequestration to Tankard until 25 April. This was renewed on 30 May for the period until 8 September. Finally, Tankard was instituted by virtue of a papal dispensation on 10 July 1306—almost exactly two years after the initial vacancy. *Reg. Gainsburgh*, ff. 26r., 28v., 29r., 40v.; pp. 86, 102, 104, 163.

[3] When Adam de Eglesfield was instituted by proxy as rector of Beverstone (13 May 1306) the church was said to be vacant by the death of the last rector, though earlier, 16 March, John de Kyrkeby had been granted custody of sequestration. *Reg. Gainsburgh*, ff. 38v., 39r.; pp. 148, 151.

[4] *Extra* 3, 8, c.2 "Nulla ecclesiastica"; ibid. 3, 38, c.22 "Eam te decet"; and ibid. 3, 38, c.27 "Quum propter". Cf. Lyndwood, p. 216 ad ver. *neutri*; *Const. Prov.* p. 2 (Oxford 1222): "Cum enim secundum apostolum" and "hoc etiam merito".

[5] In some dioceses a number of benefices remained vacant for a period as the result of "Exsecrabilis" (see above, pp. 193 et seq.), which reserved them to the pope. A bishop could not fill them but he might make grants of *custodia sequestri* as Bishop Sandale did at Winchester. *Reg. Sandale*, pp. 77–9.

profits which belonged to the latter during vacancies.[1] As we have
seen,[2] the holder of a benefice *titulo custodie* had no legal right to retain
any of the profits for himself. None the less, there was a tendency for
these distinctions to be obscured in practice. Instances can be found of
a bishop's granting custody of sequestration *graciose* to a clerk whom he
enjoined to seek institution at a later date, and who had, moreover,
been presented by the patron of the benefice.[3] On other occasions the
mandate for possession was directed, not to the sequestrator, but to the
archdeacon's official.[4] But while these exceptions tend to obscure they
do not invalidate the essential differences.

Non-residence

From time to time a special attempt was made to deal with non-
residence[5] but seldom was an incumbent deprived for unlawful absence.
In 1309 Reynolds ordered his official to compel all those beneficed in
the diocese—rectors, vicars, and other clerks who were bound by law or
custom to make personal residence—to carry out their obligations. He
empowered him to dispense with some of them so that they could for
lawful reasons leave their churches for a time, without the obligation
to reside, provided that they stayed in reputable places and that
suitable provision was made for the cure of souls.[6]

Within the framework of canonical practice the amount of non-

1 For example, Bishop Sandale's grant of Kingsclere church to the archdeacon of
Winchester (James of Florence): "Concedentes vobis nichilominus et donantes
quicquid ad nos pertinet de fructibus [et proventibus dicte ec]clesie, quousque dictum
sequestrum ad nos duxerimus revocandum" (*Winch. Reg. Sandale*, p. 114).

2 Pp. 200–1 above.

3 On 27 September 1304 Gainsburgh committed to Thomas de Ciston "clerico et
tantum primam tonsuram optinenti" the custody of his sequestration ("sequestri
sui") in the church of St John, Bristol, "ad quam per abbatem et conventum de
Teuk[esbur'] extitit presentatus, usque ad proximos ordines graciose, ita quod tunc
se faciat in acolitum ordinari et institucionem etc." (Reg. Gainsburgh, fo. 26r.).

4 "COMMISSIO CUSTODIE DE DRYEMERSTONE [Dry Marston]. VII°
Kalend' Octobris anno domini supradicto [25 September 1311] London' commissa
fuit custodia sequestri ecclesie de Dryemerston vacantis per mortem domini Willelmi
de Loriaco, certis ex causis, Petro de Gylleye diacono, quousque dominus aliud super
hoc duxerit ordinandum. Et habuit litteras induccionis directas officiali archidiaconi
Glouc' vel eius locum tenenti et ad inquirendum nichilominus super defectibus
cancelli librorum ornamentorum et defectibus rectorie et ad sequestrandum bona ad
estimacionem defectuum predictorum." Reg. Reynolds, fo. 34v.

5 In the ordinary course inquiries about absenteeism were made at times of visitation. See, for instance, the twelfth of the visitation articles in *Reg. Cobham* (fo. 126r.–v.,
pp. 225–6).

6 "COMMISSIO FACTA OFFICIALI AD COMPELLENDUM BENEFICIA-
TOS FACERE RESIDENCIAM" (Reg. Reynolds fo. 3v.). See also Cobham's
"LITTERA MONITORIA QUOD BENEFICIATI RESIDEANT IN ECCLESIIS
SUIS" (*Reg. Cobham*, ff. 80v.–81r., p. 135).

residence within a diocese depended to a large extent upon the individual bishop and the use which he made of his dispensing power. But first of all it should be borne in mind that all perpetual vicars took an oath of continual residence[1] in accordance with the constitutions of Otto and Ottobon[2] and that bishops did not consider their dispensatory power to extend to such cases.[3] What they occasionally did was to grant licences in so far as they legally could, or at the vicar's peril.[4] Very few such licences were issued and there is no evidence to suggest that they promoted any noticeable absenteeism among vicars.[5]

In practice then, licences for absence were almost entirely confined to rectors, the bishop having the canonical right to dispense *ad tempus* for reasonable cause.[6] Those licences which are to be found in the Worcester registers—usually in the form of memoranda—readily fall into certain categories. Most numerous are the licences for study ("studendi", "eundi ad scolas", "insistendi in studio litterarum" etc.). Then there are many for attendance upon some prominent layman or ecclesiastic ("insistendi in obsequiis"), and a few for pilgrimages. There is a large miscellaneous category of licences for absence ("absentandi"): in these the lawful cause is sometimes given, but more often omitted. Many of those dispensed were permitted to farm their benefices while they were away. In addition there are a number of specific licences to farm ("dimittendi ad firmam").

Licences for study were governed by the provisions of the "Constitucio Novella"—"Quum ex eo"—originally promulgated at the Council of Lyons (1274) by Gregory X but republished in 1298 by Boniface VIII.[7] Bishops were thereby enabled to dispense those who were under obligation to reside in their benefices so that they could study for a period of up to seven years. Those dispensed were to be subdeacons or to proceed to that order within a year. During their

---

[1] See Athon's glosses ad ver. *ad vicariam* (p. 24) and *continue* (p. 27)—"Hoc intellige civili modo, i.e. tempore congruo: licet non quolibet instanti."

[2] *Const. Othonis*, t. 10 c. "Ad vicariam" (pp. 24 et seq.); *Const. Othoboni*, t. 9, c. "Sacrorum canonum" (pp. 95 et seq.).

[3] Athon discusses this point in his gloss ad ver. *Residentiam* (pp. 26–7).

[4] Cobham licensed the vicar of Coughton to be absent for three months (not "years" as on p. 258 of the edition of his register). "Periculo tamen suo quantum ad iuramentum de continua residencia iuxta formam constitucionis" (Reg. Cobham, fo. 27r.). Bransford granted a special licence "quantum de iure possumus" to Hugh, perpetual vicar of Henbury (near Bristol), permitting him to visit the shrine of our Lady at Walsingham, his parents, and friends (Reg. Bransford, fo. 41r. (328): 16 June 1340).

[5] This can be stated categorically of Worcester and the fourteenth-century printed registers of other dioceses give the same impression.

[6] *Sext* 1, 6, c.14 "Licet Canon".   [7] *Sext* 1, 6, c.34.

absence vicars[1] were to be appointed, the cure of souls exercised, and divine services maintained.

The practice of individual bishops varied considerably. At Worcester Bransford (1339–49) issued forty-five licences for study involving over sixty-three years—only fourteen of them for a term of more than one year, while Cobham in less than two months of his first year as bishop (1317) issued thirteen which, with one exception, were for two years.[2] Over a decade Cobham granted 155 licences involving 217 years or more.[3] Seldom was a clerk dispensed for the full term of seven years at one time, though many must have received licences for that period *seriatim*.[4]

It is not easy to interpret evidence of this kind. The number of licences to study granted by scholar bishops such as Walter de Stapledon, bishop of Exeter; Simon of Ghent, bishop of Salisbury;[5] and Thomas de Cobham, has been taken as an indication of their zeal for learning.[6] This seems unexceptionable, though Walter Reynolds, said to have been illiterate,[7] had a rather better record in this respect than Cobham.[8] Bransford, who was not a university man, granted comparatively few such licences. This was not necessarily because he lacked interest in learning, for he had secured a papal faculty to send

[1] These, of course, were stipendiary vicars ("vicarii temporales"), who should not be confused with perpetual vicars.

[2] The exception was a licence granted for one year, and it should be added that after 1317 Cobham frequently restricted the period to a single year.

[3] This figure differs from that given by Miss Edwards in "Bishops and learning in the reign of Edward II" (*C.Q.R.* CXXXVIII, p. 79) which is apparently taken from Pearce, *Thomas de Cobham*, p. 102. The latter states that there were ninety-three licences for one year, thirty-seven for two, eleven for three, and five in which no limit is mentioned. The present writer's calculation from the appendix to Cobham's register (which was edited by Pearce but published seven years after his *Thomas de Cobham*) is as follows: ninety-two for one year, forty-three for two, twelve for three, three for nine to ten months, one for one and a half years, one for five, and three for no stated period.

[4] When Reynolds permitted John de Baskerville, rector of Combe Baskerville, to be absent for two years, he took into account the licences for two and three years respectively which his predecessor, Gainsburgh, had granted, thus bringing the total to the canonical maximum of seven years. *Reg. Reynolds*, fo. 22r., p. 87.

[5] Respectively 439 in eighteen years and 308 in seventeen and a half years, according to Miss Edwards (*C.Q.R.* CXXXVIII, p. 79).

[6] Edwards, op. cit., p. 79; Pantin, *English Church*, p. 39.

[7] See p. 77 above. For some doubts as to the alleged illiteracy of certain bishops see Pantin, *English Church*, pp. 42–3.

[8] The appendix to Reg. Reynolds records the issue over five years of seventy-eight licences to study involving 146 years: thirty-eight for two years, twenty-seven for one, six for three, two for five, two for seven, two for less than one, and one for an unspecified term. Miss Edwards' statement that Reynolds granted 156 licences during this time (*C.Q.R.* CXXXVIII, p. 79) is mistaken.

two monks from the cathedral priory[1] to a university at his own cost.[2] It could have been because he had different views as to the value of men leaving their parishes for long periods.[3] It should be remembered that the easiest way to evade the more stringent laws requiring the ordination of incumbents and their residence was to petition the bishop for a licence of absence in accordance with "Quum ex eo".[4] Episcopal complaints about vagabond scholars who neglected both their studies and their benefices are not lacking at this time,[5] and even when we have discounted much that is common form,[6] the impression remains that licences of this kind could be and were abused. Rarely do we learn of a bishop's refusal to grant a licence[7] or of his withdrawal of one.[8] This is not to belittle the importance of the fact that the number of beneficed graduates increased markedly during the fourteenth century, though the proportion actually engaged in parish work rather than administration, to which the more gifted readily gravitated, has yet to be estimated.[9]

[1] Bransford had been monk and prior when the convent (of just under fifty monks) included three Oxford scholars of some note. Richard de Bromwich and Ranulph de Cathrop both proceeded to a doctorate in Theology, while John of St Germans lectured successfully at Paris. Monk-lecturers were occasionally loaned to other houses, and Bransford as prior showed some asperity in securing the return of one of them. Little & Pelster, *Oxford Theology and Theologians* (*O.H.S.* XCVI, pp. 238–46); *Chapts. of English Black Monks* 1, pp. 181–5 (*Camd. Soc.* 3rd ser. XLV); L.A. fo. lxxxiii r.

[2] *C.P.L.* 1342–62, p. 70; Reg. Bransford, fo. 105r. al. cvi (828).

[3] Cf. p. 84 above. Another possible argument, based on the bishops' attitudes to appropriation, is given below, pp. 248, 250.

[4] John Baskerville who had exhausted his seven years' quota under Reynolds (p. 206, n. 4 above) secured a further licence from Cobham to be absent during the bishop's pleasure. An average ministry lasted for some twenty-five to thirty years (see Moorman, *Church Life in England*, p. 53), so that absences of such length were a serious matter.

[5] *B. & W. Regs. Drokensford*, pp. 227–8; and *Shrewsb.*, p. 122; *York Reg. Wickwane*, p. 308; *Reg. Cobham*, ff. 80v.–81r., p. 135. In such matters it was difficult to separate the sheep from the goats ("Nos igitur malis huiusmodi obviare et agnos ab edis quatenus possumus segregare volentes": *Reg. Cobham*, loc. cit.).

[6] The form of Cobham's mandate for the enforcement of residence (only paraphrased in the printed register) is the same as that of Ralph of Shrewsbury (see above, n. 5).

[7] In the early fifteenth century Bishop Rede of Chichester would not grant one to the rector of Bury "quia se ad studium quovismodo non disposuit nec ad alium superiorem ordinem suscipiendum quatenus intelligere potui aliqualiter preparavit" (*Chich. Reg. Rede* 1, p. 50).

[8] Cobham ordered the official of the archdeacon of Worcester to admonish all rectors and others with cure of souls to return to their benefices and to reside there before the next feast of the Purification (2 February 1323), or to show reasonable cause why they should not do so. Reynolds had made a similar attempt to enforce residence in 1309. There is no evidence that any punitive measures followed. See above, p. 204.

[9] In any case, it has been aptly remarked that "the university did not perform the function of a seminary" (Pantin, *English Church*, p. 29).

15

Roughly two thirds of all the licences granted at Worcester during the episcopates of Reynolds, Cobham, and Bransford (twenty-five years in all), were for study.[1] Apart from the miscellaneous *licencie absentandi* the next largest category was of licences to attend prominent laymen or ecclesiastics. Episcopal clerks, both those of the diocesan's own *familia* and those who served other bishops, were not bound to reside, nor could royal clerks be compelled to do so. Of them something has been said elsewhere.[2] In the case of royal clerks it is likely that the formality of issuing a licence was often foregone. At any rate few were entered in the registers.[3]

At Worcester, as elsewhere, there is no means of assessing the extent to which the canonical safeguards were enforced. For the most part the scribes have been content to enter the licences in the form of memoranda, and even when they are given in full they show little variation. Some provisory clauses are found in a small proportion of them, but they vary and are never all included in one particular licence: the church was to have its proper services, the poor their alms, and hospitality was to be maintained; the cure of souls was to be adequately discharged; a competent chaplain or vicar was to be appointed, as well as a proctor who could be held responsible by the ordinaries;[4] at the end of the term of absence an account was to be given as to how the time had been spent.[5] Occasionally a clause was inserted which declared the licence inoperative if its conditions were not fulfilled.[6]

---

[1] See the table on p. 209, n. 1 below.   [2] Pp. 90–2 above.

[3] There are none in Regs. Reynolds and Bransford, only one in Reg. Cobham, though some may be concealed under the general category of *licenciae absentandi*. For attendance on bishops six are known to have been issued by Reynolds, five by Cobham, and three by Bransford. Bransford (himself a monk) was the only one of them to grant licences (six) to attend heads of religious houses.

[4] It is an interesting fact that proctors are more often mentioned than vicars. Reynolds granted a licence (25 March 1310) for two additional years' absence to the rector of Combe Baskerville (see above, p. 206, n. 4) with the proviso: "Quod durante dicto termino per bonum et sufficientem capellanum in ecclesia predicta legitime deputandum, animarum cura salubriter excerceatur, eique deserviatur laudabiliter in divinis, oneraque eidem incumbencia agnosci facias sicut decet et tenearis iuxta canonicas sancciones". Reg. Reynolds, fo. 22r.

[5] The ultimate clause of Bransford's licence for Robert de Hasele, rector of Dyrham, to leave his church so that he could assist the prior of Lewes with his business in the Court of Canterbury, runs: "Volumus insuper quod in fine dicti bienii de tua procuracione seu promocione negociorum predictorum nobis fidem facias in forma iuris, alioquin quod dicta nostra licencia pro nulla penitus habeatur". Reg. Bransford, fo. 42v. (342): 14 August 1340.

[6] Bransford licensed John de Harewell, rector of Whichford, to leave his church for one year: "Ita tamen quod eidem ecclesie per capellanum ac alios ministros ydoneos congrue deserviri, iura episcopalia et alia onera eidem incumbencia in spiritualibus et temporalibus, causisque et negociis, per procuratorem ydoneum

Any statistical analysis of licences must be treated with caution.[1] We cannot be sure what proportion of them was recorded in the registers or whether such proportion varied from one register to another. Undoubtedly bishops held divergent views about their concession, but some degree of non-residence was inevitable if scholars were to maintain themselves at the university[2] and administrators were to be free to deal with the business of the Church in a wider sphere.[3]

Exchanges

One of the most striking trends of the fourteenth century was an increase in the practice of exchanging benefices, until an arrangement which

---

continue commorantem, quem per te specialiter ab [i]nitio constitui volumus et mandamus, agnosci facias prout decet, pauperibusque parochie tue in periculo consciencie tue subvenias medio tempore iuxta vires, alioquin huiusmodi licencia nullius penitus sit momenti." Reg. Bransford fo. 86v. al. lxxxvii (706) Cf. above. p. 208, n. 5.

[1] Tentative figures for three episcopates are given below. Under "farm" are recorded the numbers of specific licences to farm, though licences under other headings sometimes included that privilege. They are combined to give the totals in the footnote. In brackets are the numbers of years known to have been involved—though occasionally no term was recorded. The figures must be taken as indicative rather than absolute. The Cobham figures are taken—with some amendments—from Appendix 2 (pp. 250–263) of Pearce's edition of his register. They differ from those given by Pearce in his *Thomas de Cobham* (p. 109), and include two licences from Reg. Maidstone (fo. 52r.–v.) issued by Cobham's vicar-general. The Reynolds' figures also differ slightly from those given by the editor of his register (intro. pp. xvi–xvii).

BISHOP	STUDY	ATTEND	ABSENCE	PILGRIM.	FARM*	TOTALS
Reynolds 1308–13	78(146)	12(11)	6(13)	—	4(10)	100(180)
Cobham 1317–27	155(217)	19(19)†	32(37)‡	2(2)	4(5)	212(280)
Bransford 1339–49	45(63)	21(24)	34(52)	1(–)	11(23)	112(162)

* The total numbers of licences to farm were respectively 9, 36, 30.

† 8 for unstated or indefinite periods.

‡ One granted by the vicar-general until the bishop's arrival, another for 3 months (see above, p. 205, n. 4).

[2] As Miss Edwards wrote (*C.Q.R.* CXXXVIII, p. 79): "If a sufficient number of learned men could not be found for the benefices, the next best method was to give the clergy opportunities for learning after institution by licences of absence for study at universities."

[3] The position of the professional administrator is plainly stated by Roger de Otery, *clericus commensalis* of Bishop Charlton of Hereford, in the 1366 return of pluralists. After describing himself as "industriosus in temporalibus et spiritualibus et potissime circa correccionem et reformacionem morum subditorum episcoporum", he goes on to claim: "Quod persona bona et industris [*sic*] et literata posset melius et sciret regere duas ecclesias vel decem quam alius unam et altari servire intelligitur tam qui residet quam qui non residet dummodo bene vivat et bene expendat quod inde percipit." This is a considered defence of plurality and non-residence, and other clerks made protestations which were similar "in materia et quasi in forma". *Cant. Reg. Langham*, pp. 44–5.

at the beginning of the century appeared reasonable had by its close become a notorious abuse.[1]

At Worcester recorded exchanges are very few during the first two decades of the century. There seems to be no transaction of this kind in Gainsburgh's register, only a single one in that of Reynolds,[2] either none or a negligible number in Register Maidstone.[3] Pearce estimated that Cobham "gave his consent to over fifty such exchanges in the course of his decade",[4] and this total was easily surpassed during Bransford's episcopate when sixty-three were negotiated.[5] In some cases churches were exchanged with a frequency that suggests abuse, but for the most part exchanges appear to have been legitimate, though seldom are we given any indication of the lawful causes which allegedly promoted them.[6] Almost invariably the institutions can be traced, so that there is little or no suggestion of the fictitious transactions—the

[1] The increase seems to have been general and to have gathered momentum from about the second decade of the century or shortly afterwards. Part may have resulted from attempts to evade the consequences of the plurality decrees—particularly "Exsecrabilis" (see above, pp. 193–5, below, p. 212). For London diocese R. C. Fowler calculated (*Reg. Sudbury* 1, intro. pp. vii-viii) that in Gravesend's register (1318–38) 22·9% of vacancies were the result of exchanges, and that by Sudbury's time (1362–75) this had risen to 45·8%. Mrs Jenkins has shown ("Lichfield Cath.", pp. 176 et seq.) that about a fifth of the Lichfield canons obtained their benefices in this way during the century, there being seven exchanges under Bishop Langton (1296–1321), sixteen under Bishop Northboro (1322–58) and twenty-four under Bishop Stretton (1360–85). At Hereford there seem to have been very few exchanges until after Orleton's episcopate (1317–27), some thirty being mentioned in the appendix to the edition of Reg. Charlton (1327–44).

[2] So far as can be judged from the printed editions which seem to be accurate in this respect.

[3] It is impossible to be precise until all the institutions have been abstracted from the register. The mere lack of commissions for exchange does not indicate that none took place.

[4] *Thomas de Cobham*, p. 92. The present writer has traced forty-five in App. 1 of the edition of Cobham's register (for which Pearce was also responsible), and a further one, authorized by the bishop's vicar-general, in Reg. Maidstone (ff. 52r.–53v.).

[5] His register provides a rare example of a commission for an exchange (between the archdeacon of Gloucester, Roger de Breynton, and the rector of Old Radnor) which was not proceeded with. Reg. Bransf., fo. 2v. (19).

[6] An exception is provided by Reg. Bransford (fo. 75v. (654)) in the certification of an inquiry into the exchange of Mamble vicarage (Herefordshire) and St Clement's, Worcester:

"Causa vero permutacionis ex parte dicti Johannis de Curdewall est, quia propter inimicicias capitales quas habet in partibus de Momele et propter metum mortis et cruciatum corporis per inimicos capitales dicto Johanni illatos ibidem secure morari non potest; causa vero permutacionis ex parte dicti Thome est hac, quia propter corrupcionem aeris in dicta civitate compleccioni sue contrarii ac eciam propter frequentem incursum vicinorum suorum de Wych' [Droitwich] ad civitatem predictam confluencium ipsum Thomam in expensis cibariorum excessive onerancium ibidem commode commorari non potest, ut dicit inquisicio."

"chop-churches"—of the later fourteenth century.[1] During the Black Death the practice almost ceased at Worcester, and possibly elsewhere too, since with so many benefices vacant it was comparatively easy to move from one to another.[2]

The administrative details are well known from published registers. If the exchange was to be of benefices lying in different dioceses or within separate jurisdictions, one of the ordinaries empowered the other to act on his behalf.[3] The form of commission in regular use at Worcester during this period is similar to that which was current in other dioceses. The preamble recites the particulars of the proposed exchange, and the inability of the bishop to deal personally with the matter "variis et arduis prepediti negociis". In the body of the commission the bishop empowers the other ordinary to hear, examine, and fully discuss the reasons for the exchange, and if he should find himself able to approve them—in accordance with the findings of an inquiry to be held by the official of the archdeacon of Worcester (or Gloucester[4]) —to admit the resignation of the incumbent of the benefice in the Worcester diocese and to institute his successor.[5] This last with reservation of the bishop's right to induct and to receive the oath of canonical obedience. Finally comes the request for a certificate detailing the whole process. Once this was in his possession the bishop issued his mandate for induction to the Worcester benefice in the usual way. If, on the other hand, both benefices lay in the Worcester diocese the procedure was simplified, for the bishop could either deal with the matter himself or issue an *ad hoc* commission to one of his officers. The whole process was regularly carried out with commendable despatch.

Once a process of this kind had been set in motion by the petition of the parties, it almost invariably continued until an exchange was effected.[6] Since both benefices became technically vacant the patrons'

1 See *English Clergy*, pp. 107–9. Archbishop Courteney's denunciation of "choppe-churches" and of non-resident clergy (5 March 1392) is printed in *Winch. Reg. Wykeham* 2, pp. 431–5.

2 Between 1 April and 6 August 1349 141 vacancies were caused by death, eighteen by resignation, twelve by the incumbents' assumption of other benefices. There is no mention of direct exchange. A very few exchanges are recorded in the R.S.V.

3 Which one seems to have depended on the initial direction of the petition by the interested parties.

4 Certification of the inquiry is often stated to have been sent under the bishop's seal. It differed in no respect from the ordinary inquiry at times of vacancy (see pp. 55–6 above).

5 Meanwhile, on his own authority he would admit the resignation of the incumbent in his jurisdiction and institute him.

6 But see above, p. 210, n. 5 for an exception.

assent had to be secured and the fact of presentation is always mentioned. No instance of a patron refusing to present, or of a bishop
either declining to carry out an exchange himself or to send his commission for this purpose to another ordinary, is known to the writer.[1]
There are certainly no instances in the Worcester registers of this
time.

The causes of the growth of exchange require investigation. Obviously
many exchanges were made for purely personal reasons—the only ones
admitted in the Worcester examples. It is possible that financial considerations may have prompted others or, in the case of clerks engaged
in episcopal administration, the desire to have a benefice within the
jurisdiction of the bishop for whom they were working.[2] It may be that
there is some connection with the more stringent plurality regulations,[3]
but of this there is little satisfactory Worcester evidence.[4] So far as the
bishops were concerned the process seems to have become largely a
formality.[5]

Papal provisions and reservations[6]

In one respect the Worcester diocese was not a profitable field for papal
provision, there being only two collegiate churches,[7] St Mary's,
Warwick, and Holy Trinity, Westbury on Trym.[8] The deanery and
six canonries of the former were in lay patronage, that of the earls of
Warwick, whose rights were not disturbed. At Westbury the deanery
and five canonries were in the gift of the bishops. Even so, the Calendar
of Papal Letters records only three bulls of provision to Westbury

---

[1] Bishop Rede of Chichester, although he sent a long letter to Archbishop Chichele
deprecating the proposed exchange by the rector of Bury, none the less sent his commission. *Chich. Reg. Rede* 1, pp. 49–52.

[2] See p. 96 above.

[3] Churchill (1, pp. 111–12) suggests this as a possible explanation of the "very
noticeable increase of admissions by way of exchange of livings" in Archbishop
Sudbury's time (1375–81).

[4] But the exchange of Hampton Bishop (collated to him in 1341) by Robert de
Chigwell seems to provide an example. In 1344 he was granted reservation of a benefice in the bishop of Worcester's gift, but with the obligation to resign Hampton. He
did so by exchanging it (on papal authority) with M. Nicholas Janini for a canonry at
Chichester (1345). Janini exchanged it the following year for Sparham (Norwich
diocese). Reg. Bransford, ff. 48v. (410), 104v. cv (823–5); *C.P.L.* 1342–62, pp. 156,
188–9. Mollat, "La Collation des Bénéfices", p. 13 (see n. 6 below), comments on
evasions of this kind.

[5] Cf. *English Clergy*, p. 108.

[6] See Barraclough, *Papal Provisions*; Mollat, "La Collation des Bénéfices ecclésiastiques à l'époque des Papes d'Avignon" (intro. to *Lettres Communes de Jean XXII*).

[7] See above, pp. 34, n. 2, 97.   [8] See pp. 27–8 above.

canonries between 1300 and 1350.[1] This is not the whole story of course. Reservations and special graces—like the one which enabled Archbishop Reynolds in 1314 to demand the next vacant Westbury prebend for his clerk, Thomas de Teffunte,[2] further reduced the bishops' right of collation.[3]

During the last decade of our period there was a sharp rise in the number of papal reservations of benefices in the gift of the Worcester bishops. Between 1300 and 1340 there were five,[4] but no fewer than eleven in the remaining ten years of the half century.[5] Over the whole period nine bulls of provision to benefices in the diocese—six of which were in episcopal collation—are recorded in the Calendar of Papal Letters.[6]

The largest category of provisory bulls was of those issued *in forma pauperum*.[7] Bulls of this type chiefly affected benefices in monastic patronage and the Worcester diocese was for its size well endowed with religious foundations. They were not entered in the ordinary papal registers, with the exception of graces granted to graduates,[8] but were often noted in episcopal ones.[9] The diocesan was regularly named as sole executor and commonly committed his powers to a single sub-executor. An unusually full record of the formal procedure in a case of this kind is recorded in the Worcester Liber Albus. Bishop Bransford, nominated sole executor for the provision of Richard Hamslap of Tanworth to a suitable benefice in the gift of the abbot and convent of St Peter, Gloucester, at the instance of the beneficiary deputed John of Evesham, the Worcester prior, to act as sub-executor.[10] A fortnight

---

1 *C.P.L.* 1305–42, pp. 148, 185; 1342–62, p. 204. It was exchange rather than provision that deprived the bishops of their free collation of the deanery. See above, p. 28, n. 7.

2 Reg. Maidstone, fo. 7r. In this case the provision was probably acceptable to the bishop, for Teffunte was said to be Maidstone's clerk as well. See above, p. 92, n. 1.

3 For Cobham's complaint on this score, see above, p. 95, n. 4.

4 *C.P.L.* 1305–42, pp. 133, 135–6, 158, 263, 390.

5 *C.P.L.* 1342–62, pp. 62, 83, 103, 105, 106, 107, 108, 118, 156, 298–9, 323.

6 *C.P.L.* 1305–42, pp. 148, 171, 185, 319, 337, 370; ibid. 1342–62, pp. 204, 217, 259.

7 "Sub forma qua pro pauperibus clericis beneficiandis sedes apostolica scribere consuevit" (Reg. Bransf. 2, fo. 14v. (1484)). See Tihon, "Les Expectatives in forma pauperum particulièrement au xive siècle" (*Bulletin de l'institut historique Belge de Rome* V, pp. 51–118).

8 Tihon, pp. 58–62.

9 Three are mentioned in Reg. Reynolds, nine in Reg. Cobham, three in Reg. Bransford, and no fewer than six on a single folio (35v.) of Reg. Orleton 1. That there were many more is suggested by the number to be found in the Liber Albus (because the prior was sub-executor) of which there is no trace in the episcopal registers.

10 London, 13 October 1342. The bishop was attending the council at St Paul's. See above, p. 83, n. 4.

later[1] the prior ordered the dean of Gloucester to cite the abbot and convent to appear before him in the cathedral,[2] and Richard Hamslap to produce witnesses as to his good character. The dean duly returned his certificate of citation. On the day appointed, Richard Hamslap appeared in person and M. William de Abergavenny on behalf of the abbot and convent. Hamslap's seven witnesses were admitted, sworn, examined, and their depositions written down. The abbey's proctor procured copies of the apostolic rescript, the bishop's commission, and the rural dean's certification of citation. The proceedings were then adjourned and a day appointed for the publication of the attestations of the witnesses, and for the raising of objections to any of the formal instruments or to the person of Richard Hamslap himself. When the case was resumed the attestations were published and a copy secured by the abbey's proctor. A further adjournment was made to allow for the preparation of objections to the attestations or to the persons of the witnesses. At the next session a testimonial letter of the Oxford chancellor was read,[3] to the effect that Hamslap had satisfactorily pursued his studies in the faculty of Civil Law between 1334 and 1342. There follows a copy of the whole provisory process drawn up as a public instrument[4] and attested by two notaries.[5] This recites the various legal documents mentioned above and the successful outcome of the inquiry into Hamslap's eligibility to hold a benefice. Consequently the sub-executor, in accordance with the bull's provisions, declared him suitable[6] to receive one of fifteen marks' value without cure or of twenty with cure. He then conferred on him any benefice lying vacant, or failing this the first that should become so, provided it came within the terms of the bull and Hamslap accepted it within a month of the notification of vacancy.[7] The abbot and convent were warned not to

[1] 26 October 1342.

[2] On the Saturday before the feast of St Martin, i.e. 9 November 1342.

[3] Dated 18 October 1342.

[4] The sub-divisions of the *processus* accord with those given by Tihon (op. cit., p. 83) from the fourteenth-century formulary of Gaucelin de Deux: the *decretum* itself, the *reservatio*, *inhibitio*, *monitiones*, and *sententie*. Notification to the collator was termed *insinuacio*.

[5] Dated 16 December 1342. The legal proceedings had taken just over five weeks.

[6] He was said to be unbeneficed and "bone vite et conversacionis honeste, habilem, liberum et legitimum, et ydoneum ad ecclesiasticum beneficium optinendum cum cura vel sine cura".

[7] Benefices were accepted conditionally. Bransford, when conferring Broadway rectory on William de Okleye, recorded his acceptance: "Cum protestacione videlicet, quod si dicta ecclesia cuiquam alteri et non tibi debeatur de iure, aut quovis alio modo sub tua gracia antedicta minime comprehendi poterit seu includi, per huiusmodi acceptacionem tuam a gracia tua predicta seu a processibus inde secutis non

promote anyone else in violation of the process, and were ordered to put Hamslap in possession within six days after the receipt of the notice of collation or provision.[1] The usual sentences were invoked against opposers. Finally, in the prior's old hall, Hamslap was required to take an oath to the prior and convent "modo et forma quibus clerici per eos ad beneficia ecclesiastica presentati a diu consueverunt iurare".[2]

Whereas episcopal commissions to execute bulls issued *in forma pauperum*, and occasionally some details of the process itself, are to be found in diocesan registers,[3] it is seldom that other provisory bulls are so much as noted there. The process of collation and induction was in the hands of the executors (commonly three in number), or in those of the sub-executors deputed by them,[4] and was carried out without regard for the ordinary diocesan organization.[5] From episcopal registers one discovers only incidentally whether a provisor obtained his benefice[6] or, in the case of reservations and expectatives, which benefice it was that he accepted.[7]

By their very nature provisions gave rise to much litigation.[8] This might be due to the resistance of the patron affected,[9] the claims of a third party, or the importunity of the provisor.[10] There is evidence that

---

intendebas aliquatenus recedere nec in aliquo preiudicare eisdem" (Reg. Bransf. 2, fo. 15r. (1484)).

[1] In Okleye's case (see p. 214, n. 7) the bishop sent notarially attested letters to him conferring the benefice and calling upon the official of the archdeacon and all rural deans, rectors, vicars, and chaplains of the Gloucester archdeaconry to put him in possession.

[2] L.A., ff. clxxxxix r.–cci r.

[3] See above, p. 213.   [4] See pp. 195–6 above.

[5] Although sometimes a mandate for induction may have been directed to the archdeacon's official or to the rural dean.

[6] For example, there is no record in Reg. Bransford of Dunclent's provision to Tredington, but we know that he obtained possession (see above, p. 95, n. 1). This fact could explain some of the gaps which are often found in lists of institutions.

[7] This would make it difficult to carry out the investigation into "the actual historical effect of papal intervention in single churches and ecclesiastical districts" recommended by Barraclough (*Papal Provisions*, p. 177).

[8] Barraclough stressed their essentially judicial character (op. cit., pp. 93 et seq.).

[9] The prior of Worcester contested the action of Robert Tankard, dean of Warwick, appointed sub-executor of a bull *in forma pauperum* by Bishop Cobham: "Qui virtute commissionis sibi facte cognoscendo processit nos gravans in multis, quamobrem appellavimus inhibitumque est eidem per curiam Cant', qui audita nostra appellacione ad curiam Romanam suos gressus direxit nullam faciens delacionem appellacioni in forma iuris, et nos dubitamus quod ipse per maliciam et fraudem velit delacionem probare in curia per aliquod instrumentum confictum et sic causam habere in curia." L.A., fo. lxxxviii r.

[10] Of one such Prior John de Wyke wrote: "Et ille provisor fervens in prosecucione et malicia ut dubitamus". L.A., fo. lxxxvii r.

"poor clerks" sometimes waited a long time for a benefice, and some of them, in return for an undertaking not to disturb further the monastery concerned, received a small pension until one should fall vacant.[1] Occasionally a provisor is recorded to have accepted a benefice of a far lower value than that expressed in his bull.[2]

False bulls were not unknown, and possession of Saintbury church (Gloucestershire) was once obtained by such means. The forged bull was the work of William de Alveston, a clerk of the diocese, who directed it to the rector of Aston Somerville, his accomplice. On the strength of this document the rector deprived Roger Drax and inducted William de Cotes in his place. Bishop Cobham, knowing of the forgery, imposed sequestration, but this was violated. Cotes was caught in the Curia and confessed to the fraud. He and the rector of Aston Somerville were condemned by the Court of Canterbury to pay £120 in compensation to Roger Drax whom Cobham reinducted.[3]

As we have seen,[4] papal provision curtailed the amount of episcopal patronage and occasionally the bishops were unable to collate a particular benefice for some years. Blockley provides an exceptional instance of this.[5] Giffard collated the church to Peter de Escot in 1294.[6] On his death at the Curia it was given to Bartholomew de Ferentino.[7] Reynolds recovered the collation in 1310 and Benedict de Paston, his official, became rector.[8] Paston was a papal chaplain, so the disposal of Blockley was reserved to the pope who, on Paston's death in 1330, granted it to M. Armand de Rozeto, a papal notary.[9] He died before obtaining possession, and M. Gerald de Pristinio was provided in the following year.[10] On the latter's consecration as bishop of Agde, Blockley was conferred in commendam on John, bishop of Porto.[11]

[1] In 1311 John de Dowdeswell surrendered his bull in exchange for a bond whereby the abbot and convent of Tewkesbury promised him a pension of 40s. until they could provide him with a benefice (Reg. Reynolds, fo. 47v., pp. 38–9). Thomas de Bristol was likewise promised two marks a year by the abbot of Evesham until the time of his provision (Reg. Cobham, fo. 15r., p. 17: 1319).

[2] John Boter, who had been granted the reservation of a benefice in the gift of Worcester Priory in 1306, accepted Knightwick three years later, although it was "longe citra taxacionem sexaginta marcarum". In fact, Knightwick chapel with Doddenham was taxed at only £4 6s. 8d. in 1291. C.P.L. 1305–42, p. 20; L.A., fo. xxxviii v.; Tax. Eccles., pp. 216, 239.

[3] C.P.L. 1305–42, p. 246; Reg. Cobham, fo. 108v., pp. 192–3.

[4] Above pp. 94 et seq., 212–13.

[5] Cf. Wood-Legh, Studies in Church Life, p. 141; V.C.H. Worcs. 3, p. 275.

[6] Reg. Giffard, fo. 382r., p. 447.

[7] C.P.L. 1198–1304, p. 559: 8 August 1295.

[8] Reg. Reynolds, fo. 24r., p. 151.   [9] C.P.L. 1305–42, p. 319.

[10] Ibid. p. 337; Reg. Orleton 2, fo. 39v.; cf. p. 23, n. 4 above.

[11] C.P.L. 1305–42, p. 370.

Orleton secured a bull in 1333 for its appropriation to the bishops' *mensa*, and this seems to have taken effect on the bishop of Porto's death in 1348, for Bransford instituted a chaplain to the vicarage "creatam de novo" in August of the following year.[1] The similar case of the Worcester archdeaconry, held by provisors between 1289 and 1320, has already been discussed.[2] But these examples are not typical. So far as can be judged, provision seldom deprived the bishops of their right for more than one consecutive turn, and several collations of all their principal benefices—save Blockley—can be traced during the half-century.

Bishop Bransford seems to have opposed certain provisions. In 1344 both he and the archdeacon of Worcester[3] are said to have refused to execute a bull in favour of John Roger of Compton.[4] The animosity of M. Thomas Dunclent towards the bishop may have had a similar origin. Dunclent, who in 1343 had been appointed proctor of the cathedral priory at the Curia,[5] seems to have taken the opportunity of pressing a claim to the episcopal rectory of Tredington.[6] He brought a suit against the bishop who was summoned to make personal appearance at Avignon. Dunclent alleged Bransford's disobedience to the Holy See, but the King wrote urgently to Clement VI on the bishop's behalf, rebutting the charge and pointing out that if he were to make the journey it might well prove fatal, for he was in poor health.[7] These events took place just at the time when Dunclent was struggling with the king's presentee for the possession of Tredington.[8] It can hardly be that the incidents are unconnected, and a likely explanation is that Bransford had opposed the provision of Dunclent.

LICENCES AND DISPENSATIONS

Many licences and dispensations, both papal and episcopal, occur in the registers. The bishop on his own authority issued numerous licences which were permissive in character, and some of these have already been discussed.[9] There were those for the hearing of Mass outside a

---

1 Ibid. p. 382; Reg. Montacute 1, fo. 11v.–12r.; Reg. Bransford 2, fo. 19v. (1564).

2 Pp. 32–4 above.

3 Robert of Worcester.   4 *C.P.L.* 1342–62, p. 136.

5 L.A., fo. clxxxix r.

6 Three years before, Philip le Yonge, the bishop's proctor at the Curia, had done much the same thing, laying claim to the vicarage of Bromsgrove in the patronage of the cathedral priory. Bransford contested his pretensions in the Curia, but the outcome is obscure. Reg. Bransf., fo. 31v. (244).

7 *Foedera* 5, pp. 438–9; Thomas, *App.* 100–1, pp. 115–16.

8 See above, p. 95, n. 1.

9 See above, pp. 204 et seq., 209 et seq.

parish church—usually in an oratory but sometimes *in aliquo loco honesto* ("habendi oratorium", "divina officia celebrandi" etc.), for choosing a confessor ("eligendi confessorem"), for the preaching and hearing of confessions by friars in accordance with the bull "Super Cathedram",[1] for absence from benefices, for receiving orders from another diocesan ("littere dimissorie"), for celebrating matrimony elsewhere than in the parish church,[2] for the holding of sessions by secular judges during Lent, or for the begging of alms in the diocese. But even this list does not exhaust the variations which are to be found.[3] In other cases the bishop granted dispensation on account of some irregularity which had already occurred. For example, when orders had been received from the bishop of another diocese without his licence,[4] or had been assumed by virtue of a fraudulent or fictitious title.[5]

Episcopal powers of dispensation were strictly limited. When it was a matter of illegitimacy, inadequate orders, or of being less than canonical age, the bishop could dispense only on the pope's authority, usually by virtue of a mandate sent by his penitentiary.[6] Sometimes a

[1] See above, pp. 176 et seq.

[2] Instances are few, though Bransford granted a licence of this kind to the rector of Elmdon (Coventry and Lichfield diocese) for the chapel of Oversley: "Bannis tamen rite et legitime premissis, dumtamen aliud canonicum non obsistat, tibi liceat matrimonium solempnizare inter Henricum de Braylesford et Beatricem le Botiler, dumtamen parochialis ecclesie in oblacionibus et aliis iuribus parochialibus conservetur indempnitas, tenore presencium licenciam concedimus specialem." Reg. Bransf., fo. 8r. (71): 1 August 1339.

[3] Montacute licensed the prior and chapter of Worcester to renovate the small building used by the stonemasons which was in the common cemetery abutting the wall of the bishop's curia (Reg. Montacute 1, fo. 29v.; 2, fo. 22r. duplicated). Bransford licensed the prioress of the hospital of St Bartholemew, Bristol, to farm the building which, at the time when the house contained both men and women ("fratres et sorores"), had been used as a dormitory (Reg. Bransf., fo. 41r. (326)).

[4] Montacute learnt *in foro confessionis* that Richard, a canon of Fordham, had at some time prior to his entering the Order of Sempringham, received the order of acolyte from the bishop of Lincoln without the licence of the then bishop of Worcester, in whose diocese he had been born. In response to Richard's petition he ratified the order and dispensed him from any irregularity "si quam contraxisti quatenus est nobis a iure permissum". Reg. Mont. 1, fo. 8r.

[5] Simon Rogers, wishing to receive Holy Orders but lacking a sufficient title, went to his aunt and fraudulently secured possession of a portion of land. He then swore before his examiners that he had a sufficient title and proceeded to the subdiaconate and diaconate "in contemptum clavium ecclesie in sic susceptis ordinibus diucius ministrando". Bishop Hemenhale, after he had absolved him and imposed penance, granted dispensation "auctoritate pontificali" with permission to advance to the priesthood on adequate title (Reg. Hemenhale, fo. 11r.). Reynolds' dispensations of this kind seem to have been initiated by mandates from the papal penitentiary (for example, *Reg. Reynolds*, ff. 36v., 48v., pp. 83–4).

[6] See the appendix entitled "Dispensations" in *Reg. Reynolds* (pp. 78–84) and App. VI (pp. 276–8) of *Reg. Cobham*.

bishop was appointed sole executor of a bull which empowered him to grant dispensation in a particular case if he found the facts were such as the petitioners had averred.[1]

Certain bishops were granted special faculties by the pope. Reynolds,[2] Maidstone,[3] and Orleton[4] were empowered to issue commissions to persons in priest's orders for the reconciliation by water, wine, and ashes of churches or churchyards which had been polluted or violated.[5] Reynolds, moreover, received "graces" which enabled him to dispense six clerks of less than canonical age to hold benefices with cure, notwithstanding the decrees of the councils of the Lateran and of Lyons,[6] and a further six to hold two benefices.[7] Several of the bishops were authorized to create one or more *tabelliones* who had to swear an oath in the prescribed form before admission.[8] Bransford secured from Clement VI the laudable privilege of sending two monks from Worcester priory to the Schools at his own expense.[9]

RELIGIOUS HOUSES

A bishop's dealings with religious houses subject to his jurisdiction were intermittent. In the ordinary course of events he was concerned

---

[1] For example, Bishop Bransford, who was empowered to dispense Hugh le Despenser and Elizabeth, daughter of William de Montacute, earl of Salisbury, for contracting matrimony although Elizabeth's former husband, Giles de Badlesmere, had been related to Hugh in the third degree of consanguinity. Reg. Bransf., fo. 48r. (404, 405).

[2] See p. 78 above.

[3] *C.P.L.* 1305–42, p. 119 (for three years).

[4] Ibid., p. 405.

[5] Maidstone commissioned Henry, vicar of Cowley (Gloucestershire): "Ad reconciliandum ecclesiam de Hardepyr' [Hartpury] et cimiterium eiusdem que per infusionem sanguinis nuper fuerant polluta seu violata, et cetera omnia et singula faciendum que ad premissa expedienda et adimplenda pertinere dinoscuntur, habitis prius aqua vino et cinere benedictis, secundum formam et effectum privilegii a sede apostolica nobis in hac parte specialiter concessi" (Reg. Maidstone fo. 37r.: 11 October 1315). Compare Reynolds' commission to the abbot of Cirencester: "Ad impendendum munus reconciliacionis in ecclesia Sancti Johannis Cirencestr' aut alias, aquam benedictam more pontificali inibi aspergendo prout loci necessitas et negocii qualitas hoc requirit, virtute dispensacionis apostolice in hac parte specialiter nobis facte" (Reg. Reynolds, fo. 28v.: 21 August 1311). Ordinarily the diocesan either carried out such reconciliations himself or asked another bishop to do so on his behalf. For example, Hemenhale's commission to the bishop of Ossory for the churchyard of Berkeley "sanguinis efusione ut dicitur iam pollutum" (Reg. Hemenhale, fo. 9r.: 12 June 1337). For the fees levied for reconciliation see above, p. 173, nn. 2, 3.

[6] See pp. 193–4 above.

[7] See p. 78 above. Churchill (1, p. 507) gives some details of graces listed in Reynolds' archiepiscopal register.

[8] See above, pp. 134 et seq.

[9] "... non obstantibus quod dicti monachi sicut alii eiusdem ecclesie monachi per priorem dicte ecclesie creantur et sub ipsius obediencia vivunt sibique habent profiteri,

with them chiefly at times of visitation and of the election of their
heads, or when they wished to appropriate a benefice.[1] Something has
already been written about visitation,[2] and here account will be given
of the bishop's part in monastic elections. Many of the illustrations will
be drawn from the numerous and exceptionally detailed entries in
Register Bransford.[3]

The cathedral priory occupied a unique position in this as in some
other respects. By a composition of 1224 between Bishop William of
Blois and the then prior and chapter it was agreed, among other
things, that when the priorate fell vacant the convent should send some
of their number to the bishop, if he was in England, with the names of
seven monks from whom he, or in his absence his deputy, was to choose
one as prior.[4] This process can often be followed in the registers though
seldom, if ever, are all the relevant documents recorded for any
particular election. First of all the subprior and convent of the widowed
priory appointed proctors to carry news of the vacancy to the bishop.[5]
With them they carried a letter sealed with the common seal of
the priory containing their own names and those of the seven monks
who had been nominated.[6] The bishop chose one of the seven or
appointed someone to do so on his behalf.[7] He then wrote to the selected

seu aliis quibuscumque statutis et consuetudinibus ecclesie et ordinis predictorum
contrariis" (Reg. Bransford, fo. 105r. al. cvi (828)). See also, *C.P.L.* 1342–62, pp. 70,
215–16.

[1] See below under "Appropriations".   [2] Above, pp. 148 et seq.

[3] In this register are to be found the elections of three priors of Worcester (Simon
le Botiler: April 1339; Simon Cromp: November 1339; John of Evesham: April
1340), and of abbots of St Augustine's Bristol (Ralph de Assch: July 1341); Pershore
(Thomas de Pirton: November 1340); Tewkesbury (Thomas de Legh: September
1347), Winchcomb (William de Sherborne: April 1340); as well as of heads of many
lesser houses.

[4] Liber Pens., ff. 50r.–51r.; MS. Vol. XII A, ff. 59v.–61v.; Reg. Giffard, ff. 44v.–45.
Printed in Thomas, *App.* 68, pp. 74–6, and in *Anglia Sacra* 1, pp. 544 et seq.

[5] A copy of this document was usually entered in the Liber Albus of the priory along
with the details of the process of election.

[6] The process was termed *nominatio* instead of *electio* and the chosen seven were
nominati and not *electi*. Otherwise the usual election procedure was followed. In 1317
the monks acted *per viam compromissi* and delegated their powers to seven *nominatores*
who chose the seven whose names were sent to Cobham (Liber Ruber, fo. cxxxix;
Liber Albus. fo. lxxxiii). The account given by Wilson in his *Worcester Liber Albus*
(pp. 162–6) is inaccurate in some respects. Gilbert de Madeley, the subprior, was not
chosen as one of the *nominatores*, nor does the Liber Albus tell us that he was. The
"Roger de Neuwyntone" whom he lists among the final seven should be "Roger de
Stevinton".

[7] In 1317 Cobham appointed James de Cobham, who had been acting as his
vicar-general, to admit the nomination of the seven and to choose one as prior. His
choice fell on Wolstan de Bransford, the future bishop. See n. 6 above and *Reg. Cobham*,
fo. 1r., p. 1.

candidate informing him of his appointment, to the subprior and convent ordering them to be obedient and intendant to their new head, and to the official of the archdeacon of Worcester with instructions to carry out the prior's induction and installation.[1]

The system worked well in practice. There were five elections during the first half of the fourteenth century[2] and only in the first of them was there any sign of disagreement. Against John de Wyke, whom Giffard had chosen prior in July 1301, a charge of unlawful entry was preferred by some of the monks at the time of Gainsburgh's primary visitation. Special commissaries of the bishop pronounced in the prior's favour.[3]

Generally speaking the bishop took no part in the election of the heads of other religious houses, though his officers might be invited to attend the proceedings as witnesses.[4] But he had the right to confirm or quash such elections, and in the latter event to appoint someone of his own choosing. In practice, if a bishop quashed an election as uncanonical[5] he appointed the same person who had been chosen originally.[6]

---

[1] It would seem that Bransford personally inducted and installed Simon le Botiler, for in his mandate to the subprior and convent he uses the phrase: "Cum ... ipsumque in corporalem possessionem dicti prioratus cum omnibus iuribus et pertinenciis presencialiter induxerimus et installaverimus iuxta laudabilem consuetudinem dicte ecclesie ab olim pacifice obtentam et legitime prescriptam." Reg. Bransf., fo. 5v. (40).

[2] John de Wyke (1301), Wolstan de Bransford (1317). For the others see above, p. 220, n. 3.

[3] *Reg. Giffard*, fo. 468v., p. 547; *Reg. Gainsburgh*, fo. iv., p. 3.

[4] During the election at Tewkesbury in 1347 a number of secular clerks were present including Bransford's official, John de la Lowe. After the reading of the constitution "Quia propter" (Extra 1, 6, c.42) it is recorded that: "Predicti prior et ceteri monachi rogabant seculares personas, videlicet magistros Johannem de la Lowe iuris civilis professorem rectorem ecclesie de Breodon', Stephanum de Northeye rectorem ecclesie de Fayrford, et Willelmum de Assheton rectorem ecclesie de Atheriston, et Stephanum de Northeye clericum iuniorem, dicte Wygorn' diocesis tunc in eadem domo capitulari presentes, quod placeret eis interesse toti processui eleccionis per ipsos tunc ibidem faciende tanquam testes, protestantes quod non intendebant quod predicti magistri Johannes, Stephanus, Willelmus et Stephanus interesse debebant tanquam ius in eleccione eadem obtinentes" (Reg. Bransford, fo. 133r. (941)). John de la Lowe gave advice and guidance at each stage of the proceedings. This may have been because Bransford had quashed elections at two other Benedictine houses, Winchcomb and Pershore.

[5] Regulations for the conduct of elections had been drawn up at the Fourth Lateran Council—in particular the constitution "Quia Propter" (c.24: *Extra* 1, 6, c.42) which was always read out before the proceedings began.

[6] Bransford quashed the election of William de Sherborne as abbot of Winchcomb (fo. 36r. (297)), the double election of Robert de Littleton and Thomas de Pirton at Pershore (fo. 44r. (366))—where he appointed the latter, and of the abbess of the Cistercian nunnery at Cook Hill (Vol. 2, fo. 12r. (1434)). His commissary quashed the election at the Augustinian house at Studley in 1349 (Vol. 2, fo. 16r. (1504)). In each

Once an election had been made it was formally proclaimed to the clergy and people ("proclamacio eleccionis"). Meanwhile, the consent of the elected party was sought and, after a proper show of reluctance, duly obtained. A petition for confirmation of the election was then sent to the bishop, together with full details of the procedure which had been followed embodied in a public instrument ("decretum eleccionis"). With the petition were sent other documents in the form of "articles" which had to be proved at a later stage by the monastery's proctor before the bishop or his commissaries.[1] On receiving them the bishop despatched his mandate, usually to the rural dean or archdeacon's official, for the citation of any coelected persons or other opponents of the election to appear before him or his commissaries. The citation was commonly made *ad hostium cancelli deinde ad valvas ecclesie* and a certificate sent to the bishop in the usual way. On the appointed day the bishop proceeded to examine the election either in person or by deputy,[2] and to confirm or quash it *de iuris peritorum . . . assidencium consilio*. If he quashed it, he thereby deprived the electors of their rights for that occasion. If it was confirmed, the elect received the episcopal benediction and took an oath of canonical subjection and obedience.[3] The bishop directed one mandate, ordinarily to the arch-

---

case the person uncanonically elected was subsequently appointed. Hamilton Thompson found a similar state of affairs at Lincoln (*Rot. Gravesend*, intro. p. xxxi): "Usually the election was annulled *propter vitium formae, non propter defectum personae*, and the bishop proceeded to provide the elected person on his own responsibility." The same course was followed by Bishop Sutton (1280–99). See *Rot. & Reg. Sutton* 1, pp. xxiv–xxvi.

[1] For the Tewkesbury election of 1347 there are two lengthy series of articles. The rubric preceding the second runs: "Isti articuli infrascripti post examinacionem articulorum suprascriptorum in presenti eleccione fuerant ut asseritur exhibiti." Reg. Bransford, ff. 136r.–137v. (942, 943).

[2] John de Severleye, archdeacon of Worcester and Bransford's chancellor, dealt with the whole process of the election at Studley in 1349. Reg. Bransford 2, fo. 16r. (1504).

[3] The newly elected abbot of St Peter's, Gloucester, John Toky, took the following oath in 1306: "Ego Johannes Toky ecclesie Sancti Petri Glouc' electus abbas profiteor ecclesie cathedrali Wygorn' tibique patri Willelmo Wygorn' episcopo et successoribus tuis canonice int[ra]ntibus fidem reverenciam canonicam subieccionem et obedienciam promitto et hoc propria manu subscribo" (*Reg. Gainsburgh*, fo. 39r., p. 151). John of Gloucester, abbot of Hailes, a Cistercian house and so exempt from the bishop's ordinary jurisdiction (see p. 30 above), took a slightly different oath in 1305: "Ego frater J. abbas de Hayles subieccionem reverenciam et obedienciam a sanctis patribus constitutas secundum regulam Sancti Benedicti tibi domine pater W[illelme] episcope tuisque successoribus canonice substituendis et sancte sedi Wygorn' salvo ordine nostro perpetuo me exhibiturum promitto" (ibid., fo. 30r., p. 114). This must have been the general form of oath in use among the Cistercian houses, for it is *mutatis mutandis* the same as that taken by the abbot of Meaux to Archbishop Wickwane in 1280 (*York Reg. Wickw.*, p. 98).

deacon's official, for the induction and installation of the new head, and another, enjoining obedience, to the convent concerned.

In some cases letters from monastic patrons are recorded in the registers. These contain the patron's permission to hold an election, his approval of one,[1] or his presentation of the elect to the diocesan.[2] There is no evidence that they were more than a formality at this time.[3] Occasionally episcopal letters informing the king of an election and requesting restoration of the temporalities were also registered.[4] It was in response to them that the king issued his signification of assent to the election, his mandate for the restoration of the temporalities, and a writ *de intendendo*, all of which were entered on the patent rolls.

It was not unknown for some of the lesser houses, particularly nunneries, to delegate their rights of election to the bishop. Thus at Wroxall, a Benedictine nunnery, Bransford appointed Isabella de Fokerham as prioress "virtute specialis concessionis religiosarum mulierum . . . nobis in hac parte facte".[5] The bishop by letters patent declared that the concession would not redound to their prejudice in the future.[6] This may have been an easy way out of a difficulty, for at nunneries elections were often quashed because of ignorance of canonical procedure.[7]

To the alien priories of Astley, Deerhurst, and Wootton Wawen[8] the abbot of the respective mother house presented a suitable monk for admission and institution by the bishop, who then issued the usual mandate for induction. At Astley, where a vicarage had been ordained,

1 See, for instance, the *littera patroni* ("de consensu") and the *littera patroni super licencia eligendi* recorded among the entries about the Tewkesbury election. Hugh le Despenser, son of Hugh le Despenser the younger, was the patron. Reg. Bransf., ff. 128r. al. cxxix, 129r. (928, 932).

2 For example, in 1346 Maurice de Berkeley presented John de Stokeland, who had been elected master of the hospital of St Mark (Gaunt's) at Billeswick, near Bristol, for Bishop Bransford's confirmation. Reg. Bransf., fo. 98v. al. lxxxxix (784).

3 Of thirteenth-century elections Mrs Wood writes (*English Mons. and their Patrons*, p. 41): "The patron's rights became stereotyped: they were usually the right to be informed of a vacancy, and to give licence to elect; to have the elect presented to him to assent to the election, and to present him to the bishop for confirmation." See also op. cit., chap. IV "Elections" and index s.v.

4 For custody during vacancies see Wood, op. cit., chap. V.

5 Reg. Bransford, fo. 34r. (279, 280).   6 Ibid. (281).

7 Hamilton Thompson remarked that this often happened in small nunneries "where technical knowledge was insufficient and such advice as a chaplain could give was probably inexpert". He quotes four instances from Gravesend's Lincoln register (ibid., intro. pp. xxx–xxxi).

8 Dependent respectively on the Benedictine abbeys of St Taurin, Evreux; St Denis, Paris; and Conches, in Normandy.

the incoming prior swore to pay the portions due to the vicar.[1] The procedure at Deerhurst, a *prioratus curatus*, was governed by a composition of 1269 agreed between the then abbot of St Denis and Bishop Giffard.[2] By this the bishop admitted and instituted the monk presented "non racione prioratus ipsius sed tantum cure parochialis predicte dicto prioratui annexe".[3]

The bishops also admitted the resignations of heads of religious houses.[4] In 1340 William de Herwynton, the abbot of Pershore, feeling himself to be "confractum senio ac corporalibus viribus destitutum", wrote to Bransford for permission to resign. The formal resignation was dated two days later—26 September, and on the following day the bishop wrote his letter of acceptance.[5] But the abbot was not to retire so easily. A disputed election ensued and it was not until 14 November that Thomas de Pirton was appointed.[6] In the meantime the finances of the house were mismanaged, and on 21 October William de Herwynton was brought from retirement by the bishop to administer its spiritualities and temporalities.[7] When Richard of Idbury resigned as abbot of Winchcomb (1340) the monks asked the bishop to make provision for him "iuxta vires et facultates eiusdem". This Bransford did in a formal *ordinacio* which was subsequently approved by each member of the monastery.[8]

The admission of monks was ordinarily an internal matter for the monastery concerned, but in the case of the cathedral priory postulants were presented to the bishop who examined them, either in person or by deputy, before giving his approval. The diocesan also admitted the

---

1 "... idem prior iuravit solempniter tactis sacrosanctis evangeliis se soluturum et iura alia patraturum terminis constitutis porciones quascumque debitas et assignatas vicarie de Asteleye predicte et ordinatas vicario qui pro tempore fuerit absque dilacione vel fraude quacumque." Institution of William Provot in 1343: Reg. Bransford fo. 57v. (506).

2 *Reg. Giffard*, fo. 26v., p. 37; Liber Ruber, fo. lxxxvii v. An earlier composition had been confirmed by Walter de Cantilupe in 1265 (*Reg. Giff.*, fo. 12v., p. 10), but Giffard revived the dispute. In 1312 Reynolds, at the instance of the prior of Deerhurst had published "ad memoriam futurorum" all the admissions, institutions, and oaths of obedience recorded in Giffard's register. Reg. Reynolds, fo. xlix r.

3 For example, Bransford (fo. 32v. (256)): presentation by Guy, abbot of St Denis, of Ralph de Ermonvilla (9 December 1339).

4 Careful inquiry was supposed to be made in such cases. Cf. Bishop Swinfield's mandate to his official in the case of the abbot of Wigmore: "quia cessiones hujusmodi secundum canonicas sancciones nequaquam faciliter admittuntur." *Heref. Reg. Swinf.*, p. 301.

5 Reg. Bransf., fo. 43r.-v. (351-3).

6 Ibid., ff. 44r.-45r. (366-7).

7 Ibid., fo. 19v. (141). Printed in Nash 2, p. 255.

8 Ibid., fo. 38r.-v. (318).

profession of nuns and gave his blessing to women who took vows of chastity.[1]

CHANTRIES[2]

The establishment of a *perpetua cantaria*[3] followed a well-defined procedure by the fourteenth century. The founder was anxious above all to secure the continuance of his chantry. To this end the provision of an adequate endowment was of prime importance. The usual method was to grant lands and rents of a certain value together with a sum of money and sundry goods and chattels—sometimes enumerated in great detail—which were to be handed on unimpaired to each successive chaplain. If there were several chaplains the grant was made to one of them who acted as warden ("custos"), and he made provision for his colleagues. It was important too, that there should be definite rules for the presentation of chaplains, with rights devolving on second and even third parties in cases of non-presentation. Ordinarily the founder caused detailed ordinances to be drawn up. These concerned the conduct of the chaplains, the scope of their duties, and the circumstances in which they could be removed. Frequently the bishop was exhorted to make full inquiries at times of visitation.

At Worcester the stages in the formal process can be observed—to take a particular instance—in the entry recording Thomas de Berkeley's foundation[4] in the church of St Giles at Coberley.[5] The process as a whole is loosely termed *ordinacio*, although this word also has a more particular connotation which is given below. In the wider sense the *ordinacio* consists of Bishop Bransford's letters patent confirming the foundation (Blockley, 5 July 1340). These include a recension of the founder's charter (Coberley, 9 November 1337), which constitutes the *fundacio* proper. The charter recites the royal licence for the alienation in mortmain of certain lands and rents (23 May 1336),[6] and their

---

[1] One such vow is given in full in Bishop Hemenhale's register: "Ieo Isabele de Stepelton vowe a dieux et a nostre dame seynt Marie et a touz les seyntz du ciel en vestre presence Sire Thomas par la grace dieu evesque de Wyrcestr' qe ieo desores en avaunt viveray en chaste vie a servir dieux nettement en chastete." Fo. 12v.: 11 December 1337.

[2] See K. L. Wood-Legh's analysis of chantry ordinations between 1327 and 1377, which is printed in *C.H.J.* IV (1932), pp. 26–50 and, with some minor alterations, as chap. IV (pp. 89–126) of her *Church Life in England under Edward III*.

[3] We are not here concerned with chantries founded only for a period, of which there are no examples in the Worcester records of this time.

[4] This was the earlier of two chantries founded in the same church. A more ambitious one, with a warden and two chaplains, was ordained in 1347.

[5] Reg. Bransford, ff. 22v.–23v. (154).

[6] *C.P.R.* 1334–8, p. 268: 24 [*sic*] May 1336.

grant (*dotacio*) on 9 November 1337 to the chaplain and his successors. Finally comes the *ordinacio* itself, incorporating the details of the founder's wishes. After recording the institution of the first chaplain, it lays down rules for presentation at subsequent vacancies.[1] Each successive chaplain, at the time of his institution, was to take an oath to reside in person, to celebrate Mass daily, and to observe the chantry ordination. His failure to fulfil these obligations—except for reasonable cause approved by the ordinary—would entitle the patron to present someone in his stead. The Masses and offices which the chaplain was to say[2] for the good estate of the founder while living, for his soul after death, and for the souls of his parents, the benefactors of the chantry, and all the faithful departed, are then enumerated. No chaplain was to be removed merely because of age or sickness. In these circumstances he was to say such prayers as he could and two Masses a week. The chantry houses and buildings were to be kept in repair by the chaplain, but the burden of substantial rebuilding was laid upon the founder's heirs. It was hoped that at times of visitation the bishop would make inquiries and correct or remove the chaplain according to the gravity of his offences, if any such were brought to light. The document concludes with a solemn warning "sub interminacione divini iudicii in die ultionis" to the founder's kin or anyone else who should infringe the ordination.

The process was sometimes complicated by the necessity to gain the written consent of other parties, such as the patron and the rector or vicar of the church in which the chantry was to be established. The letters of the Worcester prior and convent exemplifying and confirming the foundation of the chantry of Walter de Bourton, vicar of Erdington, in the church of Bourton-on-the-Water, contain the episcopal confirmation, the licence in mortmain, that of the abbot and convent of Evesham (the patrons), the consent of the rector of Bourton, and the ordinances of the founder.[3] Thomas de Packington's plan to found a chantry in Chelmscote chapel within the parish of Brailes was agreed between himself, the prior and convent of Kenilworth (rectors of Brailes), and the vicar of Brailes, Gilbert de Withybrook.[4]

1 The founder was to be present and, after his death, his heirs, lords of Coberley. If presentation was not made within a month the right lapsed to the rector of Coberley, and after a second month to the bishop or, *sede vacante*, the prior.

2 In person or, "si legitime impeditus", by deputy.

3 L.A., ff. cxix v.–cxx v.: 1325. The chantry was to be celebrated "in capella Beate Marie ecclesie parochiali de Boroughtone contigue in honore virginis gloriose".

4 L.A., fo. cxxiiii r.–v. The agreement is dated 16 January 1322, the bishop's confirmation 10 October 1323, that of the prior and convent 30 September 1325. In 1334

Ordinarily the bishop's function was two-fold: first to approve, ratify, and confirm—so far as he could—the foundation, grant, and ordination; second, to inhibit anyone, under penalty of excommunication, from infringing them.[1] Episcopal confirmation does not seem to have been essential to the legality of a chantry ordination, and sometimes it was not given until several years after the institution of the first chaplain.[2] Only a portion of the chantries founded are known to have been confirmed.[3] On the other hand, the wise founder would seek episcopal confirmation as an additional safeguard. The assent of the prior and convent can be viewed in the same light, though whether the initiative in seeking it came from the bishop or the founder is not clear.[4] There were other precautions which could be taken. The founder might order the various chantry documents to be read aloud at fixed intervals,[5] or arrange for two, three, or even four copies of the ordination to be drawn up and delivered to the parties concerned.[6] One of them was usually given to the bishop for preservation in his archives.[7] By such means the details could be kept fresh in people's minds or doubtful points settled by reference to the originals.

---

a further (more detailed) ordination provided for two chaplains. It was confirmed by the bishop and by the prior and convent in 1335 (Reg. Montacute 1, fo. 19r.–v.). This was probably absorbed by the 1348 foundation which allowed for four chaplains, two at Chelmscote and two at Brailes. L.A., ff. cciii v.–cciiii r.

[1] For example, Bransford's confirmation of the earlier Coberley chantry runs: "Nos frater Wolstanus episcopus supradictus, laudabile propositum et pium desiderium domini Thome de Berkel' de Cubberl' predicti quo ad fundacionem, dotacionem et ordinacionem cantarie de qua in dictis litteris plenius continetur, merito commendantes, huiusmodi cantariam, ipsiusque fundacionem, dotacionem et ordinacionem quantum in nobis est auctoritate nostra ordinaria approbamus, ratificamus et ex certa sciencia confirmamus. Inhibemus eciam omnibus et singulis subditis nostris ne fundacionem, dotacionem, et ordinacionem supradictas aliquo modo maliciose infringant, capellanos–ve dicte cantarie in suis iuribus et porcionibus percipiendis impediant seu perturbent animo iniurando, sub pena excommunicacionis sentencie maioris, quam contraveniens quilibet in hac parte merito poterit formidare." Reg. Bransf., fo. 23v., (154). This was common form.

[2] See the list of chantries following this section.

[3] I.e. those in the registers. See p. 231 below.

[4] In the case of appropriations the bishop formally requested confirmation; the beneficiary sent his own petition as well.

[5] The "fundacio, dotacio et ordinacio" of the 1347 Coberley chantry were to be read out in the parish church on the eve of each of the five feasts of the B.V.M. and on that of the Nativity of St John the Baptist. This was to be done by one of the chaplains in the presence of the others. Reg. Bransford, fo. 109v. al. cx (834).

[6] Thomas de Berkeley had his (1347) ordination of Coberley chantry quadruplicated "ad maiorem securitatem et perpetuam rei memoriam". The chantry warden, the rector of Coberley, the prior and convent of Great Malvern, and the bishop each received a copy. Reg. Bransford, fo. 109v. al. cx (834).

[7] For example, Blockley chantry (1320): "Altera vero in archivis reverendi patris domini episcopi deponetur" (L.A., fo. cxii v.). Cf. n. 6 above.

Although a number of chantries were established during this period in that part of Bristol within the diocese,[1] only one finds episcopal confirmation in the registers.[2] The measures taken by the civic authorities to ensure the performance of the required duties may account for this. In the presence of the mayor and corporation every chantry priest had to take a yearly oath at Michaelmas that he would be resident and serve his chantry faithfully.[3] The chantries of Eborard le Franceys, one of which was founded in St Nicholas' church within the diocese, the other in St Mary Redcliffe in that of Bath and Wells, were safeguarded by an indenture binding on the one hand Robert Gyene, citizen of Bristol and sometime mayor, and after his death the mayor for the time being, and on the other the four chaplains of Eborard le Franceys and their successors. Under its terms the chaplains were forbidden to leave town ("devillare") for more than one night, except with Gyene's licence, and after his death that of the mayor. Such licence was not to be refused if the cause were reasonable. The chaplains had to take the customary oath to the mayor and corporation and if any should prove negligent, and after three-fold warning by Gyene— or later the mayor—should not reform himself, he was to be removed.[4]

Very occasionally the drawing up of chantry ordinances was entrusted to the bishop. This happened in the case of Adam de Herwynton's chantry in Pershore Abbey and in that of Abbot Hereward in the Augustinian abbey at Cirencester.[5] The ordination document of the former, dated 27 February 1346 from Bredon, contains a recension of the letters patent of the abbot and convent.[6] These, after enumerating the lands, rents, and money granted to the abbey by Adam de Herwynton[7] for the foundation of a chantry and the commemoration of the anniversary of his death,[8] declare the convent's willingness to submit to the bishop's ordination. They also rehearse the corresponding submission of Herwynton's executors,[9] and the monks' appointment of one of their number, Robert de Littleton, to deliver their submission and to

---

[1] Exactly how many is not known. There are thirteen mortmain licences in C.P.R. The Little Red Book of Bristol provides details of two chantries (see p. 239 below).

[2] That founded by Thomas lord Berkeley in St Augustine's Abbey (1348). Reg. Bransford, ff. 125r. al. cxxvi–126r. (907).

[3] Little Red Book 1, p. 52: "Sacramentum pro cantaria facienda." The oath itself is in Old French.

[4] "Si causa sit canonica statim sine aliqua contradiccione virtute ipsius indenture amoveatur". Little Red Book of Bristol 1, pp. 195–8 (1350).

[5] He was abbot 1334 (?1335)–1352: V.C.H. Gloucs. 2, p. 84; Monasticon 6, p. 176.

[6] Reg. Bransford, ff. 121v. al. cxxii–123r. (906).

[7] Cf. C.P.R. 1330–4, p. 250; ibid. 1338–40, p. 518.

[8] 31 March 1344.   [9] 26 February 1346, Bredon.

give assent to the bishop's decree.[1] Two further documents complete the process. The first records the procedure in the episcopal chapel at Hartlebury[2] where, in the presence of the diocesan chancellor and the official, Brother Henry de Lench swore on his own behalf, and then for each of the other thirty monks, to observe the bishop's ordination.[3] The second document is Henry de Lench's appointment as proctor for this purpose.[4] The foundation of the Hereward chantry in Cirencester Abbey is less fully documented. There are two entries. The first is the convent's submission to the bishop's ordination, dated 3 October 1346; the second, the ordination itself, which was sealed in the bishop's presence eight days later.[5] The ordinances for the (1344) Tormarton chantry were also drawn up by the bishop, after consultation with the patron of the church (the chantry's founder) and the rector,[6] but since appropriation was involved the bishop's assistance had to be invoked in any case.[7]

Once a chantry had been established, any alteration in its state, or deviation from its ordinances, was the bishop's concern. Reynolds permitted a reduction in the number of chaplains at Elmley Castle,[8] Bransford united two chantries, founded respectively in the Gloucester churches of Holy Trinity and St John, because of the diminution of their endowments.[9] Despite careful regulations on the subject, there were cases of disputed presentation. Reynolds had issued a commission for inquiry in the case of the same chantry in Holy Trinity,[10] while in

[1] 25 February 1346, Pershore: "Concedentes eidem potestatem specialem et mandatum generale quandam submissionem per nos factam voluntati, laudo, dicto, arbitrio, ordinacioni, decreto, condempnacioni ac sentencie cuicumque venerabilis patris . . . Wyg' episcopi diocesani nostri quo ad ordinacionem cuiusdam cantarie perpetue . . . presentandi, ac quamcumque conde[m]pnacionem virtute dicte submissionis nostre per eundem patrem . . . faciendam subeundi, ipsamque ordinacionem audiendi, recipiendi et eidem consenciendi."

[2] 12 April 1346.

[3] Reg. Bransford, ff. 123r. al. cxxiiii–124v. (906). Each oath is entered in full.

[4] Ibid., ff. 124v. al. cxxv–125r. (906).

[5] Ibid., ff. 109v. al. cx–111r. (835, 836). The preamble of each document recounts the good works of the abbot on behalf of his monastery. Forty days' indulgence was granted to all who should pray for his soul.

[6] "Nos igitur super premissis cum patrono et rectore predictis necnon omnibus ceteris quorum interest habito diligenti tractatu . . ."

[7] Reg. Bransford, ff. ccxxxiiii r. al. 165–ccxxxv r. (1211, 1212). See pp. 233–4 below.

[8] See p. 233 below.

[9] "Cum vix redditus antedicti in presenti sufficiant ad sustentacionem congruam unius sacerdotis." The union was effected "auctoritate pontificali, Hugonis de Chywe civis Glouc' nunc patroni predictarum cantariarum accedente consensu, concurrentibusque omnibus que in hac parte requiruntur de iure". Reg. Bransford, fo. 17r. (119): 20 March 1341.

[10] Reg. Reynolds, fo. 82r., p. 156: 1313.

Cobham's time there were disputes about the hospital or chantry in St Mary's, Droitwich,[1] and the Spagard chantry in St Helen's, Worcester.[2] In 1348 a situation arose which John Salemon, the founder of two chantries in Ripple church(1320), had not envisaged. By the terms of his ordination he was to present to both during his lifetime, and thereafter whichever chaplain remained in office was to present to the other chantry. But Salemon and both chaplains were dead in 1348, so the bishop himself made two appointments. This he did after inspecting the original ordination, a copy of which was then entered in his register.[3]

It would be impossible to discover the precise number of chantries that were established in English and Welsh dioceses at this time. As Miss Wood-Legh has shown,[4] the number of mortmain licences granted for this purpose cannot be regarded as more than a rough guide. Many of them merely augmented chantries which were already established; a few were cumulative, in which case the chantry was not founded until sufficient revenues had been collected;[5] others were never implemented. All the same, an approximation to the number of intended foundations can be made. From the Calendar of Patent Rolls covering the first half of the fourteenth century all those mortmain licences in which there is specific mention of a chantry have been abstracted. After deducting the ones which seem to concern the augmentation of existing chantries, as well as re-grants of the same licence—though without intimate knowledge of local records there is likely to be a considerable margin of error here—the resulting figures may be said to provide a rough total of projected foundations.[6] But there remain some omissions. A few chantries, either because of lacunas in the rolls, or for other reasons, are not to be traced in the Calendar. Our knowledge of them comes mainly from the episcopal registers.[7] Other chantries were

---

[1] *Reg. Cobham*, fo. 54v., p. 76 (1319): "Cantaria que wlgariter hospitale de Wichio nuncupatur." For its foundation document (1285) see Nash 1, p. 344.

[2] *Reg. Cobham*, ff. 24v., 67r.; pp. 29, 107. Bishop and rector both claimed the right to present.

[3] Reg. Bransford, ff. 142r.–143v. (969–71). "Asserens . . . quod noluit nec in futurum vellet aliquod preiudicium utilitati dicti fundatoris seu forme vel ordinacioni dictarum cantariarum imposterum aliqualiter generari. . . ." Cf. L.A., ff. cxliii r.–cxlvi r.

[4] *Church Life*, pp. 123–5.

[5] For example, the licences in favour of Worcester priory (*C.P.R.* 1334–8, p. 21; ibid. 1340–3, p. 6), which were vacated in 1378 on the acquisition of lands worth £5 a year, the sum needed to support a chantry chaplain.

[6] Where there are two or more licences for the same chantry, the first one which appears to have been implemented is counted, and not the other or others. Sometimes a person established separate chantries in the same church. It is seldom possible to be certain whether the later foundation absorbed the earlier, or not.

[7] There are six in the Worcester diocese. See p. 239 below.

founded as a consequence of grants made to monasteries. In such cases the mortmain licences do not always specify the donors' intentions.[1] But the omissions are unlikely to be so numerous as to affect the overall trend revealed by this method of calculation. The figures show a steep rise during the first four decades of the century, followed by a not so marked decline in the fifth. For the Worcester diocese the trend is much the same, except that owing mainly to the extensive foundations of Thomas de Berkeley of Berkeley,[2] there is a further slight rise in the last decade. The details can be tabulated as follows:

DECADES (INCLUSIVE)	TOTALS FOR ENGLAND AND WALES[3] (WITH WORCESTER DIOCESE)	TOTALS FOR WORCESTER DIOCESE
1300–09	61	1
1310–19	143	7
1320–29	246	11
1330–39	321	20
1340–49	270	22
1300–49	1041	61

Turning from the Patent Rolls to the Worcester records—chiefly the episcopal registers and the Liber Albus[4]—we find ordination documents for twenty-three of the sixty-one projected chantries, as well as for six others which are not mentioned in mortmain licences. The Bristol records provide two further documents: both concern chantries for which licences are recorded.[5] This suggests that local sources are more rewarding than has sometimes been thought,[6] although Worcester may be comparatively fruitful in this respect. Further research,[7] which lies beyond the scope of this book[8] would undoubtedly produce a more precise estimate of the number of those chantries on the Patent Rolls which were actually established.

[1] For example, the chantries at Pershore and Cirencester mentioned above. *C.P.R.* 1330–4, p. 250; ibid. 1338–40, p. 518; ibid. 1345–8, pp. 40–1.

[2] He established six chantries in the diocese, four of them in the name of his chaplain, William de Syde.

[3] Miss Wood-Legh's figures (*Church Life*, p. 125) are said to include all mortmain licences on the Patent Rolls "issued in each year of Edward III's reign to sanction the granting of land or rent to chantries" (ibid., p. 124). Where they are directly comparable with those in the above table—i.e. for the decades 1330–39 (289 licences) and 1340–49 (275)—they err on the low side.

[4] No original ordinations survive at Worcester.

[5] *Little Red Book of Bristol* 1, pp. 186–9, 195–8.

[6] For example, Wood-Legh, *Church Life*, p. 124.

[7] Particularly among the institutions in episcopal registers and the sixteenth-century chantry certificates.

[8] But something has been done in this direction, as will be seen from the list of chantries given below.

In the Worcester records there are only four ordination documents of chantries founded in religious houses,[1] although the Patent Rolls indicate that a further nine were at least contemplated. All four chantries were to be served by secular priests,[2] but at Bordesley, if the clerk presented was not in priest's orders, his duties were to be carried out by one of the monks until he should be so promoted.[3] Miss Wood-Legh has remarked on the number of fourteenth-century complaints about the cessation of chantries appointed in religious houses.[4] Elaborate measures to prevent this were taken by Bishop Bransford in his Pershore ordination.[5] The abbot, prior, subprior, cellarer, and *maiores* of the convent were to be *ipso facto* excommunicate in the event of their harming the chantry, and were it to cease *per maliciam* for eight days, they were bound to pay thirty shillings to the bishop for distribution as alms. During visitation, and at other times "cum clamore referente visum fuerit expedire", the religious could be called upon to give evidence—even on oath—that they had duly supported the burdens laid upon them. Not only did all the monks have to swear to maintain the ordination, but also every future monk at the time of his profession. But special penalties were not confined to monastic chantries. The same bishop imposed one of 400 shillings on the rector of Tormarton, to be paid in equal portions to the cathedral church, the diocesan, the archdeacon of Gloucester, and the patron, should he fail to perform the duties laid to his charge.[6]

The ordination documents provide much detailed information regarding chantries, although an analysis of their provisions would be out of place here. The majority of the chantries, whether actually founded or merely projected, provided for a single chaplain, though two were not uncommon. There were only three large foundations and in each case the revenues were augmented by appropriation. The

---

[1] Bordesley (Cistercian), Pershore (Benedictine), Bristol and Cirencester (Augustinian).

[2] Miss Wood-Legh (op. cit., pp. 96 et seq.) poses the problem of the preference shown by many founders for secular chaplains, although the prayers of the religious were accounted more efficacious.

[3] This chantry, in favour of Henry de Hampton, rector of Lighthorne (*ob.* 1327: *Reg. Cobham*, fo. 121r., p. 248, n. 2), seems to have been founded at the instance of the monks: "Volentes eidem Henrico caritatem sinceram quam erga eum abolim gessimus et adhuc gerimus ut tenemur operis argumento firmare." Until the presentation of a suitable clerk one of the monks was to celebrate *pro anima dicti Henrici*. The incoming chaplain was to be provided with necessaries, clothes, and shoes in the same manner as the monks. L.A., ff. cxxx v., cxxxi r. (1326). All Bordesley chantries seem to have conformed to this pattern. See Nash 2, pp. 411–14.

[4] Op. cit., p. 106.   [5] See pp. 228–9 above.

[6] Reg. Bransford, fo. 52v. (449). This was the earlier plan. See p. 233 below.

earliest of these was established at Elmley Castle where, in 1309, the rectory was appropriated to a chantry of eight chaplains and four clerks newly founded by Guy de Beauchamp, earl of Warwick.[1] Three years later, because of the heavy cost of the buildings and other initial expenses, Bishop Reynolds permitted a temporary reduction in numbers to seven chaplains and two clerks.[2] The chantry of John Stratford, bishop of Winchester, in the chapel of St Thomas the Martyr in Stratford parish church was first founded in 1331 with a warden and sub-warden as perpetual chaplains, and three temporary chaplains "pro voluntate custodis assumendi et eciam amovendi".[3] In 1336 a reordination by the founder, then archbishop of Canterbury, increased the number of chaplains to eight. This was made possible by the appropriation of the parish church, the advowson of which had been purchased from Bishop Montacute.[4] The third chantry, in Tormarton church, was founded in 1344 by John de la Riviere, a Gloucestershire knight.[5] His original plan provided for four chaplains, two clerks —one a deacon and the other a subdeacon—and three choristers, in addition to the rector who was virtually the warden and under obligation[6] to perform certain duties, among them the payment of stipends and the custody of the vestments and ornaments given by the founder.[7] Under a modified plan Tormarton church itself, of which de la Riviere held the advowson, was incorporated as a "perpetual wardenship",[8] the rector becoming in name, as he already was in fact, the chantry warden. In effect this was appropriation, although it is not called so in the register—except in one marginal rubric.[9] Immediately afterwards the neighbouring church of Acton Turville was united to that of Tormarton and appropriated to the use of the chantry wardens.[10] On the occasion of its confirmation by the pope in

[1] *Reg. Reynolds*, fo. 21r., p. 15; L.A., fo. xlv r.; printed in Nash 1, pp. 390–1. William of Wellesbourne, inst. 4 March 1309, seems to have been the first "Master" (Reg. Reyn., ff. 8r., 9r.).

[2] Reg. Reynolds, fo. 48v.: 5 May 1312. This was to last until the feast of St Michael (29 September).

[3] Reg. Montacute 1, ff. 56v.–57v.; L.A., ff. cxli r.–cxlii v.

[4] Reg. Montacute 1, ff. 50r., 53r.–56v. See pp. 242–4 below.

[5] An earlier chantry in the chapel of the B.V.M. which he had built contiguous to the church may not have been absorbed by this foundation. Reg. Montacute 1, fo. 27r.

[6] See p. 232 above.

[7] Reg. Bransford, ff. 52r.–53r. (449): crossed out and *vacat* written in the margin.

[8] Reg. Bransford, fo. ccxxxiiii r. al. 165 (1211): "Dictam ecclesiam sub nomine perpetue custodie et sub regimine custodis intitulandi in ea perpetuo incorporandam."

[9] Reg. Bransford, fo. 52r.: "Appropriacio ecclesie de Thormerton." But this entry details the earlier plan. As at Stratford later institutions were made *custodie cantarie* and no vicarage was ordained.

[10] Ibid., fo. ccxxxv r. al. 166 (1212): 3 May 1344.

1348 the chantry was said to be worth one hundred marks (£66 13s. 4d.).[1]

In each of the above foundations the chantry warden took the place of the rector. This was to the advantage of the parish in that it increased the number of clergy, particularly priests, all of whom took an oath of residence. There was contemporary awareness of this point. John Lacy, in his deposition supporting the appropriation of Stratford church, declared that the parish had a rector who was for the most part non-resident, as his predecessors had commonly been,[2] and that only two chaplains served the church. If it were to be appropriated, he argued, the number of resident ministers would be considerably increased.[3]

The relationship of the ordinary chantry priest to the parish and its rector or vicar was not always the same. That the latter were anxious to prevent any encroachment upon their income is a commonplace. In some ordination documents the chantry priest was required to take an oath of obedience or indemnity to the incumbent,[4] in others he was specifically debarred from receiving any of the parishioners' offerings or from ministering to them.[5] On the other hand, when presentation was made to the chantry chapel at Shipston "ministerio sacerdotali debito et consueto carentem", the chaplain was appointed to administer the sacraments to the parishioners as was customary

[1] C.P.L. 1342–62, pp. 300–1. Papal confirmations of chantries are uncommon at this date.

[2] The truth of his statement can be verified in part. John Stratford (the future archbishop) was rector in 1319 when two exchanges were negotiated in order to put his brother, Robert Stratford, in possession (Reg. Cobham, fo. 40r.–v., p. 41). Both were busy administrators and pluralists (see C.P.L. 1305–42, index sub nom.) and unlikely to have been resident except at infrequent intervals. John Geraud was instituted in 1334 (Reg. Montacute 1, fo. 10r.) and was rector at the time of the appropriation. But he (despite his record of absence) became chantry warden in 1349 (Reg. Bransford 2, fo. 13r. (1451)) and in 1366 was returned as a pluralist (Cant. Reg. Langham, p. 35), holding a canonry in Salisbury as well as the wardenship (taxed at thirty-five and a half marks).

[3] In theory from two to eight (see p. 233 above). Reg. Montacute 1, fo. 52r.: "Et si dicta ecclesia esset appropriata unita et annexa dictis custodi sacerdotibus et capelle et numerus ministrorum in eisdem esset augmentatus, ipsi continue resident et multum melius dicte ecclesie et parochie eiusdem ac prefati [sic] multitudini [populi] in officiis divinis et ad administracionem sacrorum ecclesiasticorum deservire quam unquam antea. . . ."

[4] For example, Chelmscote (1322). The chaplain was to take an oath to the vicar of Brailes: "Quod indempnitatem matricis ecclesie de Brailles in omnibus deservabit." L.A., fo. cxxiiii r.–v.

[5] For example Over Eatington (1316): "Nullas oblaciones parochianorum recipiat nec decimas aliquales nec sacramenta vel sacramentalia ministret eisdem." L.A. fo. lxxxxvii r.

there.[1] When a chantry was established in a chapel situated in some outlying part of a parish, and which the parishioners were licensed to attend, the chantry priest might become in effect a useful supplementary member of the parish clergy.[2] This could have been in Thomas de Berkeley's mind when he founded his chantries in chapels within Slimbridge, Berkeley, Wotton-under-Edge, and Almondsbury parishes.[3] Offerings were made by the medieval parishioner only at certain festivals.[4] On such days[5] Thomas de Berkeley's chaplains had to be in the parish church—a common arrangement—and, by implication, those parishioners who attended their Masses.[6] At Newport chapel (Berkeley parish) each of the two chaplains was to celebrate, one in the morning and the other at the third or sixth hour depending upon the season, to

---

LIST OF CHANTRIES
IN WORCESTER DIOCESE
PROJECTED OR ACTUALLY ESTABLISHED
1300–1349 (incl.)

(a) *Chantries for which there are mortmain licences but no ordination documents in the Worcester records.*

DATE OF LICENCE		PLACE	C.P.R. REF.	
24 July	1311	Longdon, St James	1313–17	p. 2
15 Oct.	1313	Evesham, St Egwin[7]		p. 28
8 July	1317	Hailes Abbey	1317–21	p. 1
16 Apr.	1321	Gloucester Abbey, Carnary chapel[8]		p. 577
8 July	1321	Gloucester, St Michael	1321–24	p. 21

[1] L.A., fo. clxxvi v.: "Ad divina celebrandum in eadem et sacramenta et sacramentalia parochianis commorantibus in dicta villa de Shipeston iuxta consuetudinem in hac parte prescriptam."

[2] How often this happened we have no means of telling, but many parishes must have lacked the priests necessary for celebrating Mass in remote chapels. It is not suggested that the chantry priest did more than this, except in special cases.

[3] Apart from the last, they were all founded in the name of his chaplain, William de Syde. See the list of chantries which follows.

[4] See Moorman, *Church Life*, pp. 126–8.

[5] At Berkeley, Slimbridge, and Wotton these were Christmas, Epiphany, the Purification, Ash Wednesday, Palm Sunday, Maundy Thursday, Good Friday, Holy Saturday, Pentecost, "et in omnibus aliis festis in quibus de iure vel de consuetudine eiusdem ecclesie parochiani offere tenetur". (For example, Reg. Bransford, fo. 77r.)

[6] Cf. the Chelmscote ordination (1322). The founder Thomas de Packington "ac dicti vicini de Chelmescote" were to go to Brailes church "servicium ecclesiasticum audituri" at Christmas, the Purification, Easter, Pentecost, St Gregory, All Saints, and on the dedication day. L.A., fo. cxxiiii r.–v.

[7] Outside the bishop's jurisdiction.

[8] The king asked the Worcester prior and convent to agree to the appropriation of Hatherop for the chantry's endowment (8 May 1321), but the prior replied that he had heard nothing from the bishop (Cobham) and was unable therefore to grant the request. L.A., fo. ci v.

DATE OF LICENCE		PLACE		C.P.R. REF.
12 May	1323	Evesham Abbey[1]		p. 285
1 Apr.	1326	Siddington, St Peter	1324–27	p. 255
2 Sept.	1329	Droitwich, Witton St Mary	1327–30	p. 437
20 Oct.	1329	Bristol, St Stephen		p. 452
28 Nov.	1329	Clopton (in Stratford)		p. 461–2
14 Feb.	1330	Bristol, Holy Trinity and prior of St Mary Magdalene[2]		p. 498
15 May	1331	Wick (Gl.)	1330–34	p. 118
22 Jan.	1332	Cold Ashton		p. 234
26 May	1332	Worcester, St Oswald's hosp.		p. 283
11 Sept.	1332	Worcester Cathedral		p. 338
26 Jan.	1333	Worcester, St Swithin		p. 404
6 Oct.	1333	Alcester, St Nicholas[3]	1330–34	p. 472
20 Sep.	1334	Bristol, St Stephen[4]	1334–38	p. 11
5 Dec.	1335	Bristol, All Saints		p. 183
22 Mar.	1337	Eldersfield		p. 401
2 May	1337	Halesowen Abbey		pp. 425, 461
18 Dec.	1337	Pucklechurch		p. 559
28 Feb.	1339	Bristol, St Nicholas	1338–40	p. 245
12 Apr.	1339	Bristol, St Augustine the less		p. 239
20 Oct.	1339	Bristol, Priory of St James		p. 322
3 Feb.	1340	Bristol, St Mark's Billeswick (Gaunt's hospital)		p. 414
19 May	1341	Cam	1340–43	p. 306
4 Apr.	1344	Bristol, St John the Bapt. and St John the Evang.[5]	1343–45	p. 256
7 July	1344	*King's Norton[6]		p. 309
1 Mar.	1345	*Bristol, St Nicholas[7]		p. 443
1 Aug.	1345	Bristol, All Saints		p. 449
27 Oct.	1345	*Staverton		p. 564
28 May	1346	Berkeley	1345–48	p. 128
12 Sept.	1346	Bristol, St Stephen		pp. 168–9
14 May	1347	Staunton		p. 539
20 June	1347	Salwarpe, St Michael[8]	1345–48	p. 336
16 Nov.	1347	Oxenhall		p. 433
14 July	1349	*Studley, St Mary[9]	1348–50	p. 343

[1] Outside the bishop's jurisdiction.

[2] Counted as one chantry for the purpose of this list and the figures in the above section.

[3] Nothing more is known of this chantry. See *V.C.H. Warwicks.* 3, p. 20.

[4] See *Little Red Book of Bristol* 1, pp. 186–9; list (*c*) below.

[5] Counted as one chantry for the purpose of this list and the figures in the above section.

[6] Identified as the chantry of St Thomas the Martyr (mentioned 1485–1500) in *V.C.H. Worcs.* 3, p. 190. But this seems doubtful. The chantry Mass was to be celebrated at the altar of the B.V.M. and Nash (1, p. 166) suggests that Humphrey Toye (*ob.* 1514) officiated in a chantry dedicated to the Virgin Mary. Asterisks in this list indicate that later evidence (commonly the record of an institution) suggests that the licence was implemented.

[7] See *Little Red Book of Bristol* 1, pp. 195–8, pp. 333–4 above, and list (*c*) below.

[8] The grant was not made. See *V.C.H. Worcs.* 2, pp. 209–10.

[9] The Middlemore chantry. It continued until the Reformation. See *V.C.H. Warwicks.* 3, p. 186.

(b) Chantries for which there are ordination documents in the Worcester records.

DATE[1]	PLACE	FOUNDER	NO. OF CHAPLAINS	REFS.
1309	Elmley Castle	Guy de Beauchamp, earl of Warwick	8 4 clks.	Reg. Reyn., fo. 21r. L.A., fo. xlv r.–v.
1316	Kempsey	John de Kempsey, Treasurer of Hereford Cath.	1	Reg. Maidst., fo. 55r.–v. L.A., ff. lxxiii r.–lxxiiii v.
1316	Over Eatington	William de Itchington, at the instance of Thomas, earl of Lancaster	1	L.A., fo. lxxxvii r.
1320[2] 1326[3]	Blockley	Ralph de Baketon, chaplain, by grant to M. Benedict de Paston, the rector	1	L.A., ff. cxii v., cxxx r. *Reg. Cobham*, fo. 65r., pp. 103–4.
1320	Ripple	John Salemon, clk. (Rector of Ripple in 1323)[5]	2[4]	L.A., ff. cxliii r.–cxliiii v.; cxliiii v.–cxlvi r. (dupl); Reg. Bransf., ff. 142r.–143r.
1322	Hartlebury	M. Richard Mayel[6] and dom. Walter Mayel further endow John de Rodberrow's chantry.	1	L.A., fo. cxxii v.
1323[7] (1322)	Chelmscote chapel, in Brailes par.	Thomas de Packington, lord of Brailes	1	L.A., fo. cxxiiii r.–v.
1335 (1334)			2	Reg. Mont. I, fo. 19r.–v.
1325 (1324)	Bourton - on - the-Water	Walter de Bourton, vicar of Erdington	1	L.A., ff. cxix v.–cxx r.
1325 (1324)	Bishampton	Robert de Somery of Bishampton	1	Reg. Cobham, fo. 46r.–v.
1325	Warwick, St. Nicholas	Robert le Purser	1	L.A., ff. cxxv v.–cxxvi v.; Reg. Orleton 2, ff. 30r.–31r.
(1326)	Bordesley Abbey	A. and C. Bordesley in favour of Henry de Hampton, rector of Lighthorne	1	L.A., fo cxxx r.–v.

[1] The date of the bishop's confirmation. When the date of the founder's charter is known to differ from this it is given in brackets.

[2] A grant made by William de Ditchford to Benedict de Paston (1314) for the support of a chaplain may have been absorbed in this foundation. *C.P.R.* 1313–17, p. 159; Reg. Maidstone, fo. 13v.

[3] A further endowment by Baketon of the same chantry.

[4] Strictly speaking two separate chantries (see p. 230 above), but for our purposes counted as one.

[5] *Reg. Cobham*, fo. 31v., p. 239.

[6] See pp. 41–2 above. Rodberrow was official in 1306 (pp. 110–11 above).

[7] It is not clear whether the original arrangement was carried out.

DATE	PLACE	FOUNDER	NO. OF CHAPLAINS	REFS.
1332[1] (1331)	Stratford church, chapel of St Thomas the Martyr	John Stratford, bishop of Winchester	5[2]	Reg. Mont. 1, ff. 50r. et seq.; L. A., ff. cxli r.–cxlii v.
1337[3]	Tormarton	John de la Riviere, lord of Tormarton.	1	Reg. Mont. 1, fo. 27r.
1338	Eastington	Isolda de Audley, widow of Hugh de Audley, kt.	1	L.A., ff. cxlviii v.–cxlix r.
1340 (1337)	Coberley, St Giles	Thomas de Berkeley, lord of Coberley	1	Reg. Bransf. ff. 22v.–23v.
1341 (1338)	Minchinhampton	William de Prestbury, rector of Minchinhampton	1	L.A., ff. clxxv v.–clxxvi r.
1343	Syde	William de Syde, chaplain, for Thomas lord Berkeley	1	Reg. Bransford, fo. 76r.–v.[4]
1343	Cambridge chapel in Slimbridge par.	idem	1	Reg. Bransf., fo. 77r.–v.
1343	Newport chapel in Berkeley par.	idem	2	Reg. Bransf., ff. 78r.–79r.
1343	Wortley chapel in Wotton-under-Edge par.	idem	1	Reg. Bransf. ff. 79r.–80r.
1344	Breadstone	dom. Thomas of Breadstone	3	L. A., ff. clxxxx-iiii r.–clxxxxv r.
1344[5]	Tormarton	John de la Riviere, lord of Tormarton	5 2 clks. 3 chor.	Reg. Bransf., ff. ccxxxiiii r. al. 165 et seq.
(1344)	Broadwas	M. John de Broadwas[6]	2	Reg. Bransf., ff. 84r. al. lxxxv–85v.
1345	Over chapel in Almondsbury parish	Thomas lord Berkeley	1	Reg. Bransf., ff. 88v. al. lxxxix–89v. L.A., ff. clxxxxvi v.–clxxxvii v.
1346	Pershore Abbey	M. Adam de Herwynton (king's clerk)	2	Reg. Bransf. ff. 121v. al. cxxii et seq.

[1] In 1336 the chantry was refounded on a larger scale. See p. 233 above.

[2] Increased to eight in 1336.

[3] The 1344 foundation is not known to have absorbed this chantry. See above, p. 233, n. 5.

[4] The Syde chantries are also to be found in the Liber Albus (ff. ccix r. et seq.). They are separately entered on a quire of four sheets (eight small folios) which has been inserted in the Liber proper.

[5] See above for the 1337 foundation.

[6] One of the cathedral priory's clerks and sometime rector of Sedgeberrow.

DATE	PLACE	FOUNDER	NO. OF CHAPLAINS	REFS.
1346	Cirencester Abbey	Abbot William Hereward	I	Reg. Bransf., ff. 109v. al. cx et seq.
1347[1]	Coberley	Thomas de Berkeley	3	Reg. Bransf., ff. 106r. al. cvii et seq.
1348	Bristol, St Augustine's Abbey	Thomas lord Berkeley	I	Reg. Bransf., ff. 125r., al. cxxvi–126r.
1348[2]	Brailes and Chelmscote chapel	Thomas de Packington, lord of Brailes	4 (2 in each)	L.A., ff. cciii v.–cciiii r.

NOTE ON LIST (*b*).

Mortmain licences are not recorded in the *C.P.R.* for the following chantries:

1323/1335	Chelmscote
1326	Bordesley Abbey[3]
1337	Tormarton
1346	{ Pershore Abbey[4]
1346	{ Cirencester Abbey

(*c*) *Documents concerning chantries in the Bristol records*

1334[5] Bristol, St Stephen. Chantry at the altar of St Catherine (two chaplains) in the chapel built by the founder, Richard le White. The grant was made to the prior and brethren of the Calendaries.

1350[6] Bristol, St Nicholas. Composition concerning the chantry (two chaplains) founded by Eborard le Franceys.

---

enable travellers, landworkers, and other labourers to hear Mass daily.[7] Much has been said about the idleness of chantry chaplains and the paucity of their official duties, but their usefulness in certain outlying parochial chapels seems to have been overlooked.

1 Not stated to have absorbed the 1340 (1337) foundation.

2 This probably absorbed the Chelmscote foundation of 1323/1335 q.v.

3 It is probable that no land was alienated. See above p. 232, n. 3.

4 In both cases grants of land, for which mortmain licences were obtained, were made direct to the monastery but without mention of the grantors' intentions. See above, p. 231, n. 1.

5 Letters patent of the founder: *Little Red Book of Bristol* 1, pp. 186–9; *C.P.R.* 1334–8, p. 11. In 1349 its vacancy was declared by the prior of the Calendaries and the mayor of Bristol presented the chaplain. Reg. Bransford, fo. 146r. (995).

6 *Little Red Book of Bristol* 1, pp. 195–8; p. 228 above.

7 "Et quia volo quod tam iter agentes quam agri cultores et alii operarii ad honorem omnipotentis Dei cotidie missam audiant, volo et ordino quod unus predictorum duorum capellanorum qui pro tempore fuerint pro disposicione dicti capellani custodis mane, et alius capellanus circa horam terciam in estate et circa horam sextam in yeme, cotidie celebrent nisi forte inexcusabilis causa eos excusat." Reg. Bransford, fo. 78v. (660).

17

APPROPRIATIONS[1]

The appropriation of parish churches was set in motion by the petition of the interested party, which during our period was normally directed to the diocesan, occasionally to the pope.[2] The bishop's function was to determine the validity of the reasons advanced by the petitioner, and if satisfied that they were "just and legitimate", to carry out the appropriation in accordance with the recognized legal procedure.[3] A necessary preliminary was the obtaining of royal licence. Failure to do this might prove expensive and troublesome, as Worcester Priory found in the case of Dodderhill.[4] Usually the appropriator already held the advowson of the church concerned, but this was not always so.[5]

[1] For a discussion of some aspects of appropriation, based mainly on entries in the printed calendars of Papal Letters and Letters Patent, see K. L. Wood-Legh, *Church Life*, chap. V, pp. 127–53 (cf. *C.H.J.* III 1929, pp. 15–22). G. G. Coulton, *Five Centuries of Religion* 3, pp. 163–78 gives a highly critical account of monastic appropriation. See also R. A. R. Hartridge, *Vicarages in the Middle Ages*, esp. chap. VII. The present writer's purpose is to cover somewhat different ground, namely the administrative details of appropriation, and in particular the part played by the diocesan.

[2] Papal bulls were obtained in seven out of thirty-six cases (see list following this section). They were sometimes used to overcome resistance, particularly that of the diocesan. See below, pp. 244–5, 246, 247, 249–50; and cf. Wood-Legh, p. 129.

[3] "Advertentes quod in concessionibus perpetuis et alienacionibus rerum ecclesiasticarum tractatus solempnis et diligens, ac certus iuris ordo quem ex officii debito observare astringimur" (L.A., fo. cxxi v: Bishop Cobham appoints commissaries to treat with the chapter about the appropriation of Snitterfield). This was only one aspect. The preambles of appropriation decrees speak of the bishop's pastoral duty to foster the growth of religion by such means. For example, Cobham, at the time of his appropriation of Wolford to the scholars of Merton, writes: "Nos fructum attendentes quem ex Dei misericordia speramus et credimus exinde perpetuis temporibus in Dei ecclesia et cultu Christiane religionis profuturum" (Reg. Cobham ff. 77v.–78r.); and Bransford, in a preamble which is common form in his register, expresses a sentiment befitting a monk-bishop: "Pastoralis officii solicitudo continua requirit, et mentem nostram velut cotidiana instancia stimulat et inducit, ut illis potissime sub iugo regularis observancie constitutis, nostre liberalitatis dexteram uberius extendamus, quibus iuxta status sui decenciam proprie non suppetunt facultates" (Reg. Bransf., fo. 91v. al. lxxxxii (750)).

[4] See p. 246 below.

[5] Miss Wood-Legh (op. cit., p. 135) argues somewhat cynically that a benefactor could grant an advowson to a monastery and secure licence for appropriation "which would give all the spiritual advantages which might be obtained by a grant of land without involving a corresponding diminution of the goods of this world". But was this often the case? As she herself points out (p. 139), the possession of an advowson meant that the lay lord could promote his clerks and relations—a common practice, as would appear from a study of the institutions in almost any episcopal register of this time. But if the advowson were to be alienated, such dependents would have to be provided for in other ways, perhaps by pensions or grants of land. The argument takes no account of the fact that advowsons had sometimes to be purchased, land and rents perhaps forming all or part of the consideration. Miss Wood-Legh instances William de Clinton's eight licences for the appropriation of churches to Maxstoke Priory (pp. 135–6). But the advowsons did not necessarily belong to Clinton; he

When enlarging his chantry foundation in 1336, Archbishop Stratford first purchased the advowson of Stratford church from the bishop and then conveyed it to the chantry warden,[1] and William de Clinton, earl of Huntingdon, had likewise to secure the advowsons of Aston Cantlow, Tanworth, and Yardley before he could carry out his intention of having those churches appropriated to his priory at Maxstoke.[2] Royal licence had to be obtained for each transfer of an advowson. Once such preparatory steps had been taken the petition was drafted and despatched to the bishop. He appointed one or more clerks (usually including the diocesan official) to hold an inquiry. The commissaries carried out this task by journeying to the church to be appropriated, summoning all whose interests were affected, and laying the articles contained in the petition before a jury of local clerks and laymen whose sworn depositions were taken down and sent to the bishop.[3] On the basis of these findings, and in accordance with the principles enunciated by Ottobon, the bishop determined the rightness of the appropriation.[4] If he approved, he sent his clerks to the cathedral priory to discuss the matter with the chapter and to secure its assent.[5] This obtained, the bishop was informed and the degree of appropriation drawn up. This

---

certainly had to acquire those of Aston Cantlow, Tanworth, and Yardley in Worcester diocese. More convincing is Miss Wood-Legh's point (p. 136) about the advantage of appropriated churches, in that as spiritual income they could not be taken into the king's hand. But the real reason for the growth of the practice of appropriation may lie deeper than this, forming one aspect of that attitude to churches which emphasized the *beneficium* to the detriment of the *officium*.

[1] See p. 233 above and pp. 242–4 below.

[2] *C.P.R.* 1338–40, p. 436; *C.P.R.* 1345–8, p. 135; Nash 2, p. 478.

[3] The procedure adopted in 1312–13 at the time of Reynolds' appropriation of Dodderhill to the cathedral priory was unusual in some respects (see p. 246 below). The bishop was in London and appointed his official to do what was necessary. The official directed the rural deans of Worcester and Droitwich (in which deanery Dodderhill lay) to cite the interested parties to come before him in the cathedral. There the four articles of the priory were put to eleven clerks (mainly incumbents of churches in Worcester and its neighbourhood) and an equal number of laymen; a far larger jury than was usual. Reg. Reynolds, ff. 96.v–97v.; L.A., fo. liv v.; Nash 1, pp. 339–40. Some churches (see p. 254 below) were appropriated to monasteries outside the diocese. In such cases the process was the same, although in one instance— the appropriation of Long Compton to Walden Abbey (Essex) in 1316—an inquiry was held by the appropriator's diocesan, Gilbert Segrave, bishop of London. Reg. Maidstone, ff. 41v.–42r.

[4] The bishop decided "de causarum legitimitate veritate ac probacione". Ottobon (Athon, p. 120) had prohibited appropriation "nisi is cui appropriare voluerit, adeo manifeste paupertatis prematur onere, vel alia legitima causa subsit, quod talis appropriacio non tam iuri contraria quam pietati consona merito censeatur".

[5] For example, Reg. Bransford, fo. 59v.: "Quia tamen alienaciones ecclesiarum sine capituli nostri consensu, tractatu et solempnitate que in huiusmodi negociis requiruntur facere nolumus sicut secundum sancciones canonicas facere non debemus . . . vobis

was later inspected and confirmed by the prior and chapter. Papal confirmation, though not necessary for the validity of the process, was procured in some cases as an added safeguard. Appropriations were made *cedente vel decedente rectore* and with the reservation of an adequate portion ("porcio congrua") for a vicar. In some cases[1] the bishop decreed that an annual pension (usually 2s.) was to be paid by the rector to the appropriators *in signum proprietatis et possessionis* or *nomine induccionis et possessionis*, they being empowered to enter on the church so soon as it fell vacant and without further formality. It was probably more usual for investiture and induction to wait upon the vacancy.[2] Bishops claimed the right to confirm—and by implication to rescind— those appropriation decrees of their predecessors which had not been implemented. Cobham told the king that at his instance he had confirmed[3] the appropriation of Long Compton to Walden Abbey "que fu nouele et repelable".[4]

The fullest process of this kind in the Worcester registers concerns the appropriation of Stratford church to the chantry in the chapel of St Thomas the Martyr there.[5] It consists of nineteen separate entries. The introductory *rubricella* records the lands and rents—including some formerly alienated by the impecunious Maidstone—which were granted to Bishop Montacute and his successors by Archbishop Stratford and his brother Robert in consideration of the transfer to the archbishop of the advowson of Stratford.[6] The eight subsequent entries are concerned with this transfer.[7] Once the warden had received livery

---

committimus et mandamus, quatenus ad capitulum nostrum Wygorn' personaliter accedentes de premissis et omnibus que in huiusmodi appropriacionibus de iure convenit intervenire cum eodem capitulo nostro vice nostra solempnem tractatum habeatis ac plene deliberetis et eiusdem capituli nostri consensum in hac parte requiratis."

1 For example, Ombersley, Pershore: Maidstone, ff. 41v.–42r.; L.A., ff. cxxx v.–cxxxi r.; Reg. Orleton 1, fo. 39r.–v.

2 For Powick, appropriated to Great Malvern, four documents are entered in Maidstone's register (ff. 16v.–17r.): the priory's appointment of Br Richard de Froma to receive the investiture (6 November 1314); the resignation of the rector, Adam de Herwynton (17 November); the bishop's letter of investiture ("per nostrum birretum") addressed to the prior and convent (18 November); his mandate for induction directed to the archdeacon of Worcester's official (18 November).

3 The MS. reading is "confermei" not "conserviei" as in the printed edition.

4 *Reg. Cobham*, fo. 101v., p. 185.   5 See p. 233 above.

6 Cf. *C.P.R.* 1334–8, p. 308. Should the bishop lose the lands by judgement of the king's court the chantry warden was to pay an annual indemnity of ten marks. Reg. Mont. 1, ff. 57v.–58r.

7 Reg. Montacute 1, ff. 50 r.–51r.

(a) Mortmain licence for alienation of the advowson by Montacute (8 April 1336). Cf. *C.P.R.* 1334–8, p. 308.

of seisin the way was open for the next step, his petition to the bishop for appropriation. This is recited in Montacute's commission for inquiry (23 July 1336) directed to the rectors of Hampton Bishop and Severn Stoke. Immediate action must have been taken, for the mandate was returned on 26 July. The return certifies the citation of all interested parties and the subsequent holding of an inquiry with the help of a sworn jury. Details of the inquiry were attached to the original and are set out in full in Montacute's register. The jurors' depositions were made on the basis of four articles put forward by the chantry warden in support of his petition. The first, which is hardly controversial, recounts the chantry's foundation; the others allege respectively that its funds were insufficient to maintain an adequate number of *servitores*; that there was a lack of houses in which, by the terms of the ordination, such *servitores* were bound to live; and that the rents and profits were too slender for the support of pious works pleasing to God and man.

The jury consisted of six clerks, including the rector of Wilmcote and the vicars of Bishopton and Luddington—all subject to the rector of Stratford,[1] the two chaplains serving Stratford parish, and one *literatus*; as well as six laymen. All save one of them were forty or more years of age. The most revealing deposition is that of John Lacy, a layman, who pointed out the advantage that would ensue if a largely non-resident rector were to be replaced by the chantry chaplains.[2]

The evidence was considered satisfactory and the appropriation decree, dated 30 July 1336, was duly sealed by Archbishop Stratford, Bishop Montacute, and the Worcester chapter. The chantry warden and his successors were to exercise the cure of souls and the special jurisdiction of the rector.[3] There were to be eight priests, instead of five, and the warden was to take an oath of perpetual residence at the time of his institution. The advowson of the chantry was then settled on the Worcester bishops by the archbishop—an exact reversal of the

---

(*b*) Montacute's letters patent granting the advowson to the archbishop (19 July 1336).

(*c*) His appointment of proctors to put the archbishop "in seisinam advocacionis" (19 July 1336).

(*d*) Stratford's appointment of his brother, Robert, to receive seisin (19 July 1336).

(*e*) The Worcester prior and convent's confirmation of (*b*) (20 July 1336).

(*f*) Royal licence for the assignment of the advowson by the archbishop to John of South Waltham, the chantry warden (12 April 1336). Cf. *C.P.R.* 1334–8, p. 308.

(*g*) The archbishop's charter confirming the grant of the advowson (21 July 1336).

(*h*) The archbishop's appointment of Robert Stratford to grant livery of seisin to the chantry warden (19 July 1336).

1 See above p. 19, n. 3.   2 See pp. 233–4 above   3 See p. 19 above.

earlier process. The arrangements were completed in December of the same year with the reordination of the chantry.[1]

When appropriation was made by papal authority the procedure differed according to the type of bull. The would-be appropriator submitted his petition, often with the support of influential persons, and if successful papal letters were issued. In some cases these were addressed to the diocesan and were technically judicial in character, containing the provisory clause *si est ita*.[2] The bishop had first to satisfy himself as to the truth of the particulars alleged by the petitioners and incorporated in the bull. This he did by holding an inquiry in the ordinary way. When Orleton executed the bull for Longdon's appropriation to Westminster Abbey, the Worcester prior and convent, the archdeacon of Worcester, and the rector of Longdon, entered *excepciones*. Their nature is not disclosed, but they probably concerned the financial interest of the parties.[3] Other bulls effected direct appropriation.[4] They did not name executors, the appropriating body being empowered to act *auctoritate propria* so soon as the rectory in question fell vacant.[5] A third class of bull was addressed to executors, commonly three in number. One or more of them, after judicial examination of the bull's contents, appropriated the church concerned and appointed sub-executors living in the neighbourhood to complete the process.[6] The Worcester chapter added its confirmation to appropriations effected by bulls of the first category, and possibly in other cases as well.

The Longdon appropriation provides an example of the delay that sometimes occurred before possession was secured. John XXII's bull is dated 23 June 1331, and in November of that year the abbot of Westminster requested the Worcester Priory's confirmation.[7] The prior replied enigmatically.[8] He must have been well aware of Orleton's

[1] Reg. Montacute 1, ff. 5or.–61v.; p. 233 above.

[2] For example, the bulls for Longdon and Dodderhill.

[3] Westm. Abb. Mun., 21256.

[4] "Diocesani ac archidiaconi loci et alterius cuiuscunque licencia et assensu minime requisitis."

[5] For example, the bull for Overbury. In 1352 Clement VI appropriated Wolverley to Worcester Priory in the same manner. See Nash 2, pp. 475–6, from Liber Pens., fo. 19v.

[6] Blockley was appropriated in this way. The bull (18 June 1333) named three executors outside England. The bishop of Agde carried out the appropriation (25 October 1333) and appointed nine English sub-executors, including two bishops, six heads of religious houses (four of them in the diocese), and the archdeacon of Gloucester. Reg. Montacute 1, ff. 11v.–12r.: printed Nash 1, pp. 106–9.

[7] Westm. Abb. Mun., 21256; Reg. Orleton 2, ff. 53v.–54r.; L.A., fo cxxxix v. See the author's 'The Appropriation of Longdon Church to Westminister Abbey' in *Trans. Worc. Arch. Soc.* XXXVIII (1961), pp. 39–52.

[8] L.A., fo. cxxxix v.

intention to use his consent to the appropriation as a bargaining counter in an attempt to recover episcopal jurisdiction over Great Malvern, relinquished by Giffard.[1] Orleton, under pressure from a further bull, eventually carried out the appropriation and his decree, dated 11 January 1334, was confirmed by the prior and chapter nine days later.[2] Meanwhile he had been translated to Winchester, and it was not until February 1335 that Montacute reappropriated Longdon.[3] In the interval the king had presented Thomas de Escrick to the church, claiming the right by reason of the vacancy at Westminster. The abbey appealed to the Holy See against Escrick, but the king withdrew his presentation and ratified the monks' estate in Longdon.[4] The presentation seems to have been a genuine error, for the king had supported the petition for appropriation and had opposed Orleton's delaying tactics.[5]

Worcester Priory's struggle to gain possession of Dodderhill was prolonged for over thirty years. Giffard appropriated the church on 21 January 1302,[6] the prior receiving investiture on the following day.[7] The bishop's death on 26 January seems to have prompted the monks to seek Archbishop Winchelsey's confirmation.[8] But Winchelsey had already shown himself critical of Giffard's appropriations and a stern visitor of the priory itself.[9] He would not recognize the appropriation, and on the priory's failure to present to Dodderhill he claimed the right by lapse.[10] After some altercation John de Middleton, the brother of one of his clerks, was inducted.[11] The new bishop, Gainsburgh, did not assume the jurisdiction until February 1303, over twelve months after Giffard's death. On consulting the documents produced by the prior in support of the appropriation, he promptly removed Middleton.[12] The struggle continued in the courts. Winchelsey cited the prior and convent to Canterbury: they appealed to Rome against

---

1 *C.P.L.* 1305–42, p. 393; pp. 29–30 above. Great Malvern was a cell of Westminster.

2 Reg. Orleton 2, ff. 53v.–54r.; Westm. Abb. Mun., 21256–21258; L.A., ff. clvii v.–clviii r.; *C.P.L.* 1305–42, p. 393.

3 Reg. Montacute 1, ff. 17r.–18r.; ibid. 2, fo. 25r.–v.; Westm. Abb. Mun., 21266–21270.

4 Westm. Abb. Mun., 21259–21261; *C.P.R.* 1330–4, pp. 543, 569; ibid. 1334–8, p. 6; Reg. Montacute 2, fo. 27r.

5 *C.P.L.* 1305–42, pp. 350, 393.

6 L.A., fo. vi v.; cf. Nash 1, p. 338   7 *Ann. Wigorn.*, p. 551.

8 *R.S.V.*, fo. 14v., p. 35 (undated). On the day of Giffard's death they made a formal appeal for protection to the Curia (L.A., fo. xiii v.).

9 See Rose Graham, *English Eccles. Studies*, chap. 15.

10 *Ann. Wigorn.*, p. 556; *R.S.V.*, ff. 18r.–v., pp. 47–50.

11 *R.S.V.* fo. 18v., p. 49. For Gilbert de Middleton see below, p. 308, n. 8.

12 *Reg. Gainsburgh*, fo. 7v., p. 21.

the archbishop's interference with their right of presentation.[1] At this juncture the king intervened, and recovering the presentation against archbishop, bishop, and presentee, secured the institution of a clerk of his own (3 August 1304).[2] The king's action was prompted by the priory's omission to secure a licence for the appropriation, but in 1305 he granted a pardon on payment of twenty marks and restored the advowson.[3] Reynolds reappropriated the church in 1313, after holding a full inquiry,[4] and five years later he confirmed the act as archbishop.[5] Meanwhile his successor at Worcester, Maidstone, had added his confirmation.[6] Finally, John XXII issued a bull of appropriation, dated 15 September 1332, which was executed by Orleton in November during his stay in Paris.[7] The king confirmed the alienation in the following year.[8] Thus after the efforts of five bishops the priory gained possession.[9]

The failure of St Augustine's Abbey, Bristol, to secure Wotton-under-Edge, appropriated in 1313, is something of a mystery. The abbey had held the advowson in 1301 when Orleton became rector, but the appropriation could not be implemented on his elevation to the see of Hereford in 1317 because of a papal bull of provision.[10] Not long afterwards the advowson somehow passed to the Berkeleys,[11] who were patrons of the abbey, and there is no further mention of the appropriation.[12]

There is no reason to doubt the contemporary awareness of the disadvantages of appropriation.[13] Richard Swinfield, bishop of Hereford, strongly resisted the demand of Worcester Priory, backed by the king,

---

[1] *R.S.V.*, ff. 18r.–19r., pp. 47, 50, 51.

[2] *Reg. Gainsburgh*, fo. 25v., p. 85: cf. *C.P.R.* 1301–7, p. 148. The official of the Court of Canterbury was inhibited from taking further action against the bishop on account of his admission of the king's presentee, William de Thorntoft (*C.C.R.* 1302–7, pp. 222–3).

[3] *Reg. Gainsburgh*, ff. 53r., 54r., 55v.; pp. 203, 205, 211: *C.P.R.* 1301–7, p. 361.

[4] *Reg. Reynolds*, ff. 96v.–97v.; pp. 75–7.

[5] Nash 1, p. 341 (from D. & C. Reg. 2, fo. 130). The archbishop's act was confirmed by the Canterbury chapter in 1330 (ibid.).

[6] Reg. Maidstone, fo. 15v.: 24 August 1314.

[7] Reg. Orleton 2, ff. 53r.–v.

[8] Nash 1, pp. 342–3; *C.P.R.* 1330–4, p. 521.

[9] During Cobham's episcopate Thorntoft (see above, n. 2) remained undisturbed and the monks even admitted him to their fraternity (1318). L.A., fo. lxxxvi v.

[10] *Reg. Giffard*, fo. 464r., p. 543; *C.P.L.* 1305–42, p. 157.

[11] See *Reg. Cobham*, ff. 27r., 30v.: pp. 237, 239; *R.S.V.*, fo. 193r., p. 345. Cf. p. 265 below.

[12] It was eventually appropriated to Tewkesbury. See p. 265 below.

[13] For thirteenth-century opinions see Hartridge, *Vicarages*, pp. 77–88.

to appropriate the rectory of Lindridge. For almost twenty-three years, he argued in a letter to Edward I (1305), he had known the dangers and losses accruing to both the living and the departed by the practice of appropriating churches. Yet when he particularizes, his main arguments concern the disadvantage to his bishopric rather than the spiritual needs of the parish. By appropriation, he contended, the church of Hereford would lose its rights of institution and deprivation, of collation after six months, and of custody; in place of a rector whose wisdom had been at the disposal of the diocesan and his chapter, the prior would present only a simple priest; hospitality and almsgiving might also be neglected and the rectory house moved to the priory's own manor "in preiudicium operum pietatis".[1] But that a decline of pastoral care tended to follow appropriation to religious houses was certainly appreciated at this time. Thomas de Seccheton (Sotheron), when bringing a suit in the Curia (1369–70) against the Premonstratensian abbey of Cockersand, the appropriator of Mitton (Lancashire), argued that the cure of souls had suffered because there was only one priest, as against the two or three commensal priests and four or five familiar clerks and laymen who had served the church in the time of William de Tatham, the late rector, and his predecessors.[2] By contrast the appropriation of parish churches to chantries maintained within them was alleged to have a favourable effect—an increase in the number of priests available for parish duties, as we have seen in the case of Stratford.[3] A church so appropriated might also benefit in other ways. At Tormarton John de la Riviere provided five sets of vestments for the high altar, three for the altar in the chapel of our Lady, and two for the nave altars of St Anne and St Joseph, as well as relics, chalices, corporals, service books, surplices, and almuces. For their maintenance he gave stock worth £20 to the chantry warden and his successors.[4]

Apart from Orleton, who had a somewhat limited purpose in mind,[5] Cobham was the only Worcester bishop known to have opposed appropriation during our period. Cobham's opposition was confined to monastic appropriations, for he was ready enough to accede to the request of Merton Hall in Oxford for the church of Wolford.[6] We learn of his resistance to three projected appropriations: those of Hatherop

---

[1] *Heref. Reg. Swinfield*, pp. 421–2, 432–6.

[2] Quoted from Arch. Vat. Collect. 417A by Barraclough, *Papal Provisions*, pp. 52–3. J. McNulty later appended the documents in the case to his article "Thomas Sotheron *v.* Cockersand Abbey" (*C.S.* N.S. Vol. 100, pp. 1–146). See also *C.P.L.* 1362–1404, p. 74.

[3] See pp. 233–4 above.   [4] See p. 233 above.   [5] See p. 245 above.

[6] *Reg. Cobham*, ff. 77v.–78r., 81r.: pp. 130, 135–6.

to Gloucester Abbey,[1] Fairford to Tewkesbury,[2] and Snitterfield to the priory of the Holy Sepulchre at Warwick. In the first two cases he was successful, although Fairford was to be appropriated by papal bull in 1334.[3]

Cobham's arguments in the Snitterfield case are instructive. To some extent they echo those of Bishop Swinfield. He was up against powerful lay interests, for the appropriation was urged by the king (Edward II), by Stapledon, bishop of Exeter and royal treasurer, and by the elder Despenser. In a letter to Stapledon, Cobham pointed out that the convent's poverty was unlikely to be alleviated by the appropriation, as had been shown in the case of a neighbouring parish;[4] that, as was well known, appropriations deprived scholars and royal and familiar clerks of the prospects of promotion; and that once an appropriation had been made bishops and chapters permanently lost the fruits at times of vacancy, as well as the counsel and help which the appropriator, and even the whole Church, had formerly derived from a rector of standing ("per discretum et potentem rectorem").[5] In another letter on the same matter addressed to the king, Cobham stressed similar points and detailed the appropriations to which he had already been forced to give his consent. Once again he makes much of the argument that appropriation harmed those at the Schools and clerks who served the king, bishops, and other lords. Such reasoning would have received the approval of administrators of Otery's stamp.[6] But although Cobham justified his resistance by urging what he considered to be the wider interests of the Church, he was not unaware, as we shall see,[7] of some of the evils of appropriation at parish level. In this instance his opposition was of no avail and he was obliged to appropriate Snitterfield in the usual way—after due inquiry and formal approval of the reasons alleged by the priory.[8]

The cathedral priory might resist appropriation merely by withholding its consent. This could be done with the bishop's connivance or occasionally, so it seems, independently. A royal request for the priory's approval of Hatherop's appropriation (1321) was circumvented on the grounds that the bishop had taken no action.[9] Doubtless

---

[1] See above, p. 235, n. 8.   [2] *Reg. Cobham*, fo. 87r., p. 151.

[3] *Reg. Orleton* 2, ff. 54v.–55r.

[4] The reference may be to Bidford or Long Compton, Warwickshire parishes the appropriation of which (1316) to Kenilworth and Walden respectively was confirmed by Cobham; or it may even be to Wolford. *Reg. Cobham*, ff. 13r., 19v.: pp. 15, 24.

[5] Ibid., fo. 101r., p. 184

[6] Ibid., fo. 101r.–v., pp. 184–5; above, p. 209, n. 3.

[7] P. 263 below.   [8] *Reg. Cobham*, fo. 103r.–v., pp. 187–8.

[9] See above, p. 235, n. 8.

the monks knew Cobham's mind well enough. In the case of Snitterfield (1325) the prior explained to the king and to Stapledon that
opposition within the chapter prevented his complying with their
demands. Five of the monks had stated that they did not wish to
consent on any account, while three or four others declared that
although for conscience' sake they had not wanted to do so they would
be guided by the bishops of Winchester (John Stratford) and Hereford
(Orleton).[1] Despite this seemingly independent show of resistance the
chapter's confirmation followed hard on Cobham's reluctant appropriation.[2] But when Evesham Abbey proposed to appropriate Saintbury (1312), the priory's attitude was not influenced, so far as is known,
by any episcopal objection. Reynolds instructed his official, Benedict de
Paston, to procure the monks' assent, but the prior for some reason
which we are not told successfully shelved the matter,[3] and the church
was not subsequently appropriated.[4]

The action of Archbishops Winchelsey and Reynolds in the matter of
appropriation, the one rescinding and the other confirming an episcopal decree, calls for additional comment. Winchelsey was initially
acting *sede vacante* at a time when the limits of his jurisdiction in the
diocese were to some extent undefined. There was no diocesan to defend
Giffard's decree until the question of Dodderhill's appropriation was
brought to Gainsburgh's notice on the occasion of his enthronement,
when he was asked to confirm it.[5] In consequence the archbishop
seems to have gained a favourable position, and later dispute revolved
round the legality of his presentation rather than of his action in
quashing the appropriation. Certainly this action was not regarded by
subsequent bishops as inhibiting reappropriation. Reynolds merely
confirmed as archbishop what he had decreed as bishop.[6] But confirmation by the metropolitan was no more a necessary stage in the
process than was papal confirmation. Resistance by archbishop or
bishop might prompt the disappointed party to petition for papal

[1] L.A., ff. cxxi v.– cxxii r.

[2] Ibid., fo. cxxii. r.–v.: 11 and 12 June 1325. Cf. *Reg. Cobham*, fo. 117r., p. 207,
where the chapter seal is said to have been affixed "propter terrorem et minas domini
W[alteri Stapledon]".

[3] He wrote to Paston ("amico suo"): "Specialiter supplicantes quatinus certifi-
cacionem super appropriacione ecclesie de Seynesbury si comode fieri possit dissi-
muletis hac vice si placet vel saltem cum modificacione quod nondum plene deliber-
avimus certificare velitis" (L.A., fo. lvi v.).

[4] William de Cotes' resignation of the church in 1314 and Maidstone's subsequent
collation by lapse could be connected with another attempt at appropriation. Cotes
later tried to regain Saintbury with the aid of forged bulls. Reg. Maidstone, ff. 18r.,
23v., 43r.; p. 216 above.

[5] *R.S.V.*, fo. 19v., p. 54.   [6] See p. 246 above.

appropriation. This, as we have seen, happened in the cases of Dodder-hill, Longdon, and Fairford.[1] At Blockley the bishop used the method to break a long series of papal provisions which had deprived himself and his predecessors of any profit from the benefice. Appropriated to his *mensa*, the rectory provided a permanent addition to episcopal income which was out of reach of papal provisors.[2] None the less, comparatively few appropriations in the Worcester diocese were carried out by means of papal bulls during our period.

Miss Wood-Legh found that of the seventy-five English churches appropriated on papal authority between 1330 and 1348 a third had been held at least twice in the preceding half century by royal clerks, papal officers, or others who did not reside.[3] This calculation suggests no more than that in a number of cases appropriation did less addi-tional harm to the parishes than has sometimes been thought.[4] But this was not the way that bishops like Swinfield and Cobham looked at the matter. In their view benefices were the appropriate recompense for the services of administrator or scholar. How else could such men be provided for? When Cobham licensed so many rectors to be absent from their benefices it seems likely that he was not thinking merely of the advantages of scholarly clergy in the parishes, but also of their value in the diocese and Church at large.[5] Appropriation, by reducing the number of suitable benefices, inflicted permanent loss not so much on the parishes themselves[6] as on the Church in general. In a way the attitude of the clerks whom such bishops sought to promote was not unlike that of the appropriators. Both wished to treat benefices as a source of income ("*beneficium*") rather than as a necessary main-tenance for the performance of a particular duty ("*officium*") for which the endowment had originally been set aside. Whereas Cobham and Swinfield considered the claim of the secular clerk to be greater than that of the monk,[7] Bransford, a Benedictine, doubtless viewed the matter from a different standpoint.

At this juncture it may be useful to glance at some of the reasons for appropriation advanced by religious houses. Many of them had become almost common form; the inadequacy of resources; propin-

[1] See pp. 244, 246, 248, above.   [2] See p. 216 above.

[3] Op. cit. pp. 140–3.

[4] With regard to Blockley (ibid., p. 141), it should have been pointed out that the ample documentation arises from the exceptional nature of the case. See pp. 216–17 above.

[5] See above pp. 206 et seq.

[6] Which would not in any case have had permanently resident rectors under Cobham's scheme of things.

[7] See pp. 247–9 above.

quity to a public highway, town, or bridge; the outbreak of murrain among the cattle, the sterility of land, the loss of manors, and the malice of the monastery's enemies. As Cobham argued, almost any religious house could prove disasters of this kind.[1] But some of the reasons do reflect particular conditions. The priory at Kenilworth alleged the losses caused by the civil war and the siege of the castle there,[2] Great Malvern Priory pleaded the burden of papal demands ("prevalens impositio summorum pontificum"),[3] Worcester Priory the need to repair the cathedral church,[4] Tewkesbury Abbey the ruin of the nave which had made it impossible to celebrate Mass on the site of the high altar.[5] Westminster Abbey complained of the destruction caused by a fire which had spread from the royal palace,[6] while at Llanthony the prior's madness ("tyrannica rabies nuper in dominum Willelmum priorem") was blamed for the financial exigencies of the house.[7] The particular plaint of Evesham was that the abbey was situated in pasture land ("in loco tam campestri") and had to spend much of its resources on the purchase of timber.[8] All this was special pleading, and one instance plainly shows how a monastic plea could be cleverly adjusted to suit altered circumstances. In 1314 the monks of Tewkesbury directed two petitions for the appropriation of Thornbury to Bishop Maidstone. The earlier one describes the monastery as having been well endowed initially with both spiritualities and temporalities by the progenitors of Gilbert de Clare, earl of Gloucester and Hertford. The later petition, by an ingenious alteration of phrasing, speaks of the slender initial endowment with spiritualities and temporalities in remote areas, and especially in Wales where they suffered from frequent enemy inroads.[9] The reason for this change is not hard to find. In the interval between the petitions Gilbert de Clare had died on the field of Bannockburn, leaving his three daughters as co-heiresses.[10]

Appropriation was an expensive business, and could have brought little financial advantage for a number of years. The cost of the royal licence was heavy. Worcester Priory paid £10 for Tibberton;[11] St

---

[1] *Reg. Cobham*, fo. 101v., p. 185.
[2] Reg. Maidstone, ff. 42v., 45r. Bidford.
[3] L.A., fo. lxv v. Thornbury.
[4] *Liber Pens.* no. 68, pp. 18–19: printed Nash 2, pp. 237–8. Overbury. The nave was being rebuilt at the time.
[5] Reg. Orleton 2, ff. 54v.–55r. Fairford.
[6] Reg. Orleton 2, ff. 53v.–54r. Longdon.
[7] Reg. Orleton 1, fo. 21r.–v.; ibid. 2, fo. 38r.–v. (duplicate). Tytherington.
[8] For example, L.A., fo. cxxvii v. Ombersley.
[9] Reg. Maidstone, ff. 7v., 17v.   [10] *G.E.C.* 5, p. 714
[11] *C.P.R.* 1313–17, p. 217.

Augustine's Abbey, Bristol, fifty marks (£33 6s. 8d.) for Wotton-under-Edge.[1] The vicarage had to be allowed for, and an annuity was some-times paid to the rector if he could be persuaded to resign. It might be cheaper to pension the rector and receive immediate investiture rather than risk the possibility of having to seek later confirmation or to oppose some royal presentee or papal provisor.[2] Tewkesbury Abbey agreed to pay the rector of Thornbury one hundred marks a year (£66 13s. 4d.) for the rest of his life; the vicarage was estimated at twenty-five marks (£16 13s. 4d.) and an indemnity of four marks (£2 13s. 4d.) was to be paid annually to the cathedral church.[3] All this from a church which was taxed at £31 13s. 4d.[4] Pensions were regularly reserved by the bishop at the time of appropriation, the burden of payment commonly being laid on the appropriators.[5] Many of them were intended to indemnify the bishop or chapter,[6] sometimes both, for the loss of the fruits of a benefice at times of vacancy.[7] Some were by way of procuration. This usually amounted to the canonical maximum of four marks[8] and became due either at times of visitation or at three-yearly intervals.[9] For Powick the monks of Great Malvern had to pay four marks' procuration and a further mark annually "in signum subieccionis et temporalis dampni recompensacionem".[10] So far as is known, the bishop ordinarily determined the amount of the indemnity

---

1 *C.P.R.* 1307–13, p. 381. The abbey did not gain possession.

2 Bulls of appropriation had a *non obstante* clause to prevent the interference of provisors.

3 Reg. Maidstone, fo. 22r.; ibid., ff. 17v.–18r.; L.A., fo. xv r.

4 The real income of a church was often well above the figure at which it was taxed. In 1342, shortly after its appropriation, a local jury valued Great Badminton at £26 8s. 2d. Including a small pension from Oldbury chapel it was taxed at £13 15s. 2d. Reg. Bransf., portion of MS. attached to fo. 53; *Valor Eccles.*, p. 220.

5 But the vicar of Tanworth had to pay 13s. 4d. a year to the bishop; the vicar of Kidderminster one mark to the bishop and another to the prior. Reg. Bransf., ff. 23v., 24v., 83v., 92v. (157, 160, 681, 753).

6 A record of the pensions due to the priory was kept in the Liber Pensionum.

7 For example, the sisters of the hospital at Maiden Bradley declared that the pensions from Kidderminster (see n. 5 above) were paid: "In recompensacionem emolumentorum que vos et quilibet successor vester loci diocesanus sede plena, ac predicti domini prior et capitulum sede vacante, temporibus vacacionum eiusdem ecclesie de consuetudine dicte Wygorn' diocesis alias habituri essetis et essent, si appropriacio huiusmodi facta non fuisset." Reg. Bransford, fo. 21v.; (153).

8 See above, p. 150, n. 5. The four marks promised by Tewkesbury Abbey to the bishop, or to the prior *sede vacante*, at times of visitation, were later increased to five. Fairford appropriation: Reg. Orleton 2, fo. 57v.; *Liber Pens.*, pp. 3–4.

9 For example, on account of Bidford Kenilworth Priory paid four marks to the bishop every three years. L.A., fo. lxxi v.

10 L.A., ff. lxv v.–lxvi r. The use of the word "subjection" is significant. The Worcester monks had not reconciled themselves to Great Malvern's new position. See pp. 29, 245.

after consultation with his chapter, though the appropriator's submission to his decree may have been a necessary preliminary.[1] But the cathedral priory's portion was sometimes arrived at by arbitration. When Hailes Abbey appropriated Longborough both parties agreed to abide by the decision of outside persons, namely the abbot of Dore and the prior of Abergavenny.[2]

Quite apart from these permanent obligations were the numerous incidental expenses incurred in the course of appropriation.[3] They must have been very heavy in the case of Dodderhill, and were probably substantial in normal circumstances, but with one exception we know little or nothing about them. Among the Westminster muniments relating to Longdon is a small roll of two membranes which details the expenses of one of the monks, R. de Beby, while engaged on the business of that church's reappropriation in 1334–5.[4] Beby's first step was to procure from Orleton's court a copy of the process of appropriation which the bishop had carried out prior to his translation to Winchester.[5] He then spent thirty-one days away from his abbey discussing the appropriation with the new bishop, Montacute.[6] During this period he seems to have had Orleton's process and the papal bull collated with the originals by the bishop's notary and to have arranged for the priory's confirmation and its registration.[7] For a further twenty-seven days he was primarily concerned with arrangements for an inquiry into the dilapidations of the buildings at Longdon. Three later journeys, occupying twelve, twenty-two, and seventeen days respectively, were made for consultations with the bishop. For each of them there is a separate account. The third includes payments to Robert de Worth, the bishop's chancellor; John de Clipston, his official; and Richard de Ledbury, his notary. It marks the completion of the process and brings the total cost to £30 17s. 11¾d. Subsequent accounts were for putting the rectory buildings in order and restocking its lands.

---

[1] Submissions of this kind are not uncommon in the Worcester records.

[2] L.A., fo. cxxv r.–v. The abbot of Dore was of course a Cistercian; the prior of Abergavenny (Richard de Bromwich) a former monk of Worcester. They decided on an annual pension of 20s.

[3] Cf. Wood-Legh, pp. 144 et seq.

[4] Westm. Abb. Mun., 21262. The story really begins with the fire of 1298 which spread from the royal palace of Westminster to the abbey. It is told in the author's "The Appropriation of Longdon Church to Westminster Abbey" in *Trans. Worc. Arch. Soc.* XXXVIII (1961), pp. 39–52.

[5] At a cost of £1 11s. 10d.

[6] See p. 245 above.

[7] The prior's notary received 3s. 4d. for writing out the confirmation, the precentor 6s. 8d. "pro feudo sigilli". The registration cost 2s. The confirmation is entered in the Liber Albus (fo. clvii v.).

During our period there would appear to have been thirty-six[1] appropriations of churches in the diocese, twenty-eight of them to religious houses. The details can be tabulated as follows:

NUMBER OF CHURCHES	APPROPRIATING BODIES
15	Monasteries in the diocese
10	Monasteries outside the diocese
4	Chantries
2	Oxford colleges (Merton, Queen's)
1	Nunnery (Cook Hill)
1	Leper hospital (Salisbury diocese)[2]
1	Hospital (St John, Warwick)
1	Collegiate church (Warwick)
1	Bishop (*mensa*)

The total represents rather less than 11% of the 335 churches which were assessed for taxation in 1291.[3] Only two churches were appropriated in the first decade,[4] six in the second. Thereafter the numbers rise steadily, reaching their highest point during Bransford's episcopate, which roughly coincides with the last decade.

DECADES	APPROPRIATIONS
1300–09	2
1310–19	6[5]
1320–29	7
1330–39	9
1340–49	12
1300–49 (incl.)	36

The amount of information about appropriations in the diocesan records is even greater than that for chantries. Appropriations, unlike chantries,[6] were the bishop's official concern except in a very few instances. In consequence they are regularly recorded in the registers, and because of the cathedral priory's right of confirmation, in the Liber Albus too. The procedure was well established and dependent upon Ottobon's ruling that poverty constituted legitimate grounds for appropriation. The truth of particular allegations was formally established, but there was no provision for a wider inquiry into the economic state of the religious bodies concerned. Episcopal resistance was comparatively rare and in the ordinary course bishops were satisfied if their sees were indemnified for the financial loss sustained. Successful resistance was even more rare, partly because of the pressure that could be brought to bear on a recalcitrant diocesan, partly because

1 Including Wotton. See p. 246 above.
2 Technically a priory of Augustinian canons.   3 Hartridge, *Vicarages*, p. 79.
4 Or three if Dodderhill is included. See p. 245 above.
5 Including Wotton. See p. 246 above.   6 See p. 227 above.

of the alternative procedure by papal bull. The Liber Albus shows that in many cases appropriation was supported by the king, or by prominent ecclesiastics and laymen, either patrons or well-wishers, whose demands it was difficult to resist.[1]

To attempt to account for the marked increase in appropriation, which Miss Wood-Legh has shown to have been general, is no part of our overall purpose. Few monasteries were founded in the fourteenth century: none in the Worcester diocese during our period. Both laymen and ecclesiastics were endowing chantries and collegiate churches in growing numbers.[2] That pious benefactions took these forms meant that religious houses stood less chance of further endowments. But it is doubtful whether the calamities of the first half of the fourteenth century, before the Black Death that is, were more severe than formerly, and it has not been proved that the growth of appropriation resulted directly from any general deterioration in monastic finances, which were already in a bad state in the thirteenth century.[3] In any case, as we have seen, the exploitation of benefices was not confined to the regular clergy.[4] However this may be, appropriation provided a useful means of increasing monastic resources, although the expense involved detracted somewhat from the immediate financial advantage.

LIST OF BENEFICES APPROPRIATED IN WORCESTER DIOCESE
1300–1349 (incl.)[5]

DATE OF EFFECTIVE APPROP.	CHURCH	APPROPRIATOR	REFS.
1302	Childs Wickham	Bordesley Abb. (Cist.)	R.S.V., fo. 34v.
1309	Elmley Castle	Elmley Castle chantry	Reg. Reyn., fo., 21r.; L.A., fo. xlv r.–v.

[1] Mrs Wood (*English Mons. and their Patrons*, pp. 138–9, 157–9) argues that appropriations were against patrons' interests. But they did urge them sometimes. A distinction should be made between the appropriation of churches long held by a monastery and new endowments in this form (p. 240 n. 5 above). Cobham declared that his hand had been forced by king and nobles (*Reg. Cobham*, ff. 87r., 101v.: pp. 151, 185); Bransford asked the chapter to comply with the earl of Huntingdon's wishes for the appropriation of Tanworth to Maxstoke "scientes profecto quod sua dileccio et benevolencia vobis et nobis ac ecclesie nostre cathedrali multum utilitatis adicere poterunt si sue in hac parte fuerit paritum voluntati" (L.A., fo. clxxiii r).

[2] Knowles (*Medieval Religious Houses*, p. 43) states that collegiate churches "became the fashion" in the century and a half after 1300.

[3] Snape, *English Monastic Finances*, p. 119.   [4] See above pp. 240, n. 5, 250.

[5] Where there are two or more appropriation decrees the latest, that is the effective one, is listed. Wotton provides the only instance of an appropriation which was not implemented.

18

DATE OF EFFECTIVE APPROP.	CHURCH	APPROPRIATOR	REFS.
1313[1]	Wotton-under-Edge	St Augustine's Abb., Bristol	Reg. Reyn., fo. 76r.–v.; cf. L.A., fo. xlix r.–v.
1314	Powick	Great Malvern Pr. (Ben.)	Reg. Maidst., fo. 16v.; L.A., fo. lxv v.
1315	Thornbury	Tewkesbury Abb. (Ben.)	Reg. Maidst., ff. 7v., 17v.–18r.; L.A., fo. xv r.
1315	Tibberton	Worcester Pr. (Ben.). Office of Precentor	Reg. Maidst., fo. 23r.
1316	Bidford	Kenilworth Pr. (Aug.)	Reg. Maidst., ff. 42v., 45r.; L.A., fo. lxxi r.
1316	Long Compton	Walden Abb., Essex (Ben.)	Reg. Maidst., ff. 41v.–42r.; L.A., fo. lxxix r.–v.
1322	Wolford	Merton Hall, Oxford	Reg. Cobh., ff. 77v.–78r.; L.A., fo. cvi x.
1324	South Cerney	Gloucester Abb. (Ben.)	L.A., fo. cxix r.
1325	Snitterfield	Warwick, Holy Sepulchre (Aug.)	Reg. Cobh., fo. 103r.–v.; L.A., fo. cxxii r.–v.
1325	Longborough	Hailes Abb. (Cist.)	Reg. Cobh., fo. 106r.–v.; L.A., ff. cxxiv v.–cxxv v.
1326	Ombersley	Evesham Abb. (Ben.)	Reg. Cobh., ff. 112v.–113r.; L.A., ff. cxxvii v.–cxxviii r.
1327	Pershore, St Andrew	Pershore Abb. (Ben.)	Reg. Orleton, 1 fo. 39r.–v. L.A., fo. cxxxi r.–v.
1329	Duntisbourne Militis	Dore Abb. (Cist.)	Reg. Orleton 2, fo. 16r.–v.; L.A., fo. cxxxvi r.
1330	Tytherington	Llanthony Sec. (Aug.)	Reg. Orleton 1, fo. 21r.–v; 2, fo. 38r.–v.; L.A., fo. cxxxvi r.–v.
1331	*Tetbury[2]	Eynsham Abb. (Ben.)	Reg. Mont. 1, fo. 12v.; L.A., ff. clii v.– cliii v.
1331	Bishampton	Cook Hill (Ben. Nunn.)	Reg. Orleton 1, fo. 23r.–v.; 2, fo. 45r.–v.; L.A., fo. cxl r.–v.
1333	*Blockley	The bishop	Reg. Mont. 1, ff. 11v.—12r.
1333	*Dodderhill	Worcester Pr. (Ben.)	Reg. Orleton, 2 fo. 53r.–v.
1334	*Longdon	Westminster Abb. (Ben.)	Reg. Orleton 2, ff. 53v.–54r.; Westm. Abb. Mun., 21256–21258; L.A., ff. clvii v.–clviii r.
1334	*Fairford	Tewkesbury Abb. (Ben.)	Reg. Orleton 2, ff. 54v.–55r.
1335	Kidderminster	Maiden Bradley Hosp. (Salisb. dioc.)	Reg. Mont. 1, ff. 20v.–21r.; L.A., ff. clix v.–clx v.
1336	Stratford	Stratford chantry in chapel of St Thomas	Reg. Mont. 1, ff. 50r.–61v.

[1] The abbey did not gain possession. See p. 246 above.

[2] An asterisk in this list indicates that appropriation was made on the authority of a papal bull.

DATE OF EFFECTIVE APPROP.	CHURCH	APPROPRIATOR	REFS.
1340	Tanworth	Maxstoke Pr. (Aug.)	Reg. Bransf., ff. 39r.–v.; L.A., ff. clxxiii v.–clxxiiii r.
1340	Campden	Chester, St. Werburgh's Abb. (Ben.)	Reg. Bransf., fo. 41r.–v.; L.A., fo. clxx v.
1340(?) (undated)	Moreton Daubeney (moiety)	Warwick, Hosp. of St John	Reg. Bransf., ff. 13v.–14r.
1341(?) (undated)	Great Badminton	Lilleshall Abb. (Aug.)	Reg. Bransf., fo. 53r.; L.A., ff. clxxvi v.–clxxvii r.
1341	Pillerton	Warwick, Colleg. ch. of St. Mary	L.A., fo. clxxvii r.–v.
1344	Tormarton	Tormarton chantry	Reg. Bransf., fo. ccxxxiiii r.–v. al. 165.
1344	Acton Turville	Tormarton chantry	Reg. Bransf., fo. ccxxxv r. al. 166.
1344	Clent with Rowley chap.	Halesowen Abb. (Premonstr.)	Reg. Bransf., fo. 83r.–v.; L. A., ff. clxxxxv v.–clxxxxvi r.
1345	Aston Cantlow	Maxstoke Pr. (Aug.)	Reg. Bransf., ff. 91v.–92r.; L.A., ff. clxxxxvii v–clxxxxviii r.; B.M. Add. Ch. 21418 (original appropriation document).
1346	*Overbury	Worcester Pr.	Liber Pens., pp. 18–19; Nash 2, pp. 237–8.
1346	*Newbold Pacey	Queen's Hall, Oxford	Liber Pens., p. 13; C.P.L. 1342–62, p. 224.
1347	Yardley	Maxstoke Pr. (Aug.)	Reg. Bransf., fo. 112r.–v.; L.A., fo. cciii r.

VICARAGES[1]

In every appropriation decree the bishop reserved a suitable portion to be assigned by himself or one of his successors to a perpetual vicar. Generally this assignment was made when the appropriator received investiture, or at any rate shortly after the institution of the first vicar.[2] Once established a vicarage might continue even if the appropriation were rescinded. This happened at Dodderhill where Giffard had ordained a vicarage in 1302.[3] Winchelsey deprived the appropriators

---

[1] The subject is treated in detail by R. A. R. Hartridge, *A History of Vicarages in the Middle Ages*. For some modification of his views see Cheney, *Becket to Langton*, pp. 131–6. All that is attempted here is a summary of the Worcester evidence with the emphasis on the administrative procedure entailed.

[2] Ottobon decreed (Athon, p. 121) that vicars were to be presented to the diocesan and a portion assigned to them within six months. This is glossed by Athon (ad ver. *spatium*): "In futurum computandum a tempore appropriationis expeditae."

[3] Printed Nash 1, pp. 338–9, from D. & C. Reg. 2, ff. 30–1.

of the church in the following year,[1] but as late as 1318 the vicar, Robert Bulfinch, was considered to be entitled to his portion. In his absence the rector, William de Thorntoft, had taken the profits for his own use on the grounds that he had had to bear the burdens of the vicarage. Thorntoft made satisfaction to the vicar and Bishop Cobham absolved him from any taint incurred in consequence of his action.[2]

In his appropriation decree the bishop usually estimated the vicarage at a certain sum. If he did not know the true value of the church, which was probably much above the figure at which it was taxed, he ordered inquiry to be made. The mandate was ordinarily addressed to the official of the appropriate archdeacon who held the inquiry in the church concerned with the help of a sworn jury of laymen and clerks.[3] At other times the inquiry involved the vicarage rather than the church as a whole, the jurors deciding whether the revenues allotted to the vicar amounted to the sum fixed by the diocesan.[4]

Although in the ordination of vicarages the diocesan acted *auctoritate ordinaria* he regularly obtained the submission of the appropriators in the first instance.[5] Ottobon had ruled that the religious themselves could assign portions to the vicars of their appropriated churches, the diocesan being enjoined to do so in cases of negligence, that is after six months.[6] The details of the vicarages of Standish (1348), anciently appropriated to St Peter's Abbey at Gloucester, and of Wellesbourne (1348), appropriated to Kenilworth Priory,[7] were agreed between the appropriators and the vicars, the bishop merely adding his confirma-

---

1 *Ann. Wigorn.*, p. 556: cf. p. 245 above.

2 *Reg. Cobham*, ff. 53v.–54r., p. 75. The editor (p. 75n) is wrong to ascribe this vicarage to Maidstone.

3 For example, Cobham's ordination of Wolford vicarage is prefaced by a note of the inquiry "facta de mandato nostro . . . per viros fidedignos in numero competenti". The portion of MS. attached to fo. 53 of Reg. Bransford, endorsed: "Venerabili in Christo patri domino Wolstano dei gracia Wyg' episcopo. Per suum clericum domini archidiaconi Glouc' officialem.", seems to be the original certification of an inquiry into the value of Great Badminton.

4 For example, Bishop Maidstone estimated Powick vicarage at twelve marks, and a jury of twelve, comprising four rectors, four vicars, two chaplains, and two laymen, gave an affirmative answer to the question: "an oblaciones, obvenciones et alie minute decime ad alteragium spectantes ad quantitatem se extenderent supradictam". Reg. Maidst., fo. 21v.

5 Submissions of this kind are often found in the registers.

6 Athon (p. 121) ad ver. *alioquin*: "i.e. Si infra sex menses praedictos diocesanis hujusmodi religiosi praesentare distulerunt, sufficientem portionem assignando".

7 Wellesbourne was probably appropriated towards the end of the thirteenth century. Cf. *V.C.H. Warwicks.* 5, p. 197. In 1303 Gainsburgh ordered the sequestration of the profits of the vicarage because the incumbent had been instituted to Strixton, Lincoln diocese. *Reg. Gainsb.*, fo. 31v., p. 118.

tion.[1] But these are exceptions, and in any case concerned the revision of existing arrangements. In the ordinary course the bishop assumed responsibility for the drawing up of the ordination documents. In some cases two or three copies of his decree were made, the appropriator and the vicar each retaining one, while the third was kept in the episcopal archives. The process was completed by the prior and chapter's confirmation, though this is recorded but rarely.

Papal intervention in the matter of vicarages can seldom be traced. Campden, where Bransford ordained a vicarage in 1343, provides an example. Although the portion was worth £20 a year question had arisen as to its sufficiency, and the pope empowered the bishop of Lincoln (Thomas Bek) to alter it at his discretion.[2] Even when appropriation was effected by papal bull to the exclusion of the diocesan, the ordination of the vicarage was almost invariably reserved to him.[3] Wolverley, appropriated after our period (1352), supplies an exception. The bull empowered the bishop of Hereford, John Trilleck, to establish the vicarage. He did so on receiving the papal letters from the cathedral priory, the appropriators, and by the usual means of local inquiry by a sworn jury.[4]

It is not easy to generalize about the relative size of the portions assigned to the rector and the vicar. Although we are seldom told both the true value of the church and that of the vicar's portion, such figures as we have suggest that the latter usually amounted to roughly a third of the whole.[5] The jury's calculation was based on common years ("communibus annis") and there was no guarantee that the vicar's portion would always reach the estimate. Cobham attempted to overcome this difficulty at the expense of the appropriators. At Longborough the vicar's portion was £10 and at Ombersley twenty marks (£13 6s. 8d.), but if in lean years the real income in either case should prove to be less, then the appropriating monastery was to pay the full amount.[6] In the Longborough ordination the bishop decreed that this was to be done on the unsupported word of the vicar.[7]

---

1 Reg. Bransf., ff. 21r.–22r., 138r.–139r. (153, 945).

2 Ibid., ff. 68r.–v. (595); *C.P.L.* 1342–62, pp. 186–7.

3 For example, Overbury (cf. above p. 244, nn. 4, 5). The vicarage was not ordained until 1368. See p. 265 below.

4 See Nash 2, pp. 476–7 (1354).

5

CHURCH	TRUE VALUE	VICARAGES	BISHOP
Elmley Castle	£12 14s. 4d.	£3 16s. 4d. + grain	Reynolds
Wolford	£17 6s. 8d.	£5 6s. 8d.	Cobham
Snitterfield	£17 14s. 9d.	£6 os. 9d. Revised	Orleton
		ordination	

6 *Reg. Cobham*, ff. 111v.–112r., 124v.–125r.: pp. 198, 223.

7 "Et si contingat quod porciones per vos assignande ob sterilitatem annorum vel ex

Ordination documents frequently contain a clause reserving the diocesan's right to alter his decree if need should arise. Complaints that vicarages were insufficient, or even over-endowed, could be made to him. The vicarage ordained at Longdon by Bishop Orleton was found to be inadequate within a year, and his successor Montacute augmented it on the vicar's petition. This was probably because of the heavy burdens imposed. The vicar had to provide for a priest celebrating our Lady's Mass daily, for a deacon and subdeacon, as well as for a priest to serve each of the chapels of "Chaddesley" and "Morton Foliot".[1] He had also to find books, vestments, and ornaments, to repair and if necessary to rebuild the chancels of Longdon and of both chapels, to pay 1s. for a lamp in the chancel, 14s. 11d. for the archdeacon's procuration, and 1s. as *senagium*.[2] Unfortunately we are not told the value of the vicarage.

It may often have been the case, as Hartridge suggests, that where the vicarage was large the burdens sustained were correspondingly great. But this was not necessarily the only factor determining its size, nor is there Worcester evidence to support the contention that appropriators received more than two thirds of the income of wealthier churches at this time.[3] Cobham, piqued by the necessity of appropriating Snitterfield, made the vicarage so substantial that only a small sum was left, and his successor had to reduce the allotment.[4] On the other hand his taxation of Wolford vicarage at £5 6s. 8d., with the obligation to repair and rebuild the chancel, was on the low side. In this case we know that he favoured the appropriation.[5] The least well endowed vicarages so far as is known were Elmley Castle, where the vicar's portion totalled £3 16s. 4d. not including an allowance of grain, and Tibberton, where it amounted to £4. At Thornbury and Kidderminster there were portions of twenty-five marks (£16 13s. 4d.), and at Dodderhill one of twenty marks (£13 6s. 8d.).[6] The best endowed

alia causa quacumque ad decem libras sterling' se annis singulis non extendant nos vicario qui pro tempore fuerit pro anno vel annis quibus porcionibus sit assignatis in principio anni vel annorum idem vicarius contentus non fuerit decem libras sterling' sine diminucione quacumque infra illum annum vel annos annuatim pro dictis porcionibus persolvemus solius vicarii assercioni stando totaliter in premissis." Reg. Cobham, fo. 112r.: the monks' acknowledgement of their obligation.

[1] I.e. Chaceley and Castle Morton.
[2] Regs. Orleton 2, ff. 56v.–57r.; Mont. 1, fo. 18r–v.; 2, ff. 25v.–26r.; Westm. Abb. Mun. 21264–5, 21270.
[3] *Vicarages*, pp. 132 et seq.
[4] See p. 263 below.
[5] See p. 247 above.
[6] See the list following this section.

vicarage was Campden, worth £20, and it is surprising that its sufficiency was questioned.[1]

It is difficult to make other than broad generalizations about the division of profits and burdens between appropriators and vicars, because each ordination was treated individually. But it can be said that it was common in the Worcester diocese, as elsewhere,[2] for the vicar to receive a house, a portion of land, the lesser tithes, the dead mortuaries, and everything pertaining to altarage, and for the rector to have the greater tithes of corn and hay together with the live mortuaries. In some instances both the ordinary and extraordinary burdens were borne by the appropriators, as at Acton Turville,[3] Campden,[4] and Tanworth;[5] in others the vicars bore the ordinary burdens and the appropriators the extraordinary ones, as at Great Badminton, Ombersley, and Wolford; a third possibility was for the parties to share them *pro rata porcionis*, as was done at Powick[6] and Tibberton.

It is not even possible to be precise about the distinction between "ordinary" and "extraordinary" burdens, but it would seem that the former included all the regular obligations, including the various episcopal and archidiaconal dues;[7] the provision of bread and wine, particularly at Easter when the parishioners communicated, and of lights;[8] as well as the repair and replacement of vestments, books, and other ornaments. The extraordinary burdens are more difficult to define, but they may have comprised procurations of papal nuncios and cardinals as well as other demands of an irregular nature.[9] The repair and reconstruction of the chancel is sometimes specifically classed as one of the ordinary burdens.[10] The responsibility was occasionally laid

---

[1] Particularly as the appropriators were responsible for all burdens (see below) save the provision of clergy (see p. 263 below) and the payment of four marks procuration at times of visitation.

[2] Cf. *Vicarages*, chaps. 3 and 8.

[3] Except 6s. 8d. for the chapter's indemnity.

[4] See n. 1 above.

[5] Except for the expense of additional clergy (see p. 262 below), of providing bread, wine, and certain lights—for which the vicar received a rent of 2s. 6d.—and an indemnity of 13s. 4d. paid to the bishop.

[6] Although most of the usual "ordinary" burdens were here assigned to the vicar in the first instance.

[7] Senagium or synodaticum, cathedraticum, auxilium, procuracio.

[8] In a number of cases lights were separately endowed.

[9] What were considered to be ordinary and what extraordinary burdens varied according to time and place as the evidence adduced by Hartridge (chap. 8) shows.

[10] For example, Great Badminton (1342): "Statuimus . . . quod vicarii prefate ecclesie . . . omnia onera ordinaria dicte ecclesie subeant, refeccione et construccione cancelli exceptis, et quod prefati religiosi omnia onera extraordinaria eiusdem ecclesie . . . subeant imperpetuum et agnoscant." Reg. Bransford, fo. 24r.

on the vicar,[1] more often on the rector[2] or the vicar and rector together.[3] Not infrequently there is no specific mention of the obligation, an omission likely to lead to subsequent dispute. Such facts reveal a very different state of affairs from that found by Hartridge in Exeter diocese, where in the fourteenth century the vicar was made responsible for the chancel in twenty-two out of thirty-two cases.[4]

In general the diocesan's aim seems to have been to ensure that all the duties and obligations incumbent upon the rector before appropriation should continue to be discharged. It is unlikely that he tried to alter or improve upon the customary arrangements. Even a slight alteration made by Bishop Gainsburgh was successfully resisted. When, in 1304, he ordained the vicarage of Childs Wickham, he decreed that the vicar should provide a suitable clerk ("clericus ydoneus"), but the official of the Gloucester archdeacon, who was doubtless aware of the former practice, brought pressure to bear on the vicar to appoint someone in deacon's orders. Gainsburgh thereupon ordered him not to molest the vicar further, arguing that anyone in minor orders was considered suitable to hold a benefice even if it involved the cure of souls.[5] He relented a few days later and declared that he had no intention of altering the pious customs already established in the church.[6]

Additional clergy, apart from a clerk[7] and a priest to act as the vicar's deputy, are seldom recorded in ordination documents. Of the three vicarages in Cobham's register, only one (Wolford) mentions even a clerk.[8] Similarly only two of the seven ordinations in Bransford's register make specific provision for extra clergy: at Tanworth the vicar was to find a parochial chaplain when not officiating himself, besides a

---

[1] For example, Thornbury, Wolford. *V.C.H. Gloucs.* 2, p. 21, includes Fairford, but the obligation does not seem to be mentioned in the vicarage ordination, though the MS. is difficult to read.

[2] For example, Great Badminton, Elmley Castle, Longborough, Ombersley, Powick, Tibberton, Tytherington, Yardley.

[3] For example, Standish, where the vicar had to pay a third but to meet the whole cost at Hardwick chapel; and Kidderminster, where the vicar's liability extended only to 40d.

[4] *Vicarages*, p. 143.

[5] "Vobis mandamus quatinus dictum vicarium si in ecclesia predicta ministrum ydoneum in minoribus ordinibus constitutum invenerit ut tenetur, hac occasione non molestetis seu molestari coram vobis de cetero permittatis, cum in minoribus constitutus ad beneficium ecclesiasticum optinendum eciam si curam habeat animarum ydoneus reputetur." L.A., fo. xxx v.

[6] "Intencionisque nostre non fuit per ordinacionem nostram consuetudinibus piis in ecclesia predicta optentis in aliquo derogare." L.A., fo. xxxi r.

[7] Who was sometimes supported at the parishioners' expense.

[8] *Reg. Cobham*, ff. 81r.–v., pp. 136–7.

clerk to give daily assistance;[1] while the vicar of Campden had to support a substitute priest when necessary, as well as a secondary priest and a deacon for daily ministrations.[2] The largest parochial staff recorded in any vicarage ordination was at Longdon, where the vicar had to maintain three priests, a deacon, and subdeacon.[3]

The only Worcester bishop during our period who is known to have decided views on the subject of vicarages is Cobham. Although defeated at Snitterfield on the main issue, that of its appropriation,[4] he postponed the investiture by instituting a rector, claiming the right by lapse. He ordained a vicarage worth twenty-four marks and reserved its patronage for himself and his successors.[5] Against these somewhat high-handed actions the prior and canons of the Holy Sepulchre, Warwick, appealed to the Holy See and to the Court of Canterbury for tuition. But their legal position was not a strong one for they had consented to abide by Cobham's taxation of the vicarage. They eventually submitted and agreed to secure the remission of the case to the diocesan.[6] This was not the end of the matter. The prior's candidate for the vicarage, Robert de Griswold, does not appear finally to have renounced his appeals until 1330, during Orleton's episcopate.[7] At that time Orleton collated the vicarage to William de Lenynton, but reopened the question of the vicar's portion.[8] A local jury declared that the value of Snitterfield was £17 14s. 9d., rather less than £5 above its taxed value of twenty marks. We can now see the reason for the priory's complaint, for Cobham's twenty-four mark vicarage had left it with precisely £1 14s. 9d. Orleton proceeded to reordain the vicarage, which in its new form did not exceed £6 0s. 9d.—that is, slightly more than a third of the church's total value.[9]

Cobham's awareness of the evils which might follow appropriation is revealed in a mandate which he addressed to the official of the Worcester archdeacon. In the preamble he wrote of the daily complaints that in some appropriated churches, as well as in others where there were perpetual vicars, so small a portion of the revenues was assigned to the vicars that they were unable to discharge the ordinary dues, to maintain hospitality, or to support the burdens incumbent

[1] Reg. Bransford, ff. 24v.–25v. (160).

[2] Ibid., fo. 68r.–v. (595).

[3] See p. 260 above.   [4] See pp. 247–8 above.

[5] Such reservation is unique at Worcester during this period, but Hartridge has come across instances elsewhere. See *Vicarages*, p. 223.

[6] *Reg. Cobham*, fo. 107r.–v., pp. 206–7.

[7] Reg. Orleton 1, fo. 21r.; 2, fo. 37r.

[8] Ibid. 1, fo. 21v.; 2, fo. 39r.

[9] Ibid. 1, fo. 22r.–v; 2, ff. 39r., 40r.–v.

upon them. What was even worse, some vicars resorted to the tables of the religious, or other rectors, abandoning the rights and office of vicar and retaining only the name, so that they had no home in which to lay their heads. The official was to make diligent inquiry into such abuses and to send the names of the churches involved to the bishop.[1]

Disputes between rectors and vicars are sometimes recorded[2] and there is a notable instance of recurring monastic encroachment on a vicarage. This was at Astley, a cell of St Taurin, Evreux, where Reynolds learnt that the monks had taken so much of the vicar's portion that he was unable to carry out his duties. The bishop cited them to produce evidence of the appropriation and of the vicarage ordination. He was in London at the time and the execution of the business was entrusted to commissaries.[3] What action they took is unknown, but the remedy was not effective as Maidstone had to institute another inquiry three years later (1316). This found that the vicar's legitimate portion was exiguous enough, but that it had been further diminished by the monks "ita quod ipsam vicariam intoller-abiliter reddunt exilem". The original portion was re-established.[4] The settlement was even then not a lasting one, for Orleton had to order the prior once again to restore the portions of which he had deprived the vicar.[5] During Bransford's episcopate, at the time of his institution the prior had to swear to render what was due to the vicar.[6]

The record of the Worcester bishops in the matter of the ordination of vicarages is a good one. Hartridge's suggestion that Giffard's legacy to his successors was a considerable number of appropriated churches in which vicarages had not been ordained will not bear examination.[7] It is true that at an episcopal council in 1300/1 the problem of providing vicars in no fewer than nine churches was brought up for discussion,[8] but not one of them was at that time appropriated.[9] Giffard was merely ensuring that there were permanent vicars in churches whose rectors were frequently absent. So far as is known, the only church which Giffard appropriated without making provision for a vicarage was Childs Wickham. This omission was somewhat ostenta-

---

[1] Reg. Cobham, fo. 81., p. 135.

[2] For example, in the preambles to the ordinations of Kidderminster, Standish, and Wellesbourne vicarages.

[3] Reg. Reynolds, ff. 86v.–87r., p. 68; cf. Nash 1, p. 47.

[4] L.A., ff. lxxxv r.– lxxxxvi r. The chapter confirmed the bishop's ruling in 1317.

[5] Reg. Orleton 2, ff. 8v.–9r.: 29 July 1328.

[6] See above, p. 224, n. 1.   [7] Vicarages, p. 221

[8] See above, p. 97, n. 4.

[9] Though Ombersley and Aston Cantlow were appropriated during our period, and there was certainly a vicarage at the latter before appropriation.

tiously pointed out by his successor, Gainsburgh, who remedied the defect.[1] But Giffard had appropriated Childs Wickham on 15 January 1302, only six days before his death, so he could hardly be accused of neglect. His successors were certainly meticulous in this matter. Ordination documents are entered in the registers for twenty-four of the thirty-two churches of which appropriators took possession during our period.[2] At Tormarton and Stratford, vicarages were not ordained because the chantry chaplains were to exercise the cure of souls.[3] In five of the six remaining cases[4] institutions to perpetual vicarages can be found, an indication that definite portions were assigned to the vicars. But the writer has not been able to trace a vicarage at Moreton Daubeney, where a moiety was appropriated,[5] although the bishop reserved a portion in the usual way.[6] Elsewhere the lack of an ordination document or of other evidence of a vicarage was occasioned by the failure of the appropriators to gain possession. Wotton, for instance, although appropriated by Reynolds in 1313 did not pass to St Augustine's Abbey at Bristol as has been supposed.[7] Rectors continued to be instituted during our period[8] and it was not until the beginning of the sixteenth century that the church was appropriated to Tewkesbury Abbey.[9] Bishampton was appropriated to the nunnery of Cook Hill in 1330 by Orleton,[10] but there were two institutions to the rectory in Bransford's time.[11] The first vicar was presented and a portion set aside by the nuns in 1356.[12] Three years later Bishop Bryan drew up a formal ordination.[13] Thoresby ordained the vicarage of Newbold Pacey in 1350,[14] but although Overbury was appropriated by papal bull in 1346[15] the last rector, Henry of Stratford, did not resign until Bishop Barnet's time (1362–3) and a vicarage of £20 17s. 4d. was ordained by his successor, Witlesey, in 1368.[16]

[1] Reg. Gainsb., fo. 1r: "Nullamque porcionem sufficientem pro huiusmodi vicarii sustentacione per dictum predecessorem nostrum aut quemquam alium fuisse vel esse aliqualiter ordinatum."

[2] The total number of appropriations was thirty-six. See pp. 254 et seq.

[3] See pp. 232 et seq. above.

[4] Aston Cantlow, Blockley, South Cerney, Long Compton, Moreton Daubeney, Tetbury.

[5] See p. 257 above. The other moiety was appropriated in 1359 (Reg. Bryan, fo. 91r.).

[6] Reg. Bransford, ff. 13v.–14r. (108).

[7] For example, V.C.H. Gloucs. 2, p. 77.

[8] For example, Reg. Cobham, ff. 27r., 30v: pp. 237, 239.

[9] V.C.H. Gloucs. 2, p. 64.   [10] See p. 256 above.

[11] Reg. Bransf., ff. 26r., 47r. (164, 393).

[12] Nash 1, pp. 91–2 (from Reg. Bryan, fo. 15v.).

[13] Ibid. pp. 93–4 (1359), from Reg. Bryan, fo. 91v.

[14] Reg. Thoresby, fo. 15r.   [15] See p. 257 above.

[16] Nash 2, pp. 238–9.

We do not know the total number of vicarages in the Worcester diocese at this time. In the 1291 *Taxatio* forty-eight were taxed[1] and two more mentioned, but this was probably fewer than half the real number.[2] In Register Bransford for example, there are institutions to eighty-four vicarages. Of these twenty-two occur in the *Taxatio*, while twenty more concern churches appropriated during our period, leaving no fewer than forty-two unaccounted for.[3] Many unappropriated churches had perpetual vicars, and Giffard's attempt to increase the number of these has already been noted. There is no evidence that further steps were taken in this direction; in fact there is some indication of a contrary movement towards the consolidation of existing rectories and vicarages.[4] Although ordinations proceeded *pari passu* with the appropriation of churches, there are no examples of the endowment of vicarages in churches served only by temporary vicars. There is no means of telling how many of these there were.

LIST OF VICARAGE ORDINATIONS
1300–1349

DATE OF ORDINATION	CHURCH	VALUE	REFS.
1302	Dodderhill	(See footnote)[5]	Printed Nash 1 p. 338, from D. & C. Reg. 2, ff. 30–31.
1304	Childs Wickham	£3 + lesser tithes and offerings	Reg. Gainsb., fo. 1r.; L.A., fo. xxx v.
temp. Gainsburgh[6]	Alcester, St Nicholas	—	L.A., fo. xxix r.
temp. Gainsburgh[7]	Spernall	—	L.A., fo. xxix r.
1310	Elmley Castle	£3 16s. 4d. + 2 qrs. of wheat and 2 of barley	Reg. Reyn., fo. 21v.
1315	Powick	£8	Reg. Maidst., fo. 21v.
1315	Tibberton	£4 5s. 6d.	Reg. Maidst., fo. 35v.

[1] This agrees with Hartridge's calculation (p. 79).

[2] Hartridge, pp. 80–1, shows some of the defects of the *Taxatio* in this respect.

[3] A corresponding search in the remaining registers would probably increase this figure considerably.

[4] In 1313 the rector of Meysey Hampton petitioned the bishop for the union of his portion with that of the vicarage, a move which was opposed by the Worcester chapter (L.A., fo. lviii v.). Bishop Cobham consolidated the portions at Weston-on-Avon in 1320 (*Reg. Cobham*, fo. 19v., p. 24).

[5] Estimated at twenty marks (£13 6s. 8d.) by Maidstone in 1314 (Reg. Maidst., fo. 15v.).

[6] Reordination with increase of portion paid to the nuns of Cook Hill. *Inspeximus* dated 1307.

[7] Reordination. Studley Priory and Cook Hill entitled to pension of 20s. *Inspeximus* dated 1307.

DATE OF ORDINATION	CHURCH	VALUE	REFS.
1315	Thornbury	£16 13s. 4d.	Reg. Maidst., fo. 36r.; L.A., fo. xv.
1316	Bidford	£10	Reg. Maidst., fo. 49r.
1316[1]	Astley	—	L.A., ff. lxxxxv r.–lxxxxvi r.
1322	Wolford	£5 6s. 8d.	Reg. Cobham, fo. 81r.–v.
1326	Longborough	£10	Reg. Cobham, ff. 111v.–112r.
1327	Ombersley	£13 6s. 8d.	Reg. Cobham, ff. 124v.–125r.
1331[2]	Snitterfield	£6 0s. 9d.	Reg. Orleton 1, fo. 22r.–v.; 2, fo. 40r.–v.
1331	Pershore, St Andrew	£8[3]	Reg. Orleton 1, fo. 39r.–v.; 2, ff. 44v.–45r.
1331	Duntisbourne Militis	—	Reg. Orleton 1, fo. 39r.; 2, fo. 43v.
1332	Tytherington	—	Reg. Orleton 2, fo. 48v.
1334	Fairford	—	Reg. Orleton 2, ff. 54v.–55r.
1335[4]	Longdon	—	Reg. Mont. 1, fo. 18r.–v.; 2, ff. 25v.–26r.; Westm. Abb. Mun. 21264–5, 21270.
1340[5]	Kidderminster	£16 13s. 4d.[6]	Reg. Bransf., ff. 21r.–22v.
1342	Tanworth	£13 6s. 8d.	Reg. Bransf., fo. 40r.–v.
1342	Great Badminton	—	Reg. Bransf., fo. 24r.–v.
1343	Campden	£20	Reg. Bransf., fo. 68r.–v.[7]
1344	Acton Turville	—	Reg. Bransf., fo. ccxxxv r.–v., al. 166
?1345	Clent with chap. of Rowley	£10	Monasticon 6, p. 929.
?1347	Yardley	—	L.A., fo. cciii r.
1348[8]	Standish	—	Reg. Bransf., ff. 138r.–139r.
1348[9]	Wellesbourne	—	Reg. Bransf., fo. 140r.

[1] Reordination.

[2] Reordination. Cobham had assigned to the vicar a portion worth twenty-four marks (£16). See p. 263 above.

[3] Estimated at this figure in Cobham's appropriation decree.

[4] Augmentation of Orleton's vicarage (1334). Reg. Orleton 2, ff. 56v.–57r.

[5] Reordination of Montacute's vicarage (1336). Reg. Mont. i, ff. 24v.–25r.

[6] Estimated at this figure by Montacute.

[7] Cf. *C.P.L.* 1342–62, pp. 186–7.

[8] Confirmation of an agreement between appropriator and vicar.

[9] *Idem.*

5

THE PART PLAYED IN ADMINISTRATION BY THE PRIOR AND CHAPTER

A. "SEDE VACANTE" ADMINISTRATION

THE BONIFACE COMPOSITION

The archbishops' claim by virtue of their metropolitical authority to the administration of vacant sees conflicted with that of the respective chapters. In consequence, during Boniface's archiepiscopate (1245–70), compositions between the archbishop and the chapters of Lincoln, London, Salisbury, and Worcester allowed for the administration of those sees by members of their chapters. It was only at Worcester that the head of the chapter, the prior, or failing him the subprior, secured the right to automatic appointment as official *sede vacante*.[1]

It may be useful to consider some of the events which led up to the Worcester composition of 1268, for this forms the *terminus a quo* for a study of the jurisdiction exercised by the priors during the vacancies of the fourteenth and later centuries.

From time immemorial, so it was claimed, the priors had exercised the *cura officialitatis* at times of vacancy.[2] But this claim did not go uncontested. With the death of Bishop Cantilupe in February 1266, the prior and chapter appointed John, master of the Carnary[3] at Worcester, to act as proctor. On the 23rd of that month at the church of St Peter,

[1] Dr Churchill (1, pp. 161–240; 2, pp. 41–118) treats the subject at length and compares the various compositions. Here it is proposed to go over as little of the same ground as possible. The following account is concerned with the working of the Worcester composition and the details of *sede vacante* administration. A shortened version appeared in *J. E. H.* (Vol. 13, no. 2, pp. 156–71) under the title: "The Administration of the Diocese of Worcester *Sede Vacante* 1266–1350". The Editor, the Reverend Professor C. W. Dugmore, has kindly given permission to reprint.

[2] *Reg. Prioratus*, fo. lxv r.–v., pp. 137b, 138a: "Vacante sede prior ex antiqua consuetudine a tempore a quo non existat memoria gerere debet curam officialitatis unde mortuo episcopo statim significetur domino Cant' de morte et de dicta consuetudine."

[3] The chapel of the charnel house was founded by Bishop Blois (1218–36). It was served by five priests, which number Giffard increased to six. See Thomas, *Account*, p. 129, and *App.* no. 61, p. 45; *Reg. Giff.*, fo. 268, pp. 308–9.

Winchcomb, in the public place of the consistory, he published an appeal to the Holy See and for the protection ("tuicio")[1] of Ottobon, the apostolic legate then in England.[2] This *provocacio* was a precautionary measure directed against any action which might be taken during the vacancy by the archbishop or his commissaries to the detriment of the prior and chapter.[3]

Such anticipation was justified, and the subsequent dispute is related at length in the preamble to Ottobon's citation of Archbishop Boniface, dated at Warwick 19 August 1266.[4] This alleges that Brother Martin de Clyve, the archbishop's vicar for the creation of officials in vacant dioceses,[5] together with M. William Rokeland, whom he had appointed official, inhibited the prior, on pain of excommunication, from entering upon the jurisdiction and administration at any future date.[6] In their presence a request was made on the prior's behalf for withdrawal of the inhibition as having issued subsequent to the appeal, which the chapter then renewed against the possibility of additional

[1] On the subject of tuitory appeals see Churchill 1, pp. 427 et seq., 460 et seq., and *Woodcock*, pp. 63 et seq. and App. VI.

[2] D. & C. MS. B.1612: "Et ego Johannes magister carnarie Wygorn' eorumdem prioris et capituli Wygorn' procurator legitime constitutus . . . die Martis proxima post festum beati Petri in Cathedra anno incarnacionis dominice M⁰CCLX quinto in ecclesia beati Petri Wy[n]checumbie in publico loco consistorii coram iurisperitorum ac testium rogatorum et aliorum fidelium ibidem multitudine congregata ad sacrosanctam sedem apostolicam antedictam et tuicionem venerabilis patris domini Ottoboni dei gracia sancti Adriani diaconi cardinalis apostolice sedis legati et insuper directe ad eundem legatum pro el[eccio]ne prosequentis in hiis scriptis solempniter et publice appellamus et apostolos petimus si forte aliquis extiterit ex parte archiepiscopi memorati qui eos nobis duxerit concedendos." The form of the document given here is the altered one. There were originally three proctors, but the names of two of them—Br W. de Bradeweye and Ralph de Pyria—were cancelled, and the whole of the rest of the document was changed from the plural into the singular. It is printed with some inaccuracies in *Worcester Charters* (*W.H.S.*), App. VI, pp. 174-6.

[3] Ibid. " . . . ne venerabilis pater. . dei gracia Cantuar' archiepiscopus seu eius officialis aut eorum vel alicuius eorum commissarius vel executor vel alius ordinarius aut delegatus occasione excercii iurisdiccionis vel administracionis predicte ipsorum prioris et capituli Wygorn' seu alic[u]ius ex eis statum immutet vel alias procedat indebite contra eos [etc.] . . . "

[4] D. & C. MS. B.1616. The date is 14 Kal. Sept. 2 Clement IV, i.e. 1266—not 1267 as given by R. L. Poole in *H.M.C.R.* 14, p. 195, and by Churchill (copying him?) in Vol. 1, p. 185, of *Canterbury Administration*.

[5] Loc. cit.: " . . . vester vicarius et ad creandum officiales in vacantibus diocesibus generalis commissarius vulgariter appellatus."

[6] *Idem:* " . . . sed predictus co[m]missarius et magister Willelmus de Rokelande quem idem commissarius in officialem de facto creaverat post [huius]modi appellaciones ad nos taliter interiectas ad partes Wygornien' personaliter accedentes prefato priori sub excommunicacionis pena inhibuerunt districcius exarupto [this unusual word occurs twice in the MS.] ne de iurisdiccione et administracione predicta se intromitterent [*sic*] aliquatenus in futurum."

encroachment. But Martin de Clyve and Rokeland persisted in their inhibition, whereupon a further appeal was made, and to this, "sano in hoc usi consilio", they paid heed. The respite was brief: Rokeland presently resumed the jurisdiction, prevented the prior from exercising it, and forbade the archdeacons and other subjects of the church of Worcester to obey him. He also excommunicated the prior and many others who supported him. As soon as this became known, yet another appeal was made to Ottobon, and the parties received absolution *ad cautelam* from the sentences. Despite Ottobon's proceedings the official of the Court of Canterbury attempted to bring the case to his audience and cited the prior, who promptly appealed. The archbishop —the citation continues—though he had approved the absolution and was aware that lawful appeal had been made, ordered the sentences against the prior to be published throughout the Worcester diocese and renewed the authority of Rokeland who, with the aid of secular power, intimidated the officers and proctors of the prior, extorted obedience from the archdeacons and from others, took the profits of vacancy, absolved the prior's subjects from his just sentences, and in other ways controverted his authority. Because of all this the legate summoned Archbishop Boniface to appear before him in person or by proxy on 2 October (1266).

Subsequently Ottobon appointed the abbot of Cirencester his executor for the excommunication of Rokeland and of his proctor, Haymo de Arvoys, who had ignored a citation.[1] The executor wrote to his fellow abbot of the Augustinian house at Bristol, reciting Ottobon's mandate and ordering him to publish the excommunication.[2]

Meanwhile the see had been filled and the new bishop, Nicholas of Ely,[3] granted faculty to the prior and chapter for the prosecution of their cause as they thought fit.[4]

In March 1267 Prior Richard Dumbleton and the chapter appointed Brother William de Broadway and M. Geoffrey de Cubberley to come to terms with Rokeland.[5] But early in the following year the see again

[1] D. & C. MS. B.1615. Coventry, 22 November 1266.

[2] Ibid. Cirencester, 7 December 1266.

[3] He was confirmed 19 June and probably consecrated 19 September 1266. See Thomas, *Account* p. 135.

[4] D. & C. MS. B.1613. *Inspeximus* (22 February 1267) of letters of the bishop dated Epiphany (6 January): "Noveritis quod in causis et negociis super iurisdiccione et administracione spiritualium in diocesi Wigorn' sede vacante pro . . . priore et capitulo Wygorn' motis pariter et movendis, cum illa iurisdiccio ad nos specialiter non pertineat, eisdem agendi administrandi et alia sicut sibi expedire viderint faciendi liberam reliquimus facultatem." Cf. *Worcester Charters*, App. VII, p. 176.

[5] D. & C. MS. B.1614. Worcester, 6 March: "Ad tractandum de pace cum magistro

became vacant with the translation of Nicholas of Ely to Winchester.[1] As a result, on 5 April, M. John de Shelsley and Walter de Hyde, proctors of the prior and chapter, renewed the appeal to the Holy See and for the protection of the cardinal. They published this further *provocacio* at Worcester in the public place of the consistory.[2] On 4 May William of Slaughter, acting as the properly appointed substitute for William de Broadway, appeared before Archbishop Boniface in the porch of his hall at Charing[3] and presented the chapter's *libellus appellatorius* by which appeal was made from the archbishop to the legate and the apostolic see.[4] But the disputants came to an agreement and less than three months later, on 28 July 1268, the archbishop published a formal composition.[5]

The Worcester composition confirmed the prior in his right to exercise the jurisdiction, while altering the basis of the authority by which he acted. This is explicit in the revised form of the letter sent to the archbishop at subsequent vacancies. It would appear that an entry in the so-called Registrum Prioratus is a pre-composition form of notification of vacancy.[6] From this it is clear that the priors had based their claim to the officiality, as is well known from other sources, on long-established practice and custom,[7] though they had none the less

---

Willelmo de Rokelaunde qui se dicebat officialem venerabilis patris B[onifacii] dei gracia Cantuar' archiepiscopi in diocesi Wigorniensi sede vacante super iurisdiccione et administracione spiritualium in diocesi Wigorniensi sede vacante et insuper ad transigendum et componendum super eisdem." Cf. *Worcester Charters*, App. VIII, pp. 176–7.

[1] Thomas (*Account* p. 135) states that he was promoted by the pope on the feast of St Matthias (24 February).

[2] D. & C. MS. B.1618. Thursday before the Resurrection 1268.

[3] D. & C. MS. B.1619. "Acta . . . in porticu aule venerabilis domini B[onifacii] dei gracia Cantuarien' archiepiscopi in villa de Cherringes coram eodem domino archiepiscopo."

[4] Ibid.: " . . . a vobis domine . . . archiepiscope Cantuar' ac officialibus et quibuscumque commissariis vestris ad predictum dominum legatum et insuper ad sacrosanctam sedem apostolicam et tuicionem domini legati quorum proteccioni et tuicioni predictos religiosos suique adherentes et sua submitto in hiis scriptis apello et peto apostolos michi dari . . . "

[5] In Register I (D. & C. MS. A4), fo. lxvi v., is a thirteenth-century transcript of this composition. It is obviously the text used at Worcester in the Middle Ages and was copied into the Liber Pensionum (fo. 30r.) in the fifteenth century, and into the volume known as MS. A XII or "The book marked ' + '" (ff. 61v.–62v.) in the sixteenth. The text is the same as that of the contemporary copy of the Canterbury prior and chapter's confirmation (October 1275: D. & C. MS. B.1617). Churchill (2, pp. 59–61) gives a transcript of Lambeth MS. 1212 which differs slightly from the Worcester version.

[6] Fo. lxv r. al. 137a.

[7] Loc. cit.: " . . . ex possessione diutina ac consuetudine longis retro temporibus optenta."

19

sought the archbishop's formal approval.[1] Under the composition the priors were to exercise jurisdiction by virtue of a commission issued by authority of the "Court of Canterbury". Whatever was in theory the precise meaning of this term, it is quite clear that in practice the priors considered their authority to proceed from the archbishop, or whoever was exercising his spiritual jurisdiction, from whom they sought help if their rights, were challenged.[2] Though they had made a substantial surrender of theoretical claims, practically their position was a much stronger one. Instead of the perennial struggle with the archbishops they had a permanent alliance against recalcitrant subjects, and in their protracted contention with some of the larger monasteries during the first half of the fourteenth century they made good use of this. There is no record of an archbishop having refused to issue a commission, but as a precaution a *provocacio* was drawn up on behalf of the prior and chapter at the beginning of each vacancy.

Whenever the see fell vacant, by the terms of the composition the Worcester prior and chapter, or if the prior were out of the realm, the subprior, had to inform the archbishop of the fact by letter, or in his absence from England, the official of the Court of Canterbury. The archbishop or official, without delay or the raising of any difficulty whatsoever, was to appoint the prior completely and irrevocably as his official for the duration of the vacancy, and in the case of the prior's death or absence the subprior was to be appointed until such time as the prior should return or a successor be elected. The prior thus appointed was to have cognizance of causes belonging to the episcopal court, with the power of instituting and depriving clerks, the examination of elections and their confirmation or annulment, the free collation of dignities and benefices by authority of the Council,[3] the receipt of wardships, fines and profits, rights of visitation and correction, the convocation and celebration of synods, and all such ordinary jurisdiction, authority, and episcopal power as could be exercised in the absence of a bishop. The prior, in person or by proxy, was to wield these powers by authority of the Court of Canterbury. Before the arrival of the archbishop's commission he could do so by the same authority and by virtue of the composition. Of the profits and emolu-

1 I *Reg Prioratus*, loc. cit. " . . . dicte officialitatis curam auctoritate vestra gratuita concurrente secundum formam prescriptam concedere dignemini. "

2 Dr Churchill (1, pp. 186–7) discusses the meaning of the term "Court of Canterbury". As far as the Worcester material is concerned one is tempted to endorse her last and most tentative suggestion that it was used as "a description of the authority of the Archbishop and the Church of Canterbury" (p. 187).

3 Third Lateran (1179), c. 8: incorporated in *Extra* 3, 8, c. 2 ("Nulla ecclesiastica").

ments of administration, excepting those procurations which were received in food and drink, one third was to be retained by the prior for his expenses, and the remainder sent to the archbishop with an account of the administration.

The later history of the composition in the thirteenth century can be briefly summarized. The prior and chapter of Canterbury confirmed it in 1275 with a saving clause: that if it so happened that the sees of Canterbury and Worcester were vacant simultaneously, they should have the same powers with regard to the jurisdiction as the archbishop would have enjoyed *sede plena*.[1] At that time the Canterbury priors' own claim to metropolitan jurisdiction *sede vacante* was being contested. The bishop of Winchester,[2] acting as dean of the suffragans of the province, and the bishops of Coventry and Lichfield, Exeter, Bath and Wells, Hereford, and Worcester, met on 16 March 1271[3] at Reading, during the vacancy of the archbishopric.[4] There, among other matters, they discussed what they alleged to be the unprecedented usurpation of the metropolitan jurisdiction by the Christ Church monks.[5] It was not until 1278 that an agreement was reached by compromise.[6]

Pope Clement IV confirmed the Worcester composition in 1268,[7] and Archbishop Pecham did so in 1283.[8]

THE FIRST VACANCY UNDER THE COMPOSITION

The episcopate of Godfrey Giffard closed with his death on 26 January 1302,[9] and the consequent vacancy provided the first opportunity to

[1] D. & C. MS. B. 1617: "Nos autem dictam composicionem sicut rite et racionabiliter facta est confirmamus, salvo iure capituli nostri sede Cantuar' [interlin.] vacante: videlicet, quod si contingat sedes Cantuar' et Wigorn' simul vacare prior et capitulum Cantuar' vel eorum officialis eandem habeant potestatem in premissis in hiis que iurisdiccionis sunt quam haberet . . . archiepiscopus plena sede."

[2] Nicholas of Ely, formerly bishop of Worcester.

[3] D. & C. MS. B.1620: " . . . in crastino Dominice qua cantatur Letare Jerusalem" 1270. Churchill (1, p. 552) gives 1270 as the adjusted date. In fact the meeting was held during a vacancy and the bishops were concerned, not with a mere contingency, but with the actuality of the prior's attempt to exercise jurisdiction.

[4] Archbishop Boniface had died 18 July 1270.

[5] Loc. cit.: "quod sede metropolitana vacante monachi ecclesie Christi Cantuar' usurpare nituntur in personis et ecclesiis, et ecclesiis suffraganeorum episcoporum provincie Cantuar', iurisdiccionem metropolitanum contingentem quam nunquam hactenus obtinuerunt."

[6] See Churchill 1, p. 553.

[7] Liber Pens. fo. 30r.–v.: undated. It must have been dated between 4 May, when the composition was published by the archbishop, and 29 November, the date of Clement's death.

[8] Reg. Pecham, fo. 110, from which Wilkins, *Concilia* 2, p. 96, and *Epist. J. Peckham* (*R.S.*) 2, pp. 632–5.   [9] *R.S.V.*, fo. 1r., p. 1.

test the practical efficacy of the composition established almost thirty-four years previously.

That the new system was not introduced entirely without friction and a certain amount of trial and error is clear from the surviving records. Our chief source of information for this, as for most of the subsequent vacancies, is the Registrum Sede Vacante.[1] It may be, however, that the notion of keeping a separate register for *sede vacante* business was not immediately conceived, for it is particularly noticeable that many of the entries in the earlier folios of the Worcester Liber Albus[2] might more properly have found a place in the R.S.V. In fact, folio vii verso of the Liber Albus is headed: "Registrum incipiens in vacacione sedis per mortem Godefridi Wygorniensis episcopi", and such a rubric is unique in the volume. It is interesting to note that Adam of Cirencester, the prior's chaplain, was responsible for the entering up of both volumes at this time.[3]

The style

The style to be used by the prior during a vacancy must at first have been the subject of much discussion at Worcester. Dr Churchill notes the style used in 1313 and remarks that the same form was current in 1433.[4] But copies of documents to be found in the Liber Albus show that it was by no means immediately adopted. The scribe commenced a number of entries for 1302: "Prior Wygorn' ecclesie cathedralis gerens curam et administracionem spiritualium in dyocesi Wygorn' sede vacante."[5] This is a variant of the more usual form: "Prior ecclesie cathedralis Wyg' curam gerens et administracionem spiritualium suo et sui capituli nomine in dyocesi Wyg' sede vacante."[6] Both styles obviously represent a survival from pre-composition times[7] and were therefore unsuitable for the prior's differently based authority. Conse-

1 D. & C. Munim. A. I. The abbreviation "R.S.V." will be used in the following pages.

2 J. M. Wilson (*L.A. Cal.*, intro. p. ix) suggests that it "probably derives its name from its having been bound in white sycamore boards till 1824, when it was rebound in white vellum by Henry Clifton, Chapter Clerk". In the sixteenth century it is sometimes referred to as the "Magnum Antiquum Registrum" (for example MS. A.XII, fo. 113, where an entry is said to be "in magno antiquo registro in fol. CCCCII").

3 His name occurs in rubrics on ff. 17r., 34v., of the R.S.V., and on ff. xviii v., xxiii v. of the Liber Albus.

4 Vol. 1, p. 186.

5 See, for instance, L.A., fo. viii v.

6 L.A., ff. vii v.–ix r.

7 Cf. D. & C. MS. B.1612 and the styles given in the *Registrum Prioratus*, pp. 137–8, which Churchill quotes (1, p. 185, n. 1).

quently a number of the outmoded forms were crossed out[1] while others were erased and rewritten.[2] On one folio[3] the words "auctoritate curie Cantuarye gerens curam offic[ialitatis] et administracionem spiritualium in cyvitate et dyocesi Wygorn' sede vacante" have been interlined. An attempt was made to regularize the position by the writing of alternative styles at the foot of two of the folios,[4] with the observation that when the prior wrote in the vacancy of the see for the jurisdiction he should assume one style or the other, and not adopt any other or others even though entered in the register.[5] The first of these is said to have been laid down by the archbishop[6] and runs as follows: "Prior ecclesie cathedralis Wygorn' auctoritate curie Cantuar' gerens curam offic[ialitatis] et administracionem spiritualium in civitate et[7] dyocesi Wygorn' sede vacante." This corresponds to the interlineation given above. The second which, according to the scribe, was to be preferred,[8] runs: "Prior ecclesie cathedralis Wygorn' venerabilis patris domini Roberti dei gracia Cantuar' archiepiscopi tocius Anglie primatis in civitate et diocesi Wygorn' sede vacante offic[ialis]."

From an entry in Archbishop Winchelsey's register we can learn something of what lay behind these changes. It is in the form of letters patent of the Worcester prior and chapter, dated 18 November 1302. Following the preamble, which includes a recension of the composition and a mention of the grant by the archbishop of his commission on the death of Giffard, is the prior's admission that through ignorance and simplicity, due to improvident counsel, he had used a style in the exercise of the administration which was inconsistent with the power given to him. By this he had pretended that the cure of the officiality and the administration of the spiritualities of the diocese during a vacancy belonged to him in his own name and that of his chapter and, moreover, by prescript and observed custom. Therefore, lest anything had been written or done contrary to the composition to the future prejudice of the archbishop or his chapter, he declared that all the documents which had been drawn up with this false style were null and

---

[1] L.A., ff. viii–ix.   [2] L.A., fo. vii v.

[3] L.A., fo. viii r.

[4] L.A., fo. vii v and viii r.

[5] *Idem:* "Et nota quod quando prior scribit in vacacione sedis pro iurisdiccione sumat stilum ex altera parte, vel istum, nec presumat alium vel alios quamvis alii scribantur in registro sumere."

[6] L.A., fo. vii v.: "Stilus prioris in vacacione sedis per archiepiscopum constitutus et ordinatus."

[7] "civitate et" interlineated.

[8] L.A., fo. viii r. "Vel stilus iste quia magis valet." But there seems to have been an attempt to scratch out the last three words.

void and incapable of redounding to the prejudice of the archbishop or of anyone else.[1]

No doubt all this helped towards the evolution of the final authoritative style which was adopted during the 1307–8 vacancy.[2] This seems to owe something to both its predecessors and runs as follows: "Prior ecclesie cathedralis Wygorn' auctoritate curie Cantuarie officialis et administrator spiritualium in civitate et dyocesi Wygorniensi sede vacante." The scribe added a caution that in the future it and none other should be written whenever the see fell vacant.[3] It certainly remained in use until the last properly documented vacancy in the register, that of 1433, and so probably until the Reformation.

So far we have observed the significance of the style as a statement of the source of the prior's authority. Its administrative use as a means of authentication was also important. The emphasis that could be placed on formality and proper procedure is revealed by the behaviour of M. Benedict de Paston, Reynolds' official. He informed the prior that he would gladly surrender the items which he had asked for, though rather out of the trust he had in him than from any obligation, since the prior should have written to him with the style appropriate to vacancies, and then he could the more safely have complied with his request.[4]

The transfer of jurisdiction to the prior and some of his administrative arrangements

On 30 January (1302) Prior John de Wyke[5] and the Worcester chapter wrote to Archbishop Winchelsey to inform him of Giffard's death four days before and to ask him to create the prior his official in the city and diocese for the duration of the vacancy.[6] The archbishop's commission of appointment was dated 17 February 1302 from Mayfield, Sussex.[7] Two days later, in London, a notarial exemplification of the commission was drawn up by William de Maldon at the request of Brother John de

---

[1] Reg. Winchelsey, ff. 91.v–92r. (*C. & Y. Soc.*, pp. 898 et seq.).

[2] It may also have owed something to the controversy with the monasteries which resisted the prior's visitation. Though not used at the beginning of the vacancy it prefaces all the mandates sent to the recalcitrant abbot and convent of Gloucester. R.S.V., ff. 64v. et seq.

[3] *R.S.V.*, fo. 97v., p. 134: "Scribatur iste stilus et non alius futuris temporibus quocienscumque sedem vacare contigerit."

[4] Ibid., fo. 8ov.: " . . . secundum stilum vestrum in vacacionibus consuetum et sic possem securius omnia vobis liberare . . . ." See pp. 281–2 below.

[5] He was prior 1301–17.

[6] L.A., fo. viii v. "Littera ad certiorandum archiepiscopum de vacacione sedis et morte pastoris."

[7] L.A., fo. x v.; Reg. Winchelsey, fo. 285r. (*C. & Y. Soc.*, p. 429).

Bromsgrove, proctor of the Worcester monks.[1] Meanwhile an appeal to the Holy See had been formulated in case the archbishop failed to grant the commission. In the event it was not published.[2]

So much for the formal commission. The prior had already been exercising the jurisdiction as he was entitled to do. His first act was to secure the seal and muniments of the officiality so as to ensure the continuity of consistorial jurisdiction. On 27 January, the day after Giffard's death, John de Wyke appointed Stephen de Witton, the subprior, and Gilbert de Maddeleye, the sacrist, as proctors and special messengers to claim from the late bishop's executors the seal of the officiality and the registers, both those of the bishop and of the consistories and courts, as well as the instruments, charters, privileges, muniments, books, chalices, and ornaments known to belong to the church of Worcester and which ought by right and custom to rest in the chapter's custody during a vacancy. The proctors were empowered to issue letters of receipt for all such articles.[3]

Two days later, 29 January, the prior wrote formally to Robert de Sutton, rector of Dursley,[4] requiring of him by Sunday next after the Purification (i.e. 4 February) the rolls and registers of the consistories of Worcester, Gloucester, and Bristol with the letters of the same which needed certification.[5]

Meanwhile on the 28th the prior had directed a commission to the Worcester archdeacon's official for convening the clergy of his archdeaconry to profess obedience in the cathedral church.[6] Doubtless a similar mandate was issued for the Gloucester archdeaconry.

[1] D. & C. MS. B.1621 A. Endorsed: "Copia commissionis archiepiscopi Cantuar' sub manu pupplica sede vacante."

[2] L.A., fo. xiiii v. (undated). In the margin is written: "Ista appellacio debuisset esse lecta si archiepiscopus non dedisset commissionem suam domino Johanni de Wyk' priori Wygorn' super iurisdiccione sede vacante. Non fuit lecta." John de Bromsgrove and John de Broadwas were appointed proctors by the prior and chapter on 30 January 1302 (L.A., fo. viii v.), Stephen de Witton and John de Bromsgrove on 11 February (ibid., fo. ix v.). The drawing up of a provocation was a regular feature of later vacancies.

[3] Ibid., fo. vii v. "Procuratorium ad petendum sigillum officialitatis et registrum et alia."

[4] This suggests that he was acting as official at the time of Giffard's death. The last appointment of an official in Giffard's register is that of Robert of Gloucester in 1297 (fo. 414v., p. 489). As late as 19 August 1300 Robert is addressed as official in a mandate empowering him, jointly with the sacrist, to visit the cathedral priory. Ann. Wigorn., pp. 545, 546–7; p. 152, n. 1 above.

[5] L.A., fo. viii v. The letters mentioned were probably mandates for citation. Cf. Woodcock, pp. 50 et seq.

[6] L.A., fo. vii v. "Littera citatoria abbatibus et aliis ad canonicam obedienciam faciendum et cetera omnia prout iusticia suadebit."

Such were the preliminaries to the exercise of jurisdiction by the prior. We find much the same process in later vacancies, though sometimes not all the documents were registered, while for certain vacancies there are, as will be seen, few or no entries.

At the end of this first vacancy Prior John de Wyke received Winchelsey's mandate for the livery of the spiritualities.[1] Its preamble informed him of the appointment of William Gainsburgh as bishop and of his profession of obedience to the archbishop and the church of Canterbury. The prior was instructed to hand over the custody of the spiritualities to whomsoever the new bishop might appoint, saving to the archbishop the decision of those unfinished cases of correction which had been brought before him or his vice-gerents during the vacancy.[2]

The day after the issue of this mandate, 8 February, the new bishop of Worcester, then in London, appointed John de Rodberrow and Robert de Sutton, rectors of Hartlebury and Dursley respectively, to take cognizance of causes, to receive canonical obedience from his subjects, to correct excesses, and to act in all matters pertaining to episcopal jurisdiction.[3]

Both the archbishop's mandate and Gainsburgh's commission were received in the prior's chamber at Worcester on 12 February, in the presence of the above-mentioned commissaries—Rodberrow and Sutton; Adam de Cirencester, the prior's chaplain; Nicholas de Broadwas, a public notary; and John de Bitterley, Henry de la Lee, and John de Bromsgrove.[4] So ended the jurisdiction of John de Wyke.[5]

There are indications that during this first vacancy the archbishop interfered with the prior's administration. Dr Churchill draws attention[6] to two relevant entries in Register Winchelsey: a notification to

---

[1] R.S.V., fo. 15v.; Reg. Winchelsey, fo. 288r.–v. (*C. & T. Soc.*, p. 447): Lambeth, 7 February 1303. A comparison of the marginal rubrics is interesting. In R.S.V.: "Dimissio prioris a iurisdiccione", and in Reg. Winch.: "Officiali Wygorniensi sede vacante quod liberet custodiam spiritualium episcopo professo et consecrato in curia Romana."

[2] Loc. cit.: " . . . vobis committimus et mandamus quatinus eidem episcopo vel cuicumque ad hoc deputando per eum custodiam spiritualium episcopatus Wygorn' liberetis integraliter sine mora, salvis nobis ac eciam nostre notioni et decisioni imposterum omnibus negociis dicte [vacantis] dyocesis coram nobis aut nostras vices gerentibus ante datam presencium inchoatis." ("Vacantis" is omitted in R.S.V.)

[3] R.S.V., fo. 15v.

[4] Ibid.: "Recepte fuerunt iste due littere precedentes ii Idus Februarii in camera prioris. Presentibus magistris J. de Rodboruwe, J. de Buterleya, H. de la Lee, R. de Suttone et J. de Bremesgrave, A. de Cyrencestr' tunc capellano et Nicholao de Bradwas puplico notario."

[5] Ibid.: "Explicit iurisdiccio fratris Johannis de Wyke prioris Wygorn' sede vacante."

[6] Vol. 1, pp. 187–8.

the justices of gaol delivery at Gloucester of the archbishop's appointment of the dean of Gloucester and M. Walter de Stratton to claim
imprisoned clerks during the vacancy,[1] and a dispensation for non-
residence and licence to study granted by Winchelsey to William le
Brun, rector of Longdon.[2]

That there had been friction can be gathered from Winchelsey's
mandate for the citation of Geoffrey de Norwyco, the prior's minister
for exercising the *sede vacante* jurisdiction.[3] It was said that in various
ways he had abused the jurisdiction and contrived, as cunningly as he
could, to deprive the archbishop of his right and authority. Geoffrey
was to appear before the archbishop on the next law day after the feast
of St Alban (22 June), but whether he came or not the archbishop
intended to proceed against him "per viam notorii" or in other ways.[4]
What this is all about is not clear, but it would seem that in Geoffrey
we can identify the giver of that "improvident counsel" which
supposedly led to the conflict over the style. Another source of friction
at this time between Winchelsey and the Worcester chapter was
Giffard's appropriation to the monks of Dodderhill church.[5]

We gain the general impression from this vacancy that the composition had by no means solved every problem. The archbishop had not
been content to issue his commission and then to leave the prior to
carry on. Yet, the encroachments were not all on Winchelsey's side.
The prior's clerks had failed to move with the times and had used
outmoded formulas which were quite alien to the composition. This is
the most favourable interpretation: at worst their action could be
attributed to a deliberate attempt to infringe the agreement. None the
less, during this period a new style was being evolved and a special
register had been started which would soon contain useful precedents
for future *sede vacante* clerks. It had been a difficult period of adjustment
to a new situation.

---

1 Reg. Winchelsey fo. 287v (*C. & T.* p. 441): 11 July 1302.

2 Ibid., fo. 288r., p. 444: 25 October 1302.

3 For the supposed letters of correction issued by him, see *Reg. Reynolds*, fo. 55r.,
pp. 47–8.

4 R.S.V., fo. 4v.: Lambeth, 7 June 1302. "Quia magister Galfridus de Norwyco
minister vester in exercicio iurisdiccionis sede vacante eadem iurisdiccione ut dicitur
multipliciter est abusus, nosque iure et auctoritate nostra defraudare callide quantum
in eo fuit presumpserit, vobis firmiter mandamus iniungentes quatinus citetis vel
citari faciatis peremptorie dictum magistrum G. quod compareat coram nobis proximo
die iuridico post festum Sancti Albani. . . . Denunciantes eidem quod sive tunc venerit,
sive non, in huiusmodi negociis per viam notorii seu aliis modis legitimis quantum in
iure poterimus procedemus."

5 See above, pp. 245 et seq.

THE GAINSBURGH-REYNOLDS VACANCY 1307-8

This vacancy began with the death of Gainsburgh at Beauvais on 7 September 1307,[1] but it was not until 9 October that William Testa, acting as administrator of the Canterbury archbishopric during Winchelsey's suspension by Pope Clement V, issued a commission from London appointing the prior his official.[2] This commission with its red pendant seal was exhibited and published in full consistory in Worcester Cathedral on the Monday after the feast of Pope Calixtus (16 October). A notarial exemplification was drawn up at Bristol on 16 December by Thomas de Stok, clerk of Exeter diocese, at the instance of John de Stratford, monk of the Worcester house and the prior's commissary for carrying out his *sede vacante* visitation.[3]

The R.S.V. does not contain the mandate for the livery of the spiritualities to Reynolds, nor is it in Register Winchelsey. The new bishop was elected on 13 November 1307[4] and consecrated at Canterbury 13 October of the following year.[5] The gap is an unusually long one, partly because of the difficulties connected with Reynolds' promotion, and partly on account of his occupation with state affairs.[6] He was the royal nominee whom the chapter had obediently elected, but the pope claimed the reservation of the bishopric. A compromise was reached with the provision of Reynolds (12 February 1308) and the bulls were published in Worcester Cathedral on 15 April 1308.[7]

The last date seems to mark the beginning of the exercise of jurisdiction by Reynolds, and it is to be noted that the prior rendered his *sede vacante* account to the archbishop for the period from 6 October 1307 to 14 April 1308.[8] Some details of the interim administration of the diocese, from the publication of the papal bulls on 15 April until the

---

[1] *R.S.V.*, fo. 50v., pp. 103 et al.

[2] D. & C. MS. B.1623. Thomas mentions a similar document running in the names of William Testa and Peter Amalinus as being an "originale penes Dec. et Cap. Wygorn" with a seal of red wax with two crossed keys between three human heads and above the Virgin Mary with the child Jesus. The date was also VII Ides (9 October) 1307. This seems to be missing from the Worcester archives. See Thomas, Corrections and Additions to the *Appendix*, p. 181. Willis Bund suggests that the entry on fo. 35 of R.S.V. is a deed of appointment "by the archbishop of Canterbury" (edition p. 80). In fact it is a partial entry of the appointment by the administrator[s] of the archbishopric.

[3] Loc. cit.

[4] *R.S.V.*, ff. 50v., 51v.; pp. 103, 107.

[5] *Anglia Sacra* 1, p. 532.

[6] See p. 78 above.

[7] *R.S.V.*, fo. 56r.–v., p. 111. For details of this election see Willis Bund's introduction to Part 2 of the R.S.V., pp. viii et seq.

[8] Ibid., fo. 79r., p. 132. From the feast of St Faith until that of SS. Tyburtius and Valerian.

first entry in Register Reynolds on 20 October, are to be found in the R.S.V.

THE REYNOLDS-MAIDSTONE VACANCY 1313-14

The see became vacant with the translation of Reynolds to Canterbury on 1 October 1313.[1] The R.S.V. contains a well-defined series of entries. First of all comes the formal heading. The request for the commission, addressed in this instance to the prior of Canterbury, recites the appointment of John de St Briavels to receive it on behalf of the Worcester prior and chapter.[2] The commission itself is dated the following day, 25 November, at Canterbury, so it must have been issued before John's arrival, four to five days being a good time for the journey from Worcester.[3] On the 27th the prior ordered the Worcester archdeacon's official to summon the clergy to appear in the cathedral church on 8 December to take the oath of canonical obedience.[4] It is noted that a corresponding mandate was sent to the Gloucester archdeaconry.

Meanwhile, on 26 November, Prior John de Wyke had written an informal letter to M. Benedict de Paston, Reynolds' official, and, tacitly assuming that the latter knew of the vacancy, he gave notice of his intention to exercise the *sede vacante* jurisdiction. He therefore asked the official to send to him at Worcester, by the feast of St Andrew (30 November), the rolls and registers of the consistory courts of Worcester, Gloucester, Warwick, and Bristol, the keys of their chests, any letters certificatory in his possession, together with the instruments and muniments of the said courts and details of the days fixed for their session. He also requested the return of the seal of the officiality by the hand of the bearer.[5]

In the reply which he sent from Blockley two days later Benedict de Paston acknowledged the receipt of the prior's letter with the news of his intention to exercise episcopal jurisdiction. From this—he went on—he conjectured that the prior had definite news of the vacancy, for though such knowledge was imputed to himself he had in fact heard nothing since leaving Worcester and what he had known then he had communicated to the prior. He would gladly have sent the rolls and other items had they been in his possession, though more on account of his trust in the prior than from any obligation, for when the latter wished to exercise the jurisdiction he ought to write specifically, as a

---

1 Cant. Reg. Reynolds, ff. 1r., 2v.–3r.
2 *R.S.V.*, fo. 8or., p. 137.
3 *Idem.*   4 *Idem.*   5 *R.S.V.*, fo. 8ov., p. 138.

judge admonishing or commanding his subject.[1] However, Master R., the clerk of the consistories, had them all with him and he anticipated his arrival from Bristol within two days. He would send him to the prior at once and, on receipt of the proper authority,[2] he would surrender everything. As to the seal he would rather it were in the prior's possession than his own, but he was unwilling to do anything which merited reproof, and since his lord who had granted livery of the seal was still living, it was safer for both parties that the prior should have livery of it through him. Foreseeing this, and being in doubt as to what to do with the seal, he had written six days before to his lord for advice, and he expected a reply within three days. Meanwhile he would put it away under his own seal.[3]

It is obvious that both Benedict de Paston and the prior had discussed the probability of Reynolds' translation to Canterbury. Paston seems to have been rather ruffled because he had not received direct news of the event, and this may well have stimulated his insistence on the exercise of due formality in the handing over of the appurtenances of the officiality.[4]

The prior wrote again—this time it was a formal letter. He told Paston that it was customary for the official or commissary of the bishop to hand over the seal and other things at the time of a vacancy and that the see had been vacant since 21 October. He commanded him to obey under canonical penalty and to deliver the seal, rolls, registers, the chests of the consistories and their keys, by the Sunday after St Andrew (i.e. 2 December).[5] What happened after that is not recorded, but the prior appointed Richard de Alcester to take cognizance of suits in the consistory courts.[6]

Bishop Reynolds' bull of translation was received in London on 21 October and this was the date which, according to the prior, marked the beginning of the Worcester vacancy. Walter Maidstone was provided to the see by a bull of the same date as that for Reynolds—

---

[1] "Quia debetis volentes iurisdiccionem exercere ut iudex monendo vel precipiendo scribere precipue subdito vestro et secundum stilum vestrum in vacacionibus consuetum et sic possem securius omnia vobis liberare." Cf. p. 276 above.

[2] Described as the prior's "mandatum in forma debita" or his "littere preceptorie".

[3] R.S.V., fo 8ov., p. 138.

[4] This would seem to be a better explanation than the remoteness of Blockley which was nearer Canterbury and only two days, at the most, from Worcester. In any case, Paston had known enough of the drift of events to write to Reynolds.

[5] This letter is undated but was probably written on receipt of Paston's own, either on 29 or 30 November. In any case it would have been difficult for Paston to have surrendered the things in Worcester by 2 December.

[6] R.S.V., fo. 81r., p. 139. Undated.

1 October. In it he is said to have been consecrated by Berengarius, bishop of Tusculum.[1] But the new bishop did not reach England until 12 February 1314, when he is recorded to have landed at Dover with the archbishop's pallium, which he delivered to him the following day at Chartham.[2]

In the meantime, on 12 January, Reynolds had reissued the *sede vacante* commission, declaring it to be common knowledge that on his provision to the archbishopric the appointment formerly made by the Canterbury prior had lapsed.[3]

Prior John de Wyke continued to exercise the jurisdiction, and as late as 2 March orders were celebrated in the cathedral at his request.[4] In an undated letter he welcomed the bishop, definite news of whose creation he had learnt from Brother John de St Briavels, and acknowledged the arrival of Stephen Bygod and John de Broadwas who had brought with them the archbishop's letters for the livery of the seal of the officiality, the registers of the consistories, and other instruments in his possession. In answer to Maidstone's request for financial aid he promised fifty marks which was all that could be spared.[5] Finally, he urged the bishop not to relax the sentences imposed during the vacancy on the abbot and *maiores* of St Peter's, Gloucester.[6] Maidstone in his reply from London on 19 March thanked the prior and gave assurances of his support.[7]

Maidstone's register began, according to the rubric, as early as 25 February.[8] His commission to John de Broadwas for the institution and induction of clerks in the diocese is dated three days earlier, but from Canterbury.[9] Though there might appear to have been some overlapping of jurisdiction, such was not really the case. The prior had arranged the Lenten ordination some time before Maidstone's arrival

---

[1] *C.P.L.* 1305–42, p. 115.

[2] Cant. Reg. Reynolds, fo. 4r.; *Anglia Sacra* 1, p. 532; Thomas, *Account*, pp. 160–1.

[3] Cant. Reg. Reynolds, ff. 5r., 6v.: "Quia tamen per provisionem ecclesie Cantuar' predicte de nobis factam huiusmodi prefeccio notorie expiravit, sitque opus nova commissione per nos super hoc facienda, vos . . . nostrum preficimus officialem [&c.]." The preambles of the two letters recorded in the Canterbury register are the same, the second continues with the appointment of the prior as official in the regular form. It is this one which is recorded in the Worcester R.S.V. (fo. 83v., p. 144) and which was received at Worcester on 26 January.

[4] *R.S.V.*, fo. 88r., p. 153.

[5] "Non quantum vellemus sed quantum valemus".

[6] L.A., fo. lxii r. See p. 307 below.   [7] L.A., fo. lxii v.

[8] Reg. Maidstone, fo. 1r: "Registrum venerabilis patris domini W. dei gracia Wygorn' episcopi incipiens V^{to} Kalen' Marcii anno domini millesimo CCC^{mo} XIII° et consecracionis sue primo."

[9] Ibid., fo. 2v. This commission was revoked on 30 March, from London (*idem*).

in England and on 15 February had ordered the Worcester archdeacon's official to summon clerks who had not secured the promotion
which the cure of their benefices required.[1] No mandate issued by the
prior in his capacity of official bears a date later than 25 February.
The actual transfer of jurisdiction must have taken place on that date
or shortly before.

THE MAIDSTONE-COBHAM VACANCY 1317

The see next fell vacant in 1317 with Maidstone's death abroad on
28 March, news of which reached Worcester on 7 April.[2] The following
day Prior John de Wyke wrote to the archbishop formally acquainting
him with the fact of the vacancy and requesting the usual commission.
This was duly issued by Reynolds on 13 April.[3]

The initial entries in the R.S.V. are such as we might expect now
that the clerks had grown accustomed to the administrative procedure.
The first four items correspond with those for the previous vacancy:
the formal heading, the request for the archbishop's commission,[4]
the commission itself, the mandate for the citation of the clergy to
profess obedience.[5] The fifth entry records the appointment of M. W. de
Ludlow and Richard de Wildmoor as sequestrators in the city and
diocese of Worcester.[6] The next but one is a mandate addressed to
M. Stephen de Northeye, the late bishop's sequestrator, for the surrender of the register, rolls, and muniments in his possession which pertained to the exercise of the prior's jurisdiction.[7] The intervening entry
is the usual one for the securing of the seal of the officiality, though the
customary demand for the muniments of the consistory courts is
omitted. It is addressed to M. J. de Oseworthe, and this is of particular
interest because no one of that name is entitled official in Maidstone's
register.[8]

Thomas de Cobham, the new bishop, was consecrated by the bishop
of Ostia at Avignon on 22 May.[9] Eight days later Archbishop Reynolds

[1] *R.S.V.*, fo. 86v., p. 151. News of the bishop's arrival could not have reached
Worcester until 17 or 18 February at the earliest.

[2] Ibid., fo. 99v., pp. 179–80. There is no confusion in the register about the date of
the bishop's death, as the editor, Willis Bund, suggests (p. 180 n.).

[3] Ibid., fo. 98r., p. 178; Cant. Reg. Reynolds, fo. 88v.

[4] *R.S.V.*, fo. 98r., p. 177: 8 April 1317.

[5] Ibid., p. 178. But in this case it is directed to the "dean of P." (Powick), so that it
would appear that mandates were sent to the individual deans rather than to the
archdeacons' officials.

[6] Ibid., fo. 98v., p. 178. The printed calendar omits Richard de Wildmoor.

[7] Ibid., pp. 178–9.   [8] Ibid., p. 178.

[9] *Anglia Sacra* i, p. 533. His bull of provision was dated ii Kal' April (31 March) 1317.
C.P.L. 1305–42, p. 140.

informed the prior of Cobham's promotion and instructed him to deliver up to James (de Cobham), the new bishop's vicar-general, the seal of the officiality of the bishopric as well as the register, rolls, and other things appropriate to the office.[1] It was not until 21 June that the vicar-general received the obedience of the clergy of the Worcester archdeaconry on behalf of the bishop.[2] Details of his activities are contained in some entries at the end of Maidstone's register.[3] Cobham's own register was begun about 16 November ("circa festum Sancti Edmundi").[4]

THE 1327, 1333, AND 1337 VACANCIES

There is only one entry for these three vacancies in the R.S.V. The first began with Cobham's death on 27 August 1327.[5] The following day Simon Cromp and Richard de Glen were sent to obtain the commission.[6] This was issued at Mayfield on 4 September.[7]

Meanwhile the Worcester monks were busy with the election of Cobham's successor. On the 31st their proctors received the royal *congé d'élire*, and signification of the king's assent to Prior Wolstan de Bransford's election,[8] dated 8 September, was sent to Archbishop Reynolds. His confirmation was announced on 3 October in the parish church of Chartham.[9] None the less, because of John XXII's provision of Orleton, Bransford was not consecrated on this occasion.[10]

A bishop elect and confirmed was entitled to administer the spiritualities of his see, and evidence that he did so can be found for a number of dioceses.[11] At Worcester the registers of both Montacute and Bransford contain a special section devoted to episcopal acts prior to consecration. A rubric in the former speaks of the "register of the bishop elect and confirmed from the time of his provision until that of his consecration".[12] Bransford's register begins on 17 February 1339 and the rubric describes him as bishop elect and confirmed.[13] A second introduction is dated 27 March—six days after his consecration at Canterbury and the day before his enthronement at Worcester.[14]

1 Cant. Reg. Reynolds, fo. 91r.
2 Reg. Maidstone, fo. 52r.
3 Ibid., ff. 52 et. seq.
4 *Reg. Cobham*, fo. 1r., p. 1.
5 *Anglia Sacra* 1, p. 533.
6 *Concilia* 2, pp. 537–8.
7 Cant. Reg. Reynolds, fo. 206r.
8 He was prior from 1317 to 1339. This was the first vacancy during his rule.
9 *Concilia*, loc. cit.; *C.P.R.* 1327–30, pp. 159, 164; Cant. Reg. Reynolds, ff. 206v.–207r.
10 See pp. 82–3 above.
11 For example, Winchester. See *Regs. Sandale*, pp. 119–24; *Rigaud de Asserio*, pp. 428–42.
12 Reg. Montacute, fo. 1r.
13 Reg. Bransford, fo. 1r. (5).
14 Ibid., fo. 3r. (20).

In view of this, we might suspect that Bransford exercised jurisdiction as bishop elect and confirmed after 3 October 1327. No record of his activities remains, but that he did exercise such jurisdiction is made quite plain by a letter of Bishop Orleton. During his visitation of the cathedral priory[1] the bishop discovered that certain monks were hesitant about their obligation to receive the mandates of Prior Bransford and to obey him in matters of discipline or of the administration of the spiritualities and temporalities of the priory, on the pretext that after the death of Cobham he had been elected bishop, confirmed by the metropolitan, and had for some time, as was well known, exercised jurisdiction in the spiritualities and temporalities of the Worcester bishopric.[2] To remove all doubts, Orleton declared Bransford's return to the priorate to be canonical and legitimate, and commanded the monks to obey him.[3]

The 1327 vacancy is also of special interest because for the first time under the composition a prior of Worcester was elected bishop. The composition, as has been shown, provided in such case for the appointment of the subprior as official. It was in compliance with this arrangement that Archbishop Reynolds wrote to the subprior and, at the request and petition of the prior, appointed him official for the duration of the vacancy.[4] It was not fit, the archbishop wrote, for the bishop elect to meddle personally or through another with the spiritualities or temporalities of the church.[5]

The only surviving entry for this vacancy is on a piece of parchment attached to the otherwise blank folio 105 of the R.S.V. It is a copy of the dean of Pershore's return certifying the citation of the clergy within his deanery in accordance with the subprior's mandate giving warning of impending visitation.[6]

It would seem therefore, that for this vacancy three registers, albeit small gatherings of folios, have been lost: that of the prior as official; that of the subprior acting in the same capacity; and that of the bishop

---

1 This would appear to be the only mention of Orleton's visitation of the priory. See pp. 155–6 above.

2 " . . . pretextu eleccionis et confirmacionis huiusmodi iurisdiccionem in spiritualibus et temporalibus Wygorn' episcopatus notorie per tempus aliquod exercebat."

3 L.A., fo. cxxxvii r: 10 November 1330, Kempsey.

4 Cant. Reg. Reynolds, fo. 206v.

5 Ibid. " . . . apparet prefatum . . . priorem vestrum in dicte ecclesie episcopum electum esse et pastorem, quem non decet iure refragante in spiritualibus vel temporalibus dicte ecclesie per se vel per alium aliqualiter immiscere . . . "

6 The subprior used the style: "Subprior ecclesie cathedralis Wyg' auctoritate curie Cant' . . . officialis et administrator spiritualium in civitate et dyocesi Wig' sede vacante priore ipsius ecclesie in episcopum Wig' canonice electo."

elect and confirmed which had his fortune been better, might have prefaced his episcopal register.

The see again fell vacant with Orleton's translation to Winchester in December 1333.[1] Montacute was provided to Worcester in the same month.[2] What happened during the period between Orleton's surrender of the administration and Montacute's assumption of it we do not know. The register of Archbishop Stratford (1333–48) is missing, and there are no entries for this period in the Worcester records. There is a gap of some two months between the latest entry in Orleton's register and the earliest in that of his successor, for although the rubric in Montacute's register asserts that it runs from the time of his provision to that of his consecration, there is no entry earlier than 11 March.[3]

The next change of bishop came with Montacute's translation to Ely by a bull of 14 March 1337. By another of the same date Thomas de Hemenhale was promoted to the Worcester see instead of that of Norwich to which he had been too hastily elected.[4] Montacute held a large ordination in Worcester Cathedral on 5 April 1337, prior to the arrival of his bull of translation.[5] On the 3rd Hemenhale, still at Avignon, had appointed three persons to act as his joint vicars-general.[6] His register is said to have begun in May,[7] and the earliest entries date from the end of that month.[8] On 21 December 1338 he died at Hartlebury.[9]

THE HEMENHALE-BRANSFORD VACANCY 1338–9

With this vacancy we can once again turn for information to the R.S.V., though the pattern of the initial entries is not quite the same as that for the 1314 and 1317 vacancies. The formal heading of the register is followed by the customary intimation of vacancy and request for the prior's appointment as official.[10] The commission which, in the absence abroad of Archbishop Stratford, was issued by the official of the Court of Canterbury, is recorded on a later folio.[11] There is no copy of the

---

[1] There are two bulls, dated 1 and 8 December respectively. *C.P.L.* 1305–42, pp. 397, 512.

[2] Again there are two bulls, dated 4 and 11 December respectively. *C.P.L.* 1305–42, pp. 405, 512. A copy of the later one is in Reg. Montacute 1, fo. 11r., and is printed by Thomas, *App.* 95, pp. 109–10.

[3] Prior Bransford was appointed vicar-general in a commission of this date. Reg. Montacute 1, fo. 1r.

[4] *Foedera* 4, pp. 714, 732–3, 744; *C.P.L.* 1305–42, pp. 540, 541, 542.

[5] Reg. Montacute 1, ff. 51r.–55r.   [6] See pp. 104–5 above.

[7] Rubric on fo. 6r. (the first folio).   [8] Reg. Hemenhale, ff. 6r.–7r.

[9] *R.S.V.*, fo. 145r., p. 256.   [10] Ibid., fo. 145v., p. 256: 24 December 1338.

[11] Ibid., fo. 151r., pp. 264–5: 29 December 1338.

20

usual mandate to the former bishop's official for the surrender of his seal and the consistory records.

Prior Bransford could only recently have received the commission at the time of his election as bishop on 4 January 1339.[1] The date of his confirmation is not known but it may have been 16 February, for the earliest entries in his register are so dated, and in them he is termed bishop elect and confirmed.[2]

We might expect that in accordance with the terms of the composition the archbishop, on receipt of the chapter's notification of Bransford's election, issued a new commission to the subprior, as had been done in 1327. Yet the R.S.V. gives no indication that the subprior acted in any such capacity during the vacancy. On the contrary, on many occasions after the prior's election as bishop he is specifically described as his commissary-general. It seems that shortly after his election Bransford left the diocese, presumably on business connected with his confirmation. Meanwhile Nicholas Morice, the subprior, described himself as the *locum tenens* of the absent prior.[3] In short, if we can judge from the style used for entries in the R.S.V., Bransford continued to act both as prior and as nominal official—despite his election—until the time of his confirmation. The R.S.V. entries bear dates up to the time of such confirmation, so that in this instance the records of the official *sede vacante* and of the bishop elect and confirmed, one and the same person, are strictly consecutive.

Bishop Bransford died at Hartlebury on 6 August 1349.[4]

THE BRANSFORD-THORESBY VACANCY 1349

The record in the R.S.V. of the last vacancy with which we are concerned bears little resemblance to earlier ones. For the most part it is made up of a series of institutions which are a continuation of those to be found in the second volume of the Bransford register. Together they provide a telling witness to the mortality among the clergy of the diocese during the Black Death.

The letter giving news of Bransford's death and asking for the

---

1 *R.S.V.*, ff. 147v.–148r, 153r.; pp. 259–60, 267–8.

2 Reg. Bransford, fo. 1r (6–9).

3 In an entry dated 22 January 1339 his style runs: "Frater Nicholaus Morice supprior ecclesie cathedralis Wygorn' reverendi patris domini prioris eiusdem auctoritate curie Cant' officialis et administratoris spiritualium in civitate et diocesi Wygorn' sede vacante commissarius generalis eiusdemque domini prioris ipso extra diocesem Wygorn' ex certis causis et legitimis existente locum tenens." *R.S.V.*, fo. 154r., p. 269.

4 Reg. Bransford 2, fo. 19v. (1568). Not necessarily of the plague, however, for he had been ill for a long time.

commission was dated 9 August.[1] On the 15th the prior issued his mandate for the citation of the clergy of the Gloucester archdeaconry to make profession of obedience.[2]

Archbishop Bradwardine died on 25 August. Nearly three weeks later (11 September) the prior of Canterbury issued the regular commission in favour of the Worcester prior. News of John of Evesham's election as bishop must have arrived on the same day, when it was confirmed by the Canterbury prior who promptly issued a fresh commission naming the subprior official.[3] In the meantime Clement VI had translated John Thoresby from St David's to Worcester.[4] Once again it is not possible to trace the intermediate exercise of jurisdiction by the subprior.[5]

The new bishop sent a letter from London, dated 4 January 1350, addressed to the Worcester prior and chapter, the custodians of the jurisdiction and spirituality or their vice-gerents, as well as all the parishioners of the church of Worcester. He informed them of the apostolic letters translating him to Worcester and of his inability, because of public business, to come to his new diocese. He was sending his familiar clerks, M. William de Fenton and M. John de Irford, as special proctors to make known to them the said apostolic letters and Archbishop Islep's mandate. In accordance with these the proctors were to secure livery and possession of the spiritual jurisdiction and of those seals, registers, and other things belonging to the spirituality which ought to be delivered up; to receive canonical obedience from the subjects of the church; to appoint ministers and officers to exercise the jurisdiction; to commit the exercise of such jurisdiction to them; and to do whatever else should prove necessary, with the power to coerce and punish the disobedient.[6]

THE DURATION OF A VACANCY

All the vacancies from the death of Giffard on 26 January 1302 until the livery of the spiritualities to John Thoresby in the same month of 1350 have now been somewhat summarily reviewed, with more particular attention to the transfer of jurisdiction at the beginning and end of each

---

[1] *R.S.V.*, fo. 120r., p. 223. Addressed to Bradwardine.

[2] Ibid., fo. 131v., p. 240.

[3] Cant. Reg. Islep, fo. 1r; D. & C. Cant. *Sede Vacante* Register G., ff. 66r., 72v.

[4] Cant. Reg. Islep., fo. 7v.: 4 September 1349.

[5] A number of commissions on fo. 132 of the R.S.V. were issued in his name, but his full title (given on fo. 131v.) shows that he was acting at that time as the prior's commissary.

[6] Reg. Thoresby, fo. 4r. But the mandate for livery of the spiritualities entered in Cant. Reg. Islep (fo. 8r.) is dated 11 January.

vacancy. Here an attempt will be made to reach some conclusions about the duration of such vacancies.

If a bishop died in the diocese, as did Giffard, Cobham, Hemenhale, and Bransford, the prior assumed the jurisdiction as soon as he heard the news. There must have been a slight delay before he secured control of the administrative machinery from the later bishop's officers, and this may explain the fact that though John de Wyke was demanding the seal of the officiality on 27 January, the day after Giffard's death,[1] he rendered his account of the profits from the feast of the Purification, exactly a week after the bishop's death.[2]

If a bishop died abroad, as did Gainsburgh and Maidstone, the same procedure was followed, though there was obviously a much greater lapse of time before the news reached Worcester.

In cases of translation there could, of course, be no administrative vacancy until the appropriate bulls reached England, when it was usual for the archbishop, or whoever was exercising the metropolitan jurisdiction, to issue the customary commission appointing the prior official.[3] Reynolds, Orleton, and Montacute were translated from Worcester to Canterbury, Winchester, and Ely respectively, during this period.

A vacancy was terminated, in the case of an election by the Worcester monks, when the bishop elect had been confirmed by the archbishop. Bransford, both in 1327 and 1339, administered the spiritualities as bishop elect and confirmed. A bishop translated to Worcester—only Orleton and Thoresby during our period—could, in normal circumstances, secure the jurisdiction on the arrival of his bulls. In Orleton's case the matter was complicated by opposition to his promotion and, though his bulls[4] were dated 28 September 1327 and appear to have been published at Canterbury in December,[5] it was not until February of the following year that he was able to take up the jurisdiction.

When a bishop was provided by the pope he was considered to be elect and confirmed, as is clear from the rubric in Montacute's register.[6] As such he was able to wield the jurisdiction as soon as

---

[1] See p. 276 above.   [2] *R.S.V.*, fo. 16r., p. 39.

[3] In 1313 the prior dated the vacancy from 21 October, the date of the receipt in London of Reynolds' bulls. See p. 281 above.

[4] *Lit. Cant.* 1, p. 259, no. 249.

[5] These, addressed respectively to the king, archbishop, the clergy and people of the diocese, and the vassals of the church of Worcester, were copied into Reg. Orleton (2, ff. 1r.–3v.).

[6] Reg. Montacute 1, fo. 1r. "Incipit registrum venerabilis patris domini Simonis dei gracia Wygorniensis ecclesie electi confirmati a tempore provisionis sibi de dicta Wygorn' ecclesia per sedem [apostolicam facte] usque ad tempus consecracionis eiusdem."

the appropriate bulls arrived and after profession of obedience to the metropolitan.[1] If he himself were abroad or at some distance from the diocese he could appoint vicars-general to secure and exercise the jurisdiction meanwhile. Gainsburgh, Maidstone, Cobham, Montacute, and Hemenhale were all appointed by the pope, but only Montacute's register claims to run from the date of his provision and this, though technically correct, is obviously inaccurate in fact.

The prior then, began to act in the diocese immediately he had definite information about the bishop's death or the arrival in England of bulls of translation. By the terms of the composition he did not have to await the arrival of the archbishop's commission, nor did he do so. But failure to send the formal intimation of vacancy coupled with the request for the prior's appointment would obviously have been looked upon with disfavour at Canterbury. There was an instance of this after the translation of Thoresby to York by a bull dated 17 October 1352.[2] Prior John of Evesham proceeded to exercise the jurisdiction but he did not trouble, so it was alleged, to inform the archbishop of the vacancy. Islep being unwilling, as he put it, to neglect his jurisdiction, but desiring rather to preserve it unimpaired,[3] committed his powers to the prior on 16 February 1353. He declared that he had no wish by this commission to detract from the composition in any way, nor did he intend to create a precedent.[4] It appears that this caution was added because he had acted *motu proprio* instead of awaiting the prior's request for the commission as laid down in the composition, and not as a protest against the prior's proceedings.[5]

The see ceased to be vacant, in cases of capitular election, with the archbishop's confirmation of the bishop elect; in cases of provision or translation, with the arrival in England of the papal bulls. In normal circumstances the archbishop issued his mandate for the livery of the spiritualities after he had confirmed a bishop elect, or when he had read the bulls of one provided or translated. It was usual for the new bishop to send representatives, armed with the archbishop's mandate as well as their own commission of appointment, to receive the jurisdiction

[1] Bishops consecrated at the Curia were to make their profession as soon as possible thereafter. *Lit. Cant.* 1, pp. 289–90, no. 276; 312, no. 304.

[2] Printed in Thomas, *App.* no. 104, pp. 118–19.

[3] Cant. Reg. Islep, fo. 64r.; *R.S.V.*, fo. 106r., p. 191. " . . . nos tamen iurisdiccionem nostram huiusmodi nolentes negligere set pocius ipsam observare illesam pro viribus cupientes . . . "

[4] "Per hanc autem commissionem nostram non intendimus dicte composicioni in aliqua sui parte quomodolibet derogare, nec ipsam in exemplum trahi volumus in futurum." Loc. cit.

[5] As Dr Churchill assumes (Vol. 1, p. 188).

from the prior, to claim the seal of the officiality, the registers and other items, and to make arrangements for the taking of the oath of canonical obedience by the clergy of the diocese. This process of transference can most clearly be seen at the end of the Giffard-Gainsburgh vacancy.[1]

Few of the vacancies were lengthy. The longest period during which the prior wielded the jurisdiction was from Giffard's death on 26 January 1302 until the arrival of Gainsburgh's commissaries at Worcester on 12 February the following year—over twelve months later. Prior John de Wyke rendered his account after the next vacancy for the period from 6 October 1307 until 14 April 1308—about six months. In 1313 the same prior probably did not assume the jurisdiction until 26 November and he relinquished it about 25 February 1314—some three months later. Prior John de Wyke resumed the administration for the last time on 7 April 1317, when he heard of Maidstone's death abroad. Reynolds' mandate for the livery of the spiritualities after Cobham's promotion is dated 30 May 1317, but the bishop's vicar-general, James de Cobham, does not seem to have been acting in the diocese until about the middle of June. The prior probably exercised the jurisdiction for some two months.

It is difficult to make calculations for the 1327 vacancy because of the lack of records. Cobham's death on 27 August 1327 must have marked the assumption of jurisdiction by Prior Bransford. The latter was himself elected bishop, and when the decree of election was brought to the archbishop on 10 September he at once issued his commission appointing the subprior official. After Bransford's confirmation on 3 October there is evidence that he resumed the jurisdiction as bishop elect and confirmed. It is probable that Orleton did not assume it until the end of February 1328—about six months after Cobham's death.[2]

The next two vacancies, if they can be given that title, are of particular interest. Each was begun by translation and terminated by provision. In 1333 only a few days separated the bulls of translation and provision, while in 1337 they were issued on the same day.[3] The R.S.V. is a blank for both vacancies, and we may wonder legitimately whether the prior assumed the jurisdiction or the commissaries of the incoming bishop took it over from the officers of his predecessor. If we take the introductory rubric literally, Montacute's register dates from the time of his provision,[4] in which case there could not have been

---

[1] See pp. 278–9 above.
[2] A few entries at the end of Orleton's Hereford register properly belong to his Worcester one.
[3] See p. 287 above.   [4] See above, p. 290, n. 6.

any interim prioral jurisdiction, although, in fact, we would have to take it as meaning—from the time of the arrival in England of his provisory bull. All the same, it is just possible that the prior did carry on the administration for some little time in each instance. Montacute appointed Prior Bransford his vicar-general on 11 March 1334 from Oxford,[1] and it may be that the latter's function was to secure the jurisdiction. In 1337 Bransford was appointed one of Hemenhale's joint vicars-general with the specific power of assuming the jurisdiction.[2] If the assumption be made that Bransford was already administering the diocese as prior, it would merely have been a matter of his continuing to do so under a different authority. Assuming that in 1334, as in 1337, the prior had been appointed to secure the jurisdiction, and that the time taken to reach England from Avignon was about four weeks, then the length of the administrative vacancy in 1333–4 could have been about two months, and that of 1337 about one.

All this is conjectural. By the terms of the composition the prior had to notify the archbishop of a vacancy, but obviously in 1337 he must have heard of the vacancy and the new appointment simultaneously. Strictly speaking there was no vacancy, but there may have been, as has been suggested, an administrative one—the prior wielding the jurisdiction until such time as the bishop's commissaries, armed with adequate powers, arrived. It should be remembered that the earliest entry in Montacute's register, despite the rubric, is that of the vicar-general's commission, and the same is true of Hemenhale's. In each case there is a significant gap between the date of the commission and that of the latest entry in the register of the bishop's predecessor.

The Hemenhale-Bransford vacancy lasted from 21 December 1338 until 16 February 1339—about two months. After Bransford's death on 6 August 1349 Prior John of Evesham exercised the jurisdiction at least until the time of his election as bishop shortly before 11 September. A commission was then issued to the subprior, but there is no proof that this was acted on. John of Evesham as bishop elect and confirmed would have continued to exercise the jurisdiction. On learning of Thoresby's provision he must still have done so, but as prior once more. He probably administered the diocese until the first fortnight in January—some five months after Bransford's death.

FURTHER ASPECTS OF ADMINISTRATION

It is not proposed to give a detailed account of entries in the R.S.V. A calendar of this volume, together with a lengthy if not altogether

---

[1] See p. 100 above.   [2] See pp. 103–5 above.

satisfactory introduction, has been available for many years. The register is not confined to *sede vacante* business; on the contrary, many items are concerned exclusively with priory affairs. Chronologically the entries often overstep the limits of the vacancies. Some of these we should have expected to find in the appropriate episcopal register, others in that of the Worcester priors, the Liber Albus. The priors' administration *sede vacante* was of necessity similar to that of the bishops *sede plena*. Consequently the R.S.V. and the episcopal registers are alike in many respects.

Episcopal elections

One of the earliest acts of the prior, though not strictly connected with the *sede vacante* administration, was the sending of notice of vacancy to the king with a petition for his *congé d'élire*. On receipt of this the election could proceed in the customary way.[1]

The elections to the bishopric during the first half of the fourteenth century are not without a somewhat special interest, although their detail need not concern us here. There is evidence that the chapter elected a candidate on five occasions: John of St Germans in 1302, Walter Reynolds in 1307, Wolstan de Bransford in 1327 and 1339, John of Evesham in 1349. The first of these was induced to renounce his claim at the Curia;[2] Reynolds, in reality a royal nominee, was content to await papal provision;[3] Bransford had to make way for Orleton, translated from Hereford,[4] John of Evesham for Thoresby, translated from St David's.[5] Of nine bishops only one, Bransford, can be said to have been freely chosen by the chapter, and he secured the bishopric only at the second attempt.[6]

Profession of canonical obedience

While messengers were on their way to king and archbishop the prior despatched mandates for the citation of the clergy to profess obedience to himself. These were ordinarily directed to the archdeacons' officials, but sometimes to individual rural deans.[7]

The preamble of a mandate of this kind recites the nature of the

[1] For details see the *Registrum Prioratus,* "De Episcopo Eligendo", fo. lxiii v., p. 134b–fo. lxiiii v., p. 136b.

[2] *R.S.V.,* fo. 13v., pp. 31–2; ibid., intro. part 1, pp. v–vii.

[3] Ibid., intro. part 2, pp. viii–xii.   [4] See p. 80 above.

[5] *Anglia Sacra* 1, p. 534; *R.S.V.,* intro. part 4, p. vii.   [6] See above, p. 83. n. 1.

[7] Two mandates addressed to the dean of Powick in 1302 and 1317 have been recorded. The rubrics suggest that they were entered as *pro forma* documents: "LITTERA DECANIS FACIENDA" (L. A., fo. ix r.); "MANDATUM PER ARCHIDIACONATUM WYG' PRO OBEDIENCIA PRESTANDA ET PREMUNICIONE IURISDICCIONIS" (R.S.V., fo. 98r.).

prior's authority and the cause of the vacancy entitling him to exercise it. The official was ordered by virtue of obedience and under penalty to cite the clergy, including those exempt from archidiaconal jurisdiction, to appear before the prior or his commissaries at an appointed time and place. In addition he was to instruct those presented to benefices or elected to dignities to seek confirmation or institution. Those with causes in the consistory courts were to appear on the days prefixed, while previously imposed sequestration was to be maintained until the arrival of a special mandate for relaxation. Executors of unproved wills, or administrators who had not presented their accounts, were to be cited to appear in the consistories to secure probate or to render such account. Finally, if the vacancy had been caused by the bishop's death, the official was to order that the office of the dead and Masses for his soul were to be celebrated in all churches.

The earliest of these mandates, entered in the Liber Albus,[1] has a preamble drawn up in pre-composition terms. Apart from a revised preamble later mandates differ only slightly.

Authority to receive canonical obedience was regularly coupled with that for the hearing of causes.

Commissions to hear causes and to receive the obedience of the diocese

Once the records of the consistory courts and the seal of the officiality had been secured[2] it was necessary to issue a commission for the hearing of causes. No such commission has been recorded for the 1302–3 vacancy. In 1307 Prior John de Wyke appointed Brother John de St Briavels and M. Robert de Sutton, jointly and severally, to hear and take cognizance of causes which had been moved or were to be moved in the diocese, both *ex officio* and at the instance of parties, and whether in the consistory or outside it; to correct and bring forward crimes and defects, and to inquire specially about them; to receive canonical obedience in the prior's name, and to implement his canonical mandates with power of coercion.[3]

In 1313 another commission empowered M. Richard de Alcester, one of the prior's clerks, to exercise similar functions. In addition he was enabled to terminate causes, a power not specifically conceded in the 1307 commission.[4]

---

[1] Fo. vii v.   [2] See above, pp. 281 et seq.

[3] *R.S.V.*, fo. 35r., p. 81: 16 October 1307.

[4] Ibid., fo. 31r., p. 139: undated. " . . . et easdem causas et negocia . . . fine debito terminandum."

The last commission of this kind was issued in 1317 to M. W. de
Ludlow, rector of Harvington. Though the arrangement of clauses is
different, it conveyed the same powers as the 1313 commission, with
the additional right of punishment.[1]

At the time of the 1338–9 vacancy authority to receive canonical
obedience, to take cognizance of and to terminate causes, was included
in a commission of much wider scope, details of which are given below.

A general commission

In 1339 Prior Bransford was elected bishop. Two days afterwards, on
6 January, he issued a commission to A. de B.,[2] the subprior; Robert de
Clifton, the precentor; Simon Crump, the sacrist; and John of Westbury, another monk. They were empowered to visit the clergy and
people of the diocese not yet visited by the prior, to make inquiries,
and to correct, punish, and reform excesses and crimes which they
found uncorrected; to institute, deprive, appoint, and remove beneficed
clerks; to receive canonical obedience; to examine, confirm, and annul
elections, and to commit the administration of the spiritualities and
temporalities to those confirmed; to take cognizance of, proceed with,
and terminate all causes pending or begun in the consistory court or
outside it, both at the instance of parties or *ex officio;* to seek out and
receive clerks from the royal justices, to keep them in safe custody,
and to free those delivered or to be delivered to the episcopal gaol;
to grant letters dimissory, admit resignations of benefices, authorize
exchanges, and to do all other things which the prior was known to
have the power to do by authority of the Court of Canterbury and by
virtue of the commission.[3]

This arrangement was an irregular one. According to the composition the proper course was for the archbishop to issue a new commission to the subprior appointing him official, instead of which, Bransford,
even though bishop elect, had appointed commissaries-general of his
own and retained the officiality.

Sequestrators

Sequestrators were regularly appointed at the beginning of vacancies
and a number of such commissions were entered in the R.S.V. By the

---

[1] *R.S.V.*, fo. 98v., p. 178: undated. It is not likely that "puniendum" has merely
slipped out of both the earlier commissions.

[2] Possibly the initials of Alexander de Brerhulle. If so, he ceased to hold the office
shortly afterwards, for later in the month Nicholas Morice is frequently described as
subprior. Morice is entitled "commissary-general" and he would seem to have exercised powers comparable to those conceded by the commission. See p. 288 above.

[3] *R.S.V.*, fo. 151v., p. 265.

earliest of these, dated 20 March 1302, M. Wolstan of Worcester was appointed to exercise the office of sequestrator during the vacancy, to keep the goods which he had sequestrated in safe custody, to give details of their value, location, and quantity, and to answer for them to the prior's commissaries. He also received the power of canonical coercion and his commission was to remain in force until revoked.[1]

At the next vacancy M. Robert de Sutton was appointed by a similar commission, dated 4 October 1307.[2] No commission has been recorded for the 1313 vacancy.

In 1317 Prior John de Wyke in a letter to Stephen de Northeye, formerly Maidstone's sequestrator, instructed him to send to the church of St Nicholas at Gloucester any registers, rolls, or muniments in his possession which were known to pertain to the exercise of the prior's jurisdiction in this respect.[3] He then proceeded to appoint M. William de Ludlow, rector of Harvington, and Richard de Wild-moor, jointly and severally, as his sequestrators. The body of the commission is in the usual form and is undated.[4]

There is no record of an appointment during the 1338–9 or 1349 vacancies, but a commission of 1349 empowered the archdeacon of Gloucester to receive the fruits of vacant benefices and the goods of intestates within his jurisdiction—duties which were appropriate to the office of sequestrator.[5] It may be that this was an exceptional measure on account of the Black Death.

Visitation

Early in each vacancy the prior made arrangements for visiting the diocese. He did not have to await the arrival of the archbishop's commission as is clear from details of the first and of a later visitation. Archbishop Winchelsey issued his commission at Mayfield, 17 February 1302, and it could not have reached Worcester before the 21st, probably later. Yet on 31 January the prior had written to the dean of Worcester warning him of his intention to visit the churches of St Nicholas and St Helen on 5 February, and of Kempsey on the 7th.[6] Similarly in 1338, Prior Bransford warned the monks of the cathedral priory on 26

---

1 *R.S.V.*, fo. 34r., p. 79. He was not a monk, as Willis Bund suggests (ibid., p. 79, n. 4), but one of the prior's secular clerks.

2 Ibid., fo. 35v., p. 81. See his appointment to hear causes on p. 295 above.

3 Ibid., ff. 98v.–99r., pp. 178–9.

4 Ibid., fo. 98v., p. 178. Cf. p. 284 above.

5 Ibid., fo. 132r., p. 240.

6 L.A., fo. ix r. Willis Bund is inaccurate when he writes (R.S.V., General intro. p. lvii): "On receipt of the commission the Prior at once began a visitation."

December of his intention to visit them the following Wednesday, the 30th.[1] The visitation duly took place that day,[2] although the archbishop's commission, which was issued at London on the 29th, could not have reached Worcester before 2 January 1339 at the earliest. It is a fact however, that in both 1307 and 1313 the commission had arrived before the commencement of visitation.

Undoubtedly the prior relied on the authority of the commission when his right to make visitation was disputed. In 1307 Brother John de Stratford, the prior's commissary for exercising the office of visitation, had the commission issued by the administrator of the archbishopric exemplified by a notary at Bristol.[3] Likewise the contemporary summary of the relevant documents in the prior's case, drawn up after the refusal of the monks of St Peter's, Gloucester, to admit him in 1313, includes the *sede vacante* commission.[4] In fact, it was regularly produced when disputes arose with religious houses.

Visitation proceedings began with the despatch of the prior's *premunicio visitacionis* to the subprior and chapter of the cathedral priory, whom he invariably visited first and in person. As regards the clergy, it would seem that mandates for their citation were sent, not to the archdeacons' officials, but to the individual rural deans. No doubt the jurisdiction of the archdeacons was suspended temporarily in the usual way. One specific mandate for this purpose has survived from the 1349 vacancy. It was directed to the archdeacons' officials and inhibited them from holding corrections, issuing citations, or doing anything else to the prejudice of the prior's visitation.[5]

During our period seven of the eight deaneries of the Worcester archdeaconry were subjected to prioral visitation. Blockley, an episcopal manor, was not visited, nor did the prior receive procurations there.[6] All the deaneries of the Gloucester archdeaconry were visited. So too were many monasteries.

From the surviving evidence we can see that *sede vacante* visitation was a somewhat rapid affair. The prior, understandably in view of his many commitments at such times, did little of the actual visiting himself, seldom more than the cathedral priory, the Worcester deanery, and perhaps one or two religious houses. The bulk of the work was carried out by special commissaries, both monks from his priory and

---

[1] *R.S.V.*, fo. 145v., p. 257.   [2] Ibid., fo. 155v., p. 272.
[3] D. & C. MS. B.1623.   [4] D. & C. MS. B.1627.
[5] *R.S.V.*, fo. 134v., p. 244.
[6] Although in the late fourteenth and fifteenth centuries the priors accounted for the rents of the rectory which was appropriated to the bishopric (see pp. 23, 216–17, 250 above).

secular clerks. Even so, it would be unwise to dismiss such visitation as "the usual *sede vacante* formality which cost little trouble and brought in rich fees".[1] The efficacy of visitations as a whole may perhaps be called into question, but there is at least some evidence that they were taken seriously. That this is only fragmentary cannot be denied, but the scribes of the R.S.V. were not as a rule concerned with the recording of visitatorial corrections and injunctions. We do know that during the 1338–9 visitation detailed and carefully prepared injunctions were sent to the nunnery of Wroxall[2] and that the vicar of the church of St Thomas at Great Malvern was deprived.[3] And these are not the only examples of action which went well beyond the bounds of formal visitation.

There are few details of the earliest visitation undertaken in 1302. Citations were issued for the deaneries of Worcester[4] and Winchcomb.[5] M. Geoffrey de Norwyco was probably one of the prior's commissaries, though the only evidence is that he was instructed to spare the impoverished nunnery of Westwood.[6] The most interesting entry in the R.S.V. is that of a commission empowering John de Bromsgrove to visit the clergy and people of Alvechurch, an episcopal manor.[7] Although the prior was within his rights, in practice the bishops' manorial churches were seldom visited *sede vacante*.[8]

We know more about the prior's process of visitation in 1308.[9] This began with the cathedral priory and the Worcester deanery, which were both visited on 8 January. Nothing further is recorded about the Worcester archdeaconry, but a citation is said to have been issued for every deanery in the Gloucester archdeaconry.[10] The deaneries of Bristol, Hawkesbury and Bitton, Stonehouse, Dursley, Gloucester, and Fairford, are specifically mentioned as having undergone visitation, as are the churches of Childs Wickham and Didbrook in Campden

---

1 Coulton, *Medieval Panorama*, p. 749. He was writing about the 1349 vacancy.

2 *R.S.V.*, fo. 157r., pp. 275–6.

3 Ibid., fo. 150r.–v., pp. 263–4. Cf. p. 300, n. 3 below.

4 L.A., fo. ix: 31 January 1302. But only the churches of St Helen and St Nicholas in Worcester, and of Kempsey are mentioned.

5 L.A., fo. xii r.: 1 March 1302.

6 *R.S.V.*, fo. 22v., p. 62.

7 L.A., fo. xii v.: 2 March 1302.

8 Prior John de Wyke also planned to visit Kempsey in 1302 (above, n. 4). The point is discussed above, p. 20, n. 3.

9 According to the rubric on fo. 61r. of the R.S.V. the visitation was during the vacancy "a XV Kalen' Septembris anno domini M^mo CCC^mo septimo usque XVII Kal' Maii proximo sequenti" (i.e. 18 August 1307–15 April 1308). Probably XV Kalen' Octobris (17 September), the date of Gainsburgh's death was intended.

10 *R.S.V.*, fo. 61v., p. 117.

deanery.[1] Most of the work was entrusted to commissaries, among whom were Ralph de Cattrop, John de Stratford, John de Harley, John de St Briavels, J. de Grimley—all monks of Worcester, and M. John de Broadwas and M. Simon de Woncote, the prior's secular clerks.

On 29 November 1313 Prior John de Wyke once again announced his intention to visit the priory, this time on 13 December. He likewise warned the dean of Worcester, and similar mandates were sent to the remaining deaneries in the archdeaconry.[2]

Brother Richard de Bromwich, a Worcester monk, and M. Richard de Alcester were appointed to visit the diocese on the prior's behalf, and the former was also associated with M. Simon de Woncote in another commission of the same date—24 January 1314. The commissaries were empowered to visit the prior's subjects in his name, to correct and bring forward their crimes and defects, and if necessary to inquire especially about them, as well as to proceed against and to deprive any incapable, unlawful, or unworthy holder or detainer of an ecclesiastical benefice. They were entrusted with powers of coercion and their commission was to stand until revoked.[3]

We learn little about the prior's visitation of the deaneries in 1317. Only the warnings sent to the deans of Worcester and Powick are entered in the R.S.V.[4]

Our sole glimpse of the 1327 vacancy reveals that the subprior, on Prior Bransford's election as bishop, commanded the dean of Pershore to summon the clergy of his deanery to undergo visitation.[5]

By contrast, the records of Prior Bransford's 1338–9 visitation are fairly detailed.[6] The itinerary omits only Blockley from the deaneries of the Worcester archdeaconry, and Hawkesbury and Bitton from those of the southern archdeaconry. But it is likely that the latter were visited for we know that a citation was sent.[7]

The prior himself visited only the cathedral priory and the deaneries of Worcester and Powick. The remainder of the Worcester archdeaconry was largely visited by his commissary Brother Robert de

---

1 R.S.V., fo. 64r.–v., pp. 120–1. The MS. has "Dudibrok", not the "Audibrok" of the edition (p. 121).

2 Ibid., fo. 82r., pp. 141–2. "Similis tenor dirigebatur ad ceteros decanatus archidiaconi [sic] Wygorn."

3 Ibid., ff. 82r., 90r.: pp. 142, 169. Bromwich was responsible for the deprivation of the rector of Broadwas, William de Stanway. M. Richard de Glen was reinducted after an appeal to Canterbury in which Bromwich's decision was upheld. See Reg. Maidstone, ff. 27v.–28r.

4 R.S.V., fo. 99r., p. 179.   5 Ibid., fo. 105r., p. 190.
6 Ibid., ff. 155v.–156v., pp. 272–5.   7 Ibid., fo. 150v., p. 264.

Clifton, the priory precentor; the rest of the diocese by his fellow monks Nicholas de Stanlak, Simon Crump, John de Westbury, and by M. Henry de Neubold, a secular clerk.[1]

The visitation of Prior John of Evesham in 1349 is equally well recorded. Only the deaneries of Blockley and Stow are left out of the itinerary as written in the register. The prior visited the Worcester chapter in person; the remainder of the visitation was carried out by his commissaries, John de Lyce the subprior, Nicholas de Clanefeld, John de Leominster, Robert de Weston, his fellow monks, and M. Robert de Nettleton.[2]

"SEDE VACANTE" JURISDICTION
TABLE OF RECORDED VISITATIONS OF DEANERIES[3]

ARCHDEACONRY OF WORCESTER	1302	1308	1313–14	1317	1327	1338–9	1349
Deaneries							
Worcester	C	V	C[4]	C		V	V
Powick				C	C	V	V
Pershore						V	V
Droitwich						V	V
Kidderminster						V	V
Blockley						—	—
Warwick						V	V
Kineton						V	V
ARCHDEACONRY OF GLOUCESTER							
Deaneries:							
Gloucester		V				V	V
Stonehouse		V				V	V
Dursley		V				V	V
Bristol		V				V	V
Bitton		V				C	V
Hawkesbury		V				C	V
Cirencester		—				V	V
Fairford		V				V	V
Stow						V	—
Winchcomb	C					V	V
Campden		CH				V	V

C = Citation only recorded
CH = Only individual churches known to have been visited.
V = Record of visitation having taken place.

[1] For a commission issued at this time which included powers of visitation, see p. 296 above.

[2] *R.S.V.*, ff. 140r.–142v., pp. 250–4.

[3] In effect this is a revision of the inaccurate table given by Willis Bund in his general introduction to the *R.S.V.*, p. lv.

[4] Similar citations are said to have been sent to all the deans of the archdeaconry.

A table of those deaneries known to have been visited has been compiled, but it cannot be said to tell the full story of the activities of the priors or their commissaries. This is because the information given in the R.S.V., supplemented by the Liber Albus, is only partial. For some reason the 1302 and 1313–14 visitations were ill recorded, though they may have been no less extensive than some of the others.[1] It is most unlikely that a visitation was held in either 1333 or 1337.

Monastic resistance to prioral visitation

So far we have examined prioral visitation of the secular clergy, which was effected without incident. Certain monasteries, on the other hand, offered resistance from the time of the first vacancy under the composition.

When Prior John de Wyke attempted to visit the Benedictine abbey of Tewkesbury on the morrow of St Gregory (13 March) 1302, he was refused admittance.[2] Claiming that the diocesan had exercised visitation less than two years before,[3] that the metropolitan had done likewise,[4] and that therefore the abbey should not be burdened again after so short an interval, M. W. de Benham published a provocation and tuitory appeal on the abbot and convent's behalf.[5] Despite this, the prior excommunicated the abbot and greater officers and petitioned the archbishop for his support.[6] The abbot and convent then appealed on the grounds that the prior had exceeded the scope of his commission by demanding a visitation in temporals when he was the archbishop's official only in spirituals.[7] They further complained that he had excommunicated them after provocation and appeal had been made to the Holy See and the Court of Canterbury, due notification of which had been sent to him.

In the same manner the abbot and convent of the near-by Benedictine house of St Peter, at Gloucester, twice refused to admit the prior.[8]

---

[1] £12 5s. 8d. was received during the first vacancy for corrections and the perquisites of visitation. See p. 311 below.

[2] R.S.V., fo. 23r.

[3] Giffard had held a visitation in 1300. *Reg. Giffard*, fo. 450v., pp. 530 et seq.

[4] For an account of Winchelsey's 1301 visitation see Rose Graham, *English Eccles. Studies*, pp. 330–59.

[5] *R.S.V.*, fo. 23r., p. 62.   [6] Ibid., ff. 23v., 24r.: pp. 62–3.

[7] "Quia vos domine prior fines commissionis excedentes in eo quod religiosis viris dominis meis abbati et conventui monasterii Theuk' in temporalibus demandastis quod eosdem voluistis visitare cum solum sitis constituti officialis domini archiepiscopi Cant' in spiritualibus" (R.S.V., fo. 23v.: appeal by the abbey's proctor).

[8] *R.S.V.*, fo. 23v., p. 62. "Et in tercia sancti Gregorii visitavit apud Gloucestriam et habuit ibi secundo repulsum."

The subsequent process of provocation, excommunication, and appeal paralleled that at Tewkesbury.[1]

In April the inhibitions of the Court of Canterbury arrived and on the 26th the prior acknowledged their receipt. They prevented his proceeding further while the appeals were being considered in the superior court. Meanwhile he released the abbots and *maiores* from his sentences of excommunication.[2] The appeals proved unsuccessful and remissions, dated 27 March 1303, were sent to the prior by the Dean of Arches, commissary-general of the official of the Court of Canterbury. These removed the inhibitions and left the prior free to proceed.[3] The abbots were considered to be excommunicate,[4] and formal sentence was published in Worcester Cathedral on the octave of the Ascension (23 May).[5]

But there was another factor in the case. During the vacancy a certain amount of friction had been caused by the prior's adoption of a style alien to the composition.[6] In November 1302 Prior John de Wyke had declared null and void all mandates, sentences, and other instruments which had issued under this style. Thereby he must have invalidated the sentences against the abbots of Gloucester and Tewkesbury. It appears that the archbishop had written to the Gloucester archdeacon's official directing him to declare publicly that all those sentences etc. of the prior and his ministers exercising the jurisdiction which had been issued in a form, manner, or style inappropriate to the composition were null and void. When Winchelsey had so written is not clear, but his words echo those of the prior's notification of November 1302.[7] This general denunciation had not satisfied the abbots who petitioned the archbishop for a more specific declaration. Winchelsey, therefore, wishing to remove all trace of the ill fame and scandal that had arisen, commanded the official to announce publicly that those sentences against the abbots and others of their monasteries which had been published during the late vacancy by the prior or his

---

1 In addition, the abbot of Gloucester was cited to appear before the prior on 21 March at Winchcomb, and a list of questions which were to have been put to him is given on fo. 26r. (p. 64) of the *R.S.V.*

2 *R.S.V.*, ff. 6r.–v., 27v.: pp. 11–12, 69.

3 Ibid., fo. 19r., p. 50. But by that time he had ceased to exercise the jurisdiction.

4 "Littere decani London' per quas patet quod abbates Gloucestr' et Teukesbur' sunt excommunicati quia non admiserunt priorem in sua visitacione" (ibid.).

5 " . . . similiter puplicata fuit sentencia in oct' Ascenc' predicte contra abbates Gloucestr' et Teukesbur'" (ibid.).

6 See above, pp. 274 et seq.

7 These details are contained in the preamble of the mandate referred to below. Cf. p. 275 above.

21

ministers, by unwarranted or usurped authority, were contrary to the composition, null, of no effect, and unable to bind the abbots or their brethren.[1]

The prior's visitation was also resisted at Cirencester and Winchcomb.[2] At Cirencester, an Augustinian house, a list of exceptions was drawn up. The argument that both diocesan and metropolitan had recently made visitations was repeated.[3] It was further contended by the abbey's proctor that a general commission did not in itself confer power to visit monasteries, and though the prior might be able to do this of right he had given too little warning of his intention. Because of the brevity of the term assigned by the prior arrangements appropriate to a solemn act of this kind could not be made.[4] Another reason for refusing him admittance was that a visitation should be full and complete, yet this could not be so as long as there was no bishop in the diocese, for the act of consecration might be necessary.[5] Moreover, if any dispute arose it could not be settled *sede vacante* because at such times the Worcester monks were without a head.[6]

It will be observed that the *excepciones* are of both a particular and a general character. Following them in the R.S.V. is the formal *provocacio*, but further proceedings are not recorded.

The abbot of the Benedictine house at Winchcomb, although he had initially resisted the visitation, finally consented to admit the prior whenever the see fell vacant.[7]

1 D. & C. MS. B.1622: Fulham, 13 July 1303. Endorsed: "Revocacio specialis sentencie late per Wygornenses."

2 R.S.V., fo. 24r.: "Similiter habet prior repulsum apud Cyrencestr' et Wynchycumbyam."

3 Ibid., fo. 27r.: "Et bis eodem anno visitari de iure non debent, maxime cum aliqua nova non emerserint racione quorum nova indigent visitacione . . . ."

4 Ibid., fo. 27r.: " . . . quis habeat generalem administracionem in spiritualibus sibi commissam ab aliquo superiore non potest visitare monasteria et aliqua loca religiosa nisi specialiter sibi committatur, et licet vos dicte domine . . . prior possetis hoc facere de iure, quod omnino diffiteor ad presens, tamen minus breve tempus ad huiusmodi actum solempnem exercendum michi et dominis meis assignastis . . . nam in huiusmodi actu solempni multa sunt providenda que propter dicti termini brevitatem provideri non possunt [&c.] . . . ." By the terms of the composition the prior had the right to visit the diocese.

5 Ibid.: " . . . sed talia in visitacione vestra possunt inveniri que ministerium consecracionis desiderarent et talia per vos sine presencia alicuius episcopi expediri non possent, et nullum constat nobis esse assistentem episcopum, nec aliquem esse presentem in diocesi Wygorn' sede vacante. . . . " But this was equally so *sede plena* when an absent bishop visited by commissaries.

6 Ibid.: " . . . nam si inter vos et dictos religiosos dominos meos in dicta visitacione aliqua questio . . . oriretur, non posset terminari nec in iudicio deduci sede vacante cum vos domine . . . prior et monachi Wygorn' dicimini acephali ipsa sede vacante".

7 Ibid., fo. 22r., p. 61.

At the next vacancy trouble came from another source—the Augustinian abbey at Bristol. Prior John de Wyke warned the abbot of his intention to visit the monastery on 16 January 1308.[1] On the 8th Ralph de Catthrop and John de Stratford, Worcester monks and commissaries of the prior, published the composition in full consistory in the lesser church of St Augustine at Bristol.[2] But when the commissaries arrived at the abbey gates on the appointed day they were refused admittance on the grounds that the prior had not come personally, that the fact of his jurisdiction was unknown, and for other reasons.[3] John de Stratford eventually excommunicated the abbot and *maiores* who neither responded to later citations nor acceded to the request for a copy of their appeal, if any. Details of this lengthy process of attempted visitation were set down by a notary on the commissaries' behalf.[4] A subsequent memorandum reveals that provocation and tuitory appeal were made on account of the many *gravamina*,[5] but, both because there was an error in the above process and because the abbot prevailed in the proof of his tuitory appeal by reason of the number of his witnesses, the Worcester prior failed in the matter of the appeal for protection,[6] and a suit was in process in the Court of Canterbury on the principal issue.[7]

The prior's commissaries again encountered opposition at Cirencester, although they successfully visited Tewkesbury.[8] The small Augustinian priory of Horsley offered resistance and its prior appealed to Canterbury against sentence of excommunication. Later he renounced the appeal and submitted to visitation.[9]

There was further resistance at Gloucester. Prior John de Wyke

1 *R.S.V.*, fo. 61v., p. 117.

2 "Cuius composicionis virtute sic eisdem licuit visitare."

3 R.S.V., fo. 61r.: "Et eodem die dicti commissarii abbatiam sancti Augustini ibidem visitare volentes resistenciam habuerunt, eo quod dictus prior non venit personaliter nec de sua iurisdiccione innotuit et propter quedam alia sicuti fuerat allegatum. . . . "

4 Ibid., ff. 61v.–64r., pp. 117–20.

5 Woodcock (p. 64) distinguishes between appeal following definitive sentence and that arising from a *gravamen*.

6 The first thing to be established in the Court of Canterbury was whether tuition should be granted or not.

7 R.S.V., fo. 64r. "Et memorandum quod provocacio et appellacio hinc inde ob multa gravamina ["ob·gravamina" interlin.] ad curiam Romanam et ad curiam Cant' pro tuicione, tum quia erratum fuit in prescripto processu, tum quia dictus . . . abbas sancti Augustini propter testium multitudinem in tuitorii probacione prevaluit, prior Wygorn' in tuitorio subcumbebat, et pendet lis in curia Cant' super principali."

8 *R.S.V.*, fo. 61v., p. 117.

9 Ibid., fo. 64r.-v., p. 120. The priory was a cell of Bruton and, according to *Knowles & Hadcock* (p. 140), had only a prior and one canon.

twice warned the abbot that he intended to make personal visitation.
The abbot demurred, arguing that the prior had not given adequate
warning, that many of the monks were far away on essential business,
and that the day chosen—the eve of Palm Sunday—was unsuitable
owing to their preoccupation with religious worship.[1] The abbot and
principal officers were excommunicated by the prior and tuitory
appeal was promptly made. In his inhibition the official of the Court of
Canterbury recited the *suggestio* of the abbot and convent. They
claimed immunity from the visitation of any save the apostolic legate,
the archbishop, or their diocesan. In any case, they pointed out,
Bishop Gainsburgh had held a visitation less than two years before.
Furthermore, it was common knowledge that the see of Worcester had
been filled by the promotion of Reynolds.[2] The prior's proctor answered
these points individually and claimed that the prioral right of visitation
rested on the composition.[3]

The archbishop persuaded the parties to submit the suit to his
decision.[4] Their submissions, the *libellus* of the Worcester prior and
convent and the *contestacio* of the abbot and convent of Gloucester, are
recorded in the R.S.V. So too are the proceedings, terminated by the
pronouncement of Archbishop Winchelsey's definitive sentence, which
took place at Mayfield on 18 January 1309. A notarially attested copy
of these was sent by the archbishop to the Worcester prior.[5] Later,
another copy was sent to the diocesan official for publication.[6] The
sentence decreed that the priors had and ought to have at times
of vacancy the right of visiting the monastery of St Peter, Gloucester.[7]

---

[1] *R.S.V.*, fo. 64v., p. 122: " . . . brevitatem temporis vestri mandati . . . longinquam
absenciam nostrorum confratrum ex causis necessariis absencium . . . occupacione
divini cultus in vigilia dominice sancte in Ramis Palmarum. . . . "

[2] Ibid., ff. 66r.–67r., p. 123. The prior's mandate to the dean of Gloucester for the
publication of the excommunication was dated the eve of Palm Sunday—the day of
the projected visitation.

[3] Ibid., fo. 67v.–68r., p. 124.

[4] Ibid., fo. 68r.–v. "Littera archiepiscopi suadentis . . . priori Wyg' quod litem
suam sue ordinacioni submittat."

[5] D. & C. MS. B.1624 (seal and tag missing): Mayfield, 18 January 1309.

[6] D. & C. MS. B.1626 (seal tag, but seal of brown wax lost): Charing, 9 August
1309. Entered on ff. 69v.–72r. of the R.S.V. (summarized on p. 125 of the edition).
A general notification of this sentence, dated 12 March 1310 at Lambeth, is also
among the Worcester MSS. (D. & C. MS. B.1625).

[7] This is marked by a marginal "hic" in D. & C. MS. B.1626 and runs: " . . . predictum . . . priorem et administratorem spiritualium episcopatus Wygorn' sede
vacante auctoritate nostre Cant' ecclesie deputatum, et . . . priores eiusdem Wygorn'
ecclesie qui pro tempore fuerint eadem auctoritate futuris vacacionibus deputandos,

Even this did not end the controversy. When Prior John de Wyke at the next vacancy announced his intention of visiting the abbey on 15 December 1313 the abbot replied evasively that he would obey only in so far as he was bound by law, and saving his right and that of the monastery.[1] When the prior arrived on the day assigned the abbey gates were closed against him and after a further ineffectual attempt at visitation, he excommunicated the abbot and *maiores* and later pronounced sentence aggravatory against them.[2] The abbot appealed to the Holy See, claiming that the prior had himself been under sentence of excommunication since before the vacancy because he had failed to pay procuration to certain papal nuncios. This, if true, would have rendered the prior's action nugatory. Subsequently both parties agreed to abide by the decision of arbiters. These decreed that the sentences should be relaxed, whereupon Bishop Maidstone, with the assent of the parties, duly absolved the abbot and monks from the prior's censures and sentences.[3]

The canons of Cirencester also opposed the prior in 1313, asserting that they were exempted from visitation by a special privilege and bringing forward other reasons whereby they claimed immunity in that instance. The prior declared his determination to proceed, but no further details are given in the register.[4]

At the next vacancy Prior John de Wyke declared his intention to visit Gloucester Abbey on the third juridical day after the Ascension (12 May).[5] Abbot Toky, it was discovered, had failed to observe certain injunctions of Archbishop Winchelsey.[6] Nothing more is recorded except that the abbot and convent showed their title to churches,

ius habuisse et habere debere sede predicta vacante Sancti Petri Glouc' predictum monasterium visitandi, in scriptis per nostram diffinitivam sentenciam duximus declarandum et ipsis ius huiusmodi adiudicare curavimus . . . (etc.)."

1 D. & C. MSS. B.1627 and B.1628: " . . . vestro igitur mandato si prout et quatenus de iure tenemur et non alias parere intendimus, iure nostro et monasterii nostri predicti semper salvo. Dat' in capitulo nostro Glouc' VIto Idus Decembris anno domini supradicto." (B. 1628; cf. transcript in *H.M.C.R.*, p. 197.)

2 *R.S.V.*, ff. 73r., 84r.: pp. 126, 145–6.

3 D. & C. MS. B.1632 A: Kempsey, 22 August 1314. Endorsed: "Relaxacio sentencie illorum prioris Wygorn' fulminate in ipsos de Glouc' sede vacante per episcopum Wygorn'."

4 *R.S.V.*, fo. 73v., p. 126: " . . . dicti religiosi se privilegio munitos fuisse allegarunt quominus visitari debuissent et quasdam alias raciones proposuerunt quarum pretextu dicebant se ea vice inmunes fuisse a visitacione nostra predicta."

5 Ibid., fo. 99v., p. 179. The monition is dated 15 April 1317.

6 R.S.V., fo. 103v. " . . . et specialiter quo ad non observanciam iniunccionum seu statutorum domini Roberti dei gracia quondam Cantuar' archiepiscopi." Willis Bund (*R.S.V.*, p. 189, n. 1) suggests Kilwardby, but the reference is more probably to Winchelsey's 1301 visitation.

portions, and pensions as required by the prior.[1] We know nothing about the visitation of other monasteries.

During the 1338–9 visitation of Prior Bransford, Tewkesbury and Gloucester abbeys were successfully visited by commissaries.[2] The proctor of William Hereward, abbot of Cirencester, professed canonical obedience to the prior in the person of the latter's commissary, Nicholas Morice, but although a day was assigned for discussion of the proposed visitation, nothing seems to have come of it.[3]

In 1349 Prior John of Evesham is not known to have encountered any difficulty at Tewkesbury or Gloucester,[4] but this was not the case at Cirencester. A later inhibition of the Court of Canterbury recites the abbey's claim to be free from any visitation save that of papal legate, archbishop, or diocesan.[5] Gloucester Abbey had asserted as much in 1308 but the continued resistance of Cirencester had its reward in a composition which can only be described as extremely favourable to the abbey. In future the prior could conduct visitation but with only one monk and one secular clerk. His inquiries were to be confined to two points: whether Mass of our Lady was daily celebrated with devotion and whether a daily chapter was held for corrections. The prior was to have four marks by way of procuration, but his *familia* was to lodge outside the abbey. The composition was confirmed by Bishop Thoresby on 1 March 1350.[6]

With this composition ended the struggle of some of the larger monasteries to resist prioral visitation *sede vacante*. It had lasted for nearly half a century. Only an outline of its course has been given, but enough to show that whatever the priors' claims might have been in former years, in the fourteenth century they based their right to visit religious houses squarely on the Boniface composition. Because they were deputed by authority of the church of Canterbury[7] they had the ready support of the archbishops. As a practical indication of this we find that during the first vacancy Archbishop Winchelsey sent M. Gilbert de Middleton, one of his clerks, to the prior.[8] He, on the

---

[1] *R.S.V.*, fo. 100v., pp. 181–2   [2] Ibid., fo. 156r., p. 273.

[3] Ibid., fo. 153v., p. 269.   [4] Ibid., ff. 140v.–141r.: pp. 252–3.

[5] Ibid., ff. 141v.–142v., pp. 253–4. " . . . et sunt privilegiati sufficienter muniti per sedem apostolicam quod nove exacciones seu consuetudines aut nova eis imponi nequeant a quocumque." (fo. 142r.)

[6] Ibid., fo. 143r., pp. 254–5. Dated 29 November by the abbot and convent, 2 December 1349 by the prior and convent.

[7] See above, p. 306, n. 7.

[8] His letters of credence are in *R.S.V.* (fo. 34r., p. 79). He was granted a pension of five marks by the prior and chapter (ibid., fo. 33r., p. 77). For his later career see Churchill, index sub nom.

archbishop's behalf, counselled the prior to deal gently on that occasion with those who resisted his visitation. What is more, the prior sent to the archbishop for his inspection a copy of the *forma* which, after much discussion, had been adopted for the visitation process at Gloucester and Tewkesbury.[1]

There is more than a hint of preconcerted action in the resistance of the monasteries, particularly those of Tewkesbury and Gloucester. Their contentions are similar, and it may be that they took the opportunity of withstanding a newly based authority before it hardened into custom. For the Worcester priors it was a period of experiment, of working out suitable formulas for warning of visitation, excommunication on resistance, and the like.[2] It is possible that the evolution of the *sede vacante* style was not unconnected with the struggle to subject the recalcitrant monasteries to visitation.[3] In his judicial proceedings the prior was at a great disadvantage owing to the system of tuitory appeal. Once tuition had been granted the case was removed from his jurisdiction, and the consequent inhibition of the Court of Canterbury prevented his taking further action during any particular vacancy, for not one was long enough to allow a prior to act after sentence. All the same, in the long run the Worcester priors established their claims with the exception of those concessions forced from them by the Cirencester canons.

Assistant bishops

Despite the necessity for regular performance of episcopal functions, evidence of the employment of bishops during fifty years of *sede vacante* administration is slight. The lack of a bishop must have caused inconvenience, but only once, in 1301-2, was the see vacant for more than six months, and then provision was made for the holding of an ordination.

Prior John de Wyke seems to have been on friendly terms with John de Monmouth, bishop of Llandaff (1297-1323), for he invited him

---

1 *R.S.V.*, fo. 22r., p. 61: "Quia discretus vir magister Gilbertus de Middeltone nobis et conventui nostro litteras vestras credencie exhibendo ex parte vestra consilium nobis dedit ut visitacioni nostre volentes resistere ista vice cum omni mansuetudine tractaremus, propter quod ut forma quam de Glouc' et de Theuk' monasteriorum abbatibus ac eorundem conventibus post aliquos tractatus inter nos habitos optulimus vestram non lateat scantitatem [*sic*] eam inspiciendam si placeat dominacioni vestre mittimus hiis inclusam."

2 Evidenced by such rubrics as: "Littera ad archiepiscopum super forma visitandi porrecta abbatibus Gloucestr' Teuk' et aliorum" (R.S.V., fo. 22r.); "Excommunicacio preferenda in abbatibus et prioribus non admittentibus visitacionem" (ibid., fo. 23v.).

3 The final style was used in the visitation mandates of 1308 (see p. 276 above).

to his installation as prior in 1301.[1] Copies of a number of letters which passed between them during the first vacancy have been entered in the R.S.V. In one of them the prior asked the bishop to hold an ordination in the Worcester diocese, adding to his style a phrase which proclaimed his right to invite neighbouring bishops to perform episcopal functions.[2] The bishop was not impressed by this but promised to come if it would not prejudice anyone, though he feared it might conflict with the rights of the bishop to be elected.[3] The prior wrote again in July (1302) urging the bishop to come at the priory's expense and pointing out that there was no need to secure the archbishop's consent. To support his contention he sent a copy of the composition and of Winchelsey's commission.[4] Even this did not convince the cautious bishop, though in his letter of 14 August he expressed his willingness to come should the archbishop prove agreeable.[5] Finally, being reassured that it was the archbishop's wish, he consented to come if his services were still required.[6] Thereupon the prior issued mandates for the citation of all those with cure of souls who had not yet proceeded to the appropriate orders.[7] The ordination duly took place on the Saturday in Embertide after the feast of St Matthew (22 September).[8]

During the same vacancy Prior John de Wyke also approached the bishop of Hereford, Richard Swinfield (1283–1317), whom he asked for consecrated chrism and oil.[9]

At the next vacancy but one Gilbert, bishop of Annaghdown, celebrated orders on Saturday in the first week of Lent (2 March) 1314 at the prior's request.[10] He had introduced himself to the prior in 1310[11] and Bishop Reynolds had made use of his services.

Of the remuneration of assistant bishops at this time we learn little save that they stayed at the prior's expense.[12]

[1] L.A., fo. 4r.

[2] *R.S.V.*, fo. 34r., p. 79: " . . . cum potestate vicinos episcopos ad ea que sine episcopali presencia expediri non poterunt cum cautele studio invitandi [interlin.] vocandi sede predicta vacante."

[3] Ibid.: 20 March 1302.

[4] Ibid., fo. 8v., p. 16: 18 July 1302. "Et prior misit sibi copiam commissionis et composicionis."

[5] Ibid., fo. 8v., p. 16.

[6] Ibid., fo. 9v., p. 18.

[7] Ibid., fo. 9r., p. 18 (Gloucester archdeaconry), and fo. 9v., p. 19 (Worcester archdeaconry).

[8] Ibid., fo. 11r., pp. 21–6.   [9] Ibid., fo. 33v., p. 78.

[10] Ibid., fo. 88r., p. 153.

[11] L.A., fo. 46v. See also *Worcester Liber Albus*, pp. 104–5.

[12] *R.S.V.*, fo. 34r.: "nostris sumptibus". But see p. 173 above. In York diocese suffragans are known to have received stipends. See *V.C.H. Yorks.* 3, p. 44.

The rendering of the account

By the terms of the composition the prior had to surrender two parts of the profits of jurisdiction to the archbishop. There are only two accounts in the R.S.V. for vacancies during our period and each of these is compiled on a different system, neither giving us detailed information.

On 23 February 1303 Prior John de Wyke notified Archbishop Winchelsey of his appointment of John de Broadwas to answer to him or his commissaries for the accounts of the archdeacons and their officials and for other perquisites.[1] A later notification, of 30 May 1303, records the appointment of Brother John de Bromsgrove as well as John de Broadwas.[2]

The account itself is for the period from 2 February 1302 to the 12th of the same month in the following year.[3] The major part of it is divided into archdeaconries. The deaneries of the Worcester archdeaconry are all mentioned, save Blockley which in practice seems to have been exempt from payment. The Warwickshire deaneries of Kineton and Warwick are taken together, the remainder separately. For each deanery two totals are given, one for the summer and the other for the winter account.[4] In the Gloucester archdeaconry the deaneries of Hawkesbury and Bitton are taken together, the other nine deaneries separately.

After the receipts from the archdeaconries[5] a few items are listed individually, and the whole account can be summarized as follows:

Archdeaconry of Worcester		£37 10s. 0d.
Archdeaconry of Gloucester		£46 8s. 10d.
Church of Down Ampney	48s.	
Church of Bibury	48s.	
		£ 4 16s. 0d.
Visitation, corrections, and perquisites	£12 5s. 8d.	
Various emoluments and perquisites	£13 7s. 5d.	
		£25 13s. 1d.
TOTAL		£114 7s. 11d.

[1] *R.S.V.*, fo. 16r., p. 39: "De compotis archidiaconorum et eorum officialium eiusdem diocesis quam aliis perquisitis."

[2] Ibid., fo. 19r., p. 52.

[3] Ibid., fo. 16r., p. 39. "Compotus fratris Johannis de Wik' prioris Wigorn' de receptis de spiritualitate in episcopatu Wygorn' sede vacante a die Purificacionis Beate Marie anno domini M⁰CCC primo usque ad diem Martis proximam post octavas Purificacionis Beate Marie anno domini M⁰CCC^mo secundo."

[4] "De compoto estuali": "de compoto hyemali".

[5] Cf. pp. 58, 71–2 above.

At the next vacancy the prior rendered the account for the period from 16 October 1307 to 14 April 1308.[1] He must have been somewhat dilatory for Archbishop Winchelsey wrote on 4 December 1308 and cited him to appear in person or by proxy to render the account in accordance with the composition.[2] It was probably in response to this mandate that Brother John de St Briavels was deputed to do all that was necessary in the matter.[3]

This time the account is given in a different form, the receipts being divided into the two categories of perquisites and synodals, although in the Worcester archdeaconry only Powick deanery is credited with the payment of synodals.

Kineton deanery is apparently omitted from the account for the Worcester archdeaconry, but its figures are almost certainly included in those for Warwick deanery. Blockley is omitted as before. The total for the deaneries of the Gloucester archdeaconry is inaccurate; it should be £13 12s. 5d. and not £15 13s. 5d.—if the items have been accurately listed.

The account is summarized below:

Archdeaconry of Worcester	£16 9s. 10d.	
Archdeaconry of Gloucester	£15 13s. 5d.	£13 12s. 5d.
		recte
Probate of wills,[4] corrections, and other emoluments and perquisites	£27 4s. 3d.	
TOTALS	£59 7s. 6d.	£57 6s. 6d.
		recte

From the Canterbury registers we learn that Prior John de Wyke paid £8 19s. 10½d. in 1314,[5] and Prior John of Evesham £24 1s. 5d. in 1350.[6] The latter sum was sent after Archbishop Islep had cited the prior to render account.[7]

We can now calculate that in round figures the total income from the deaneries and from visitation fees and sundry emoluments—in

[1] *R.S.V.*, fo. 79r., p. 132. "Compotus fratris J. de Wyke prioris ecclesie cathedralis Wygorn' de receptis omnium synodalium et perquisitorum de episcopatu Wyg' sede episcopali vacante per mortem bone memorie domini Willelmi de Geynesburgh quondam episcopi Wyg' a festo Sancte Fidis virginis anno domini M^mo CCC^mo septimo usque ad festum sanctorum Tyburtii et Valeriani anno domini M^mo CCC^mo octavo."

[2] Ibid.   [3] Ibid. (undated).

[4] Ibid., fo. 79v., p. 134. "Item idem compotum reddit de probacionibus testamentorum et correccionibus in visitacione et aliis emolumentis et perquisitis de tota iurisdiccione per predictum tempus." The scribe began to write down the amounts received for probate of individual wills but then scored out the entries.

[5] Cant. Reg. Reynolds, fo. 9v.   [6] Cant. Reg. Islep, fo. 18v.

[7] Ibid., fo. 12v.

short the profits of jurisdiction—amounted to £114 in 1302–3 (twelve months), £57 in 1307–8 (six months),[1] probably £13 10s. in 1313–14 (about three months), and £36 in 1349–50 (about five months).[2] The prior was entitled to retain one third of these sums; respectively, £38, £19, £4 10s., and £12. The figures for the first two vacancies give the same monthly average of £3 3s. 4d., and this is the maximum for any vacancy. Moreover, because in these cases we have the full accounts, the figures are the most reliable of those which survive. It will be appreciated that such a sum by itself could hardly have constituted a handsome profit. In view of the many additional expenses incurred by the prior as a direct result of his exercise of jurisdiction, not to mention the cost of the legal processes which it engendered, we should probably be right to assume that so small a sum as £3 3s. 4d. a month was soon swallowed up and that financial profit was out of the question.

But these accounts do not mention a number of items which yielded profit to the Worcester priory at times of vacancy. There were the indemnities paid on account of appropriated churches,[3] the bishop's share of the offerings at the shrine of St Oswald and St Wulfstan,[4] and the procurations in food and drink received during visitation.[5]

CONCLUSION

It is hoped that a not too inadequate account has been given of the main features of *sede vacante* administration, of the establishment of the composition, and of the difficulties which were experienced in putting it into effect.

No special section has been devoted to the administrative staff of the priors in their exercise of the jurisdiction, although those who were chiefly employed have been mentioned under the appropriate headings. This is because there was no specialist staff for *sede vacante* business. The prior took over the administrative reins from the former bishop's

1 Willis Bund in his general introduction to the R.S.V. (pp. xvii et seq.) confuses the issue. For some reason he assumed that the 1307–8 vacancy lasted for fifteen months and so was at a loss to explain the apparent discrepancy between the monthly averages for the first two vacancies.

2 The last two are calculated from the figures given above, which are taken from the Canterbury registers. They are arrived at by adding the prior's third to the sum received by the archbishop.

3 There is a list in the Registrum Prioratus on the dorse of the first folio and they are also entered in the Liber Pensionum

4 In 1302 the *custos* of the temporalities of the bishopric attempted to secure both these offerings and also certain pensions paid in lieu of procurations for visitation. The prior complained to the king's chancellor, apparently with success. L.A., fo. xii v.

5 By the terms of the composition the prior did not have to account for them.

clerks and handed them back to those of his successor. In the interim he employed clerks who were in any case in the service of the cathedral priory, as well as a number of his fellow monks. Sometimes he had the help of an outside expert, such as M. Gilbert de Middleton, one of Archbishop Winchelsey's clerks,[1] but this was exceptional. The often unspecialized records of the R.S.V. and the Liber Albus show that there was considerable overlapping of prioral and strictly diocesan business. None the less, after a somewhat muddled start, which was not without a hint of bad faith on the prior's part, administrative experience was gained and many difficulties were resolved. By the end of the half century the priors had firmly established their *sede vacante* style, regularized their position *vis à vis* the archbishops, crystallized methods of procedure, worked out appropriate forms, and had overcome the considerable opposition to their right of visitation.

B. CHAPTER AND BISHOP

A number of *causes célèbres* involving bishops and their chapters, such as the dispute between Bishop Bek of Durham and Prior Hoton,[2] have tended to obscure the extent of their common interests. According to John de Scalby, the registrar of Oliver Sutton, bishop of Lincoln, the diocesan could not exercise jurisdiction without his chapter's consent.[3] In practice this meant that certain episcopal acts, particularly those touching the alienation of rights or property, were regularly confirmed by the chapter, which may account for the considerable survival of documents of this kind in capitular archives.

Outstanding disputes between Worcester cathedral priory and the diocesan had been settled by a composition of 1224. This regulated the method of electing the prior,[4] the division of the profits from the shrine of SS. Wulfstan and Oswald,[5] and the manner of episcopal visitation.[6] Nominally the bishop was abbot of the cathedral priory,[7] but over its

[1] See p. 308 above.   [2] See pp. 151–2 above.

[3] Linc. Archives Comm., Archivist's Rpt., March. 1952–March 1953 (typescript), p. 41; *L.C.S.* 2, p. lxxxvii. Cf. *Extra* 3, tit. 10: "De his quae fiunt a praelato sine consensu capituli".

[4] See pp. 220–1 above.

[5] Convent and bishop were to share the proceeds equally. Two tumbaries were to be appointed, one by each party. Appointments of the bishop's tumbary are not uncommon in fourteenth-century registers.

[6] See p. 152 above.

[7] The canons of Cirencester declared this to be the case when resisting the prior's visitation *sede vacante* (see above, p. 304, n. 6.). The contention was not uncommon in the fourteenth century, though it usually amounted to special pleading. A full statement of the argument ("raciones quod episcopus est abbas") is to be found in

everyday affairs he had no control. He nominated its head, appointed the sacrist and one of the tumbaries, and admitted those who wished to become monks. Beyond this, episcopal action would have been interpreted as interference.

The 1224 composition did not end all friction between prior and bishop, in fact the episcopate of Giffard marked one of the stormiest periods in their relationship. In the fourteenth century there were lesser disputes about the bishop's appointment of the sacrist,[1] and the procuration in kind exacted by the diocesan official at times of the consistory.[2] While engaged in the latter quarrel, Prior John de Wyke roundly declared that the bishop (Reynolds) unless prevented would reduce everyone in the diocese to slavery.[3] But this was written in the heat of the moment, and on the whole their relations were good.

In the field of diocesan administration, the farming of episcopal manors,[4] the alienation of lands or rights, the appropriation of churches,[5] and the ordination of vicarages,[6] were matters for the bishop and chapter in common. To formal episcopal documents embodying arrangements of this kind the confirmation of the prior and chapter had to be appended, otherwise their legality might be called in question. It was with this in mind that Bishop Gainsburgh advised the chapter not to confirm certain grants of land made "sub modico vel nullo annuo censu" by his predecessor Giffard, so as not to aggravate the injury already done to the church of Worcester.[7] The withholding of capitular confirmation might also be used as a weapon against the bishop himself. It proved successful in thwarting Giffard's attempt to make episcopal churches prebendal to Westbury.[8]

Close study of diocesan administration leaves an impression of co-operation between bishop and chapter. Jealousy of their respective

---

Winch. Reg. Pontissara, p. 678. At Durham the notion was adapted to impugn the legality of the bishop's visitation (for example, *York Reg. Wickwane*, p. 163).

[1] See the *Calendar of the Liber Albus*, pp. xxvi–xxvii, and *Worcester Liber Albus*, pp. 277–8.

[2] See p. 108 above.

[3] L.A., fo. xxxvi r.: "Et nos omnes et singulos de episcopatu predicto in perpetuam redigeret servitutem, nisi obstaculum affuerit repressivum."

[4] See p. 98 above.

[5] See pp. 241, 248 above. Chantries were sometimes confirmed, but this was not essential for their legality (see p. 227).

[6] See p. 259 above.

[7] Reg. Gainsburgh, fo. 32r.: "Quod si fieret in nostri et dicte ecclesie sponse nostre gravamen et preiudicium redundaret." Cf. the attempt of the chapter of Wells to restrict episcopal grants save those for the life of the grantee and his wife. *H.M.C.R.* X, App. pt. 1, p. 154.

[8] *Ann. Wigorn.*, p. 504. Cf. p. 28 above.

rights was balanced by awareness of common interests and responsibilities. In general the diocesan considered it proper to consult his chapter about matters affecting the status of the see, its financial position, or the limits of his jurisdiction.[1] At times of vacancy the prior assumed the spiritualities and handed them on unimpaired to the next bishop. The "ecclesia Wygorniensis" was a unity to which they both owed allegiance and which it was their common duty to preserve unharmed.

[1] See, for instance, p. 107 above.

EPILOGUE

Jurisdictionally the thirteenth century in the Worcester diocese had been a time of final definition and limitation. It had been punctuated by a series of disputes and tedious legal processes, most of which were terminated by the establishment of agreed compositions. The Evesham jurisdiction had been irrevocably detached, Great Malvern priory had secured immunity from the diocesan's control, while the peculiar of the archbishops of York at Churchdown had successfully withstood his assault. Outstanding differences between bishop and cathedral priory had been settled in 1224, the *sede vacante* composition followed in 1268, and the vexed question of the bishop's rights at Deerhurst was finally resolved in 1269. In the last few years of the century the claims of the Gloucester archdeacon ended with his submission to Bishop Giffard, and the latter's scheme to make churches in his collation prebendal to Westbury was abandoned in the face of the priory's stern opposition.

With Giffard's death at the beginning of 1302 a notable, if somewhat belligerent figure, was removed from the scene. There followed, as it were, a period of quiescence broken, *sede vacante*, by the priors' struggle to impose their visitation on the larger monasteries. Few bishops held the see for long, fewer still gave their undivided attention to it; but disputes were comparatively rare and short-lived. There was little serious attempt to upset established jurisdiction, though Gainsburgh tried to reopen the question of Churchdown, and the Worcester archdeacon's authority in Warwick was challenged by deans of the collegiate church.

The thirteenth century had also been a time of reform,[1] marked by the publication of diocesan constitutions and by attempts to enforce them. A related development was the expansion of the episcopal curia. By the following century this comprised a comparatively small number of specialized clerks, some of whom occupied the established offices of vicar-general, official, and sequestrator-general, or exercised judicial powers as commissary-general or adjutor. The local administration of archdeaconry and rural deanery remained important, but much more of the initiative had passed to the centre. It is this central administration

---

[1] See Gibbs and Lang, *Bishops and Reform*, part 3.

which seems to be such a notable feature of the fourteenth-century diocese.

The origin of the two principal offices of vicar-general and official has been the subject of much research by French scholars. Paul Fournier regarded the official as, in essence, the bishop's officer for the exercise of his contentious jurisdiction.[1] The official's institution, he claimed, was a consequence of the bishops' struggle against the archdeacons on the one hand, and the increased study and practical application of the Justinian compilations on the other.[2] Edouard Fournier, while rejecting the first part of this hypothesis, argues that the increase of legal business and its growing technicality had (in the twelfth century) forced the bishop to delegate judicial power to an official. In other words, his appearance was really due to the needs of the episcopal curia.[3] This theory, it may be remarked, is close to that enunciated in the (common form) preamble of Orleton's commission to Robert de Worth.[4]

Paul Fournier regarded the official as the bishop's substitute, corresponding to the later vicars-general,[5] but Edouard Fournier insists that the two offices were essentially distinct both in origin and in their later development. The vicar-general, the latter argues, was at first the proctor-general of a bishop who was absent or otherwise occupied. He was not, any more than the official, created to curb the archdeacon's jurisdiction. He acted on the bishop's behalf in all matters touching the spiritualities or temporalities of the see.[6] By contrast the official had only a limited sphere of action, he was "un fonctionnaire à compétence bornée".[7] If the bishop were absent the official continued to carry out the functions of his office as before, while the vicar-general acted *loco episcopi*. That is to say, the vicar-general had powers of surveillance over the official but left him undisturbed in the exercise of the bishop's contentious jurisdiction, and in general collaborated closely with him.[8]

The Worcester evidence which we have reviewed does not conflict with Edouard Fournier's basic analysis of the evolution of the two offices, even though this is drawn mainly from French sources. But

1 *Les Officialités*, p. 22.   2 Ibid., p. 8.

3 This forms part of the general thesis of *Les Origines du vicaire général* (see particularly chaps. 3–5 and the summary on pp. 129–30), which is reasserted in the relevant chapters of the later *L'Origine du vicaire général* (3me. part. pp. 283–365).

4 See pp. 111–12 above.   5 *Les Officialités*, pp. 21–2.

6 This is worked out in chaps. 5–7 of *Les Origines* and the argument summarized on pp. 129–30.

7 See, for instance, *Les Origines*, pp. 69–70; *L'Origine du vicaire général*, pp. 325–6.

8 *Les Origines*, pp. 97, 103, 115.

because, so far as Worcester is concerned, the fourteenth century is in some of these respects transitional, the picture is not always so well defined.

That such thirteenth-century conflict as there was at Worcester between episcopal and archidiaconal jurisdiction may have resulted from the growth of the bishop's curia has already been suggested.[1] But certain episcopal arrangements for the exercise of judicial functions imply that this was no longer an issue in the fourteenth century. In 1318 Cobham temporarily entrusted both consistorial and archidiaconal courts within the Gloucester archdeaconry to a single clerk.[2] Bishop Reynolds deputed William de Birston, the Gloucester archdeacon, to act as commissary-general, and a later archdeacon, Roger de Breynton, was one of Orleton's vicars-general.[3] John de Severleye, archdeacon of Worcester, functioned as chancellor and commissary-general in Bransford's time, and as official during the episcopate of his successor, Thoresby.[4]

At Worcester the continuous history of the vicar-general's office dates from the fourteenth century. No appointment of this kind is known to have been made by Giffard (1268–1302). During our period the vicar-general is usually concerned only with the spiritualities of the see, and to that extent at least his power was limited.[5] He remains a temporary officer, seldom holding office for long, whose appointment (as a general rule) followed upon two contingencies: the bishop's personal inability to assume the jurisdiction at the beginning of an episcopate, and his absence from the realm. In the first case the bishop sometimes preferred to appoint a commissary-general.[6] At any time, rather than appoint a vicar-general he could extend the powers of his official or of some other of his clerks.[7] Montacute's commission appointing M. John de Hildesle official in 1334 empowered him to exercise all the bishop's ordinary and spiritual jurisdiction—which seems to involve a concession of authority no less extensive than that made to a vicar-general in spirituals.[8] Why arrangements of this kind became less common, while the number of commissions to vicars-general increased, cannot perhaps be fully explained. The practice of other dioceses may have had an influence, as well as the need, in view of the considerable augmentation of administrative business, for a separate officer who

---

1 See p. 62 above.   2 See p. 54 above.
3 See pp. 38, 130; 39, 103, n. 4; above.   4 See pp. 36, 127, 130 above.
5 Exception was also regularly made of the right to confer benefices in the bishop's collation.
6 See pp. 130–1 above.   7 See pp. 99–100 above.
8 See p. 112 above and App. B, p. 332 below.

would be responsible for the exercise of the bishop's gracious jurisdiction. Officials, it is true, were appointed vicars-general, but this was rare in the Worcester diocese at this time, and in such cases the commission was usually a joint one. Fundamentally the development seems to have been due to administrative convenience.

The registers of the late thirteenth and fourteenth centuries reveal the increased provision made for the exercise of the bishop's office of correction, which had become even more prominent with the practice of triennial visitation. The sequestrator was regularly empowered to deal with corrections, and the official had undoubtedly taken part in such work during the thirteenth century, but since the publication of Sext (1, 13, c. 2) the latter could not act *ex officio* but only by virtue of a special mandate, which was commonly conceded in practice. The commissary-general also exercised such powers, as did Bransford's adjutor or special commissary, and commissaries to administer corrections after visitation occur from time to time in the registers.[1] A complementary development was that of the penitential system.

The fourteenth century saw a remarkable expansion in the volume of diocesan business. Regular visitation (inherited from the previous century) involved—when conscientiously carried out—careful planning, constant attention to every kind of business while keeping to a pre-arranged schedule, and an aftermath of correction and reformation. Chantries rarely figure in Giffard's register,[2] but their number grows rapidly after the first decade of the new century. Here the bishop's function was mainly that of confirmation, but in cases of appropriation, where the growth was no less striking, his duties were far more arduous. The Longdon expense account shows that appropriation might involve protracted discussions about which we learn little from the formal documents. The necessary corollary was the ordination of vicarages, a duty which the Worcester bishops assiduously performed. Exchanges brought a more frequent "turn-over" of benefices, and as in the case of certain types of provisions—which were also on the increase—appropriate arrangements had to be made by the diocesan.

Contemporary with the unparalleled growth in the pious endowment of chantries is the mounting evidence of a secular and materialist attitude to benefices, manifested in the prevalence of exchanges, provisions, farming, absenteeism, and appropriations. Boniface VIII,

---

1 In France there emerged the "promoter", attached for this purpose to the courts of official and archdeacon: (for example, Rheims, 1329) "Un 'procurator curie' ayant pour fonction essentielle d'assurer la poursuite des délits, le déroulement des causes d'office." See Fournier, *L'Origine du vicaire général*, chap. 5.

2 See *Reg. Giffard*, intro. pp. cxii–cxiii.

in a decretal directed against the farming of the benefices of those who occupied themselves in business remote from their cures, lamented the diminution of the "cultus divinus" and the disregard of the "officium . . . propter quod beneficium ecclesiasticum datur".[1] Secular clerks—and this was no new phenomenon—were inclined to lose sight of real spirituality in their anxiety to provide for the Church's higher administration with a growing body of learned men. Cobham's attitude to benefices—a typical one for his day—is revealed by his early pluralism and the fact that at the time of his election to Canterbury he was only in subdeacon's orders. As bishop he licensed numerous rectors to leave their churches for the Schools—Reynolds' record in this respect was even better—but was his main purpose the spiritual benefit of the parishioners? His arguments against appropriation suggest that it was not. So far as appropriation itself is concerned, Cobham reveals the fundamental issue as a struggle between regulars and seculars to secure a vital source of income. To set against all this we have a decline in the holding of benefices by the title of commend or custody and only a moderate amount of pluralism.

Most noticeable is the diocesan's inability to curb the importunity of petitioners once a particular legal procedure had been established. Exchanges increased to such an extent that they became an abuse, but the process once begun seems to have been carried through almost as a formality. Much the same is true of appropriation. Cobham's largely ineffectual resistance to monastic demands, backed by influential laymen and ecclesiastics, demonstrates the impotence of the diocesan in the face of such powerful tendencies.

To sum up, the fourteenth-century diocese lacked the jurisdictional conflicts of the thirteenth; in few respects was it a time of innovation, but it was none the less one of evolution. The synod had ceased to be a regular organ of diocesan government. Its decline may have been due to various changes, among them the introduction of regular visitation, the development of episcopal courts, the frequent use of the machinery of archdeaconry and rural deanery for the publication of episcopal mandates and for local inquiries, and the enlargement of the bishop's staff of specialized clerks with duties extending to every part of the diocese. The period of large-scale diocesan legislation had passed, but attention could be drawn to points of law and their interpretation by the use of special mandates, a number of which were copied into the registers.

There emerges from the episcopal records of the first half of the

[1] *Sext* 1, 3, c. 15.

century the picture of a firmly established diocesan organization and a well-tried and remarkably efficient administrative system. Although there were to be further developments—particularly in the episcopal curia[1]—both were to continue substantially unchanged until the time of the Reformation.

[1] For example, in the offices of vicar-general and of the commissaryship.

LISTS OF
BISHOPS, VICARS-GENERAL,
OFFICIALS, SEQUESTRATORS,
AND CHANCELLORS

BISHOPS OF WORCESTER
1300–1350

BISHOP	PROBABLE DATE OF ASSUMPTION OF JURISDICTION	DATES OF ELECTION, PROVISION OR TRANSLA- TION, CONSECRATION, DEATH OR TRANSLATION
Godfrey Giffard		ob. 26 Jan. 1302
William Gainsburgh	12 Feb. 1303	prov. 20 Oct. 1302
		cons. 28 Oct. 1302
		ob. 17 Sept. 1307
Walter Reynolds	15 Apr. 1308	elect. 13 Nov. 1307
		prov. 12 Feb. 1308
		cons. 13 Oct. 1308
	(to Canterbury)	trans. 1 Oct. 1313
Walter Maidstone	25 Feb. 1314	prov. 1 Oct. 1313
		cons. 7 Oct. 1313[1]
		ob. 28 Mar. 1317
Thomas Cobham	21 June 1317	prov. 31 Mar. 1317
		cons. 22 May 1317
		ob. 27 Aug. 1327
Adam Orleton	Feb. 1328	trans. 28 Sept. 1327
		(from Hereford)
	(to Winchester)	trans. 1 Dec. 1333[2]
Simon Montacute	11 Mar. 1334	prov. 11 Dec. 1333[3]
		cons. 8 May 1334
	(to Ely)	trans. 14 Mar. 1337
Thomas Hemenhale	May 1337	prov. 14 Mar. 1337
		cons. 30 Mar. 1337[4]
		ob. 21 Dec. 1338

1 From Handbook of British Chronology (1961). [This work wrongly dates Orleton's translation 25 September.]

2 There was another bull dated 8 December.

3 An earlier bull is dated 4 December, but it is the later one which is recorded in Reg. Montacute.

4 See n. 1, above.

Wolstan de Bransford	16 Feb. 1339	elect. 4 Jan. 1339
		cons. 21 Mar. 1339
		ob. 6 Aug. 1349
John Thoresby	Jan. 1350	trans. 4 Sept. 1349
		(from St David's)
	(to York)	trans. 17 Oct. 1352

VICARS-GENERAL

DATE OF COMMISSION	BISHOP	PERSONS APPOINTED
17 Oct. 1305	Gainsburgh	M. Walter de Wotton
16 Mar. 1309	Reynolds	M. Benedict de Paston
17 Jan. 1317	Maidstone	M. Richard de Clara
		M. Richard de Chaddesley
Not extant (1317)	Cobham	M. James de Cobham
29 Feb. 1328	Orleton	Adam de Herwynton
15 May 1328	Orleton	Adam de Herwynton
		M. William de Fowehope
18 Jan. 1331	Orleton	M. Robert de Worth
		Adam de Herwynton
		Roger de Breynton
20 Apr. 1332	Orleton	Adam de Herwynton
		M. William de Fowehope
9 Nov. 1332	Orleton	Roger de Breynton
		Adam de Herwynton
11 Mar. 1334	Montacute	Prior Wolstan de Bransford
(Revoked June 1334)		
3 Apr. 1337	Hemenhale	Prior Wolstan de Bransford
		M. Stephen de Kettlebury
		M. Andrew Offord

DIOCESAN OFFICIALS

DATE OF COMMISSION	BISHOP	PERSONS APPOINTED
25 Oct. 1297	Giffard	Robert of Gloucester
None	Giffard	(?) Robert de Sutton (See above, p. 277, n. 4.)
27 Dec. 1306	Gainsburgh	M. John de Rodberrow
20 Oct. 1308	Reynolds	M. John de Rodberrow
1 Jan. 1309	Reynolds	M. Benedict de Paston
None	Maidstone	M. John de Bloyou
None	Maidstone	(?) M. J. de Oseworthe (See p. 284 above)
31 Jan. 1318	Cobham	M. John de Bloyou
(Sept. 1320)	Cobham	M. Nicholas de Gore
		M. John de Broadwas (But see p. 111 above)
None (acting 1328)[1]	Orleton	M. William de Fowehope
Sept. 1330	Orleton	M. Robert de Worth
None (acting 1332)	Orleton	John de Karselegh (al. "Cassele")
None (acting 1334)	Montacute	John de Clipston
3 Apr. 1334	Montacute	M. John de Hildesle
19 Sept. 1339	Bransford	M. John de la Lowe (ob. 1349)

[1] Judging from an entry in *Heref. Reg. Charlton* (p. 12), which probably dates from shortly after 23 October 1331, Fowehope continued to act as official.

"DEPUTY OFFICIALS"

20 Sept. 1315	Maidstone	M. Richard Mahel (al. "Maiel")
8 June 1316	Maidstone	M. Nicholas de Gore
None (acting 1330)	Orleton	John de Usk
25 May 1334	Montacute	M. William de Bosco

SEQUESTRATORS

DATE OF COMMISSION	BISHOP	PERSONS APPOINTED
8 Oct. 1305 (He had been acting in 1303)	Gainsburgh	M. R. de Sutton
20 Oct. 1308	Reynolds	M. John de Broadwas
18 Aug. 1309	Reynolds	M. John de Broadwas
21 Sept. 1315	Maidstone	M. John de Broadwas M. Stephen de Northeye
None (Acting in 1317 and 1319)	Cobham	M. John de Broadwas
29 Feb. 1328	Orleton	Nicholas de Kaerwent
None (Acting in 1334 and 1335)	Montacute	John de Stanford
7 Dec. 1335	Montacute	M. Henry de Neubold
7 Dec. 1335	Montacute (By this second commission he was appointed commissary-general and sequestrator.)	M. Henry de Neubold
16 Feb. 1339	Bransford	M. Henry de Neubold
30 Mar. 1339	Bransford (Reissued after the bishop's consecration. Neubold was acting as Thoresby's sequestrator in 1350: see above, p. 171, n. 3.)	M. Henry de Neubold

CHANCELLORS

DATE OF TRANSFER OF SEALS	BISHOP	PERSON APPOINTED
30 Sept. 1303	Gainsburgh	M. Walter de Wotton (ob. 1306)
Not known	Cobham	M. John de Renham
Probably 5 June 1334 (See p. 125 above)	Montacute	M. Robert de Worth
Not known	Hemenhale	M. Andrew Offord
Not known	Bransford	M. John de Severleye

SELECTED COMMISSIONS

VICARS-GENERAL

See pp. 101–2

No. 1 17 Oct. 1305

Bishop Gainsburgh appoints M. Walter de Wotton, archdeacon of Huntingdon and canon of Westbury.

Reg. Gainsburgh, fo. 9v.

COMMISSIO VICARII GENERALIS DOMINI WYG' EPISCOPI

Frater W[illelmus] permissione divina Wyg' episcopus &c. dilecto in Christo filio magistro Waltero de Wotton archidiacono Hunt' et canonico ecclesie nostre collegiate de Westbur', salutem graciam et benediccionem. Cum pro diversis et arduis nostris et ecclesie nostre negociis serenissimum principem dominum Edwardum dei gracia regem Anglie illustrem et regnum Anglie contingentibus[1] in curia Romana et alibi procurandis, nedum a nostra diocesi sed eciam a regno Anglie ad tempus aliquod oporteat nos abesse; ad examinandum elecciones et personas electas in abbates priores abbatissas et priorissas confirmandumque electos, ac ad recipiendi munus benediccionis huiusmodi electis a quocumque episcopo Cant' provincie suffraganeo licenciam concedendum, ac ad recipiendum quoscumque clericos idoneos ad quecumque beneficia ecclesiastica nostre diocesis presentatos, instituendumque eosdem, et quocumque iuris titulo eosdem in corporalem possessionem huiusmodi beneficiorum per te vel alium inducendum, et preficiendum ac providendum monasteriis seu ecclesiis de personis idoneis in casibus quibus ad nos dinoscitur pertinere de consuetudine vel de iure, necnon eligendum et preficiendum priorem in ecclesia nostra Wygorn' iuxta formam composicionis inter bone memorie dominum Willelmum quondam Wygorn' episcopum predecessorem nostrum[2] et capitulum nostrum Wygorn' initum et hactenus pacifice observatum, si ipsum prioratum nobis absentibus a regno Anglie vacare contigerit quoquomodo, et quoscumque illicitos deten-

---

[1] "Serenissimum—contingentibus" added later but in a contemporary hand.

[2] William of Blois (1218–36).

tores beneficiorum ecclesiasticorum administracionum seu dignitatum quorumcumque, iuris ordine servato ab eisdem, necnon ministros nostros quoscumque in spiritualibus et temporalibus a suis ministeriis officiis et ballivis amovendum pro tue libito voluntatis, et alios subrogandum; beneficia quecumque ad nostram collacionem qualitercumque spectancia, beneficiis nostre collacionis proprie patronatus nostri dumtaxat exceptis, personis ydoneis conferendum;[1] necnon alium ad premissa loco tui substituendum et substitutum revocandum quociens videris expedire: tibi de cuius fidelitate et industria confidenciam gerimus specialem in nostra absencia a regno Anglie vices nostras committimus per presentes, teque in premissis ac ceteris (fo. 10r.) omnibus et singulis que ad administracionem spiritualium et temporalium nostrorum pertinere noscuntur, aut nos seu ecclesiam nostram predictam tangunt seu tangere poterunt quoquomodo, eciam si mandatum speciale requirant, nostrum vicarium generalem tenore presencium facimus constituimus et eciam ordinamus, tibique ad premissa ac omnia alia ad officium vicarii predictum pertinencia pleniter exequenda et cetera omnia libere excercenda que iurisdiccionis episcopalis existunt, generalem plenam et liberam concedimus potestatem cum cohercionis canonice potestate. In cuius rei testimonium sigillum nostrum presentibus est appensum. Dat' London' XVI Kalen' Novembris anno domini M°CCC^mo quinto.

See p. 103, n. 5

No. 2 29 Feb. 1328

Bishop Orleton appoints Adam de Herwynton, canon of Hereford, his vicar-general in spirituals.

Reg. Orleton 2, fo. 3v.

COMMISSIO VICARIATUS

Adam permissione divina Wygorn' episcopus discreto viro dilectoque in Christo filio domino Ade de Herwynton canonico Heref', salutem graciam et benediccionem. Quia extra nostras civitatem et diocesem Wygorn' in remotis agentes, administracioni spiritualium in eisdem ad presens intendere non valemus, de vestra circumspecta prudencia et probata fidelitate plenam in domino fiduciam obtinentes, vos in absencia nostra nostrum vicarium generalem ordinamus et constituimus per presentes, ac vobis in hiis que ad officium vicarii pertinent vices nostras committimus cum cohercionis canonice potestate. In cuius rei testimonium presentes litteras sigillo nostro munitas fieri

---

[1] The clause "beneficia—conferend." is written at the bottom of the folio and its proper position indicated by *vacat* marks.

fecimus has patentes. Dat' Ebor' II Kalen' Marcii anno domini M°CCC°° XXVII, et nostre translacionis primo.

No. 3 11 Mar. 1334   *See pp.* 100, 103

Bishop Montacute appoints Brother Wolstan de Bransford, prior of Worcester, his vicar-general in spirituals.

Reg. Montacute 1, fo. 1r.

COMMISSIO VICARIATUS

Simon permissione divina Wygorniensis ecclesie electus confirmatus, reverende discrecionis viro domino priori ecclesie cathedralis nostre Wygorn', salutem in omnium salvatore. Cum ex quibusdam causis legitimis a diocesi Wygorn' aliquamdiu oporteat nos abesse, de vestris fidelitate et prudencia fiduciam plenam habentes, vos spiritualitatis Wygorniensis diocesis nobis sic absentibus facimus et constituimus nostrum vicarium generalem, vobisque ad faciendum excercendum et expediendum omnia et singula que ad huiusmodi officium de iure vel consuetudine pertinere noscuntur committimus vices nostras cum cuiuslibet cohercionis canonice potestate. In cuius rei testimonium sigillum officii nostri archidiaconatus Cantuar' presentibus apposuimus. Dat' Oxon' XI die Marcii anno domini millesimo trecentesimo tricesimo tercio.

See pp. 100, 103

No. 4 Undated[1]

Revocation of the above commission

Ibid., fo. 8r.

REVOCACIO COMMISSIONIS

Simon permissione &c. reverende discrecionis viro domino priori . . . ecclesie nostre Wygorn', salutem graciam et benediccionem. Quia nuper variis et arduis negociis prepediti vos spiritualitatis nostre diocesis nostrum vicarium fecimus generalem, necnon ad excercendum et expediendum omnia et singula que ad huius[modi] officium de iure et consuetudine pertinere noscuntur, vices nostras commisimus cum cohercionis canonice[2] potestate: nos tamen ad presens certis et legitimis de causis nos moventibus nostrum propositum mutare volentes ipsam commissionem nostram vobis concessam revocamus. Mandantes quatinus dicta commissio et potestas sic ut premittitur vobis facte ultra

---

[1] The preceding entry is dated XI Kal' Junii (21 June) 1334, also from Crookham.
[2] "Canonice" interlineated.

diem confeccionis presencium nullatenus durare valeant, nec robur
aliquod habeant firmitatis. Inhibentes insuper ne quicquam circa
premissa attemptetis donec a nobis aliud habueritis in mandatis. Dat'
apud Crokham &c.

No. 5 3 Apr. 1337   *See pp.* 103–4

*Bishop Hemenhale appoints Prior Wolstan de Bransford, Stephen de
Kettlebury, and Andrew de Offord his vicars-general in spirituals.*

Reg. Hemenhale, fo. 6r.–v.

COMMISSIO VICARIATUS

Frater Thomas permissione divina Wygornien[sis] episcopus dilectis
nobis in Christo fratri Wolstano priori ecclesie nostre Wygorniensis et
magistris Stephano de Kettlebury et Andree de Offord, salutem et
sincere dileccionis affectum. Suscepte servitutis iugum propensius nos
invitat et quadam urgentis consciencie necessitate compellit, ut ad ea
excercenda que circa iniuncti oneris execucionem iure nobis permittente
incumbunt, cum nequeamus ea per nos ipsos presenciali ministerio
excercere, tales evocemus et eligamus personas quarum presencia
defectus quos nostra prebere posset absencia suppleantur et iuris
observanciam prebeant in subiectis. Ne autem nobis agentibus in
remotis ecclesia nostra Wygorniensis et populus nobis commissus in
spiritualibus [racione] nostre absencie sustineant detrimenta, attendentes quod persone vestre de quibus quarumque fide et virtutibus nobis
notis fiduciam in domino gerimus specialem tam morum gravitate
quam sciencia commissum nobis in hac parte onus iuvante domino
scient et poterunt supportare, quodque subiecto clero et populo erunt
non modicum fructuose: ideoque vos et vestrum quemlibet in solidum
nostros et dicti episcopatus nostri Wygorn' in spiritualibus generales
vicarios facimus constituimus ac ordinamus. Dantes et concedentes
vobis et vestrum cuilibet in solidum plenam et generalem administracionem et omnimodam facultatem per vos vel alium seu alios
statuendi nostro nomine et reformandi inquirendi visitandi personas
ecclesiasticas, monasteria, prioratus nostre iurisdiccioni subiectas seu
subiecta, et earundem personarum excessus puniendi, interdicendi,
suspendendi et excommunicandi, ammovendi imperpetuum vel ad
tempus ab ecclesiis vel beneficiis quibuscumque quos inveneritis illud
culpis exigentibus demereri; elecciones quorumcumque abbatum et
priorum et aliorum quorumcumque factas seu faciendas ad quascumque
ecclesias seu monasteria seu alia beneficia nostre civitatis et diocesis
Wygorniensis cum diligencia examinandi, de vita et conversacione

electorum et aliis circumstanciis inquirendi, et si ipsas elecciones vel
earum aliquam [rite et canonice factas seu factam] et electos bone vite
et honeste conversacionis ac sufficientis sciencie esse reperieritis, super
quibus vestram volumus conscienciam onerare, confirmandi, et eciam
elecciones factas et faciendas secundum canonicas sancciones impugn-
andi et infirmandi, quibuscumque eciam abbatibus auctoritate nostra
faciendi munus benediccionis impendi per quemcumque archiepiscopum vel episcopum catholicum graciam et communionem apostolice
sedis habentem; pueros et clericos civitatis et diocesis nostre Wygorniensis quibuscumque episcopis catholicis ad sacramentum crismatis,
primam tonsuram, et omnes tam minores quam sacros ordines presentandi, eisque super hoc litteras concedendi; ecclesias autem et beneficia
cum cura vel sine cura que in civitate et diocesi predictis per cessionem,
renunciacionem vel mortem seu alio quovis modo vacant ad presens vel
vacabunt imposterum quorum ad nos collacio seu disposicio spectat seu
pertinet nobis nostreque collacioni specialiter reservamus. Dantes
eciam vobis et cuilibet vestrum in solidum auctoritatem, potestatem et
mandatum speciale adipiscendi, petendi, recuperandi pro nobis et
nostro nomine iura, census et iurisdicciones, primicias, et quecumque
alia bona ad nos et episcopatum nostrum spectancia de consuetudine
vel de iure, et si aliqua alienata vel occupata inveneritis vel distracta
ad ius et proprietatem ecclesie nostre revocandi; et generaliter omnia et
singula faciendi et excercendi que veri, legitimi et generales vicarii
facere possunt et que nosmet possumus facere si personaliter presentes
essemus. Ratum et gratum atque firmum habere promittimus quicquid
per vos vel vestrum aliquem et substitutum vel substitutos a vobis vel
aliquo vestrum actum fuerit in premissis et quolibet premissorum sub
ypotheca obligatione omnium bonorum nostrorum et ecclesie nostre
Wygorniensis predicte. In quorum omnium testimonium presentes (fo.
6v.) litteras per Nicholaum North notarium nostrum mandavimus
publicari et sigilli nostri appensione muniri. Dat' Avinion in hospicio
habitacionis nostre III° die mensis Aprilis anno domini millesimo
CCC^{mo} tricesimo septimo et consecracionis nostre primo. Presentibus
discreto viro magistro Johanne de Redyngg' rectore ecclesie de
Aldebergh et[1] Roberto de Belagh' ac Philippo de Brom clericis testibus
ad premissa vocatis specialiter et rogatis.

Notarial attestation

Et ego Nicholaus North clericus Wygorniensis diocesis publicus
apostolica auctoritate notarius dictis constitucioni, ordinacioni,

---

[1] "Et" interlineated.

potestatis dacioni, concessioni et commissioni ac omnibus aliis supradictis una cum dictis testibus presens interfui eaque omnia et singula
prout supra scribuntur fieri vidi et audivi, scripsi, et de mandato
reverendi in Christo patris et domini domini Thome dei gracia Wygorniensis episcopi supradicti huius commissionem sive litteras sigillo suo
sigillavi et in dictorum testium presencia publicavi sub anno, die
mensis et loco predictis, indiccione quinta, pontificatus sanctissimi in
Christo patris et domini nostri domini Benedicti pape XII^{mi} anno
tercio, dictasque litteras signo meo consueto signavi rogatus in fidem et
testimonium veritatis. Constat de illis diccionibus 'vel sine cura'
interlineatis super decima octava linea descendente scriptis ante signi
apposicionem per me notarium supradictum.

OFFICIALS

No. 6 27 Dec. 1306   *See pp.* 110–11

   Bishop Gainsburgh appoints M. John de Rodberrow,[1] *rector of Hartlebury.*

Reg. Gainsburgh, fo. 11r.

COMMISSIO OFFICIALITATIS EPISCOPI WYG'

Frater W[illelmus] etc. dilecto in Christo filio magistro Johanni de Rod'
rectori ecclesie de Hertlebur' nostre diocesis, officiali nostro, salutem
graciam et benediccionem. In hiis omnibus et singulis que ad officialitatis officium in nostra Wygorn' diocesi pertinent, vobis vices nostras,
necnon specialem potestatem inquirendi corrigendi puniendique
subditorum nostrorum quorumque excessus, ac eciam clericos de iure
privandos a suis beneficiis et administracionibus amovendi, committimus per presentes cum cohercionis canonice potestate. Dat' apud
Hertilbur' VI Kalen' Januarii anno domini M°CCC^{mo} sexto, consecracionis vero nostre quinto.

No. 7 ?1 Sept. 1330   *See p.* 111

   Bishop Orleton appoints M. Robert de Worth, canon of Salisbury.

Reg. Orleton 2, fo. 12r.

COMMISSIO OFFICIALITATIS

Adam permissione divina Wygorn' episcopus, discreto viro filioque in
Christo dilecto magistro Roberto de Worthe canonico Sar' officiali
nostro, salutem graciam et benediccionem. Ad audiendum et fine
debito terminandum causas et lites in consistoriis nostre civitatis et

---

[1] Rodberrow, or something near it, is the usual form in the registers—probably for
"Rodborough".

diocesis motas et movendas seu eciam agitandas, necnon ad inquirendum corrigendum et puniendum quorumcumque subditorum
nostrorum excessus, vobis vices nostras committimus cum cohercionis
canonice potestate. In cuius rei testimonium litteras nostras fieri
fecimus has[1] patentes. Dat' apud Bellum [?primo][2] die mensis Septembris anno domini millesimo CCC°tricesimo et translacionis nostre
tercio.

No. 8 3 Apr. 1334   *See p.* 112

Bishop Montacute appoints M. John de Hildesle, canon of Chichester.
Reg. Montacute 1, fo. 4v.

COMMISSIO FACTA MAGISTRO JOHANNI DE HILDESLE AD INQUIR-
ENDUM CORRIGENDUM

Simon permissione divina Wygorn' ecclesie electus confirmatus,
dilecto nobis in Christo magistro Johanni de Hildesle canonico Cicestr',
salutem cum benediccione salvatoris. Cuncta nobis incumbencia
expedire personaliter non valentes, illis quorum mores et sciencia
diuturna rerum experiencia manifestat nonnulla committere nos
oportet. De vestra igitur fidelitate et prudencia multipliciter approbatis
plenam in domino reportantes fiduciam, vos cum potestate inquirendi
corrigendi puniendi quorumcumque subditorum nostrorum excessus in
nostrum officialem preficimus per presentes, ac vobis in omnibus que
ad nostram ordinariam et spiritualem iurisdiccionem spectare noscuntur cum cohercionis canonice [potestate][3] committimus vices nostras.
Mandates quatinus equitate pensata iusticiam prout vobis dominus
inspiraverit exhibere curetis: et commissionem seu commissiones nostras
magistro Thome de Wyche sub quacumque verborum forma conceptas
penitus revocamus. Dat' apud Crokeham sub sigillo officii nostri
archidiaconatus Cant' tercio die mensis Aprilis anno domini supradicto.

"DEPUTY OFFICIALS"

No. 9 20 Sept. 1315   *See p.* 113

*Bishop Maidstone empowers Richard Mahel to act in all matters pertaining
to the officiality during the absence of the official [John Bloyou].*
Reg. Maidstone, fo. 26v.

COMMISSIO FACTA MAGISTRO RICARDO MAHEL

Walterus permissione divina Wygorn' episcopus dilecto filio et clerico[4]
nostro magistro Ricardo Mahel, salutem graciam et benediccionem.

---

[1] MS. "has" interlineated.   [2] MS. δ
[3] MS. "predicte".   [4] "Et clerico" interlineated.

In hiis omnibus et singulis que ad officialitatis officium, officiali nostro absente, in nostra Wygorn' diocesi pertinent, vobis de cuius fidelitate et industria confidenciam gerimus specialem, vices nostras committimus cum cohercionis canonice potestate. In cuius rei testimonium sigillum nostrum presentibus est appensum. Dat' apud Alvech' XII Kalen' Octobris, anno domini M°CCC°XV°, consecracionis vero nostre secundo.

No. 10 8 June 1316   *See p.* 113

> *Bishop Maidstone empowers M. Nicholas de Gore to deal with all causes pertaining to the officiality during the absence of the official [John Bloyou] and to inquire into, correct, and punish excesses.*

Ibid., fo. 45r.

COMMISA [*sic*] FACTA MAGISTRO NICHOLAO DE GORE

Walterus permissione divina Wyg' episcopus dilecto nobis in Christo magistro Nicholao de Gore clerico nostro, salutem graciam et benediccionem. De vestra circumspeccione et industria non modicum confidentes, ad cognoscendum et procedendum terminandum et diffin[i]endum in omnibus causis et negociis motis seu movendis que ad nostre officialitatis officium, nostro officiali absente, qualitercumque spectare dignoscuntur, necnon ad inquirendum cor[r]igendum et puniendum subditorum excessus quorumcumque in nostra civitate et diocesi Wygorn' memorata, vobis vices nostras committimus cum cuiuslibet cohercionis canonice potestate. Non intendentes potestates aliis nostris commissariis primitus factas per presentes aliqualiter revocare. In cuius rei testimonium sigillum nostrum &c. Dat' apud Wythindon VI^to Idus Junii anno domini M°CCC° sexto decimo.

ADDITIONAL COMMISSIONS TO OFFICIALS

(a) SPECIAL AUDITOR

No. 11 18 Apr. 1312   *See pp.* 127, *n.* 2., 131

> *Bishop Reynolds appoints his official, Benedict de Paston, to hear the case brought* ex officio *against M. Robert de Wych.*

Reg. Reynolds, fo. 55r.

COMMISSIO OFFIC[IALI]

W[alterus] permissione divina &c. dilecto filio . . . magistro Benedicto de Paston officiali nostro, salutem graciam et benediccionem. In negocio correccionis ex officio nostro contra magistrum de Wych qui se dicit rectorem ecclesie de Alvynechirch moto vobis committimus vices nostras cum cohercionis canonice potestate, vos in premissis auditorem nostrum constituentes tenore presencium specialem. Dat' apud Hertle-bur' XIIII Kalend' Maii anno M°CCC°XII°, consecracionis nostre quarto.

(b) CORRECTION AND PROBATE

No. *12* 12 June 1314   See p. 112

Bishop Maidstone appoints his official, M. John Bloyou, to inquire into, correct, and punish excesses; to impose suspension from the administration of spiritualities; and to grant probate etc.

Reg. Maidstone, fo. 12v.

COMMISSIO FACTA J. BLOYOU AD CORRIGENDUM EXCESSUS SUBDITORUM ET PROBACIONES TESTAMENTORUM RECIPIENDUM

Walterus permissione divina Wygorn' episcopus dilecto filio magistro Johanni Bloyou officiali nostro, salutem graciam et benediccionem. Ad inquirendum corrigendum et puniendum excessus subditorum nostrorum quorumcumque et eosdem si ipsorum protervitas hoc exegerit ab eorundem administracionibus in spiritualibus suspendendum, necnon insinuaciones testamentorum quorumcumque in nostra diocesi decedencium recipiendum et compota testamentorum huiusmodi et acquietancias super eisdem audiendum faciendum, vobis vices nostras committimus cum cohercionis canonice potestate. Dat' apud Hembur' in Salso Marisco II Idus Junii anno domini M°CCC°XIIII°, consecracionis vero nostre primo.

(c) AUDITOR OF RURAL DEANS' ACCOUNTS

No. *13* 25 July 1334   See p. 71[1]

Bishop Montacute empowers M. John de Clipston, his official, to audit the accounts of the deans of the diocese; if necessary, to remove both them and their apparitors, and to appoint others.

Reg. Montacute 2, fo. 2v.

COMMISSIO AD AUDIENDUM RACIOCINIUM DECANORUM WYGORN' DIOC'

Simon permissione divina Wygorn' episcopus, dilecto filio magistro J. de Clipston officiali nostro, salutem graciam et benediccionem. De vestre

---

[1] Cf. p. 66 above.

circumspeccionis industria plenam in domino fiduciam obtinentes, ad audiendum raciocinium singulorum decanorum omnium decanatuum nostre diocesis de quibuscumque proventibus nos in dicta diocesi concernentibus quovismodo, ac ad allocandum seu disallocandum allocanda vel disallocanda prout raciocinii huiusmodi exitus ex hoc requirit, et ad faciendum acquietancie litteras in hac parte, necnon ad ammovendum decanos et apparitores eiusdem nostre diocesis et loco ammotorum alios subrogandum prout vestre circumspeccioni faciendum esse videbitur, vobis cum cohercionis canonice potestate vices nostras committimus per presentes, quas in testimonium sigilli nostri impressione fecimus communiri. Dat' apud Crokham VIII Kalen' Augusti anno domini supradicto.

SEQUESTRATORS

No. 14 8 Oct. 1305   *See p.* 116

   Bishop Gainsburgh appoints M. Robert de Sutton, rector of Dursley.

Reg. Gainsburgh, fo. 9r.

COMMISSIO SEQUESTRATORIS

Frater W[illelmus] permissione &c. dilecto in Christo filio magistro R. de Sutton rectori ecclesie de Duresleye clerico nostro, salutem graciam et benediccionem. De vestra fidelitate ac circumspecta industria plenius confidentes, vos sequestratorem nostrum generalem facimus et constituimus, vobisque huiusmodi officii excercium [a variant of "excercicium"] ac omnia et singula ad idem qualitercumque spectancia in tota nostra diocesi Wygorn' et in singulis partibus eiusdem cum cohercionis canonice potestate committimus per presentes. Dat' apud Hylyngdon VIII Idus Octobris anno domini M°CCC^moquinto, consecracionis vero nostre tercio.

No. 15 18 Aug. 1309   *See p.* 116

   Bishop Reynolds appoints M. John de Broadwas, rector of Himbleton.

Reg. Reynolds, fo. 12v.

COMMISSIO SEQUESTRATORIS

W[alterus] permissione &c. dilecto filio magistro Johanni de Bradewas rectori ecclesie de Humelton, salutem &c. Cum fructus et obvenciones ecclesiarum nostre diocesis vacancium tempore vacacionis ipsarum

23

provenientes de iure et consuetudine ecclesie nostre Wyg' ad nos nostramque disposicionem spectent, ac eciam ad diocesanos episcopos predecessores nostros qui pro tempore fuerant pertinere consueverint ab antiquo, nos de vestra fidelitate circumspeccione et industria plenius confidentes, ad sequestrandum fructus proventus et obvenciones huiusmodi et eosdem colligendum et recipiendum per omnes partes nostre Wyg' diocesis, vobis tenore presencium specialem tribuimus auctoritatem, et officii huiusmodi exercicium cum canonice cohercionis potestate committimus per presentes. Dat' Lond' XVI Kal' Septembris anno domini M°CCC^mo^nono.

No. 16 21 Sept. 1315 *See p.* 116

> *Bishop Maidstone appoints M. John de Broadwas and M. Stephen de Northeye to exercise the office of sequestrator-general and to punish and correct his subjects.*

Reg. Maidstone, fo. 36v.

(UNTITLED)[1]

Walterus permissione divina Wygorn' episcopus, dilectis in Christo filiis magistris Johanni de Bradewas et Stephano de Northeye clericis nostris, salutem graciam et benediccionem. De vestris fidelitate et industria circumspecta plenius confidentes, vos sequestratores nostros generales facimus et constituimus, vobisque huiusmodi officii excercium [a variant of "excercicium"] ac correccionem et punicionem excessuum subditorum nostrorum ac eciam omnia et singula premissa qualitercumque contingencia in nostra dyocesi Wyg' cum cohercionis canonice potestate coniunctim committimus per presentes. Dat' apud Alvechurch' XI° Kalen' Octobris, anno domini M°CCC^mo^ quinto decimo.

COMMISSARY-GENERAL AND SEQUESTRATOR

No. 17 7 Dec. 1335 *See pp.* 117, 128

Reg. Montacute 2, fo. 17r.

> *Bishop Montacute appoints M. Henry de Neubold, rector of Hethe.*

COMMISSIO COMMISSARII GENERALIS ET SEQUESTRATORIS

Simon permissione divina Wygorn' episcopus dilecto nobis in Christo magistro Henrico de Neubold' rectori ecclesie de Hethe, salutem &c. De vestra fidelitate et circumspecta industria plenius confidentes, vos

---

1 A post-medieval (? seventeenth-century) rubric runs: "Commissio facta Johanni de Bradewas et Stephano de Northeye . . . sequestratores suos."

commissarium nostrum generalem facimus et sequestratorem constituimus, vobisque huiusmodi officii excercicium ac correccionem et[1]
punicionem excessuum subditorum nostrorum, insinuaciones et
probaciones testamentorum quorumcumque in nostra diocesi decedencium, et si alibi fortassis decedant bona in eadem nostra diocesi obtinentes, suorum testamentorum approbaciones recipiendi, et bonorum
huiusmodi administracionem legitime committendi, raciocinia administracionis eorum audiendi et acquietancie litteras prout iuris fuerit
faciendi, yconomos et custodes quarumcumque dicte nostre diocesis
ecclesiarum vacancium quando et quociens eas vacare contigerit,
earum vacacione durante, per vos alium vel alios constituendi et
legitime deputandi et ipsos quando et quociens expedire videritis
revocandi, et alios subrogandi, ac omnia alia faciendi et expediendi
que in premissis et ea tangentibus necessaria vel oportuna fuerint,
eciam si mandatum exigant speciale, vobis cum canonice cohercionis[2]
et sequestri interposicionis potestate vices nostras donec eas duxerimus
revocandas committimus per presentes, quas nostri impressione sigilli
fecimus in testimonium communiri: commissiones nostras quibuscumque aliis in hac parte factas ex certa sciencia revocantes. Dat'
apud Alvech' VII Idus Decembris anno domini supradicto.

AUDITOR OR COMMISSARY-GENERAL

No. 18 13 June 1312   *See pp.* 128, 130

Bishop Reynolds appoints William de Birston, archdeacon of Gloucester.

Reg. Reynolds, fo. 56r.

COMMISSIO GENERALIS

W[alterus] permissione &c. dilecto filio magistro Willelmo de Byrston,
archidiacono nostro Glouc', salutem graciam et benediccionem. In
omnibus causis et negociis coram nobis ex officio nostro vel ad partis
instanciam motis seu movendis, necnon ad inquirendum corrigendum
et puniendum excessus nostrorum quorumlibet subditorum, vobis
committimus vices nostras cum cohercionis canonice potestate, et vos
auditorem seu commissarium nostrum deputamus generalem. Nolentes
per commissionem seu deputacionem huiusmodi iurisdiccioni seu
nocioni officialis nostris in aliquo derogari. In cuius rei testimonium
sigillum nostrum presentibus duximus apponendum. Dat' apud Bredon'
Id[ibu]s Junii anno domini MᵒCCCᵐᵒduodecimo, consecracionis
nostre quarto.

---

[1] "Correccionem et" interlineated.   [2] "Potestate" crossed out.

ADJUTOR OR SPECIAL COMMISSARY

No. 19 1 July 1339   *See p.* 132

Bishop Bransford appoints M. Hugh de Penebrugg [Pembridge].

Reg. Bransford, fo. 7v. (*65*).

COMMISSIO

Frater W[olstanus] &c. dilecto nobis in Christo magistro Hugoni de Penebrugg clerico, salutem graciam et benediccionem. In omnibus causis et negociis coram nobis ex officio nostro vel ad partis instanciam in curia nostra motis vel movendis, necnon ad inquirendum corrigendum et puniendum excessus nostrorum subditorum, vobis committimus vices nostras cum cohercionis canonice potestate, et vos adiutorem seu commissarium nostrum in curia nostra predicta deputamus specialem. Nolentes per cessionem seu deputacionem huiusmodi iurisdiccioni seu nocioni officialis nostri seu commissarii generalis in aliquo derogari. In cuius rei testimonium sigillum nostrum fecimus hiis apponi. Dat' apud Broedon' primo die mensis Julii anno domini supradicto etc.

THE HEARING OF CAUSES

No. 20 20 Sept. 1303   *See p.* 131

Bishop Gainsburgh appoints M. Walter de Wotton and M. Benedict de Feriby to act in all causes ("coram episcopo"), with powers of inquiry, correction, and punishment.

Reg. Gainsburgh, fo. 4v.

COMMISSIO PRO W. DE WOTTON ET B. DE FERIBY

Frater W[illelmus] permissione divina Wyg' episcopus dilectis nobis in Christo magistris W. de Wotton et B. de Fer', salutem graciam et benediccionem. In omnibus causis et negociis tam ex officio nostro quam ad instanciam partium coram nobis motis vel movendis, necnon ad inquirendum corrigendum et puniendum excessus nostrorum quorumlibet subditorum, vobis coniunctim et divisim vices nostras committimus cum cohercionis canonice potestate. Valete. Dat' apud Bredon XII Kalen' Octobris anno domini M°CCC™otercio, consecracionis nostre primo.

No. 21 11 Apr. 1315   *See p.* 131

Bishop Maidstone appoints M. Simon de Walpole, M. Richard de Chaddesleye, and M. Gilbert de Kyrkeby, his clerks, to act in all causes, with powers of inquiry, correction, and punishment: saving the jurisdiction of the official.

Reg. Maidstone, fo. 25v.

COMMISSIO MAGISTRORUM S. DE WALEPOL, R. DE CHADDESLEY, ET G. DE KIRKEBY.

Walterus permissione divina Wygorn' episcopus dilectis filiis magistris Simoni de Walpole in sacra pagina professori, Ricardo de Chaddesleye et Gilberto de Kyrkeby, clericis nostris, salutem graciam et benediccionem. Ad inquirendum cor[r]igendum et puniendum excessus subditorum nostrorum quorumcumque, necnon in omnibus causis et negociis ex officio nostro vel ad partis instanciam motis seu movendis qualitercumque [que] ad officium nostrum pertineant, ac eciam in omnibus aliis et singulis premissa qualitercumque contingentibus, vobis coniunctim et divisim vices nostras committimus per presentes cum cohercionis cuiuslibet canonice potestate. Nolentes per commissionem huiusmodi iurisdiccioni seu nocioni officialis nostri in aliquo derogari. In cuius rei testimonium sigillum nostrum presentibus est appensum. Dat' apud Hertelbyri tercio Idus Aprilis anno domini millesimo CCC^{mo} decimo, consecracionis nostre secundo.

No. 22 10 Dec. 1342   *See pp.* 127, 130

Bishop Bransford appoints M. John de Severleye, the diocesan chancellor, to deal with all cases pertaining to his audience outside the consistory court, with the power of punishment and correction in accordance with the comperta *of the recent visitation.*

Reg. Bransford, fo. 64r. (*566*).

COMMISSIO MAGISTRI JOHANNIS DE SEVERLEY

Frater Wolstanus permissione divina Wygorn' episcopus dilecto filio magistro Johanni de Severleye cancellario nostro, salutem graciam et benediccionem. Ad audiendum cognoscendum et fine debito terminandum omnes causas et lites presentes et futuras ad audienciam nostram extra consistorium nostrum qualitercumque spectantes in ipsa motas vel movendas, una cum potestate canonice puniendi et corrigendi omnia et omnimoda comperta in visitacione nostra nuper in diocesi nostra Wyg' per nos et nostros exercita, tibi committimus[1] vices nostras cum cohercionis cuiuslibet canonice potestate. Dat' apud Hertlebur' decimo die mensis Decembris anno domini millesimo CCC^{mo} quadragesimo secundo, et nostre consecracionis quarto.

---

[1] "Et firmiter iniungendo mandamus" crossed out.

No. 23 4 Oct. 1342   *See p.* 127

Bishop Bransford appoints M. John de Severleye, with powers of inquiry, correction, and punishment.

Reg. Bransford 2, fo. 2r. and fo. 8r. (duplicated) (*1330, 1366*)

COMMISSIO GENERALIS IN OMNIBUS CAUSIS ET NEGOCIIS

Frater Wolstanus [&c.] . . . dilecto filio magistro Johanni de Severleye cancellario nostro, salutem graciam et benediccionem. Ad inquirendum corrigendum et puniendum crimina quecumque et excessus quorum-cumque subditorum nostrorum, necnon ad cognoscendum in causis quibuscumque ad nostram iurisdiccionem sive nocionem qualiter-cumque spectantibus, tam matrimonialibus quam aliis, motis seu movendis, et ad ipsas causas discuciendum et fine debito terminandum, vobis de cuius discrecione fidelitate et industria plenam in domino fiduciam optinemus, vices nostras committimus cum cohercionis canonice cuiuslibet potestate. Dat' apud Wythindon' IIII die Octobris anno domini MCCCXLII^{do.}, et nostre consecracionis quarto.

APPENDIX C

"SEDE VACANTE" DOCUMENTS

THE BONIFACE COMPOSITION

No. 1   *See pp. 271 et seq.*

28 July 1268

The composition of Archbishop Boniface regulating the exercise of jurisdiction during vacancies of the see of Worcester.

D. & C. Register 1, fo. lxvi v. (thirteenth century and probably contemporary). Collated with Lambeth MS. 1212 (L.) as printed in Churchill 2, pp. 59–61. See above, p. 271, n. 5.

COMPOSICIO ARCHIEPISCOPI CANTUAR' SEDE VACANTE (later hand)

Omnibus sancte matris ecclesie filiis ad quos pervenerit hec scriptura, Bonifacius miseracione divina archiepiscopus Cantuar' tocius Anglie primas, salutem in domino sempiternam.[1] Inter pacis et discordie tranquillitatis et dissensionis semitas quamdiu laboramus in via positi libenter advertimus quam dulce sapiat in pacis pulcritudine delectari quantumque amaritudinis afferat molesta dissensio. Caritatis enim quam pax nutriverat refrigerium abicit, cogitaciones malas immittit, cor impellit et elevat, ex hoc lites et iurgia suboriri contingit, expense fiunt inutiles, lites ex litibus oriuntur, bona pauperum que presertim[2] ecclesiastici viri multo precio deberent redimere, ut ipsis pauperibus que sua sunt redderent consumuntur. Hiis igitur animum nostrum pulsantibus, eum habentes pre oculis Jesum Christum qui ut pacem emeret sanguinem suum fudit pacem amplectimur, ut ad pacis vinculum verbo pariter et exemplo dissidencium animos invitemus. Eapropter cum inter nos ecclesie nostre Cantuar' nomine ex parte una et religiosos viros . . priorem et capitulum Wygorniensis ecclesie ex altera[3] super iurisdiccione et potestate episcopali in civitate et diocesi

[1] L. "Ricardus Wigorn. ecclesie prior humilis et eiusdem loci capitulum salutem . . . " (Richard Dumbleton was prior 1260–72.)

[2] "Presertim" interlin. in later hand.

[3] L. "Eapropter cum inter reverendum patrem Dnm. Bonifacium dei gracia Cant. archiepiscopum tocius Anglie Primatem nomine ecclesie sue Cant. ex parte una, et nos pro nobis et ecclesia nostra Wygorniensi ex altera . . . "

341

Wygorn', sede Wygorn' vacante, mota fuisset materia questionis, et in domini . . . legati presencia dum esset in partibus Anglicanis aliquantulum agitata, tandemque ad examen curie Romane[1] usque perducta, non absque multis hincinde laboribus et expensis; demum invitante pacis auctore domino, mediantibus bonis viris et amatoribus unitatis, talis inter nos composicio intervenit; videlicet quod: Quocienscumque et quandocumque sedem Wygorn' vacare contigerit . . . prior et capitulum eiusdem loci,[2] vel supprior mortuo priore vel extra regnum absente, quam primum comode poterunt, vacacionem huiusmodi domino . . . archiepiscopo Cantuar' si in Anglia fuerit, alioquin officiali curie Cantuar' litteratorie intimabunt. Et statim idem dominus[3] archiepiscopus vel eius officialis sine mora et difficultate quacumque . . . priorem Wygorn' qui pro tempore fuerit, vel eiusdem loci suppriorem priore mortuo vel extra regnum absente, donec prior redeat vel creetur, et postmodum illum redeuntem vel creatum priorem irrevocabiliter et in solidum officialem suum creabit in civitate et diocesi Wygorn' toto tempore vacacionis illius, quo ad cognicionem causarum ad forum episcopale spectancium, institucionem et destitucionem clericorum, eleccionum examinacionem, et confirmacionem ac infirmacionem earum, dignitatum et beneficiorum liberam collacionem, auctoritate concilii et alias racionabiliter faciendam, custodiarum emendarum ac proventuum percepcionem, visitacionem, correccionem, sinodi convocacionem et celebracionem, vicinorum episcoporum invitacionem cum canonice cautele studio, censuram ecclesiasticam, et omnem penitus ordinariam iurisdiccionem imperium et potestatem episcopalem que sine presencia episcopali poterunt excerceri, per dictum priorem aut[4] suppriorem et alios quos sibi in hiis duxerit subrogandos, auctoritate curie Cantuar' plene et integre excercendas. Que omnia et singula ac ea qualitercumque contingencia dictus prior vel supprior per se et alios auctoritate predicta Wygorn' sede vacante[5] libere excercebit. Interim autem ab inicio vacacionis huiusmodi usque ad recepcionem specialis commissionis predicte dictus prior vel supprior per se et alios quos sibi in hiis duxerit subrogandos auctoritate curie Cantuar' ex virtute presentis composicionis ne civitas et diocesis Wygorn'[6] iudicis presencia careant, premissa omnia et que ea contingere poterunt libere integre et plenarie excercebit. Et proventuum et emolumentorum omnium, exceptis procuracionibus quas in esculentis

---

[1] L. "Romane curie".   [2] L. "eiusdem loci capitulum".
[3] "Dominus" interlineated.   [4] L. "vel".
[5] L. "sede Wigorniensi vacante".
[6] "Wygorn" slipped out of "L" but has been supplied by the editor.

et poculentis percipiet, tercia parte sibi pro laboribus et expensis retenta, domino . . . archiepiscopo Cant' qui pro tempore fuerit, administracionis sue per se vel alium reddita racione fideliter restituet duas partes. Nos igitur[1] composicionem huiusmodi ratam et gratam habentes eam pro nobis et successoribus nostris imperpetuum bona fide promittimus observare et contra eam per nos vel per alium nullo modo venire. In cuius rei testimonium[2] et perpetuam firmitatem sigillum nostrum presentibus est appensum. Datum apud Thenham die Sabbati proxima post festum Sancti Jacobi apostoli anno gracie millesimo CC° sexagesimo octavo.

THE REQUEST FOR THE COMMISSION

No. 2   *See pp. 274 et seq.*

Undated

Pre-composition form of letter to be sent to the archbishop for the officiality sede vacante.

Registrum Prioratus, fo. lxv r., p. 137a (in Hale's edition, q.v.).

LITTERE DIRIGENDE DOMINO CANT' PRO OFFICIALIT[ATE]

Reverendo domino et patri in Christo karissimo N. dei gracia Cant' archiepiscopo, tocius Anglie primati, devoti filii sui N. prior Wigorn' et humilis eiusdem loci conventus, salutem et tam devotam quam debitam cum obediencia reverenciam. Cum vacante sede Wigornie ecclesie eiusdem loci priores officialitatis curam in episcopatu ipso ex possessione diutina ac consuetudine longis retro temporibus optenta hactenus optinuerunt; sancte paternitati vestre duximus supplicandum, quatinus cum per decessum venerabilis patris nostri N. Wigorn'

---

[1] L. "Nos vero predicti prior et capitulum Wigorn."

[2] L. "In cuius rei testimonium nostrum commune sigillum de communi consensu nostro presentibus est appensum. Datum die Sabbati proxima post Festum beati Jacobi Apostoli anno gracie MCC sexagesimo octavo. Item alia de eodem de verbo ad verbum usque ad clausulam illam videlicet. In cuius rei testimonium et perpetuam firmitatem sigillum communitatis nostre presenti scripture duximus apponendum. Dat' in Capitulo Wigorniensi in festo Nativitatis beate Marie virginis Anno Incarnacionis dominice Millesimo Ducentesimo Sexagesimo Octavo."

NOTE ON THE ABOVE.

The footnotes have not been burdened with details of slight differences in spelling: L. has pul*ch*ritudine, W*i*gorn' (usually extended adjectivally by Dr Churchill); exerceri, exercendas, exercebit, rather than ex*c*erceri etc.; quociescun*q*ue, quandocu*n*que, in*p*erpetuum, instead of quociescumque etc.

The Worcester text approximates to that of the Registrum Album (of Lambeth), the "A" of Churchill's collation.

episcopi ecclesie Wig' sedes vacans sit, dicte officialitatis curam auctoritate vestra gratuita concurrente secundum formam prescriptam concedere dignemini. Valeat sancta paternitas vestra semper in domino.

No. 3   *See p. 276*

30 Jan. 1302

Prior John de Wyke informs Archbishop Winchelsey of Giffard's death on 26 January and asks for his appointment as official in accordance with the composition.

Liber Albus, fo. viii v.

LITTERA AD CERCIORANDUM ARCHIEPISCOPUM DE VACACIONE SEDIS ET MORTE PASTORIS

Reverendo in Christo patri et domino Roberto dei gracia Cant' archiepiscopo [&c.] . . . frater J. prior ecclesie cathedralis Wyg' et eiusdem loci capitulum promptum pariter et devotum obediencie spiritum et reverencie debitum cum honore. Paternitatem vestram credimus non latere modum et formam composicionis super iurisdiccione et potestate episcopali in dyocesi Wyg' sede ipsa vacante dudum inter felicis recordacionis dominum Bonifacium quondam archiepiscopum Cant' predecessorem vestrum ex parte una et nos ex altera post varios litis amfractus inite, et tam successorum eiusdem quam capituli Cant' et sedis apostolice confirmacione roborate. Cuius effectui et tenori quatenus in nobis est innitentes, sanctitati vestre litteris presentibus intimamus, quod in crastino conversionis Sancti Pauli ultimo preterito infra noctis tenebras bone memorie dominus Godefridus nuper episcopus Wyg' diem suum clausit extremum. A vestra igitur sanctitate petimus humiliter et devote, quatinus iuxta ipsius composicionis formam dictum priorem nostrum irrevocabiliter et in solidum officialem vestrum creare dignemini in civitate et dyocesi Wyg' supradicta toto tempore vacacionis instantis quo ad institucionem et destitucionem clericorum, cognicionem causarum ad forum episcopale spectancium, et cetera omnia que in composicione memorata plenius continentur. Nos vero parati erimus dante deo iuxta ipsius composicionis exigenciam de proventibus et emolumentis vobis aut hiis quos ad id duxeritis assignandos pro tempore respondere. Valeat sancta paternitas vestra diu ad regimen ecclesie sancte in filio virginis gloriose. Dat' Wyg' III⁰ Kal' Februarii anno domini M⁰CCC⁰primo.

No. 4   *See p.* 281

24 Nov. 1313

On account of Archbishop Winchelsey's death the Worcester prior and chapter direct their request for the commission to the prior and chapter of Canterbury and appoint Brother John of St Briavels to receive it.

R.S.V., fo. lxxx r.

LITTERA UNA CUM PROCUR[ATORIO] . . . PRIORI ET CONVENTUI
ECCLESIE CHRISTI CANT' PRO COMMISSIONE IURISDICCIONIS
HABENDA

Reverendo in Christo patri domino Henrico dei gracia priori ecclesie Christi Cantuar'[1] et eiusdem loci capitulo venerando, vestre subieccionis filii devotiores, frater J. humilis prior ecclesie cathedralis Wygorn' et eiusdem loci capitulum, obedienciam et reverenciam debito cum honore. Advertentes pericula et iacturas que ecclesie vestre Cantuar' et nostre Wygornien' accidere poterunt per vacacionem ecclesie nostre predicte per absolucionem reverendi patris domini Walteri dei gracia Cantuarien' electi nuper ministrantis in ea contingentem quam vos credimus non latere, preminencie vestre dominanti cui subici gratulamur preces affeccione devotissima fundimus supplicantes, commissionem nobis fieri iuxta composicionem super iurisdiccione sede vacante predicta inter bone memorie dominum Bonifacium quondam Cantuar' archiepiscopum et nos initam et de vestra gracia confirmatam, ut sic nobis mediantibus nanciscamini possessionem emolumentorum iurisdiccionis iuxta formam composicionis predicte quam vos nec predecessores vestri habuistis hucusque, et nos vestro suffulti adiutorio quod est nostrum liberius exequamur. Ad quam quidem commissionem petendam et recipiendam vice nostra dilectum nobis in Christo confratrem nostrum J[ohannem] de Sancto Briavello procuratorem nostrum facimus per presentes. Dantes eidem potestatem alium vel alios loco sui substituendi et procur[atoris] officium reassumendi si viderit opportunum, necnon omnia alia faciendi que qualitas predicti negocii in forma iuris requirit etiamsi mandatum exigat speciale. Ratum habituri quicquid idem frater Johannes substitutus suus ve substituti fecerint in premissis. In cuius rei testimonium has litteras nostras apertas et clausas nostro sigillo communi fecimus consignari. Dat' in capitulo nostro Wyg' VIII Kalen' Decembris anno domini M°CCC° terciodecimo.

[1] Henry of Eastry (1284–1331).

THE COMMISSION

No. 5 *See pp.* 276–7

19 Feb. 1302

Notarial exemplification of the appointment by Archbishop Winchelsey of Prior John de Wyke as official *sede* vacante *(Mayfield, 17 February).*

D. & C. MS. B.1621 A.

Endorsed: COPIA COMMISSIONIS ARCHIEPISCOPI CANTUAR' SUB MANU PUPPLICA SEDE VACANTE

In nomine domini amen. Hoc est exemplum quarundam litterarum vero sigillo venerabilis patris domini R[oberti] dei gracia Cantuar' archiepiscopi tocius Anglie primatis cera viridi pendente sigillatarum, non cancellatarum, non abolitarum, nec in aliqua earum parte viciatarum, quarum tenor talis est: Robertus permissione divina Cantuar' archiepiscopus tocius Anglie primas, dilecto filio . . . priori ecclesie cathedralis Wygorn', salutem graciam et benediccionem. Durante vacacione sedis episcopalis Wygorn' iam pridem per mortem domini Godefridi Giffard pastoris solacio destitute, que per denunciacionem vestram et capituli vestri Wygorn' nobis plenius innotescit, vos officialem nostrum in civitate et diocesi Wygorn' secundum formam et effectum composicionis dudum habite inter felicis recordacionis dominum Bonifacium predecessorem nostrum ex parte una, et vos et capitulum vestrum ex altera, ad exercendum tempore vacacionis predicte ibidem omnem iurisdiccionem et potestatem episcopalem in eadem composicione contentam, creamus et preficimus per presentes. In testimonium vero premissorum sigillum nostrum presentibus est appensum. Dat' apud Magefeld' XIII Kal' Marcii anno domini millesimo trecentesimo primo, consecracionis nostre octavo. Et Willelmus de Maldon' London' diocesis, publicus *(Notarial sign)* apostolica et imperiali alme urbis prefectorie dignitatis auctoritate notarius, predictas litteras sanas et integras diligenter examinavi, easque fideliter exemplavi et in hanc publicam redegi formam, London' sub anno domini ab Incarnacione millesimo trecentesimo primo, indiccione XV, die Lune, videlicet XI Kal' Marcii, ad instanciam fratris Johannis de Bremesgrave commonachi et procuratoris dictorum religiosorum meoque signo consueto et nomine signavi rogatus.

No. 6   *See p.* 281

25 Nov. 1313

Henry of Eastry, prior of Canterbury (1284–1331), appoints Prior John de Wyke official, the sees of Canterbury and Worcester being vacant simultaneously.

R.S.V., fo. lxxx r.

COMMISSIO IURISDICCIONIS PRIORI WYGORN'

Henricus permissione divina prior ecclesie Christi Cantuar' et eiusdem loci capitulum venerabili viro domino . . . priori ecclesie cathedralis Wygorn', salutem in eo qui est omnium vera salus. Durante vacacione sedis episcopalis Wygorn' de qua nobis per denunciacionem vestram et vestri Wygorniensis capituli innotescit, vos officialem nostrum in civitate et diocesi Wygorn', secundum formam vim et effectum composicionis inter nos et ecclesiam nostram ex parte una et capitulum vestrum ac ecclesiam Wygorn' ex altera dudum inite, ad excercendum toto tempore vacacionis eiusdem ibidem omnem iurisdiccionem et potestatem episcopalem de quibus in eadem composicione fit mencio creamus et preficimus per presentes. Dat' in capitulo nostro die Sancte Katerine virginis anno domini M°CCC° terciodecimo.

No. 7   *See p.* 283

12 Jan. 1314

Archbishop Reynolds, claiming that on account of his provision to Canterbury the appointment made by Prior Henry (no. 6) had expired, appoints Prior John de Wyke his official.

Cant. Reg. Reynolds, fo. 5r.

COMMISSIO EXERCICII IURISDICCIONIS DIOCESIS WYGORN' SEDE VACANTE

W[alterus] dei et apostolice sedis gracia &c. religioso viro . . . priori ecclesie cathedralis Wygorn', salutem cum gracia et benediccione salvatoris. Licet dilecti filii . . . prior et capitulum ecclesie Christi Cantuar' . . . custodes spiritualitatis archiepiscopatus Cantuar' sede vacante, vos iuxta vim et effectum composicionis in hac parte edite . . . officialem Wygorn' dicta Wygorn' sede vacante prefecerint; quia tamen per provisionem ecclesie Cantuar' predicte de nobis factam huiusmodi prefeccio notorie expiravit, sitque opus nova commissione per nos super hoc facienda, vos ex nunc in eadem iurisdiccione nostrum

preficimus officialem, et ad exercendum officium officialitatis huiusmodi iuxta tenorem composicionis predicte vobis committimus vices
nostras cum cohercionis canonice potestate. Dat' apud Lamheth' II Idus
Januarii, anno domini &c. ut supra.

No. 8   See p. 283

12 Jan. 1314

Another commission issued by Archbishop Reynolds in the regular form.

Cant. Reg. Reynolds, fo. 6v.

Walterus [&c. as in 7] . . . facienda, vos officialem nostrum in civitate
et diocesi Wyg', secundum formam et effectum composicionis dudum
habite inter felicis recordacionis dominum Bonifacium quondam Cant'
archiepiscopum ex parte una et vos ac capitulum vestrum ex altera, ad
exercendum tempore vacacionis predicte ibidem omnem iurisdiccionem
et potestatem episcopalem secundum formam in eadem composicione
contentam, creamus et preficimus per presentes. In cuius rei &c. Dat'
apud Lameh' II Idus Januarii anno domini M°CCC°XIII°.

No. 9   See p. 286

10 Sept. 1327

*Archbishop Reynolds, on Prior Bransford's election as bishop of Worcester,
appoints the subprior his official.*

Cant. Reg. Reynolds, fo. 206v.

ALIA PREFECCIO[1] OFFICIALITAT' SEDE WYGORN' VACANTE

Walterus &c. dilecto filio . . . suppriori ecclesie cathedralis Wygorn',
salutem graciam et benediccionem. Cum nuper priorem ecclesie
predicte durante vacacione sedis episcopalis Wygorn' iam pridem per
mortem bone memorie magistri Thome de Cobham pastoris solacio
destitute que per denunciacionem ipsius . . . prioris et capituli
Wygorn' nobis plenius innotescebat et adhuc innotescit . . . officialem
nostrum in civitate et diocesi Wygorn', secundum formam et effectum
composicionis dudum habite inter felicis recordacionis dominum
Bonefacium predecessorem nostrum ex parte una et priorem et
capitulum Wygorn' ex altera, ad exercendum nomine nostro tempore
vacacionis predicte ibidem omnem iurisdiccionem et potestatem
episcopalem contentam in composicione antedicta creaverimus et

---

[1] The appointment of Prior Wolstan de Bransford is on fo. 206r.

prefecerimus, et iam per decretum eleccionis ex parte vestra et capituli predicti nobis presentatum apparet prefatum . . . priorem vestrum in dicte ecclesie episcopum electum esse et pastorem, quem non decet iure refragante in spiritualibus vel temporalibus dicte ecclesie per se vel per alium aliqualiter immiscere, vos officialem nostrum in civitate et diocesi antedictis, secundum vim formam et effectum composicionis memorate, ad exercendum nomine nostro istius vacacionis tempore omnem iurisdiccionem et potestatem episcopalem, ad rogatum et peticionem partis prioris supradicti, creamus et preficimus per presentes. In cuius &c. Dat' apud Otteford IIII^{to} Idus Septembris anno domini millesimo CCC^{mo}XXVII^{mo}. Commissionem dicto priori per nos prius factam penitus revocantes.

No. 10   *See p.* 291

16 Feb. 1353

Archbishop Islep appoints Prior John of Evesham his official, although he had not been informed of the vacancy on the translation of Thoresby to York or asked for the commission in accordance with the terms of the composition.

Reg. Islep, fo. 64r.; R.S.V., fo. cvi r.

COMMISSIO AD EXERCENDUM IURISDICCIONEM IN EPISCOPATU WYGORN' SEDE VACANTE

Simon &c. dilecto filio . . . priori ecclesie cathedralis Wygorn' sede ibidem vacante, salutem graciam et benediccionem. Licet vacacionis huiusmodi ut supponimus ignari, pro commissione nostra habenda iuxta formam composicionis inter predecessores nostros ac priorem et capitulum ecclesie Wygorn' inde facte habite et hactenus observate ad nos minime declinastis, seu eciam transmisistis; nos tamen iurisdiccionem nostram huiusmodi nolentes negligere set pocius ipsam observare illesam pro viribus cupientes, ad exercendum omnem iurisdiccionem in civitate et diocesi Wygorn', sede eiusdem ecclesie per translacionem venerabilis fratris nostri domini Johannis nuper Wygorn' episcopi ad ecclesiam Ebor' apostolica auctoritate nunc factam vacante, secundum vim formam et effectum composicionis huiusmodi, vobis committimus vices nostras cum cohercionis canonice potestate. Per hanc autem commissionem nostram non intendimus dicte composicioni in aliqua sui parte quomodolibet derogare, nec ipsam in exemplum trahi volumus in futurum. Dat' apud Lamheth XIIII Kalen' Marcii anno domini millesimo CCC^{mo} quinquagesimo secundo, et consecracionis nostre quarto.

ARCHIEPISCOPAL MANDATES
FOR THE LIVERY OF
THE SPIRITUALITIES

No. 11   *See p. 285*

30 May 1317

Archbishop Reynolds orders Prior John de Wyke to surrender the seal of the officiality of the bishopric, as well as other items, to James de Cobham, vicar-general of Thomas de Cobham who had been appointed bishop by Pope John XXII.

Cant. Reg. Reynolds, fo. 91r.

Walterus &c. dilecto filio domino . . . priori Wygornien', officiali iurisdiccionis spiritualis civitatis et diocesis Wygornien' sede inibi vacante per nos nuper prefecto, salutem &c. Quia sanctissimus in Christo pater et dominus noster dominus Johannes divina providencia papa XXII ecclesie Wygornien' per modum reservacionis de persona venerabilis viri magistri Thome de Cobeham sacre pagine professoris providens, ipsum in eiusdem loci prefecit episcopum et pastorem, curam et administracionem ipsius in spiritualibus et temporalibus committendo, prout in litteris suis apostolicis quas nobis inde mittere dignabatur plenius est expressum, vobis iniungimus et mandamus, quatinus discreto viro magistro Jacobo, dicti domini electi vestri in administracione spiritualium vicario in eius absencia constituto, ipsius domini electi vestri nomine, sigillum officialitatis eiusdem episcopatus necnon registrum rotulos ac omnia alia penes vos residencia officialitatis officium concernencia liberetis. Valete. Dat' apud Lamhethe III Kalen' Junii anno domini millesimo CCC^{mo} septimo decimo.

No. 12   *See p. 289*

11 Jan. 1350

Another mandate sent by Archbishop Islep to Prior John of Evesham after the translation of Thoresby from St. David's to Worcester by Pope Clement VI.

Cant. Reg. Islep, fo. 8r.

LIBERACIO SPIRITUALITATIS EPISCOPATUS WYGORN'

Simon permissione divina ecclesie Cant' electus consecratus, dilectis filiis . . . custodibus seu custodi iurisdiccionis spiritualis et spiritualitatis ecclesie Wygorn' nuper vacantis, salutem graciam et benediccionem. Cum sanctissimus in Christo pater dominus noster, dominus Clemens divina providencia papa sextus, venerabilem fratrem dominum Johannem pridem Meneven' episcopum ad dictam Wygorn' ecclesiam transtulerit, ipsum eidem preficiendo in episcopum et pastorem et sibi curam et administracionem plenarie committendo, prout in litteris apostolicis inde nobis directis plenius continetur, vobis quatenus ad nos attinet iniungimus et mandamus, quatinus eidem episcopo vel procuratoribus suis spiritualitatem predictam, sigilla, registra, et omnia alia et singula que episcopo dicti loci de iure vel consuetudine pro exercicio iurisdiccionis spiritualis huiusmodi liberari debeant sine dilacione quacumque liberetis, sibique ut episcopo dicti loci intendatis, obediatis, et reverenciam debitam impendatis. Taliter vos habentes quod ex hoc vestra debeat humilitas merito commendari. Dat' London' sub sigillo quo utimur III Id' Januarii anno domini millesimo CCC^{mo}XLIX°, et consecracionis nostre primo.

THE PRIOR'S REQUEST FOR
THE LIVERY OF THE SEAL OF THE OFFICIALITY,
THE REGISTERS, ETC.

No. 13   See p. 277

27 Jan. 1302

Appointment of Stephen de Witton, the subprior, and Gilbert de Maddeleye, the sacrist, to secure the seal of the officiality and other items on behalf of the prior.

Liber Albus, fo. vii v.

PROCURATORIUM AD PETENDUM SIGILLUM OFFICIALITATIS ET REGISTRUM ET ALIA

Pateat universis quod nos frater Johannes prior ecclesie cathedralis Wygorn' et eiusdem loci capitulum, dilectos fratres et commonachos nostros Stephanum de Witton suppriorem nostrum et Gilbertum de Maddeleye sacristam nostrum divisim et sub alternacione eorum quemlibet, ita quod non sit melior condicio occupantis, facimus ordinamus et constituimus procuratores nostros et nuncios speciales, ad petendum exigendum et recipiendum ab executoribus et ministris bone memorie domini Godefridi nuper episcopi nostri sigillum offic[ialitatis] Wygorn' registra tam ipsius patris quam consistoriorum et curiarum quarumlibet, instrumenta, cartas, privilegia, et munimenta, libros calices et ornamenta quecumque que ad statum ius vel possessionem ecclesie Wygorn' pertinere noscuntur, et in capituli Wygorn' custodia vacante sede debent de iure aut consuetudine residere, et ad faciendum super

24

receptis litteras dividendas aut alias que ipsa liberantibus in testimonium liberate sufficere debeant in hoc parte, et omnia alia faciend[a]
que in premissis et eorum quolibet fuerint oportuna. Ratum et firmum
habituri quicquid se aut unus eorum egerit in premissis. In cuius rei
testimonium sigillum nostrum commune fecimus hiis appendi. Dat' in
capitulo nostro VI⁰ Kal' Februarii anno domini M⁰CCC⁰primo.

THE RENDERING OF THE ACCOUNT

No. 14 *See p.* 312

4 Dec. 1308

*Archbishop Winchelsey cites the prior (John de Wyke) to appear before him
on the next juridical day after 1 January to render the account of his
administration.*

R.S.V., fo. lxxix r.

CITACIO DOMINI . . . ARCHIEPISCOPI AD COMPOTUM REDDEN-
DUM

Robertus permissione divina Cantuar' archiepiscopus tocius Anglie
primas, dilecto filio . . . priori ecclesie cathedralis Wygorn', salutem
graciam et benediccionem. Vacante nuper Wygorn' ecclesia per
mortem bone memorie domini W. de Geynesburgh dudum Wyg'
episcopi tam noster vicarius generalis quam administratores nostre
Cantuar' ecclesie per[1] sedem apostolicam deputati[2] vobis sub certa
forma administracionem spiritualium episcopatus eiusdem duxerant
committendam, verum quia prout debetis nondum administracionis
predicte nobis raciocinium reddidistis, vos tenore presencium peremptorie citamus, quod compareatis coram nobis proximo die iuridicco
post festum Circumcisionis Domini ubicumque tunc in civitate diocesi
seu provincia nostra Cant' fuerimus per vos seu per[3] procuratorem
sufficienter instructum administracionis vestre predicte raciocinium
reddituri et de veritate dicenda in ea parte si necesse fuerit iuraturi,
necnon et reliqua iuxta vim et effectum composicionis inter nostram
Cantuar' et vestram Wygorn' ecclesias in hac parte initam reddituri,
ulteriusque facturi et recepturi in premissis et premissa contingentibus
iuxta naturam et qualitatem dicti negocii cum continuacione et

---

[1] "Per" interlineated.
[2] There is no record, it would seem, of the commission issued by the archbishop's
vicar-general.
[3] "Per" interlineated.

prorogacione dierum usque ad finalem expedicionem eiusdem quod iusticia suadebit. Quid autem in premissis duxeritis faciendum nobis dictis die et loco intimare curetis per vestras litteras patentes harum seriem continentes. Dat' apud Leuesham II Non' Decembris anno domini M^{mo}CCC^{mo}octavo, consecracionis nostre XV°.

No. 15 *See p.* 312

Undated (1308)

Prior John de Wyke informs the archbishop of his appointment of Brother John of St Briavels to render the account.

R.S.V., fo. lxxix r.

PROCURATORIUM PRIORIS AD REDDENDUM COMPOTUM

Reverendo in Christo patri et domino domino Roberto dei gracia Cantuar' archiepiscopo tocius Anglie primati, suus humilis et devotus frater Johannes prior ecclesie cathedralis Wygorn' eiusdem patris in dicta diocesi nuper sede vacante officialis, debitam et devotam in omnibus obedienciam et reverenciam cum honore. Ad calculandum et reddendum raciocinium vice nostra vobis aut aliis quos ad id duxeritis deputandos, de proventibus exitibus et emolumentis quibuscumque iurisdiccionis predicte pro tempore vacacionis eiusdem perceptis, iuxta modum formam et tenorem composicionis super ipsa iurisdiccione inter bone memorie Bonifacium tunc Cant' archiepiscopum ex parte una et priorem ac conventum dicte Wygorn' ecclesie ex altera dudum facte, satisfaciendum prout iustum fuerit, de eisdem acquietancias et litteras de soluto recipiendum, prestandum si sit opus in animam nostram quodlibet licitum iuramentum, et omnia alia faciendum que in premissis fuerint oportuna, dilectum nobis in Christo fratrem et commonachum nostrum Johannem de Sancto Briavell' nostrum procuratorem verum et legitimum facimus et constituimus per presentes.

APPENDIX D

SOME WORCESTER MANDATES

In the Worcester records there are a number of mandates which, though prompted by particular abuses, draw the attention of the recipients to general points of law, sometimes with instructions to make them known. See p. 89.

No. 1   *See pp.* 63, 107, *n.* 4.

18 May 1301

Archbishop Winchelsey,[1] *having found during his visitation of the deanery of Bristol that money had been extorted at baptisms and for the probate of wills etc., forbids such practice under penalty of excommunication, and orders the dean to publish his inhibition and ordinances throughout the deanery.*

Reg. Gainsburgh, fo. 3r.

CONSTITUCIONES ARCHIEPISCOPI IN DECANATU BRISTOLL'

Robertus permissione divina Cant' archiepiscopus tocius Anglie primas decano Bristoll', salutem graciam et benediccionem. Quia visitacionis nostre officium in decanatu Bristoll' excercentes invenimus, quod pretextu cuiusdam consuetudinis, que pocius dicenda est coruptela, pro sacramento baptismatis in municipio Bristoll' per rectores vicarios et presbiteros parochiales passim et indistincte pro singulis parvulis baptizatis duo denarios exiguntur pertinaciter ab invitis, et quod infra ecclesias fiebant violente inpignoraciones inhumaniter pro eisdem; insuper quod pro probacionibus testamentorum raciociniorum et compoti reddicionibus de bonis defunctorum et liberacionibus ab onere administracionis huiusmodi bonorum et pro litteris acquietancie super hoc concessis solebat per ordinarios locorum gravis pecunie summa hactenus extorqueri; ita quod in hiis magis lucrum et commodum pecuniarum quam debita et salubris correccio querebatur: volentes sicut debemus huiusmodi vicia extirpare ut sacramenta

1 Although not an episcopal mandate—as the editor of Gainsburgh's register thought (see above, p. 63, n. 3)—there is nothing unusual about the process involved, except for the instruction to make a copy at the request of the mayor and commonality of Bristol.

ecclesiastica decetero pure gratis et devote qualibet exclusa cupiditatis labe iuxta sanctorum patrum et sacrorum canonum instituta exhibeantur ibidem, inhibemus publice et districte ne pro sacramento baptismatis pretextu alicuius consuetudinis vel pocius abusus prioris aliquid ab invitis per quoscumque inposterum exigatur, sed quod parentes vel alii huiusmodi parvulos deferrentes, absque omni exaccione vel coaccione, offere voluerint, devote recipiatur, sub pena excommunicacionis maioris per nos late, quam contravenientes incurrere volumus ipso facto. Ordinariis eciam publice inhibuimus ne pro testamentorum probacionibus, administracionis commissionibus, raciociniis reddendis, vel acquietancie litteris, quicquam extorqueatur aliqualiter inposterum ab invitis, nec ea occasione municipes et habitatores eiusdem municipii extra ipsum municipium ad loca remota sint maliciose pro aliquorum vexacionibus nimis voluntariis et iniustis [sicut] hactenus factum fuisse comperimus trahantur inviti, sub eadem pena quam contravenientes poterunt non inmerito formidare. Quocirca tibi committimus et mandamus quatinus huiusmodi inhibiciones et sentencias ac ordinaciones nostras in singulis ecclesiis tui decanatus facias temporibus oportunis sollempniter publicari, ne per ipsarum ignoranciam inposterum malivoli aliqui se valeant excusare. Denunciari insuper facias publice infra municipium predictum quod mercatores in una parochia commorantes et in alia seldas ubi sua de die excercent mercimonia optinentes quoad decimas et oblaciones eo pretextu faciendas et solvendas id communiter observent quod per loci diocesanum super hoc dudum fuerat ordinatum, donec cum maiori deliberacione super hoc equitatis tramite pro conservacione iuris cuiusquam loci aliter duximus ordinandum. Maiori vero et communitati eiusdem municipii quorum principaliter interest in hac parte huiusmodi mandati copiam sub sigillo tuo facere non differas requisitus. Et quid feceris in premissis cum ex parte eorundem congrue requisitus extiteris distincte et aperte nos certificetis per litteras tuas patentes harum seriem continentes. Dat' apud Cyrencestr' XV Kalen' Junii anno domini MᵒCCCᵐᵒprimo, consecracionis nostre septimo.

No. 2 *See p.* 63

10 Feb. 1304

Bishop Gainsburgh orders the dean of Worcester to warn priests not to grant absolution in reserved cases, for which recourse was to be made to the bishop's penitentiaries in the cathedral church and in the house of the Friars Minor at Worcester.

Reg. Gainsburgh, fo. 2v.

LITTERA AD COHIBENDUM CAPELLANOS WYG' NE ABSOL[VANT]
OMNES INDISTINCTE A P[ECCATIS]

Frater W. &c. dilecto in Christo filio decano Wygorn', salutem graciam
et benediccionem. Fama vehementi referente didicimus evicino
visitacionis nostre officium excercentes quod quidam vicarii et presbiteri in civitate Wyg' et in suburbio commorantes non sane sapientes sed
proprie salutis immemores, plus temporali commodo quam animarum
saluti dampnabiliter insistentes, ad se venientes undecumque et sua sibi
commissa confiteri volentes indistincte audiunt et a peccatis quorum de
iure nobis absolucio reservatur absolucionem verbalem impendunt
absque nostra licencia speciali, et sic multorum animas dampnabiliter
decipiunt quas solvere nequiunt vel ligare, in nostri iuris episcopalis
preiudicium, animarum periculum, et grave scandalum plurimorum.
Quocirca vobis mandamus firmiter iniungentes, quatinus duobus
diebus Dominicis et festivis in singulis ecclesiis parochialibus dictorum
civitatis et suburbii intra missarum sollempnia inhibeatis seu inhiberi
per alios faciatis ne quis rector, vicarius seu sacerdos huiusmodi penitentes in casibus nobis reservatis audiat confitentem [sic] aut manum
apponat absolutoriam nisi in casu a iure permisso, sed ad nostros
penitenciarios in ecclesia nostra cathedrali Wyg' et in domo fratrum
Minorum Wyg' deputatos habeant omnes huiusmodi penitentes pro
debite absolucionis beneficio optinendo, quibus in hac parte sub certa
forma litterarum nostram concessimus potestatem. Valete. Dat' apud
Bybur' IIII Idus Februarii, consecracionis nostre anno secundo.

No. 3   *See p. 63*
  30 Jan. (1309)

*The bishop instructs the official of the Worcester archdeacon to ascertain the
names of those beneficed in the deanery of Warwick who had not proceeded to
the priesthood within a year in accordance with a regulation of the Council of
Lyons (1274).*

Reg. Reynolds, fo. 6v.

LITTERA MISSA OFFICIALI ARCHIDIACONI WYGORN'[1] AD
INQUIRENDUM DE NON ORDINATIS INFRA ANNUM

W[alterus] permissione divina &c. dilecto filio officiali[2] archidiaconi
Wygorn', salutem graciam et benediccionem. Licet in generali concilio

---

[1] "Archidiaconi Wygorn" interlin.   [2] "Nostro" crossed out.

provide sit statutum,[1] quod assumpti ad regimen parochialium ecclesiarum ut diligencius gerere possint sibi crediti gregis curam infra
annum a sibi commissi regiminis tempore numerandum se faciant ad
sacerdocium promoveri, et si id non fecerint anno eodem elapso ipso
iure dictis ecclesiis sint privati, nisi ipsos causa racionabilis excusaret,
plerique tamen rectores parochialium ecclesiarum decanatus Warr' se
prout debuerunt cessante impedimento canonico infra annum huiusmodi non procuraverant in presbiteros ordinari sicut fama referente
ad nostram audienciam est delatum. Quocirca vobis de quo fiduciam in
domino gerimus pleniorem committimus et mandamus, quatinus de
nominibus rectorum non ordinatorum huiusmodi in decanatu predicto
per viros fidedignos et iuratos quos credideritis nosse melius veritatem
inquisicionem faciatis diligentem. Et nomina ipsorum quos infra annum
non esse ordinatos repereritis per eandem nobis per vestras litteras
patentes harum seriem continentes citra festum Sancti Valentini
martiris[2] studeas fideliter intimare. Dat' London' III° Kalen' Februarii.

No. 4

26 April 1314

*Bishop Maidstone instructs the sacrist to take action against those dese-
crating the cathedral precincts and despoiling church property.*

Reg. Maidstone, fo. 5r.

COMMISSIO CONCESSA SACRISTE WYGORN' AD CASTIGANDUM ET
PUNIENDUM DIVERSOS MALEFACTORES ET DILAPIDATORES
RERUM ECCLESIASTICARUM

Walterus &c. dilecto in Christo filio sacriste ecclesie nostre Wygorn'
vel cuicumque eius locum tenenti seu ad hoc per ipsum deputato vel
deputando, salutem &c. Acclamante fama gravi ac ex conquestione
multiplici recepimus, quod nonnulli sue salutis immemores ab illicitis
abstinere nescientes set pocius flagiciis se conferentes ecclesie cathedrali
Wygorn' iniuriari non verentur, ludos theatrales, ductu corearum,
proiectu lapidum, armorum delacione, palestrizacione, ac alias illicitos
et inhonestos in eadem ecclesia et eius cimiterio temere excercentes,
idemque cimiterium spurciciis variis multipliciter fedantes et enormiter
deformantes. Nonnulla eciam bona ipsius ecclesie ac tenencium suorum
precipue infra fines eiusdem cimiterii seu limitaciones habitancium
iniuriose contractant et violenter asportant, ac ad eadem loca licet
hactenus immunitate plena gaudere solebant et debeant confugientes

---

[1] Lyons II, c. 13; *Sext* 1, 6, c. 14.   [2] 14 February.

abstrahere, indebitas exacciones et insolitas tenentibus eiusdem inponere, ac inquietaciones multiplices ab eisdem tenentibus facere et eos alias indebite molestare non formidant. Quamplures eciam ballivi ac ministri temporales maneria eiusdem ecclesie temerarie ingredientes, de maneriis domibus grangiis vel locis aliis ipsius ecclesie et religiosorum virorum inibi deo famulancium contra voluntatem ipsorum vel custodum rerum eiusdem bona varia diripiunt, auferunt, et iniuriose contractant, aliasque multipliciter ipsos in suis et prefate ecclesie iuribus et possessionibus decimis et porcionibus decimarum ad eandem ecclesiam pertinentibus, ipsas detinendo ac eciam subtrahendo, maliciose impediunt impediri-ve faciunt seu procurant in ecclesiastice libertatis lesionem, exempli perniciem, ac scandalum plurimorum. Et quia pluries nos abesse contingit, adeo quod huiusmodi sceleribus quod absit occurrentibus pro remedio celeri adhibendo de facili nequimus adire, iccirco de vestra circumspeccionis industria plenam in domino fiduciam optinentes, vobis tenore presencium committimus iniungimus et mandamus, quatinus in huiusmodi[1], si quod absit quicquam attemptari contingat, cautelam celerem adhibentes omnes huiusmodi nequiciarum patratores eorumque fautores et aux[ilia]tores canonice coherceatis et contra eosdem per omnem censuram ecclesiasticam procedatis. Super quibus omnibus et singulis et ea contingentibus vobis vices nostras committimus cum cohercionis canonice potestate. Dat' in manerio nostro de Kemeseye VI[to] Kalen' Maii anno domini M[mo]CCC[mo]XIIII[o], et consecracionis nostre primo.

No. 5   *See p.* 182

26 July (1334)

Bishop Montacute gives instructions to the deans of Kineton and Warwick about the claiming of criminous clerks.

Reg. Montacute 2, fo. 2r.[2]

[3] QUI CLERICI SUNT [?] EXIGENDI A IUSTICIARIIS ET QUI NON. COMMISSIO [?] DECANO

Simon permissione &c. dilecto filio decano [sic] de Kyngton et Warr', salutem graciam et benediccionem. Cum vos ad exigendum clericos et alios iuxta sancciones canonicas exigendos in comitatu Warr' deputaverimus per nostras alias litteras inde factas, pro vestra informacione ad vestram deducimus noticiam per presentes, quod non omnes qui se

---

[1] *Sic.* Perhaps for "hiis", or a word may have been omitted.
[2] This mandate is in the precedent book called "Register Bryan 2" at folio xliiii v.
[3] This rubric is difficult to read because the writing has faded.

clericos pretendunt gaudere debeant privilegio clericali, quodque in huiusmodi privilegio coniugati clerici distinguendi sunt multipliciter a solutis sicut habetis expresse de clericis coniugatis, Extra: DE CLERICIS CONIUGATIS c. unico Li° VI^{to}; et de solutis in eodem libro DE SENTENCIA EXCOMMUNICACIONIS, SI JUDEX LAICUS.[1] Vobis igitur iniungimus et mandamus quatinus in exigendis clericis ita circumspecte vos habere curetis quod nullos de cetero exigatis ut clericos nisi qui dicto privilegio gaudere debent de iure, scientes quod si secus facere vos contingat, quod absit, nedum vobis immo nobis per hoc grande preiudicium poterit generari. Et ideo vos in hac parte caucius et diligencius habeatis considerando iura predicta et alia per que poteritis, si ea inspicere volueritis, plenius informari. Ceterum cum huiusmodi per vos exactos clericos ad nostrum carcerem principalem vos deinceps destinare contigerit, scribatis custodi eiusdem carceris vel illi cui eos liberaveritis nomina et cognomina huiusmodi clericorum ac causas seu crimina pro quibus vobis liberati fuerint per iusticiarios domini nostri regis Anglie, adeo quod si se purgare voluerint ipsi de eisdem criminibus et non de aliis futuris in nostre, quod absit, iurisdiccionis ordinarie elusionem, sicut alias fieri audivimus, valeant se purgare. Hoc mandatum nostrum in exigendis clericis semper habeatis vobiscum ne predicta vel eorum aliqua [sic] oblivioni tradatis quin pocius recentiori memorie commendetis. Valete. Dat' apud Crokham VII Kalen' Augusti anno domini ut supra.

No. 6 *See pp.* 186 *et seq.*

Undated

Bishop Bransford instructs the dean of Pershore to pronounce those defaming the character of Celestra, wife of Richard Hayl, ipso facto excommunicate by reason of a decree of the Council of Oxford (1222).

Reg. Bransford, fo. 8r. *(72)*

SENTENCIA GENERALIS CONTRA DIFFAMATORES

Frater W[olstanus] &c. decano de Pershora, salutem graciam et benediccionem. Querelam Celestre uxoris Ricardi Hayl gravem recepimus continentem, quod quidam iniquitatis filii quorum nomina ignorantur penitus et persone ipsam falso nequiter et maliciose apud bonos et graves diffamarunt, cum prius apud eosdem nullatenus extiterat diffamatum, crimen incontinencie cum presbiteris diversis commissum eidem imponendo, pretextu cuius diffamacionis eidem

---

[1] *Extra* 3, t. 3; *Sext* 3, 2, c.1; *Sext* 5, 11, c. 12.

fecimus purgacionem indici et ipsa ad arbitrium commissarii nostri in hac parte specialis de crimine predicto legitime se purgavit, quos omnes in sentenciam excommunicacionis maioris a venerabilibus patribus in consilio Oxon' contra huiusmodi diffamatores provide latam non est dubium incidisse.[1] Quocirca tibi in virtute obediencie firmiter iniungendo committimus et mandamus quatenus omnes huiusmodi diffamatores sic excommunicatos esse publice et solempniter denuncies et per alios facias solempniter [de]nunciari in ecclesia Sancti Andree[2] de Pershora et aliis vicinis[3] quibus per partem dicte Celestre congrue fueris requisitus diebus dominicis et festivis intra missarum solempnia quando maior in eisdem aderit populi multitudo, pulsatis campanis, candelis accensis et extinctis, cruce erecta, et aliis solempnitatibus adhibitis in hac parte fieri consuetis. Quid autem feceris in premissis nos cum per partem &c.

No. 7   *See pp.* 187, 188, *n.* 5.

    6 Feb. 1344

Bishop Bransford orders the dean of Warwick to pronounce excommunicate those responsible for removing candles from Ipsley church after Candlemas, contrary to a decree of the recent council at St Paul's.[4]

Reg. Bransford, ff. 68v.–69r. (*597*)

LITTERA CONTRA OCCUPANTES CANDELAS IN ECCLESIIS OBLATAS

Frater Wolstanus permissione divina Wygorn' episcopus dilecto filio decano de Warr' nostre diocesis, salutem graciam et benediccionem. Ex relacione multorum fidedigna ad nostrum [non] sine displicencia grandi pervenit auditum, quod [?] licet quicunque laici oblaciones quascunque in ecclesiis vel capellis aut cuiusvis earum porticu vel cimiteriis seu quocunque loco alio divino intuitu in Cantuariensi factas seu faciendas provincia, occupantes, aufferentes, seu disponentes quovismodo de ipsis, pretextu eciam cuiusvis operis, consuetudinis, aliove colore, nisi de consensu ecclesiasticarum personarum ad quas oblacionum huiusmodi percepcio pertinet, et ex causa sufficienti et legitima per episcopum loci primitus approbanda, ex decreto et deliberacione concilii provincialis in ecclesia Sancti Pauli London' ultimo celebrati maioris excommunicacionis sentencie subiaceant eo

---

[1] *Const. Prov.*, p. 1: tit. "Item Excommunicamus".
[2] "Apostoli" crossed out.   [3] "Locis" crossed out.
[4] It met in October 1342 and Bishop Bransford was there in person. See above, p. 83, n. 4.

ipso,[1] quidam tamen iniquitatis filii laici sue salutis immemores quorum nomina ignorantur pariter et persone quadraginta novem candelas (fo. 69r.) cere in ecclesia parochiali de Ippesley nostre diocesis et provincie memorate ad altaria et ymagines in eadem existentes in festo Purificacionis Beate Marie ultimo preterito[2] ac post prefati concilii publicacionem et efficacem ipsius artacionem divino intuitu oblatas, in casu eisdem non permisso temere occuparunt, abstulerunt ac de eisdem pro libito suo disposuerunt, maioris excommunicacionis sentenciam in eos et eorum quemlibet ut premittitur provide latam ipso facto dampnabiliter incurrendo, in animarum suarum grave periculum aliorum pernisiosum [sic] exemplum et scandalum plurimorum. Quocirca tibi committimus et in virtute obediencie firmiter iniungendo mandamus quatinus omnes et singulos prefatas oblaciones ut prefertur occupantes, aufferentes seu de eisdem disponentes, predicta maioris excommunicacionis sentencia fuisse et esse involutos, in dicta ecclesia de Ippesley ac in singulis ecclesiis decanatus tui diebus dominicis et festivis intra missarum solempnia cum maior in eisdem aderit populi multitudo, cruce erecta, campanis pulsatis, candelis accensis et in signum perdicionis in terram proiectis et extinctis, publice, solempniter et in genere denuncies seu facias per alios sic denunciari; ab huiusmodi denunciacione non cessans donec a nobis super hiis aliud habueris in mandato. Inquiras insuper de nominibus malefactorum huiusmodi, et si quos in premissis culpabiles seu denunciacioni tue inveneris reclamantes cites seu citari facias eosdem peremptorie quod compareant coram nobis seu nostro commissario in ecclesia parochiali de Hertlebury proximo die iur[id]ico post festum Sancti Petri quod dicitur[3] Cathedra[4] proximo futurum, dicti culpabiles quare in dictam excommunicacionis sentenciam incidisse nominatim minime debeant denunciari, ipsique reclamantes reclamacionis sue causas proposituri et ostensuri ulteriusque facturi et recepturi quod iusticia suadebit. Et quid feceris et inveneris in premissis una cum nominibus per te citatorum in hac parte nos aut nostrum commissarium dictis die et loco reddere cures cerciores litteris tuis patentibus habentibus hunc tenorem. Dat' apud Hertlebury sexto die mensis Februarii anno domini millesimo CCC^{mo}XLIII°, et nostre consecracionis quinto.

---

[1] *Const. Prov.* p. 45 (John Stratford): tit. "Immoderatae temeritatis praesumptio". The passage "in ecclesiis . . . approbanda" is a direct quotation from the constitution.

[2] 2 February.   [3] "Quod dicitur" interlineated.   [4] 22 February.

BIBLIOGRAPHY

The following list is not intended to be exhaustive. Where appropriate, books and MSS. have been adequately identified in the footnotes. The primary sources for the study of Worcester diocesan administration are the episcopal registers themselves, supplemented by the Registrum Sede Vacante and the Liber Albus. These have been examined in the originals, as has all the Worcester material, any printed transcripts, extracts, or calendars being used merely as a guide to the whereabouts and contents of the entries concerned. Worcester has been unfortunate in the editors of her records. With few exceptions the editions and calendars of the registers and other MSS. must be treated with caution. References to the pages of such editions have been given for the reader's convenience, in each instance the original manuscript has been consulted.

MANUSCRIPT SOURCES

An asterisk denotes that the MS. has been edited in some form.

(a) *Dean and Chapter Library, Worcester*

A *Class MSS.* (Bound volumes)

A 1 Registrum Sede Vacante* (*W.H.S.*)
A 2 Registrum Prioratus* (ed. Hale. *Camden Soc.* No. 91. 1865. The proper title of this volume is not known.)
A 3 Liber Pensionum* (*W.H.S.*)
A 4 Register 1.
A 5 Liber Albus* (*W.H.S.*)
A 6 Ledger 1.
A 12 "The book marked +" (There is an incomplete card index to this volume in the library.)

B *Class MSS.* (Loose MSS. placed flat in boxes)

As a whole these are unindexed, but some of them are noted, and a very few transcribed, by J. H. Bloom in *Charters relating to the City of Worcester* (*W.H.S.*). References to the individual MSS. are given in the footnotes of the present work.

C *Class MSS.*

C 885a A roll of corrections made in the deanery of Droitwich.* (*W.H.S.*)

(b) *The Worcestershire Record Office*

The MSS. formerly in the custody of the bishop's registrar have now been transferred to the County Record Office and are housed in St Helen's repository.

The episcopal registers

(The dates in brackets are those of the registers themselves and not necessarily of the bishops' episcopates.)

1. Godfrey Giffard* (1268–1302)
2. William Gainsburgh* (1303–7)
3. Walter Reynolds* (1308–13)
4. Walter Maidstone (1314–17)
5. Thomas Cobham* (1317–27)
6. Adam Orleton (1328–33)
7. Simon Montacute (1334–7)
8. Thomas Hemenhale (1337–8)
9. Wolstan de Bransford* (1339–49)

   (The writer has edited this register and has written *A Calendar of the Register of Wolstan de Bransford: Bishop of Worcester 1339–49.* H.M.S.O./W.H.S., 1965. In the footnotes of this book the edition number is added in brackets after that of the folio.)

10. John Thoresby (1349–52)

Other MS. volumes

"Liber Albus sive Extenta 9 R. Hen. IV et Chartae Regum et alia." Otherwise known as the "Liber Ruber". (This is the volume called "Lib. Alb. Episc. Wigorn." by Nash and others. It is bound in rough calf and is entitled "Liber Ruber" on the outside. It is so called in the present work. It should be distinguished from the "Red Book of Worcester" (*W.H.S.* 1934–50, ed. M. Hollings), the original of which has not survived, and from the priory Liber Albus.)

17th–18th cent.

Price, John (*ob.* 1705), Notitia Dioecesis Wigorniensis.
  Price, who was chancellor of the diocese, had a keen interest in diocesan administration. Unfortunately his notes are far more difficult to read than the medieval MSS. from which they are derived.

(c) Lambeth Library

Archiepiscopal registers
Robert Winchelsey (1294–1313)* (*C. & T. Soc.*)
Walter Reynolds (1313–33)* (*C. & T. Soc.*)
Simon Islep (1349–66)
  No registers are extant for the episcopates of Simon Mepham (1328–33), John Stratford (1333–48), and Thomas Bradwardine (1349).

(d) Bodleian Library

MS. Rawlinson C 428. A book of constitutions presented to the cathedral priory by Henry Fouke (professed 1302), and written *c.* 1330. On fo. 70r.–v. is entered a mandate of Bishop Montacute dated 8 April 1334.
MS. Glouc. Ch. 2. Original will of John de Botynton with endorsements certifying probate.

(e) Westminster Abbey Muniments

Great Malvern

Documents relating to the visitation of the priory 1282–6: Nos. 504, 22930, 22942, 32633–32643.

Longdon

Documents concerning the appropriation of the church and the ordination of the vicarage: Nos. 21256–21270.

(f) Dean and Chapter Library, Canterbury

Sede Vacante Register G.

PRINTED BOOKS

(a) Worcestershire Historical Society

Episcopal registers (cf. section (b) above)

Giffard, ed. J. W. Willis Bund. 1898–1900
Gainsburgh, ed. J. W. Willis Bund. 1906
   Introduction, R. A. Wilson. 1928
Reynolds, ed. R. A. Wilson. 1927
Cobham, ed. E. H. Pearce. 1929–30
   (This is the only scholarly edition of a Worcester register that has been printed.)

Other registers

Sede Vacante, ed. J. W. Willis Bund. 1893–7
Liber Albus, ed. J. M. Wilson. 1919
   (A calendar covering the priorates of John de Wyke 1301–17 and Wolstan de Bransford 1317–39. Some further details are given in the same author's *Worcester Liber Albus*. S.P.C.K., 1920.)

Various

Bloom, J. H., *Charters relating to the City of Worcester.* 1909
Hamilton, S. G., ed., *Collectanea.* 1912
   (This includes F. S. Pearson's transcription of MS. C 885a; see above under C Class MSS.)
Price, C., *Liber Pensionum.* 1925

(b) Collections of documents

Nash, T., *Collections for the History of Worcestershire.* 2 vols. (1st ed. 1781–2; Supplement 1799.)
   (Invaluable for the lengthy extracts from episcopal and capitular archives.)
Thomas, W., *Survey of the Cathedral Church of Worcester;*
   An Account of the Bishops thereof;
   An Appendix of Original Papers and Records. 1737

(c) Monastic Chronicles, Cartularies etc.

Dugdale, W., ed. Caley, J., Ellis H. and Bandinel, B., *Monasticon Anglicanum*, 6 vols. in 8. 1817–30

Hale, W. H., *Registrum Prioratus Wigorniensis, Camd. Soc.*, Vol. 91. 1866 (Cf. A Class MSS.)

Hart, W. H., *Historia et Cartularium Monasterii Gloucestriae*. 3 vols., *R.S.* 1863–7

Luard, H. R., *Annales Monastici, R.S.* 1864–9
Vol. 1, Annales mon. de Theokesburia
Vol. 4, Annales prioratus de Wigornia

Royce, D., *Landboc sive Registrum Monasterii de Winchelcumba*. 2 vols. 1892–3

(d) Catalogues etc.

Atkins, I., and Ker, N., *Catalogus Librorum Manuscriptorum Bibliothecae Wygorniensis*. 1944

Floyer, J. K. and Hamilton, S. G., *Catalogue of Cathedral Library MSS.* (*W.H.S.*). 1906

Historical MSS. Commission, 14th Report, Appendix pt. VIII.
Muniments in the possession of the Dean and Chapter of Worcester, pp. 165–203
The Muniments of the Bishop of Worcester preserved in his registry at Worcester, pp. 204–5 (R. L. Poole) (Referred to as *H.M.C.R.* with addition of page number)

Survey of Ecclesiastical Archives 1946. Pilgrim Trust. London 1952.

(e) The bishops

Haines, R. M., "Bishop Bransford." (Unpublished M.Litt. thesis. Univ. of Durham, 1954.)
— "Wolstan de Bransford, Prior and Bishop of Worcester, *c.* 1280–1349", in *University of Birmingham Historical Journal*, Vol. 8, No. 2 (1962), pp. 97–113.

Pearce, E. H., *Thomas de Cobham*. S.P.C.K., 1920

Thomas, W., An *Account* of the Bishops. . . . 1737 (See section (*b*) above.)

(f) Diocesan organization and administration

Addleshaw, G. W. O., *Rectors, Vicars and Patrons in 12th and 13th century Canon Law*. St Anthony's Hall publications, No. 9.

Barlow, F., *Durham Jurisdictional Peculiars*. 1950

Cheney, C. R., *English Bishops' Chanceries*. 1950

Churchill, I. J., *Canterbury Administration*. 2 vols. 1933

Dansey, W., *Horae Decanicae Rurales*. 2 vols. 2nd ed., 1844

Foster, J., "The activities of Rural Deans in England in the 12th and 13th cents." (Unpub. M.A. thesis. Univ. of Manchester, 1955.)

Fournier, E., *Les origines du vicaire général*. Paris 1922
— *Le vicaire général au moyen âge*. Paris 1923. (In reply to the criticisms of M. Mollat.)
— *L'origine du vicaire général et des autres membres de la curie diocésaine*. Paris, 1940

Fournier, P., *Les Officialités au moyen-âge*. Paris 1880

Gréa, A., "Essai Historique sur les Archidiacres", *B.E.C.* 3me ser., t. 2, pp. 39–67, 215–47.

Haines, R. M., "The Administration of the Diocese of Worcester *Sede Vacante* 1266–1350", *J.E.H.* Vol. 13, No. 2, pp. 156–71.

Hill, R.M.T., "Bishop Sutton and his Archives", *J.E.H.* Vol. 2, No. 1, pp. 43–53

Jacob, E. F., Introduction to the *Register of Henry Chichele (1414–43)*. 4 vols., 1943–7

Morris, C., "The Commissary of the Bishop in the Diocese of Lincoln." *J.E.H.* Vol. 10, No. 1, pp. 50–65

— "A Consistory Court in the Middle Ages", *J.E.H.* Vol. 14, No. 2, pp. 150–9

Storey, R. L., *Diocesan Administration in the 15th cent.*, St Anthony's Hall Publications, No. 16

Thompson, A. H., "English Clergy and their Organization in the Middle Ages: Archdeacons and Rural Deans" (Raleigh Lecture, *P.B.A.* 1943)

— *The English Clergy and their Organization in the later Middle Ages.* 1947

Wood-Legh, K. L., *Studies in Church Life in England under Edward III.* 1934

(g) Legal works

Friedberg, E., *Corpus Juris Canonici.* 2 vols. Leipsic 1879, 1881.

Gibson, E., *Codex Juris Ecclesiastici Anglicani.* 2 vols. 1713

Lyndwood, W., *Provinciale etc.* Oxford 1679. Containing:

   1. *Provinciale (seu Constitutiones Angliae)*

   2. *Constitutiones Legatinae (Othonis et Othoboni)*, with the gloss of John de Athon

   3. *Constitutiones Provinciales*

   (These are referred to in the footnotes as Lyndwood, Athon, and *Const. Prov.*, respectively.)

Maitland, F. W., *Roman Canon Law in the Church of England.* 1898

Makower, F., *Constitutional History of the Church of England.* 1895

Pollock, F. and Maitland, F. W., *A History of English Law before Edward I.* 2nd ed. 2 vols. 1952

Woodcock, B. L., *Medieval Ecclesiastical Courts in the diocese of Canterbury.* 1952

(h) Reference

Cheney, C. R., ed., *Handbook of Dates.* Royal Hist. Soc., 1948

Emden, A. B., *A biographical Register of the University of Oxford to* A.D. *1500.* 1957–9

Eubel, C., *Hierarchia Catholica Medii Aevi.* 1898

Gams, P. P. B., *Series Episcoporum Ecclesiae Catholicae etc.* Leipzig 1931

Jones, W. H., *Fasti Ecclesiae Sarisberiensis.* 1879

Mansi, J. D., *Sacrorum Conciliorum Nova et Amplissima Collectio.* Venetiis 1759 on

Le Neve, J., rev. Hardy, T. D., *Fasti Ecclesiae Anglicanae.* 3 vols. 1854

Powicke, F. M. and Fryde, E. B., ed., *Handbook of British Chronology.* 2nd ed., Royal Hist. Soc., 1961.

Rymer, T., *Foedera, Conventiones*, etc. 1704–35

Rymer, T. and Sanderson, R., ed. Clarke, A., Holbrooke, F. and Caley, J., *Foedera etc.* (with additional material). 1816–69

Tout, T. F., *Chapters in the Administrative History of Mediaeval England.* 6 vols. 1920 on. (Vols. 1 and 2 rep. 1937)

Wharton, H., *Anglia Sacra, sive Collectio*, etc. 2 vols. 1691. (Abbreviated *A.S.*)
Wilkins, D., *Concilia Magnae Britanniae*, etc. 1737

(i) *Various*

Barraclough, G., *Papal Provisions*. 1935
Blomefield, F., *An Essay towards a Topographical History of the County of Norfolk*.
11 vols. 1805–10
Cheney, C. R., *From Becket to Langton*. 1956
— *English Synodalia of the 13th cent.* 1941
— *Episcopal Visitation of Monasteries in the 13th cent.* 1931
Coulton, G. G., *Five Centuries of Religion*. 4 vols. 1929–50
Deeley, A., " Papal provision and rights of royal patronage in the early 14th
cent.", *E.H.R.* XLIII (1928), pp. 497–527
Denholm-Young, N., *Vita Edwardi Secundi*. Nelson's Medieval Classics. 1957
Douie, D. L., *Archbishop Pecham*. 1952
Edwards, K., *The English Secular Cathedrals in the Middle Ages*. 1949
Feltoe, C. L. and Minns, E. H., *Vetus Liber Archidiaconi Eliensis*, *C.A.S.* 8° Vol.
xlviii. 1917
Fraser, C. M., *A History of Antony Bek, Bishop of Durham 1283–1311*. 1957
Frere, W. H., *Visitation Articles and Injunctions of the period of the Reformation*,
Vol. 1. *Alcuin Club Coll.* xiv. London 1910
Gabel, L. C., " Benefit of Clergy in England in the later Middle Ages", Smith
College Studies in History, Oct. 1928–July 1929
Gibbs, M. and Lang, J., *Bishops and Reform, 1215–72*. 1934
Haigh, G., *The History of Winchcombe Abbey*. 1947
Hartridge, R. A. R., *A History of Vicarages in the Middle Ages*. 1930
Jenkins, H., "Lichfield Cathedral in the 14th cent." (Unpub. B.Litt. thesis.
Univ. of Oxford, 1956.)
Mollat, G., *The Popes at Avignon 1305–78*. 1963
Moorman, J. R. H., *Church life in England in the 13th cent.* 1946
Pantin, W. A., *The English Church in the 14th cent.* 1955
Salter, H. E., ed., *Snappe's Formulary*, *O.H.S.* LXXX. 1923
Stubbs, W., *The Constitutional History of England*. 3 vols. 1875–8
Tout, T. F., *The History of England 1216–1377* Vol. 3 of the *Political History of
England*. 12 vols. 1905
Wood, S., *English Monasteries and their Patrons in the 13th cent.* 1955

NOTE

The definitive work of F. M. Powicke and C. R. Cheney, *Councils and Synods
II*, parts 1 and 2 (1964), became available only after this book had gone to
press

INDEX

ABBREVIATIONS

A. & C.	abbot and convent	hosp.	hospital
Abb.	abbey		
abb.	abbot	jurisd.	jurisdiction
abp	archbishop		
approp.	appropriation	kt	knight
archd(y).	archdeacon(ry)		
Aug.	Augustinian	ld	lord
Ben.	Benedictine	m.	monk
bp	bishop	M.	*magister*
		man.	manor
can.	canon		
card.	cardinal	N.	nunnery
cath.	cathedral		
celebr.	celebrated	offic.	official
ch(s).	church(es)		
chanc.	chancellor	P. & C.	prior and convent
chant(s).	chantry, chantries	par.	parish
chap.	chapel	Pr.	priory
chapl.	chaplain	pr.	prior
Cist.	Cistercian	preb(s).	prebend(s)
clk	clerk	Premonstr.	Premonstratensian
Clun.	Cluniac	present.	presentation
const(s).	constitution(s)	pss	prioress
comm.	commissary	pst	priest
ct(s)	court(s)		
		r.	rector
D. & C.	dean and chapter	rect.	rectory
deany	deanery	reg.	register
e.	earl	sequest.	sequestration
fam.	family	v.	vicar
fder	founder	vic.	vicarage
gen.	general (vicar-gen.)	w.	wife
Gilbert.	Gilbertine	wid.	widow
gtd	granted		

INDEX

26